# The MYSTERY of HISTORY

## Volume III

### The Renaissance, Reformation, and Growth of Nations

Linda Lacour Hobar

Dover, Delaware

Library of Congress Control Number: 2008926075
ISBN: 978-1-892427-08-3
First Edition



Printed in the United States of America

Published by Bright Ideas Press
Dover, Delaware

www.BrightIdeasPress.com
1.877.492.8081

17 16 15 14 13 12 10 9 8 7 6 5



**Design and Production by Aptara Corp.**
Design: Carole Allen, Christine Corcoran, Matthew Salerno
Photo Research: Morgan Floyd, Caitlin Underdahl
Production: Joe Antonio (Project Manager), David Fulk, Lori Brice
Maps: John Ott

**Other Production Credits**
Copyediting: Kathryn Dix, Kathryn Dix Publishing Services
Proofreading: Andrea Howe, Blue Falcon Editing
Illustrations: Amy Pak, Home School in the Woods; Nicole Petersen

**PHOTO CREDITS**
**Cover and Title Page:** Galleries des Batailles, Palace of Versailles, © Massimo Listri/Corbis; Inset from study for *Leda and the Swan* by Leonardo da Vinci, © Alinari Archives/Corbis; Inset of St. Basil's Cathedral, Moscow, © Steven Vidler/Eurasia Press/Corbis; Inset of Portuguese bronze astrolabe, © The Granger Collection, New York.

***Photo, illustration, and map credits continue on page 440, which constitutes an extension of this copyright page.***

With love and great sentiment,
I dedicate this book to my parents,
Ray and Marilyn Lacour,
who not only gave me life
but breathed into it the sweet language of love.

*"And though I have the gift of prophecy,*
*and understand all mysteries and all knowledge,*
*and though I have all faith, so that I could remove mountains,*
*but have not love, I am nothing."*

1 Corinthians 13:2

# CONTENTS



## Semester I

## The Renaissance and Reformation

### Quarter 1 – The Age of Rebirth (1455–1521)

## Week 6



## Week 7



# Quarter 2 - The Age of Reform (1522–1572)



## Week 8



## Week 9



## Week 10



## Week 11

## Week 12



## Week 13



## Week 14



# Semester II

## The Growth of Nations

### Quarter 3 – The Age of Reason *(1572–1632)*



## Week 15



## Week 16



## Week 17

# Acknowledgments

First and foremost, I acknowledge my Lord and Savior, Jesus Christ, who is the Mystery of all history. Jesus says in the Scriptures, "apart from me, you can do nothing." (John 15:5, NIV) This couldn't be truer in my life. While completing this Volume, I have been spiritually and emotionally beaten, bruised, torn, tormented — and humbled. It is all to the glory of God. I realize with a new sense of brokenness that I could not write of God's glorious grace in history had I not been in the lowly position of needing it myself. But I have. With inexpressible gratitude, I thank the Lord for allowing me the privilege of suffering under my sins that I might know His grace and the mystery of redemption. "I want to know Christ and the power of his resurrection and the fellowship of sharing in his sufferings, becoming like him in his death, and so somehow, to attain to the resurrection of the dead. Not that I have already obtained all this, or have already been made perfect, but I press on to take hold of that for which Christ Jesus took hold of me." (Phil. 3:10–12, NIV)

Now, as I pull myself together from such transparency, let me thank the wonderful people God has placed in my life to journey with me through the production of *The Mystery of History.*

My Family — Thank you for granting me time to write. This project takes the most from you, as is evident by the leftovers and piles of laundry. Nonetheless, you have helped with photos, binders, shipping, conventions, and listening to my history stories at dinner. I love you all "the most." Apart from seeking to please my Savior, you remain my greatest inspiration for living the Christian life.

Bob and Maggie Hogan — Thank you for publishing this work and for being dear friends along the way. I admire the principles by which you live and appreciate the grace you regularly extend. I've needed it this year.

Kathy Dix — You are far more than an editor to me. You are a dear friend. Thank you for taking my words and making them so much better. I could not have imagined this Volume without your input and wisdom.

Aptara's Design, Photo Research, and Production Teams — Thank you for pouring beauty into these pages through your skills and expertise.

Reed Depace — Thank you for your biblical and historical input. It's been wonderful, challenging, and entertaining to work with you.

Lisa Arce — Thank you, my dearest friend, for being Jesus to me in grace, truth, and love. I would not be who I am apart from God working through you.

Anne Lassy — Thank you for your heartfelt devotion, not only to *The Mystery of History* but to me. There are no words to express my thanks for your prayers, concern, and help.

Regina Sanchez — Thank you for shipping books all over the country and all over the world with great efficiency. I appreciate your good heart and your understanding through the growing pains of this series.

Tara Bentley — Thank you for contributing to the convention life and sharing your soul with me. We needed each other.

Amy Pak — Thank you for blessing us all with your artwork and creativity.

Test Families — Thank you for using your own kids as guinea pigs for my lessons and half-developed activities. Your enthusiasm helped to keep me going.

GPS Class at Hope Church — Thank you for letting me teach you in raw form and for lifting me up along the way of life as true brothers and sisters in Christ.

MOH Families — Thank you to all the teachers, moms, dads, and students who take time to say hi, to say thanks, and to let me know you've learned something new. You inspire me more than you'll ever know.

Tim and Sue — Thank you for serving the body of Christ like skilled surgeons who know how to resuscitate the near-dead. Thank you for detecting my pulse and providing life support when needed. I'm grateful.

# Preface

Welcome to *The Mystery of History.* It is an honor and a privilege to be presenting you with *Volume III* in this series — this time we are spanning *The Renaissance, Reformation, and Growth of Nations.* I have personally developed a new love and fascination for this era. But here are a few important disclaimers and an explanation of the new format.

First, though I have spent years in the research of this book, I would like to apologize ahead of time for any inaccuracies, discrepancies, or errors that lie within this text. None are intentional. But invariably, archaeologists, Bible scholars, and expert historians will dig, discover, and develop new ideas and facts that will outdate the information contained here. With an ever-expanding sea of knowledge at my disposal, I will strive to modify this work accordingly and ask your patience as I do so.

Second, it would be negligent of me not to mention that though this is a "world" history course, there is a greater amount of attention given in this Volume to the history of the Western world through the accomplishments and failures of its men and women. This imbalance is in no way meant to imply superiority of any race, color, sex, or culture, but rather it is a reflection of the history most pertinent to the majority of my readers.

Third, without reservation, this book is written from a Christian perspective. I have sincerely tried to discuss other faiths with dignity and respect while at the same time pointing my readers to what I believe is the true Gospel of Jesus Christ according to the inspired Word of God.

Fourth, the time period of this Volume includes the Protestant Reformation. I have prayerfully sought to write with sensitivity toward Protestants and Catholics alike in regard to this piece of tumultuous history. I have approached the Reformation by presenting doctrine and theology of both Protestants and Catholics, along with the history of disagreement and bloodshed between them. I have included "heroes of the faith" in both Protestant and Catholic circles. However, the differences between these groups are vast and divisive. It is beyond the scope of this book to bridge them. As I am a Protestant, I have undoubtedly written with a bias toward Protestantism, though I have tried to in no way offend or attack modern-day Catholicism. Forgive me if I have. I hope all my readers will take the information contained here and use it for its historical value and for examining their own faith, whatever it may be.

As for the format, this Volume of world history is written for all ages. If you are 8 years old, or 80 years old, I hope you will enjoy the stories. However, for those who are interested in this material for meeting particular academic requirements, please know that the accompanying *Companion Guide* now contains everything you need for making *The Mystery of History, Volume III,* a complete world history course.

Pretests, quizzes, mapping exercises, timeline work, hands-on activities, research projects, and more can be found in the paperback *Companion Guide* (which is also available on CD). One special feature is a long list of supplemental books and literature for all ages that will greatly enhance any study of world history. Even more resources can be found on my Web site or on that of my publisher (www.themysteryofhistory.com or www.brightideaspress.com). The *Companion Guide* will provide you with a framework for teaching "Younger, Middle, and Older Students," with attention given to high school requirements. To personalize this book for my broad audience of students, I've written letters to three different age groups in the pages that follow this Preface. Please read the letter(s) that applies to you and/or your students.

Last, for additional resources, encouragement, fellowship, or questions to the author and publisher, please visit any of *The Mystery of History* Yahoo support groups. To subscribe, visit:

Volume I: http://groups.yahoo.com/group/MysteryofHistory1
Volume II: http://groups.yahoo.com/group/MysteryofHistory2
Volume III: http://groups.yahoo.com/group/MysteryofHistory3

Linda Lacour Hobar

# Letters to the Students

Dear Younger Student Friends (Elementary School Age),

Before you start this history book, I want to write you a personal note and say hi. Maybe that seems strange to you. History books don't usually begin this way. But to me, *The Mystery of History* isn't just a book. It's an adventure in time and travel and that makes me your personal tour guide on a long and amazing journey!

With that thought in your mind, let me tell you of the exciting things to come on this adventure. In our first quarter together, I'm going to take you to meet the queen of Spain, to see the works of a famous artist named Leonardo da Vinci, and to sail around the Cape of Good Hope, where it was once thought that ships would fall off the edge of the world! In our second quarter, we'll scale the Swiss Alps, ride elephants in India, and steer boats across the city of Venice. Does that sound like fun? It gets better!

In our third quarter, we'll meet ninja fighters in Japan, visit the wild outback of Australia, and witness the wedding ceremony of Pocahontas. And in the last quarter, we'll fight civil wars in England, attend a masquerade party with Louis XIV, and watch an apple drop with Isaac Newton, a scientist who helped explain gravity.

Of course, our adventures are usually going to be on paper. I can't really take you to fight ninjas or hike the Swiss Alps. I wish I could! But since I can't, I've additionally written a *Companion Guide* full of ideas about how you can experience history with your own hands, eyes, feet, and taste buds. You can pretend we are together on some of these adventures. With or without the *Companion Guide*, I think you'll like the stories here.

Unfortunately, not all of history is fun. Some of my stories are sad or even gory in places. Others involve great danger! They are about massacres, murder, and revenge. But you see, ever since sin entered the world, man has struggled against all kinds of wickedness and evil. Some of it we see, and some of it we don't see. But it's there. Our world has many problems, and history is full of mistakes that people have made. Some mistakes are little — but some, sadly, are very, very big!

There is good news, though! The good news is that God knew ahead of time that man would struggle with living right. And so, by sending his son Jesus Christ to die for our sins, He has a plan to help us live! I hope you know this plan. We call it the Gospel. If you aren't exactly sure what the Gospel is, please read more about it in the section titled "Would You Like to Belong to God's Family?" that comes right after Quarter 4 in the back of this book. One of the reasons I write history is to share the story of the Gospel with boys and girls just like you. The Bible says, "My purpose is . . . that they [meaning you] may know the ***mystery*** of God, namely, Christ, in whom are hidden all the treasures of wisdom and knowledge." (Col. 2:2–3, NIV. Words in brackets are mine. Bold type is mine for emphasis.)

So, are you ready? Are you ready to learn the treasures of wisdom and knowledge found in Christ? Are you ready to see God's hand in history? I hope so because I love teaching these things. Just know ahead of time that this book is for all ages, so parts of it will be too hard for you. Don't worry. Learn what you can for now and come back to this book one day when you're a little older. Now, let's get going!

For the sake of the Mystery,
Linda Lacour Hobar

Dear Middle Student Friends (Middle School and Junior High Age),

Hi! Before you delve into this book, I want to say a couple of personal things. First, I want to welcome you to *The Mystery of History*. Whether you like history or not, I think you'll find *something* interesting here. This Volume not only covers fifteenth- and sixteenth-century "world history," but it also includes famous artists of the Renaissance, some of the greatest names in science, and a few of the toughest explorers ever to circle the globe. On top of that, this Volume grapples with the infamous Inquisition, the bloodshed of the Reformation, and the horror of the Atlantic slave trade. I don't think you'll find this book to be "light."

But second, I want you to know that there is more going on behind the scenes than just my telling you stories about art and science, exploration and discovery, and yes, wars, mutinies, and treaties! I am striving throughout these pages to guide you into truth — the truth of the Gospel, that is. You see, as a follower of Jesus Christ, I believe that history is more than a string of events in time. I believe that history is *the* story of God revealing Himself to mankind so that we might be redeemed. God's plan to redeem us is really a very *personal* story and one that I hope you already know. We call this plan the Gospel.

If you are not sure you know the Gospel, please read more about it in the section titled "Would You Like to Belong to God's Family?" that comes right after Quarter 4 in the back of this book. I've provided some Scriptures to help explain God's plan of salvation. I came to understand it myself at 17. It changed my life, and I've not yet quit talking about it! That's how much the Gospel means to me.

Now, with all that said, it's time for you to get started on this course. I've geared this book to use "as is" for your age group. This means you should try to use every component of *The Mystery of History* as provided in this *Student Reader* and in the accompanying *Companion Guide* to get the most out of it. But please feel the freedom to make adjustments where needed. I would never expect you to finish all the activities or to read all the supplemental materials in the *Companion Guide*. There's a lot to choose from! But please do read all the lessons in this *Student Reader* in the order in which they are written, and if possible, complete at least the tests and worksheets in the *Companion Guide*. They are great tools for review to help you retain the vast amount of information presented here. There is so much to know about this rich and provocative time period, and I'm praying for you as you journey through it.

I'll end on this note taken from Scripture. "For though I am absent from you in body, I am present with you in spirit and delight to see how orderly you are and how firm your faith in Christ is. So then, just as you received Christ Jesus as Lord, continue to live in him, rooted and built up in him, strengthened in the faith as you were taught, and overflowing with thankfulness." (Col. 2:5–7, NIV)

For the sake of the Mystery,
Linda Lacour Hobar

Dear Older Student Friends (High School Age),

Hi! If you are new to *The Mystery of History*, or a returning student, I want to personally welcome you to this program. I've a few important things to share with you before you get started.

For one, this program is written "as is" for Middle School students. This means that for you to receive a high school credit for the course, you will need to put more time into it than just reading what appears on these pages. Hopefully, that will be easy because the hundreds of activities in the accompanying *Companion Guide* give you the freedom and ability to explore in more depth the parts of history that *you* find interesting. In reality, you can design this course to be your very own. I hope you find that appealing.

So, to make the MOH your very own course, I suggest you do two things. First, choose the activities in the *Companion Guide* that will really engage you. You've got only so much time. Choose activities that will complement your learning style, further your mind and spirit, and challenge your research skills. Second, with those same criteria, choose to read supplemental books and literature from lists in the *Companion Guide* that are going to broaden your thinking, expand your knowledge, *and* stir your heart. There is so much to choose from — I hope it's hard to decide what NOT to read.

Now keep in mind that a high school credit generally consists of 135–180 hours of instruction in a school year. This means you should be putting in at least four to five hours a week on this course. (It may take more.) So, once you've got the basics done (with or without some younger siblings to slow you down), roll up your sleeves and keep going. If you are home educated, use your integrity to keep track of the hours it takes you to work on your activities and supplemental reading — so that you might genuinely fulfill your requirements. That is what's expected of you.

And second, please know that there is much more to this course than "world history." The premise of *The Mystery of History* is that God is behind the scenes revealing Himself to mankind. I don't know where you are in *your* thoughts about God and spiritual things. But wherever you are, I hope you're growing in your faith and solidifying that in which you believe. I would like to be a long-distance mentor of sorts and assist you in your spiritual journey as you shape and define your own convictions. If you're not sure where you are in relation to knowing Christ personally, please read the section titled "Would You Like to Belong to God's Family?" that comes right after Quarter 4 in the back of this book. The Scriptures contained there might answer some questions for you. I was 17 before I gave my own life to Christ. So I understand if you're new to this concept.

Well, I've laid out a tall order for us here. I'm expecting a lot from you and hoping to give a lot in return. I sincerely believe, though, that there is *much* to learn from this time period of the Renaissance and beyond — knowledge that will shape your worldview and become part of your very life.

I'll close with this Scripture, which sums up my prayer for you. "See to it that no one takes you captive through hollow and deceptive philosophy, which depends on human tradition and the basic principles of this world rather than on Christ. For in Christ all the fullness of the Deity lives in bodily form, and you have been given fullness in Christ, who is the head over every power and authority." (Col. 2:8–10, NIV)

For the sake of the Mystery,
Linda Lacour Hobar

# Semester I

## The Renaissance and Reformation

### Quarter 1

### The Age of Rebirth 1455 – 1521



### Quarter 2

### The Age of Reform 1522 – 1572

*In* School of Athens, *Raphael captured the images of Plato and Aristotle, ancient Greek philosophers, strolling under Roman archways and surrounded by great thinkers, writers, and artists. This scene portrays the essence of the Renaissance, which was to glorify the classical age of the Greeks and Romans.*

# The Age of Rebirth
## 1455–1521

If history were a graceful landscape of valleys, hills, and winding streams, then the *Renaissance* would be a snow-peaked mountain jutting out of the horizon, begging for attention. You can't help but notice it. Compared to some parts of history, the Renaissance glitters and twinkles in places. You see, it was a rich time period when the achievements of mankind soared very high. Like a mountain stretching into the highest part of the sky, so mankind reached upward, too. What was he reaching for? What did he attain? Well, I can't reveal the whole story to you now. It will take us weeks to gaze at the accomplishments of the Renaissance. But here are a few things to note as our breathtaking scene unfolds.

First, the word *Renaissance* means "rebirth." It refers to the rebirth of ancient Greek and Roman thought. In the fifteenth and sixteenth centuries, these thoughts triggered a surge of creativity in the arts. *Leonardo da Vinci, Michelangelo,* and *Raphael* studied the Greeks and Romans to produce some of the world's most beautiful works of art. It was to our benefit that these three artists lived near each other in time and place, for it resulted in their trying to outdo one another with brilliant masterpieces. In reality, they all succeeded in some areas and failed in others.

Second, it was during this time period that mankind gave birth to the exploration of the sea. Through the voyages of *Bartolomeu Dias, Christopher Columbus,* and other explorers, men sailed to new and exotic places. They were driven by a quest for gold, glory, and the proclamation of the Gospel. The world would be forever changed by these seafaring adventurers.

Third, while the Renaissance rose to new heights, new faith was being born, too. A fiery preacher named *Savonarola* and a monk named *Martin Luther* would seek to draw men and women into fresh faith in God. They hoped to rekindle hearts for the Holy One. In many ways, they did.

In my opinion, much of history is just that. It is the Lord breathing life into the souls of his created and rekindling hearts for Him. I hope you see that in these stories. I'm titling this quarter "The Age of Rebirth" in honor of the arts, the exploration, and the faith that flourished from about 1455 to 1521. These are the 66 years of unforgettable history that we'll be looking at in Quarter 1. I hope you enjoy it!

# WEEK 1

## Lesson 1 — 1455–1485

# The Wars of the Roses

Though the title of our lesson might make you wonder, roses don't really have wars. We all know that. So what were the "Wars of the Roses"? Well, they were a long series of struggles between two ruling groups of families in England. We call these ruling groups "houses." For thirty years, the **House of Lancaster** fought with the **House of York** over who would be the king of England. What does this have to do with roses? It's really quite simple. The House of York used a *white rose* for their royal emblem. The House of Lancaster used a *red rose* in their coat of arms. So, the clashes between these two houses became known as the "Wars of the Roses."[1]

Before I get into the details of these wars, I'd like to review the history of England with you. (Some of you have already studied this information in other volumes of *The Mystery of History*. If you didn't, don't worry. I'll get you caught up very quickly! Younger Students may opt to skip this review.)

### A Brief History of England

For such a small island, England has had a great influence on our world. Its people are a melting pot of great cultures. Going far back in time, you would find that England was occupied by the amazing people who built **Stonehenge**. England was settled later by the **Celts** (Keltz) — until **Julius Caesar** brought over the **Romans**. The Celts and the Romans lived side by side in England until 476 when the Roman Empire collapsed. With that collapse, the Romans left England. They left the Celts stranded against the invading tribes of the **Angles**, the **Saxons**, and the **Jutes**. Those were the legendary days when **King Arthur** and his knights fought the Saxons to protect their homeland.

As a reminder of history, ancient Roman ruins like these can still be found in the English countryside.

But worse than the invading Saxons were the **Danish Vikings**.

During the 700s they pillaged, plundered, and attacked the coast of England to make parts of it their home. **Alfred the Great**, a Saxon king, did his noble part to keep the Vikings in one place. Alfred was a strong Christian king who tried to make peace with the Danes by telling them about Jesus. For the most part, Alfred was successful. Under his rule, the threat of the Vikings lessened and the strength of England grew.

England was just coming together as a nation under the Saxons when a powerful man from Normandy, France, decided to make it *his* home. That man was **William the Conqueror**. In 1066, he invaded England at the famous **Battle of Hastings** and crowned himself king. With him came a rush of Frenchmen into England *and* the idea of feudalism. (Feudalism is a system of rule by kings and landowners.) England was then subject to a host of kings and queens throughout the period of the Middle Ages. I'm sure you've heard of that era.

Some kings and queens were magnificent, like **Eleanor of Aquitaine** and her son **Richard the Lionhearted**. Some were ill tempered and cruel, like **King John** from whom the tales of **Robin Hood** are derived. King John was in fact so evil that the English forced him to sign the **Magna Carta** to put limits on his power. It was a concept that shaped history.

Eventually, England and France began to fight each other because the English wanted complete freedom from the French. This long and fearsome struggle was called the **Hundred Years' War**. It included the tragic death of **Joan of Arc**, a brave young girl who fought for France and was burned at the stake.

## *The House of York Takes England*

This leads us to our present study of the Wars of the Roses in England, which spanned the years **1455–1485**. Shortly after the Hundred Years' War, the House of Lancaster was ruling the nation. This house included a line of three kings named Henry IV, Henry V, and **Henry VI**. (There were a lot of kings named Henry in English history. You can keep them straight by the Roman numerals that appear after their names.) It was Henry VI who had problems that led to the Wars of the Roses. You see, Henry VI was quite feeble and from time to time showed signs of insanity. He probably suffered from catatonic schizophrenia (skitz oh FREN ee ah). Because of his condition, Henry VI really wasn't a good ruler for England.

If Henry's mental issues weren't bad enough, Henry's officials were corrupt and his queen was power hungry. With all these problems, the country grew ripe for civil war. It was then that a rival family of nobles — called the House of York — decided to take action. The House of York had hoped for years to gain control of the nation. In 1455, the first blood was shed over the matter at the small **Battle of St. Albans**. In that battle, the Yorkists defeated the Lancastrians (meaning they beat them). Though the Yorkists won, the House of York failed in making their leader, the duke of York, the next king. The English Parliament kept Henry VI in place as the king. They made the duke of York the "Lord Protector" of the nation. It was a sort of compromise. Though he was not made king, the duke of York had a lot of power. He more or less ran the country during Henry's episodes of mental illness.

This arrangement might have continued awhile and worked just fine had it not been for the queen. Henry's wife, **Queen Margaret**, was afraid that *her* son would never inherit the throne of England with the duke of York having so much control. So, Queen Margaret raised up forces to fight against the duke of York. In 1460, at the bloody **Battle of Wakefield**, Queen Margaret got what she wanted. The duke of York was slain in combat! In prideful victory, Queen Margaret had his head mounted on the town gates of York. (Disgusting, isn't it?) She left his head to rot in public as a reminder that the House of Lancaster, *not* the House of York, was still on the throne of England. (Remember, I told you that the queen was power hungry!)

The message of the queen, however, wasn't as clear as she hoped. Completely against her wishes, Parliament declared that the *son* of the duke of York would be the next king of England! His name was Edward. Now, keep in mind, Henry VI wasn't dead; he was just incompetent. So, to get Henry out of the way, Edward had him locked up in the Tower of London! The queen fled to Scotland, and Edward was crowned **Edward IV**, the new king of England. He was only 19. Edward IV was, of course, of the House of York. After a few more bloody battles, the House of Lancaster was officially out. But this is still not the end of the story!

## *The House of Lancaster Retaliates*

The earl of Warwick was nicknamed "the Kingmaker."

The House of York had great confidence in their new king, Edward IV, but they greatly underestimated the House of Lancaster. The **earl of Warwick**, who was nicknamed "the Kingmaker," manipulated the royalty to put Henry VI *back* on the throne of England! Unstable and bemused, Henry VI was let out of the Tower of London to once again be the king. His rescuer, the earl of Warwick, secretly hoped to rule England through him. Poor Henry. He was being used and didn't even know it. Still suffering from mental illness, he held on to the throne for only a few months. But it was long enough for the civil war to start up all over again.

The conflict erupted again in 1471, when Edward IV declared war against Henry. In a confusing battle in the fog, the Lancastrians accidentally fought their own men! The earl of Warwick, the kingmaker, was killed. After two gruesome battles, Edward won. He immediately claimed the throne of England *again* for the House of York. To prevent Henry VI from ever being king again, Edward threw Henry back into the dark and dreary dungeon of the Tower of London and days later had him executed. The queen, who had by then returned from Scotland, was spared death, but she was kept in prison. For England, it was a soap opera that seemed to have no end — because you see, there's even more to this tangled story!

## *An Evil Plot*

If it weren't bad enough that the houses of Lancaster and York warred *against one another*, the House of York had a battle going on within itself. Edward IV of the House of York had two young sons who were in line to become king after his death. But Edward also had a brother named Richard, who wished to become the next king. Can you see the problem? There was serious rivalry in the family.

As the story goes, in 1483, Edward IV died unexpectedly. His oldest son was immediately named king. But this was not to last long! Richard (who was Edward's brother and the boys' uncle) locked up the boy king and his younger brother in the Tower of London. They were only 12 and 9! Some would say this happened because Richard was wretched and ruthless. Others would say he was only "protecting" the boys from other rivals by locking them away. No one knows for sure, but the boys seemed to "disappear" for good, and Richard was crowned **King Richard III** of England.

After the strange disappearance of his nephews, Richard was crowned the king of England.

As an intriguing side note, most would say that the young princes were never seen or heard from again and that they were murdered or starved to death in the Tower of London. But, in the seventeenth century, a workman found their supposed bones while repairing an old stairwell. The true fate of the boys remains quite a mystery. To add to it, a few years *after* the disappearance of the boys, a young man *claimed* to be one of the two princes who had escaped! If his story were true, it would have made *him* the rightful king of England! But most people didn't believe him. They thought he was an imposter whose real name was **Perkin Warbeck**. Most of England assumed that the poor princes were dead, and England continued to acknowledge Richard III as the king.

## *The House of Tudor*

Now, after all this turmoil in the House of York, what do you think the House of Lancaster thought about Richard III? I think they were terrified of him. If Richard had been ruthless enough to lock up his own nephews for life, what else was he capable of? They couldn't afford to wait and find out. The House of Lancaster made a plan. Their plan involved yet another Henry. This was **Henry Tudor**, the son of Edmund Tudor and Margaret Beaufort. (Henry is worth remembering now, for he became the father of the very famous Henry VIII!)

Henry Tudor first used force against Richard III in the **Battle of Bosworth Field**. Richard had a chance of winning the battle until one of his own lords traded sides in the war and joined the Lancastrians! With that turn of events, Richard III was killed in battle and that was the end of him *and* the line of York kings.

To change the lineage of kings for good, Henry Tudor went a step beyond the battlefield. Going against all Lancaster tradition, he married a woman from the House of York! His idea was to unite the feuding families once and for all. The woman he chose to marry was — believe it or not — the daughter of Edward IV and the sister of the disappearing princes! And you know what? The outrageous plan worked. The marriage *did* bring peace between the houses. Henry dropped the names of Lancaster *and* York and renamed his family the **House of Tudor**. His new title became **Henry VII**.

To help keep the peace that he created, Henry VII did something else special. He created a unique group of bodyguards to protect him from assassination. These bodyguards were named **Yeoman Warders**, but most know them as **"Beefeaters."** Why were they nicknamed Beefeaters? There are two theories — either they really ate a lot of meat, which was their daily ration, or the name was modified from the French word for guard, which is *buffetier*. (Buffetier – Beefeater. I think you can hear the likeness.) Either way, the name Beefeaters has stuck for centuries. The Beefeaters still guard the Tower of London today and are known for their elaborate costumes and great knowledge of English history.

Modern-day Beefeaters educate tourists of all ages with their vast knowledge of English history.

In closing, let me tell you about one more thing that Henry VII did to help keep peace in England. He made the royal emblem of the House of Tudor a *two*-color rose. He made it both red *and* white to symbolize the new union. You will learn later in this volume that the House of Tudor, with its red and white rose emblem, gave England some of its most famous and infamous kings and queens.

## Lesson 2 — 1464

# Cosimo de' Medici and the Rise of the Italian Renaissance

The rise of the Renaissance in Italy just can't be understood without knowing about **Cosimo de' Medici** (KO zee mo deh Meh DEE chee *or* MEH de chee). Cosimo was considered the "Father of His Country," but many in his family were famous. Cosimo's grandson was nicknamed "the Magnificent"; three Medici men became popes; and two Medici women became queens in France. That's not bad for one family! Though eventually I will tell you more about all of them, today we will look at just Cosimo and a few of his close friends. With money, ideas, and talent, Cosimo and his friends were *all* influential in ushering in the time period known as the **Renaissance**.

Italy, just so you know, was not yet a unified country in the 1400s. It was divided into city/states that were usually ruled by rich, powerful families rather than by kings. **Florence** was one of these city/states, and it was the home of the Medici family. The Medicis were bankers. Through wealth and power, they ruled Florence for nearly three centuries.

As for Cosimo, he was the second Medici to rule Florence. Cosimo was not only rich and powerful, he was brilliant and *loved* to learn. He particularly enjoyed studying ancient texts written by the Greeks and Romans. Because he was rich, Cosimo could afford to buy these texts from scholars who had escaped Constantinople after it was overrun by the Turks.

Plato, an ancient Greek philosopher, lived about 400 years before Christ.

Being not far from Greece, scholars in Constantinople had for centuries preserved ancient Greek manuscripts. I'm talking about books written by ancient Greek philosophers like **Plato** and **Aristotle**. Do you remember them from your past studies? Cosimo spent a fortune collecting and reprinting their old books and other classics. He invested in thousands of books written in Latin as well as in Greek. Cosimo was generous enough to share these rare books with the scholars of Italy. In fact, just to ensure that others had access to the writings of Plato, Cosimo started the first **Platonic Academy** in 1445.

The men who studied these old classic texts in their original languages were labeled **"humanists."** They were called this for studying *umanita* (ooh ma NEE ta), or "the humanities." A humanist, as the name implies, favors the study of mankind. Some humanists of old *so* favored the study of mankind that they left God out. Others didn't and tried hard to integrate their faith with Greek philosophy. Either way, *most* humanists of the Renaissance promoted the greatness of mankind above all else. This greatness was particularly noticeable in the achievements of the Renaissance.

## *Brunelleschi the Architect*

What were mankind's achievements during the Renaissance? They were too numerous to describe here. But I will tell you about four of Cosimo's friends who achieved a great deal. The first was **Filippo Brunelleschi** (Fuh LEE po Broo nayl LAYS kee). Brunelleschi was an architect. (That means he designed buildings.) It seems that he, like other Renaissance architects, didn't care at all for the Gothic style of building that had once been popular across Europe. They thought Gothic cathedrals like Notre-Dame were a bit "overdone" with all their dainty detail, flying buttresses, and pointy spires. For inspiration, Brunelleschi looked instead to the bold, columned structures of the

Gothic architecture was intricately designed to rise and climb so that it might draw one's attention toward heaven.

ancient Greeks and Romans. Are you beginning to see why Brunelleschi and Cosimo were great friends? They both admired ancient Greek and Roman works.

For a time, Brunelleschi moved to Rome to observe the old ruins there. From that experience, he was inspired to build his most famous work, the **dome of Santa Maria del Fiore** in Florence. (This cathedral dome is more commonly known as the Dome of Florence.) A story is told of Brunelleschi that to get hired to build the dome, he challenged other architects to make an egg stand on its end. None of them could do it. Brunelleschi bragged that he could. He then broke an egg, took the empty blunt end of it in his hand, and successfully stood it on a table. The other architects argued that Brunelleschi cheated, but his cleverness got him the job. He was hired to build the great dome — though it was, of course, far more difficult than getting an egg to stand on its end!

This replica of the Parthenon is in Nashville, Tennessee, and testifies to the bold, classic look that inspired Renaissance architects.

It took Brunelleschi 14 years to build the Dome of Florence. Few to this day stand more perfectly. So marvelous is this dome that not even Michelangelo wanted to compete with it. When he was asked to build a similar dome at the Vatican, Michelangelo protested that he would make one larger but *not* more beautiful.

## *Donatello the Sculptor*

Another of Cosimo's close friends was **Donatello** (Dahn uh TELL oh). He was a sculptor. And just like Cosimo and Brunelleschi, Donatello liked to study ancient works for inspiration. What better masters to study than — you know who — the ancient Greeks and Romans. In fact, Donatello traveled to Rome along with Brunelleschi to be inspired by the classical ruins there. Donatello copied the graceful, flowing look of ancient Greek sculpture but improved upon it with his knowledge of anatomy. (Anatomy is the study of the human body.) Donatello used anatomy to make his figures look even *more* lifelike than the Greeks did.

There is a humorous story about just how lifelike Donatello's work could be. It seems that one of Donatello's "not-so-attractive" customers ordered a statue of himself, but upon seeing the completed work, was insulted at how ugly it was. The customer didn't want to admit that he was unattractive, so rather than fuss about the statue's ugliness, he complained that it was too expensive. When Donatello found out, he smashed the sculpture into a thousand pieces! Seems to me they both lost on that deal.

Eventually, Donatello left Rome and moved back to Florence. Cosimo had endless money to sponsor projects for Donatello and Donatello had endless talent to complete them. His work spread all over Florence. His best works include the statue *St. George*, the *Equestrian Statue of Gattamelata* (which is a man on horseback), and the bronze statue *David*. It is the statue of David that Donatello is probably most famous for, though Michelangelo would later outdo him.

It has been said that Cosimo took such good care of his friend Donatello that Donatello had no real need for money. Because of this, Donatello kept his money hanging in a basket in his studio. He insisted that his friends help themselves to his money *whenever* they needed it — without asking! Donatello and Cosimo were such good friends that before Donatello died, he asked to be buried next to Cosimo. The two lie side by side at the church of San Lorenzo.

## *Religious Art of the Renaissance*

Before I introduce you to two more friends of Cosimo de' Medici, I want to stop and explain something about art in the Renaissance. Although Cosimo was influencing the *scholars* of his time toward Greek philosophy and humanism, *artists* of the same time period were s-l-o-w to reflect humanism. Why? Well, most artists were being paid by the church to make religious scenes about God.

You see, the churches of the Renaissance weren't designed just to gather worshipers. The buildings themselves were designed to teach. Doors, arches, and ceilings — indeed, all parts of the church — were decorated to tell the stories of the Bible. Paintings, sculptures, and reliefs (which are one-sided sculptures) were carefully conceived to inspire the masses. For example, it took an artist named **Ghiberti** (Gee BEARR tee) 48 years to carve a bronze relief for the doors of a baptistery! It contained 38 panels of Bible stories from both the Old and the New Testament. Young people, old people, smart people, even those who couldn't read — all could learn from seeing the works of the artists.

Now, if the artists of the early Renaissance were Christians, or humanists, or a little of both, most of their work *was* very religious because of the role of the church. Does that make sense? It should. I'll bring this topic up again later because we will see changes in this religious theme in art.

## *Fra Angelico and Fra Filippo Lippi*

Now that I've explained the *reason* for religious art in the Renaissance, I have examples of two artists who painted the same scenes of the Bible — but for very different reasons. Both artists were monks, but one seemed to sincerely paint for the glory of God and the other didn't.

Let's start with the sincere one. His nickname was **Fra Angelico** (Frah An JELL ih ko), which means "Angelic Brother." As his name implies, he was a gentle, peaceful, humble man. Fra Angelico is said to have "painted in much the same mood in which he prayed, and he never painted without praying first."[2] No wonder he was nicknamed an angel.

I think you would agree, when you see samples of Fra Angelico's work, that it is inspiring. His work is delicate, gentle, and lovely in every detail. Though he was invited to live the comfortable life of an archbishop, Fra Angelico chose to remain a simple Dominican monk. He spent most of his life painting stories of the Bible in the monasteries where he lived. In every

In *The Annunciation* by Fra Angelico, the arches and columns are smaller in the background than in the foreground. Fra Angelico used this form of "perspective" to create rich depth.

situation, Fra Angelico painted his favorite scenes of Mary, Christ, the Crucifixion, and the Transfiguration.

One of the most inspiring of Fra Angelico's paintings was made for Cosimo, who from time to time retreated to a monastery for rest. On the walls of Cosimo's small room, Fra Angelico painted the *Crucifixion* and the *Adoration of the Kings*. We may never know how Fra Angelico touched others with the story of the Gospel, but it seemed to be his intent. Because of his strong faith, Fra Angelico is considered the last of the great medieval artists.

In contrast, there was the other monk. His name was **Fra Filippo Lippi** (Frah Feh LEE po LIP pee). Now I don't mean to be judgmental, but he was hardly the angel that Fra Angelico was. Though his work was excellent, and in fact beautiful, Filippo Lippi seemed much more enamored with this present world than with eternity. Like Fra Angelico, he enjoyed painting numerous scenes of Mary — but it was probably because he enjoyed the pretty ladies who modeled for him! Filippo had a bad reputation for mingling with nuns and even took one to be a girlfriend. For his misconduct, Filippo had to leave his monastery, but he did keep the title of a monk for the rest of his life.

A story is told that Cosimo once locked up his friend Filippo to help keep his mind off women and on to finishing an art project. But Filippo tied sheets together from his bed and snuck out the window to visit a young lady or two. Cosimo pardoned Filippo's poor behavior and promised never to lock him up again. The church apparently pardoned the artist, too, because priests, nuns, and bishops continued to hire Filippo Lippi for his great ability to paint.

### *Pater Patriae, Father of His Country*

As for Cosimo de' Medici, his last years were tranquil ones (that means "peaceful"). When in the quiet countryside of Italy, he enjoyed his old books and close friends. When in the busy city, he enjoyed his vast collection of art and antiquities. His rule over Florence had been a good one. He raised the standard of the middle class and when he died in **1464**, both the rich and the poor grieved over his death.

Cosimo was so greatly appreciated for all he had done for Italy that he was given the title **Pater Patriae**, which means **"Father of His Country."** Indeed he was, because of his great influence. And in an unusual way, Cosimo's passion to buy and sell "old things" is still honored today. Pawn dealers (those who buy and sell used items) often display three decorative balls on their signs and in their advertisements. These three balls are an adaptation of the numerous balls on the Medici coat of arms! Check it out for yourself. I love it when history shows up in unexpected places.

## Lesson 3 — 1469

# *Ferdinand, Isabella, and the Spanish Inquisition*

You might have heard of **Ferdinand and Isabella**. They are the royal couple who sponsored Christopher Columbus on his famous voyage to the New World. We're going to look at that important event soon. But Ferdinand and Isabella are well known for something else. Unfortunately, they are also the ones who started the **Spanish Inquisition**. This was a dreadful court created to weed heretics out of the church. (I'll explain what "heretic" means later.) Sadly enough, the Inquisition grew to be one of the cruelest institutions ever set up by man. Let me explain how it came to be.

At this time in history, Spain was divided into a handful of kingdoms — each ruled by its own royal family. Ferdinand was the prince of the kingdom of **Aragon**. Isabella was the princess of the kingdom of **Castile**. She was strong and devout in her faith. She never missed Mass or the celebration of holy days recognized by the Medieval Church.

Well, the Spanish kingdoms of Aragon and Castile were destined to merge into one. Can you guess how? Young Ferdinand and Isabella got married. They were only teenagers, but their marriage in **1469** brought together the two largest kingdoms of Spain. The wedding was a grand event that lasted six days and nights. Though their marriage was political and arranged, the teenagers seemed to genuinely care for one another. As a token of his love, Ferdinand gave Isabella a beautiful pearl and ruby necklace that had once belonged to his mother. The newlyweds grew older and within 10 years inherited the titles of king and queen of their kingdoms. They had much to accomplish in holding their union together.

Isabella is shown here wearing the pearl and ruby necklace given to her as a gift by Ferdinand. The necklace had belonged to his mother.

## The Reconquista

Even before the marriage of Ferdinand and Isabella, the kingdoms of Spain were rich and advanced. During the Middle Ages, Spain was, in fact, in its Golden Age. It attracted merchants, scholars, and inventors from all over the world. For its prosperity, Spain was nicknamed "the Ornament of the World." Spain was also heavily populated with Muslims, Christians, and Jews. (It is important to remember that!) It was during the *later* Middle Ages that Christians began to drive Muslims to the south of Spain during what was called the ***reconquista*** (rrray kon KEE sta). That word means to "reconquer," which is what the Christians believed they were doing. They believed they were *reconquering* Spain in the name of Christ.

Under Ferdinand and Isabella, this concept of reconquering Spain was taken to the extreme. To raise money for fighting the Muslims, Isabella sold her special pearl and ruby necklace! Then, the royal couple took it upon themselves to drive out of Spain *anyone* they believed was opposed to Christianity — particularly anyone who was Jewish. They did this by instituting the Spanish Inquisition.

The Spanish Inquisition was not really a "thing." Rather, it was a process. It was the process of putting someone on trial in a court. The name Inquisition comes from the word *inquire*, which means "to ask." The court "asked" questions of people on trial to prove their guilt or innocence in crimes against the church.

The idea of the church placing people on trial goes back to the 300s. That is when the Roman Empire was "Christianized" by Constantine. Though Constantine freed Christians from persecution through the **Edict of Milan**, he — as a downfall — shifted much of the *authority* of the Roman government to the church. That is how and when the church first became involved in running trials. Jesus didn't teach that the church should do such a thing, but it seemed to make sense to the Romans. They continued to use the church as a means to run civil matters long after the collapse of the Roman Empire.

I hope you can grasp that difficult concept about the church because I think it is important to understand. (You may even want to reread the last paragraph.) Some would say that the Medieval Church was in error for becoming so political. I would agree. But that's another topic.

## *Torquemada and the Dominicans*

As for the *Spanish* Inquisition, this particular court system was patterned after one started in the 1300s by the **Dominicans**, a religious order founded by St. Dominic in the Middle Ages. I believe the early intentions of the Dominicans were good. They would claim that they were trying to protect the church from falsehood. Banners of the Inquisition carried the words "Mercy and Justice" to describe the court process. However, in promoting justice, the Dominicans got carried away. They used harsh measures to try to turn the hearts of heretics. A heretic was someone who disagreed with the teachings of the church.

Ferdinand and Isabella got carried away in the whole process of turning the hearts of heretics. They placed their court in the cruel hands of **Tomás de Torquemada** (Toe MAS day Tawr kay MAH dah). Torquemada was Isabella's strict childhood priest. He was a Dominican friar who thought nothing was wrong with actually *torturing* people to make them confess sins against the church! A common torture device was the rack, which stretched and pulled the arms and legs of the supposed heretic.

On his behalf, some would say that Torquemada believed he was saving souls from *eternal* punishment by punishing them here on earth. Perhaps he was hoping to soften hardened hearts. Perhaps he cared so much for the souls of the lost that he would do anything for their salvation. I don't know his exact thoughts.

Regardless of one's opinion of Torquemada, here is an account of what occurred under his leadership as the head inquisitor in Spain. Between 1478 and 1483, the Spanish Inquisition was most often directed at Jews who *claimed* to have converted to Christianity — but didn't. Apparently it was common for Jews in Spain to do this. To avoid persecution, they claimed to be Christians but secretly practiced their Jewish faith. For supposedly converting, they were called *conversos*.

During the Spanish Inquisition, these "secret" Jews were arrested, put on trial, and sometimes put to death. The World Book Encyclopedia states that at least 2,000 people were put to death during the 18 years that Torquemada was head inquisitor.[3] Other sources state that as many as 32,000 perished through the system and that perhaps as many as 341,000 people were punished![4] We may never know the exact number who suffered, but most who died were strangled to death and then burned. The dirty work was performed by soldiers rather than by the inquisitors themselves. This might explain why the inquisitors grew callous toward the killings and ordered so many. They literally kept their own hands clean of the bloodshed.

In 1492, Ferdinand and Isabella made persecution even more official when they signed the **Edict of Expulsion**. This edict forced Jews to leave Spain within three months if not willing to be baptized. As a result, as many as 800,000 Jews fled Spain! They took with them their businesses, their skills, their books, and their families. Some historians believe it was a great loss to Spain. But who could blame the Jews for fleeing? This was the largest mass exodus of the Jews in Europe before the Holocaust under Adolf Hitler. The last date that most Jews left the country was August 2, 1492.

In knowing all of this, perhaps you can understand why I would call the Spanish Inquisition one of the cruelest institutions of mankind. I don't believe Jesus ever intended for Christianity to be promoted through torture or execution. But unfortunately, the Inquisition, in one form or another, continued across Europe for centuries.

The royal flag of Spain used under Ferdinand and Isabella, and carried by Christopher Columbus, reflects the previous union of the kingdoms of Castile ("castle") and León ("lion") in 1230.

As for Ferdinand and Isabella, they continued to rule Aragon and Castile to form the nation of Spain. Their daughter would grow up to make history by marrying Henry VIII of England. Their granddaughter would grow up to be nicknamed "Bloody Mary." (These are interesting stories to come!) Other than their harsh treatment of supposed heretics, Ferdinand and Isabella ruled wisely and had great vision for the future. That fact is probably why they are more "kindly" remembered as the king and queen who sponsored Christopher Columbus. But we'll get to that later.

# WEEK 2

## Lesson 4 1480

# *Ivan the Great*

There have been a lot of "greats" in history. Can you think of some? How about Ramses *the Great*, Alexander *the Great*, Herod *the Great*, or Alfred *the Great*? Those are just a few. Today we will add another "great" to our studies. He is **Ivan the Great** of Russia (also known as Ivan III). Let me tell you how he earned his "great" nickname.

When Ivan III was a child, Russia wasn't yet its own country. It was under the rule of outsiders called the **Tatar Mongols**. The Tatar Mongols were a ravaging group of warriors from Mongolia. They were descendants of the "great and terrible" **Genghis Khan** (GING gus Kawn) who was rumored to have eaten his captives! To say the least, the Tatar Mongols were feared. Well, it was the *grandson* of Genghis Khan who first claimed Russian lands for the Mongols. His name was **Batu Khan** (Bah TOO Kawn) and his army was the **Golden Horde**, named for their gold-colored tents that glistened in the sun along the Volga River.

The Tatar Mongols were descendants of Genghis Khan who, in the 1200s, ravaged large portions of Asia.

Now, at the time of our story, though Russians were ruled by the Tatar Mongols, they had a prince of their own. His name was Ivan, the main character of our lesson today. Ivan was actually the prince of Muscovy, which is a region in Russia that includes Moscow. Ivan was not the least bit impressed with the Golden Horde and desperately wanted to free Russia from their harsh rule. It was expected that someone, someday would revolt against the Mongols. They had been there for 240 years! Being that Ivan was nicknamed the Great, you may be guessing already that he was the one who freed Russia. And you're right — he was.

But before we get into that, let me back up to something very significant in Ivan's personal life. You see, before Ivan freed Russia from the Mongols, he did something that gained him more power. He married a very important girl. Her name was **Sophia**, and she was the niece of the last Byzantine emperor. Why was she important? Let me stop and explain the Byzantine Empire all over again for you to understand.

### *The Eastern Orthodox Church of the Byzantine Empire*

During the Middle Ages, the Byzantine Empire was actually the *Eastern* Roman Empire. This empire separated from the Western Roman Empire *and* the Western Roman Church.

In doing so, the Byzantine Empire created its own church, the *Eastern Orthodox Church*. Though different from the Western Church in many ways, the Eastern Orthodox Church did something just like the West. It blended the power of the church and state. The leader of one was the leader of the other. We just discussed that issue in our last lesson. Though Jesus never taught this model for the church, it existed.

The picturesque domes on top of most Eastern and Russian Orthodox churches are a clear example of Byzantine style passed down through the ages.

Now, this is where Sophia became so important. When the Byzantine Empire collapsed at the close of the Middle Ages, Sophia was one of the last royal members still alive from the former empire. Her uncle, the last Byzantine emperor, was killed in battle. With his death, Sophia inherited the remaining power of her uncle, which *included* the power of the Eastern Orthodox Church! Did you follow that? The leadership of the church rested in the hands of Sophia. So, when Ivan married Sophia in 1472, the leadership of the church shifted to him. The marriage was very important.

With this marriage, Ivan appointed himself "the protector" of the Eastern Orthodox Church. Whether or not he was a sincere follower of Christ, I do not know. But I do know that Ivan took his role in the church very seriously. As the protector of the church, he took on the attitude of a crusader, aiming to take back ancient Russian lands from the Mongols, who were Muslim. Ivan also fought off Polish armies that were creeping in from the west. Ivan III had the vision of creating a free Russia — free from outside rule.

In 1453, the Christian city of Constantinople was conquered by the Ottoman Turks. In 1930, it was officially renamed Istanbul.

And it happened. With the fall of Constantinople and the marriage of Ivan to Sophia, Russians began to see themselves as *the New Rome*. They claimed to be the "third" great Rome. Why the third Rome? Well, they thought the "first" Rome was the ancient Roman Empire. They thought the "second" Rome was the Byzantine Empire. That made them the "third" Rome. A Russian historian put it this way: "The Church of Old Rome fell because of its heresy; the gates of the Second Rome, Constantinople, have been hewn down by the axes of the infidel Turks; but the Church of Moscow, the Church of the New Rome, shines brighter than the Sun in the whole Universe . . . Two Romes have fallen, but the Third stands fast; a fourth there cannot be."[1]

This is the proud Russia that Ivan began to lead. It was a new Russia seeing herself as Rome come back to life. Ivan put it this way: "By God's grace we have been lords in our land since the beginning of time, since the days of our earliest ancestors. God has elevated us to the same positions which they held, and we beg him to grant it to us and our children."[2] Right or wrong, Ivan carried what he believed to be his "God-given" power very effectively.

## *Ivan's Success*

As for tackling the Mongols, Ivan started his conquest in **1480** by *refusing* to pay tribute (meaning tax money) to the Golden Horde. Sophia agreed with him on this bold move. Surprisingly, the Mongols didn't bother to wage war over this insult. Ivan then took the city of **Novgorod** (NAHV gah rod), which had been held by the Mongols. Through these bold acts and many more, Ivan shook Russia free of the Mongols. He began to call himself the ruler of *all* Russians, not just those of Muscovy. He revised a code of laws for Russia, moved his capital to Moscow, and had buildings in the **Kremlin** rebuilt in his honor.

The Kremlin is a magnificent fortress containing palaces and cathedrals. Parts of it had been damaged by fire. Do you want to guess what kind of architects Ivan invited to rebuild the palaces? They were Italian architects — the ones who were bringing back the classic style of the Greeks and the Romans. The fit couldn't have been more perfect since Ivan saw himself as a successor of the Romans through his Byzantine bride.

During the Renaissance, the Kremlin in Moscow was beautified by Italian architects. At dusk, it is a breathtaking sight.

In fact, Ivan behaved a lot like a Byzantine emperor. He made his seal that of the Byzantine double-headed eagle, which looks east and west to guard both Europe and Asia. He also dressed in Byzantine garb. In fact, up to 1894, all Russian tsars (zarz) were crowned with a Byzantine-style cap and clothed with a jacket of Byzantine design — all from Ivan's influence. The term **tsar** even comes from ancient Rome as a derivative of the name *Caesar*.

### *Feudalism in Russia*

Of course, oftentimes bad comes along with good. It seems that in Ivan's zeal to lead Russia, he abandoned the counsel of the nobility. That means he no longer asked his governors for advice. In fact, he greatly *lessened* the power of the nobility by creating another class of landowners. He gave power and land to those who would work for him in *military* service. As a result, Ivan basically started **feudalism** in Russia.

You may be familiar with feudalism from studying the Middle Ages. Under this system, peasants or serfs "work" for their lords or landowners in exchange for food and shelter. In Russia, the work of the serfs appeared more like slavery. Landowners became so powerful that they collected taxes from their own serfs and bought and traded their peasants as if they were property. It was nearly impossible for the poor to ever get out of debt. This harsh economic system lasted for hundreds of years. It wasn't until 1861 that serfdom in Russia came to an end!

And so, the poor working class of Russia grew. While Western Europe had left the Dark Ages, Russia seemed to be entering it. The results of feudalism would haunt Russia for centuries to come. Some say they still do because Russia has a rather large, poor working class today. And, burned deep into Russian minds, was the idea of an *absolute ruler* as started by Ivan the Great.

Truly great or not, Ivan III died in 1505. We are done with our study of him for now, but we are not done with Russia. We will look at her history again when I introduce you to Ivan the Great's grandson. His nickname was "the Terrible"! As you will learn, it was terribly fitting!

## Lesson 5 — 1487, 1497

# *Dias and da Gama Round the Cape of Good Hope*

**Note to Teacher:** *Students may follow this lesson more easily with a globe or atlas at their fingertips.*

It would take a brave soul in the 1400s to board a rickety wooden ship and sail into the deep unknown. Some people back then still believed the earth was flat. And so sailing out to sea toward the distant horizon might mean falling off the edge of the world. If that weren't frightening enough, there were rumors of giant sea monsters, bottomless whirlpools, and boiling oceans to scare away the timid. Sailors knew they risked their lives to fight storms, sickness, shipwrecks, and starvation. It's a wonder that *anyone* attempted to explore the world by sea. But of course, some did and their names and stories have survived. Today we will learn of two of the more daring explorers of the late 1400s. They were **Bartolomeu Dias** (Bar TOLL a mew DEE us) and **Vasco da Gama** (VAS koh duh GA muh). Both were from **Portugal**, a country on the west coast of Spain.

To appreciate the stories of Dias and da Gama, you have to know what happened to the Portuguese explorers *before* them. For 12 years, explorers tried to sail from Portugal all the way down the coast of Africa and around its southernmost tip (the tip is also called a "cape"). Fourteen different expeditions tried and failed! Not one made it even *halfway* down the coast for fear that the sun at the equator would boil them alive or that monsters would consume them from the "Green Sea of Darkness" (as the Atlantic Ocean was called). Now before I jump into the success of Dias and da Gama, let me explain why the Portuguese were so *eager* to get around the southern tip of Africa. There were three good reasons.

## *Why Round the Cape?*

*First,* the Portuguese wanted to sail around Africa because they were looking for trade routes. You see, when Constantinople fell to the Turks in 1453, it closed a doorway of trade between Europe and Asia. The Europeans were quite upset about this. They had begun to enjoy many things from the East, such as spices, silks, rubies, and pearls. Spices were important because there was no refrigeration back then. Meat was heavily salted to keep it fresh. Spices made meat taste much better, and it helped hide the odor of spoiled food. Pepper was especially valued for its strong flavor and was almost as valuable as gold. With trade routes closed in Constantinople, Europeans wanted to create new ones. It seemed only logical to the Portuguese that if their sailors could get *around* Africa, they could surely reach India and its eastern neighbors where spices and treasure were plentiful.

But there is a *second* reason why some Portuguese wanted to reach the East by sailing around Africa. Many of the Christians of Portugal believed it their duty to share the Gospel of Jesus Christ with others around the world. At least that was the case with **Prince Henry the Navigator**. Henry was the son of the king of Portugal. He was devout in his faith and part of a religious group called the **Order of Christ**. Members of the Order of Christ saw themselves much like the crusading knights of the Middle Ages. They feared the spread of Islam and sought to convert Muslims. They abhorred, or hated, the idea of taking slaves, which was common practice among other traders of the sea. Their interest in exploration had to do with spreading Christianity.

Henry the Navigator was the son of the king of Portugal and a member of the Order of Christ.

Prince Henry the Navigator was so dedicated to exploration that he invested in it personally. Though he seldom left the shores of Portugal, he made sure that the crews who did were well trained. Henry joined the smartest astronomers, shipbuilders, and cartographers (which are mapmakers) to make Portugal the leader of exploration in Europe.

Though more unusual, there is a *third* reason why Henry and others were drawn toward sailing around Africa. Some were trying to find the whereabouts of a mysterious Christian king named **Prester John**. Prester John, which could be translated as John "the priest," supposedly owned kingdoms somewhere in India or Ethiopia, Africa. It was believed that Prester John sent a letter to the West asking for help because he was being overrun by barbarians. This vague but intriguing letter was translated into several languages and circulated across Europe. In the process, the stories of Prester John grew to be more and more fanciful. Some believed that the priest king was rich and a descendant of the magi who presented the Christ child with gifts! Others claimed that he had the treasures of Solomon's Temple. Many wondered if he existed at all. Nonetheless, searching for Prester John was one more exciting reason to sail around the southern tip of Africa.

## *The Success of Dias*

As for Bartolomeu Dias, I'm not sure what his motivation was for exploring. But in **1487**, he was asked to sail around the cape of Africa by **King John II of Portugal**. The king paid for the trip, which included three of the finest ships of that day. Each ship was a *caravel*, which is a sturdy sea vessel made especially easy to maneuver because of its square- and triangular-shaped sails. The latter are called *lateens*.

Dias's first success was that he sailed farther south than Cape Bojador near the Canary Islands. Because of fear, that is where the last 14 expeditions had stopped. But not Dias. He and his men bravely sailed down the coast of Africa, keeping their eyes carefully fixed on land. To their amazement, there were no bottomless whirlpools to engulf them. There were no sea monsters to eat them. And the oceans weren't boiling at the equator as had been believed. Relieved and excited, they continued their way down south.

However, near the tip of Africa, a terrible storm overcame Bartolomeu Dias and his men. For two weeks it pelted and tossed and tormented them. So great were the winds that they blew Dias and all three of his ships far out into the ocean and slung them *around* the tip of Africa without their ever seeing land! Thrilled with their survival, Dias wanted to sail farther. He wanted to venture up the east coast of Africa and into the Indian Ocean. But his men weren't so thrilled. They staged a sit-down strike, demanding that Dias turn the ships toward home. The courage of the crew had run out.

Without a crew to lead, Bartolomeu Dias gave in to his men and turned back for Portugal. But this time, he maneuvered the ships close enough to the shore that he and his men could see with their own eyes the southern cape of the huge continent of Africa. For all they had been through, Dias named it *Cabo Tormentoso* (KAH bo Tor men TOE so), meaning **"Cape of Storms."**

## The Cape of Good Hope and Vasco da Gama

To reach India for spices and treasures, Vasco da Gama sailed all the way around the Cape of Good Hope from Portugal.

Soon after the return of Bartolomeu Dias, King John of Portugal renamed the southern tip of Africa the **Cape of Good Hope**. He thought the name was more inviting and would inspire others to return. His idea worked. Ten years later, the Cape of Good Hope lured another brave explorer to try the difficult journey. He was Vasco da Gama.

By this time Portugal had another king, **Manuel I**. He was as eager as any other king to find a successful route to the East. In **1497**, he commissioned Vasco da Gama for the job. Do you want to guess who Vasco invited to go along? It was Bartolomeu Dias, of course. It only made sense that Dias help out the new team. But for unknown reasons, Dias made only part of the journey. Upon reaching Cape Verde on the west coast of Africa, Dias returned to Portugal while da Gama continued south.

Da Gama had four ships and a crew of 170. Most of the men were former convicts. (That means they had been in jail.) Though accused of corruption, these men were tough and proved to be quite brave. To reach the cape faster, they dared to sail far into the Atlantic Ocean where they couldn't see the coastline of Africa at all. They did so to catch stronger winds that could whip them around the cape. Their plan worked! When they reached the Cape of Good Hope, they kept their momentum and kept sailing where no Portuguese had sailed before. They ventured up the east coast of Africa and headed into the Indian Ocean. With the help of a native guide, they crossed the Indian Ocean and arrived on the shoreline of India at the city of **Calicut**.

The trip had not been easy. At least 100 of da Gama's sailors suffered from **scurvy** — a disease brought on by not getting enough vitamin C in fresh food. (Fresh food is hard to keep on long sea voyages.) In fact, so many men died of scurvy that Vasco had to burn one of his four ships. There simply weren't enough men to steer all four.

Knowing this, you can only imagine the thrill of finally setting foot on the beach of India. The tired crew of former convicts had been at sea for 10 months with only a few stops in Africa.

But unfortunately, their elation didn't last long. They weren't the least bit welcome in India. Arabs had control of the trade industry there. They were threatened by the Europeans and made it impossible for them to stay. After three months, da Gama and his men headed for home with only a few spices as their reward.

Nonetheless, back in Portugal, da Gama and his band of sea-weary sailors were greeted like war heroes. Da Gama was named *Admiral of the Sea of the Indies.* For 20 years, he served as an adviser to the king. Now, you might think that this is the end of the story of Vasco da Gama, but it's not. I've a little more to tell you.

In 1503, Vasco da Gama returned to India by once again sailing around the Cape of Good Hope. This time, he went prepared to fight the Arabs because he was determined to open up a trade route. Like pirates, da Gama and his men blasted their way through the harbor at Calicut, demanding to be received. In a cruel frenzy, da Gama sank an Arab ship holding 300 Muslim pilgrims journeying toward Mecca. This unnecessary violence gave da Gama the victory he wished for. His demands were heard, and trade routes were again opened between the East and the West.

Now you may be wondering whatever happened to Bartolomeu Dias. Well, sadly enough, in 1500 he was shipwrecked and drowned on a return trip to the Cape of Good Hope. As for Vasco da Gama, he died in 1524 in India, where he was living as viceroy for the king of Portugal. (That means he was the king's representative.) I find it interesting that both explorers died at the places where they had become famous. Had they a choice in the matter, I wonder if that's exactly what they would have wanted.

## Lesson 6 — 1492

# *Lorenzo the Magnificent*

Of all the Medici who were famous during the Renaissance, only one was called "the Magnificent." It was **Lorenzo de' Medici**, the grandson of Cosimo. I hope you remember Cosimo de' Medici, the wealthy patron of classical art and literature. Well, as you might expect, Lorenzo was just like his grandfather. He also loved the classics and deeply appreciated the arts. Lorenzo was equally passionate for music and poetry. Everything about him reflected his cultural interests and genuine charm, which I'm sure is why he was called "the Magnificent."

In his youth, Lorenzo studied Greek and philosophy. At age 19, he won first place in a war tournament. The French phrase *Le Temps Revient* (Leh TAW Reh VYEH) was etched on his armor. It means "The Age Returns." Do you know what "age" was "returning"? It was the *Golden Age* of classic Greece and Rome. Like his grandfather, Lorenzo helped usher in the "Renaissance," or the "rebirth" of Greek and Roman thought.

## Vivano le palle!

It wasn't easy for Lorenzo to follow in the footsteps of his grandfather. Though he was tall and strong, Lorenzo had a few serious enemies. His main enemies were members of a rival family of bankers and an archbishop of the church. Though *most* of Florence welcomed Lorenzo and his brother as leaders, his enemies didn't. These enemies plotted an assassination (meaning murder) of the Medici brothers on Easter morning in 1478. However, things didn't exactly go as planned.

The awful plan was that both Lorenzo and his brother would be killed during a Sunday morning church service. In the middle of worship, Lorenzo's brother never saw his attacker coming. He was stabbed in the chest, fell to the ground, and was struck again and again by his attacker, who was one of the bankers! Lorenzo, however, was far more fortunate and received only a cut in the attack. His friends quickly surrounded him and led him safely out of the church. You can only imagine the riot that broke loose after that!

The archbishop used this opportunity to try to rouse the crowd *against* the Medici family. "Freedom!" he yelled, wishing Florence were free of the Medicis.[3] But in shock from the murder that so many had witnessed, the crowd chanted in *favor* of the one Medici who escaped. (That was Lorenzo, of course.) They shouted, "*Vivano le palle!*" meaning "Long live the balls!" — the symbol on the coat of arms of the Medici family.[4]

Having spoken in favor of Lorenzo, the rioting crowd moved quickly against the murderers. One banker and the archbishop were captured and hung. The other banker was stripped naked and drawn by horses through the streets! Others were pushed out of windows to meet the stone-cold pavement below. By their riotous actions, the masses made it clear that they were devoted to Lorenzo.

Tall, strong, and passionate toward the arts, Lorenzo de' Medici helped usher in the Renaissance in Italy.

When **Pope Sixtus IV** of Rome heard about the hanging of the archbishop, he was furious. The pope excommunicated (meaning banished) Lorenzo from the church and punished the city of Florence! If this weren't harsh enough, the pope waged war against Florence with the help of Ferrante I, the king of **Naples**. (Naples was another city/state in Italy, south of Rome.)

Well, if this story isn't interesting enough, it's about to get more interesting. In response to this crisis, Lorenzo did something very unusual — but very brave. Without weapons or a bodyguard, Lorenzo went to Naples to talk face-to-face with King Ferrante, the very king who had declared war against him with the help of the pope.

King Ferrante would never have expected a friendly visit from Lorenzo. He could have had Lorenzo killed on the spot. But King Ferrante was intrigued with Lorenzo's courage in coming to talk to him, and so he gave Lorenzo a chance to explain his predicament with the pope and the citizens of Florence. Lorenzo's good character, charm, and intelligence must have impressed the king because for three months, Lorenzo stayed there in Naples. He wasn't there as a prisoner of war but rather as an honored guest! The king and Lorenzo grew to have great respect for one another, and so the "war" between them was canceled. Yes, canceled! Pope Sixtus eventually gave up on his "war" against Florence, too. Lorenzo returned to his home as the uncontested ruler of Florence, free from war with Naples or Rome.

## *Lorenzo the Politician*

During his lifetime, Lorenzo continued to show wisdom when it came to politics. He selected a council of 70 men to help him run the affairs of Florence.[5] And they did so very well. Under the **Council of Seventy**, crime went down and prosperity went up. Though Lorenzo had the power and authority of a dictator, he kept his character clean and fair. One Italian put it this way, "If Florence was to have a tyrant, she could never have found a better or more delightful one."[6] Lorenzo kept his good temper at home as well. He had a large family and took good care of them, just as he did the citizens of Florence. Lorenzo was well loved, crooked nose and all.

## *Lorenzo the Poet*

Lorenzo governed Florence with perhaps even more flare than his grandfather. He was a little less of a scholar and more of a socialite than Cosimo had been. Though Lorenzo once claimed he would sell off his furniture for the sake of buying books, he was quick to join every parade, sporting event, and carnival in the city. It was custom in Florence to celebrate historic events through glamorous parades with floats and colorful costumes (much like a Thanksgiving Day parade). Lorenzo so enjoyed these events that he employed special artists and musicians to make them even more spectacular. Lorenzo himself wrote carnival songs to celebrate the frolic and fun. The citizens of Florence loved him for this and performed his songs in the streets.

But Lorenzo's passion for music and poetry ran deeper than carnival songs. In Italian, he wrote love sonnets, nature poems, and sacred hymns. Though not a religious man, Lorenzo wrote biblical plays for his children. Through his many writings, Lorenzo took Italy back to the romantic language of Italian and away from old-fashioned Latin. (Cosimo would have been disappointed in that.) But the masses were fond of their native tongue and found Italian to be one of the most beautiful languages for song. For that reason, opera music is still quite often written in Italian.

## *Lorenzo the Patron*

Like Cosimo, Lorenzo had a strong influence on the artists of Florence. With his great wealth, he, too, shared his collection of Greek and Roman relics to inspire painters, architects, and sculptors. Probably none were more influenced than **Sandro Botticelli** (SAHN dro Bo tih CHEL lee). At a young age, Botticelli proved himself a masterful painter and was soon employed by the Medici family for numerous projects. Naturally, these projects were Greek and Roman looking. Botticelli brought ancient mythology to life through paintings like *Primavera (Spring)*, *Pallas and the Centaur*, and *Venus and Mars*. So graceful are the goddesses in these masterpieces that in viewing them, you can nearly feel the wind that blows their gowns and sweeps the tousles of their hair. In my opinion, they are breathtaking.

Before I get back to Lorenzo, I do want to tell you a little more about Botticelli because he is one of *my* favorite artists of the Renaissance, and his spiritual life is quite interesting. After years of painting mythological scenes for Lorenzo, Botticelli had a change of heart. A powerful preacher by the name of **Savonarola** (Sav uh nah ROLL uh) had something to do with it. Savonarola saw that Florence had become worldly and humanistic under the Medicis. As bold as John the Baptist, Savonarola preached for sinners to repent and seek the kingdom of God. Botticelli listened and responded. He quit painting anything that had to do with mythology and for the rest of his life painted scenes of the Christian faith. His later works include *Madonna of the Pomegranate*, *Annunciation*, and *Mystic Nativity*.

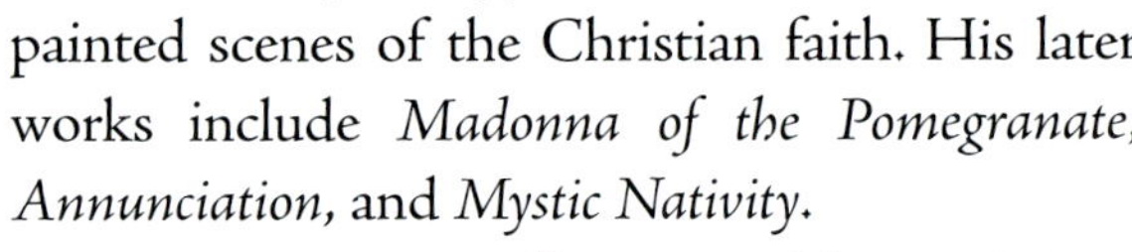

In *Mystic Nativity*, Sandro Botticelli used his talent for portraying movement to paint heavenly dancing angels above the Christ child.

It is especially noticeable in *Mystic Nativity* that Botticelli transformed the wind-swept "goddesses" of his earlier works into heavenly angels dancing above the manger of Jesus. Botticelli also painted scenes to illustrate Dante's *Divine Comedy*, a poem describing heaven and hell. (See Volume II of *The Mystery of History*.) The themes of these works were quite different than those Botticelli once painted for Lorenzo.

## Lorenzo's Death

Since Lorenzo was so well loved, I wish I could write that he lived a long life. But he didn't. At only 43, Lorenzo fell deathly ill. On his deathbed, he called for Savonarola, the fiery preacher of Florence, to hear his final confession of sins and pray over him. On April 9, **1492**, Lorenzo de' Medici died. The entire country grieved at the sudden loss. A famous philosopher said ". . . there had never died in Florence — nor yet in Italy — one for whom his country mourned so much, or who left behind him so wide a reputation for wisdom."[7] Through politics, poetry, and patronage, I believe Lorenzo did do *magnificent* things for Florence.

# WEEK 3

## Lesson 7 — 1492

# Christopher Columbus Sails to an "Other World"

**Note to Teacher:** *Due to the historical significance of Christopher Columbus and the raging debates that exist over him, the content of the next two lessons is lengthier and has more detail than most lessons in Volume III. Please excuse my excessiveness and paraphrase as needed for Younger Students. All students may need more time than usual to adequately cover the next two lessons.*

**Christopher Columbus** is quite famous for navigating the *Niña* (NEEN ya), the *Pinta* (PEEN ta), and the *Santa Maria* to the New World. A well-known rhyme tells us the date of this historic voyage. It says, "In fourteen hundred and ninety-two, Columbus sailed the ocean blue." Though we know a lot about the seafaring journeys of Columbus, his life is full of riddles.

For one, scholars don't agree on the ancestry of Christopher Columbus. (That means we're not sure where he came from.) Second, it's unclear as to exactly *where* Columbus landed on his first voyage across the Atlantic. And third, over the course of his life, his actions would appear to contradict his faith, causing all sorts of problems. With these mysteries to consider, it will take us two lessons to study Christopher Columbus.

### The Heritage of Christopher Columbus

Though it might have been forged (meaning faked), Christopher Columbus wrote in a document that he was born in **Genoa.**[1] Some believe he was referring to the Republic of Genoa in Italy and that he was related to a family of Italian wool weavers. There seems to be a lot of evidence in Genoa to support this, and most history books claim that he was Italian.

However, some scholars believe that Christopher Columbus was Greek, a Spanish Jew, or Portuguese. Those believing he was Portuguese think he might have served as a spy to King John II of Portugal! Isn't that an interesting concept? According to the spy theory, Columbus was actually Portuguese and sent to Spain as a decoy to lure Spanish sailors away from Portuguese trade routes around Africa. Hmmm!

Unfortunately, the name of Christopher Columbus is of no help in solving the riddle of his ancestry because it has been translated into many languages. It might even be that he changed his name while living in Portugal.[2] In original documents, Columbus used the name

Christopher Columbus, as he is traditionally known, was a man of many unsolved mysteries.

Cristóval (Kree STAW ball) Colón (which is most commonly written as **Cristóbal Colón**, with a "b"). Those holding to the spy theory speculate that Cristóbal Colón and Christopher Columbus from Genoa were two different people! Traditional historians disagree.

To add to our confusion, there is no known portrait of Columbus painted in his lifetime. Those that were painted later don't necessarily match his description as a graying blond with a ruddy complexion. So, who exactly was Columbus? His signature won't help us answer this question either. It has perplexed historians for years because it's made up of Greek and Latin letters on four lines in the shape of a pyramid. Who signs their name on four different lines? Columbus did! Why he did so, nobody knows for sure. But the last line, *X po Ferens*, is properly translated "Christ bearer."

A man who admired Columbus, named Bartolomé de Las Casas, wrote this about him: "He was called Cristóbal, which is to say, *Christum Ferens*, which means the bearer of Christ. And it was this way that he often signed his name, for the truth is that he was the first to open the gates of the Ocean Sea in order to bear our Savior Jesus Christ over the waves to those remote realms and lands."[3]

To sum up the controversies thus far, historians don't agree on the heritage of Columbus, his motives for sailing west, his true portrait, or the meaning of his signature. But one thing is certain — in 1492, he crossed the ocean blue! And according to Bartolomé de Las Casas, Columbus was a messenger of Christ. Putting aside all mysteries, let's look now at how this adventure started. And from this point on, I'll refer to Columbus as Cristóbal Colón to be true to the name that *he* used.

## *Enterprise to the Indies*

The plan of Cristóbal Colón, or so it would appear, was to reach the East by sailing west. You already know a few reasons why Europeans were anxious to reach the East. For one, they sought spices and jewels from China, Japan, and India. They also hoped to find gold, the whereabouts of Prester John, and to share the Gospel with other nations. For whatever reason Colón was sailing, he called his adventure his "Enterprise to the Indies."

Cristóbal Colón wasn't the first to come up with the idea of reaching the East by sailing west. Colón was familiar with ancient Greek thought to support the idea; he'd been on the sea since the age of 14; and he knew the minds of other navigators who had tossed the plan about for years. Furthermore, while living in Lisbon, Portugal, he and his brother **Bartholomew** made, studied, and sold maps and books on the subject. It was also in Portugal that Cristóbal was promoted to captain, married a Portuguese noblewoman, and fathered a son named Diego.

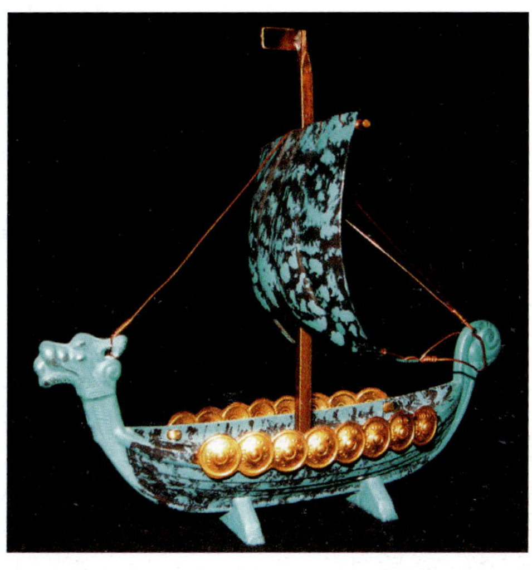

Long before Cristóbal Colón sailed to the New World, the Vikings had made landfall in North America.

To further his research, it's believed that Cristóbal Colón made a trip to Great Britain, Ireland, and Iceland to investigate the stories of other mariners. In particular, he studied the stories of **Leif** (Leaf) **Ericsson**, a Christian Viking nicknamed "Leif the Lucky." Why would he study a Viking? Well, as far back as A.D. 1000, Leif "the Lucky" Ericsson *had* sailed west! What Leif found was North America, but he called it **Vinland**. Though new to the Vikings and Europeans, Vinland wasn't really new at all. North America had been home to native peoples since before the time of Christ! Nonetheless, from a European point of view, the "discovery" of Vinland was important evidence showing that new lands could be reached by sailing west.

The next part of our story is less clear. Tradition tells us that Cristóbal Colón, while living in Portugal, sought the help of several kings to sponsor his voyage across the Atlantic. (Ships were expensive, and Colón needed money for supplies.) One of his appeals was to the king of Portugal, King John II. Supposedly, King John turned him down because he was satisfied with the trade route opened by Bartolomeu Dias. Do you remember him? By sailing around the Cape of Good Hope, Dias created a pathway for Portuguese traders to reach treasures in the East.

But there are those who wonder . . . did King John really turn down Cristóbal Colón? Did he employ him as a spy? Did he use Colón as a decoy to keep the Spanish occupied? At the time of my writing, I don't believe it is clear enough to say. But it would appear that *without* funding from King John II, Cristóbal Colón left Portugal and moved with his son to Palos, Spain. (His wife had died by this time.)

Once in Spain, Colón was relentless in seeking the help of Ferdinand and Isabella. This famous king and queen were busy with many matters, including the *reconquista*. I'm sure you remember that from Lesson 3. Ferdinand and Isabella listened many times to the plan of Colón, but they also listened to their advisers who thought the enterprise was a bad idea. Poor Cristóbal! It would take him six years of pleading, with a lot of maps, to convince Ferdinand and Isabella to sponsor him. But finally, Isabella said yes! She was the same age as Colón and shared his zealousness. Ferdinand agreed to the plan, and the Enterprise to the Indies was made official.

## *First Voyage*

With funds from Spain, and money from Italian investors, Cristóbal Colón acquired three ships and 90 men for his first voyage across the Atlantic. (He made four voyages in all.) At the harbor in Palos, Spain, Colón and his crew boarded their ships on August 2, **1492**, and set sail the following day.[4] The *Niña* and *Pinta* were small caravels. With triangular-shaped sails, these ships were easy to maneuver and steer. They were captained by two brothers, **Martín Alonso Pinzón** and **Vicente Yáñez Pinzón**. The *Santa Maria* was a bigger ship called a nao. With large, square sails, it was more awkward to manage but held a larger cargo. Being no more than 70 feet long and 12 feet wide, none of the ships were very big for crossing the unknown waters of the Atlantic. But Cristóbal Colón would travel on the *Santa Maria* and be the "Admiral" (as he called himself in his journal) of the fleet.

From Spain, Colón and his crew stopped first at the **Canary Islands** just off the coast of Africa. After taking on fresh "water, wood, [and] meat,"[5] they left the Canaries on September 6. For three days they could still see land on the horizon behind them. But after that? It would be three *weeks* before land would be seen again! The ships were surrounded by nothing but deep blue sea. Keep in mind that as far as we know, no other European had ever sailed these waters!

Cristóbal Colón had great faith in his dream, but his crew grumbled a lot and complained. To try to keep up the spirits of his crew, Colón fibbed to his men about their progress! He told them they weren't as far away from home as they really were. To cover the truth, he kept two journals — one fabricated for his men, and one kept accurately for himself.[6] On September 9, the Admiral confessed in his private journal, "I have decided to log less than our true run, so that if the voyage is long the crew will not be afraid and lose heart."[7]

The false information that Cristóbal fed his crew was not enough to keep them from murmuring mutiny. After weeks at sea, the crew feared they would never see home again and begged the Admiral to turn around. The downtrodden sailors seriously considered tossing their stubborn Admiral overboard! But Colón could not be swayed. On October 10, Colón wrote in his journal, "[We have traveled] sixty-two and a half leagues in the twenty-four hours; [but] I told the men only forty-six and a half. They could contain themselves no longer, and began to complain of the length of the voyage. I encouraged them as best I could . . . I also told them that it was useless to complain; having set out for the Indies I shall continue this voyage until, with God's grace, I reach them."[8] (Words in brackets are mine for clarity.)

Strangely, sailors from the voyage would later report that there were vague sightings of land from time to time — but the Admiral would not steer toward them. Some suspect that Cristóbal Colón had a secret map that told him exactly where to sail and where not to sail! Where would he get a secret map? Had someone sailed this route before him? No one really knows. But Cristóbal was overly determined at times to sail in the direction he wanted. And his actions were strange as he maneuvered his way across the Atlantic, catching winds that he should *not* have had any knowledge of. His journal would later appear to be scrambled and out of order. Perhaps he did have secrets he was protecting! But back to our voyage.

To encourage his men to keep a good lookout, on October 11, Colón offered a gift of silk and gold to the man who would first sight land. All eyes were fixed fast on the horizon. They saw birds, but no land. Anxiety mounted and the men grew more restless. Leafy sticks were seen floating on the waters around them, but still no sight of land.

A full-scale model of the *Santa Maria* sits on the river in downtown Columbus, Ohio, a city named in honor of the explorer.

At ten o'clock that evening, Colón, who always had an eye on the sea, claimed that he saw from the *Santa Maria* a distant fire in the night — which had to mean there was land in sight! Others gazed deeply into the darkness, but the flame was only a flicker "like a wax candle rising and falling."[9] For this sighting, Colón rewarded himself the promised gift of silk and gold! His men grumbled about this self-reward and questioned the stubbornness of their Admiral. What *was* driving Cristóbal so strongly? Was it his faith? Was it sheer determination? We may never know.

But the *Pinta*, being smaller and swifter than the *Santa Maria*, sped forward into the night. Then, at two o'clock in the morning on October 12, it happened. **Juan Rodriguez**, a lookout on the *Pinta*, saw actual land and signaled back to Colón. Slowly and steadily the sailors saw white cliffs emerge in the distance and glimmer in the moonlight. After weeks on the sea, can you imagine how they felt? With surges of hope racing through their veins, I doubt that the crew slept the rest of the night while the ships pointed for shore.

Cristóbal Colón named his first place of landfall **San Salvador**, which means "Holy Savior."[10] He wrote to a friend, "To the first of these I gave the name of the blessed Savior, on whose aid relying I had reached this as well as the other islands."[11] With great ceremony, and excitement I'm sure, Colón first stepped ashore with the Pinzón brothers. Colón carried the royal standard of Spain, and his captains each carried a banner from their ships marked with a "Green Cross" and royal letters. They knelt and prayed, thanking the Lord for their safety and the opportunity that lay before them.

Filled with curiosity, the native inhabitants of the island came forward to greet the light-skinned newcomers. What a spectacle it must have been! I don't think we can imagine the scene properly, but it must have given an eerie sensation to all who were there. Colón wrote, "Soon many of the islanders gathered around us. I could see that they were people who would be more easily converted to our Holy Faith by love than by coercion, and wishing them to look on us with friendship I gave them red bonnets and glass beads which they hung round their necks." He further wrote, "They go about as naked as the day they were born . . . all well built, finely bodied and handsome in the face."[12]

I wonder, what did these handsome, gentle, naked people think of the sunburned sailors with their heavily armored clothes and banners blowing in the wind? Were these bearded gods or were these humans from afar? What was the meaning of the cross hammered into the sandy soil, and what words were they speaking with eyes closed and heads bowed?

The Europeans and the islanders had much to learn about one another. None knew then that they were experiencing one of the most pivotal events in history as members of the Old World stared into the eyes of the New. And just where had Cristóbal Colón and his crew of 90 landed? Believe it or not, Colón didn't exactly know and historians still disagree. But the landing of Cristóbal Colón would change the handiwork of mapmakers and the perspective of mankind toward his world. I'll tell you about this mysterious place of landfall and much more in our next lesson as we trace the rest of the voyages of Cristóbal Colón and consider his loss of reputation.

## Lesson 8 — *1493–1502*

# *The Return of Cristóbal Colón*

As promised, we're going to pick up where we left off with Cristóbal Colón. There is so much to tell about this seafaring Admiral that it will be hard to narrow it down! But in this lesson, we'll look at where Colón most likely was when he landed in the New World — and where he thought he was. Then, we'll reflect on his varied ambitions and on how later voyages would tarnish his reputation. I'll tell you ahead of time that in the end, "discovery" wasn't that glamorous for Cristóbal Colón.

### *Cruising the Caribbean*

As mentioned before, there is great debate as to what tiny island Cristóbal Colón actually first stepped on when he reached the New World. Normally, the landfall of a ship of malodorous (meaning smelly) sailors wouldn't be so important. But the event was so historic in bringing two foreign worlds together that scholars are likely to keep arguing over it until the matter is solved. If Colón traveled as it appears in his journal, he may have landed on **Watling Island** (later named San Salvador), the **Plana Cays**, or **Samana Cay**. All are islands of the **Bahamas**, a few hundred miles from the coast of Florida.

If Cristóbal Colón scrambled his journal to protect some secrets, he may have sailed a more southern route and landed at **Grand Turk Island**. Wherever he was, it is certain that the *Niña*, the *Pinta*, and the *Santa Maria* were cruising the waters of the **Caribbean Sea**. Colón would eventually touch down in the *West Indies*, *Central America*, and *South America*. Though often implied, Colón never set foot on the continent of North America.

The interesting thing about the first voyage of Cristóbal Colón is that he was lost and didn't know it! Colón seemed to believe that he had landed somewhere off the coast of Asia. Over and over in his journal, he referred to his landing in **Cuba** as *Cipango*, which is the name that Marco Polo had given to Japan! If you can picture this on a map, Colón envisioned himself in the ocean near China and Japan. He had mistakenly estimated the world to be about two-thirds smaller than it is, and he thought Asia was broader and wider than it is. He couldn't have been more wrong.

With letters in hand from the king and queen of Spain, Cristóbal sent sailors inland to search for the emperor of China. On October 21, he wrote, "I am still determined to continue to the mainland . . . and to give Your Majesties' letters to the Great Khan and return with his reply."[13] This means that Colón thought he was near China and he had no idea that the continents of North and South America lay *between* Europe and Asia.

Cristóbal Colón called the people he found living on these islands "Indians." Why? Because he thought that if he weren't on the coast of China, then he might be on some outlying islands of India. To this day, native peoples of the Americas are often called "Indians" — all because of this honest mistake by Cristóbal. And for the same reason, the islands he circled in the Caribbean are still called the "West Indies."

## *The Gospel and Gold*

Cristóbal Colón was at first compassionate toward the local people he encountered. (He landed on at least five islands before reaching Cuba.) He wrote in a letter, "They show greater love for all others than for themselves; . . . all understand each other mutually; a fact that is very important for the end . . . that is, their conversion to the holy religion of Christ, to which . . . they are very ready and favorably inclined . . . Let Christ rejoice on earth, as he rejoices in heaven, when he foresees coming to salvation so many souls of people hitherto lost."[14]

The gentle people Cristóbal Colón was describing were most likely the **Arawak** (AIR uh walk), a Caribbean group who greatly declined in number after the arrival of the white man. According to Colón, the natives were trusting, generous, and "had no god." By his writings, Colón appeared truly concerned for sharing the Gospel of Christ with the Indians. He wrote on November 27, "God willing . . . I shall have the language taught to one of my people, for I can see that so far the same language is spoken everywhere. Then it will be possible to find out which things are useful and to convert these people to Christianity. It will be easy, for they have no faith and do not worship idols; Your Majesties will have a city and a fort built here and these lands will be converted."[15]

But let me be clear about something else. Cristóbal Colón also wrote, without apology, that he was seeking gold and a way to profit from the new land. On October 23, while leaving one island to sail to another, he wrote, "It is only sensible to go where there is good potential for trade. To my mind there is no point in lingering when one can set off and explore a large area until one finds a country which offers profit."[16] On November 1, from another island, Colón wrote, ". . . more than sixteen canoes came out to the ships with cotton thread and other small items. I gave orders for none of this to be taken, so that they would know that I am seeking only gold."[17]

Though "seeking only gold" may sound greedy, Colón *also* wrote that his quest for gold was inspired by a crusade to the Holy Lands! He wrote to Ferdinand and Isabella that he hoped the discovery of gold mines in the East would fund further conquests of Jerusalem. (The city of Jerusalem in the Holy Lands was under Muslim control.) Colón's journal entry for December 26 reads, "I trust in the Lord that when I return . . . I shall find . . . the gold mine and spices, and all in such quantities that Your Majesties will be able to make your preparations to go to recover the Holy Sepulcher, for Your Majesties may remember my request to you that all the proceeds of this voyage of mine should be used for the conquest of Jerusalem."[18]

So, the journals of Colón reveal something of his dual ambitions. He *did* seek the conversion of the natives and he *did* seek gold for himself and the king and queen of Spain. But, as a true explorer, he also sought the thrill of discovery. He wrote on December 26, "My constant aim has been discovery, and I was resting no more than a day in any one place except for lack of wind."[19]

To piece it all together, like most adventurers, Cristóbal Colón had numerous ambitions. If he sailed for the Gospel, for gold, or as a spy, he was elated at what he discovered in the West Indies. He made endless comments in his journal on the beauty of the land and the gentle ways of the people. He recorded the trees, the terrain, and the gorgeous weather that he compared to pleasant days back home in May. He also wrote of his loss of the bulky *Santa Maria*. It hit a bank on Christmas Eve and had to be abandoned. The remaining sailors and supplies were crowded onto the *Niña* and *Pinta,* making for a difficult trip back home.[20]

In fact, the trip back to Spain was very difficult. Once out in open sea, both the *Niña* and *Pinta* were caught in a terrible storm and tossed out of sight from one another. The men prayed and offered themselves to holy pilgrimages if they could just make it safely back home. With the amazing navigational sense of Colón, he and his men safely reached the **Azores**, which are small islands off the coast of Portugal. Without fancy instruments, Colón depended greatly on his knowledge of the stars and the sea. Modern sailors would describe his "dead-reckoning" instincts as phenomenal.

After leaving the Azores, Cristóbal Colón made one interesting stop before heading home to Spain. He dropped in to visit King John II in Portugal — the king who turned down the opportunity to sponsor him! Many still wonder if King John was up to mischief and using Colón as a spy. For now it remains a mystery. But upon his arrival in Spain, Cristóbal Colón was given a hero's welcome. He was given everything he had requested from Queen Isabella, which was a lot! He received a tenth of the riches he found, the title "Admiral of the Ocean Sea," the rank of nobility, and a promise to govern newly discovered lands. He was also granted the privilege of wearing his hat in front of the king and queen because it was a sign of royal favor.

Perhaps all this reward was the beginning of the downfall of Cristóbal Colón. Perhaps fame and fortune went to his head or he was pressured to find gold and slaves. For on the next voyages of Colón, his actions would appear cruel and careless.

Upon his return from the New World, Cristóbal Colón was granted everything he requested from Queen Isabella.

## *Second and Third Voyages*

On his **second voyage in 1493**, Cristóbal loaded 1,000 settlers onto 17 ships. Under the leadership of his brother, these Spaniards started the first permanent European colony in the New World. This is historical fact. They were on the island of **Hispaniola** (which holds the modern-day countries of **Haiti** and the **Dominican Republic**). The European settlers were poorly prepared for the hardships they faced. To survive their new home, and believing that they were superior to the natives, the settlers began to make slaves of the local people. It was cruel and one-sided because the Spaniards had guns and horses to fight with. The natives didn't. They had no fair way to protect themselves.

Nevertheless, the natives did their best to turn against the Spaniards and fight for their survival. Unfortunately, Cristóbal didn't resolve the conflict peacefully. Rather than negotiate, he stepped in with weapons, and many natives were killed. And somewhere along the way, Cristóbal Colón began to *demand* gold! Taking charge over the Indians, he required the natives to bring him a payment of gold dust every three months. Those who did were marked with a bronze band. Those who didn't had arms lopped off or were killed!

After some time, Colón headed back to Spain, but his people weren't so proud of him this time. His reputation as a cruel taskmaster had spread, and the Spanish weren't quite sure what to think of him. But, with his usual tenacity and determination, Colón left Spain for a **third voyage in 1498.** He sailed in a southerly direction and made it to present-day **Trinidad** and the coast of **Venezuela** (Ven uhs ZWAY la). (Venezuela is a country in South America.) It was there that Cristóbal said, "I believe that this is a very great continent which until today has been unknown."[21] He called it an **"Other World."**

In the meantime, a new governor was sent to Hispaniola by the order of Ferdinand and Isabella. They were concerned with the problems facing the colonists and thought new leadership might help. But when Colón landed there, he wasn't welcome. In the very colony that he first helped to establish, he was arrested and placed in chains! In humility, Cristóbal Colón was shipped back to Spain as a prisoner. Ferdinand and Isabella were alarmed to find their "Admiral of the Ocean Sea" bound like a common criminal. They immediately set him free and fired the governor of Hispaniola for having arrested their Admiral.

It was after the third voyage of Cristóbal Colón that he edited a collection of writings called the *Book of Prophecies*. In this book, he and a monk recorded verses from the Bible and wrote commentary to defend Colón's "Enterprise to the Indies." I suppose after being in chains, he felt the need to explain himself! He might have feared, too, that his mission was on shaky ground and could be canceled at any time. Out of pages of Bible passages, here are three verses as found in his *Book of Prophecies*.[22]

- "Sing his praise from the ends of the earth, you who sink into the sea and his plentitude, the islands and their inhabitants." (Isaiah 42:10, **as quoted in the *Book of Prophecies*, p. 189**)
- "When you cross the waters, I will be with you and the floods will not overwhelm you . . . for I am the Lord your God." (Isaiah 43:2, 3, **as quoted in the *Book of Prophecies*, p. 191**)
- "I will send ones who have been saved to the ocean peoples in Africa, in Lydia, the ones with arrows, in Italy and Greece; to the distant islands, to those who have not heard of me and have not seen my glory." (Isaiah 66:19, **as quoted in the *Book of Prophecies*, p. 341**)

As for making mistakes, Colón admitted that he was a sinner, but he believed he was still fulfilling prophecy. He wrote, "I have greatly sinned. Yet, every time that I have asked, I have been covered by the mercy and compassion of Our Lord. I have found the sweetest consolation in throwing off all my cares in order to contemplate his marvellous [*sic*] presence. I have already said that for the voyage of the Indies neither intelligence nor mathematics nor world maps were of any use to me; it was the fulfillment of Isaiah's prophecy."[23]

Considering the controversies that surround Colón as to why he sailed and for whom, I think these words are powerful. Perhaps they contain clues to the real heart and soul of the Admiral. Unless he was protecting

> *"I have already said that for the voyage of the Indies neither intelligence nor mathematics nor world maps were of any use to me; it was the fulfillment of Isaiah's prophecy."*
> —Cristóbal Colón [Christopher Columbus]

his reputation, or trying to impress the king and queen, Cristóbal Colón sounds like a man on a mission for God — torn by his own selfishness. Whatever his intentions, he made one last voyage to the New World.

## *The Fourth and Final Voyage*

Ferdinand and Isabella furnished Colón with funds and supplies for one more trip. On this **fourth and final voyage in 1502**, Colón chose his 13-year-old son to accompany him to the New Word. In fact, most of the crewmen were mere teenagers. They may not have had much experience, but they were a little less prone to grumble than the older sailors. The goal of this trip was to find a passage through Central America to reach the seas and the shores beyond. The young sailors scoured the coasts of **Honduras** and **Panama** looking for a shortcut that didn't exist. Colón, though wrong about this passageway, was right that he wasn't far from another great ocean. The Pacific Ocean lay just on the *other* side of Central America, which would have led him to Asia. But the difficult conditions of sea travel never allowed Cristóbal to prove he was right. This fourth voyage was the most challenging of all.

The country of Honduras is lush and beautiful, but it does not provide a shortcut to the Pacific Ocean as Colón was hoping for.

On that dreary journey, the clothes of the crew remained soaked from bad weather. They chose to eat their hardtack biscuits at night so they wouldn't have to see the worms that had infested their supplies! Besides that, the ships stalled; the crew faced hurricanes; and the sailors had troubles with the natives. As before, this trouble led to bloodshed — lots of bloodshed. As if Colón was no longer concerned with the conversion of the Indians, thousands were killed.

Going further against his Christian faith, Cristóbal later told lies about his powers to gain the trust of the remaining natives. You see, he knew that an eclipse of the moon was coming, and he used this knowledge to appear to have supernatural powers in front of the Indians! Maybe it was self-protection because hostilities had grown out of control. Maybe it was plain deceit. I don't know the motive for his lying. But before it was all over, Colón took a tribal chief as a hostage, and his crew slaughtered *more* natives. Why? I can't explain this either. But, on these later voyages, greed and survival seemed to crowd out grace and the desire to fulfill prophecy.

Colón's final trip back to Spain was terribly rough. Worms bore so many holes through the planks of his ship that the crew was forced to sail slowly and close to the coast. For a year, they were marooned in **Jamaica** before another ship came to their rescue. By the time Cristóbal reached Spain, Queen Isabella was dying and unable to meet with him. King Ferdinand had lost interest in the "Enterprise to the Indies" and withdrew his support. The voyages of Cristóbal Colón were over!

Though the memory of Christopher Columbus draws mixed reactions, many statues have been built in his honor.

If that weren't disheartening enough, Cristóbal had other issues to face. He had trouble with his estate and he fought severe arthritis. At just 53, he died in Spain, with little if any recognition. He had no idea of the impact he had made on history. Neither did those around him.

From all of this, what would you conclude about the life of Cristóbal Colón? Is he to be admired for his tenacity and navigational genius? Is he to be scorned for his treatment of the natives and his quest for gold? Is he to be credited with discovering an "Other World"? I think it's safe to say we could admire, scorn, and credit the Admiral of the Ocean Sea. As is true for most people, his life was a mixture of good and bad. I think our views of him can be a mixture, too. Besides, until more facts are certain, there will remain a mixture of opinions about the man who dared to sail the ocean blue.

In closing, I've one last note to share. Though most credit "Christopher Columbus" with discovering the Americas, they were not named after him. **Amerigo Vespucci** (Ves SPOO chee) was given that honor. He was an Italian explorer funded by none other than the Medici family. When Amerigo identified what he believed to be a whole new continent, a German geographer used his name on a map. Thus, both North and South America were eventually named in history after an Italian, and that is an undisputed fact!

## Lesson 9 — 1493

# *Ghana, Mali, and Songhai: Empires of West Africa*

The world is a big place, and it's been here for thousands of years. As much as I'd like to, I'll never cover the history of it all! That would be impossible. But I will keep telling you stories from *all* over the world when they stand out in history for one reason or another. Today's story is about three West African empires. They are **Ghana** (GAH nuh), **Mali** (MAH lee), and **Songhai** (Song GUY). Each empire covered about the same territory in West Africa, but they arose at different times over a few centuries. Starting in the Middle Ages and lasting through the Renaissance, each stood in the spotlight of history just long enough to get some attention.

## *Africa in Ancient Times*

As I usually do, I first want to glance back at the early history of the land we're discussing — in this case, Africa. It will help give you a big picture of the history of this continent. Ancient Africa is most famous for the incredible accomplishments of the early Egyptians who lived along the Nile River. As you probably know, Egypt is in the far northeast corner of Africa. We remember the ancient Egyptians most for pyramids, mummies, and multiple gods. That is, except for a pharaoh named **Amenhotep IV**; his wife, **Nefertiti**; and their son-in-law, **King "Tut."** They worshiped only *one* god, the sun god they called Ra.

Over a thousand years ago, builders in Great Zimbabwe erected impressive stone houses without the use of mortar.

Other ancient kingdoms of Africa would include the **Kush**, who lived along the southern part of the Nile River. Like the early Egyptians, the Kushites (or Nubians) were very advanced and used the great Nile as a means of trading with others. They remained prosperous for nearly a thousand years. Next in line, the peoples of the **Nok** culture stand out in Africa's ancient history. They lived south of the Sahara in present-day Nigeria. Like the Kushites, they were artistic and left interesting terra-cotta statues behind so we can know what they looked like.

Though the Sahara was once lush and green, it grew to become a vast desert. This change in climate drove people to settle farther and farther south in Africa. One of the most developed cultures of southern Africa was found in Zimbabwe (Zim BOB way). It was called **Great Zimbabwe** during the Middle Ages because of the amazing stone structures the people built there. *Zimbabwe* means "houses of stone." Around the year A.D. 1000, large amounts of gold and other rich resources were traded through the streets of Great Zimbabwe.

So what about the rest of Africa? What was going on there? Well, of course there were tribes of people living *all* over the large continent for thousands of years. We know that these tribes were hunting, farming, trading, and fighting, but we don't have written records of the details of their lives. We don't have a record of exactly who lived where and when — except in western Africa.

In western Africa, there were special men named **griots** (GREE otz) who were chosen to memorize the history of their people. Like walking

> *"We are the vessels of speech. We are the repositories which harbor secrets many centuries old; without us the names of kings would vanish into oblivion, we are the memory of mankind; by the spoken word we bring to life the deeds and exploits of kings for younger generations."*
>
> *–Words of a griot*

history books, the griots were storytellers of the past. (Some still are.) One modern griot put it this way, "We are the vessels of speech. We are the repositories which harbor secrets many centuries old; without us the names of kings would vanish into oblivion, we are the memory of mankind; by the spoken word we bring to life the deeds and exploits of kings for younger generations."[24] Isn't that neat? Because of the griots, we do have stories of western Africa from long ago. That should help explain why we will study this area today.

## *The Ghana Empire*

As far back as A.D. 750, western Africa was home to the dark-skinned **Soninke** people. They called their ancient empire **Ghana**. (Though it was near present-day Ghana, it is not the same place.) The capital of ancient Ghana was **Kumbi Saleh**. It sat near the **Niger River** (NYE jer), which winds its way through western Africa and spills into the North Atlantic Ocean.

Now, in a smart way, this small empire grew to become very wealthy. The Soninke rulers of Ghana charged high taxes on those who passed *through* their empire with gold and salt. You see, there was a lot of gold just *south* of Ghana. And there was a lot of salt just *north* of Ghana. Traders of both items had to pass *through* Ghana to sell their products. Though you would think that gold was far more valuable than salt, it wasn't. The people around Ghana would perish without salt in their diet. Salt protected them against dehydration brought on by the hot climate near the equator. So, both gold *and* salt were in great demand and sold at high prices. And the higher the prices were, the richer the empire of Ghana grew. It was good business.

In the hot, dry climate of West Africa, salt was valuable in helping to prevent dehydration.

To protect their treasure and wealth, the Soninke of Ghana built a large army. Because iron was plentiful too, it was easy to equip this army with strong weapons. With money and power, the Ghana Empire remained strong for over 300 years. That means it was older than the United States is today.

## *The Mali Empire*

But as we see over and over in history, empires do fall. Ghana was no exception. In 1070, it fell to Muslims of the **Almoravid dynasty**. Muslims captured the capital and defeated the army. Though the Soninke tried to rebuild, their supply of gold began to dwindle in the south. Without it, the Soninke lost their power and wealth.

In time, the Mali Empire began to take shape in the same region. The success of Mali was due in part to one thing — a *new* source of gold was discovered along the Niger River. This new gold helped boost the area back into business — *really* good business.

Gold was again so plentiful that an Arabic historian said this about the king of Mali: "He sits in a domed pavilion around which stand ten horses covered with *gold*-embroidered cloths. Behind him stand ten pages holding shields and swords decorated with *gold;* and on his right are the sons of vassal kings of his country, wearing splendid garments with *gold* braided into their hair. At the door of the pavilion are dogs of an excellent breed . . . around their necks they wear collars of *gold* and silver."[25] (Italics are mine for emphasis.) Did you notice all the gold? There was so much there that even dogs wore it around their necks!

The founder of the Mali Empire was named **Sundiata** (Soon dee AHT ta). The griots have passed down an interesting story of Sundiata. In his early childhood, Sundiata couldn't walk. Though he was strong, his legs wouldn't bend properly. For seven years this condition forced him to crawl from one place to another. But legend says that Sundiata was cured by the hands of a blacksmith. By the time he was 10, he was an able hunter and a respected leader. By 18, he was a warrior and a trusted adviser to the king. In 1240, Sundiata defeated an enemy and proceeded to make the *Kingdom* of Mali into the *Empire* of Mali. For overcoming his disability, Sundiata has been remembered as the "Lion of Mali." His story is an inspiration to others.

Seventy-five years later, another king rose to fame in Mali. He was **Mansa Musa** (MAHN sa MOO sa). He has an entirely different story than the Lion of Mali. It seems that Mansa Musa was impressed with the Muslim traders he came to know. He was so impressed with their customs that he decided to make a very big trip into the Muslim world. He chose to visit Mecca, the holy city of the Muslims, in Arabia. Thousands of Muslims make a pilgrimage every year to Mecca to visit the Kaaba, a square-shaped Muslim temple. Mansa Musa joined them.

Do you remember the vast source of gold that I told you about near the Niger River? Well, that gold is part of this story. To impress others on his journey to Mecca, Mansa Musa took lots and lots of gold with him, passing it out freely to those he met. Because of his generosity, Europeans and those in the Middle East paid great attention to Mansa Musa and the Mali Empire.

One historian recorded this about Mansa Musa: "He was a young man with a brown skin, a pleasant face, and a good figure . . . He appeared among his companions magnificently dressed and mounted, and surrounded by more than 10,000 of his subjects. He brought gifts and presents that amazed the eye with their beauty and splendor."[26]

This splendid king of Mali made such an impression on others that it put him and his country "on the map." Literally. Mali appeared on a map made in 1375, with a picture of Mansa Musa holding a large nugget of pure gold. As the map was circulated, his generous reputation spread even more. As a result, hundreds of curious tourists showed up in Mali, hoping to find more of the gold that seemed to be so abundant.

Though the empires of West Africa have changed since the Renaissance, the marketplaces still bustle with people buying and selling goods.

What the curious tourists found in Mali was far more than gold. They found Mali to be an amazing center of culture, learning, and trade. The city of **Timbuktu** (TIM buck too) was particularly magnificent. (Younger Students: Isn't it fun to say "Tim - buk - tu"?) When Mansa Musa returned from the Middle East, he brought back with him Muslim scholars, architects, philosophers, and writers. They launched a center for learning that had never been seen before in western Africa. They built mosques, started schools, and set up courts. With strict laws in force, Mali was a safe place to live and so attracted more and more people to live there.

Oddly, Mansa Musa himself never adopted the religion of Islam. Though he admired many Muslim customs and the style of learning, he kept his traditional African beliefs. Like many Africans of that time, he had superstitious beliefs about nature and the gods. Western Africa became a strong blend of these traditional African beliefs and Islam. It remains so today.

## *The Songhai Empire*

I have yet one more empire to introduce you to, so stay with me here. First there was *Ghana*, known for trading gold and salt. Then there was *Mali*, started by Sundiata and influenced by Mansa Musa, gold, and Islam. Now, we will look at the *Songhai Empire*, which has its own particular story.

The clothing of these children reflects a blend of Islamic and African traditions that still exists in Africa today.

Though the Songhai slowly took over the empire of Mali, it was **1493** that stands out in history. That was the year that **Askia Muhammad I** (Ah SKEE uh Muh HAHM med) took control of the empire and just one year after Columbus sailed to the New World. Askia Muhammed made Songhai by far the strongest empire that western Africa had ever seen. Like the leaders before him, he kept the gold industry moving. He also continued to promote learning and education.

But Askia went a step further than most of the kings before him. He adopted Islam as his own faith and appointed Muslims to most of the government positions. Though 97 percent of the people of the Songhai Empire were NOT Islamic, the government was. The major cities would also appear to be Islamic by their architecture, courts, and mosques. It was a unique situation.

Askia Muhammed used this situation to build a very strong *central* government. He standardized weights and measures and promoted Islamic thought to connect hundreds of small cultures that existed in the region. It proved to work for centuries and create great stability for the Songhai Empire.

The city of Timbuktu itself grew to a population of 100,000. It grew so large because it was home to the **University of Sankore**, which drew students from all over the world to study law and medicine. So difficult was this school that even the brightest of Arab students were turned away. Black African students proved to be well educated and many went on to teach as professors in other high-ranking universities. Hand-copied books were of so much value at the university that I think even the Medici family would have been impressed with the library at Sankore. It was as if western Africa was experiencing its own "renaissance" during the rich reign of Askia Muhammed.

This golden age of learning lasted through the 1500s in the Songhai Empire. It's an impressive record. While many parts of Africa were loosely organized, this region was getting worldwide attention. Historian Leo Africanus used the word "sumptuous" to describe the success of the Songhai. Sumptuous means something "luxurious, splendid, and lavish." He said, "It is a wonder to see what plenty of Merchandize is dayly brought hither, and how costly and sumptuous all things be."[27] I think Leo wrote a fitting summary of western Africa. With great wealth, strong culture, and prominent schools, it was *sumptuous* for decades to come.

# WEEK 4

## Lesson 10 — 1498

# The Death of Savonarola

There are many ways a person could be executed. Though horrible to think about, a person could be hung, burned, or stoned to death. But even worse, a person could undergo *all* those methods and then be dumped into a river on top of that. Unfortunately, that is what happened to **Girolamo Savonarola** (Jih ROLL uh mo Sav oh nuh RO luh) and two of his friends in **1498**. They were executed without any mercy. Theirs is a sad but inspiring story that unfolds in the heart of the Renaissance.

Savonarola was born in Italy of a noble family. Even as a young boy he was very serious. Rather than play sports with other boys his age, Savonarola read books. He read and reread works by Thomas Aquinas (Uh KWINE us) and Augustine, both strong men of faith. He was largely influenced by their godly lives. Savonarola went on to attend a university but found the experience disheartening. He was quickly appalled at the loose, immoral, and godless lives of many of the students. Clearly, Savonarola was different. He left school and went back home to live with his parents.

If you remember, Italy was slipping into a period of humanism during the Renaissance. Humanism, again, glorified mankind more than God. In the fifteenth century, this trend toward humanism started with Cosimo de' Medici when he brought ancient Greek thought to Italy. It was expanded through his grandson Lorenzo. Through the Medici, the Renaissance was soaring. But, as men took their eyes off God, Italy grew in immorality and excessive luxury.

Though at first Savonarola was not well received, thousands would later crowd into the city of Florence to hear him preach the Gospel.

Savonarola took it upon himself to straighten out his wayward countrymen. He was particularly eager to straighten out the church, which had grown terribly rich and immoral. The ambition of Girolamo Savonarola is to be admired. His pure and tender heart ached for the lost and the misguided. In hopes of making a difference, Savonarola joined the Dominican friars when he was 23 years old.

Savonarola continued to be serious minded. At the Dominican monastery, he asked only for the most menial of jobs of cooking and cleaning. But he was quickly identified as a powerful preacher. Indeed he was powerful, but when he was transferred to Florence to preach, things didn't go so well. The people of Florence were not the least bit responsive to his sermons. Savonarola preached way over their heads and failed to connect with their hearts. His voice was weak and shrill. He went back to his monastery, a more humble man than before. He was about 38 years old.

I find it interesting that Savonarola experienced this kind of "failure." It appears to me that God used this time in Savonarola's life to better define his message. And once he did, he was unstoppable. When Savonarola returned to Florence a few years later, his preaching was amazing. Thousands packed the enormous cathedrals just for a chance to hear him. So moved were his followers that they were nicknamed "the weepers" for all the tears they shed.

What was the clearer message that made so many cry? It was the Gospel, actually. Savonarola preached straightforward truth about Jesus to the people of Florence. And they were moved. His greatest emphasis was on personal holiness through the Spirit of God. He stressed the fear and judgment of God that was to come. Savonarola preached, "You Christians should always have the Gospel with you, I do not mean the book, but the spirit, for if you do not possess the spirit of grace and yet carry with you the whole book, of what advantage is it to you?"[1]

## *Turning the Hearts of Florence*

Through his bold preaching Savonarola urged people to rid themselves of worldly things and to be more like Jesus. What were "worldly things" in that century? According to Savonarola, that included gambling, cursing, cards, and dice. He opposed carnivals, horse races, pagan books, sensuous art, and acrobatic events. Savonarola frowned on makeup, excessive jewelry, and any immodest clothing.

The amazing part of the story is that so many people listened and submitted to Savonarola. The poor people loved the preacher because he fussed so much at the rich. Corrupt businessmen and bankers turned over money they had gained by cheating. Famous artists like Botticelli and Michelangelo changed the themes of their artworks to better glorify God.

People of all classes collected their "vanities," as they were called, and threw them into great bonfires built in the city's main square. These vanities included wigs, mirrors, lipsticks, perfumes, carnival masks, and all sorts of trinkets, along with pagan books and godless works of art. Imagine these things going up in smoke!

Large bonfires were built in the city square of Florence where citizens burned their worldly "vanities."

On the downside, there were extremists. There were groups of boys known as "bands of hope" who went door to door as "moral police," *demanding* these items for burning. Neighbors began to spy on neighbors and report one another for gambling and playing cards. Unfortunately, the zeal for holiness gave way to fear and intimidation. According to one observer, Florence was "so full of terrors and alarms, cries and lamentations, that everyone went about the city bewildered, speechless, and, as it were, half dead."[2]

Considering how drastic the situation got, can you imagine the backlash from those who were *not* so holy? Though many listened to Savonarola and heeded his teachings, there were many who didn't. In time, it cost Savonarola his life for trying to impose his strict lifestyle on everyone.

One of the people upset with Savonarola was Lorenzo de' Medici. Naturally, he was fond of the art, the carnivals, and the literature that Savonarola so freely condemned. Lorenzo tried to bribe the preacher with gifts of gold to tone down his message. But it was a useless gesture on Lorenzo's part. With his heart set on eternal things, Savonarola couldn't be bribed with anything of this world.

After Lorenzo de' Medici died, his son followed him in office. But the masses soon overthrew Lorenzo's son and looked to Savonarola to rule and govern Florence! It was quite an experiment, to place a government in the hands of a zealous Dominican friar. It had never been done before.

Savonarola took his role very seriously. He selected a council of men to help him govern Florence. Politically, he proved wise enough to avoid a war with France. This helped others respect him as a leader. It also gave him confidence to pursue his vision. And what was Savonarola's vision for Florence? He imagined a city with Christ as its head. He imagined a city with high morals and a Christian government. He imagined a little bit of heaven on earth. In hopes of being an influence to the whole world, he proclaimed, "O Florence! Then wilt thou be rich with spiritual and temporal wealth; thou wilt achieve the reformation of Rome, of Italy, of all countries; the wings of thy greatness shall spread over the world."[3]

Unfortunately, Savonarola's grand vision had problems. You see, Christ never taught that mankind should or would establish His kingdom on earth. The Bible teaches that the kingdom of heaven is something of God that will occur in *His* timing, in *His* way, and by *His* hand. (See Matt. 25:34.) Was this kingdom to be set up on earth by one man in Florence? Was one city going to save the world? No, only Jesus can save. (See Matt. 18:11; Luke 4:43.) But Savonarola believed that he was to create a Christian utopia in Italy. Though his intentions were sincere, they were not completely biblical.

## *Pope Alexander VI*

Savonarola's greatest threat turned out to be **Pope Alexander VI**. Oddly enough, the pope (who was voted into the "holiest" of offices) wasn't the least bit holy himself. Pope Alexander VI was probably one of the most immoral men to ever fill the papacy. Though he never married, Alexander fathered five children and supported the use of murder to get things he wanted! He was hardly a saint. When Savonarola began to preach to the pope, it wasn't a pretty scene. When he spoke of the church, Savonarola quite boldly said, "O prostitute Church, thou hast displayed thy foulness to the whole word, and stinkest unto heaven."[4]

In 1495, Pope Alexander VI pressured Savonarola to stop preaching. The pope certainly didn't want to hear Savonarola refer to the church as foul and stinky! For about a year, Savonarola heeded the pope's wishes and toned things down a bit. But when the season of Lent came around, Savonarola returned to the pulpit with more authority than ever. He again

Pope Alexander VI offered Savonarola the high position of cardinal in the church, but Savonarola turned it down to preach.

stirred the crowds to burn their "vanities" in a massive bonfire in the heart of Florence. The fire was 60 feet high and 240 feet around. It was huge, to say the least, and drew a great amount of attention to the preacher who started it.

The pope then tried to bribe Savonarola to pipe down. He offered him the high position of a cardinal (where the pope could keep a closer eye on him and keep him busy with church affairs). Savonarola wanted no part of it. Pope Alexander then concluded that the only way to shut up Savonarola was to excommunicate him. (That means to cut him off from the church entirely.) This caused a great deal of confusion among Savonarola's followers. Why would the pope condemn a man of God? The masses wondered if maybe Savonarola wasn't the man of God they thought he was.

Savonarola appealed to leaders in other countries for help. He pleaded with them to take the pope out of office. He called the pope, "a Devil" and "a monster" presiding over a "harlot" church.[5] No one joined in on his cause. I think Savonarola knew that his own life was in danger for warring against the pope. But I also think he was prepared for it. On numerous occasions he predicted that he would die a martyr's death. I suppose it was evident by the strong message he preached that he would draw enemies. And he did.

## *Trials and Tests*

One group of Savonarola's enemies was the Franciscans. They regularly bickered with the Dominicans over petty matters. On one occasion, they challenged Savonarola to a ridiculous test. They proposed that he be set on fire in the city square along with one of their friars! This test was called an "ordeal by fire." It was believed that the most "innocent" man would be spared by God. Savonarola took on this challenge and predicted that he would win — but he changed the rules and allowed a friend to stand in for him!

Of course, this switch made Savonarola appear to be a coward. His followers were more confused than ever. Where was the faith of their powerful preacher? A debate went on throughout the day as to whether or not the two men should really be set on fire and what the rules would be. Finally, after rain fell and both sides grew weary of arguing, the ordeal by fire was canceled. The disappointed crowd raised a ruckus and then returned to their homes.

When the pope found out about the ordeal by fire, he was furious. Apparently Savonarola had a reputation for making prophecies and predictions. Some came true and some didn't. It appeared to the pope that this fire incident was one more failed prediction of the preacher — though it was the Franciscans who had started the debate! This time, the pope had Savonarola arrested and taken to Rome.

In Rome, Savonarola was at the complete mercy of the pope. Be he godly or not, Pope Alexander had great power. Savonarola was put through the court of the Inquisition with two other friars and told to admit that he was a liar and a blasphemer — or suffer the consequences of torture! He chose torture, as did his friends.

Though Savonarola was sincere in his faith, physical torture *did* get the best of him. Several times, he broke under the pain and confessed things he really didn't believe. When the tortures ceased, Savonarola took back his words and the process started all over again. It was inhuman.

"The Lord has suffered much for me."
–Savonarola

Though weakened beyond our imagination, Savonarola (who was then 45 years old) ultimately withstood the torture of the Inquisition and held to his beliefs. His beliefs were that he was teaching the true Gospel of Jesus Christ. He was teaching personal holiness at the very height of the Renaissance and in an era of humanism. In doing so, he and his fellow friars knew that they would be declared heretics and die. I just don't think they knew how deplorable their deaths would be.

On May 23, 1498, Savonarola and the two friars were dragged into the same town square where, ironically, the large bonfire of vanities had been set. The men were publicly stripped of their garments all the way down to their shoes. While one of the friars sang hymns, a mean group of boys gathered and threw stones. In his last words, Savonarola simply stated, "The Lord has suffered much for me."[6] After the men were hung and strangled to death, their bodies were burned. After they were burned, their ashes were collected and thrown into a river.

I can't grasp the mind-set of those who performed these extreme executions. The only way I can make sense of it is to remember that there is a dark enemy opposed to the Gospel. The Bible says, "The thief does not come except to steal, and to kill, and to destroy." (See John 10:10.) Such seems to be the case with Savonarola and the friars who died that day in May. They were killed and their bodies destroyed. On their behalf, a bronze plaque was later erected in the square of Florence.

The good news is that death isn't the end for those who believe in Jesus. It is just the beginning of spending an eternity with Him. Destroying the body of a saint doesn't give the enemy the upper hand. Though tragic, the death of Savonarola wasn't the end of his message. Many would follow in his footsteps with the Gospel message of Jesus Christ.

## Lesson 11 — 1501

# The Safavid Empire of Persia

Long, long ago there was a land called **Elam**. This land existed so long ago that it was named after the grandson of Noah! That's right. Elam was one of Noah's many grandsons. The land of Elam was just east of the Tigris and Euphrates rivers — otherwise known

About 500 years before Christ, Darius organized Persia into 20 provinces called "satrapies" and started one of the first postal services.

as Mesopotamia (Mess uh po TAME ee uh). By 2000 B.C., the Elamites were overrun by the Medes and the Persians, and the land of Elam grew to be called **Persia**.

In later centuries, mighty men such as **Cyrus the Great**, **Darius**, and **Xerxes** (ZERK sees) ruled Persia. Xerxes is the king in the Old Testament who married **Esther**, meaning she had a hand in the history of Persia, too. In later times, **Alexander the Great** and **Genghis Khan** each took a turn ruling over Persia. Are you impressed? You should be. Persia has a long and amazing history. (Much of it is recorded in the Bible.) Today, Persia is renamed the **Islamic Republic of Iran**. But we're not ready for that story. Right now, we're going to look at one of the strongest Persian empires that ever existed. It was the **Safavid** (sah FAH weed) **Empire**.

## *The Sunnis and the Shiites*

In order for you to grasp the importance of the Safavid Empire, I need to introduce you to two groups. They are the **Sunnis** (SOO knees) and the **Shiites** (SHEE ites). You may or may not have ever heard of them before, but they are the names of two divisions of Islam. Why are there two? It seems that right after Mohammed (the founder of Islam) died, a great debate arose among his followers as to who was going to lead the movement of Islam. This debate was so great that it eventually split Mohammed's followers into the Sunnis and the Shiites.

The Sunnis believed that the next Islamic leader should be the closest, wisest *friend* of Mohammed. The man who best fit that was his friend and father-in-law, **Abu Bekr**. When Mohammed died, Abu Bekr claimed to be the next Islamic leader. The highest leader in Islam is called a **caliph** (KAY liff).

The Shiites, however, believed the next leader or caliph should be a *relative* of Mohammed. His closest relative was **Ali**, the husband of one of Mohammed's daughters. When Mohammed died, Ali wanted to be the next caliph. It didn't work out right away, but he waited his turn and served as the fourth caliph. After that, the two groups fought bitterly over their differences, and in time each claimed its own leaders.

Can you imagine the problems this created? Over the years, there have been wars and assassinations between the Sunnis and the Shiites over their beliefs. The two groups *still* haven't settled their differences. And so, there are two "brands" of Islam so to speak. One way to better understand this is to consider the differences between Roman Catholics and Protestants. Though both consider themselves Christians, they hold to some very different views. In the same way, the Sunnis and the Shiites both consider themselves Islamic but hold to very different views. (In reality, the differences between all these groups are very complicated. My short comparison here is simply for your better understanding.)

Despite the differences between the Sunnis and the Shiites, Islam spread like wildfire. It was first introduced to the Persians in the 600s. Before Islam, many of the Persians held to

Before Islam, Persians held to the religious beliefs of the ancient Babylonians.

old Babylonian beliefs or were followers of **Zoroaster**. Zoroastrians believed in one god and the presence of good and evil. But they didn't know the one God of the Bible or the god of Mohammed. One reason that Islam may have spread easily to the Persians is that it was more than a religion. Islam was a form of government, too. To oppose it was difficult. To accept it was to bring unity and strength to Persia. And so it did.

But which brand of Islam was to unite Persia? Would it be the Sunni brand of Islam or the Shiite brand? Believe it or not, some debate still exists over which group got things started in Persia. But it is clearly the Shiites who won the battle. Their domination officially started in **1501** under the leadership of a young man named **Ismail I**. So, let's get to know him.

## *Ismail I*

Ismail was born of a very important family. His ancestors were leaders of a religious order. When Ismail was a boy, he received a special education. His education is an important part of the history of Persia because he was tutored by a Shiite. From that experience, he became very strong in his Shiite beliefs. And it was his Shiite beliefs that shaped the Safavid Empire, which eventually shaped Iran.

It's important to know that the Shiites view their leaders very differently than the Sunnis view theirs. The Shiites believe that their *first* 12 leaders (who are called **Imams**[7]) had supernatural abilities. They believe the Imams were without sin and that they could intervene between Allah and man. (Allah is believed to be God in Islam.) Why only the first 12? Well, the 12th Imam had no sons and so the supposed chain of "supernatural leadership" stopped after him. Furthermore, Shiites believe that the 12th Imam didn't completely die and will one day return to give knowledge and direction to the Shiites.

Now, I've shared a lot of new information with you. Most of you are not familiar with these details of Islam. I suggest you review the last paragraph to absorb it. Once you've done that, continue on. As you do, remember that according to the Bible, Jesus was the only sinless man because He was Divine. That means He claimed to be God. (See 2 Cor. 5:21; Heb. 4:15; John 8:19, 10:30, 12:44–45.)

When Ismail was only 13, he made some important decisions. Unlike his ancestors, he wanted to be more than the leader of a religious order. He wanted to be the *king* of an empire. And so he claimed himself to be the ***shah***, which means king. He named his empire Safavid after one of his ancestors, Safi od-Din. Know this though — in becoming the shah,

Ismail wasn't claiming to be one of the special Imams. He wasn't claiming to be without sin or to have supernatural abilities. He believed, like other Shiites, that one day an Imam would return who had those special abilities. But, in the meantime — as the shah of Persia — Ismail believed that he was the *highest* spiritual and political leader of the land.

This new style of leadership changed Persia forever. With a *spiritual* king, it became a true **theocracy**. A theocracy is a government that is completely based on a religion. For example, the courts of the land were run by religious men known as *clerics* of Islam. And the brand of Islam was clearly Shiite. To this day, Iran is 89 percent Shiite and 10 percent Sunni. Though many Shiites live around the world, Iran is presently the *only* country in the world that is a theocracy based on the Shiite faith.

So, did Ismail make an impact on Persia? Yes he did. But unfortunately, he wasn't very gentle about it. Apparently there were still many Sunnis in Persia when Ismail took over. Some were killed and others were forced to convert to Shiism. Despite this harshness, Ismail proved to be a capable military leader as well as a strong spiritual leader. His warriors wore red hats to represent their loyalty to him. Because of their hats, they were called the **Qizilbash** (KEE zil bash), which means "red-heads" in Turkish.

Some members of the Qizilbash (also spelled Kizilbash) army had so much confidence in Ismail that they didn't wear any armor in battle! They believed that Ismail's spiritual power would protect them. With the help of the loyal Qizilbash, Ismail easily expanded the borders of Persia to include most of Mesopotamia; he made **Tabriz** (Tah BREEZE) the

In modern-day Baghdad in Iraq, an abandoned army truck sits in front of a mosque. It is a sober reminder of war in the twenty-first century.

capital of Persia; and he captured the most important city of his enemies — who I am about to introduce.

Ismail's enemies were the **Ottoman Turks**. The important city he captured was **Baghdad**, which is in present-day **Iraq**. Why were the Ottoman Turks his enemies? The answer is simple: The Ottomans were Sunnis. To the Shiites, the Ottoman Empire was a 300-year-old enemy. So, in 1508, when Ismail conquered Baghdad, he made quite a reputation for himself. (We will learn more about the Ottomans later.) Ismail was also successful in conquering the **Uzbeks** (OOZE beckz) to the east. And you know what? The Uzbeks were also Sunnis! Considering the fact that Sunnis surrounded Persia on *every* side and dominated most of the Islamic world, Ismail and his fellow Shiites were turning history upside down.

## *Abbas the Great*

But, as we often see in history, Ismail's sons and grandsons weren't as capable or victorious as he was. One son was nearly blind; one was too young to rule well; and one was insane and, on top of that, switched his loyalties to the Sunnis. With that instability, the Ottomans eventually took back their beloved Baghdad, and the size of the empire shrank.

However, there was *one* descendant of Ismail who proved to be remarkable. His name was **Abbas** (Ah BOSS *or* AH boss). As Abbas I, he came to power in 1587 when he was only 17 years old. For his abilities, he has been remembered as **Abbas the Great**. One of the smart things he did was move the capital city from Tabriz to **Isfahan** (Is fuh HAHN). This city was centered in the heart of Persia and far from the borders of his enemies. Abbas turned Isfahan into a work of art. He adorned it with fine architecture, magnificent palaces, and enormous mosques. The arts grew and prosperity rose. The making of Persian rugs and tapestries became more widespread. As a result, Abbas opened trade with the English, selling them Persian tapestries. These beautiful tapestries are still popular around the world today.

But Abbas was far more than a man of fine taste. In a great victory, Abbas took Baghdad back from the Ottoman Turks in 1603. By 1629, he returned the borders of Persia to where Ismail had first pushed them.

Later on, it would appear that one flaw led to the downfall of the legacy of Abbas the Great. He was terribly paranoid and insecure. He was fearful that his own sons would overthrow him, as he had his father. So, Abbas had his eldest son killed in 1615 and left his other sons to be raised in a harem. The boys never received the education they needed to be good leaders. It is speculated that he had one of them blinded. For these reasons, the Safavid Empire was short-lived compared to others. By 1722, the Persians were overrun by their neighboring enemies. But nonetheless, the Shiite empire, in its glory, shaped the future of Iran.

## Lesson 12 — 1503

# *Leonardo da Vinci Paints the* Mona Lisa

**Note to Teacher:** *This is one of the longest lessons in Volume III and may need to be broken up for younger audiences.*

What is it about the ***Mona Lisa***? Is it her timid smile, her mysterious eyes, or just the pleasant look on her face? For centuries, art lovers have asked themselves these questions about the most famous painting in the world. I don't think I can explain it. But I can tell you a lot about the genius who painted her. He was **Leonardo da Vinci** (properly pronounced LAY oh NAR do).

Leonardo was born on April 15, 1452, in a small village near Vinci, Italy.[8] (April 15 happens to be my birthday, too!) His early years were unstable because his mother never married his father. Being poor, she gave Leonardo up to be raised in the home of his wealthy father. For awhile he lived with his grandparents and spent time with an uncle who cared a great deal for him. Despite the ups and downs of moving around, Leonardo was charming and attractive in every way, according to what those who knew him have written. A friend of his named Vasari wrote, "The radiance of his countenance, which was splendidly beautiful, brought cheerfulness to the heart of the most melancholy."[9]

Leonardo was also a genius. In school he excelled in math and music. With intense curiosity, he was always drawing something with great detail. Supposedly when he was just a boy, Leonardo brought dead lizards, toads, and snakes into his house as models for sketching. He was so absorbed in the details of his drawings that he never noticed the rotten smell of his subjects as they decayed!

### *Life in Florence*

Leonardo's father eventually moved him to Florence to expose him to much better opportunities. I'm sure you remember from other lessons what Florence was like in those days. Lorenzo de' Medici — just three years older than Leonardo — was in power and opportunity was everywhere.

When Leonardo was about 15, his father arranged for him to become an **apprentice** in the shop of **Andrea del Verrocchio** (Vair RAWK kyoh). Andrea was a master goldsmith, painter, and sculptor. As in medieval times, an apprentice was someone who learned a trade under a master. Rather than being paid, an apprentice was given food and lodging for learning a trade. This arrangement between Leonardo and Verrocchio must have been a good one because it lasted 13 years.

Though it may or may not be true, an interesting story has been passed down about Verrocchio. It seems that when Leonardo was about 18, he was asked by master Verrocchio to paint one of the two angels that appear in *The Baptism of Christ*. (His angel is the one on the left.) Supposedly, Leonardo's angel was so superb, so mystifying, and so perfect compared to his master's, that Andrea del Verrocchio said he would never paint again! Whether he ever did make this statement or not, I think Verrocchio realized that his finest pupil was going to surpass him. And the truth is, he did.

While in Florence, Leonardo painted something peculiar that began to reflect the mind of this genius. Leonardo began a scene titled *The Adoration of the Magi* (MAY jie). In it, the artist experimented with breaking the rules of perspective. "Perspective" in art is the science of making objects appear their real size. A good example of this is drawing things smaller when they are far away because that is how our eyes see them. Well, Leonardo enjoyed playing mind games with perspective. In *The Adoration of the Magi*, he drew stairs that lead to nowhere, horses larger than life, and the mother of Jesus as if she were suspended in time and space. In awe of her Son, she appears unaware of all kinds of chaos around her.

According to the artist himself, Leonardo was using "abundance and variety" to spice up *The Adoration of the Magi*. He continued to make abundance and variety one of his distinguishing traits. (You might want to remember that fact for tests!) He once said, "He is but a poor master who makes only a single figure well."[10] Even in serious portraits of his patrons, he added real and imaginary landscapes to the background. Though distant and hazy, they were full of detail. Again, he was using perspective to create depth. (You will want to hunt for depth and fine details when studying any of Leonardo's paintings.)

Unfortunately though, Leonardo never finished *The Adoration of the Magi*. This too became one of his distinguishing traits! It took him years and sometimes decades to finish his projects, if he finished them at all. In most cases, Leonardo was either too much of a perfectionist to consider his works "done," or he was too easily distracted by all the things on his brilliant mind to finish what he started.

So what was on the brilliant mind of this genius? The list is long and his notebooks were full. Leonardo filled over 7,000 pages in notebooks of drawings, sketches, and notes. Some were only random thoughts, which give us snapshots into Leonardo's thinking. Incidentally, his notes were all written backward — from right to left! It may be that it was easier to write this way because he was left-handed. (Moving his hand from right to left prevented him from smudging the ink.) Or it may be that his "mirror-image" handwriting helped protect his notes from being read and stolen.

Regardless, it is from these backward notes and endless drawings that we know what preoccupied Leonardo. He wrote of weapons, geometry, fabulous machines, the movement of water, and the anatomy of the human body. He illustrated levers, cameras, parachutes, bicycles, flying devices, water canals, crossbows, flying saucers, and helicopters — which he cleverly referred to as "air screws." Just for fun, the artist and scientist even wrote down a few jokes.

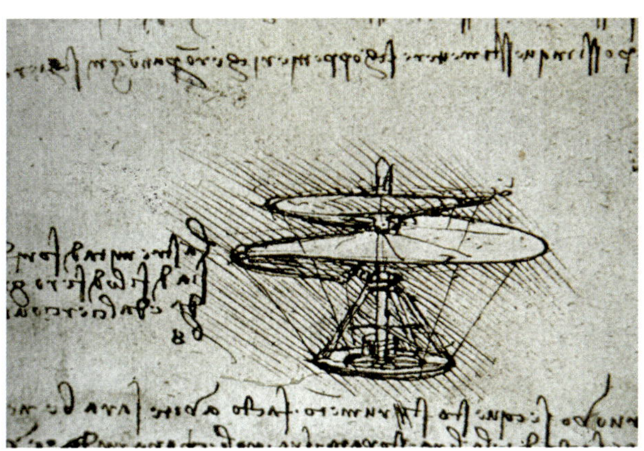

Though these items were not yet invented, Leonardo illustrated parachutes, flying saucers, and helicopters — which he cleverly named "air screws."

Besides that, Leonardo also conceived the idea of cars, tanks, and two-tiered cities. He wrote, "These cars take the place of elephants . . . one may put carabineers in them to break up every company."[11] He envisioned machine guns, mechanical chariots, and water mechanisms to prevent floods — or to create them in times of war. Leonardo was equally fascinated with plants, architecture, rock formations, and grotesque deformities. (Though the church frowned on it, the scientist cut open dead bodies to draw the insides!) In other words, just about everything visual that the world had to offer ran across Leonardo's mind, through his pen, and onto his paper. When that ran out, he used his own imagination to invent things to draw! And though it didn't happen in his lifetime, the writer in him hoped to be published. The name for one of his nature books was going to be *Of the Sky and of the Earth*.

Besides that, Leonardo had a knack for designing jewelry, costumes, banquet decorations, and music machines. Does that surprise you? Let me elaborate on this lesser-known fact. For several years, Leonardo worked exclusively for the duke of Milan, who hired him not only to work as an engineer and an architect, but also to create stables, carnival props, and dresses and girdles for his wives. Though it may sound strange to us to find this brilliant man designing a woman's wardrobe, it might have been just one of many creative outlets for the artist. He worked for the duke for 17 years.

## *Life in Milan and* The Last Supper

Of course, while in Milan, Leonardo also started some bigger-than-life projects. Some were so big that, as you might expect, he didn't finish them. The best example of this was the building of a 26-foot bronze statue of a horse. Leonardo spent over 10 years just crafting the clay model of it! Even unfinished, it was lovely. Poets wrote of it and visitors flocked to see it. The clay horse was elegant enough to decorate the wedding processional for the niece of the duke of Milan. Unfortunately, though, the bronze for the horse statue was never cast. Eventually enemy soldiers destroyed the clay horse when they invaded Milan in 1499. In complete disrespect, the soldiers used it for target practice! The original was never seen again. In 1999, however, an American used Leonardo's sketches to construct the horse exactly as Leonardo had designed it. It was presented as a gift to the city of Milan — 500 years after the disaster. I think Leonardo would have been delighted!

It took Leonardo da Vinci 20 years to complete two paintings of *The Virgin of the Rocks*. This lovely version is found in the National Gallery in London.

I'll mention here, too, that before Leonardo left Milan, he started two versions of *The Virgin of the Rocks*. It took him 20 years to complete, but at least he did. In the version that is located today in London, Leonardo captures the baby Jesus in the position of blessing John the Baptist, also depicted as a baby, while his mother and an angel gaze peacefully nearby. Behind them, in awesome detail, lies a rugged world that would soon mistreat both the Messiah and his messenger. The delicate smiles and the tender lighting of the characters are clearly the touch of Leonardo.

But soldiers and his own slowness weren't the only obstacles that Leonardo faced. One of his most famous works was destroyed by his own experimentation. Before Leonardo even completed painting *The Last Supper*, it began to erode! The artist had experimented with tempera paints and varnish to try to achieve a substance easier to use than plaster paints. (Plaster paints dry quickly, which was a terrible problem for the s-l-o-w-working Leonardo.) Despite the near-complete loss of *The Last Supper*, it has remained one of the greatest masterpieces of the Renaissance. So that you can fully appreciate this work of art, let me tell you more about it.

First of all, in *The Last Supper*, Leonardo again broke the rules of perspective. It would have been impossible for the 12 disciples to have clustered on one side of a table in the posture in which the artist painted them. But he did so for a reason. Using his mathematical mind, Leonardo positioned the disciples in groups of three. Each group is alive with expression as they react to the moment that Jesus announced that one of them would betray him.

The use of perspective and the addition of background detail are undeniable characteristics of Leonardo da Vinci's work found in *The Last Supper.*

A story is told that Leonardo sorted through the faces of countless citizens of Milan for the proper models to capture the expression of each of the disciples. Hunting a model for Judas was particularly difficult but finishing the face of Jesus was supposedly the most difficult task of all. It may even be the work of another artist. In the end, the look on Jesus' face is a calm one as He appears to accept his coming fate. And the background? It is unmistakably the work of Leonardo da Vinci because it is filled with details to mystify the viewer. The geometric perfection of the room draws the viewer both to Christ in the center and to the world beyond Him that waits for salvation. *The Last Supper* is a true masterpiece.

## *The* Mona Lisa

In 1499, Leonardo left Milan. With his distinctive long hair and flowing beard, he traveled for awhile, enjoying the countryside where he was free to create, dream, and capture nature on the pages of his notebooks. In time, Leonardo returned to Florence — after Savonarola had died. (I don't think the two would have mixed well. Leonardo possessed far too many "vanities" and fancy clothes for the approval of Savonarola.) It was there, in **1503**, that Leonardo began his most famous work, the painting of *Mona Lisa*. There is so much to say about this work of art.

Art historians would praise the *Mona Lisa* for many things. As a great example of lighting, the fair skin of the model radiates almost three dimensionally from the darker background. But the change is gradual, giving the edges of the portrait a smoky look. Leonardo named this technique ***sfumato*** (sfoo MAH toe), meaning "smoke-like" in Italian. And of course, the background is filled with an "abundance and variety" of natural structures.

Leonardo da Vinci painted the *Mona Lisa* with a *sfumato*, or smoke-like, hue radiating from the calm, gentle face of Madonna Elisabetta.

In case you weren't sure, most historians think that Mona Lisa was a real person. Most likely she was **Madonna Elisabetta**, the third wife of **Francesco del Giocondo** (Joe KAHN doe). In Italian, the portrait is called *La Gioconda* (La Joe KAHN da) — after the feminine version of Elisabetta's married name. Francesco asked Leonardo to paint the picture of Elisabetta, or Lisa. The request came perhaps after the couple had lost a child. The odd thing about the portrait is that Leonardo kept it in his possession for years. Every once in a while he would add a layer of paint here and a layer of paint there to give it more depth or less depth — or whatever Leonardo desired. Over the course of three years, the artist called Lisa back and forth to pose in his studio. Legend says Leonardo hired clowns and jesters to keep Lisa smiling. It may be that she was still grieving the loss of her baby and needed a little help in making that famous smile.

After that, it's believed that Leonardo carried the painting with him and slept with it by his side. Perhaps the genius in him *was* pleased and knew he had created a masterpiece. Perhaps he felt he had captured the broken heart of a mother in mourning. The story is not fully known. But, many, many years later, the *Mona Lisa* made it into the hands of Napoleon, who hung it in his own bedroom! Fortunately for us, it was retrieved and now hangs in the **Louvre** (Luuve) — a very large and beautiful museum in Paris. The painting is heavily guarded behind bulletproof glass where millions can admire it. (I saw it once myself. To my surprise, it's not very large.)

One of my favorite paintings by Leonardo da Vinci is called *The Virgin and Child with Saint Anne and Saint John the Baptist*. There are two versions of this scene, which Leonardo painted as an altarpiece for a group of monks. One was never finished, but in simple brown ink it still remains beautiful. One historian wrote, "men and women, young and old, flocked for two days to see it, as if in festival time."[12] In this cartoon sketch, Mary sits on the lap of her mother while doting over baby Jesus. A young John the Baptist is nearby and Saint Anne (Mary's mother) points toward heaven. The print is famous for the "Mona Lisa–looking" smiles on the women and the interesting position of their feet. (It's hard to tell whose feet are whose.) Geometrically, Leonardo used the shape of a triangle to draw perfect attention to Jesus.

In another version of the same scene, John the Baptist is replaced with a symbolic lamb. The heads of Anne, Mary, and Jesus line up to direct the viewer to the lamb, which represents the coming sacrificial death of the Messiah. The background was finished with creative details as was typical of Leonardo. The portrait was finished properly by Leonardo and to this day remains vibrant with color.

Unfortunately, one of Leonardo's other works from this time in his life doesn't remain with us at all, but it has an interesting story behind it. It seems that Leonardo and his greatest rival, Michelangelo, were each asked to paint a large fresco in memory of a battle in Florence. The patriotic murals were to be across from each other in the new city hall. (The city hall was built to house Savonarola's large council.) Now, these two artists — Leonardo da Vinci and Michelangelo — were *not* friends at all. As true rivals, they worked in separate studios, each trying to outdo the other. The public cheered on their favorite artist as if the two were in some kind of sporting match. Many would say that Leonardo's rough sketch was the most lifelike battle scene of the two. It was greatly admired. But something awful happened!

Though never painted, the brown-ink sketch of *The Virgin and Child with Saint Anne and Saint John the Baptist,* by Leonardo da Vinci, captures tenderness and reverence for the Christ child.

On the day that paint was applied, there was so much moisture in the air that it ruined Leonardo's mural! In his own words, Leonardo said, "I was just picking up my brush when the weather took a turn for the worse . . . and the cartoon began to come apart, and water went everywhere."[13] Poor Leonardo! After working on the sketch for a year and a half, it began to disintegrate right before his very eyes. He tried to repair it but eventually gave up. Michelangelo didn't finish his mural either. (All of Florence was upset with these finicky artists!) Others did their best to duplicate the masterpieces. **Peter Paul Rubens** was the most successful in re-creating Leonardo's mural, which is titled *The Battle of Anghiari* (UN gear are ee).

## Later Years

Some of Leonardo's last years were spent in Rome. He and his rivals Michelangelo, Raphael, and Bramante, were all invited by the pope to live there. They spent most of their time beautifying the Church of St. Peter and other buildings at the Vatican. (This was when Michelangelo painted the famous ceiling of the Sistine Chapel, which is our next lesson.) Even in Rome, Leonardo continued to pour his fascination with science into his work. In his leisure, he created a robotic lizard with flapping wings! He used quicksilver to power it.

But Leonardo's final years were spent in France. The king of France offered him the life of a prince if he would move there. I suppose that was an appealing offer. In his official contract, Leonardo was hired as a painter, engineer, architect, and mechanic of the state.

He enjoyed it all. Leonardo settled in at the castle of Cloux near Amboise for the last three years of his life. At an old age, he said, "As a day well spent makes it sweet to sleep, so a life well used makes it sweet to die."[14] Leonardo died in France on May 2, 1519. He was 67 years old.

**(Middle and Older Students)**

In closing, let me share these further comments. I referred to Leonardo da Vinci as a "genius" five times in this lesson. I hope by now you would agree. But being a genius doesn't make one perfect. Twice in 1476, Leonardo and a few other young men were arrested in Florence for immoral behavior. The charges were dropped, but Leonardo was insulted over the matter and probably left Florence because of it. It is doubtful that the issue of immorality was ever resolved for Leonardo.

Because of all the religious works Leonardo painted, I would conclude that he knew *of* the Savior. But outwardly, he did not appear to *follow* the Savior. In many ways his lifestyle failed to demonstrate one who was called and saved by Christ. In my opinion, that would be all the more reason to view Leonardo da Vinci as the epitome, or true example, of a Renaissance man.

# WEEK 5

## Lesson 13 1508

# Michelangelo

Stop right now and look at your ceiling. What do you see up there? Probably not much. Most of us don't do much with our ceilings. But this was not the case with **Pope Julius II**. In 1508, he commissioned an artist to paint the most spectacular ceiling in the world. It was the ceiling of the **Sistine Chapel** in Rome, Italy. But strangely enough, the painter who painted it didn't like to paint at all! In fact, he despised it. This artist was **Michelangelo** (Mike kuhl AN juh loh *or* Mick kuhl AN juh loh).

Michelangelo's full name was Michelangelo di Lodovico Buonarroti Simoni. For obvious reasons, most folks just call him by his first name. Michelangelo was born near Florence, Italy, in 1475. Think about that for a minute. It's hard not to believe that the time and place that Michelangelo was born had something to do with his destiny. He was born during the lifetime of Lorenzo de' Medici in the highest city of the Renaissance. You will learn later that Lorenzo and Michelangelo became good friends.

Much like Leonardo da Vinci, Michelangelo started his career as an apprentice. He was set up to work for **Domenico Ghirlandaio** (Geerr lahn DAH yo), who was not only a painter but also a sculptor. He has been given credit for first teaching Michelangelo how to use a chisel (which is a tool for sculpting). However, Michelangelo would later say (with some pride) that he never had a teacher. In a way, that was true. What Michelangelo accomplished was far beyond what anyone could teach him.

After only three years with Domenico, Michelangelo moved to the workshop of **Bertoldo di Giovanni** (Joe VAHN nee). His studio happened to be part of the famous Medici gardens, which were filled with Greek and Roman statues. Do you think this had something to do with Michelangelo's future? Of course it did. He had access to some of the finest statues ever created, including a bronze statue of David carved by **Donatello** that would inspire Michelangelo's greatest work. These three-dimensional masterpieces burned a love for sculpture into Michelangelo's heart that would last a lifetime.

Lorenzo de' Medici was quick to notice the talent and passion of the young artist and invited Michelangelo to live in his home. Lorenzo provided him with a room and paid him a modest salary. The young artist regularly dined with Lorenzo and other politicians and artists. It was there that Michelangelo became good friends with the Medici family and was naturally shaped by the ideas of the Renaissance.

In the *Pietà*, Michelangelo sculpted sorrow on the face of Mary and serenity on the face of Jesus, her Savior and son.

Unfortunately, Michelangelo's nose was shaped during this time as well. (Yes, his nose!) It was during his stay with Lorenzo that someone punched him *so* hard in the face that it left his nose broken and disfigured for life. This didn't help Michelangelo's disposition any. He was known for being temperamental and having a lot of self-pity. His broken nose seemed only to add to it.

But the young artist was soon to be famous, and for a time, his self-doubt was pushed aside. Michelangelo's two greatest statues were created early in his career and brought him more recognition than he could imagine. Each statue is so amazing that I'm going to take the time here to describe them.

The first masterpiece was the *Pietà* in St. Peter's Basilica in Rome. It is a deeply moving piece portraying Christ after his death lying across the lap of his mother, Mary. She is blanketed in layers of a robe that help hold the Savior on her lap. Mary gazes sorrowfully upon the crucified body of her Son, who had taken upon Himself the sins of the entire world. The face of Jesus is serene and seems to whisper to the viewer, "It is finished." I personally find it to be Michelangelo's most beautiful work.

But Michelangelo's most famous statue would be *David*. Created in Florence, this 18-foot nude male is so remarkably lifelike, it nearly breathes. Every muscle, every vein, every curl on David's head seems alive. Michelangelo approached the position of his marble giant this way — the right side is firm and steadfast to represent the strength of man under the guidance of God. The left side, however, is relaxed and unguarded, reflecting the weak and sinful side of man. It is toward this direction that the statue gazes and is fixed in time. As you will learn later, Michelangelo — then only 27 years old — knew all too well this weak side of mankind.

It was near this time that Michelangelo was asked to paint the battle scene for the city of Florence alongside his rival, Leonardo da Vinci. Do you remember what happened to

Leonardo's work? Bad weather made it drip right off the wall. Though both Leonardo's and Michelangelo's works were left incomplete, they made a major impact on art for capturing intense *action*. Many artists after them tried to do the same. While Leonardo chose to depict the fury of soldiers on horseback, Michelangelo chose to paint soldiers caught in the act of bathing! Yes, apparently in the real battle of Florence, soldiers were bathing in the river when word came that they were under attack. And so Michelangelo created an unusual scene showing men rising out of a river, pulling up their socks, and running for their clothes and weapons. The artist would say it expressed the "bestial folly" of war.[1]

This unusual battle scene also allowed Michelangelo to express his deepest-felt fascination — the movement and anatomy of the human body. Like Leonardo, Michelangelo dissected dead bodies to better understand muscles, limbs, and torsos. In marble or on canvas, Michelangelo used his understanding of anatomy to bring mankind to life. He applied the same techniques to mythological characters and heavenly beings, like sibyls and cherubs. Most of his models were men, however, which explains why the women in Michelangelo's paintings are extremely masculine. Muscle-bound figures became one of his trademarks.

Now, unlike Leonardo, Michelangelo practically ignored landscapes, still portraits, or issues of perspective. He said of painting landscapes that it was "a game for children and uneducated men."[2] In content and style, his works were *quite* different from Leonardo's. In fact, as much as Leonardo loved painting, Michelangelo hated it. He once said of painting that it was only "suitable for women . . ."[3] He cared for it only when it looked like the sculpture that he loved. Michelangelo said, "The more painting resembles sculpture, the better I like it, and the more sculpture resembles painting, the worse I like it."[4]

So, how was it that Michelangelo, who despised painting, went and *painted* one of the greatest masterpieces of all time? That is a good question. The short answer is — he was coerced by the pope! Let's move now to that part of the story.

## *Pope Julius II*

The perilous story of Michelangelo painting the Sistine ceiling can't be appreciated until you know a little more about Pope Julius II. He was a stern, arrogant, ill-tempered man who wished to be well remembered by the world. For this reason, he first invited Michelangelo to Rome to build a magnificent burial tomb for him. Well, Michelangelo was arrogant and ill-tempered himself. The two men, very much alike in pride and bad moods, found it hard to agree on anything. This was especially true in the building of Julius's elaborate tomb, which originally was to contain 40 statues in all.

After Michelangelo spent eight months in the mountains collecting tons of stone suitable for the tomb, the pope changed his mind about the whole thing and put the entire project on hold! This made Michelangelo furious! So, one Saturday, Michelangelo demanded a meeting with Julius, but it didn't go very well. The two quarreled over money. Michelangelo went back on Monday but was turned away. He went back on Tuesday, on Wednesday, on Thursday, *and* on Friday — but the pope refused to see him. With that final blow, Michelangelo fled on horseback to Florence, angry and insulted.

Stirring the emotions, the painted hand of God the Father reaches out to touch man on the ceiling of the Sistine Chapel by Michelangelo.

It took an official letter and three forceful letters from Pope Julius II to get Michelangelo to return to Rome. But he did, with the intention of building the tomb. Unfortunately though, only one of the 40 statues was brought to life at that time. It was later melted down to form a cannon! After so much bickering and disappointment, things were not good between the pope and the artist.

It was then that Julius II came up with the extraordinary idea of painting the ceiling of the Sistine Chapel, a private chapel in the Vatican. By then Michelangelo felt he could not refuse. Though the artist dreaded picking up a paintbrush, he was weary of arguing and tired of being disappointed. In fear of the pope and in need of money, he agreed to paint the enormous vaulted ceiling in **1508**. He grumbled all the way through it.

I hardly think anyone could blame Michelangelo for grumbling. He was being asked to paint 10,000 square feet from 70 feet off the ground! For more than four years, the artist painted in agony. Mounted on scaffolding, Michelangelo either reclined on his back or stood with his arms stretched over his head going numb. At times he painted alone through the night with no more than a few feet between his face and the gigantic fresco. The job was so consuming that the artist hardly changed his clothes or took a bath. He slept in his boots and ate only what was on hand. The constant nagging of the pope made it worse. (The pope was known for his impatience. At least once he struck the artist with a stick just to hurry him along!)

Perhaps it was Michelangelo's pride that kept him going. (He wasn't going to do a poor job for the pope to criticize!) If not his pride, it was perhaps the content of his masterpiece that fueled his determination. Michelangelo designed the biblical mural to contain 343 muscle-bound figures — his favorite thing to create. Most of the figures were human or made to look it. Michelangelo portrayed the Creator of the Universe in the form of a gray-bearded man floating in the heavens. And, with the mindset of the Medicis, he added characters of Greek mythology to the biblical stories. (These female mythological characters, called *sibyls*, were thought by the Greeks to be prophetesses.)

In the pure style of Michelangelo, every muscular being he designed appeared to be in action. Probably the most famous scene of the entire ceiling is the hand of God reaching out toward the hand of Adam. There is something moving about the Creator drifting tenderly toward humanity. As if in slow motion, the mind of the viewer is left to imagine the two hands touching while man breathed his first breath.

The artist continued to show action by portraying the fall of Adam and Eve, a swirl of sinners in the flood, the triumph of David over Goliath, and other Old Testament stories.

In every panel, there appears no landscape but rather, multitudes of faces and bodies flying in midair. Between the panels, some figures sit as eternal guardians or onlookers of the stories being told.

Sadly enough, Pope Julius II lived only four months after the ceiling was completed. It was hardly enough time to appreciate the greatness of the work. But Michelangelo must have felt rewarded. For *after* Julius died, Michelangelo attempted to build him a tomb. Can you believe it? He returned to the very project that drove the two men to quarreling! Though the final tomb wasn't anything like the original plan, Michelangelo sculpted a figure of *Moses* for the entrance that is staggering, to say the least. Depicting Moses seated on a throne with flowing beard and robe, this is one of the most superb sculptures of all time. The Jews of the community were enamored with the piece and flocked to see it.

Despite the difficulty of working with Pope Julius II, Michelangelo sculpted the dramatic statue of *Moses* in his honor.

## *Last Years in Rome*

In his late fifties, Michelangelo returned to Rome. He lived there for 32 more years. A lot of his work focused on beautifying the Vatican through architecture. But something special happened to the artist during those last years in Rome. He made friends with a widow named **Vittoria Colonna** (Kuh LOW nuh). Though they were never romantically involved, Michelangelo loved her. Vittoria was a strong Christian woman who cared a great deal for the aging artist. The two visited on Sundays at a convent and spent hours and hours discussing their faith.

Michelangelo needed this kind of spiritual guidance because his life had not been well balanced. Having been consumed by his work, he had not made much time for friends or family. He may even have turned to immoral behavior to fill some emptiness in his life. If that was indeed the case, it would appear that he later repented of it. Some claim that Michelangelo was influenced by the teachings of Savonarola, whom he had heard in his younger years. Others say the Waldensians (see Volume II of *The Mystery of History*) shared the salvation message with the artist. Regardless of the influences on him, the struggle in Michelangelo's soul is most clearly seen in one of the last works he ever did. He went back to the Sistine Chapel and painted a scene titled *The Last Judgment*.

As a reflection of weariness or repentance, in *The Last Judgment* Michelangelo painted his self-portrait in the hanging flesh of St. Bartholomew.

*The Last Judgment* tells a sobering story. In it, Michelangelo portrays the folly of man's sin and the consequences of it in the end. Many believe that the goriness of the scene was inspired by Dante's poem *Inferno*. This could be true because Michelangelo himself wrote poetry and admired the work of Dante. As if he were confessing his own depravity, Michelangelo painted himself as an obscure figure in *The Last Judgment*. He painted his face in the flailing hollow of St. Bartholomew's skin dangling before the Lord Jesus Christ. (Bartholomew was skinned alive and died a martyr for Christ.) Some would say the hanging flesh expressed the emptiness of the tired artist, worn out and spent of creativity. Others would say it expressed his abandonment of the sins of his flesh. Maybe it reflects both. He was 66 years old by this time and regretful of much of his past.

When Vittoria died in 1547, Michelangelo was plagued with unbearable grief. It led him to a deeper change of heart. Though he continued to paint and sculpt, he did so only for the glory of God. He wrote, "Neither painting nor sculpting can any longer quieten my soul, turned now to that divine love which on the cross, to embrace us, opened wide its arms."[5] In 1550, he carved a statue of Nicodemus holding the dying body of Christ. In this sculpture (known as the *Florentine Pietà* or *The Deposition*), the statue of Nicodemus is actually a portrait of himself. Older, wiser, and finally at peace with himself, Michelangelo embraced the Savior in spirit — and in stone. In February of 1564, the worn-out artist passed away.

Unlike Leonardo da Vinci, Michelangelo was not an example of a true Renaissance man, in my opinion. (Many historians, however, would say he was.) I think his interests were too narrow and his faith in God too strong to be compared to other humanists of his time. I think Michelangelo stands alone in what he accomplished. The *Pietà, David,* the Sistine Chapel, *Moses, The Last Judgment* — these incredible works surely place Michelangelo in a category all by himself. That is why Giorgio Vasari, the great art historian, claimed that Michelangelo surpassed them all.

*"Neither painting nor sculpting can any longer quieten my soul, turned now to that divine love which on the cross, to embrace us, opened wide its arms."*

*–Michelangelo*

# Artists of the Northern Renaissance

Italian artists weren't the only ones rising to prominence in Europe during the Renaissance. In the **fifteenth and sixteenth centuries, Flemish** and **German** artists were on the rise, too. Though a few of them were trained by Italians, most found fame on their own. Today, I will introduce you to four outstanding artists who helped make *northern* Europe famous during the Renaissance. Rather than elaborate on their personal lives, I'll tell you about their most famous works. (Our study on the Renaissance just wouldn't be complete without them!)

## Jan van Eyck (c. 1390–1441)

The first Flemish artist we'll look at is **Jan van Eyck** (Yahn van IKE). He lived in Flanders, which today is part of Belgium, the Netherlands, and France. (The people of Flanders called themselves "Flemish.") Jan van Eyck had a special gift for creating detail. He did this exceptionally well in the portrait of a couple titled *The Arnolfini* (ARR no fee nee) *Marriage* (also known as *The Arnolfini Portrait*).

In *The Arnolfini Marriage*, husband and wife hold hands in a room surrounded with details that tell us more about everyday life in the fourteenth century. There is a dog in the room, fruit on the table, a pair of slippers strewn on the floor, and the name of a saint finely engraved on a chair. Of great interest to art historians is the image that lies in a small convex mirror in the back of the room. The mirror shows the back of the couple and introduces us to two more people standing right in front of them but not in the actual portrait. But we don't know who they are! They appear only as tiny reflections in the mirror. Some think they are wedding attendants. Others think it is Jan van Eyck and a priest. Either way, the convex mirror is a very clever approach to *perspective*.

As a clever use of perspective, Jan van Eyck added a convex mirror to the back wall in *The Arnolfini Marriage.*

Based on today's standards, it is doubtful that the Arnolfinis would win a beauty contest, but their pale skin and delicate features would have been popular back then among the Flemish. Interesting, too, is the fact that the woman in the portrait appears to be expecting a child. Some believe she was not pregnant, but rather was holding up her dress as was tradition. Perhaps it was in hopes of having a fruitful union. Regardless, the painting of this couple in everyday surroundings is a clear example of the **realism** that Jan van Eyck is known for.

Besides realistic portraits, Jan van Eyck painted numerous scenes from the Bible. His largest was a 20-panel altarpiece known as the *Adoration of the Lamb* or the *Ghent Altarpiece*. And much like Leonardo, he included amazing landscapes and creative depth in his work. But Jan van Eyck died 10 years before Leonardo was ever born, and so he could *not* have been influenced by Leonardo. (If anything, it was the other way around.) Jan van Eyck was a master painter by his *own* merit and way ahead of his time. By going beyond religious works, to portraits of real people, Jan van Eyck was steering northern Europe toward a Renaissance of its own.

In *The Ship of Fools,* Jerome Bosch portrays the folly of mankind, traveling through life always chasing after something.

## *Jerome Bosch (1450–1516)*

Another Flemish artist to bring fame to northern Europe was **Hieronymus Bosch**. (In English, his name translates to "Jerome.") He lived 60 years later than Jan van Eyck, but he kept up the Flemish tradition of bringing great detail into his work. His detail, however, wasn't the least bit real like Jan van Eyck's. Jerome's details were strange and sometimes grotesque. In *The Garden of Earthly Delights,* the artist crammed three panels with images of heaven, hell, and earth. It is his portrayal of hell that is most bizarre. Jerome created weird and horrifying creatures of all shapes and sizes to depict the torture and torment of eternal doom. His imagination went wild with monsters, strange instruments, giant ear-like creatures, and odd mechanical devices! I'm not sure of the intentions of his imagination, but it seems he was depicting hell to be a pretty scary place. It was sure to make one think!

In *The Ship of Fools,* Jerome Bosch pokes fun at man's foolishness. He painted a ship of people going about life like a boat on a river. Each person appears to be a fool for chasing after something in "life." Bosch was a religious man and was probably challenging people to think about their own lives when viewing *The Ship of Fools*. It is thought provoking, as were most of his strange works. In an eerie way, his paintings are very similar to works of modern artists like **Salvador Dalí**. We call them **surrealists**. This fact places Jerome Bosch *way* ahead of his time.

## *Albrecht Dürer (1471–1528)*

In Germany, art wasn't appreciated as much as it was in Italy during the high Renaissance. It was only considered a craft. But a German artist named **Albrecht Durer** (al breckt DOO rawr) helped to change that. His great skill as a painter and engraver caused the Germans to take notice of the arts. You could say that Dürer was to Germany what Leonardo was to Italy. Dürer was an educated man who studied anatomy and perspective. He went to Italy to learn firsthand some of the techniques of the great masters.

One of Albrecht Dürer's most famous paintings is that of a pair of praying hands. The story behind the hands is touching. Legend says that Albrecht and his brother *both* wished to study art. But being from a family of 18 children, they were too poor to afford it. The two brothers agreed that one would work the mines while the other went to study art for a few years — and then they would switch places. But that's not how things worked out.

The well-worn hands clasped together in *Praying Hands* are supposedly those of Albrecht Dürer's brother.

As the story goes, Albrecht went first to study art and won quick fame for his talent. When he returned home to trade places with his brother, his brother wouldn't hear of it. He claimed that he could in no way take Albrecht's place since Albrecht's hands were skilled and refined, and his were gnarled and twisted from working the mines. Albrecht's brother insisted that Albrecht stay in school while he continued to work the mines. In gratitude for his brother's sacrifice, Albrecht supposedly painted his brother's hands — well worn and clasped in prayer. Whether this tender story is true or not, the praying hands are famous all over the world.

Albrecht Dürer did continue on as his brother wished. He painted and learned the skilled craft of engraving. One of his most outstanding engravings is titled *Knight, Death, and the Devil*. The knight in the scene is armed with spiritual weapons to fight sin and death. The artist used some imagination to symbolize spiritual truths. But many of his engravings were lifelike representations of simple things like rabbits and tufts of grass. Through paintings and engravings, Dürer captured the lives of peasants, animals, relatives, and himself in great detail and liveliness.

Dürer's own self-portraits are convincingly real. To help with realism, Dürer created unusual devices to help him visually change the size and shape of objects. Using glass panes, pulleys, and strings for measurement, Dürer invented something like a primitive overhead projector to reflect and copy images. For all of this and more, Albrecht Dürer is considered one of the greatest German artists to ever live.

## *Pieter Bruegel the Elder (c. 1525–1569)*

I've saved one of my favorites for last. That would be **Pieter Bruegel** (BROI guhl *or* BROO guhl), another Flemish artist. It is his painting of *The Tower of Babel* that I like best of all the works of the northern European artists. Here's why. In this scene, Pieter Bruegal integrated lots of things we've talked about in art. He used *perspective* to cause the tower to rise toward heaven. He added *detailed landscaping* in the background. He made the scene *realistic* with a group of builders discussing their plans in the foreground. And he portrayed *action* as the Tower of Babel appears to still be under construction in the sixteenth century!

This oddity presents the viewer with something moral to think about. It leads one to wonder, "What are *our* modern-day Towers of Babel"? In what ways do *we* build our lives apart from God? It's something to reflect on.

In *The Tower of Babel*, Pieter Bruegel used perspective, detail, realism, and action to portray mankind's foolishness in building their lives apart from the power of God.

Other works of Pieter Bruegel focused a great deal on ordinary life. He loved to capture harvesters, hunters, and peasants doing everyday things. Bruegel especially liked to paint realistic scenes from winter. His seasonal works are the ones that most of us can relate to. Though the people he painted lived a long time ago, we can relate to hunters trudging home in the snow, ice skaters on the pond, and those tending the fire on a gray day. Since there were no cameras back then, we can thank artists like Pieter Bruegel for giving us these portraits of real life.

## Lesson 15 — 1511

# *Erasmus Writes* In Praise of Folly

We have looked closely now at many artists of the Renaissance. I hope you haven't forgotten *early* Renaissance artists such as Fra Angelico, Botticelli, and Donatello. I hope you have burned in your memory the *high* Renaissance works of Leonardo da Vinci and Michelangelo. (Real quick — which one painted the *Mona Lisa*? Which one sculpted *David*? Remember that!) And I hope the northern European artists are still fresh in your mind. You'll be glad one day to have become acquainted with these masters because the works they produced are classics. That means they'll be remembered for a long, long time.

I'm going to shift gears today to a different kind of Renaissance man. This man wasn't an artist, a sculptor, or an architect. This man was a writer. His name was **Desiderius Erasmus** (Des a DIR ee us Ih RAZ mus). His name means "desired beloved" (a name he may have given himself). His most famous work was ***In Praise of Folly***. Some people loved it; some despised it. It had something to do with *worldview*. I'll talk more about that as we get to know Erasmus.

Erasmus was born in the Netherlands about 1469. Sadly, both of his parents died while he was still young. His new guardians steered him toward living in a monastery. Erasmus didn't really want to go there, but he agreed to it so he could have access to books — lots of books. They were his favorite thing and continued to be most of his life.

Erasmus eventually took the vows of an Augustinian monk. But it never suited him very well. He didn't like fasting, which was required, and he hated eating fish during Lent. (Some Christians fast from red meat during Lent to remember the sacrifice of Christ.) To escape the rigid rules of the monastery, Erasmus eagerly took the position of a secretary. He was ordained a priest in 1492 (the same year as the voyage of Columbus).

Though they didn't suit him well, Erasmus took the humble vows of an Augustinian monk.

## *Classics and Controversy*

I don't think that being a priest suited Erasmus any more than being a monk did. He never had his own church but went to a university in Paris where he could pursue his real love — books and literature. It was there that he was immersed in reading the classics. It was, of course, the rage of the Renaissance to read classic works of the ancient Greeks and Romans. He was particularly enamored with **Plato**. To better enjoy Plato and others in their original language, Erasmus taught himself Greek. He already knew Latin. Both of these languages were important when it came to doing one of the things that made him famous. And that was to update the **Latin Vulgate**.

The Latin Vulgate was a translation of the Greek and Hebrew Bible into the Latin language. It was first translated by **Jerome** in the Middle Ages. (See Volume II of *The Mystery of History*.) According to Erasmus, the Vulgate had errors and wasn't accessible to the common man. But his "updates" became very controversial. Admirers of Jerome's older work didn't appreciate the new edition. Those who did like the new edition criticized Erasmus for not better applying the Word of God to his "personal life." Apparently his life wasn't the holiest.

During the Middle Ages, Jerome spent 23 years translating Greek and Hebrew scriptures into the Latin Vulgate.

But controversy didn't stop Erasmus from reading and writing more. He tutored students to pay for his love of books. His tutoring took him back and forth to England where he met other scholars, including **Thomas More**, and his fame as an intellectual grew. He regularly wrote letters to kings, emperors, and popes who admired his writings. Back in Paris, he wrote a best-seller that actually provided him with a salary. His best-seller was a collection of more than 800 quotes from classical authors, with extra comments from Erasmus himself. The ***Adagia*** (Uh DAH zhee uh), as it was called, was incredibly popular. It was so popular that it was translated into English, Italian, German, French, and Dutch. The *Adagia* provided a crash course in the classics for those wanting to keep up with the Renaissance. Erasmus's fame spread even more.

At one time Erasmus was offered a position at a university, a place at the Vatican, and many other jobs. But he chose to remain a "freelance" writer, which allowed him the freedom to write what he wanted when he wanted. It was a bold move on his part because few people were full-time writers back then, but it seemed to work. He kept very busy traveling, writing, and translating. He did accept one full-time job in the court of King Henry VIII of England, but the king ignored Erasmus and the job proved to be rather dull.

## *The Satire of* In Praise of Folly

It was in **1511**, during his stay in England, that Erasmus was inspired to write his most famous work, titled *In Praise of Folly*. As mentioned earlier, some people loved it, but others despised it. To better understand why, you need to understand the term *satire*. A satire is a work of literature that points out the weaknesses and foolishness of mankind. And that is what Erasmus did in *In Praise of Folly*. He poked fun, which is why *some* people didn't like the work at all.

In the story, *Folly* is the name of a female character who represents all mankind. In the beginning of the story, Erasmus just pokes a "little" fun at the foolish ways of mankind. He starts with amusing remarks about grammarians and writers like himself. He then slams merchants, lawyers, and philosophers for their greed and ego. But by the end of the book, he flat-out ridicules the behavior of just about everyone he could think of. He especially attacked members of the church. Erasmus lashed out at evil priests, immoral monks, and greedy popes. He spewed at those who worshiped shrines or argued over theology or "paid" for their sins to be pardoned.

The powerful thing about the satire is that Erasmus was right about most of it. According to the Bible, the heart of man *is* foolish. (See Eccl. 9:3; Jer. 17:9; Rom. 1:21.) Many of man's ways *are* nonsense. And some of the practices of the church *had* become ridiculous. As one example, Pope Julius II distributed "indulgences" for money to help pay for the painting of the Sistine Chapel. Indulgences were letters that *appeared* to forgive people of their sins! The Bible teaches that only the blood of Jesus can pay for our sins. (See Rom. 5:9; Eph. 1:7; Heb. 9:12–14; Rev. 5:9.) But out of fear and superstition, people traded money for indulgences anyway. This was just one of many ways the church was out of line. (We will look more at that in later lessons.)

The famous German artist Albrecht Dürer sketched this image of Erasmus busy at his writing desk.

In another publication by Erasmus, titled *The Handbook of a Christian Knight*, he urged Christians to return to the moral teachings of Christ. He especially encouraged acts of charity. But before I make Erasmus sound too noble, there were those who found fault with his teachings about Christ. Why? Well, Erasmus was a humanist in his thinking. And a humanist generally gives more credit to man than God. You could say Erasmus promoted Christ as a good "role model" rather than as God in the flesh. He thought that people would benefit from following Christ's example as a *man*, but he wasn't so sure about Christ as *Lord*. Erasmus wasn't even sure if he himself was a Christian. That's how far his humanism had taken him.

Erasmus continued to write and mingle with the top scholars and intellects of the Renaissance up until his death in 1536. Over the years, he received permission to quit wearing the clothes of a monk, though for a long time he was still considered to be one. He spent time in Rome, Germany, Paris, and Oxford. Because he had ties to so many different countries, he wasn't loyal to any one nation. He in fact began to think that patriotism, or nationalism, was ridiculous, too. Erasmus marveled instead at the rate of mankind's achievements at this time. (I imagine he saw firsthand the works of Leonardo da Vinci and Michelangelo.) He wrote, "All over the world, as if on a given signal, splendid talents are stirring and conspiring together to revive the best learning."[6]

The observations of Erasmus were certainly accurate. Splendid talents *were* stirring during the Renaissance. But something else was stirring across Europe. And that was the **Reformation**. It was very near this time that **Martin Luther** spoke out to "reform" the ways of the church. Some would say that Erasmus was part of the Reformation. But that's not quite accurate. Erasmus was disgusted with the church, but he never tried to "reform" it. In fact, Erasmus disagreed with Martin Luther on many things. For Erasmus, his issue with the church was the *behavior* of Christians, not their *beliefs*. (Though truthfully, *his* behavior wasn't much to be admired!)

But what Erasmus did do for the Reformation was to make people aware. Through the satire of *In Praise of Folly*, Erasmus boldly pointed out the shortcomings of the church. In a way, he paved the way for reformers like Martin Luther. Because of Erasmus and others, it was no secret to Europeans that the church had grown corrupt in many of its ways. As if to retaliate, the church banned the books of Erasmus 23 years after his death.

So, was Erasmus a good guy or a bad guy? Well, I don't think anyone is entirely good or bad, but generally speaking, I think the answer to my question depends on your *worldview*. For those who view the world through the eyes of man, Erasmus was a "good" guy. He was considered one of the smartest men of the Renaissance, and he wrote things to stimulate others to think very deeply. Furthermore, his translation of the New Testament was a huge accomplishment.

But if one has a Christian worldview, Erasmus wasn't so good. As a humanist, he analyzed the world through the eyes of man rather than through the eyes of God. In regard to Christ, Erasmus confessed that he viewed Him as a "good man" more readily than as Lord. As Christians, any teaching that lessens the Lordship of Christ ought to alarm and concern us.

Lesson 16 1513

# *Niccolò Machiavelli and* The Prince

Men and women live and die, but sometimes their names go on. This is quite true of **Niccolò Machiavelli** (NEEK ul LOW MAH kyah VEL lee). He died in 1527, but his last name has lived on as a political term. The term is ***Machiavellian***. Do you know what Ma-chi-a-vel-li-an means? Probably not. It's a very big word. It usually refers to tricky, deceitful, or dishonest politics. I'm going to teach you more about that today and a little about the man behind it.

Niccolò Machiavelli was an Italian through and through. He was born in Florence during the rule of Lorenzo de' Medici. By now, you should have a good picture in your mind of Florence, Italy, during the Renaissance. Florence was a strong and vibrant city/state under Lorenzo. Humanism was also strong in the thought of the time and influenced the arts and sciences. But by 1492, Lorenzo had died, and for a time Savonarola led the city in a spiritual revival. Six years later, however, Savonarola was executed — as you should remember — and the remaining Medici family was overthrown. Now stay with me here because we are getting to Machiavelli.

The name of Machiavelli has lived on to refer to evil politics.

It was after Savonarola died and the Medicis were overthrown that Niccolò Machiavelli was hired to work for the Republic of Florence. The Renaissance was in full force, and the great Leonardo da Vinci had returned to Florence and was starting his work on the *Mona Lisa*. Machiavelli's job was to be the first secretary of the council of Florence. What does that mean? It means that Machiavelli spent hours every day working in government affairs and politics. His duties were numerous.

### *The Borgia Family*

One of Machiavelli's duties was to work for a man named **Cesare Borgia** (SAY zar BORE zhee uh). To help you understand Machiavelli, I need to introduce you to the **Borgia family**. They were a sinister clan from Spain who rivaled and hated the Medici family. (Both families were rich and powerful.) It was a member of the Borgia family who became Pope Alexander VI, the pope who ordered Savonarola's execution. Do you remember him? He was not a very good pope. In fact, Pope Alexander VI broke his vows of purity and fathered several children. One of those children was Cesare Borgia.

So, what do you do if you are the son of the pope? (It's a rather odd position to have in life since the pope doesn't usually have children!) Well, Cesare Borgia chose to follow in the "corrupted" footsteps of his father. With charm, good looks, and intelligence, Cesare lived it up. He took advantage of his father's position as pope and used it to get things he wanted. Because of his father, Cesare was appointed to serve as a cardinal in the church, which is a very high position.

When Cesare grew weary of church business, he had his father get him out of the position, which was unheard of as well. Cesare spent a great deal of time leading military campaigns that proved to be more exciting than his marriage or his earlier work as a cardinal. But Cesare Borgia was known for terrible things, like shooting prisoners for sport. It was rumored that he was in love with his sister and murdered her husband! In fact, there were several murders, poisonings, and unsolved mysteries that clouded the life of Cesare Borgia. He was one scary guy!

Well, this scary guy had a large influence on Machiavelli, our main character today. As a governmental secretary, Machiavelli could watch the life of Cesare "up close and personal." Machiavelli watched the power that Cesare possessed. He watched as Cesare seemed to get his way everywhere he went. And something in Machiavelli believed this power was "good." We'll talk more about that later.

For 14 years, Machiavelli served as a secretary to Florence. His friend Cesare didn't last so long. When his father (the pope) died in 1503, Cesare Borgia was sent to prison in Spain. There Cesare died. For Italy, it was good riddance. But for Machiavelli, it wasn't good at all.

With Cesare Borgia gone, the Medici family came back. (Remember, the Borgia and the Medici families were enemies.) When the Medici family came back to Florence, they had Machiavelli arrested for being part of a conspiracy! Not only was he arrested, he also was tortured and then sentenced to exile at his country estate. And so Machiavelli, the one-time secretary of Florence, was destined to live the rest of his life in exile in the country. It's not where he wanted to be.

## The Prince

Niccolò Machiavelli had dreams for Florence and for all of Italy. He wanted to see the country unite as a whole nation. There was no unity because Italy was ruled by rival city/states like Florence, Venice, and Milan. Machiavelli likened it to ancient Greece, which had *also* been run by warring city/states such as Athens and Sparta. He wished Italy would come together as a *whole* nation the way that Spain, England, and France each had.

Now you may still be wondering what all this has to do with Cesare Borgia or Machiavellianism. We're getting to that. While Niccolò lived in exile in the country, yearning

Cesare Borgia, the son of Pope Alexander VI, was one of many characters who inspired Machiavelli in writing *The Prince*.

to unite his beloved Italy, he began to write. His writings were powerful, and it was from them that his name — as well as his ideas — grew famous.

In **1513**, Machiavelli wrote a long essay titled ***The Prince***. The essay was about how Machiavelli *personally* thought the problems of Italy ought to be solved. In particular, the essay was about how the power of one person, or one prince, could shape an entire nation. Do you want to guess who was one of the role models for Machiavelli's "perfect" prince? It was Cesare Borgia! Aha. Now we're getting somewhere.

Machiavelli, after all his years in politics, had concluded that the only way a nation could be run well was through power, like that of Cesare. Never mind that Cesare Borgia was a ruthless murderer! Never mind that he was unstable and conniving. Machiavelli focused not on the *character* of Cesare, or of any prince, but on how much *power* one person could have. And Machiavelli believed it was *power* that could solve political problems.

Here are a few quotes straight from *The Prince*:[1]

- "The art of war is all that is expected of a ruler." (p. 61)
- "It is far better to be feared than loved if you cannot be both." (p. 71)
- ". . . because men are wretched creatures who would not keep their word to you, you need not keep your word to them." (pp. 74–75)
- "Cesare Borgia was accounted cruel; nevertheless, this cruelty of his . . . brought . . . unity and restored order and obedience." (p. 70)

**(Middle and Older Students: Please read some more. Words in brackets are mine.)**

- ". . . he [a prince] should not deviate from what is good, if that is possible, but he should know how to do evil, if that is necessary." (p. 76)
- "Violence must be inflicted once for all; people will then forget what it tastes like and so be less resentful." (p. 40)
- "[A prince] will find that some of the things that appear to be virtuous will, if he practices them, ruin him, and some of the things that appear to be vices will bring him security and prosperity." (p. 66)
- ". . . princes who have achieved great things have been those who have given their word lightly, who have known how to trick men with their cunning, and who, in the end, have overcome those abiding by honest principles." (p. 74)

**(Younger Students: Resume reading here.)**

Now, that's a lot of words I just gave you, but I think if you read them slowly enough, the ideas of Machiavelli will begin to sink in. He basically wrote that it was okay for a prince to be bad, use evil, or lie — as long as the goals of the country were achieved. Rather alarming, isn't it?

And like Erasmus, Machiavelli saw clearly all the faults and foolishness of mankind. He thought the Italians were in a mess because they weren't smart enough to get out of it. From his own experience with the classics, Machiavelli thought that ancient people were perhaps smarter. He blamed the church for being one of many things that had ruined the spirit of the Italian people. He thought men had grown weak under the firm hand of the church and forgotten how to fight for one's country.

Before I make Machiavelli sound any worse, I should note that historians don't agree on the intent of *The Prince*. Some would say Machiavelli wrote his essay in the form of a satire, meaning that he was just poking fun at how some princes lived. Others disagree and think that Machiavelli was simply writing down things the way he saw them. In other words, Machiavelli didn't "invent" the role of a dictator. He just observed that dictatorship happened in history, and when it did, nations united.

I find it interesting to know that, over the years, many a dictator has appreciated the work of Machiavelli. Napoleon studied it, and so did Hitler. It would only make sense that those who had ruthless power would hold *The Prince* in high regard. The essay would serve to back them up and help them justify *any* cruel methods used to hold a nation together.

## Later Years in Exile

I'm not sure what the full intentions of Machiavelli were, but he did dedicate the essay to the new Medici family. He was hoping to get in good with them and get his job in the government back. His plan failed and he remained exiled.

There were other books that Machiavelli wrote while in exile that almost seemed to contradict *The Prince*. In his book titled *Discourses on Livy*, Machiavelli insisted that a sound government could only be run "by the people."[2] He stated in *Discourses* that the people of a nation know better than a prince what is good for a nation. It's a bit confusing as to why he would claim that after writing what was practically a "handbook" for a dictator. Some think his views changed over the years. Some think it's because *The Prince* really was a satire. Regardless, it's his theories in *The Prince* that remain the most well known.

The beauty and love of Italy helped sustain Machiavelli during his exile and inspired his writing of politics, poetry, and comedy.

In time, the name of Machiavelli was used to describe eeee-vil politics. Whenever a dictator rose to power — using *whatever* means necessary to keep that power — he or she was described as having "Machiavellian tendencies." The term became so common that it has been placed in the dictionary. Webster's defines Machiavellianism as "the view that politics is amoral and that any means however unscrupulous can justifiably be used in achieving political power."[3]

As for Niccolò Machiavelli, he continued to write politics, poetry, and comedy while in exile. Two significant works were *The Art of War* and *The History of Florence*. His love for Italy sustained him. His desire to see Italy *unified* consumed him, but he failed to see it happen in his lifetime. Machiavelli died in 1527, and his name remains associated with ruthless politics, whether he meant it to be or not.

## Lesson 17 — 1514

# Raphael

What do you think happens when you cross Leonardo da Vinci with Michelangelo? You get **Raphael**! Well, not exactly, but it's a good way to look at this master artist. Raphael is considered one of the greatest artists of all time, and he was clearly influenced by both Leonardo and Michelangelo.

Raphael's full name in Italian is Raffaello Sanzio. He was born in **Urbino**, a city in the Papal States of Italy. Raphael first learned to paint from his father, who was very talented. But when Raphael was only 11, his father died. He was sent to study under an artist named **Perugino** (Peh rue JEE no).

Working under Perugino was great for the young artist. Raphael became so good at what he did that to this day some people mistake his works for those of his master. While Perugino was away, Raphael painted in his place. And his fame grew.

By 1504, Raphael moved to Florence, where of course he could learn from the best. Leonardo da Vinci was in and out of Florence, as was Michelangelo. It's been said that Raphael learned *gracefulness* from Leonardo and *anatomy* from Michelangelo. If you put the two specialties together, you have the **"Divine Raphael."** That was Raphael's nickname. His works were so amazing that people believed God was working through him.

Raphael painted a great number of glorious scenes for the church. To name just a few, he painted *The Small Cowper Madonna* in 1505, *St. George and the Dragon* in 1506, *The Madonna of the Goldfinch* in 1507, and *The Alba Madonna* in 1510. (Unlike Leonardo, Raphael finished his projects in a reasonable amount of time!)

You have probably seen a sample of Raphael's work and not even known it. I'm referring to two little cherubs that appear on the bottom of Raphael's *Sistine Madonna*. They are so cute and popular that they show up today on blankets, purses, umbrellas, coffee mugs, and address labels. Legend says that Raphael painted the two cherubs after seeing a pair of street children lean against the window of a bakery. That might explain why the hat in the left corner of the full portrait looks a lot like a cake!

In painting the famous cherubs found in *Sistine Madonna,* Raphael was supposedly inspired by street children peering into a bakery window.

Besides the cute angels, Raphael became famous for the beautiful and graceful way he painted women, especially Mary, the mother of Jesus. Of course, there is a little bit of scandal behind that story. Apparently, Raphael had countless girlfriends throughout his life who he claimed were his inspiration for painting beautiful women! In fact, the face of Mary in *Sistine Madonna* is the face of one of Raphael's loves. (She was the baker's daughter. That may better explain why Raphael was taking notice of children at the bakery! He was probably visiting his girlfriend.)

## *Pope Julius II*

Raphael's talent was soon recognized by Pope Julius II. This is the same pope who asked Michelangelo to paint the Sistine ceiling. As you may recall, Julius was an impatient man and very demanding, but he did have vision. He envisioned the Vatican as one of the most beautiful places in the world. Pope Julius knew that to achieve his dream, he would need the best of the best artists and architects. And that included the young Raphael. He was invited to Rome in 1508.

What Pope Julius first desired from Raphael was that he paint the pope's private chambers. It was these chambers that became Raphael's claim to fame. He started by painting the room known as *Stanza della Segnatura*. That's Italian for the "Room of Signatures." It was called this because the pope sometimes used this room to sign important papers. This room also contained the pope's private library. On one wall, the pope stored all his books on *theology*. On another wall, he kept all his books on *philosophy*. It was on these two opposing walls that Raphael would become forever famous — because on these two walls he captured the essence of the Renaissance through the eyes of the church. Let me explain.

On the wall that was dedicated to *theology*, Raphael painted a scene titled *Disputa*, or *The Dispute of the Sacrament*. Like a "Who's Who of the Bible," it could serve as a history lesson of the Gospel. It includes the three persons of the Trinity and Bible characters such as Abraham, Moses, David, Peter, Paul, and James. Below this realm of Bible figures are gathered great theologians, such as Jerome, Augustine, Aquinas (Uh KWINE us), and Savonarola. They appear to be debating the teachings of the Bible, as the title of the fresco would suggest.

In this great work, Raphael included faithful men of the arts like Dante and Fra Angelico. Hardly a soul could view this masterpiece and not see the hand of God working

*The Dispute of the Sacrament* by Raphael presents a colorful gathering of historic figures — artists, theologians, and Bible characters — who appear to be debating the teachings of the Bible.

through history to reveal Himself. (Something I really appreciate!) And besides being magnificent in theme, *The Dispute of the Sacrament* is magnificent in *how* it's painted. It contains the background and action in the style of Leonardo and the movement and "floating" characters in the style of Michelangelo. It is superb.

## School of Athens

But back to Raphael's fame. It was the next wall in the Room of Signatures that would prove to be his best. On the wall dedicated to *philosophy*, Raphael painted a scene titled *School of Athens*. Before I describe it, I have to tell you a little story about the title. Before Raphael moved to Rome, there was a preacher who gave a sermon in the Sistine Chapel. (Though the ceiling wasn't finished yet, the chapel was still used from time to time.) In that sermon, the preacher praised Pope Julius II for bringing the best of learning to Rome. And what was considered the "best learning" at that time? You should know this — the ancient works of the Greeks and Romans. The preacher said, "You, now, Julius II, Supreme Pontiff, have founded *a new Athens* when you summon up that . . . world of letters as if raising it from the dead." (Italics are mine for emphasis.)[4]

You see, by this time, the church had *strongly* embraced the Renaissance way of thinking. It was not just seen in the minds of the humanists, but it was seen in the collection of the pope's library and his emphasis on the classics from the city of Athens in Greece. Though he was a pope, Julius II wasn't all that different from Cosimo and Lorenzo de' Medici. And so

In *School of Athens*, Raphael portrayed Plato as Leonardo da Vinci with a long, flowing beard, walking and talking alongside Aristotle. (See also the full view of this painting in Quarter 1's Around the World section.)

Raphael captured this Renaissance "way of thinking" in the painting he titled *School of Athens*. The title was inspired by the words of the sermon. Do you see the connection? The title said it all because the church was giving way to humanism and trying to blend ancient thought with theology.

In *School of Athens*, Raphael brought together more than 50 characters from history, representing all the classic thinkers of the past. (Some of these names you'll recognize.) And what makes some of these men more interesting is whom Raphael painted them to look like. In some cases, he used fellow artists as his models. It's pretty cool.

In the very middle of the scene, Raphael painted *Plato* and *Aristotle* walking and talking side by side. His model for Plato was none other than Leonardo da Vinci, the greatest genius of the time. Raphael painted Plato to look just like Leonardo, with a long, flowing white beard and hair below his shoulders. The ironic thing about this is that Plato thought very little of artists and would not have been flattered. Raphael probably made Plato look like Leonardo because of the artist's brilliance in so many *other* fields.

On the far left side of the painting, Raphael inserted *Alcibiades* (Al suh BYE a deez), a pupil of Socrates'. He's wearing the clothes of a soldier. The seventh figure from the left is *Socrates* himself, wearing a purple robe and busying himself in conversation. *Pythagoras* (Pi THAG or us), an ancient Greek mathematician, is shown working in a notebook on the floor. He is wearing an orange-and-white robe and has a beard.

Alone on the steps to the right reclines a man meant to be *Diogenes* (Die AH jih neez), a cynic from ancient times. He was a loner in his lifetime and sits alone in the painting. To the far right are clustered a few more celebrities. Raphael painted himself as a young man looking straight at the viewer. You can only see his face. He portrays himself as a student of *Ptolemy* (TOL uh mee), a once-great geographer. Ptolemy stands across from *Zoroaster*, an astronomer from long ago. Near them, bending on the floor and working, is *Euclid* (YOU clid), the father of geometry. With a bald head, he is painted to look like **Donato Bramante**, a good friend of Raphael's and the head architect of the Vatican.

But of all the figures in *School of Athens*, I find the one of *Heraclitus* to be the most intriguing. It seems that after Raphael saw half of the Sistine ceiling completed, he was in awe. It inspired him to go back to his *School of Athens* and add Heraclitus. Why? Well, in history, Heraclitus was a grumpy old philosopher who hardly got along with anyone. He must have reminded Raphael of the temperamental Michelangelo. So, as either an insult or a compliment,

Raphael painted Heraclitus to look just like Michelangelo! The figure has the same color and posture as the characters on the ceiling of the Sistine Chapel, except Heraclitus is wearing boots — just like those of Michelangelo.

It was well known that Michelangelo was a loner. Unlike Leonardo and Raphael, he didn't mix and mingle with other artists. One time Michelangelo and Raphael passed each other in the halls of the Vatican. Michelangelo sneered at Raphael, saying, "You with your band, like a bravo." Raphael retorted, "And you alone, like the hangman."[5] Their personalities were very different, and Raphael cleverly revealed this in *School of Athens*.

Another funny story has been told about these two rivals. Though not confirmed, there is a story that Michelangelo left the Vatican one day in haste. (He was probably angry with Pope Julius.) While he was away, Raphael and Bramante supposedly snuck into the Sistine Chapel to peek at the ceiling. This infuriated Michelangelo, who thought the two were out to ruin him. Michelangelo accused Raphael of repainting a portrait of *Isaiah* after peeking. (It may be true because the style of *Isaiah* is very similar to Michelangelo's!)

Except for his rivalry with Michelangelo, Raphael got along with just about everyone. He was charming, sociable, and eager to teach. Giorgio Vasari said of Raphael, "He was never seen to go to court without having with him, as he left his house, some fifty painters, all able and excellent, who kept him company in order to do him honour."[6] It was this kind of discipleship between master and apprentice, or teacher and pupil, that Raphael captured so well in *School of Athens*. He captured it well because he lived it. He served his time as a pupil and went on to become a master teacher.

While painting more apartments in the Vatican, Raphael also produced magnificent tapestries and engravings. Before Julius II died, Raphael honored him greatly by producing one of the most realistic portraits of a pope ever painted. It's very majestic. Like Leonardo, portraits were one of Raphael's specialties. (His *Portrait of Bindo Altoviti* and *La Donna Velata* are exceptional.) Furthermore, Raphael tried his hand at architecture. In **1514**, Pope Leo hired Raphael to take the place of Bramante, who had died. Raphael was given the enormous task of trying to finish what Bramante had started. The challenge put Raphael at the height of his career.

## *Secrets*

In the midst of his busy professional life, the private life of Raphael proved to be very interesting — yet it is in many ways still a mystery to art lovers today. A powerful cardinal insisted that Raphael marry his niece Maria. Out of obligation, Raphael agreed to the engagement, but he kept coming up with excuses to put off the wedding. Some believed the idea of marriage frightened him because it would put an end to his busy dating life. Others think he was already secretly engaged to a pretty young woman named **Margherita Luti**. I mentioned her earlier as the daughter of a baker. She is the one whose face appears as Mary in the *Sistine Madonna*. She is also the lovely woman in *La Donna Velata*.

Why was Margherita a secret? It remains a mystery. It may have been because she was loved by many men and had a poor reputation. Or it may have been that Raphael loved her,

It was probably Margherita Luti who posed for Raphael's *La Donna Velata*, which means "woman with a veil." The woman and the artist may have been secretly engaged.

but after six years, he wouldn't commit to marrying her for the same reason he wouldn't marry Maria. Perhaps he simply didn't want to be tied down.

But the real mystery lies in one of Raphael's paintings. Hundreds of years after Raphael painted a seductive portrait of Margherita, X-ray analysis showed that a large ruby ring was originally painted on her finger. It may have been an engagement ring! It is believed that Raphael (or one of his pupils) painted over the ring to keep the relationship a secret. Some claim it is the wedding portrait of a completely different woman, but most think it is Margherita.

Sadly enough, Maria, Raphael's official fiancée, died before she and Raphael could settle on a wedding date. Some believe Maria died of a broken heart, knowing she wasn't really loved. Not long after her death, Raphael died too. He was only 37! Though nobody knows for sure, he might have died from receiving the wrong medicine for a high fever. Regardless of what killed him, Raphael knew he was dying beforehand and, according to Vasari, had enough time to distribute his belongings, write a will, and prayerfully repent of any misdeeds.[7] Margherita, the secret girlfriend, signed herself over to live in a convent that took in repentant women.

Raphael died on the same date that he was born, April 6, which in the year of his death was Good Friday. Legend says that the walls of the Vatican wept for him because they started to crack after his death. Raphael was buried next to Maria, who would appear in death to have finally gotten her man. Inscribed on his sarcophagus were the words, "Here lies that famous Raphael by whom nature feared to be conquered while he lived, and when he was dying, feared herself to die."[8]

Raphael's early death was a tragic fate for this talented artist. He had so much potential. Had he lived longer, the world would surely have more of his masterpieces. I hope that somewhere along the way he understood the Gospel, which he so gloriously captured and painted.

# *Martin Luther Posts His "Ninety-five Theses"*

**Note to Teacher:** *The Protestant Reformation is a difficult piece of history to understand. I suggest that all students read Part I of this lesson, which covers the historical backdrop of the Reformation. I challenge Older Students (and parents or teachers) to read Part II of this lesson, which addresses theological issues. Though modern practices have changed since the start of the Reformation, to some degree Protestants and Roman Catholics remain divided on the issues presented here. It is beyond the scope of this book to bridge these differences. I pray that all my readers will benefit from this lesson and allow it to serve as a springboard for their own spiritual growth and understanding of God.*

## Part I

The town of Wittenberg, Germany, was busy with activity. It was October 31, **1517**. Villagers were going about their usual business. They were buying and selling vegetables, exchanging silver and gold, and dodging dogs in the street. But on this day, there was extra excitement in the air. Tomorrow would be All Saints' Day, a day on which the local church and all the churches across Western Europe remembered their heroes and martyrs.

On this particular All Saints' Day, there was going to be a special exhibition. "Holy" relics were going on display for the public to see. As townsmen gathered, hardly anyone noticed a young monk named **Martin Luther**. Hardly anyone noticed him pass through the crowds to post a document on the door of **All Saints' Church**. Hardly anyone, including Martin Luther, realized that this day, with the posting of this document, was going to be considered the start of the **Protestant Reformation**. But it was.

So what was this document that was being nailed to the door? It was a document containing 95 thesis points (or short paragraphs), and so it has been remembered as the **"Ninety-five Theses"** of Martin Luther. The points were written to invite the upper clergy of the church into a debate. For that reason it was written in Latin, which was understood only by higher members of the church. Did you know it was common practice back then to post news and debates on the doors of busy places? It was. A door such as the one at Wittenberg was like a bulletin board for the entire community. And so Martin Luther posted his debate and went about his day.

What was the topic of debate? The topic was *indulgences*. I've mentioned indulgences in the church before, but I think they're hard to understand. Let me briefly define them again. An indulgence is a favor or blessing granted by the pope or his representative. Roman Catholics would say that, once granted, an indulgence lessens one's "temporal punishment due to sin" here on earth or in purgatory. (Protestants disagree, but that's not the point right now.) As early as the twelfth century, indulgences were being offered to the public in *exchange* for a donation to the church. These indulgences were written in the form of a tangible document and signed by the pope or his representative. Let's look now at what was going on in the sixteenth century regarding indulgences that prompted Martin Luther to host a debate on the topic.

In 1517, Martin Luther posted his Ninety-five Theses on the doors of All Saints' Church in Wittenberg, Germany.

## *Johann Tetzel*

During Martin Luther's time, **Pope Leo X** was the head of the church in Rome. He happened to be the son of Lorenzo de' Medici, which should mean something to you. Much like his father, Pope Leo X embraced humanism and the arts. The pope just before Leo was Julius II. Remember him? He commissioned Michelangelo to paint the ceiling of the Sistine Chapel. Both of these popes worked on rebuilding St. Peter's Cathedral at the Vatican in Rome. Both employed numerous artists and architects, including Leonardo da Vinci and Raphael, to make the Vatican one of the most spectacular sights in the world. We've already covered all of that. But something we haven't covered is that in making these improvements, the popes spent *a lot* of money. One way for them to collect money for these projects was to offer indulgences to members of the church.

In the 1500s, a Dominican friar named **Johann Tetzel** was hired by Pope Leo X for this very job. He was to offer indulgences across the Holy Roman Empire. Apparently, Johann Tetzel was very good at his work. With great ceremony, Tetzel and his helpers would parade through the towns of the Holy Roman Empire with bright banners and fanfare to stir the interest of the crowds. An indulgence, written on paper, was propped on a velvet cushion and held up high for the crowds to see while church bells rang, organs played, and candles were lit. Johann Tetzel proclaimed (words in brackets are mine for better understanding):

> May our Lord Jesus Christ have mercy on thee and absolve [forgive] thee by the merits of His most holy Passion. And I, by His authority, . . . and of the most holy Pope, . . . do absolve [forgive] thee . . . from all thy sins . . . how enormous soever they may be . . . I remit to you all punishment which you deserve in purgatory . . . so that when you die the gates of punishment shall be shut, and the gates of the paradise of delight shall be opened.[9]

Johann Tetzel, a persuasive Dominican friar, was hired by the pope to offer indulgences across the Holy Roman Empire.

Like a high-powered salesman, Johann Tetzel was quite persuasive. He came up with a jingle that went like this: "So soon as coin in coffer rings, the soul from purgatory springs!"[10] His jingle implied that when a coin was dropped in the offering box, someone was released from purgatory, which according to Roman Catholics is a temporary state between heaven and hell.

In 1517, the money coins that Johann Tetzel collected went to two things. The money went to help build St. Peter's Cathedral in Rome, and it went toward the debts of an archbishop. Most Protestants and Roman Catholics today would agree that Tetzel was "abusing" the system. In his efforts to raise a lot of money, he was excessive in granting indulgences. He took advantage of the common people who gave large amounts of money for them.

Keep in mind that most commoners couldn't read the indulgences they obtained because they were written in Latin. Many people didn't understand them. By Tetzel's words, many were led to believe they were "buying" a pardon for their sins. Many were led to believe they were escaping *all* guilt and punishment of sin for themselves and their loved ones in purgatory by the indulgences they received for a donation to the church.

Now stay with me here. Martin Luther was a monk and a priest of the Roman Church. He was part of the system that was being abused! Luther wasn't the first to raise his eyebrows and question the exchange of indulgences for money. Many before him were concerned over what *appeared* to be the "selling" of forgiveness.

Martin Luther, who was more outspoken than most, chose an appropriate method by which to raise his concerns for the members of his beloved church. By posting his Ninety-five Theses, he called for a debate between theologians on the topic of indulgences. In 1517, he wasn't trying to start a revolt. He wasn't asking people to leave the church. Martin Luther was just hoping to *reform* a system that was misleading. Let's focus now on Martin Luther's background and what stirred his deep convictions.

## Martin Luther's Convictions

Martin Luther was raised in a strict family. He planned on being a lawyer. But one day he was caught in a bad thunderstorm. Fearing for his life, he cried out a prayer to Saint Anne. He prayed that if his life were spared, he would become a monk. His life *was* spared, and he soon enrolled in an Augustinian monastery. He was 22 years old. By 1507, he was ordained a priest.

Having grown up in a strict home, Martin was used to serious work habits such as those of the monks and priests. However, his soul was restless. He found that no matter how hard he tried to make up for his sins, he was still a sinner. Martin spent great amounts of time in prayer, fasting, and inflicting himself with pain in order to deal with his sins. For inspiration, he went on a pilgrimage to Rome where he visited the shrines of saints and saw the Vatican firsthand. Still, he felt discontent. He said of himself, "I was a pious monk, and so strictly observed the rules of my order that . . . if ever a monk got into heaven by monkery, so should I also have gotten there . . . If

I had lasted longer I should have tortured myself to death with watching, praying, reading, and other work."[11]

Other caring monks suggested that Martin read the Bible more carefully. Martin Luther did. He came to a passage in Romans that says, "The just shall live by faith." (See Rom. 1:17.) According to Martin Luther, in understanding this verse, his faith was transformed and his soul born again. He understood the passage to mean that faith in Christ alone, not *any* good works, would atone for his sins. Of his experience, he wrote, "Night and day I pondered until I saw the connection between the justice of God and the statement 'the just shall live by his faith' . . . I grasped that the justice of God is that righteousness by which . . . grace and sheer mercy God justifies us through faith . . . I felt myself to be *reborn* and to have gone through open doors into paradise. The whole of Scripture took on a new meaning."[12] (Italics are mine.)

> *"Night and day I pondered until I saw the connection between the justice of God and the statement 'the just shall live by his faith.'"*
> *–Martin Luther*

With deepened faith, Martin Luther continued his work as a priest and gave lectures on theology at the University of Wittenberg. Knowing his personal experience, you may now better understand why the actions of Johann Tetzel and the offering of indulgences were so bothersome to him. It greatly disturbed Luther that people might misunderstand the marvelous grace of God. So, in 1517, he did something about it by asking theologians to join him for a debate.

**Younger and Middle Students**: I suggest that Younger and Middle Students now end your reading. But in just a few lessons, I will bring you back to the life of Martin Luther and what happened *after* he posted his Ninety-five Theses.

**Older Students**: I recommend that Older Students continue reading. For you, I have some theology to explain. Why? Well, it was the issue of indulgences, *and many things related to this issue*, that divided the Christian faith into two main groups. It divided Protestants from Roman Catholics. I think it wise to learn more about the issues behind such a historic event, don't you? Of course, I can't thoroughly explain all the differences between these groups, but I hope to bring a little understanding to both sides.

**Part II**

## *The Catholic View on Indulgences*

As recently as the 1960s, Pope Paul VI of the Roman Catholic Church wrote, "An indulgence is a remission before God of the *temporal* punishment due to sins whose *guilt* has already been forgiven."[13] (Italics are mine for emphasis.) This means (according to the Roman Catholic Church) that the *guilt* of sin, which is eternal, has already been forgiven by the death and resurrection of Jesus. But the *punishment* of sin, which is temporary, is still attached to sinners. Let me give an example.

Let's say that a thief breaks into a store and steals money. He is caught and put on trial. At his trial, the thief confesses his crime and is truly sorry for having committed it. The judge is glad to see that the man is remorseful of the crime, but being a just judge, he still sends him to jail for two years. Catholics would say that God is much like that. He forgives us but requires restitution for our wrong deeds.

In more theological terms, Catholics would teach that only the blood of Jesus can cleanse the thief of the *guilt* of his crime. However, they would say that the thief still carries the *punishment* for his crime, or more specifically, the *temporal punishment*. In our example, the thief has to make amends for his crime by returning the money and spending time in jail. That is a Catholic example of his "temporal punishment." Now hold that thought as I explain something else.

Roman Catholics believe that the pope has been granted special abilities. They base this belief on a Bible passage where Jesus says to Peter, "And I also say to you that you are Peter, and on this rock I will build My church, and the gates of Hades shall not prevail against it. And I will give you the keys of the kingdom of heaven, and whatever you bind on earth will be bound in heaven, and whatever you loose on earth will be loosed in heaven." (See Matt. 16:18–19.)

From this passage, Catholics conclude that the church, through the pope, has the ability to forgive "temporal punishment" of sin. Think of the example of the thief. In that case, it means that the pope (or his representative) could pardon the thief of the *punishment* that is due to him. The pope, like a judge in this case, could let the thief go free based on the authority of the pope as Catholics interpret Matthew 16:18–19. Of course, the pope would only do so if he saw that the thief was a repentant man who was not going to steal again. Modern Roman Catholic doctrine puts it this way (italics are mine):

> An indulgence is obtained through the Church who, by virtue of the power of binding and loosing granted her by Christ Jesus, intervenes in favor of individual Christians and opens for them the treasury of the merits of Christ and the saints to obtain from the Father of mercies the remission of the *temporal punishments* due for their sins.[14]

If you wrap these two beliefs together — the belief that a sinner bears "temporal punishment" and the belief that the church can forgive "temporal punishment" through the pope — you might begin to understand the concept behind indulgences. An indulgence is granted to reduce the "punishment" of sins. Sometimes an indulgence is an act of charity performed to negate the consequence of sin. Other times an indulgence is a written document signed by the pope (or his representative) who, according to Roman Catholics, has the authority to take away the punishment of sin.

Roman Catholics would say that this teaching was always a part of the church. However, it was not until the 1100s that the Roman Church offered indulgences in the form of documents to its members. Catholics would say that written indulgences are not "sold." However, in the course of history, it would *appear* that they were sold because money was usually donated to the church in exchange for an indulgence.

According to the Roman Catholic Church, an indulgence of any sort is considered good only if a sinner is truly sorry for his sin. In history, this belief developed into all kinds of ways that a person could *show* he was sorry. Like the thief in our example, he would want to prove to the judge or the pope that he would never steal again by returning the money and expressing remorse. In medieval times, repentance was demonstrated by things like visiting holy shrines, viewing holy relics, giving money to the poor, or praying to a saint. These were considered expressions of repentance.

I hope you followed all of that. But there's a little more I want to explain. It became a practice in the Medieval Church for members to acquire indulgences for those who had already died. It is believed by Roman Catholics that because of the need to be *punished* for sins, the dead spend a certain amount of time in **purgatory**. Purgatory to Catholics is a state of being between heaven and hell where a person waits for judgment and does penance (meaning makes up) for the "temporal punishment" of his sins. Since indulgences are thought to "lessen" the punishment of sin, then according to Catholics, an indulgence can "carve off" the amount of time one has to spend in purgatory for one's sins.

In medieval times it became the custom that an actual number of days was assigned to acts of charity and indulgences. For example, for seeing a holy relic (like the bones of a saint), it was believed that someone could carve off "160 days in purgatory." For going on a pilgrimage, it was believed that someone could carve off "300 days in purgatory."

Okay. That was the historical and modern Roman Catholic viewpoint of indulgences. Please bear in mind that many of my examples are from the Medieval Church and are not necessarily practiced in the same manner today. Now, let us look at what Protestants would say about indulgences.

## *The Protestant View on Indulgences*

Protestants do not separate the *guilt* of sin from the *punishment* of sin. They believe the Bible says that guilt and punishment go together. (See Rom. 3:24–26.) They believe that no one, except Jesus Christ, can pay for sin, and He does so as a gift. The Bible says, "For the wages of sin is death, but the *gift* of God is eternal life in Christ Jesus our Lord." (Italics are mine. See Rom. 6:23.) The Bible also says, "For by grace you have been saved through faith, and that not of yourselves; it is the *gift* of God, not of works, lest anyone should boast." (Italics are mine. See Eph. 2:8–9. See also Rom. 6:23; 1 Cor. 15:3–6; Col. 1:21–22.)

Protestants interpret these passages to mean that sin is taken care of as a *gift* from God. The gift is salvation and eternal life. It is given by grace and received through faith in Jesus Christ alone. On a further note, Protestants don't believe in purgatory. Since they do not believe that "temporal punishment" exists separately from the guilt of sin, then they don't see the need for dealing with temporal punishment after death. In part, it is for this reason that Protestants don't pray for those who have already died.

Because the Bible teaches that salvation is a gift, a person can't do anything to earn it. Let's go back to our example of the thief. A Protestant would say that if the thief prays and repents to God, the guilt *and* punishment of his crime are covered through the blood of Jesus.

Does that mean the thief shouldn't spend time in jail? No. Protestants would consider that a logical consequence for breaking the laws of a society. But as for God's genuine forgiveness, Protestants would emphasize that it cannot be earned.

In regard to forgiveness of sins and salvation, most Protestants would agree to the following points: First, Jesus died for sinners. The Bible says in Romans 5:8, "But God demonstrates his own love toward us, in that while we were still sinners, Christ died for us." Second, one can receive forgiveness of all sin by asking for it. In 1 John 1:9, it says, "If we confess our sins, He is faithful and just to forgive us our sins and to cleanse us from *all* unrighteousness." (Italics are mine. See also Rom. 10:9–10.) Third, someone can come into a personal relationship with God by believing in Jesus and receiving Him as Savior and Lord. John 1:12–13 says, "But as many as *received* Him, to them He gave the right to become children of God, to those who *believe* in His name: who were born, not of blood, nor of the will of the flesh, nor of the will of man, but of God." (Italics are mine.)

In our example of the thief, a Protestant would agree that the thief *ought* to repent of his crime, return the money he stole, and spend time in jail for his crime as ordained by a judge. The Old and New Testaments support this. (See Ex. 22:1–4; Lev 6:1–7; Matt. 5:21–26; Eph. 4:28.) But these acts, or works, would in no way help him obtain true and full forgiveness from Christ. The thief is *fully* forgiven if he repents. His forgiveness comes to him as a gift of God.

Martin Luther was a monk and a priest of the Roman Church who sought "reform." It led to a great division in Christendom.

In closing, you may be wondering why I've spent so much time elaborating on these issues. Well, I think they're important because once Martin Luther began to question indulgences, the floodgates opened. So many people left the established church over the matter that it led to a great division in Christendom. Modern Protestants and Catholics would generally agree that there were abuses in the Medieval Church, but one group left it and the other group stayed to correct it. Tragically, the differences between the groups led to bloodshed. The power struggle grew to include politics and became a war between the faiths.

But be encouraged by this. We don't live in the sixteenth century anymore. It is history. In most parts of the world, Protestants and Catholics have learned to exist in peace. Do they agree on everything? No. But there is far more harmony than disharmony between these groups today.

# WEEK 7

## Lesson 19 *1519, 1531*

# *Cortés and Pizarro: Conquistadors of Spain*

I have a confession to make. I don't care much for the practices of **Hernán Cortés**. Nor do I like the actions of **Francisco Pizarro**. Though some commend these two for being *brave* and *successful*, they were also *cruel* and *greedy*. To elaborate, Cortés and Pizarro were *brave* for exploring Mexico and South America, and they were *successful* in conquering the **Aztecs** and the **Incas** (also spelled *Inkas*). But Cortés and Pizarro were *cruel* in their methods and *greedy* in their motives. Let's take a closer look at these two Spanish conquerors and separate the good from the bad.

As you know from previous lessons, the fifteenth century was a time of great exploration. Bartolomeu Dias and Vasco da Gama each had explored the coast of Africa and rounded the Cape of Good Hope. Cristóbal Colón had sailed to the New World and back. It was an exciting time for European explorers who had just begun to realize that two continents lie between the East and the West.

With every voyage that set sail, more rumors and stories were created. Every nugget of gold seen in the New World was cause for more excitement. There wasn't an explorer in Europe who didn't wonder if just maybe there was a huge fortune of gold yet to be discovered. And these eager explorers grew to be *conquistadors*, which is Spanish for "conquerors."

### *Hernán Cortés*

As you know, Colón started colonies in the West Indies. These colonies were ruled by governors. The Spanish governor of the colony of **Cuba** was very curious about the land to the west of him. That land was Mexico. The governor wondered if Mexico might have gold or treasure waiting for him. He just had to know. And so the governor of Cuba asked Hernán Cortés — who was then serving as a mayor in Cuba — to explore lands to the west. Cortés said yes.

With 650 men, Hernán Cortés founded the settlement of Veracruz on the east coast of Mexico.

In **1519**, just after the start of the Protestant Reformation, Hernán Cortés loaded 11 ships. With 650 men, he sailed to the coast of **Mexico** and founded the settlement of **Veracruz**. To keep his men committed to the settlement, Cortés did something rather drastic in my opinion. He burned all but one of his ships! He spared one for the sake of running messages back and forth to Spain. With the loss of 10 ships, the crewmen were prisoners to the new, mysterious land of Mexico. Cortés hoped to make it worth their while. He hoped to find gold for himself, for the governor of Cuba, and for Spain.

The people Cortés first met were the Tabascans from the city of **Tabasco**. Does that name sound familiar? It might. The makers of *Tabasco sauce* were inspired by the hot peppers that grow in the area. But that would be later in history. The Tabascans of the sixteenth century had never seen men as light-skinned as Cortés. They certainly had never seen anything like their ships, their horses, or their weapons. The Tabascans thought perhaps the "white men" were gods. In both awe and fear, the Tabascans catered to the needs of these white men and helped them establish their new settlement.

In awe of the stories he heard about the newcomers, Montezuma sent gifts of gold and silver to Hernán Cortés.

Among the Tabascans was a woman who could speak the language of other tribes in Mexico. The Spanish called her *Doña Marina*, which we would translate as **"Lady Marina."** Lady Marina knew the language of the legendary Aztecs, the most warlike group on the mainland of Mexico. (We learned a great deal about the Aztecs in Volume II of this series.) Hernán Cortés found himself very interested in the Aztecs and the rumors of their gold. For months he learned all he could about them with the help of Lady Marina. Some sources say the two were actually in love. I don't know if that's true or not, but it might explain why Lady Marina was happy to help Cortés!

In the meantime, the Aztecs were just beginning to learn something of the white man who had landed on their shores. The head chief of the Aztecs, whose name was **Montezuma** (Mon teh ZOO muh), was intrigued to hear stories of these white men on horseback. You see, Aztec legend said that "white gods" would one day come to earth. Montezuma wondered if perhaps Cortés and his men were these white gods! As a good gesture toward Cortés, Montezuma did something he would later regret. He sent Cortés a large gift of gold and silver. It was, of course, exactly what Cortés was looking for.

For a closer look at the source of this treasure, Cortés made his way to the main city of the Aztecs in central Mexico. It was the city of **Tenochtitlán** (te nowch tee T'LANN), which is present-day Mexico City. The city was *more* than impressive to Cortés and his men. It was magnificent. Cortés wrote this about seeing Tenochtitlán:

> The city has many open squares in which markets are continuously held . . . and completely surrounded by arcades where there are daily more than 60,000 folk buying and selling. Every kind of merchandise such as may be met . . . whether of food and victuals, or ornaments of gold and silver . . . There is a street of herb sellers . . . there are houses . . . of apothecaries and . . . there are barbers' shops where you may have your hair washed and cut . . . the manner of living among the people is very similar to that in Spain, and considering that this is a barbarous nation shut off from a knowledge of the true God or communication with enlightened nations, one may well marvel at the orderliness and good government which is everywhere maintained.[1]

Set on an island in the middle of a lake, the city of Tenochtitlán glistened and gleamed before Hernán Cortés and his men. Highly advanced roads bridged the sparkling city to other parts of the Aztec empire. Streets were lined with elaborate palaces and temples. Bright-colored clothing was everywhere. Montezuma was honored that Cortés came to visit. He welcomed his guests with great fanfare and offered them luxurious palaces to sleep in. Thinking they might be gods, some Aztecs went so far as to kiss the ground the Spaniards walked on!

But all this hospitality backfired. The more Cortés saw, the greedier he got. Though he saw with his own eyes a marvelous nation, he had no compassion for those who built it. To him, the culture was pagan and meaningless. So, in a short time, Cortés completely turned against Montezuma and took him for a prisoner. Cortés used Montezuma as a puppet to govern over the city of the Aztecs.

The Aztecs were furious! In time they rose up against Montezuma and stoned him to death! Why would they kill their own leader? They killed him for *appearing* to submit to the white man. Aztec armies then rose up against the Spanish invaders, who they no longer believed were gods. On their first attempt, the Aztecs were victorious. In what the Spanish called *la noche triste*, which means "the sad night," all but 100 Spaniards were killed. Defeated and humiliated, Hernán Cortés left.

This Aztec calendar attests to the advanced culture of the Aztecs before they were conquered by the Spanish.

But, less than a year later, Cortés returned with a full army. This time, the Aztecs stood little chance against the Europeans. This time, thousands of Aztecs lost their lives on the plain of Otumba. Their spears and arrows were just no match against Spanish guns and cannons. And on top of that, the Spanish had spread smallpox to the natives! Millions died of disease in just a few years. By 1521, the city of Tenochtitlán was completely taken and the Aztec nation was no more. In the end, the Aztecs lost their nation, and the Spanish got their gold.

In my opinion, this method of conquest is nothing to be proud of. However, I will say on behalf of the Spanish explorers that some of them were good people. Some were concerned with the cruel practice of human sacrifice that was common among the Aztecs. Horrified by the human blood poured out for the Aztec gods, some Spaniards tried to turn an Aztec temple into a church. Some Spaniards genuinely cared enough about the Aztecs to share the Gospel. Unfortunately, they were overshadowed by the greed of most of the sailors and explorers who were there for gold, not for God.

I will also add that some of the smaller tribes of Mexico were sincerely grateful to the "white man" for stopping the terrifying reign of the Aztecs. The Aztecs were feared far and wide for their methods of warfare. They were feared for the pagan practice of cutting out the hearts of their prisoners for human sacrifice. Some would definitely consider Hernán Cortés a hero for toppling the pagan Aztec empire. There is that angle to consider when pondering the harsh conquest.

On a much lighter side, it is believed that Hernán Cortés was the first to bring chocolate from Mexico to Europe! He learned of chocolate through the Aztecs, who had mastered the harvesting of cacao (keh KAY oh *or* keh KOU oh) beans. Millions would appreciate Cortés for paying attention to that.

## *Francisco Pizarro*

While Cortés was off conquering the Aztecs, a young man named Francisco Pizarro was taking care of pigs. Literally. Francisco grew up in a poor family, raising pigs for a living. Francisco dreamed of more. He served as a soldier and joined the crew of **Vasco Balboa**, a Spanish explorer. One of Vasco Balboa's main missions was to find the legendary Incas, a rich and sophisticated empire. All that Balboa ever found was the Pacific Ocean, which was new to the Europeans. For a time, stories of the Incas — and all their gold — remained a mystery.

After his travels with Balboa, Francisco settled in **Panama** in Central America. On a voyage down south, he met a rich man from Peru, which is in South America. As it turned out, the rich man was one of the Incas! Finally, Francisco found proof of this wealthy empire. It *wasn't* just a legend. He took gold back to Spain to show **King Charles I**. Of course, with the promise of finding *more* gold, Charles I sent Pizarro back on a well-planned expedition.

Francisco Pizarro was sent by King Charles I of Spain to find treasures of gold in Peru.

In **1531**, Pizarro took three ships and 180 men to Peru. It was there that history seemed to repeat itself. Like the Aztecs, the Incas had myths about "white gods." Like the Aztecs, the Incas thought that just maybe these "white men" were gods. Like the Aztecs, the Incas welcomed the Europeans. And, like the Aztecs, the Incas made the mistake of trusting them. This is where the story gets ugly.

Pizarro first took over the city of **Cajamarca** by luring the emperor into the city square. It was a trap. What was supposed to be a meeting turned into a blood bath. The Spaniards shot cannons into the city square, killing thousands of Incas at one time. The emperor, whose name was **Atahualpa**, was taken prisoner.

Doesn't this story sound familiar? Just like Cortés capturing Montezuma, Pizarro captured Atahualpa. But the rest of the story is fuzzy. Some sources say that Pizarro held the emperor for ransom and promised to let him go if the Incas would bring him ninety million dollars' worth of silver and gold! Other sources say that Atahualpa offered a vast treasure to Pizarro as a bribe for his release. Either way, as a ransom or a bribe, the Incas brought forth gold. They filled a room 22 feet long and 17 feet wide with treasures of unimaginable worth.

You would think that Pizarro would have been satisfied. But, when the treasure was collected, Pizarro ordered the execution of the emperor! Atahualpa was strangled to death. Some sources say Atahualpa embraced Christianity before his death, but that part of the story is unclear.

Over the course of a few years, the Inca Empire fell apart. By 1533, Pizarro took over the capital. He later built the city of **Lima** (LEE muh), Peru. The name means the "City of

Today, the Incan ruins of Machu Picchu stand hauntingly empty and quiet.

Kings." It probably referred to Pizarro and one of his partners who each lived like a king. They ruled over what *had* been the amazing Inca Empire.

As fate would have it, Pizarro was later murdered — not by revengeful Incas but by Spaniards from his partner's camp. Apparently, Pizarro and his partner had clashed many times over the years, and the death of one led to the death of the other. In the end, it would seem that treachery caught up with Pizarro and that he died as a victim of cruelty. How very ironic.

The brightly dressed people of Peru are proud descendants of the once great Inca Empire.

It is not easy for me to write a conclusion to these stories of "conquest." Some view the conquest of pagans as admirable and necessary. Some don't. Some see the conquistadors as brave and successful. Others can't see past their cruel and greedy ways.

The good news is that whether we understand it or not, the Bible says that God is in control of the rise and fall of nations. Psalm 22:27–28 says, "All the ends of the world shall remember and turn to the Lord. And all the families of the nations shall worship before You. For the kingdom is the Lord's, and He rules over the nations." In that I find great comfort.

## Lesson 20 — 1519–1522

# Ferdinand Magellan Sails West

**Note to Teacher and Students:** *Before you start this lesson, I recommend that you have a globe or world map handy as you read along. No matter your age, this lesson will make more sense if you use your finger to trace ships traveling east and west.*

In 1519, no one in history had sailed around the world. In 1519, no one in history was *planning* to sail around the world. But through a series of treacherous events and dangerous voyages, it happened. A ship named the *Victoria* left Spain in **1519**. It was heading west with four others. Three years later, in **1522**, the *Victoria* returned home alone from the East, having sailed all the way around the world! Of course, this huge accomplishment wasn't the work of just one man. It took hundreds of men to pull it off. But, in my opinion, the navigator who started the trip deserves the most credit for it. He was **Ferdinand Magellan**.

## *A Squire in the King's Court*

Ferdinand Magellan was a short man with dark features. He grew up in Portugal, which of course was a good place for a young navigator to be. If you remember, both Bartolomeu Dias and Vasco da Gama were from Portugal, as were many others who dared to explore the world by sea. As for Ferdinand, his parents died when he was only 10. At 12, he went into service for King Manuel of Portugal. Ferdinand worked his way up to become a squire. Through all of this, he went to school and found that he loved geography and astronomy. And as part of the king's court, Ferdinand Magellan was surrounded by those who dreamed of exploration and discovery. For Magellan, this was the perfect environment in which to dream.

By the time he was 20, Ferdinand Magellan was entrusted by King Manuel to sail back and forth to India for business. Of course, he sailed to India in the same direction that other Portuguese had gone. He sailed around the Cape of Good Hope at the southern tip of Africa. (If you have a map or globe, you might want to find this route now.) From there, Magellan headed east to India. It wasn't an easy trip because he encountered battles along the way with Muslim fighters.

But the trip was significant to Magellan because it gave him vision. From his travels, he learned more about the **Spice Islands** and the value of reaching them. The Spice Islands are really the **Moluccas** (Muh LUCK uz) **Islands** of Indonesia. (You will find that Indonesia is a chain of large islands between China and Australia.) The Moluccas Islands are nicknamed the "Spice Islands" because cloves and other spices grow so plentiful there. I'm sure you remember how important spices were to the Europeans during this era. They were valued almost as highly as gold!

Ferdinand Magellan's ambition was to reach the Spice Islands in the East by sailing west beyond the New World.

With this in mind, think about the options that lay before Ferdinand Magellan. He knew that Cristóbal Colón — his boyhood hero — had sailed west to reach the East. He knew that Colón had discovered the New World while trying to find this passage. Magellan put this information together with his own experience. Why not sail *west* from Portugal to reach the Spice Islands? Maybe it would be easier than sailing around Africa. Maybe the Spice Islands were just beyond this "New World." (Follow this on your globe or map. Magellan was right about the *location* of the Spice Islands. But he didn't realize how big the Pacific Ocean is or how far away those islands are!)

Magellan's dream to sail west didn't come together easily. During his years of service to the king of Portugal, he was wounded in battle. It caused him to walk with a limp for the rest of his life. Furthermore, he got in trouble for taking a ship without permission and trading illegally with

Muslims. In 1514, the king of Portugal fired him! Though discouraged, humiliated, and lame, Magellan didn't stop dreaming.

Like Colón, Magellan went to Spain with his dream. The king of Spain was **Charles I**, the *grandson* of Ferdinand and Isabella. It only made sense that he might be more sympathetic to explorers after the success of Cristóbal Colón. Charles I was only a teenager at the time and easy to convince. In a serious race against Portugal, Charles was eager to claim new lands and open trade routes for Spain. After Magellan changed his nationality from Portuguese to Spanish, Charles employed him in the service of Spain. It was a big deal to the Portuguese that Magellan switched his loyalties to Spain because the two nations were in a bitter rivalry.

In 1519, Magellan was granted five ships to hold about 270 men. Since Charles I was such a young king, and not very rich, the ships he provided were in terrible shape. They needed new coats of black pitch to prevent them from leaking, and lots of other repairs. Even then, it took a lot of convincing from Magellan to find the crew he needed. Because Magellan was originally Portuguese, the Spanish weren't even sure they could trust him.

But with the promise of riches and adventure, sailors were found from all nations and all walks of life. At least one man was no more than a curious tourist. His name was **Antonio Pigafetta**. Fortunately for us, he kept a detailed diary of the entire voyage. The fleet was called the *Armada de Molucca*. The ships were by name the *Trinidad*, the *San Antonio*, the *Concepción*, the *Santiago*, and the *Victoria*. Magellan took the *Trinidad* as his own.

On September 20, after Mass, Magellan and the Armada de Molucca plunged into the Atlantic Ocean from the city of Sanlúcar de Barrameda. It must have been difficult leaving family and friends behind. The sea was known to be unkind and sometimes fatal. Magellan had to say goodbye to his wife, who was pregnant, and his young son. Like many others, Magellan's wife didn't know if she would ever see her husband again. I imagine she cried at the last sight of the sails disappearing from the harbor. She would have to wait years to know of his fate.

Magellan's plan was to return his fleet to Spain the *same* way they came. Like Colón, he sailed west toward the New World. By November, he veered the fleet far enough south to cross the equator near South America. By December, the armada reached Brazil but stayed only briefly as that land had been claimed by Portugal.

One of Magellan's dreams was to find a passage *through* South America to the Spice Islands. He knew from having sailed around the Cape of Good Hope that it would be difficult to sail all the way *around* South America. And so for months, he and his men sailed along the eastern coast of South America in shark-infested waters looking for a shortcut to the other side. (Using your map or globe, see if you can you find any shortcuts across South America. There is only one, but it is very far south!)

What you have to realize is that the farther south the ships sailed, the colder it got. Do you know why? The tip of South America gets very close to the South Pole. Both the North and South poles are colder than the rest of the earth because they point farther away from the sun. (It all has to do with how the earth tilts.) The point of my sharing this is to help you imagine the agony and the fear of the crew. It's bad enough to nearly always be wet onboard a ship. But to be wet and cold is miserable!

The coast of Argentina pictured here was nicknamed "Patagonia" by Magellan's crew because of the "big feet" of the natives living there.

It grew so cold on the journey that the crew chose to camp on the mainland for the rest of the winter. They camped in what now is **Argentina**. The sailors named it *Patagonia*, which means "big feet," because the natives there were very tall and, in fact, had very big feet. On a cruel note, some of the gentle giants were tricked to go onboard the ships. There they were locked up as prisoners — forced to endure the rest of the long voyage ahead! Pigafetta, the diary keeper, did his best to learn their language and calm their fears.

Those bitter cold months in Patagonia were tense. Hunting was difficult and fresh food scarce. The main sources of food were sea lions and penguins, which were certainly new and unusual to the Europeans. The men were always cold and grew lonely for the warmth of home.

To scout out better living conditions, Magellan sent the *Santiago* out to sea. With the weather against it, the ship was caught in a storm and destroyed! Two survivors made it back to the base camp on foot, and Magellan sent a rescue squad for the others. The rattled survivors salvaged what they could from the wreckage.

Believe it or not, this tension was made worse by the fact that the king of Portugal had apparently tried to sabotage the voyage beforehand. (To "sabotage" something is to secretly plan to ruin it.) Why would the king of Portugal try to sabotage the trip? Well, he was pretty upset that Magellan switched his loyalties to Spain for sponsorship. (It certainly made the Portuguese look bad.)

So, before the expedition had ever started, the king offered a lot of money to the other ship captains to ruin the journey through a mutiny! The king's plan failed. Through a series of tricks and battles, Magellan outsmarted the other captains and stopped the mutiny. Two captains were tortured and executed. As a cruel punishment, another captain and a rebellious priest were left stranded on the coast of South America, never to be seen or heard from again. After that, the crewmen grew more afraid of Magellan than of the dangers of the sea. So they pressed on.

## The Strait of Magellan

It would be October of the next year (1520) before Magellan found what he was looking for. Far down the coast of South America, there was indeed a passage to the other side! Magellan named it *Estreito de Todos los Santos*, which means "All Saints' Channel." It was named that because the ships sailed through the channel on All Saints' Day, November 1. The passage was later named the **Strait of Magellan** after Ferdinand Magellan, who never gave up believing that this waterway existed. (Find it on your globe or map.)

This waterway, however, turned out to be quite treacherous. Though it was a shortcut across the continent, the narrow, winding canal was difficult to sail, with steep, snow-covered mountains on either side of it and winds cutting in between. Through patches of fog, the sailors could see fires at night on the lands to their left, so they named this land *Tierra del Fuego*, meaning "Land of Fire." The fires were started either by lightning or by the natives.

Maneuvering through the 330 miles of the strait took the Armada de Molucca over a month. The captain of the *San Antonio* avoided the danger by refusing to sail through it at all. His ship was the largest. He turned it around and headed back to Spain, taking a great deal of food and supplies with him!

Finally, on November 28, 1520, the three remaining ships — the *Concepción*, the *Trinidad*, and the *Victoria* — reached the Pacific Ocean. With tears in their eyes, the sailors looked out over the vast sea. In surviving their passage through the strait, they had accomplished one of the greatest feats in the history of sea travel. I wonder if they knew it. It was Magellan who named the ocean before them *Pacifico*, which we call the **Pacific**. It means "peaceful." The wide-open waters appeared much calmer and more peaceful than the tortuous channel they had just passed through.

This aerial view of the Strait of Magellan shows the channel that cuts through the tip of the continent. Can you find Tierra del Fuego?

However, peaceful is hardly the best word to describe the rest of the journey. Magellan had no idea how far away he was from reaching any land at all across the Pacific. Unknown to him, the Pacific Ocean covers one-third of the earth's surface! It is more than 63 million square miles. Though Magellan was headed in the right direction to find the Spice Islands, he greatly underestimated how long it would take him to get there. For this mistake, he and his crewmen would suffer greatly.

First, the fleet ran out of fresh food. This resulted in the spread of scurvy, the disease that comes from not having enough vitamin C. (Scurvy leads to swelling of the gums and makes eating almost impossible. In time, it makes the body lose skin and deteriorate.) Then the fleet ran out of dried foods. Then they ran out of rats to eat. Then they resorted to eating sawdust and leather just to stay alive! What little water they had was discolored and tainted. In January, the crew found two deserted islands where there were crabs and other sea creatures to eat. But by then, a large number of men had already starved to death or died from scurvy.

Antonio Pigafetta wrote this in his diary: "We were three months and twenty days without getting any kind of fresh food. We ate biscuit, which was no longer biscuit, but powder of biscuits swarming with worms, for they had eaten the food. It stank strongly of the urine of rats. We drank yellow water that had been putrid for many days. We also ate some ox hides . . . and sawdust from the boards."[2]

Finally, on March 6, after 98 straight days on the ocean, Magellan and his ships reached the **Marianas** (Mar ee AHN uhs), a small group of islands just east of the Philippines. Can you even imagine the sight of land on that day? Can you imagine the men falling to their knees and kissing the ground? Can you imagine them eating real food after having had nothing but sawdust and rats to eat? Of the 270 men who started on the incredible voyage, only 150 had made it to that point. At least 20 men perished from starvation just before crossing the Pacific.

As great as landfall was, something awful was yet in store. Upon reaching the **Philippines**, Magellan made a mistake that would cost him his life. After converting a local chief to Christianity, Magellan joined him in a fight against another tribe. It was foolish to get involved in a battle that wasn't his, but Magellan had bonded with the leader. Caught up in this civil war, Magellan and about 40 of his men were attacked on the beach. Magellan himself was speared to death and left dead in the surf. Antonio Pigafetta recorded this in his diary (the words in brackets are mine):

> An Indian hurled a bamboo spear into the Captain General's face . . . they all hurled themselves upon him . . . [Magellan] turned back many times to see whether we were all in the boats . . . [they] caused the Captain General to fall face downward, when immediately they rushed upon him with iron and bamboo spears . . . until they killed our mirror, our light, our comfort, and our true guide. Thereupon beholding him dead, we, wounded, retreated as best we could to the boats, which were already pulling off.[3]

Ferdinand Magellan died on April 27, 1521, before ever seeing the Spice Islands. He never knew that his name would be despised among the Filipinos. Nor did he know that his name would be great in the West. Magellan never knew that at least one of his ships would continue to sail all the way around the world and forever change history.

## *Juan Sebastián de Elcano*

In the meantime, the *San Antonio* drifted back to Spain in disgrace. Remember, the *San Antonio* was the ship that abandoned the Armada de Molucca when it came time to sail through the Strait of Magellan. Members of the *San Antonio* returned to Spain full of lies to cover up their desertion. According to them, the expedition had failed. Friends and family concluded they would never see the rest of the armada again. They were wrong.

Back in the Philippines, the remaining crew scrambled for their own safety. After much disagreement between the sailors, three men were chosen as captains. But it was **Juan Sebastián de Elcano**, the captain of the *Victoria*, who would unofficially take charge. He had tough shoes to fill. Juan Sebastián de Elcano was faced with the fact that Magellan, their brilliant leader, was dead and the Filipinos had all turned against them. He took charge of the men who were left, and they fled back to the sea.

For months, the three remaining ships sailed around the islands of Indonesia under the direction of Juan Elcano. The crewmen saw many new and amazing things. They saw tamed elephants, pearls the size of eggs, and spectacles — which were only just getting popular in Europe. But maneuvering through the islands was tricky with so few men. So, Elcano and his crew abandoned the worm-infested *Concepción* and burned it. The *Trinidad* and the *Victoria* became their new homes.

Finally, on November 6, 1521, the *Trinidad* and the *Victoria* reached the Spice Islands. With 115 men, two of the five ships that started the voyage had actually reached their destination! Pigafetta wrote, "So we thanked God, and for joy we discharged all our artillery [guns]. And no wonder we were so joyful, for we had spent twenty-seven months less two days in our search for the Moluccas."[4] (Word in brackets is mine.)

As planned, the armada bought and loaded their remaining ships with 26 tons of cloves and other spices. Magellan would have been thrilled. His vision had been fulfilled.

With ships fully loaded, Elcano knew it was time to head home. Despite the loss of men and ships, their mission had been accomplished. But rather than sail home the way they came, Elcano made a historic decision. He pointed their ships west! This was historic because never before had ships sailed all the way *around* the world in one direction. And just when you would think this story is over, one more tragedy occurred. The *Trinidad* began to leak! It would have to be grounded awhile for repairs. This left Elcano and his crew on their own to cross the Indian Ocean and complete their circle around the globe.

The trip across the Indian Ocean proved almost as dangerous as the trip across the Pacific. You see, Elcano couldn't sail the *Victoria* safely near the coast of India or Africa because of hostile traders. The Arabs and the Portuguese ruled those water routes like pirates. Elcano was forced to steer the *Victoria* far out into the Indian Ocean for 10,000 miles. In doing so, once again the sailors suffered. Food rations were short, and the men had to battle again with scurvy. By May 1522, the *Victoria* finally rounded the Cape of Good Hope with little but rice to eat. Twenty more men died of starvation before the ship landed at the Cape Verde Islands. To protect the valued cargo, 13 crewmen were left behind at that point and the ship sailed on.

Finally, finally, finally, on September 6, 1522, almost exactly three years since their departure, the *Victoria* arrived in Spain. With tattered sails and half-starved men, the Armada de Molucca arrived home. Of the original 270-man crew, only 18 weather-beaten sailors pulled into port that day. Though barely alive, these skeleton-sized men had much to tell.

To some degree, Juan Sebastián de Elcano was rewarded during his lifetime for his heroic efforts. After all, he was the one who navigated the *Victoria* back home. (It was 15 times farther than Colón's first trip to the New World!) Elcano had officially circumnavigated the globe. (That means he circled it.) And Elcano *was* the one who brought Spain a wealthy cargo of cloves. There was quite a celebration for that. But over time, Elcano's fame faded. When he tried a second time to circumnavigate the globe, he died crossing the Pacific Ocean.

As for the *Trinidad* (the ship that started to leak at the Spice Islands), after repairs were made, it set sail again. But the ship chose to head *east* with its cargo, returning the way it came. That proved to be a bad decision. The *Trinidad* never made it back to Spain. It faced terrible storms and was attacked by the Portuguese. Its cargo full of precious cloves sank to the bottom of the sea. The ship splintered into driftwood, never to sail again.

Historians today can't help but give a lot of credit to Ferdinand Magellan. He was a brilliant navigator and a fine leader. He was certainly persistent in following his dream and making it happen. But historians are inaccurate when they say that he "circumnavigated the world." For one, Magellan never planned to. Second, he only made it halfway around the world before his tragic death. But had it not been for Magellan, Juan Elcano and the *Victoria* would never have accomplished what they did. In my opinion, Magellan, Juan Elcano, and the other 17 survivors of the *Victoria all* deserve credit for the first circumnavigation of the world.

## Lesson 21 — 1521

# Martin Luther and the Spread of the Protestant Reformation

The last time we looked at **Martin Luther**, he had posted his Ninety-five Theses to the door of a church. The theses invited theologians into a debate over indulgences. Though posting an invitation to debate was an ordinary thing to do back then, the result was not the least bit ordinary. The result was one of the biggest events in the history of the church. The result was the **Protestant Reformation**.

Shortly after Martin Luther posted his theses, copies of the document were made in German and circulated throughout the region. This started a debate that was no longer just between theologians. The debate moved into the streets, the shops, the taverns, and the churches. Everyone was talking about it. Though many of the commoners didn't understand the theology of indulgences, they did understand the part about their money going to the Vatican in Rome — and to the debts of the archbishop. The Germans didn't like that at all.

Germans during the Renaissance were concerned about the high cost of building the beautiful structures of the Vatican in Rome.

For the next several years, numerous letters, documents, and sermons were written about the good and the bad of the church. One such document was written by Johann Tetzel (the monk who collected indulgences for Pope Leo). Tetzel wrote a 106-point "anti-thesis" to counter the debate started by Martin Luther. It wasn't well received by the Germans, who had come to love and support Luther. Eight hundred copies of the anti-thesis were burned in the market square of Wittenberg! Tetzel was fired from his job, retired to his monastery, and died in 1519. He never knew what an impact he had on history.

Interestingly, the early letters that Martin Luther wrote to Pope Leo X were sympathetic (that means nice). He admired the finer attributes of the pope and encouraged him in his difficult position. But things were not going to stay smooth between them. The issue of indulgences became only one of many things that Luther and the pope differed on. Over time, Luther offered less and less support to the pope and, in fact, questioned his authority altogether.

## The Debate at Leipzig

In 1519, the same year that Magellan started his historic voyage, a formal debate was held in the city of **Leipzig**. It was there that Martin Luther joined others in a debate against **Johann Eck** (EK). In the debate, Luther publicly stated three very important beliefs. Read or listen to these carefully: First, Martin Luther stated that the pope was *not* infallible. (That means he was only human and thus capable of making mistakes.) Second, Luther stated that the church of Rome was *not* supreme over other churches. Third, Luther stated that the Bible is the ultimate authority for Christians, not the teachings of the church (which he believed were no longer in line with the Bible).

Johann Eck argued against every point that Luther made. First, he would distinguish that the pope could make human mistakes. Certainly he might forget his umbrella one day or order the wrong size shoes. However, Eck would say that the pope, as Christ's representative, is incapable of making errors in spiritual matters.

Second, in regard to the supremacy of the church in Rome, Eck would point to the passage in Matthew 16:18–19, which Catholics believe gives the church its authority. Third, Eck would point out that the church existed before the canon of the Bible was compiled, thus demonstrating the church's integral role in guiding its members.

In concluding the debate, Johann Eck declared Martin Luther a heretic and accused him of holding to the same beliefs as **John Huss** (Hoos), who had been burned at the stake 100 years before. Eck was a powerful debater, but not powerful enough to shut Luther down. Though he would have had Luther arrested, too many people were paying attention to him. Too many were joining Luther in questioning the role of the pope in the sixteenth century.

There were some very good reasons for raising questions. For centuries, the power and authority of the pope had grown. Popes were doing more than giving spiritual leadership. They were living like kings. That's why popes and emperors fought in the Middle Ages over who was in charge. (Some of you will remember that from Volume II.) Popes acted very much like kings in launching wars, making treaties, living in luxury, and falling into immorality.

For example, during the Renaissance, Pope Alexander VI and Pope Julius II had illegitimate children. (That means they broke their vows of chastity, as well as the Seventh Commandment.) Pope Julius II also led wars against neighboring city/states in Italy. Pope Leo X, the son of Lorenzo de' Medici, embraced humanism. Both Pope Julius and Pope Leo overused the offering of indulgences to help pay for their extravagant improvements on the Vatican. To many, the power and position of the pope had been corrupted.

All these things and many more set the stage for the Protestant Reformation. Questions were being raised far and wide — but mostly by the Germans. Germany (though still part of the Holy Roman Empire) was pulling further and further away from Rome and the pope. By 1520, Pope Leo X thought it time to take action. He issued a special letter called a **bull** against Martin Luther. (The letter is called a bull because it is sealed by the pope with a round lead device called a *bulla.*) In this particular bull, titled *Exsurge Domine,* Martin Luther was condemned. The pope ordered that his writings be burned. Furthermore, Luther was given 60 days to report to Rome and repent of his teachings or face excommunication (which is being banned from the church).

In a special letter (a "bull") titled *Exsurge Domine*, Pope Leo X condemned Martin Luther and banned his writings.

The threatening bull backfired on the pope. Rather than quiet Martin Luther down, it spurred him to speak more strongly of his views, which he believed were in line with the Bible. Luther ignored the deadline to report to Rome and chose instead to write three small books. Each one carried a strong message.

**(Middle and Older Students: Read the summaries that follow.)**

In *An Open Letter to the Christian Nobility,* Luther stated:

- There is no special ranking in God's eyes between members of the clergy and the masses. In other words, every Christian is equal before God. (See Gal. 3:28.)
- If every Christian is equal before God, then each has the right to read and interpret the Bible.
- The Bible is the final authority for Christians.

In *The Babylonian Captivity of the Church,* Luther wrote:

- As the Israelites were once in captivity in Babylon, so the church is in "captivity" under the pope.
- The bread and the wine of communion are not changed into the real body and blood of Christ through the prayers of a priest of the church.
- Baptism and communion are the only true sacraments of the church.
- Marriage is not a sacrament and should not be forbidden for clergy.

In *A Treatise on Christian Liberty,* Luther proclaimed:

- Faith in Christ alone, not good works, provides salvation.
- Good works should flow from the believer whose faith is in Christ, not because he has to do good works but because he is free to. (See Eph. 2:10; Phil. 2:12–13.)

**(Younger Students may resume reading here.)**

After writing these small books, Martin Luther burned the bull from the pope in a public square in Wittenberg. It was outward defiance of the pope. For this, and for ignoring the bull, Luther was excommunicated. But it didn't seem to matter to him or to his followers. Many of his students followed him in burning other books that represented the authority of the pope. Luther continued to preach, teach, and write.

## *The Diet of Worms*

Now, I hope you can see how difficult the situation was. Germans everywhere were protesting against the pope. This led to yet another turning point in history, the **Diet of Worms**. Let me clarify what those words mean. A "diet" is a special meeting, and "Worms" is the name of a city. (In German, it is pronounced with a "v" to sound like *Vermz*.) The Diet of Worms was a meeting called by the Holy Roman Emperor. And do you know who had become the Holy Roman Emperor? It was Charles I, the young king of Spain who had sent Magellan to the Spice Islands. (Charles's new title was **Emperor Charles V**.)

For many reasons, Charles V was disturbed by the German protests. Germany was not yet a country but was still a part of the Holy Roman Empire. Charles wondered how he could keep his empire together with a rebellion such as this. To get to the bottom of it, he called nobles, princes, and churchmen to the Diet of Worms. The meeting started in January of **1521**. But it was not until March that Luther was invited to attend. The emperor promised him safe travel there and back.

Friends of Luther begged him not to go. They were afraid for his life. John Huss had been offered safe travel 100 years before him but was thrown into prison and burned at the stake! Luther had a hard decision to make. His answer was this, "Though there were as many devils in Worms as there are tiles on the roofs, I will go there."[5] And so he went. The meeting proved to be one of the most historic events in history.

Two thousand people greeted Luther in Worms. Knights rode out to protect his entry into the city. Everyone wanted in on the scene. On April 17, Luther stood before the council. Johann Eck was there to publicly accuse him of heresy. There, in front of everyone, Luther was asked to recant or deny his own beliefs and teachings. Luther was unprepared for this attack. He thought he was going to have a chance to debate with Johann Eck, like he had before. But the council skipped the debate and asked him to deny everything he believed.

Luther asked for another day to prepare. In fairness, Charles V granted it to him. The next day, Martin Luther appeared before the council. With confidence, this is what he said:

> Your Imperial Majesty and Your Lordships demand a simple answer. Here it is . . .[6] Unless I am convinced by the testimony of Scripture or by clear reason (for I trust neither pope nor council alone, since it is well known that they have often erred and contradicted themselves), I am bound by the Scriptures I have cited, for my conscience is captive to the Word of God. I cannot and will not recant anything since to act against one's conscience is neither safe nor right. I cannot do otherwise. Here I stand, may God help me. Amen.[7]

In other words, Luther stood his ground regardless of whether it would cost him his life or not. Charles V was stunned, as was most of the council. Charles V didn't know what to do with this man who was so bold as to stand against the pope, the church, the council, *and* the Holy Roman Emperor. But the emperor was generally mild tempered and very busy with war. (He was constantly battling the French and the Ottoman Turks.) Distracted and disgusted, Charles said only that he wished to have nothing more to do with Martin Luther. He declared him a heretic and forbade him to preach. But rather than condemn him to death (as had been the custom), Charles V only condemned Luther's writings and teachings. He was afraid that putting Luther to death would set off a revolt. With too many problems already, a revolt would be one more problem that Charles didn't need. Besides that, he had promised not to harm Luther. The emperor kept his word, and Luther was allowed to leave — alive. Considering the times, it was a miracle.

At the Diet of Worms, Charles V (the Holy Roman Emperor) declared Martin Luther a heretic but did not condemn him to death.

Luther's friends and supporters were not convinced that his life was safe. With masked horsemen, they arranged a fake capture of Martin Luther and placed him in the **Castle of Wartburg** for protection. Luther lived in hiding for almost a year. From time to time, he left the castle disguised as a knight with a beard. He called himself "Junker George." It was there, at the Castle of Wartburg, that Luther had the freedom to do something that would become one of his greatest accomplishments. Using the works of Erasmus, he translated the New Testament into common German for the sake of his own beloved countrymen. It was a great gift to the common people who now could read, understand, and apply the Word of God to their lives. With the invention of Gutenberg's printing press, thousands of copies of God's Word were circulated.

## Changes

In 1522, Luther shed his disguise and left his place of hiding. With his rivals cooled down, he was no longer in fear for his life. He went back to the church he loved in Wittenberg. He eagerly returned to give direction and bring order to his congregation. It led to a lot of changes. For one, Luther encouraged his members to attend church on a voluntary basis, rather than as a required mass. (For this reason, Protestants today do not call their church services a "mass" as Catholics do.) Secondly, Luther conducted his services in German instead of Latin for people to better understand the sermon. Third, he distributed communion differently than the Roman Church. Fourth, Luther did away with indulgences and prayers to Mary and the saints. Fifth, Martin Luther added congregational singing. He loved music and wrote many hymns himself. The most famous hymn he wrote was "A Mighty Fortress Is Our God." It is still sung by Protestants and Catholics today.

There were many other changes that Martin Luther made. But one more to mention is this: In order to "practice what he preached," Luther got married! In 1525, he married **Katharina von Bora**, a young former nun. Luther, along with hundreds of other monks and priests, left the monastery, married, and had a family. In fact, Luther had six children with Katharina. He was very proud of them and proved to be a wonderful husband and father. When his daughter died at 13, it grieved him deeply. But it didn't dampen his faith in the sovereignty of God.

Luther was glad for the changes in his church and all across Germany. But he was also concerned. He feared that changes made too fast would be made for the wrong reasons and create confusion. He was right. The attitude of rebellion against the pope led to other rebellions. The *spiritual* reformation also became a *social* and *economic* reformation. Knights rose up against rulers. Peasants rose up against their landowners. For two years, it was a fight between the rich and the poor. Luther sided with the peasants at first, for their lives were very harsh.

But over time, Luther switched his loyalties to the wealthy landowners. He held to the biblical teaching that believers should honor those in *political* authority over them. (See Rom. 13:1–2; Eph. 6:5–8.) It was a messy controversy that almost squelched the Reformation. Thousands of peasants were killed in the uprisings. It was difficult for the commoners to understand the difference between *spiritual* freedom and *social/economic* freedom. But that's a different lesson in history.

It was not until 1529 that "Protestants" completely adopted a new name and identity. It happened as the result of another diet, or meeting. At the **Diet of Spires**, the princes of the Holy Roman Empire were each given the right to determine if their region would follow the pope or follow Luther. However, limits were placed on those who followed Luther but *not* on those who followed the pope! Because of the unfairness of it, the followers of Luther "protested." In Latin, *pro testans* is a legal term for "bearing witness" or "declaring" — thus the princes and those they represented have been called "Protestants" ever since. (However, it would take 26 more years, and lots of quarreling, before the empire would officially "recognize" the Protestant Lutherans.)

As for Martin Luther, he lived for 20 more years. He spent the rest of his life preaching, teaching, and writing. By the time he died, he had written at least 400 publications and 37 hymns. Upon his death, his body was buried at Wittenberg, the place where it all started for him. In his memory, the doors of the church where he posted his theses were replaced with bronze. On them are carved his Ninety-five Theses. They remain a symbol of the courage and conviction of Martin Luther, one of the most remarkable men of the Renaissance.

Before he died, Martin Luther denied that he had been the least bit remarkable. In modesty he wrote, "I simply taught, preached, wrote God's Word: otherwise I did nothing. And then, while I slept . . . the Word so greatly weakened the Papacy that never a Prince or Emperor inflicted such damage upon it. I did nothing. The Word did it all."[8]

*Pictured here is John Calvin's Bible on display in Geneva, Switzerland. Calvin, a leader in the Protestant Reformation, lived by the motto* Prompte et sincere in opera Dei, *which means "Ready and wholehearted work for God."*

# The Age of Reform
## 1522–1572

I hope you enjoyed Quarter 1 and our look at the high Renaissance. I told you that compared to some other parts of history, the Renaissance "glitters and twinkles in places." I hope you agree, now that you've seen some of the glorious artworks produced in that time period. But we're not quite done with the Renaissance. This quarter we will learn of one more master artist who contributed to the beauty of this era. He was *Titian* of Venice, Italy. His watery homeland would inspire him toward a graceful, colorful style.

However, our main focus this quarter will be on the *Protestant Reformation*. For you see, in half a century, the ideas of the Reformation spread to *Switzerland, Moravia, England, Scotland,* and to the tiny kingdoms of *Navarre* and *Béarn* near France. All these countries and more would be influenced by the spiritual movement sparked by Martin Luther in 1517.

For this reason, I'm titling this quarter "The Age of Reform." We will span only 50 years in the next 21 lessons — from 1522 to 1572 — but they were a tumultuous 50 years! This part of the sixteenth century was loaded with conflict, bloodshed, and heroism from both sides of Christendom.

In the middle of it, you will get a chance to meet *Henry VIII,* one of the most famous kings of England, and his equally famous daughters, *"Bloody Mary"* and *Elizabeth I.* I think you'll agree that they are one of the most fascinating families in history. Elizabeth herself held the throne for one of the longest and most prosperous reigns in England's history.

As notable as Elizabeth I was, she was not the only woman to leave an impression on Europe. We will meet seven other outstanding women of the Renaissance and Reformation. Through their talents, their passions, and their femininity, each left a mark in history worthy of our consideration.

We will also get a glimpse of the *Turks,* the *Mughals,* and the *Russians* in this quarter. Though not a part of the Reformation per se, they have their own histories we'll want to look at. The same goes for a group of *explorers to North America,* an astronomer named *Nicolaus Copernicus,* and a great humanitarian named *Bartolomé de Las Casas.* Through conquest, sea travel, stargazing, and diplomacy, the world would never be quite the same after the sixteenth century.

# WEEK 8

## Lesson 22 1522

# *Suleiman and the Ottoman Turks*

Several lessons ago, I introduced you to the Safavid Empire of Persia. We learned then of two extraordinary rulers of Persia — **Ismail I** and **Abbas the Great**. Their religious faith greatly influenced present-day Iran. Do you remember their religion? Ismail I and Abbas the Great were Islamic. More specifically, they were Shiites, one of the two major divisions in Islam. Today, we will look at the *other* division of Islam, the Sunnis. One of the greatest Sunni leaders who ever ruled was **Suleiman** (like the name Solomon of the Bible but pronounced "Sue le MAN"). While Europeans were embracing the Renaissance and battling over the Reformation, Suleiman was taking over the world! (Well, almost.)

In 1520, one year after Charles was made emperor of the Holy Roman Empire, Suleiman was made an emperor, too. He was made ***sultan*** of the **Ottoman Empire**. The center of this empire was the city of Constantinople, which had fallen to the Ottoman Turks back in 1453. Right from the beginning, Suleiman had a lot going for him. His father, who was the emperor before him, left him a lot of money, a lot of land, and a lot of people to govern. But like other rulers, Suleiman wanted more. He spent the rest of his life expanding the Ottoman Empire. And he did it quite well.

Before I tell you how Suleiman went about expanding his empire, let me tell you what he had to begin with. (It was a lot!) When his father died, he inherited lands along the edges of three continents:

1. In Europe, Suleiman inherited Greece and several countries on the Balkan Peninsula.
2. In Asia, he inherited parts of Russia around the Black Sea, as well as Anatolia (An uh TOLL ya, which is present-day Turkey) and the Holy Lands.
3. In Africa, Suleiman inherited Egypt.

### *Expanding the Empire in Europe*

On each of these continents, Suleiman pushed his borders farther. Let's look first at what he accomplished in **Europe**. In 1521, the same year that Charles V called for the Diet of Worms (Vermz), Suleiman was on the move. He traveled north and attacked the city of **Belgrade**, the present-day capital of Serbia. With this victory, Suleiman left Europe alone for awhile, but it marked the beginning of a long struggle between Europeans and the Ottoman Turks. We'll come back to it later.

Suleiman then looked toward the Mediterranean Sea. He had good reason to pay attention to the Mediterranean. It was the center of trade between Europe, Asia, and Africa. Whoever could rule *this* sea could rule the trade *across* this sea — and become very rich. That made the islands of the Mediterranean strategic (meaning important) places to conquer. So, in **1522**, Suleiman went after **Rhodes**, an island in the Mediterranean Sea off the coast of Anatolia.

Toppled by an earthquake in 226 B.C., the Colossus of Rhodes was one of the Seven Wonders of the Ancient World.

Rhodes was an interesting island. In ancient times, a huge statue of a man guarded the harbor. It was called the **Colossus of Rhodes** and was one of the Seven Wonders of the Ancient World. (I hope you remember it from Volume I of *The Mystery of History*!) During the Crusades, Rhodes had become home to the **Knights of St. John** (also known as the **Knights Hospitallers**). These special knights were established in Jerusalem during the Middle Ages. Their role was to protect Christians visiting the Holy Lands. When crusaders failed to win the Holy Lands, the Knights of St. John fled from Jerusalem and moved to the island of Rhodes. Rhodes was the last Christian stronghold in the eastern Mediterranean Sea. The Knights of St. John took this position seriously and pirated the sea around them, attacking Muslim fleets. In time, they grew rich and powerful. To Suleiman, they were a nuisance.

But as much as Suleiman wanted to take Rhodes from the Knights, he did so very cautiously. After beating them in a long battle, Suleiman began to feel sorry for the Knights. When it was time for them to surrender, Suleiman allowed the Knights to leave the island safely. Suleiman was especially concerned for the grand master of the Knights, who was an older, wiser gentleman. On Christmas Day, Suleiman asked for a meeting with the grand master. In an unusual display of honor, Suleiman congratulated the old knight for having fought bravely against him. He then showered him with gifts. One historian recorded this of Suleiman, "It caused him great sorrow to be obliged to force this Christian in his old age to abandon his home and his belongings."[1] This story shows us that there was a noble side to Suleiman.

Regardless of how noble he was, Suleiman continued to push the borders of the Ottoman Empire. He looked again at invading Europe. In a strange twist of fate, the French practically begged him to do so. They asked Suleiman to attack southern Europe! Why would they do that? It's a long story, but the short version is this: The king of France, who was **Francis I**, was enemies with Charles V. (They were enemies because both wished to be the Holy Roman Emperor. It was ultimately awarded to Charles.) Charles and Francis battled back and forth for years over everything imaginable. In one such battle, Francis was captured by Charles and put in prison! In desperation, the French pleaded with Suleiman for help. Though King Francis I was a Christian king, he had no problem partnering with Muslims. Francis was desperate to be free from Charles V.

Suleiman responded to the call from Francis I and sent help. He had been planning on attacking the country of **Hungary** anyway. So, in April of 1526, Suleiman set out with 100,000 men. The Hungarians might have had a chance against the Turks had the Europeans been better united. But they weren't. Lutherans were at odds with Catholics, and the pope

was at odds with Charles V. This left the Hungarians without much help. At the **Battle of Mohács** (MOH hatch), which lasted only an hour and a half, the king of Hungary was drowned; 25,000 Hungarians were killed; and 100,000 Hungarians were captured. A large part of Hungary was lost that day to Suleiman and his forces.

This victory gave Suleiman more confidence. In 1529, he decided to be so bold as to invade **Vienna**, which at that time was the capital of the Holy Roman Empire! With 200,000 men, he dared to threaten the very heart of Europe. To say the least, all of Europe was shaken. Though probably not true, rumor spread that Suleiman would force Europe to convert to Islam. Interestingly, it was eight centuries before this that Charles Martel had stopped Muslims from invading Europe at the **Battle of Tours**. It was believed that if Europe were to remain Christian, history was going to have to repeat itself.

In a way, it did. Just as Charles Martel kept the Muslims out of Europe, so did Charles V. Twice the troops of Suleiman tried to take Vienna. Twice they failed. They were forced to retreat and try harder. In 1532, Suleiman gave it all he had. In a great spectacle this is what happened: Suleiman marched from his capital in Constantinople with a parade of 120 cannons; 8,000 **Janissaries** (JAN ih sair eez), who were specialized soldiers; 1,000 camels; 2,000 horsemen; thousands of Christian slave boys; and an army of 200,000 well-trained men. Suleiman joined the parade on a chestnut-colored horse. He wore a red velvet robe laced with gold trim and a brilliant white turban that was studded with jewels. It was a spectacular display of magnificence, which led to his being remembered in the West as **"Suleiman the Magnificent."**

But the fancy display of finery and all the fanfare didn't help Suleiman's cause. Charles V, the pope, and Lutherans put their differences aside and rallied together against the Turks. In a small town outside Vienna, the Europeans stopped Suleiman and his troops. Humiliated by the defeat, Suleiman backed away. He took the captives he had and headed back home. Not all was lost, however, because he kept Belgrade in his possession and he still had an alliance with France. His friendship with France would later serve to open up trade between them.

## Expanding the Empire in Asia and Africa

There is still *more* to Suleiman's expansion of the Ottoman Empire. After failing to take any more of Europe, he looked to his east. Ah ha! There to his east was the Safavid Empire of Persia, which you should remember is present-day Iran. The Safavid Empire became Suleiman's next target on his list of places to conquer.

If you remember, the Persians had become quite powerful under Ismail. Earlier in history the Persians had invaded the Ottoman Empire and taken slices of it. Of particular interest, the Persians had taken the city of Baghdad. Well, Suleiman took it back — along with a lot of other land to the east of his empire. The struggle between the two empires lasted many years. At one point, the Hungarians even got involved, urging and pleading with the Persians to attack the Ottomans. It didn't help the Hungarians. The Ottomans were strong enough to defend both their eastern and their western borders.

Pirate ships scourged the Mediterranean Sea for years under Barbarossa, giving great power to the Ottoman Empire.

In Africa, Suleiman pushed his empire to the west of Egypt. He conquered a great amount of northern Africa, including the city of **Tunis** (Too NEESE). Now, this was very strategic because it secured the Ottoman stronghold over the Mediterranean Sea. Remember, Suleiman had the island of Rhodes in the *eastern* half of the sea. By gaining the city of Tunis, he now had the *western* half of the sea. By dominating the entire Mediterranean Sea, the Ottoman Empire grew even richer.

## Pirates and Captives

While we're on the subject of the Mediterranean Sea, I want to stop and tell you a true pirate story. Much of Suleiman's success in the Mediterranean had to do with a Greek pirate named

**Barbarossa**. That wasn't his real name, but that's what the Europeans called him because Barbarossa means "red beard." This red-bearded pirate first became a hero to the Islamic world when he ferried 70,000 Muslim refugees from Spain to the coast of North Africa. Because of his help, Suleiman made this heroic pirate the admiral of the Turkish navy! With highly organized fleets, Barbarossa scourged the Mediterranean Sea for years. He bullied the shores of Italy, France, and Spain, taking thousands of Christian captives along the way. Had Barbarossa not been such a menace, the Ottoman Turks might not have kept their stronghold over the Mediterranean. Through this bloodthirsty Greek, they did.

Since I mentioned that thousands of Christians were taken captive by Barbarossa, let me tell you what happened to captives in the Ottoman Empire. It's a strange thing. It seems that the Turks took their younger captives (infants and boys, that is) and trained them to be specialized soldiers and bodyguards for the sultan. These special soldiers were called Janissaries. I mentioned earlier in this lesson that Suleiman marched on Vienna with 8,000 Janissaries! That's a lot of bodyguards. The name came from the Arabic words *yueni cheri*, meaning "new soldiers." These new soldiers were trained at a young age in the ways of Islam and in the service of the sultan.

To assure their loyalty to the sultan, the Janissaries lived and were trained in special schools. They were forbidden to marry, to have contact with people outside the school, or to have other jobs. Though it would appear to us that they were prisoners, the Janissaries were treated well and considered an elite class. It's hard for us to imagine that a sultan would surround himself with converted Christians as bodyguards, but the Janissaries spent *so* many years being programmed in the ways of Islam, they were loyal to their leader. With this built-in security system, the Ottomans maintained one of the most efficient armies in the world.

## *Suleiman the Lawgiver*

Suleiman and the Ottoman Turks remained a world power throughout the Renaissance and Reformation. When not expanding the empire, Suleiman was improving it. Though he was strongly Islamic, he gave religious freedom to Jews and Christians alike. He bowed to all on his way to temple, where he prayed for two hours every Friday. Suleiman built a great mosque in Istanbul that still bears his name, and he codified the laws of his land. The laws gave much strength to the Ottoman Empire and led to Suleiman's Arabic nickname, *Kununi*. It means "Lawgiver." Suleiman's people admired

As a spectacular display of architecture, Suleiman commissioned the building of the Süleymaniye Mosque in Istanbul.

him and loved him. Even those he conquered would say he did so honorably because Suleiman never allowed his troops to plunder or pillage the cities he added to his empire.

Unfortunately for Suleiman's sons, some of the laws of the empire were harsh. A law was made that allowed one prince to kill another prince if both were in position to be the next emperor. The practice is called **fratricide**. Of course, this kind of murder happened behind closed doors all around the world between royal family members. But it was the Ottoman Turks who made it legal!

The practice of fratricide led to genuine tragedy in Suleiman's family. His favorite wife, **Roxalena**, was jealous of the rising popularity of Suleiman's first son from another marriage. Roxalena convinced Suleiman that he should kill his firstborn son to guarantee the lives of *her* children. In a heart-wrenching struggle between power and love, Suleiman agreed to the pleas of Roxalena and had his first son strangled to death! As hoped by Roxalena, this allowed *her* son to later become the sultan, though he wasn't a strong one.

In closing, do you think Suleiman was much different from his European counterparts? In faith, I would say yes. But in intentions, I would say no. Suleiman, just like Francis I and Charles V, tried to expand and improve his empire. Though some of his methods were cruel, many were not. Suleiman successfully took the Ottoman Turks to their highest level, and they remained a strong empire for hundreds of years.

## Lesson 23 — 1523

# Ulrich Zwingli Leads the Swiss Reformation

The history of the Protestant Reformation is so messy. After this lesson, I think you will agree. It was messy because Protestants not only found fault with the Roman Church, but they also found fault with one another. Leaders in the business of "reforming the church" didn't agree on what they were doing — or how they were doing it. You will see this clearly in the life of **Ulrich Zwingli** (UHL rick ZWING lee), an ambitious reformer from Switzerland.

Switzerland is a small, peaceful country situated in the heart of Europe. But it wasn't always peaceful. The counties of Switzerland, which are called *cantons*, had to fight for their independence. They fought the nearby Austrians, and then they fought the Holy Roman Empire. The story of **William Tell** comes from that time period. He is the character who supposedly used a bow and arrow to shoot an apple off the top of his son's head! Whether that legend is true or not, by 1499 the Swiss were "free." However, the 13 cantons that remained were very separate from one another. Like the city/states of Greece and Italy, the cantons of Switzerland were not at all united. This fact led to the early death of Ulrich Zwingli. So pay attention to it!

## *Swiss Reforms*

Ulrich Zwingli was born in a valley near the large city of **Zürich** (ZOOR ick). Zürich was the name of both a city and a city/state. Ulrich was one of 10 children, but his father was a mayor and could afford a good education for his children. By age 10, Ulrich learned Latin, and at 14, he was in college. By 22, he had his master's degree and was ordained a priest. Obviously, he was smart!

One of the smartest things that Ulrich did was to teach himself Hebrew and Greek. For one, he enjoyed the Greek classics that were popular during the Renaissance. But mainly, he wanted to study ancient languages so he could better understand the Bible (which was originally written in Hebrew and Greek). Ulrich also read translations of the New Testament written by Erasmus. (Do your remember him?) Erasmus was one of Zwingli's favorite authors.

The reading of the Scriptures proved to be life-changing for Ulrich Zwingli. The more he read the Bible, the more he understood it. And the more he understood it, the more his personal faith in Christ grew. And the more his faith in Christ grew, the more concerned he was for the church. The things he read seemed not to match up with what was being practiced in the church he was a part of. Remember, he was an ordained priest.

But it was not until Zwingli was invited to be the "people's priest" of Zürich that he did something about his convictions. It was in 1518, at the Grossmünster (Gross MOON ster) church of Zürich, that Zwingli started a new tradition in the pulpit.[2] Instead of leading Mass in the traditional style of the Roman Church, Zwingli taught straight from the Scriptures. Starting with the book of Matthew, Zwingli taught his congregation the meaning of the words in the Bible one by one. (Older Students: We call that *expository* preaching, or the *exegesis* of the Scriptures.) Sometimes Zwingli referred to the Greek because he knew it so well. This impressed the educated folks. But the simple folks were impressed with Zwingli, too, because he managed to break down the Scripture to their level of understanding. It took him six years to teach through the entire New Testament verse by verse, leaving out only the Book of Revelation.

Ulrich Zwingli battled symptoms of the plague for three months but recovered to preach his Christian views in Zürich, Switzerland.

Two years into his teaching, Zwingli and one-third of Zürich were struck by the plague! Rather than flee, Ulrich remained in the city to teach, tend to the sick, and comfort his grieving countrymen. It nearly cost him his life. For three months, he battled high fever and infection. But he survived to be a stronger preacher than before. His near brush with death only fueled his passion more for teaching the Word of God.

As church members paid more attention to the Word of God, they began to question some of the church's traditions. For example, some church members concluded that the tradition of *not* eating meat for Lent was unbiblical — meaning that this practice was not mentioned in the Bible. To make their point, church members gathered on

Ash Wednesday, which is considered the first day of Lent, and ate fried sausages! Though it wasn't exactly a riot, it was a gesture of defiance against the Roman Catholic Church. Zwingli supported these believers by writing a pamphlet on Christian liberties.

Besides that, under the influence of Zwingli, the Bible was translated for the common man and study groups were formed for members of the clergy. The pure study of God's Word led to the questioning of more traditions. Believing the Roman Church was practicing idolatry, church members tore down statues of saints from church altars and whitewashed images of Mary from the walls. Even musical instruments were removed because they are not mentioned in the New Testament. This may sound very radical, but these believers were seeking to line themselves up with the New Testament as closely as possible.

In time, church services shifted their emphasis from a Mass said in Latin to a sermon spoken in German (the language of most of the Swiss). And priests and nuns left the monasteries to marry and have families of their own. Zwingli followed along and publicly married a woman who had been his "secret" wife for years. He openly admitted that he had struggled with celibacy (which means being unmarried).

Now, let's stop and make an important observation. With solid biblical preaching, it would appear that Switzerland was going through the same kind of Reformation that Germany went through. But it was much easier than what Martin Luther had faced. Why was that? Well, there is a very good reason for it. You see, earlier in history, in the year 1510, **Pope Julius II** had "released" the city/state of Geneva, Switzerland, from his rule. That means the Swiss were free to govern their *own* church affairs.

So, when Zwingli began to make reforms, he didn't have to contend with the pope as Martin Luther had. In fact, when Zwingli began to fuss about a monk selling indulgences in *his* area, **Pope Leo** simply called the monk home! Apparently some lessons *had* been learned from Martin Luther's outrage over Johann Tetzel, and those same problems were avoided in Switzerland.

But back to our story. Though Zwingli didn't have to tangle with Pope Leo, he was accused of heresy by the next pope, **Adrian VI**. But Pope Adrian, in his concern, asked only that Zwingli quit preaching. Not wanting to resign, Zwingli appealed to his own city council to back him up in **1523**. Upon hearing his 67-point thesis of needs for reform, the council agreed with everything. They completely supported Zwingli's ideas!

That sounds like good news, doesn't it? Well, it was and it wasn't. It was good that council members agreed to embrace biblical teachings. But it was not good that they agreed to *enforce* them. For in doing so, the city council crossed lines of authority. They failed to practice what we call the "separation of church and state."

As a result, Ulrich Zwingli unofficially became both a spiritual *and* a political leader in Zürich. He "ruled" the city/state of Zürich much like Savonarola had previously "ruled" the city/state of Florence. Civic matters became church matters, and church matters became civic matters. (For example, church salaries were paid by the state, not by the church itself.) The problem? Though Zwingli's heart was in the right place, his authority wasn't. Rather than following New Testament guidelines, he followed the Old Testament. He patterned Zürich after the nation of Israel and created a theocracy. This meant his spiritual leadership was enforced by the government. Unfortunately, it led to bloodshed and persecution. (Sigh!) That's why I stated earlier that the history of the Reformation was "messy."

## *The Anabaptists (or Swiss Brethren)*

The first mess that Zwingli found himself in was against a group he called the **Anabaptists**. The Anabaptists were strong believers who read the Scriptures diligently. In their study, they interpreted the Bible differently than Ulrich Zwingli did. The Anabaptists believed that the Bible taught *full* separation of church and state. With that, they wished for simpler rules and greater discipline *within* the church. They didn't want the government involved.

But most important to this group was the issue of baptism. The Anabaptists believed in baptizing only those who were old enough to understand sin and salvation. This means they didn't (and still don't) baptize infants. Zwingli did. Though infant baptism does not appear in the New Testament, Zwingli believed it represented a covenant sign between God and man. He viewed baptism much like circumcision in the Old Testament.

Because the Anabaptists felt so strongly about baptism, they banded together over the matter. They followed the leadership of **George Blaurock**, **Conrad Grebel**, and **Felix Manz**. In one historic gathering, on January 21, 1525, George Blaurock asked Conrad Grebel to baptize him as an adult. Then George proceeded to baptize the other men present. For this act, they were nicknamed the "Anabaptists," which means "re-baptizer." However, the term was *not* appreciated by these folks. They believed that their first baptisms as infants were not legitimate. So, in their minds, they were not being *re*-baptized at all. They despised the term *Anabaptist* and instead called themselves the **Swiss Brethren**. Well, they were "Swiss" and they did choose to live as brethren in Christ. (You may want to stop and read this paragraph again. It's important.)

The Swiss Brethren grew in number. They grew strong enough to be of great concern to Ulrich Zwingli. He so disagreed with their interpretations of Scripture, that he used his political power to try to stop them. Did you catch that? He used his *political* power against them. Why did he have political power? Because he had created a theocracy and used the city council to enforce his teachings. Under Zwingli, Swiss Brethren were arrested, tortured, and even put to death! It was tragic.

The first arrested were Blaurock, Grebel, and Manz, the men who had first gathered for adult baptism. They managed to escape, but not for long. Manz was eventually drowned for his views. Grebel died naturally from the plague. Blaurock was stripped half naked, dragged, and beaten in the cold streets of Zürich. He was later burned at the stake by Roman Catholics.

As beautiful as they are, the Alps were not a safe home for the Swiss Brethren, who faced persecution under Ulrich Zwingli.

These are difficult atrocities to understand. The horrible situation forced most of the Swiss Brethren to flee their mountainous homes in the Swiss Alps. The strong emotions felt by the Swiss Brethren during their age of persecution have been preserved in numerous hymns of faith. These hymns are still sung by their descendants today.

## *Martin Luther*

Ulrich Zwingli had another messy encounter. It was with Martin Luther. Though Zwingli and Luther shared *many* of the same ideas for reform, they disagreed on one major thing. They disagreed over the exact meaning of the Lord's Supper, or Communion. Though Luther thought differently than Roman Catholics, he believed as they do that the bread and wine of Communion were *literally* the body and blood of Christ. Zwingli disagreed. He believed that the bread and wine were mere *symbols* of Christ's body and blood by which to remember Him. It led to a great division between the reformers.

The division was such an ordeal that an outsider named **Philip of Hesse** (HESS uh) tried to fix it. In 1529, Philip of Hesse invited both Zwingli and Luther to his castle in Marburg, Germany. There he hoped to iron out their differences and bring unity to the movement. It was a good effort, but it failed. Martin Luther defended his point by chalking on the table, "*This* is My body," as found in Luke 22:19. (Italics are mine.) He could not — or would not — negotiate his interpretation of the passage. Zwingli refused to budge on *his* interpretation, quoting over and over again, "Do this in *remembrance* of Me," as found in the rest of Luke 22:19. (Italics are mine.)

In the end, Luther left the castle in Marburg in a huff. He was so disturbed by Zwingli's differing views that he labeled him a heretic and a heathen! On Luther's behalf, he believed that communion represented Christ's "dual" nature as both God and man — both a spiritual and physical being. On Zwingli's behalf, he believed so strongly in the Divine nature of Christ that he was insulted to imagine Christ in the form of bread or wine. So deep ran their convictions that the two never spoke again face-to-face. They continued their "war" of words through numerous pamphlets written back and forth. They and their followers were divided and remain so today.

## *Battle of Kappel*

The next mess I'll mention would be Zwingli's last. It involved the cantons, or city/states, of Switzerland. Six of them were faithful to Zwingli. Five were not. These five opposing cantons wanted to remain Roman Catholic. It led to war when a follower of Zwingli was burned at the stake for preaching in Roman Catholic territory. The first battle between the cantons ended by negotiations. But the negotiations weren't satisfying to Zwingli. He wanted freedom for his preachers across every canton in Switzerland. So, serving as a chaplain in the army, he joined troops in preparation for another battle.

Zwingli's plans came too late. A surprise attack by the five warring cantons caught Zwingli and his troops unprepared. A second battle, called the **Battle of Kappel** (1531), had a gloomy ending. In this civil war of Swiss fighting Swiss, 50 city councilmen and pastors were killed. Zwingli was fatally wounded. His enemies dismembered his dying body and burned it to ashes. Today, there stands a statue of Ulrich Zwingli in the city of Zürich. Fittingly, the figure holds a Bible in one hand and sword in the other. Both represent his passions.

The movement started by Zwingli didn't end with his death. A devout believer named **Heinrich Bullinger** (HINE rick BULL ing er) picked up where Ulrich left off — but he did so *without* a sword. Bullinger was a sincere pastor and a wise scholar. The only sword he carried was the Word of God. He wrote more theological works than any other reformer of his time. Bullinger's devotion to the Scripture laid a strong foundation for later branches of the "Reformed church."

## Lesson 24 1525

# The Anabaptist Movement and Menno Simons

As we step deeper into our study of the Protestant Reformation, let me share some things in my heart. In our last lesson, I introduced you to the Anabaptists. Their story is a difficult one because so many were persecuted. You will learn of more persecutions today. For that reason, *my* heart is concerned with *your* heart. I'm imagining the questions about God that may run through your mind when you learn today of *more* Christians harming other Christians. You may be wondering where God was (and is) in the midst of the suffering of his saints. I've wondered it, too.

Let me assure you that though it is sometimes hard to see, the Lord promises never to abandon his followers. (See Matt. 28:20.) On the contrary, Jesus *predicted* the suffering and persecution of believers. (See also Matt. 10:16–23.) We don't see all Christians suffering bodily persecution, but during the Protestant Reformation, there were many who did suffer greatly.

I will proceed with telling you the amazing stories of some of the persecuted. But don't lose heart. Don't think for a minute that their deaths were in vain. God was very much in control of the spread of the Gospel. In losing their lives, the persecuted gain the kingdom of heaven. (See Matt. 5:10.) Jesus said, "Blessed are you when they revile and persecute you, and say all kinds of evil against you falsely for My sake. Rejoice and be exceedingly glad, for great is your reward in heaven." (See Matt. 5:11–12.) With that said, let's look more closely at the Anabaptist movement and the extraordinary life of **Menno Simons**.

As mentioned in our last lesson, George Blaurock, Conrad Grebel, and Felix Manz gathered one historic day in **1525** to baptize each other as adults. This act labeled these men and their followers as Anabaptists. They called themselves the Swiss Brethren. A man named **Michael Sattler** was greatly attracted to the new group and joined them that same year. Michael Sattler saw the need for writing down the things the Swiss Brethren believed that made them different from Roman Catholics, Lutherans, *and* the followers of Zwingli. He didn't write down everything the Swiss Brethren believed, but he narrowed it down to seven points. Sattler wrote these points down while in the Swiss-German border town of Schleitheim and so they are called the **Schleitheim Confession**. Here are the seven points:

1. *Baptism* — is only for adults who have professed Christ as their Lord and Savior.
2. *Discipline* — of sinful believers belongs within the church.
3. *Communion* — is only for those who have been baptized.
4. *Separation* — from evil and the world is necessary.
5. *The Duties of Pastors* — are outlined in the New Testament.
6. *The Sword* — is never to be used, and believers shall not serve as judges or magistrates.
7. *Oaths* — are forbidden by Jesus.

Michael Sattler and his wife paid a great price for their firm beliefs. Within months of writing the confession, both were arrested and killed. One of the main reasons Sattler was put to death was his view toward pacifism (meaning not going to war). At a time when the Ottoman Turks were breathing down Europe's neck, it made no sense at all to Roman Church officials that a Christian would "turn the other cheek." But the Swiss Brethren would say, "The worldly are armed with steel and iron, but Christians are armed with the armor of God, with truth, righteousness, peace, faith, salvation, and with the Word of God."[3] On matters of war, Christians remain divided even today.

But back to our Swiss Brethren, who were forced to flee because of persecution. Many headed east to Moravia under the leadership of **Jan Hut** (Yahn Hoot), who died in prison for his beliefs. Leadership was picked up again by **Jacob Hutter** (HOO ter). For years, the Brethren in Moravia were persecuted off and on. During good times, Moravia was nicknamed "the promised land of the Anabaptists." But as kings would come and kings would go, persecution resumed. The Brethren barely survived under the harsh treatment of **King Ferdinand of Bohemia and Moravia**. Under King Ferdinand, Jacob Hutter was whipped, stretched on a rack, and burned to death. Two years later, his wife was also executed.

Despite all of this, and this is amazing, the **Hutterites** (as they were named) were more evangelical than most. This means that they continued to go out, two by two, and share the Gospel, using tracts and Bibles to help explain the marvelous story of Jesus. If they lost property because of persecution, they shared with one another. Following the New Testament example in Acts 4:34–35, they literally laid down their possessions and shared everything in common. Their collective homes were called the *bruderhof* (BROO der hohf), or "brother farms." This form of "communal" living is still evident today in the Hutterite settlements of South Dakota, Minnesota, and Canada.

## *Disaster*

But unfortunately, not all the Swiss Brethren followed good leadership. Instead of fleeing east, some groups traveled north under **Melchior** (MEL key or) **Hoffman, Jan**

**Matthys**, and **Jan van Leiden**. Each one of these men went astray from biblical teachings, and the results were disastrous. Melchior Hoffman tried to predict the end of the world and claimed to be the prophet Elijah. His followers were set up for disappointment and disillusionment every time a prediction of Christ's return failed to be met. In Matthew 25:13, Jesus says that man cannot know "the day nor the hour in which the Son of Man is coming," but Hoffman tried to guess it anyway. Authorities put him in jail for 10 years.

Jan Matthys resorted to using the sword to force his beliefs on the citizens of Münster.

Jan Matthys violated the Anabaptist view about using the sword. He took over the city of Münster, Germany, and forced his views on the town. Those who didn't follow? They were executed! Thus, under Jan Matthys, the once-persecuted Anabaptists became the ones to persecute! Like Zwingli, Matthys died in battle. Some would say that it fulfilled Jesus' words that "all who take the sword will perish by the sword." (See Matt. 26:52.)

But the most embarrassing mistakes in the Anabaptist movement were made under Jan van Leiden. He went so far away from New Testament teachings as to take 15 wives and call himself the king of Münster! His followers were the **Münsterites**. Jan van Leiden believed that the city of Münster was the New Jerusalem and a haven for Anabaptists. He justified having many wives as a way of taking care of widows. As absurd as that was, he also set himself up to live in luxury while his community went hungry. This ridiculous arrangement lasted less than two years. Jan van Leiden was captured, tortured, and hung to death from a bell tower. Many of the citizens of Münster were cruelly executed, too.

Because Jan van Leiden was *associated* with Anabaptists, his pitiful reputation stained the movement for centuries. *Anyone* believing in adult baptism was connected to the crazed "king" of Münster and hunted down and persecuted. Some were labeled "hedgepreachers" for hiding behind hedges and out in the fields. The Münsterites, unfortunately, did great damage to the reputation of the Anabaptist movement.

This leads us to Menno Simons. You'll be glad to hear that he was a good guy. In the midst of turbulent times for the Anabaptists, God appeared to be raising a leader to point believers back to the Bible.

## *Menno Simons*

The testimony of Menno Simons is to be admired. He was born in the Netherlands of a peasant family. He enrolled in a nearby monastery and began his career under the Roman Catholic Church. He soon became a priest. But he admitted that, even as a priest, he didn't read the Bible! In fact, he was almost afraid of it. He had heard stories of Martin Luther and Zwingli who left the church after reading the Bible. He had no intention of following them. Menno wrote, "I had not touched them [the Scriptures] during my life, for I feared, if I should read them they would mislead me. Behold! Such a stupid preacher was I for two years."[4] (Brackets contained in original source quote.)

Menno Simons got past his fears and did begin to read the Bible. With the Word of God in his head *and* his heart, Menno found he was bothered by the same issues that bothered the first Anabaptists. He had questions about the Lord's Supper, baptism, and church membership. Though he remained a priest in the Roman Church, he began to preach and teach like an Anabaptist. Many listened and were drawn to his calm and gentle spirit.

For preaching Anabaptist views, Menno Simons was forced into hiding and became a "night preacher."

But it was not until 1535 that a tragedy really changed Menno's life. A man thought to be his brother was killed, along with 300 other Münsterites. This deathblow forced Menno to study his convictions more closely. In doing so, he preached more boldly against both the Roman Church *and* the misguided Münsterites. This made him very unpopular with both groups. Within a year he was forced to go into hiding. He lived on the run most of the rest of his life.

Menno Simons was married and had three children. His entire family went into hiding with him. They moved from place to place to avoid imprisonment. Charles V, the Holy Roman Emperor, issued an edict to destroy all Anabaptists! So Menno Simons became a "night preacher," teaching believers in odd places in the middle of the night. Sometimes he wore disguises. Menno Simons eventually fled to Germany where he and his family were safe.

Despite all the challenges, Menno's ministry flourished. For 25 years he taught others from the Bible. His most important work is titled *The Book of Fundamentals*. On everything he wrote about faith, he started his page with 1 Corinthians 3:11. It says, "For no other foundation can anyone lay than that which is laid, which is Jesus Christ."

Menno Simons died of natural causes in 1561. In humility, he did not want his name used for his followers. But it stuck anyway. The **Mennonites**, as they are called, grew in great numbers through times of peace and persecution. (Some branched off later to become the **Amish**. We will study them in Quarter 4.) There are 1.2 million Mennonites around the world today — many live in the United States. Perhaps you know a Mennonite family or you are Mennonite yourself. In my opinion, the simple, godly lifestyle of the Mennonites gives much honor to the Lord and to Menno Simons, for whom they are named.

> "For no other foundation can anyone lay than that which is laid, which is Jesus Christ."
>
> —1 Corinthians 3:11

# WEEK 9

## Lesson 25 1526

# Babur, Akbar, and the Mughal Dynasty of India

We're going to take a short break from the Protestant Reformation and return to our study of Islam. We've already studied Islam in three different regions. Can you remember them? We learned first of *West African* empires. Two of the three we studied were Islamic. Try to name them. (They were the **Mali Empire** and the **Songhai Empire**.) We then learned about the **Safavid Empire** of *Persia* where the Shiites overcame the Sunnis. Last, we looked at the **Ottoman Empire** in *Turkey*. The Ottomans bravely tried to invade Europe under Suleiman the Magnificent. Remember him? He was stopped by Charles V. And now, we're adding another Islamic region to our study. The region is *northern India*. It was conquered by **Babur** (BAH bur) of the **Mughal dynasty** and his grandson **Akbar** (ACK bar). We'll look first at India, then at the achievements of the Mughal dynasty.

### India

We have only briefly looked at India in this volume. I mentioned India when we learned about Vasco da Gama. Do you remember why? He was the Portuguese explorer who rounded the Cape of Good Hope and eventually moved to India. He was there for the sake of trade. Southern India was inhabited by lots of traders who pushed the Indians aside to get rich. Both Europeans and Arabs were guilty of taking advantage of India's resources.

Northern India was getting pushed around, too. It had seen its golden age under the Gupta dynasty during the Middle Ages. But after that, it was invaded over and over again. The Huns, the Persians, and the descendants of Genghis Khan — all pushed their way into India bringing their culture and beliefs with them. Hinduism, the primary religion of India, was mixed with Islam. Very few Christians lived there and the Word of God was not heard. No one in India was arguing over methods of baptism or Communion, for they did not know the scriptures of the Bible.

### Babur

Let me tell you now about Babur. He is a very interesting guy. His full name was **Zahir-ud-din Mohammad Babur**, but history remembers him mostly as Babur, which means either "tiger" or "beaver" (depending on whom you ask). Apparently, Babur was unusually strong. It's been said that he could race with two men on his shoulders and swim upstream the many rivers of India! On his mother's side, Babur was related to Genghis Khan, the first of many fearless Mongol warriors. On his father's side, he was related to **Tamerlane** (TAM er lin), or "Timur the Lame." Tamerlane was a ferocious Mongol Turk who blazed a path of destruction across India in the Middle Ages. Tamerlane slaughtered many to expand his territory. Remember that!

After losing his homeland of Turkistan, Babur set out to conquer northern India.

When only 11 or 12, Babur inherited a small kingdom in **Turkistan** in central Asia. Can you imagine being a king at 12? Though he was young, Babur was very dedicated to his small Turkish kingdom and to his faith, which was Islam. All he knew was the Koran, the holy book of Islam. He followed it closely.

Babur first expanded his kingdom by invading parts of Afghanistan. However, in doing so, he lost cities of his kingdom back home in Turkistan. For several years he went back and forth, winning a city here and losing a city there, until he finally lost his kingdom entirely. It was then that Babur set his eyes on India.

## *Babur Conquers India*

With an army of only 12,000 men, Babur eventually crossed into India to stay. At the **First Battle of Panipat** in **1526**, he easily conquered the sultan of Delhi. I say he "easily conquered" because Babur had one thing that the sultan of Delhi didn't. That one thing was gunpowder! Babur had learned the secret of gunpowder from the Ottoman Turks and used it to defeat an army of 100,000 men and at least 100 war elephants at the First Battle of Panipat. Babur's bullets could not penetrate the thick hide of the war elephants, but the sound of the guns scared the large beasts into trampling their own army. With this success, Babur also took the nearby city of Agra.

However, winning would not always be so easy. An army twice that of Delhi's set out to attack Babur. **Rana Sanga of Mewar** gathered 210,000 men for the onslaught. Not even Babur thought he had a chance. His troops were hot, tired, and on foreign soil. But, against all odds, Babur and his men overcame Rana Sanga at the **Battle of Khanua** in 1527. This enormous victory made Babur the supreme ruler of northern India.

In his triumph, Babur officially started the Mughal dynasty. It was probably named "Mughal" to not be associated with the "Mongols." If you remember, Tamerlane was a cruel Mongol Turk whom the Indians despised. Babur wished to be loved and so didn't use the Mongol name.

Babur was not only a military man, he also had heart. Babur was passionate for the arts and loved to read and write. His language was Persian. A journal he kept through his battles remains a favorite to Central Asians today. Babur wrote stories not only of battles and bloodshed, but he wrote of plants, nature, and the customs of others. When homesick for Turkistan, he built gardens to resemble the ones of his forefathers.

But Babur's reign was short-lived. Only three or four years after his conquest of northern India, Babur died of disease. Legend says that he wished to die in place of his son, who contracted the disease first. As it turned out, Babur did die, and his son recovered, just as he had wished.

## *Akbar "the Great"*

Unfortunately, Babur's son didn't prove to be the leader that Babur was. In time, he lost everything his father had gained. He fled back to their Turkish kingdom, where he raised his son Akbar. Akbar was strong like Babur and when old enough, he went *back* to India to claim the land his grandfather had conquered.

In Arabic, Akbar's name means "the Great." In one particular way, I would agree. Akbar granted religious freedom to the people of India. He allowed them the freedom to practice their faith, which was largely Hindu. To show his favor toward the Indian people, he married a Hindu princess. Now, I'm not promoting Hinduism as the best religion for India. But I am promoting *freedom* of religion. That's what Akbar gave to India. It helped restore peace between the mixed cultures.

As an example of his open-mindedness, Akbar held debates every Thursday night between men of various faiths — Hindu, Islam, Zoroaster, and even Christian. He listened carefully and invited Catholic priests to translate the Bible into Persian for his people. He attended Mass and wore a medallion of Mary around his neck. But according to the priests, Akbar was *too* open-minded. He refused to settle on one faith, thinking perhaps they all had something to offer. He tried to create a mixed religion, but it didn't catch on in India.

Symbolic of his tolerance, Akbar built a magnificent palace that blended Islamic and Hindu architecture. The palace, **Fatehpur Sikri** (Fat tay POOR SICK ree), was built in beautiful red sandstone near the capital city of Agra. Its towers, courtyards, and bridges stand fixed in time as one of the greatest artistic accomplishments of the Mughal dynasty. But unfortunately, the palace was abandoned in Akbar's lifetime because it didn't have a good water supply. Today it is open to tourists.

Still following Hindu tradition, Birla Mandir, a Hindu temple, was built in the 1930s in New Delhi, India.

Akbar the Great brought stability to India in other ways. He built schools and forbade young children to marry, as had been the custom. Akbar freed women from harsh conditions and put an end to the old custom of *sette*, which forced the act of suicide on widows. He centralized the government and increased the trade of rice and silk. Under Akbar the Great, northern India became as strong as it had been under the ancient Gupta dynasty. But one thing Akbar lacked was the ability to read or write. Since he loved to learn, he hired others to read and write for him. Day and night, he listened and dictated. With a library of 24,000 books, he became the most learned leader of the Mughal dynasty, despite the fact that he was illiterate.

## *The Building of the Taj Mahal*

I'll close with one more thing about India that might already be familiar to you. Have you ever seen or heard of the **Taj Mahal** (Tajz Muh HALL)? It is by far one of the most beautiful tombs in the world. It stands perfectly symmetrical before a large reflection pond in Agra, India. Well, it was Akbar's grandson who built it. His name was **Shah Jahan** (Shah Ja HAHN). He was very wealthy and admired fine architecture. So, when Shah Jahan lost his favorite wife in 1621, he began a 22-year project to build her an elaborate tomb and an architectural image of Islamic belief.

At least 20,000 workers were hired for the job. The magnificent tomb is made of white marble embedded with jewels. Its large dome stands 120 feet high. The marble was imported on elephants and practically all of Asia was searched for the gemstones to adorn the structure. Though many would think of the Taj Mahal as a great example of Indian architecture, it is clearly Islamic. Much like a mosque, the dome of the Taj Mahal is circled by towering minarets and inscribed with passages from the Koran. The inscriptions are more than decorative; they speak of Islamic beliefs of paradise and judgment. Muslims do not worship there, however, because the Taj Mahal is a tomb and does not face Mecca as almost all other mosques do.

As a monument, the Taj Mahal stands as one of *the* most sentimental. From all accounts, Shah Jahan truly loved his wife and grieved so deeply when she died that his hair turned gray. They had married when she was 19. The wedding had been extravagant, with parades in the streets and fireworks into the night. The bride's title was **Mumtaz Mahal**, which means *pride of the palace*. Thus, the Taj Mahal bears the name of Shah Jahan's most beloved. She died giving birth to her 14th child. (Only 7 of her 14 children survived.)

The Taj Mahal also symbolizes the decline of the Mughal dynasty. Though others tried to copy it, the Taj Mahal was the last great monument erected under the Mughals. Shah Jahan's son stole the throne out from under him and locked him away for nine years. Sadly enough, from his confinement, Shah Jahan could see the outline of the Taj Mahal where he had laid his beloved wife to rest. I imagine it reminded him of her every day. Upon his death, his body was laid to rest next to hers.

The breathtaking Taj Mahal honors Shah Jahan's beloved wife and stands as a monument to the Mughal dynasty.

After Shah Jahan, later Mughal kings failed to be strong. And they failed to give religious freedom to the people of India. Muslims heavily taxed the Hindu people and their poverty grew. Later in history, Europeans joined Muslims in oppressing the people of India and the nation continues to battle poverty today.

# *Henry VIII and His Many Wives*

To know **Henry VIII** is to know the story of his love life. Not that his love life was great. It really wasn't. But it was most certainly complicated and unusually dramatic. I would say that Henry's love life was in fact *so* complicated and dramatic that it affected the **Reformation in England**.

Henry VIII was the son of Henry VII, who started the House of Tudor. You should remember the House of Tudor from our lesson on the Wars of the Roses. Henry VII is the one who married Elizabeth of York to end the "family feud" *between* the houses of Lancaster and York. Is it coming back to you? Henry's new family line was the House of Tudor. When he started that line, I doubt that Henry had any idea just how much his son was going to impact the history of England — but believe me, he did.

Henry VIII never thought he would be king. He had an older brother named **Arthur** who was first in line for the position. But Arthur died at just 15. After that happened, Henry not only took his brother's place to be the next king of England, he also took his brother's wife, **Catherine of Aragon**. Well, that is, Henry was engaged to her. He was only 11. Catherine was 15. It would be a few years before they actually married. But when they did, it was sweet. They were childhood friends who grew up to be both husband and wife, and king and queen.

## *Wife #1 — Catherine of Aragon*

There is much to know about Catherine of Aragon. She was the daughter of Ferdinand and Isabella of Spain. They are the ones who sent Christopher Columbus across the Atlantic and used the Inquisition against Muslims and Jews. But remember this too — they were strongly attached to the Roman Church.

Well, their daughter, Catherine of Aragon, had long golden hair, a Spanish accent, and a great deal of patience. She and Henry VIII were married for almost 20 years and were well loved as the king and queen of England. Catherine gave birth to many children, though only one survived. Her name was **Mary** — later to be known as "Bloody Mary." (You'll definitely want to remember that.) Henry cared for his daughter Mary, but he really wished she had been a boy to carry on his name and wear the crown of England. It haunted Henry day and night that he had not one "legitimate" son to grow up to be king.

After 20 years of marriage, Henry concluded that God was punishing him by not giving him a son. He based this on a passage in Leviticus that reads, "If a man takes his brother's wife, it is an unclean thing . . . They shall be childless." (See Lev. 20:21.) Henry believed that he had been wrong to marry Catherine to begin with and that they were without a son because she had been his brother's wife. Remember Arthur, who died at 15? Catherine *had* in fact been married to him first.

So, based on that fact, Henry petitioned **Cardinal Wolsey**, the head of the Church of England, to annul his marriage. An annulment is similar to a divorce except it declares a marriage to have *never* been real or valid. Poor Catherine! She was crushed at the idea of "dissolving" her marriage of 20 years. She deeply loved her husband and never agreed that the passage in Leviticus applied to them. According to her, and many others, she was *never* wrongly married to Henry and God was *not* punishing them to give them no son. She married Henry as a young widow and was free and clear of wrongdoing.

But Henry was adamant about the matter and persisted in petitioning Cardinal Wolsey for an annulment. Now, this petition put Cardinal Wolsey in a terrible predicament. In order to give the annulment, Cardinal Wolsey had to get the approval of Pope Clement VII. But, now follow this closely — the pope was in a war at that time with the Holy Roman Emperor, who just happened to be the nephew of Catherine of Aragon! Did you follow that? The pope was fighting against the emperor — and the emperor's aunt was Catherine of Aragon. The pope could not — or would not — hurt Catherine with the annulment and provoke the Holy Roman Emperor he was at war with. For the record, the emperor I'm referring to was Charles V. Yes, you know Charles V. He was the one who declared Martin Luther a heretic. As you can see, the situation was complicated and went far beyond the shores of England.

Now, listen carefully to the next part of this story. When Henry learned that he was refused an annulment by the pope, he was furious. In order to get what he wanted, he fired Cardinal Wolsey in **1529** and had a small court give him a "secret" annulment. In that same year, he hired **Thomas More** to take Wolsey's place as the Lord Chancellor of England. Henry fully expected Thomas More to back him up and grant him the official annulment he wanted through the pope. But this didn't happen! No matter how hard he tried, Henry could *not* convince Thomas More to extend him an annulment.

Henry's fury raged on. In another attempt to get the official annulment from Catherine, he resorted to blackmail. He coerced a group of bishops to pass a bill declaring that he was the new head of the Church of England! Forget the pope, thought Henry. Forget the cardinal. Forget Thomas More. Henry declared *himself* to be in charge of the Church of England so that he didn't need *anyone's* approval for an annulment or a divorce. Thomas More, a very devout man, didn't believe in divorce. He resigned from his position as chancellor and was later beheaded for standing up against the king. I'll tell you more about this devout man in our next lesson. His strong ethics are worth our examination.

## *Wife #2 — Anne Boleyn*

Finally, it was an archbishop named **Thomas Cranmer** who gave Henry the official annulment he wanted on paper. That was in 1533. Catherine of Aragon was tucked away to live out her life quietly as the "ex-queen." (Her loss of royalty was a fact she never accepted.) Before the annulment was official, Henry VIII remarried in secret! Apparently, the *whole* time he went on and on demanding an annulment, he had his eye on a lively, petite 15-year-old named **Anne Boleyn**. Anne was strong in character. Her spirited personality also had something to do with shaping the history of England.

You see, for years Anne refused to become a mistress, or girlfriend, to the king because he was married to Catherine. Some would say Anne took this stance because she was strong in her Christian faith. Others would say she wanted to be queen and "manipulated" the king into marrying her! I don't know her heart. But Anne was certainly the reason that Henry was so emphatic about getting an annulment from Catherine.

A lively 15-year-old, Anne Boleyn captured the heart of Henry VIII, one of the most famous kings of England.

Henry was obsessed with Anne Boleyn and could hardly spend an hour without her. He wrote her numerous love letters expressing his infatuation. But the only way he could have Anne was through marriage. She refused to be his woman otherwise. It drove Henry nearly crazy and into bizarre behavior — like firing the cardinal, beheading Thomas More, and defying the pope!

Unfortunately though, Anne did not remain strong in her moral convictions. Once she believed she *would* marry the king, she moved in with him and loved him as a wife. Anne became pregnant right away. It was then that Henry "secretly" married her. Eight months after that, Anne gave birth to a daughter named **Elizabeth**, another fact to remember for later.

After the annulment, Henry enjoyed his new wife and he enjoyed his new power. In 1534, he solidified his position of newfound authority through the **Act of Supremacy** and the **Act of Succession**. In these two acts Henry persuaded the English Parliament to grant him these three things:

1. The act declared that the King of England (not the pope) was the *Supreme Head* of the Church of England.
2. It stated that Mary, Henry's daughter with Catherine, would *not* inherit the throne.
3. It required all the king's subjects to sign an oath giving Elizabeth, and any of Henry's future children, the right to the throne.

Yet, after all the fuss of getting an annulment and making himself the head of the church, Henry's marriage to Anne didn't last long. As fast as he had fallen in love with her, he fell away from her. He in fact began to despise her. It seems Anne Boleyn was not nearly as patient and forgiving as Catherine had been. Anne raged with jealousy when Henry noticed other women — which he did a lot. The English despised Anne, too. They called her a home wrecker and accused her of being a witch for having a growth on her hand that looked like a sixth finger! Anne could hardly walk down the streets without hearing jeers and insults and gossip.

Only three years into their marriage, Henry decided to do away with Anne. This time, he wouldn't choose an annulment. He instead charged Anne with committing adultery (which is unfaithfulness in marriage) and plotting to kill the king! For her crime Anne was locked in the Tower of London and given the death penalty. Her supposed "boyfriends" were sentenced to die first — a fact that tormented Anne greatly because *she* knew they were innocent. Before they were killed, she appealed to Henry's heart with these final words from prison (word in brackets is mine):

> My last and only Request shall be, That my self may only bear the Burthen [burden] of your Grace's Displeasure, and that it may not touch the Innocent Souls of those poor Gentlemen, who (as I understand) are likewise in strait Imprisonment for my sake. If ever I have found favour in your Sight; if ever the Name of Anne Boleyn hath been pleasing in your Ears, then let me obtain this Request; and I will so leave to trouble your Grace any further . . . From my doleful Prison in the Tower, this 6th of May.
>
> Your most Loyal and ever Faithful Wife, Anne Boleyn[1]

Though filled with emotion, the letter made no impact on Henry. Anne's innocent gentlemen friends were executed from her viewpoint in the Tower. Henry hardly acted remorseful over the ordeal, but he did respond to Anne's request for a French executioner. Why would she want a French executioner? Well, Anne had been raised in France. She knew that the French method of execution was swifter and less painful than English execution because the French used larger, sharper chopping blades for the task. It's a true but gruesome detail, and Henry arranged for it.

Anne died saying her prayers at the hands of a French executioner. As is custom, she forgave him beforehand. Her lips were said to still be moving in prayer even after the deed was done. And wouldn't you know, less than a week later, Henry married again! It was fairly evident then that Anne *was* falsely accused of adultery so that Henry could remarry without all the hassle he had been through before!

## *Wife #3 — Jane Seymour*

Wife #3 was named **Jane Seymour**. Interestingly, she at one time was a maid in the king's court, which may make you wonder just how long the king had his eye on her. But Jane stood for purity when it came to "dating" the king. She would visit him only with a chaperone.

The English had great respect for her. Seventeen months after their wedding, Jane gave birth to a royal son — the one thing that Henry wanted most of all. Church bells rang! Feasts were held! All of England celebrated the birth of the baby prince. The newborn's name was **Edward.** But, in gaining a son, Henry lost Jane in the process. Tragically, she died from complications of childbirth just 12 days after Prince Edward was born.

Henry's heart was truly broken. He said later in life that Jane Seymour had been his best queen. She had always been proper, gentle, and submissive to Henry. (She learned how important that was from Anne Boleyn!) Jane also worked very hard during her short reign to mend Henry's relationship with his daughter Mary. Jane was a great friend to young Mary and invited her to their court. It was a teary reunion for Henry and Mary — they had been separated for six years because of the messy annulment with Catherine. Yes, Henry benefited greatly from Jane Seymour. Her calm dignity was a good influence on him.

Meanwhile, aside from all this drama, there were other important things going on in Henry's court. Archbishop Cranmer (the one who gave Henry his annulment) and a secretary named **Thomas Cromwell** were getting very involved with the Protestant Reformation. They wanted Henry to break even *further* from the Roman Church than he had. But Henry was not really a "Protestant." He didn't agree with Martin Luther about anything except limiting the power of the pope. Ironically, earlier in his career, Henry was nicknamed the "Defender of the Faith" for his *support* of the Roman Church! Isn't that confusing? Henry defended the Roman Church and then broke away from it.

Nonetheless, Thomas Cranmer and Thomas Cromwell managed to push Protestantism toward England. They dissolved hundreds of Roman Catholic monasteries in England. Henry went along with this because *he* got the land and the wealth of the old monasteries! As you can see, Henry made changes in the church that seemed to be for *his* own good. His interests were not on true reform.

## *Wife #4 — Anne of Cleves*

Thomas Cromwell, however, did care about reforming the church, though it may have been more for political reasons than spiritual reasons. He hoped England would become more like Germany and completely break away from Rome. So, after the death of Jane Seymour, he came up with the idea for Henry VIII to marry a German princess. Her name was **Anne of Cleves.** Perhaps *this* marriage, according to Cromwell, would benefit England and unite it with German reformers. It was a good idea on paper, but in real life, it proved to be a disaster.

Henry agreed to marry the princess because he was told she was young, beautiful, and sophisticated. He also had seen a portrait of Anne by **Hans Holbein** (Hahnz HOL bine) **the Younger**, Henry's favorite artist. Hans Holbein painted Anne to be quite lovely and impressive. But Anne of Cleves was not beautiful, nor was she refined. Her upbringing had been simple and her interests were narrow. She had no musical background at all — something of great importance to Henry. Anne was older than expected, dreadfully unattractive, and could hardly speak English. When Henry first laid eyes on her, his face fell with disappointment.

Hans Holbein the Younger embellished this portrait of Anne of Cleves by giving great detail to her dress and portraying her to be quite lovely and impressive.

Poor Anne of Cleves. Though others found her very nice in personality, Henry was not the least bit impressed. Henry went through with the wedding ceremony, but he never loved Anne as a wife. They ate dinner together and played cards at night. But that was about as far as their relationship went. They parted as "friends" and their marriage was annulled six months later. When Martin Luther heard about it, he retorted in disgust, "Squire Harry [referring to Henry] wishes to be God, and do as he pleases!"[2] (Words in brackets are mine.)

That may have been true. But Henry was at least kind enough to have Anne provided for. She continued to live in England on a nice budget. She accepted her fate well because it was far better than that of Henry's other wives. Hans Holbein fared well, too. He was forgiven for misrepresenting Anne in her portrait. But Thomas Cromwell — the man who came up with the plan for Henry to marry Anne of Cleves? Henry had him beheaded for his "brilliant" idea to unite Germany and England through a wedding. Cromwell begged for mercy — but didn't get it.

## *Wife #5 — Catherine Howard*

On the same day as Cromwell's execution, Henry married again. (Can you believe it?) This time he married a teenager named **Catherine Howard**, "Wife #5." Believe it or not, in less than two years, this marriage failed, too! But this time, it was against Henry's wishes. It seems Catherine Howard was foolish and immature. The attention she received as queen went to her pretty little head. Though she flattered Henry with the attention he craved, she gave her heart to someone else and was unfaithful.

No one knew what Catherine was up to. Thomas Cranmer stumbled upon the story when snooping around her personal life. You see, Thomas Cranmer didn't like Catherine. She was Roman Catholic, and he was trying to reform the church in England toward Protestantism. He thought she stood in the way. Cranmer set out to ruin Catherine's reputation and push her aside by stirring up a scandalous story about one of her *old* boyfriends. In doing so, what he found instead was something worse. What Cranmer found was that Catherine was secretly involved with a man right there in the court!

Once the secret was discovered, Catherine confessed that she was guilty of adultery. In 1542, she was beheaded for her crime, as were her lover and a maid who covered up the secret. Because he had been unfaithful to his other wives, you could say Henry was getting "a taste of his own medicine." It must have tasted pretty terrible. Henry felt especially foolish because just before Catherine's secret affair was discovered, he had thrown a big party in her honor. At the party he boasted that the young, beautiful Catherine was the fairest, most wonderful queen in the world. He called her his "rose without a thorn." Henry had been duped.

## *Wife #6 — Catherine Parr*

Henry's love life would eventually settle down. A year and a half after Catherine Howard's execution, Henry met another Catherine. She was **Catherine Parr**. This 31-year-old woman was warm, caring, practical, and very intelligent. She had been widowed twice. Perhaps the loss of love was something she and Henry had in common. Henry and Catherine were married in 1543, and she became "Wife #6." Catherine Parr took in all three of Henry's royal children (Mary, Elizabeth, and Edward) and treated them as her own. She saw to their education and made their house a home.

This stable marriage lasted the rest of Henry's life. It was almost cut short by the fact that Catherine was a "Protestant." Though Henry broke from the Roman Church, he wasn't in support of the Protestants. Catherine began their marriage by bringing up the views of the reformers to try to convince Henry of their ways. For that, she was temporarily confined! Her fate dangled by a thread. But she learned to keep her views to herself and gave Henry *no* excuse for sending her to the Tower and cutting off her head!

That incident passed, but Henry wasn't well. He overate; he fought a bad infection in his leg; and he struggled against disease. Henry VIII died only four years after he and Catherine Parr were married. He was 55 years old. He is buried at Windsor Castle near Jane Seymour, the wife he probably had loved the most. Catherine Parr married again a short time after Henry's death. Ironically, it was to Jane Seymour's brother! But that's another story.

Though stubborn and selfish in character, Henry VIII had the reputation of being a "Renaissance man" because he was well educated, athletic, musical, and fun loving.

## *Henry's Legacy*

So what had Henry VIII accomplished by the end of his life? Most would agree that he didn't accomplish as much as he could have. When young, he showed potential for more. Red-headed and good looking, Henry was fun, athletic, musical, and trained in the classics. He knew three languages and was one of the most educated kings to ever sit on the throne of England. Ambassadors from Venice "believed him to have few equals in the world" because he was "so gifted and adorned with mental accomplishments of every sort."[3]

Henry professed to be very "religious" and attended mass as often as six times a day. He even wrote a few hymns that are still sung in the English church. Most expected him to be England's finest "Renaissance man." For this he had quite a reputation. Hans Holbein, the artist, spent most of his career in the service of the king. He painted numerous flattering portraits of Henry and his many wives playing "king and queen" in all their fancy attire. And believe me, their attire was fancy. Henry and his wives had the finest of gowns, furs, jewels, and lavish palaces.

But, unfortunately, Henry left matters of administration to other men. His chancellors practically ran the country for him because politics was not his strength. Though he warred against Scotland and France, and tried to unite England and Wales, Henry never set foot on the battlefield. He spent most of his career dancing, hunting, entertaining, building ships — and chasing women. Most of England adored him and forgave his ruthless ways.

Some would say that Henry VIII brought reform to the Church of England. But that's not quite accurate. Though Henry ordered English Bibles to be placed in the churches, it wasn't for spiritual reasons. He issued the Bibles to promote nationalism and independence from Rome. Henry wasn't interested in *reforming* the Roman Church. He only wanted England to be free of the pope. In fact, in 1539, Henry wrote **Six Articles** that he wanted enforced in England. The articles were similar in thought to Roman Catholic practice. They outlined the Lord's Supper, Mass, confession, and more. Anyone who failed to abide by the Six Articles could be condemned as a heretic and burned at the stake! Under the Six Articles, both Protestants *and* Catholics were executed! No, Henry VIII was not a reformer; he was a tyrant. Under him, thousands of people from all walks of life were put to death.

Henry's children are another story — and a complicated one. I won't finish that story here. But I'll tell you this much. Henry VIII wrote in his will that Prince Edward would be the next king. If he died, Mary would replace him. If she died, Elizabeth would replace her. And that's exactly what happened. Edward VI, "Bloody" Mary, and Elizabeth I each ruled England in that order.

I'll prepare you ahead of time — each change on the throne was messy because Henry's children all had different religious beliefs! Edward was strongly Protestant; Mary was strongly Roman Catholic; and Elizabeth reinstated the Anglican Church. As you will learn later, it led to a tragic amount of bloodshed. Sad but true, many would be executed before England would settle on a state church.

## Lesson 27 — 1529

# Sir Thomas More

I've already introduced you to **Sir Thomas More**. I mentioned him in our last lesson as one who served in the court of Henry VIII. Do you remember how he died? He was beheaded for *not* signing an oath in favor of the king. His bravery alone is worth remembering. But there is much "more" to Thomas than that. Sir Thomas More is also remembered for his warmth, his skill as a lawyer, and *Utopia* — a creative story about a perfect place.

Thomas More was born in London and went to school there. While serving as a young page, he was predicted to become a "marvelous man" by an archbishop who knew him well. He studied at Oxford and filled his time there writing comedies and studying Greek and Roman classics. Thomas had a good sense of humor and was well liked.

Thomas More attended the prestigious University of Oxford, the first university in the English-speaking world.

One of Thomas More's favorite authors was our old friend Erasmus, the well-known humanist of Europe. The two were great friends. It's no wonder they got along so well. Both loved the popular classics of the Renaissance. Thomas enjoyed humor and Erasmus liked to poke fun. If you remember, he poked fun at just about everyone in his famous satire titled *In Praise of Folly*.

In fact, Erasmus dedicated the satire to Thomas More — that tells you what good friends they were. Erasmus wrote this about his friend Thomas: "He seems born and framed for friendship, and is a most faithful and enduring friend . . . In a word, if you want a perfect model of friendship, you will find it in no one better than in More . . . In human affairs there is nothing from which he does not extract enjoyment, even from things that are most serious . . . As a rule, in talking with women, even with his own wife, he is full of jokes and banter."[4]

*"In a word, if you want a perfect model of friendship, you will find it in no one better than in More."*

*–Erasmus*

Though great friends, Thomas More and Erasmus were different in one area. Thomas was more serious about his Christian faith. He read St. Augustine's *City of God* and was moved to be more virtuous with his life. He considered joining the monks and spent a great deal of time around them. Eventually, though, he decided that marriage was a better option for him, and he never took the vows of a monk.

Thomas More's other great interest was law. Because of his strong faith and convictions, he made an excellent lawyer and judge. Others appreciated the fact that he was fair, gracious, and uncompromising. These were qualities that never left him and ultimately contributed to his tragic death. We'll come back to that later.

## *Thomas More Writes* Utopia

Before Thomas More joined the court of Henry VIII, he wrote an unusual piece that became his claim to fame. In 1516, he wrote a fictional story titled *Utopia*. The title itself was a play on Greek words. *Ou* means "not" and *topos* means "place." Putting these together, More created a word meaning "no-place." Why did he write a story about No-place? That was the funny thing. More wrote about an imaginary place that was so perfect, it could never truly exist. But there was a point behind writing it.

Thomas More used *Utopia* to bring to light the ups and downs of civilization. On one hand, he made some great suggestions about how a perfect place *ought* to be governed — at least in his opinion. On the other hand, he made fun of the impossible efforts of mankind to make such a perfect place.

The story line of *Utopia* is comical in places. More wove real characters (including himself) and fictional characters together so that it's hard to tell which parts of the story are made up. It opens with a sailor talking to Thomas More and his friends about his journey to the New World. On the journey, he supposedly lands on the island of Utopia, where everything is nearly "perfect."

For one thing, the imaginary "Utopians" don't just punish thieves, they prevent theft altogether. How does a society do that? According to the sailor in the story, the Utopians are prevented from stealing because money and possessions are spread evenly among them. Thomas More debates with the sailor whether this is logical or whether a society could ever improve without some people wanting to be richer than others. The debate is left for the reader to think about.

Other philosophical debates are presented to the reader. The sailor points out that in Utopia, everyone is happy when they follow the Golden Rule. Thomas More states that this is good and fine, but he points out that there is no personal freedom in Utopia. Everyone is told what to do and when to do to it for the betterment of all. The Utopians work six hours a day, sleep eight hours, and are allowed leisure time in between, which nearly always includes reading.

Oh, the Utopians are fine citizens indeed. They all grow gardens; they aren't allowed to litter; and they move to the country every few years so all can learn to farm. War is frowned upon except for self-defense, and gold and silver are used for everyday things so people won't grow greedy for the precious metals.

Thomas More writes this of the imaginary Utopians:

> So you see there is no chance to loaf or kill time, nor pretext for evading work; there are no wine-bars, or ale-houses, or brothels; no chances for corruption; no hiding places; no spots for secret meetings. Because they live in the full view of all, they are bound to be either working at their usual trades or enjoying their leisure in a respectable way. Such customs must necessarily result in plenty of life's good things, and since they share everything equally, it follows that no one can ever be reduced to poverty or forced to beg.[5]

The rest of *Utopia* deals with slaves, travel, religion, marriage, clothes, and other real-life things. Are you wondering what Thomas More thinks is a "perfect" wardrobe? More describes the

Utopians as having one sturdy work outfit made out of leather that would last seven years. These work outfits are covered with inexpensive woolen garments all the same color. In addition to that, every Utopian is content with one comfortable outfit of any color to wear while relaxing; this outfit is to last at least two years.

Sounds too good to be true, doesn't it? Thomas More would agree. But he is making the point that some rulers would try to completely run other people's lives if they could. Some results would be good and practical, but some would be rigid and ridiculous.

Ambrosius Holbein created this intricate woodcut design of the legendary land of Utopia for the cover of Thomas More's *Utopia* (the 1518 edition).

## *Politics*

After writing *Utopia,* Thomas More had more serious things to preoccupy him. His life became very political as he moved up the ranks in England. As a strong member of the Roman Church, he got involved with putting down heretics and reformers. (Personally, I don't admire him for condemning reformers, but I admire him for his strong convictions.) Thomas was noticed by the king himself and "knighted" for his fine service. This gave him the title "Sir" Thomas More. Eventually he was hired by Henry VIII to be Lord Chancellor in **1529**. Of course, Henry VIII was not exactly a "Utopian" kind of a king. He was far too selfish. Henry "used" Thomas More to help him write the theological piece that earned Henry VIII the title "Defender of the Faith."

Now that you've come to know Thomas More's warm heart, his sense of humor, and his sense for right and wrong, you may better understand his death. You see, when Henry *insisted* that his advisers sign an oath *agreeing* to his annulment and marriage to Anne Boleyn, Thomas More refused. He was a man of principle and held deep religious convictions. He would not bend to the king's wishes. He resigned as Lord Chancellor.

As a lawyer, Thomas More tried to use the laws of the land to protect him from the king's court. He did so by remaining silent. In other words, when asked *why* he wouldn't sign the oath for the king, Thomas said nothing. He chose not to say anything that could be used to condemn him for treason. For this, Thomas More spent an entire year in prison. Without a full case of treason against him, he could not be put to death!

The year Thomas More spent in the Tower of London was hard. He saw his family only briefly. When he did, his wife cried and cried. She never fully understood his silence on the matter of the king's marriage. She and the rest of the family grew poorer as time went by. But Thomas stood his ground. He *would not* sign the oath or speak out against the king.

Remember when I described Thomas More as "fair, gracious, and uncompromising"? He was all of these. By not bending to the king, he was being "fair" to Catherine of Aragon — who he believed was the rightful queen. He was "gracious" to Henry by not speaking treason against him. And he was "uncompromising" by not signing an oath he didn't believe in.

In time, Thomas More's enemies found a way around the system to put him to death. They found a man willing to lie about Thomas More in court. The man claimed that he heard Thomas speak treason against the king. This was enough for the court to condemn Thomas More to die! In great humility, Thomas said to the liar, "In faith, Mr. Rich, I am sorrier for your perjury [lie] than for my own peril."[6] (Word in brackets is mine.)

Thomas went to his execution bravely. It fell on July 6, 1535. In his final words, Thomas More referred to himself as "the King's good servant, but God's first." Above all, Thomas More *has* been remembered as God's servant. The Roman Catholic Church declared him a saint in 1935. Schools and universities around the world bear his name in honor. You could say that Thomas More's "silent" witness probably spoke louder than his words ever could have.

# WEEK 10

## Lesson 28 1530

# *Titian and the Rise of Venice*

There is no other city in the world quite like **Venice**. During the Renaissance, Venice was rich, inspiring, and perplexing. It was rich because nearly all the world's trade from the East to the West passed through its elegant ports. It was inspiring because it was built upon thousands of tiny islands that were connected by intricate canals and waterways. It was perplexing because it withstood wars, water, and would-be tyrants. All of this to say: Venice was something special in the sixteenth century. And a Venetian artist named **Titian** (TISH un) was special too. He rose to fame right alongside this mystical city of water.

Before I elaborate on Titian and his masterful works of art, I want to tell you more about Venice and what made it so special. If you don't already know, Venice is in northeastern Italy on the coast of the Adriatic Sea. Do you know how Italy looks like a boot? The **Adriatic Sea** is the body of water on the east of that boot. The coastline there is nestled away from the big winds of the Mediterranean Sea making it perfect for trade ships. These days Venice is a city overrun with tourists. But during the Renaissance, Venice was a large city/state. In fact, it was so large that it hardly considered itself part of Italy. It would be later in history before it officially became a city of Italy.

Being on the coast, Venice had to make the most of the water that lapped at its edges. To some degree, the builders of Venice got carried away with the idea. They trapped the sea on their behalf and used it to maneuver boats from one tiny island to another. The idea caught on, and Venice grew more gorgeous from the 400 stone bridges that connected it. Of greatest beauty is the **Grand Canal** that winds through the city of Venice in an S-shaped curve. The Venetians used every excuse to decorate the Grand Canal and other waterways for festivals and regattas. The greatest feast of all was *Sposalizio del Mare*, when Venice was supposedly "married" to the Adriatic Sea. It was a dramatic ceremony welcoming the waters of the sea into the streets of the city.

Where Venice couldn't spread out, it spread upward through the addition of tall palaces, cathedrals, and monuments. Every corner of the city was made ornate. Every form of architecture was welcomed. Gothic spires blended with Roman arches and Byzantine domes. Mosaics mingled alongside frescoes and canvas oil paintings. Venice had it all and the people loved it.

The wealth of Venice should come as no surprise. It was all based on trade. It had to be. The Venetians had to import most of their food because they couldn't grow it there. They traded their leather, cloth, lumber, and metal for food and all kinds of finery. The city was

Venetian artists of the Renaissance were inspired by the deep-colored skies over Venice and the lights glimmering off its many waterways.

perfectly situated between the East and the West and so it had the best of both worlds. Marco Polo helped make that happen hundreds of years before when he left Venice to travel to China. After his travels, Venice was forever changed. It quickly opened routes to the Far East, bringing silks, spices, and rare jewels to Venice. It grew to be home to many wealthy people. This was evident by the mansions that lined the streets.

Even without its wealth, Venice would still be lovely. There's something about the way the city lies against the misty water that makes it shimmer. Venice is well known for its orange and bluish purple sunsets. It's probably these sparkling colors mirrored on the sea that began to inspire artists a little differently than those in Florence. Venetian art schools were all about *color* and *light*.

## *Titian*

Titian, the famous artist of Venice, was born near the Alps. His full name was Tiziano Vecelli (Vih CHELL lee) da Cadore (Ca door aye). (Now that's a beautiful Italian name! Cadore, by the way, is a place.) Tiziano moved to Venice when he was very young because he showed such promise as an artist. He first studied under **Gentile** (Zhen TEEL) and **Giovanni Bellini** (Jee oh VAHN nee Bell LEEN knee). Titian was joined in the studio by an artist named **Giorgione** (Johr JOE knee). The two young students were about the same age, but Giorgione was far advanced in his skill. Unfortunately, Giorgione died from the plague when he was only 34. Giovanni Bellini, the master instructor, died six years later. This left the door wide open for Titian to take the lead as a master artist. He, in fact, surpassed his teachers.

When Titian began to finish the projects that Giorgione had left incomplete, others found it hard to tell who had painted what. To this day, some of their works are confused because Giorgione didn't always sign his work.

Once Titian was recognized for his talent, he was commissioned for big projects like the painting of three frescoes in the *Scuola del Santo* in the city of Padua. (Padua was part of the city/state of Venice.) It led to a long and satisfying career. Titian wasn't a genius like Leonardo, a poet like Michelangelo, or a socialite like Raphael. He was just a great painter. But he lived well into his nineties and so left a long trail of masterpieces behind him.

To add to his fame, Titian began to break some painting traditions. In *Madonna with Saints and Members of the Pesaro Family* (also known as the *Pesaro Madonna*), he moved the main figures, Mary and Jesus, to the side of the painting instead of centering them in front. That was unheard of back then. But he used light to draw attention to Mary and Jesus and create balance. He did the same in *Noli Me Tangere* (No lie Me TAN jer ee) and in *The Three Ages of Man*. Look for these rule breakers yourself. It was a refreshing change of style that many would later copy.

Though Mary and Jesus are off-center in the *Pesaro Madonna*, Titian drew attention to them through gentle and delicate lighting.

Titian didn't seem to have a favorite subject to paint. He painted portraits, Bible stories, mythological scenes, beautiful women — and himself. He even left behind some mysterious paintings that no one can really explain. I suppose because he lived so long, he had the chance to paint a little bit of everything. Probably one of his greatest works is the *Assumption of the Virgin*. The light rays from heaven are absolutely mesmerizing — especially when they shine down on hovering cherubs and clouds. To me, the painting gives the impression that we're catching only a glimpse of what lies beyond this world.

But it was Titian's skill at portraits that gave him the most fame during *his* lifetime. He painted more portraits than I have room to write about. But of course, I'll tell you of a few. One of my favorites is the *Portrait of Isabella d'Este* (DES stay). It seems that Isabella was unhappy with growing old. So, she asked Titian to paint a portrait of her looking about 40 years younger than she was! He did. Isabella was flattered and claimed that Titian had made her far prettier than she ever was, which she didn't mind a bit.

Another favorite of mine is the portrait of young *Ranuccio Farnese* (Rah NEW chee oh Far NIECE). He's a handsome boy wearing a Maltese cross on his jacket. He was probably in training to be one of the Knights of St. John. He is as stunning to me as the

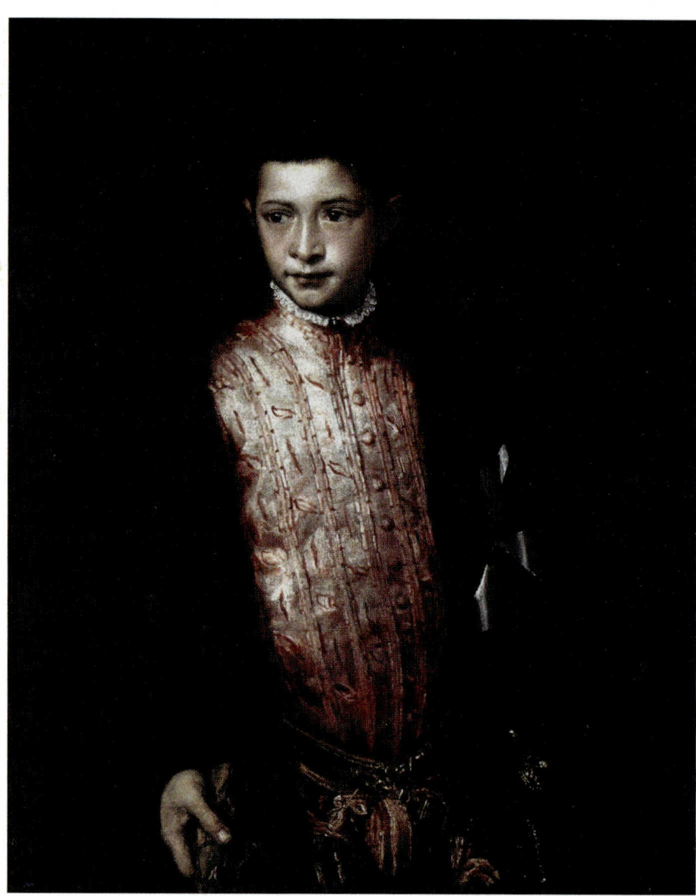

Titian grew famous for his stunning portrait work, like this painting of *Ranuccio Farnese*, a young boy probably in training to join the Knights of St. John.

woman who posed for *La Bella*. The woman in *La Bella* wears a beautiful Renaissance gown to show us just how rich the Venetians really were. And to be different from Leonardo's *Mona Lisa*, Titian added no landscaping in the background. All eyes are drawn instead to the lovely woman in her elegant dress.

## Court Painter

Titian's big break came in **1530** when he was introduced to Charles V, the Holy Roman Emperor. Charles was so impressed with Titian that just a few years later he was knighted and made the court painter. This was a good offer for Titian. His wife had died in 1530, so he needed a change of scenery and accepted the opportunity to travel. Over the years and in different cities, Titian painted Charles in every pose possible: Charles on a horse; Charles with his dog; Charles in fancy clothes; etc., etc. I think you get the idea. With these great works, Titian made full-length poses quite fashionable. It was the height of his career.

One of the more touching portraits Titian produced for Charles was of his Portuguese wife, Queen Isabella. It was touching because she had been dead several years when Charles asked Titian to paint her. Using a simple sketch of her, Titian managed in art form to bring her back to life. Some say his painting makes her far more beautiful than she was. But the emperor didn't seem to mind since it was all he had left of his queen.

When Charles V resigned as Holy Roman Emperor, Titian was employed by his son, **Philip II of Spain**. The two became great friends. Titian painted Philip many times and gave him numerous mythological paintings. Coincidentally, Philip II married one of Henry VIII's daughters — Mary. We'll get to that later. But I point it out now because artists like Titian and Hans Holbein became important historians. They captured the lives of many famous kings and queens long before cameras were invented. I'm glad they did.

Titian was such a popular artist that the pope wanted his services, too. In 1545, when Titian was 68 years old, he went to Rome to paint **Pope Paul III**. At that time, Michelangelo was still alive. The two got along pretty well. It is evident in Titian's version of *David and*

Goliath and the *Sacrifice of Isaac* that he had been influenced by Michelangelo. The floating muscle-bound figures are a definite giveaway. But these were painted *before* Titian's trip to Rome, so he didn't "steal" the ideas straight from Michelangelo as it might appear.

The great wealth of Venice declined in the sixteenth century when trade routes opened elsewhere, but the canals today remain busy and intriguing.

As Titian grew older, his style began to change. Like summer fading into autumn, so did the colors in Titian's work. He used gloomy hues to depict dark stories like the *Martyrdom of St. Lawrence*. From mythology, he borrowed a story to create the *Flaying of Marsyas* (MAHR see us) — a sobering image of torture. To soften the goriness of the scene, he used a technique similar to later Impressionists. (An Impressionist painting is one that looks blurry close up but clear from far away.) In some ways, Titian was ahead of his time.

The last scene Titian started was the *Pietà*, in 1576. It, too, has the look of an Impressionist painting. In this final masterpiece, which someone else finished, Titian paints himself kneeling before Jesus. I hope it indicates the place of Jesus in his heart. But the historical record is unclear about Titian's faith. Though he lived through the height of the Renaissance and the Reformation, the artist kept his religious views mostly to himself.

Titian passed away in 1576. As his life faded, the sun began to set on Venice, too. Through a gradual decline, the wealth of Venice dwindled away. As explorers like Vasco da Gama, Columbus, and Magellan opened trade routes around the world, Venice was no longer the hub of it all. Eventually this city/state was absorbed by Austria and Italy. Italy in time kept the city of Venice as its own. There it remains — one of the most enchanting cities the world has ever known.

## Lesson 29 — 15th–16th Centuries

# Women of the Renaissance and Reformation

History is made up of all kinds of people. Young and old, rich and poor, male and female alike — they're all part of the story. But since I've already discussed a number of men in this volume, I want to stop and focus on a few special women of the Renaissance and the Reformation. I chose these women because in one way or another, they were exceptional. By their status, their determination, or their giftedness, they did more than most. I'll share their lives

Isabella d'Este was not satisfied with a portrait of herself until Titian painted this one of her looking about 40 years younger than she was.

as if they were part of a scrapbook. Pretend I'm sitting next to you on the sofa, showing you snapshots and telling you a little bit about each one. It's the best I can do without writing another book!

## Isabella d'Este

The first woman in my scrapbook is **Isabella d'Este** (DES stay), born in 1474. I find her to be the epitome of a Renaissance woman. She was gracious, modest, fun-loving, and surpassed many a man in intelligence. Poets and artists loved her as much as popes and statesmen. Isabella married to become an Italian duchess, but her marriage was not a happy one. She found peace in having deep friendships and devoting herself to literature and the arts.

Isabella devoted herself also to fashion and fine taste. In trying to be beautiful, she hired artists like Leonardo, Raphael, and Titian to paint her, sculpt her, or craft her profile in gold. She was rarely satisfied until Titian finally painted her looking about 40 years younger than she was. I mentioned her in our lesson on Titian. Now you know a little bit more.

## Lucretia Borgia

Another famous woman of the Renaissance was **Lucretia Borgia** (Lew CREE sha BORE JZEE ah), born in 1480. She's an interesting one. Do you remember Machiavelli, who wrote *The Prince*? He based it in part on the ways of Cesare Borgia, the illegitimate son of the pope. Well, that same pope had another child — Lucretia, a lovely girl with long blonde hair. Much like Cesare Borgia, Lucretia was spoiled by her father. But unlike Cesare Borgia, Lucretia wasn't spoiled so "rotten."

Lucretia suffered much because of the murder of her second husband — who was probably killed by her brother Cesare. She married again and became one of the most notable

During the Renaissance, Lucretia Borgia was considered one of the most notable women in Italy for sponsoring the arts and giving to charity.

women of Italy. Lucretia educated her own children, wrote poetry in several languages, sponsored the arts, and gave generously to charity. One servant wrote of her, "She is modest, lovable, and decorous. Moreover, she is a devout and God-fearing Christian . . . She is very beautiful, but her charm of manner is still more striking."[1] Lucretia died when she was only 39 years old after the birth of her seventh child. Lucretia was far from perfect, but she was a bright spot in the Borgia family tree.

## *Vittoria Colonna*

The third woman in my scrapbook is **Vittoria Colonna**, born in about 1490. Her name has come up in this book before. She was the kind Christian widow who befriended Michelangelo during his later years. Her strong faith had a great influence on the famous artist. But let me tell you a little bit more about Vittoria.

Vittoria's husband didn't amount to much — he was away at war most of their married years, and he was in love with another woman. Regardless, Vittoria honored him in life and death. While he was living, she spoke only good of him. After he died in battle, she wrote tenderly of her love for him. Many would have liked her to remarry, but she said, "My husband Ferdinand, who to you seems dead, is not dead to me."[2] Instead of chasing romance, Vittoria spent her widowhood writing deep and meaningful poetry and studying the works of the reformers. Her friendship with Michelangelo was a tremendous ministry. I think Vittoria was an extraordinarily virtuous woman who grasped the best of the Renaissance and the Reformation.

Though a queen, Margaret of Navarre associated with people from all walks of life by caring for the poor, mingling with scholars, and supporting her family.

## *Margaret of Navarre*

Fourth in my scrapbook is **Margaret of Navarre**, born in 1492, the same year as the voyage of Columbus. Margaret had violet blue eyes and was full of life. As a young girl, she was extremely well educated.

She mastered Latin, the Bible, and Greek. After the death of one husband, Margaret remarried to become the queen of Navarre. (She was French, but Navarre was its own small kingdom just between France and Spain.)

As the queen of Navarre, Margaret used her warm heart and intelligence to influence many. One of her roles was to support her brother, whom she greatly loved. He was Francis I, the king of France, mentioned many times already in this book. As a genuine people lover, Margaret not only cared for the royal family, but she did a lot to care for the poor. Anyone on the street could approach her. At the same time, Margaret was intelligent enough to be invited to mingle with Erasmus and other fine scholars of the Renaissance. She herself was an excellent writer. Her favorite subject was romance, which some greatly frowned upon. Others frowned upon her tolerance. Margaret supported humanists, Catholics, *and* reformers. She was too kindhearted and far too popular to want to exclude anyone from her court. Margaret of Navarre had a heart for all. Later, we will study her daughter, *Jeanne d'Albret*, who was quite a woman of influence herself.

## *Teresa of Avila*

The next woman in my scrapbook, **Teresa of Avila**, has an entirely different story. Born in 1515, Teresa threw herself into reforming the Catholic Church but remaining a part of it. As a nun, Teresa's ambition was to take her fellow nuns back to strict servanthood. She saw that too many nuns had fallen into immorality and worldliness. Teresa opened a convent in Spain nicknamed the "shoeless" convent because of her strict guidelines for poverty. Teresa's methods were so drastic that even the Inquisition questioned her. But her convictions prevailed, and Teresa committed her life to writing of her experiences and promoting spirituality.

## *Anne Askew*

Moving through time, our next snapshot is of **Anne Askew**. Her life was short but very dramatic. She lived from 1521 to 1545. Of course, those were the years that the Protestant Reformation was brewing. That is why Anne's life was so short. Anne was a devout follower of Martin Luther but was forced by her father to marry a Catholic. The marriage failed. Anne moved to London to preach. There she became friends with Catherine Parr, the last of Henry VIII's wives, who was secretly a Protestant, too.

More than once, Anne Askew was arrested for preaching and distributing Protestant literature. But worse than that, she was tortured to give authorities the names of other reformers. Anne never gave in to the pain. She protected her Protestant friends, especially Catherine Parr. Anne Askew was tortured so brutally on a stretching rack that she couldn't walk to her own execution — or stand for the duration of it. Anne was burned at the stake sitting in a chair. She was only 24 years old.

## *Sofonisba Anguissola*

On the lighter side, I'll tell you last about **Sofonisba Anguissola**. She was born in 1532. I like Sofonisba because, as a woman, she beat the odds in becoming a famous portrait artist. Of all the famous artists of the Renaissance, there were only about 40 women who succeeded. Of those, Sofonisba was probably the most famous. She and her four sisters were all good artists and well educated, but Sofonisba surpassed them all. She studied under some of the great masters and was eventually hired by a duke in Spain.

Sofonisba Anguissola was one of the most famous women artists of the Renaissance and hired by the king and queen of Spain to be a court painter.

Sofonisba's talent was later spotted by the king and queen of Spain, where she was invited to live for many years as a court painter. Along the way, she married a ship captain. Between their two careers, Sofonisba led a very exciting life. Among her great works, she painted a beautiful self-portrait to help us know exactly what she looked like. She had big brown eyes, a gentle smile, and soft brown hair. Sofonisba lived and painted well into her eighties.

I hope you've enjoyed this scrapbook. It is only a short tribute to some of the exceptional women of the Renaissance and Reformation. There will be more to come. But as for these women, I hope you noticed something they had in common. That was their education. I point that out to inspire you, boy or girl, man or woman, to take advantage of the education that is available to you! All the women mentioned today were patrons of learning, and it made a huge difference in their lives. So, study the classics, write poetry, learn a new language, or take a class in painting. Who knows — as a result, you may make history!

## Lesson 30 — 1533

# John Calvin

We're going back to our study of the Protestant Reformation today. Before doing so, let's review what we've learned so far. (If you're short on time right now, skip this review for later and begin reading below at "Young Calvin.")

During the Middle Ages, godly men like **John Wycliffe** and **John Huss** (Hoos) read the Bible carefully and began to question some of the traditions of the Roman Church. John Huss was put to death for his beliefs, as were many of Wycliffe's followers. It was just the beginning of bringing reform to the church.

Years later, **Martin Luther** "officially" set off the Protestant Reformation when he posted his Ninety-five Theses on the door of the chapel in Wittenberg. He was interested in debating the issue of indulgences. The debate, of course, was never resolved. Protestants and Catholics still disagree on this matter, as well as on many others.

While Luther was preaching and teaching in Germany, **Ulrich Zwingli** was stirring things up in Switzerland. He, too, questioned practices of the Roman Church, but he and Luther didn't see eye to eye on everything. They mainly disagreed over the Lord's Supper. It created division between Lutherans and other Protestants.

The "other" Protestants who followed Zwingli had disagreements, too. They differed on the practice of baptism and the separation of church and state. **Menno Simons** and others were labeled **Anabaptists** for their views. Many Anabaptists were persecuted and fled to other parts of Europe.

While the Anabaptists were organizing themselves into communities, **Henry VIII** shook the foundation of the church in England. Of course, his interest in reforming the church was based on wanting an annulment from his first wife. He made himself the supreme head of the Church of England and broke away from the pope entirely. Henry's right-hand man, **Thomas Cranmer**, was behind the scenes seeking true reform for the Church of England.

Can you back away from each of these snapshots and see the big picture? Can you see all that was happening across Europe? While humanism and the Renaissance were sweeping across the land, so was the hand of the Lord. Through Wycliffe, Huss, Luther, Zwingli, Simons, Cranmer, and many others, the Word of God was being proclaimed. Hebrews 4:12 says, "For the word of God is living and powerful, . . ." and so it brought change. The nations of Slovakia, Germany, Switzerland, England, and the Netherlands were being transformed. As you can see, the Protestant Reformation was fairly widespread by the sixteenth century.

That leads us to **John Calvin**, the main character of our lesson today. More than any of the men before him, John Calvin solidified the Protestant movement. You could say he laid down a concrete highway where others had started a path. How did he do it? John Calvin yielded his life fully to God and worked very hard at preaching, teaching, and writing. He worked so hard that he nearly worked himself to death.

## *Young Calvin*

John Calvin was born in northern France. His father pushed him toward church work at a very young age. For his service in the Roman Church, he received a small salary that helped toward his education. At only 11, John went to college in Paris. By 17, he had his master's degree and considered becoming a priest. However, he veered toward the study of law instead, which suited him even better. John Calvin was brilliant with words, and he would use them one day to greatly shape the Protestant movement.

As a young man, John Calvin was influenced by the humanists of his time. Like so many others during the Renaissance, he flourished in Greek and the study of the classics. But something happened to him around **1533**. In his early twenties, Calvin would say he experienced a "sudden conversion." In his words, "God himself produced the change. He instantly subdued my heart to obedience . . . Only one haven of salvation is left open for our souls, and that is the mercy of God in Christ. We are saved by grace — not by our merits, not by our works."[3]

This conversion drew John Calvin toward the reformers. Hearing from them a clear message of salvation by grace, Calvin joined their cause. In a short time, John Calvin was teaching Protestantism among his peers in France.

France at this time, however, was not kind to Protestants. **King Francis I** was a devout Roman Catholic and very disapproving of the movement. Two hundred Protestants had been captured and at least 20 executed. One of Calvin's closest Protestant friends was forced to flee France for his life. Calvin left right behind him.

John Calvin was on his way to Strasbourg when the course of his life was changed. While passing through Geneva (Juh NEE va), Switzerland, he was introduced to **William Farel**. Farel was a Protestant preacher in Geneva. He enjoyed his work but was having a hard time with it. He begged John Calvin to stay in Geneva and give him a hand. Though somewhat reluctant, Calvin stayed in Switzerland.

John Calvin and William Farel were a strong team. Both were appointed as town pastors — Farel was the senior pastor and Calvin, the junior pastor. But in a short time, Calvin passed Farel in popularity. Farel was never jealous. He loved to see Geneva embracing the new young pastor and did everything he could to help Calvin in his success.

John Calvin was a humble man. "Success" by the world's standards wasn't anything he was looking for. He refused a raise in his pay, kept very few possessions, and never owned a home. His joy was found in teaching the Word of God. He started with Paul's letters to the Romans and continued to work his way through the New Testament verse by verse. Though from the outside, John Calvin was small and appeared weak and sickly, he was anything but that on the inside. His strong and powerful preaching brought many thirsty souls to Geneva.

But of course, Calvin and Farel were not perfect men. In their zeal, they rubbed some people the wrong way. In 1537, the two men drafted a confession of faith and set of rules that every citizen in Geneva was *required* to sign and abide by. Those who didn't were punished! Can you imagine what that led to?

For a three-year span, Calvin and Farel were kicked out of Geneva by members of the city council. They found the preachers and their moral code a bit too harsh to follow. Farel moved to Basel, where he finished out his preaching career. Calvin moved to Strasbourg, where he settled down and married a kind widow.

## *Geneva*

But back in Geneva, things weren't going very well. The town preachers who were chosen to replace Calvin and Farel were ineffective. The government was unstable and crime

Though hesitant at first, John Calvin returned to Geneva, Switzerland, to teach and preach. Pictured here is a serene harbor on Lake Geneva.

was on the rise. A more conservative group of council members came into office and begged John Calvin to come back. They apologized for having kicked him out in the first place and insisted he return. Calvin was hesitant. He said, "There is no place in the world which I fear more; not because I hate it; but because I feel unequal to the difficulties which await me there."[4] John Calvin realized that there was a lot of work to be done in Geneva, but he agreed to face the challenge and do it.

Calvin returned to Geneva and resumed his preaching on the letters of Paul. He also reinstated a strict moral code for all the citizens of Geneva. The city desperately needed to clean up its morals. Calvin raised the standards of godly living by forbidding drinking, dancing, gambling, swearing, indecency, and all kinds of other questionable activities. Following Old Testament guidelines, Calvin declared adultery, blasphemy, and idolatry as punishable by death. Other crimes received fines, torture, or prison — or maybe all three.

In case you are wondering, John Calvin *did* believe in the separation of church and state, but he didn't separate them very far. You could say he saw the church and state as two arms on the same body. He believed each should support the other.

To pull this off, John Calvin created a special group called a consistory. Members of the consistory were from both the state *and* the church. (The "state" in Geneva was the city council.) He believed that this one group of both church and state officials should oversee the enforcement of the strict moral code. John Calvin himself was *not* a city council member, but he was part of the consistory.

For those who agreed with biblical teaching, the moral code — and the enforcement of it — was great. It made Geneva a wonderful place to live. Crime went down; good morals went up. John Knox, a famous Scottish preacher, said that Geneva was "the most perfect school of Christ since the days of the apostles."[5]

However, there were some drawbacks to this system. Enforcing the moral code led to rigid legalism. Here are some examples: To help against the sin of gluttony (which is overeating), the council regulated the number of dishes allowed on one's dinner table! It was forbidden for parents to name their children after saints of the Roman Church. A woman was fined for wearing her hair "too high." Three men were imprisoned for laughing in church. Some children were punished for eating cake when they should have been in church. One man, accused of writing a bad note about John Calvin, was tortured twice a day for a month and then executed. Overall, between the years 1542 and 1546, 58 people were executed and 76 banished from Geneva for some sort of violation of the moral code.

## *Michael Servetus*

Of all the executions that took place in Geneva, there is one that stands out in history. It is the case of **Michael Servetus** (Ser VEE tuhs). Of great significance is the fact that, according to most, Servetus *was* a true heretic. He taught that Jesus wasn't fully God. Servetus wasn't Protestant, Catholic, or Anabaptist. He and his teachings were confusing many Europeans over the issue of Christ's deity, a fundamental belief of the Christian faith. Michael Servetus was also a brilliant doctor and one of the first to understand the circulatory system of the body. But his medical reputation didn't count for much in Geneva.

While Servetus was passing through the city one day, he was supposedly recognized by John Calvin and arrested. The two had written harsh letters to one another over their theological differences. Calvin believed that the church had the right to condemn heretics like Servetus and that the state had the right to execute them. (This is where he didn't separate church and state very far.)

Though it wasn't Calvin's fault, the subsequent trial of Servetus was quite unfair. He wasn't given a lawyer or a chance to defend himself. Judgment was quickly passed. Servetus was condemned to burn at the stake. Now, on behalf of John Calvin, I must include that he begged the city council *not* to burn Servetus. He suggested that Servetus be beheaded instead because it's considered a less painful way to die. But Calvin was overruled on the matter. Servetus died a very slow and cruel death at the stake because the wood used to burn him was green. It took 30 minutes for him to perish by flames.

The unfair trial of Michael Servetus and his slow painful death would leave a dark cloud over the name of John Calvin for years. Though it wasn't Calvin's intent that Servetus suffer so greatly, history books still make mention of it today and oftentimes portray John Calvin as cruel and unforgiving. But was he? According to his friends, he was not.

John Calvin was loved by those who knew him well. He loved people, nature, books, and above all, Jesus. John was devoted to his wife and grieved deeply when she died after only nine years of marriage. Calvin's personal emblem was that of a heart held by a large hand. It carried the motto *Prompte et sincere in opera Dei* (Prompt aye et sin keh ray in op er ah Deh ee), which means "ready and wholehearted work for God."

In my opinion, if John Calvin was guilty of anything, it was of working too hard. He slept only four hours a night and ate but one meal a day. He wrote volumes of commentaries on the Bible and preached almost every day of the week. He also set up the Geneva Academy, which later became the **University of Geneva**. The school became famous for training pastors and evangelists. Out of his deep love for God, John Calvin was hard on himself. He didn't want the Lord to return to find him idle. Calvin taught and lived that God was everything, and man was nothing. His greatest theme in life was the knowledge of God.

## *The Legacy*

To convey this theme, John Calvin wrote a remarkable piece. It was titled *Institutes of the Christian Religion*. Calvin started the work when he lived in France, and in fact, he dedicated it to Francis I. He hoped it would open the king's heart to the message of the Gospel. Calvin rewrote the *Institutes* many times over the years to improve it. Apparently, he did a great job. The Scripture-based book is still considered the most classic statement of Protestantism today. It contains deep points of the Christian faith regarding predestination, the sovereignty of God, original sin, and salvation by grace.

Because of his widespread influence on Protestantism, many would identify John Calvin as one of the most remarkable men of the Reformation.

The effects of John Calvin's writings are what is most amazing. You see, Calvin's teachings were so clear that they were identified by his name. "Calvinists" grew to describe those who adopted John Calvin's interpretations of the Bible. In France, Calvinists were called **Huguenots** (HYOOH guh nots); in Scotland, they were called **Presbyterians**; in the Netherlands, they were called the **Dutch Reformed**; and in England, they were **Puritans**. Last but not least, brave Calvinists who fled to the New World were called **Pilgrims**. Yes, the same Pilgrims who sailed on the *Mayflower* for religious freedom were "Calvinists" in their doctrine.

So, as you can see, John Calvin has had a widespread impact on history, perhaps more than any other man during the Renaissance. But he wouldn't say so. At his death he begged forgiveness for any of his weaknesses. He asked that his grave remain unmarked so others would not look to *him* for their salvation but rather to Jesus Christ alone.

# WEEK 11

## Lesson 31 1533

# *Ivan the Terrible*

I think you would agree that history has its bad guys. Such is the case with **Ivan the Terrible**. Though he had a few strong points, Ivan the Terrible, as his name would suggest, has gone down in history as one of the cruelest murdering monarchs ever to rule Russia. So, listen up. I think you'll find this guy "interesting" and pretty scary.

The last time we looked at Russia was during the reign of Ivan III, better known as Ivan the Great. If you remember, Ivan the Great took control of the Eastern Orthodox Church by marrying a Byzantine princess. The marriage had a great impact on Russia. According to the Russians, their nation became the "new Rome" as it absorbed the best of Byzantine culture.

When Ivan the Great died, his son Vasili ruled in his place. When Vasili died, Ivan the Great's *grandson* took the throne. He was Ivan IV, the subject of our lesson today who was later nicknamed "the Terrible." It's no wonder he grew to be named the terrible. Ivan IV had one tough childhood. He was only 3 when his father died in **1533**. Everyone knew that Ivan was the next true prince of Muscovy and the king-to-be. But he was treated poorly by rival members of the court. Behind closed doors, Ivan was clothed in rags and barely fed. When important people came to visit, he was dressed up and fed like a king. It was a cover-up for a secret power struggle in the palace.

To make Ivan's situation worse, his mother, **Elena** (EL uh nuh *or* Eh LAY nah), was murdered by family rivals when he was only 7 or 8. At the same time, his favorite nurse was taken away. She was probably closer to him than his real mother. With the loss of *both* his nurse and his mother, Ivan grew more "terrible" by the day.

Life around Ivan was cruel. Abuse and murder were common. Plots and conspiracies raged. In response, Ivan threw cats and dogs out of tall towers! Why he bullied animals, I don't know. But perhaps he was scared and terrified by his environment and acted mean to hide it.

By 13, Ivan's rage turned from animals to people. He had a fellow prince thrown to a pack of wild dogs. It seemed to be his way of declaring that he was of age to take the throne. He did so with full force. Just a few years later, in 1547, Ivan IV had himself crowned the official first tsar (zar) of Russia.[1] Ivan considered himself an "autocrat," which means he paid tribute to no one. He was only 17.

One of Ivan's first interests as tsar was in finding a beautiful wife. He invited hundreds of young maidens from across Russia to his palace. From them he chose **Anastasia Romanovna**

(ROW muh noff). Though he would eventually have as many wives as Henry VIII, it would appear that he loved Anastasia the most. We'll come back to her later.

The other thing Ivan did early in his reign was to strengthen his power. He gathered together a "national assembly" called *zemski sobor*. On paper, the zemski sobor would be a good thing. Similar to other parliaments, it was supposed to represent the people and guide the ruler of the country. But that's not what happened. After one meeting, the zemski sobor was powerless under Ivan IV. He took matters in his own hands and quickly became a dictator. What Ivan the "autocrat" said was law.

Now, in all fairness, Ivan's laws weren't too bad at first. He rewrote old laws and centralized the loose ends of his kingdom. He also took troops to outlying areas and extended the borders of Russia. You could say he completed the crusade against Muslim Tatars that his grandfather had started. In doing so, he added **Kazan** (Kuh ZAN) to his territories in the East. It was an important city on the **Volga River**. He also added **Astrakahn** to his kingdom on the edge of the **Caspian Sea**. This did a lot for trade.

## *Tears and Celebration*

Before I go on, we have one snapshot of a soft spot in Ivan IV. It seems that when he conquered the people of Kazan, he wept. Upon seeing so many of the dead, Ivan said, "They are not Christians, but they are men."[2]

I don't know where Ivan's pity came from that day or where it went afterward because three years later he *celebrated* his victory over the Tatars. He celebrated by ordering the construction of **St. Basil's Cathedral**. St. Basil's is the colorful onion-looking structure that would become Russia's most famous landmark. Pictures of the bright-colored cathedral domes appear nearly everywhere that Russia is mentioned.

Legend says that Ivan hired Italian architects to design St. Basil's. After they did, he supposedly had their eyes gouged out so they could never build anything more beautiful! Other historical records say that two Russians designed the cathedral. We may never know the full story.

It was after the victories over the Muslim Tatars that the Russians nicknamed Ivan "the Terrible." But the term has been poorly translated. In Russian, he was Ivan *Groznyi*, which more accurately means "awesome" or "inspiring fear." That is what the Russians *first* thought of Ivan and thus nicknamed him. It was later that the Russians would consider him "terrible," as *we* would translate the word.

While still in good standing with the Russians, one of Ivan's ambitions was to open trade between Russia and western Europe. A daring British explorer named **Richard Chancellor** made this possible. He sailed from England to Russia through the frigid waters around Scandinavia. Ivan signed a treaty with Chancellor and trade was opened. But the trade route was more of a window into Russia than a door. The Russians remained suspicious of other Europeans for centuries and just barely let them in and out.

Nonetheless, Ivan's conquests in the East and trade moves in the West made him one of the wealthiest men of his time. But you couldn't say that about his country. Russia suffered

St. Basil's Cathedral is a cluster of nine intimate chapels found in the Red Square of Moscow, Russia, just outside the walls of the Kremlin.

greatly under the feudal system that was started by Ivan III. Peasants remained poor. Roads were unpaved. The masses were illiterate (meaning they couldn't read). Though the Renaissance in Europe was practically "next door" to Russia, only those at the top of Russian society were exposed to any learning at all.

But things were going to get worse. In 1560, Anastasia died. Ivan believed she was poisoned. He may have been right about that. Forensic scientists have recently found large amounts of mercury present in the hair of her corpse. But whatever her cause of death, after it, Ivan seemed to go crazy. Feeling ill himself, in 1564 he moved the rest of his family out of town and sent two letters to Moscow. In one letter he resigned as the tsar of Russia saying he had been overthrown by the nobility and the church. In the other letter, he assured the masses that he loved them and he hoped they would do well without him.

Now, if you think about it, this was a strange thing for a tsar to do. Most tsars don't resign and they don't send farewell letters to the public! It might be that Ivan was paranoid and afraid that he, too, would be poisoned. It might be that in his grief over Anastasia, he wasn't thinking clearly. Or it might be that Ivan was manipulating the lower class to miss him and want him to take even more control over Russia. Oddly enough, that is exactly what happened. In trying to resign, Ivan won the hearts of the poor people of Russia. They begged him to return to power — and he did! Though he was staunch in his ways and sometimes cruel and paranoid, Ivan's leadership was perhaps more appealing to the masses than that of the unknown.

## *Secret Police*

Over the next few years, Ivan took control of Russia like no one had ever done before. In his paranoia to protect himself from being overthrown or assassinated, he created a whole new class of citizens to surround him. It was almost eerie! Old members of the nobility were literally moved out of their neighborhoods and replaced by Ivan's new protectors. This new class was called the ***Oprichnina***, or the "separate estate." Individual members were called the *oprichniki*, or the "separate class." They started out about 1,000 strong and quickly grew to 6,000 members. These protectors were the beginning of Russia's famous "secret police." They had few rules to follow except to protect Ivan. They enslaved peasants, murdered conspirators, and plundered the old nobility.

The oprichniki were a private class of citizens subject only to Ivan himself. The rest of Russia remained under "public" authority. As a result, Russia became a two-class society. Nearly half the land was taken by the private class of the Oprichnina. The rest of the public was pushed into serfdom. Between the two classes, living districts and neighborhoods were confused and divided. This disunity would ruin the economy and dampen the spirit of Russia for a very long time.

The worst of Ivan's terror fell on the city of **Novgorod** (NOV guh rod). It was rumored that a revolt was brewing there against Ivan. It probably was! But without investigating the matter, the oprichniki went on a rampage of destruction that lasted for five weeks. Shops, farms, and monasteries were destroyed. Hundreds of citizens were murdered. So many dead bodies were thrown into the river that it clogged and overflowed. By the time the massacre was over, at least 3,000 were dead. Some claim that 30,000–60,000 were slain! Of course, Ivan reported much less, so we may never know the truth.

A peculiar thing about Ivan is that throughout his reign he proclaimed to be a very religious man. Ivan's closest bodyguards were moved into an old monastery where Ivan joined them for singing and prayer. Supposedly Ivan spent so much time lying facedown in prayer that he bruised his forehead in the act.

At the same time, Ivan did everything to instill fear in those around him, and he drank excessively. He dressed his secret police in black robes and skullcaps. These police used the symbol of a broom and a dog — the broom symbolized the clean "sweep" of the old nobility, the dog symbolized the soldiers' loyalty to Ivan. If you can envision it, the secret police served the tsar as private watchdogs would serve their master.

Ivan the Terrible claimed to be a religious man, but by his actions and through his secret police he instilled great fear in those around him.

As for Ivan, some say he drooled like an animal and was mad. I do wonder. He once nailed a messenger's foot to the floor because Ivan didn't care for the message he carried! He created torture chambers to resemble hell where victims were roasted, fried, or impaled. Ivan allowed his troops to brutalize the women they captured in war, and he himself was unfaithful to his wives. Many of them died "mysterious" deaths. I don't know if Ivan was insane or just power-crazed. But something happened toward the end of his life that really put him over the edge.

In a fit of anger, Ivan struck his pregnant daughter-in-law for dressing immodestly. It caused her to lose the baby she was carrying in her womb. Naturally, her husband, who was Ivan's grown son, reacted to the scene. In a scuffle, Ivan struck him, too. In fact, he struck his son *so* hard that he killed him.

Ivan never forgave himself for his rage. He wailed day and night in the halls of his palace over the loss of his son and his unborn grandchild. Three years later, he died of a strange disease. Some believed he was poisoned by a member of the court for indecency. We may never know what killed him. But just before his death in 1584, he asked to take the vows of a monk and be buried as such. Perhaps he was looking to absolve his conscience.

I think Ivan's life is a reminder that being outwardly "religious" (as Ivan appeared to be) isn't the same as knowing Jesus personally and being obedient to the Spirit of God. You see, the Bible says, "Now the works of the flesh are evident, which are: adultery . . . hatred, contentions, jealousies, outbursts of wrath, selfish ambitions . . . murders . . . and the like . . . But the fruit of the Spirit is love, joy, peace, longsuffering, kindness, goodness, faithfulness, gentleness, self-control." (See Gal. 5:19–23.) From these verses, what do *you* conclude of Ivan's life?

# Explorers of North America

I thought this lesson would be an easy one. Being a North American myself, I thought I could easily retell the stories of a few well-known Europeans and how they first explored **North America**. But there is nothing simple about the early history of this continent. Knowing my compassion, you can probably guess what's troubling me. That would be the story of the Native Americans who found themselves suddenly "invaded" by the curious white man. The history that unfolded is tragic. We will only scratch the surface today.

To stay on track with our main study of the Renaissance and Reformation, I'm going to start with the Europeans and their "side" of the story in exploring North America. To them, North America was a land of opportunity. It was rumored to be full of gold, silver, and the "fountain of youth." To Europeans, North America was a land free for the taking. It was just waiting to be "claimed" by whichever nation could get there first. (Of course, according to the Native Americans, this land wasn't "available." But we'll get to that later.)

## Juan Ponce de León

One of the first Europeans ever to set foot in what is presently the United States was **Juan Ponce de León** (Wahn Ponce day Lee on). You might have already heard of this Spaniard. He made himself famous by his quest for the "fountain of youth." Ponce de León had traveled with Cristóbal Colón on his second voyage to Central America. He settled there and was made the governor of Puerto Rico. He was told by local people there that just north across the sea lay the secret to staying young. He was told that there was a fountain of water that would restore youth to the old and give eternal life.

The likely truth is that the local people of Puerto Rico probably didn't want Ponce de León there. So they told a story they had heard from other Europeans about a fountain of life in the East. That story might have originated with Christian missionaries trying to teach Native Americans about the Garden of Eden and eternal life. Regardless of the exact origins, the story sent Ponce de León on a wild-goose chase! In 1513, Ponce de León sailed to Florida looking for a miracle.

Of course, an eternal fountain of youth can't be found on the coast of Florida. The story was a myth. What Ponce de León *did* find was the thick, green foliage of Florida with flowers blooming everywhere. Because it was Easter Sunday when Ponce de León claimed the area he found, he named it *Pascua florida*, which is Spanish for "flowery Easter." Of course, the term *Florida* has stuck ever since.

Eight years later, Juan Ponce de León made another trip to Florida. He was still hoping to find the fountain of youth. Though some would say he founded the city of **St. Augustine**, Ponce de León failed at starting a permanent colony there. He was wounded in a battle against

In 1513, Juan Ponce de León sailed to Florida seeking the legendary "fountain of youth."

Native Americans and died in Cuba. The French Huguenots (meaning Protestants) would later try to settle St. Augustine as a safe refuge from persecution. But the Spanish returned to claim it for themselves and had to fight the English for it! The fighting over St. Augustine was just a taste of what was in store for North America. Everyone wanted to claim it as their own.

## *Jacques Cartier*

In the meantime, the French had their eyes on other parts of North America. Not to be outdone by the Spanish, the French sent explorers to the "New World," too. But their goal was to find a northern passage to China. You know why, don't you? They were still looking for better trade routes to the Far East. So Francis I of France sent **Jacques Cartier** (Zhahk Car tee AYE) toward North America seeking a northern shortcut to the spices and riches of China. Jacques Cartier never found this shortcut because he bumped into Canada, a huge landmass covering nearly 4 million square miles!

Jacques Cartier made three trips to Canada. On his first trip in **1534**, he sailed beyond **Newfoundland** (NEW fun land) to the Gulf of St. Lawrence. It is near the present-day province of Quebec. He and his crew were greeted warmly by 50 canoes of **Micmac Indians**, who said, *napeu tondamen assurtah*, which means "we want to make friendship." You might want to remember that these Native Americans were at first friendly.

On his first trip to the New World, Jacques Cartier sailed beyond Newfoundland to reach the Gulf of St. Lawrence.

Jacques Cartier bartered with the Micmac for furs and sailed farther along to find the opening of the St. Lawrence River. Cartier hoped that *this* great river would lead him to China. But of course, it didn't. The St. Lawrence River actually flows into the Great Lakes of the United States. China was still a long ways away.

In Quebec, Cartier met over 200 Huron (or Wyandot) Indians and their chief named **Donnacona**. While there, Cartier built a large 30-foot cross and claimed the land for France. The Huron, who had been friendly, were now confused at this gesture. This was *their* home. Why was it being "claimed" by France? Cartier sensed their hostility and so he lied to them about the cross, saying that it was just a landmark. In my opinion, that was the first of a few mistakes that Cartier would make.

After making friends with Donnacona, Cartier convinced the chief to send his two sons to France. Some would say the boys were captured. The arrangement is a little unclear. Regardless of the agreement, Cartier sailed home with Donnacona's boys to teach them French. He hoped they would make good tour guides when he returned. In less than a year, Cartier worked his plan. He went back to Canada with Donnacona's boys, who now spoke French. He used them as guides to maneuver down the St. Lawrence River, which they knew quite well. Cartier reached the Huron settlement of Stadacona where chief Donnacona was happily reunited with his boys.

On this trip, Jacques Cartier visited the Huron village of **Hochelaga**. It was a well-organized town much bigger than Stadacona. Cartier climbed a nearby mountain for a better view of the area. He named it "Mount Royal." The words later blended together to become **Montreal**, which is one of the largest cities in Canada today. The name Canada, by the way, came from the Huron word for village, which is *kanata*.

The winter proved to be harsh for Jacques Cartier and his men. The snow in places was 4 feet deep. Their ships were frozen in thick layers of ice. And to make matters worse, scurvy broke out among them and nearly wiped out the entire crew, but Chief Donnacona's son kindly provided a remedy made from tree bark and other plants. Apparently the remedy contained vitamin C because it worked to revive the sick crewmen.

Donnacona may have lived to regret that. When Jacques Cartier was ready to sail back to France, he captured Chief Donnacona and nine other Huron with him! Cartier wanted them to stand before the king of France to testify of cities filled with gold. Cartier hoped these stories would make him look good and give him an excuse to return to the New World.

While in France, Donnacona was treated fairly well at the expense of the king. I can't help but wonder, though, what he thought about France. Imagine the new sights, the new sounds, and the new smells. All would have been quite different from his homeland. But

Though he never found gold or diamonds, Jacques Cartier established a strong fur trade between Native Americans and the French.

unfortunately, the chief soon died in France, as did every other Huron — except one little girl. Her fate is unknown. We can only guess that the little Huron girl grew up far from home to live out the rest of her life in the foreign land of France.

The next time Jacques Cartier went back to Canada, he had to sail under another captain. It is unclear why he was "demoted," but it caused tension between him and the other men. To make matters worse, the Huron weren't the least bit friendly anymore. Cartier told them their leader was alive and well back in France, but they suspected he was lying — which of course, he was. Chief Donnacona had passed away.

Jacques Cartier had numerous troubles on his third and last trip to Canada. He was stopped by rapids on the St. Lawrence River, and many of his men were attacked and killed by Native Americans. Cartier went back to France with quartz rocks and fool's gold, thinking he had diamonds and real gold. After realizing his mistake, Cartier retired.

Though he never found gold or riches as desired, Jacques Cartier did open up fur trade between Native Americans and the French. And many Jesuit priests followed in his footsteps to teach the Native Americans about the Catholic faith. Generally speaking, the French were far kinder to the native inhabitants than were the Spanish or the English.

## Hernando de Soto

While Jacques Cartier was exploring Canada, Spanish explorers were scouting out the *southern* parts of North America. If you live on the Gulf Coast of the United States, your state history will certainly include **Hernando de Soto**. Twenty-five years after Juan Ponce de León reached Florida, Hernando de Soto returned in the name of Spain. However, unlike Ponce de León, he wasn't looking for a fountain of youth. De Soto was looking for gold.

Hernando de Soto's cruel methods of exploration would make Jacques Cartier look like a pretty nice guy. De Soto sought to enslave the Native Americans of Florida to help him in his elaborate treasure hunt. His large crew included blacksmiths who were brought along to make chains and collars for the Indians. He also brought along bloodhounds for tracking any slaves who might run away. I find it sad that he thought that far ahead. But on the opposite end of the spectrum, de Soto also brought along priests and monks to care for the spiritual welfare of the Native Americans.

To understand this mixture of both cruelty and compassion, you have to understand that Hernando de Soto had originally joined Francisco Pizarro in wiping out the Incas of Peru. In that setting, Pizarro would have served as a role model to de Soto. However Pizarro justified *his* poor treatment of the Incas in South America, de Soto did the same with the Indians in North America. That means he befriended some and ran over others, believing it an acceptable way to deal with "pagans."

Hernando de Soto first landed in Florida in **1539**. For two years, he blazed his way through thick brush and soggy swamps looking for gold. Swarms of mosquitoes nearly ate his men alive. Blood and sweat ran thick down their backs as they fought their way through. Conditions worsened when they encountered Native Americans. Battles broke out and in the conflict at least 11,000 Indians were killed.

The irony of the situation is that Native Americans were *partly* responsible for Hernando de Soto's quest. You see, to keep de Soto on the move, they told stories of gold that didn't exist. Their hope was to get rid of him. But the tales of gold would eventually hurt all Native Americans who were subject to the white man's greed. In the short term, it worked to keep de Soto wandering.

Hernando de Soto eventually wandered over what in the future would be six or more of the most southern states in the United States, from Alabama to South Carolina. He saw the Blue Ridge Mountains, the Ozarks, and parts of Tennessee. More than likely he encountered Cherokees, Seminoles, Creeks, Appalachians, and Choctaws. These native tribes were at one time some of the most advanced in North America. Some were related to the ancient Mound Builders discussed in Volume I. But no two tribes were alike. Each had its own distinctive culture and still does today.

Generally, however, these Native Americans built rectangular homes around a central meeting area similar to a town hall. They built ballfields, temples, and pyramids. They farmed, and hunted, and celebrated. My point in adding this to our lesson is to remind you that these were real people with real homes and real families — something that de Soto pretended *not* to notice when he sought to overrun them. He did *not* see these people for who they were.

Something that Hernando de Soto *did* see on his journey was the Mississippi River. But even that he didn't appreciate! De Soto saw the wide river as just another barrier to his riches. Ironically, the Mississippi River would later serve as his grave. You see, de Soto died from a high fever in 1542. His crewmen first buried him in an old Indian hole. But they realized that de Soto had told the Indians he was immortal. If the Indians found his body, they might think him a liar and grow in their hostility toward the white man. So, de Soto's crew carved a casket out of a hollow tree, weighted it down with their captain's body, and submerged him in the Mississippi River at night. It was as if he just disappeared.

With Hernando de Soto dead and no signs of gold, the crew was eager to return home. Still dodging Native Americans, the men made crude boats and sailed out as fast as they could down the Mississippi River and made their way to a Spanish settlement in Mexico. For the most part, Hernando de Soto's expedition ended a failure.

## *Francisco de Coronado*

Now stay with me here — we've one more explorer. His name is **Francisco de Coronado**. He, too, was Spanish. His expeditions from **1540** to 1542 led him over the future states of New Mexico, Arizona, Texas, and Oklahoma. Like the other white men we've studied, he was duped! The Pueblo Indians of the region told a legend of **Seven Cities of Cibola**

In search of the Seven Cities of Cibola, Francisco de Coronado and his men traveled through vast areas of America's Southwest.

(SEE buh luh). Supposedly, the houses of Cibola were made of gold and the doors inlaid with jewels. It was, of course, just another tale the natives told, but the Spaniards fell for it.

The legend of the Seven Cities of Cibola lasted long enough to lure Francisco de Coronado. He gathered 300 Spaniards and hundreds of Native American slaves to trek through the Southwest region of North America. Through cactus-filled deserts, the travelers battled thirst and scorpions and snakes. They sighted large beasts they called "hump-backed cows," which we know now were wild buffalo.

One reward for their difficult task was stumbling upon the sight of the **Grand Canyon**. Can you imagine describing that to the people back home? I'm sure it was as breathtaking then as it is now. Coronado and his men also discovered the **Continental Divide**, a natural division of the east from the west that runs through the magnificent Rocky Mountains.

In the end, Francisco de Coronado never found the Seven Cities of Cibola. Instead of houses made of gold and jewels, he found "pueblos" made of clay and pebbles. Not exactly the same thing. Defeated and discouraged, Coronado retired in Mexico City. There he was declared a failure and in 1544, he was actually charged by the Spanish with "poor treatment" of the Native Americans.

I hope you caught that. Francisco de Coronado was charged as a criminal for having enslaved hundreds of Indians while on his treasure hunt! Though many explorers were guilty of such abuses, at least some Spaniards were paying attention and tried to make slavery a crime. In fact, many good and caring priests would seek to improve the lives of Native Americans by teaching blacksmithing, shoemaking, methods of farming, and the Gospel. As stated earlier in this lesson, this is just scratching the surface of 200 years of American history. We're just getting started!

Lesson 34 1536

# William Tyndale: Father of the English Bible

"Open the eyes of the king." Those were the dying words of **William Tyndale** in **1536** just before he was strangled and burned to death. Do you want to guess what king he was praying for? It was Henry VIII. William Tyndale prayed that Henry VIII would open his eyes to the Word of God. Though William Tyndale didn't live to see it, his prayer was answered to some degree. Let's travel back to England today, back to the days when Henry VIII was still alive and wrestling with his faith. There we will find William Tyndale risking his life to translate the Bible into English.

William was born in England near the border of Wales. He went to school in Oxford, was ordained a priest, and later transferred to Cambridge. It was at Cambridge that William Tyndale was exposed to some of the best Greek scholars in Europe. These scholars had been trained in the Greek classics at the Platonic Academy started by Cosimo de' Medici in Italy. Remember Cosimo? Though long dead, he was still influencing history.

Before I go on, stop and picture something with me. Picture in your mind a Renaissance man. Can you see him? Now picture in your mind a reformer. Do you see him? Generally speaking, each represents a completely different mind-set. The Renaissance man, if you pictured him correctly, is focused on the glory of man and his marvelous achievements. He is considered well-rounded, lives for the here and now, and appreciates art, literature, and the classics. The reformer, if you pictured him correctly, is focused on the glory of God and His Word rather than on things of this world. He lives for the kingdom of God *yet* to come and risks his earthly life for an eternal one.

But there was at least one common thread between the Renaissance man and the reformer. Can you guess what it was? It was the Greek language. Think about it. The masters of the Greek language were the ones who brought Greek thought and humanism to the Renaissance man. He was stimulated to dwell on the wisdom of the ancient Greek philosophers who lived before the days of Christ. But it was also the Greek language that was used to write most of the New Testament.[1] It was the renewed learning of Greek that brought clearer understanding of the Word of God to those who chose to study it. I find it fascinating that those of the Renaissance and the Reformation met at the crossroads of the Greek language.

William Tyndale used his extensive knowledge of the Greek language to study the original words of the New Testament.

## *Tyndale Translates the Bible*

Now let me take you back to William Tyndale. Do you remember what he was studying at Cambridge? It was Greek. He was instructed by the Italians. But Tyndale didn't follow the course of the Renaissance thinkers. He used his knowledge of Greek to deeply study the New Testament. It would affect many generations to come — even ours.

At this time in history, the Word of God was still not readily available to the English. Though John Wycliffe had translated most of the Bible into English in the 1300s, his version never made it to the printing press. It was still being hand-copied and distributed by the Lollards. These hand copies were expensive and hard to come by.

Besides that, Wycliffe's version wasn't as accurate as it could have been. Here's why. Jerome first translated Greek into Latin to make the Latin Vulgate. Then Wycliffe took the Latin Vulgate and translated it into English. That made it a "second-generation" translation. In translating three languages (Greek to Latin to English), Wycliffe lost some accuracy and the original meaning of some words.

So William Tyndale, with his great knowledge of Greek, set out to fix this problem. He made it his goal to give the English-speaking world a Bible based on the *original* language of Greek, Hebrew, and Aramaic. He said, "It was impossible to establish the lay people in any truth, except the Scripture were laid before their eyes in their mother tongue."[2] But this would be no small task.

William Tyndale first approached the bishop of London to sponsor his project. Though the bishop was fond of Greek, he wasn't so fond of the idea of the common man handling the Word of God. The bishop was of the mind-set of the Roman Church authorities at that time in history. They had no confidence in men or women reading the Word and properly understanding it. They wished instead that the Bible remain in the hands of priests to teach to commoners.

After being turned down by the bishop, William Tyndale realized that he was up against some serious conflict. England was a hotbed of controversy at that time as Henry VIII was making himself the supreme head of the Church of England and breaking away from Rome. It was safer for William to leave his homeland and work abroad. So he sailed to mainland Europe. He would never see England again.

## *An Escape to Europe*

While in Europe, William Tyndale probably had the chance to meet Martin Luther. He was a big fan of Luther's and used his notes to make comments throughout his translation work. William published his first New Testament in 1525 in the city of **Cologne** (Kuh LONE).

Thousands of New Testaments were smuggled into England in everyday items like barrels, sacks of flour, and bales of cloth.

It was an exciting time but a dangerous one, too. A customer at the print shop caught wind of what was being printed there. This customer blew the whistle on Tyndale and sent for the authorities. Tyndale was given short notice about the raid. He quickly ran through the printing press gathering every precious page he could. He escaped to the town of Worms (Vermz).

Tyndale was a little safer in Worms. He managed to have 6,000 copies of the New Testament printed there. Only two still exist today. Do you know why so few can be found? The rest were smuggled into England. They were hidden in crates, barrels, sacks of flour, and bales of cloth. Because authorities were still in conflict over the Word, the Bible had to be smuggled in. Many would risk their lives in printing, packing, shipping, unloading, and distributing the dear Word of God.

One of those "authorities" against the printing of the Bible might surprise you. It was Sir Thomas More, who was still alive at this time. He sent Tyndale letters criticizing his work and pointing out errors in translation. If you remember, Thomas More was good with words and knew his Greek pretty well, too. He used his knowledge of Greek as a way to discredit William Tyndale.

Now, as you know, Thomas More was also a good man. So, it may be hard to understand why he didn't want the Bible distributed. Well, look at Thomas More this way — he and many others *did* view the Bible with great respect. They just didn't trust that common people could understand it. They deeply believed it was the role of the church to interpret it. They weren't haters of the Word of God. Rather, they saw themselves as protectors of it. Remember, this was one of the dividing issues between Protestants and Roman Catholics.

The bishop of London and the archbishop of Canterbury were of the same mind-set as Thomas More. They, like Thomas More, thought the Bible should be taught only in the Roman Church. They also thought that Tyndale made errors in his translation work. They convinced the cardinal of England to issue a decree for Tyndale's arrest and sought to stop all the smuggling of the New Testaments.

Now, something ironic happened. In order to prevent William Tyndale's New Testament from hitting the streets of England, the archbishop of Canterbury tried to buy them all himself so he could burn them. The ironic part of the story is that the buying of the Bibles put money into the hands of William Tyndale to print even *more* Bibles! I guess you could say that the plans of the archbishop backfired.

In time, William Tyndale moved to the city of Antwerp in the Netherlands.[3] There he began translating the Old Testament from Hebrew to English. For the most part, Antwerp was a city of safe refuge. Many Protestants were there. But over his seven-year stay in Europe, Tyndale had to hide most of the time because he was a "wanted" man. It was difficult to know who was friend or foe.

Henry Phillips pretended to be a friend to William Tyndale, but on the streets of Antwerp he turned Tyndale over to authorities for his arrest.

Unfortunately, in 1535, Tyndale was tricked. A man who claimed to be his friend and who was staying in his boardinghouse, turned out to be an enemy. This man was named **Henry Phillips**. Phillips eased his way into the private life of William Tyndale in order to "rat" on him. Henry Phillips drew William out into the streets of Antwerp one evening simply to have dinner. Once outside, Phillips pointed to authorities to arrest Tyndale. He was sent to prison in Brussels, another city of the Netherlands.

William Tyndale spent 16 to 18 months in the dark, cold dungeon of the castle of Vilvorde. Ironically, it was during this time period that Thomas More was arrested and put to death back in England. I wonder how it made Tyndale feel to hear of Henry VIII turning his back on Thomas More. More and Tyndale had been enemies — now it appeared they would share the same fate.

While in prison, William Tyndale requested three things: a warm coat, the Hebrew Bible, and a candle to read by. He hoped by candlelight to finish translating the Old Testament. But his trial came before that could happen.

William Tyndale was written up for many offenses. Throughout the ordeal, he claimed to be "saved by faith alone" and would not relent of that faith. William was only in his early forties when the court in Brussels condemned him as a heretic. Like many other martyrs of the faith, he was to be strangled to death and his body burned.

Before his death on October 6, 1536, William uttered one last prayer, the one that opened this lesson. He prayed for the king of England to open his eyes. We know he was praying for Henry VIII. This is where the story gets really interesting.

Back in England, Henry VIII was surrounded by many reformers. Two of those were Thomas Cranmer and Thomas Cromwell. They approached Henry with the idea of printing the Bible in English. At the time, Henry had heard that William Tyndale was a heretic and would have nothing to do with Tyndale's Bible. So, Tyndale's Bible was disguised! Cranmer and Cromwell sent Henry a copy of the **Matthew's Bible** for review.[4] But you know what? The Matthew's Bible was primarily the work of William Tyndale! In fact, on the last page of the Old Testament, William Tyndale's initials were included in 2½-inch block letters. It was a secret tribute to Tyndale, who by then had been put to death. Henry VIII had no idea that this Bible was mainly the work of William Tyndale.

The Matthew's Bible was later improved upon by **Miles Coverdale**, another Bible translator and close friend of Tyndale's. It grew in size to be called the Great Bible. Finally, in 1539, Henry agreed that it was a good idea to circulate the Great Bible throughout his country. He stated, "In God's name let it go abroad among the people."[5] This full-sized English Bible was placed in every parish church with a chain on it to prevent its being stolen. Henry saw it as a way to promote the pride of the English who had recently broken from Rome.

We see it differently, don't we? I think it was an answer to William Tyndale's prayer and the culmination of his lifelong work. The English *were* going to get the Bible in their mother tongue. At least for a time, Henry's eyes *were* open to the Word of God.

Believe it or not, Tyndale's translation work was so excellent that years later, when King James authorized another translation of the Bible, 90 percent of it was the work of William Tyndale. Very little was changed. Seventy-five percent of Tyndale's words make up the Revised Standard Version of the Bible today. Though it cost him his life, William Tyndale's work was remarkable. Those of us who use English as our everyday language should be grateful for his sacrifice. Of this man, John Foxe wrote, "There is no grander life in the whole annals of the Reformation than that of William Tyndale — none which comes nearer in its beautiful self-forgetfulness to His who 'laid down His life for His sheep.'"[6]

Lesson 35 1543

# *Nicolaus Copernicus*

Finally. We have finally reached a lesson that isn't terribly depressing. This lesson, unlike so many others, does not contain violence. Nor does it contain greed, murder, envy, or conspiracy. I think you'll find this lesson refreshing. It's the straightforward story of **Nicolaus Copernicus** (Koh PUR nih kus). He was a Polish astronomer who dared to think differently about the heavens. He was the first astronomer to publish the idea that the earth revolved around the sun. And you know what? He was right.

Nicolaus Copernicus was born in **Poland**. We haven't talked much about Poland yet. It became an independent nation in 1025, but for 300 years, it suffered through wars and invasions. In the 1300s, Poland finally experienced a time of peace, and the culture began to blossom. In 1364, the **University of Krakow** (CRACK koff) opened. That was a good thing for Nicolaus Copernicus. He was fortunate to attend the university in 1491. There he discovered a love for mathematics and astronomy that would last him a lifetime.

Also to last Copernicus through his lifetime was his employment with the Roman Church. (By the way, we've backed up in time here, so the Roman Church is not yet called the Roman Catholic Church.) Through his uncle, Nicolaus was appointed to be a canon in the cathedral of his hometown. (A canon is a high position in the church but not as high as a priest.) The church job continued to pay Nicolaus even when he took a three-year leave of absence to study in Italy. The cathedral was generous and so Nicolaus never turned his back on the Roman Church — even when his ideas disagreed with theirs.

## *Questioning the Movement of the Stars*

Early in his studies, Nicolaus questioned the way the stars appeared to move in the night sky. It was believed back then that the earth was the center of the universe and that all the heavenly bodies spun around it. A Greek astronomer named **Ptolemy** (TOL uh mee) had made this theory popular around A.D. 150 in his work titled *Almagest*. We call it the **geocentric theory**. (*Geo* stands for "the earth" and *centric* stands for "the center.") Under this theory, the earth was believed to be stationary. The stars were thought to be lights splattered across a concave dome rotating around the world.

But Nicolaus Copernicus thought differently, as had a few other scientists before him. As far back as 300 years before Christ, some scientists wondered if the earth revolved around the sun. **Archimedes** (Ar kih MEE deez) thought so, as did **Seleucus** (Si LOO kuhs) **of Babylonia**. Even Leonardo da Vinci suspected that the sun stood still. But Copernicus was the first to officially propose what we call the **heliocentric theory** of the heavens. (*Helio* stands for "the sun.") In this theory, the sun is the center of the solar system and all the planets spin around it.[7] He also theorized that the earth spins on its own axis every 24 hours, giving us different views of the sun and the stars.

In his work titled *Almagest*, Claudius Ptolemy mistakenly wrote that the earth was the center of the universe.

Now, all you students, young and old, should know that Nicolaus was right. The earth does revolve around the sun, as do the other planets. And the earth does spin on its axis every 24 hours. But it wasn't so obvious back then. Think about this: When you look at the stars at night, it could *appear* that they are moving around the earth. For thousands of years, people tracked the paths of the stars and gave names to the constellations, believing that they were circling the earth. Because the sun rises in the east and sets in the west, it would *appear*, too, that the sun is moving around the earth. But actually, *we* are the ones moving. (We move with the earth, so we don't feel it.) Nicolaus called this phenomenon "real motion" versus "apparent motion."

One way to understand this is to think about sitting in a parked car and watching a train go by. You know in your mind that the train is whizzing by. But sometimes your eyes play tricks on you, and you get this funny feeling inside that *you* are moving, not the train. Have you ever felt that? I have. That is what we call "real motion" versus "apparent motion." It's an optical illusion between a moving object and a stationary one.

Now back to Nicolaus. It was 1522 when he first wrote a small pamphlet about his heliocentric theory. Think about the year 1522. This was just five years after Martin Luther posted his Ninety-five Theses. And as you know, this document triggered the Protestant Reformation and a lot of questions over the authority of the church. For this reason, Nicolaus was a little shy about making his theories widely known. He knew that the Roman Church would disapprove of his ideas. Let's talk about that for a moment because this issue explains the rest of the story of Nicolaus Copernicus.

The Roman Church at this time was, as you know, very powerful. The church played the role of overseeing what was taught in all kinds of areas, including science. So when a scientist came up with a new idea, the church gave its opinion on the matter. When the Roman

Without the use of a telescope, Nicolaus Copernicus tracked the movement of Mars, his favorite planet to study.

Church disapproved of something, the Inquisition got involved as the ruling body to investigate. This means that when someone came along with a new idea that *challenged* the view of the church, that person could be arrested and questioned before the Inquisition. And you know what that meant! The Inquisition had a reputation for burning heretics at the stake along with their books and ideas.

Now, I don't know if Nicolaus was wise or a coward, but he did *not* have his ideas published right away because it would have put him in front of the Inquisition. And, more than likely, the inquisitors would have declared his ideas heresy. That might sound crazy to us in the twenty-first century, but that's the way things were back then. A radical new idea, like the earth circling the sun, would have been scorned for sure. Both Martin Luther and John Calvin thought that Copernicus was talking nonsense! Calvin quoted Psalm 93:1 to make his point. It says, "Surely the world is established, so that it cannot be moved." (Of course, the Bible is not wrong; Calvin simply misinterpreted the passage. The Scripture is not referring to the physical movement of the earth but rather, to the will of God, which nothing can move.)

To avoid the obvious conflict, Nicolaus Copernicus worked on other projects for awhile. He studied medicine, worked for his uncle, and improved the money system in Poland while continuing to serve as a canon in the church. But Copernicus never lost his love for studying astronomy. Whenever possible, he got away to observe the stars and planets. His favorite planet to follow was Mars. It provided him with a lot of information. But keep this in mind — Nicolaus was tracking the planets and the stars *before* telescopes were invented! It's impressive that he figured out as much as he did.

## Developing a New Theory

What Nicolaus Copernicus figured out was a major flaw in Ptolemy's theory. Ptolemy taught that the stars and planets were circling the earth in invisible bands following a cyclical pattern. (Ptolemy was right about the invisible bands. We call those orbits.) But Ptolemy was wrong about the number of them that existed and what they were circling. The math behind Ptolemy's theory wasn't adding up.

At the insistence of a friend, Nicolaus Copernicus agreed near the end of his life to publish his brilliant work on the heliocentric theory.

This puzzled Nicolaus Copernicus until he developed his heliocentric theory. In his theory, the orbits were renumbered and redirected around the sun. His calculations also made the universe much larger than it was thought to be. It would be years before some of these ideas were fully developed. For example, Nicolaus still thought the planets traveled in round orbits when in fact they are elliptical, or oval shaped. But at least his theory was heading in the right direction, literally.

Now, we may never have heard of Nicolaus Copernicus except for the fact that he had a very persistent friend. His friend was a bright professor at the University of Wittenberg. In 1542, the professor insisted that Nicolaus publish his works. By then, Nicolaus was in his seventies. Having lived a full life, he was ready to risk his life if need be in front of the Inquisition. But he never had to. Legend says that Nicolaus Copernicus was on his deathbed when his book came out in **1543**. Supposedly he was just able to leaf through the pages of his book before he drew his last breath.

The book by Nicolaus Copernicus was titled *Concerning the Revolutions of the Celestial Spheres*. It laid out the heliocentric theory as best as Copernicus understood it. And as feared, the theory did *not* go over well with the Inquisition. The Roman Church was mostly upset that the ideas were presented as fact rather than as theory. No matter what it was called, it was beyond their understanding, and eventually condemned as heresy. In 1615, the book by Copernicus was banned.

It would be decades before the theories of Copernicus were accepted. Other great scientists, such as Kepler, Galileo, and Newton, would expand on them and start what has been called the Scientific Revolution. This was just the beginning of a whole new age for mankind.

## Lesson 36 1550

# Bartolomé de Las Casas

Imagine you are a 9-year-old boy. (I'm sure some of you are.) Pretend you are watching a parade go through your town. Streamers and banners cloud the sky, loud music is playing, and sweet smells of food fill the air. Everyone is celebrating. They are celebrating the return of Cristóbal Colón from the New World. While you watch him go by, you are in complete awe. But what really grabs your attention is not Cristóbal Colón but the seven Indians who are walking behind him like trophies on display. You're drawn to their long black hair and fierce-looking eyes. By your culture's standards, they are barely dressed. And their decorations of tiny shells and beads, as well as the beaten-gold ornaments they carry, also catch your eye.

As the crowd gawks and presses in, you wonder what the Indians are thinking and feeling. Are they scared and embarrassed? Or are they as proud and strong as they appear? You wish you could speak to them. Deep down inside, your spirit is touched and after that day, you're never quite the same.

If you can imagine that scene in your mind, then you're seeing **Bartolomé de Las Casas** (Bar toll oh MAY day Las CAH sahs). In 1493, when he was just a boy, he really *did* attend a parade for Cristóbal Colón held in Spain. And he really *did* see Indians who were put on display like spoils from a victory. As a result of this and many other experiences, Bartolomé de Las Casas would grow up to be one of the greatest humanitarians of the sixteenth century. He became known as the "Protector of the Indies" for fighting for the rights of the indigenous people of the Americas.

The word *indigenous* means "natural." It refers to the people of the New World who were naturally living there *long* before Europeans began to immigrate. We might also use the words *natives, locals,* or *Indians* when speaking of the indigenous people of America. (Of course, the term *Indian* came from Cristóbal Colón.) No matter what you call these folks, they were people. And Bartolomé de Las Casas cared a great deal for them.

Bartolomé grew up in Spain in a family of farmers and merchants. He excelled in Latin and other academics. He was only 18 when he made his first trip to America. He traveled to Hispaniola in the West Indies with the governor. For his services, Bartolomé was granted an **encomienda** (en co mee IN duh). I doubt you know what that is, but it's very important that you understand the term. So let me stop and explain.

## The Encomienda System

As the Spanish settled in the Americas, they patterned things after the ways of life in Spain. Spain in the fifteenth century was still under the influence of the old feudal system. Do you remember the feudal system from the Middle Ages? It's a system in which wealthy landowners give portions of their land to the *less* wealthy in exchange for their services. This system gave protection to the poor and provided places to live and farm. Though the poor usually stayed poor, it was a decent system when practiced fairly.

Well, in the West Indies, the Spanish took the same idea of feudalism and applied it to the Indians. They renamed it the **encomienda system**. It was supposed to be a fair way to employ Indians in their own land and teach them the Christian faith. As wealthy Spaniards came to the West Indies and took large portions of land, they "hired" the Indians who lived on the land to work for them. The landowners, or *encomenderos* (en co men DARE ohs) provided protection and Christian training for services. Unfortunately, the Indians didn't have much say in the matter and were usually overworked and poorly taught. It was practically slavery, though nobody wanted to call it that.

Now, let's go back to Bartolomé de Las Casas. As I mentioned before, when he arrived in the West Indies, he was given an encomienda — which was a small tract of land with Indians who lived on it. According to the system, it was "his" to manage. But Bartolomé wasn't like most wealthy Spanish landowners. He saw the Indians as people rather than as a source of cheap labor. He would spend the rest of his life trying to change the unfairness of the system.

Bartolomé had a spiritual experience that was one of his sources of inspiration. In 1511, he listened to the preaching of a Dominican priest who based his message on the Bible verse that reads, "I am 'The voice of one crying in the wilderness: "Make straight the way of the Lord."' " (See John 1:23.) The Dominican priest believed he was speaking the voice of the Indians who were crying out in their despair. Bartolomé was moved in his heart and returned his encomienda to the governor!

A year later, in 1512, Bartolomé de Las Casas was ordained a priest in the Roman Church. He was the first to be ordained in the Americas. In 1513, Bartolomé took part in the conquest of Cuba. And do you want to know what he received for his services? Once again, he received an

Bartolomé de Las Casas, the first ordained priest in the Americas, devoted his life to fair treatment of Native Americans.

encomienda of land and Indians! The system was still alive and well in the West Indies despite the preaching of the Dominicans.

So, in 1515, Bartolomé decided to fight for the Indians. He went back to Spain to speak to King Ferdinand about the matter. The king listened and sent Las Casas back to the West Indies for a full investigation of the treatment of Indians. Las Casas provided that and came up with a better plan to employ and teach the natives.

Well, the next king of Spain, Charles I, was not as optimistic as King Ferdinand. He wanted Bartolomé to *prove* that his plan could work. He allowed Bartolomé to set up an experimental farming colony in Venezuela just the way he wanted it — with more freedom for Native Americans. Part of the experiment was proper teaching of the Gospel to the natives. Bartolomé must have been excited to show others that there were better ways than slavery to settle a land.

I wish I could report that the "better way" of Bartolomé was successful. But unfortunately, not everyone in the colony cooperated. Oppressive neighbors made it almost impossible for the new colony to get established. The encomenderos were resistant to change. They liked the old system as it was because it allowed the colonists to work very little, yet get very rich!

## *Bartolomé Joins the Dominicans*

Naturally, Bartolomé was discouraged at the failure of his colony, but he didn't give up his fight for the American Indians. When he was 36, he joined the Dominicans and turned to the power of the pen. That means he directed his energy into writing books. His books would expose the terrible treatment of the Indians to all who could read. He wrote gruesome stories of natives being butchered and burned alive. He wrote of seeing thousands die from laboring in the gold mines. He wrote of thousands more who were being massacred by the Spanish. Bartolomé saw these crimes firsthand and believed they were ultimately a result of man's sin and selfishness. Few could argue that.

By 1537, Bartolomé would gain the attention of the pope in the matter. The pope agreed with Bartolomé that the Christian faith ought *not* to be forced on the Indians in exchange for labor. He also recognized the humanity of the American Indians, declaring that they were "rational beings" who should be protected. As normal as that might sound to us in the twenty-first century, it was a new view back then.

Finally, in 1542, Bartolomé de Las Casas experienced some victory. He convinced Charles I to sign what were called the "New Laws." They prohibited slavery of the American Indians and limited the encomienda system. In particular, the New Laws limited the employment of serfs to one generation. It was progress.

Two years later, Bartolomé was made a bishop in Guatemala. He was joined by 45 Dominican friars in a large-scale mission to evangelize the Indians. He was there also to oversee that the New Laws were followed. Unfortunately, they weren't. Because of racism and greed, Native Americans were *still* being treated cruelly. Bartolomé got the cold shoulder from wealthy landowners and made enemies trying to set things straight. So many colonists broke the New Laws that they were impossible to enforce. Bartolomé resigned as bishop but pressed on in yet another way. (This man was amazingly persistent!)

Serving as a bishop, Bartolomé de Las Casas ministered to Native Americans through the Roman Catholic Church of Guatemala.

In **1550**, Bartolomé petitioned Charles I, the king of Spain, to host a debate. The king agreed. The debate over slavery was held at the **Council of Valladolid** (Val uh duh LID) in Spain. Bartolomé's opponent was a persuasive man named **Juan Ginés de Sepúlveda**. Though no official verdict was given, most would say that Bartolomé *won* the debate at Valladolid. His strong views were heard.

But you know what? When all was said and done, the encomienda system stayed in place! The views of Sepúlveda and the colonists won in the long run and were practiced in the Indies and Americas. Slavery was kept alive and fed by greed. The promise of gold found in Peru was especially damaging to the Incas — who were enslaved to collect it. (Remember Francisco Pizarro?) But Bartolomé kept writing. He believed that the treasure tombs of the Incas belonged to the Incas, not to the Spanish. Bartolomé continued to speak at councils and give his voice to the American Indians until he died in 1566. He was 82 years old.

Do you think the long fight of Bartolomé de Las Casas matters today? I think it does. Our world is not free of racism, slavery, or oppression. It exists in many forms. I'm glad that Bartolomé de Las Casas had the courage to address these difficult issues as far back as the fifteenth century. I believe we need voices like his today to speak out for those who can't be heard.

# WEEK 13

## Lesson 37 1553

# *Mary Tudor ("Bloody Mary")*

**Note to Teacher:** *This is a long lesson. You may wish to divide it into two parts.*

There are times I wish we could rewrite history, especially the last few years that **Mary Tudor** sat on the throne of England.[1] Why do I feel so strongly? Well, as you may have gathered from the title of our lesson, Mary Tudor was also known as "Bloody Mary." She was nicknamed that for the 300 or more people that she sent to burn at the stake toward the end of her reign. The stories are excruciating. But equally sad to me is the story of Mary herself. Her life was one of sickness, anguish, and rejection. So, both sides of this story are sad to me. In doing my research, I couldn't help but shed a few tears for Mary and for those who died under her.

To understand this story, let's place Mary Tudor back in time. Let's place her back in her childhood where her heartache first began. Mary was the red-headed daughter of Henry VIII and Catherine of Aragon. By the time she was 8 years old, her father was demanding an annulment from her mother. It was an ugly scene, as you know. Mary was tossed to and fro during the breakup of her family. She was shuffled away from her mother in England to live in Spain, where her mother had been raised.

In Spain, Mary was surrounded by her mother's heritage and faith. It was the heritage of Ferdinand and Isabella, the Catholic king and queen of Spain who created the Spanish Inquisition. Do you see the lineage clearly? Mary's grandparents were Ferdinand and Isabella, the ones who put the Inquisition in place to rid Spain of those whom they deemed to be heretics, as well as of Jewish and Muslim converts they judged to be insincere. Remember that! The Inquisition was part of her heritage.

Now, let's fast-forward just a bit to the end of Henry VIII's reign. If you recall, at his death, he made a will. It stated that when he died, his three children would rule in the order of (1) Edward, (2) Mary, and (3) Elizabeth. Those were Henry's wishes, and that is exactly what happened.

After Henry died, Edward VI became the next king of England. In faith, Edward was a strong Protestant. In health, Edward was weak and sickly. When only 15, he showed signs of a mysterious disease that caused him terrible pain and discomfort. It was probably tuberculosis. He knew he was dying and faced a great dilemma. He knew that, according to his father's will and wishes, Mary was next in line to rule England. He also knew that she would naturally bring Roman Catholicism with her. Mary was extremely devout in her Catholic faith, as her mother and grandparents had been. It was inevitable that she would undo everything that had been done in England to promote Protestantism.

So, on his deathbed, Edward VI was persuaded by his counselors to go against Henry's will and appoint a young Protestant girl named **Lady Jane Grey** to the throne. She was only 16 years old and the granddaughter of Henry's sister. She was also a brand new bride. Jane's husband would not be made the king because she had "royal blood" and he didn't. Anyway, when Lady Jane Grey was approached to become the next queen, she fainted with anxiety! She really didn't want to be the queen, especially after seeing the fate of Henry's wives! But out of respect for her parents and husband, she agreed to the plan.

Of course, as soon as word reached Mary that her brother was dead, she made her move to take over the throne of England, which was rightfully hers! By this time Mary was 37 years old. Her red hair was streaked with silver; she had never been married; and she had never been very happy. Let me fill you in on the pitiful life she had endured up to this point.

## *Mary's Childhood*

In Mary's childhood, she was, as I said earlier, separated from her mother. Even when Mary was very ill, which she was a lot, Henry refused to allow Catherine to visit. The mother and daughter had only a few chances to ever see and know one another. When Catherine lay dying in England, Mary was refused the right to see her! I suppose it was a control issue for Henry. He had hardly acknowledged Mary throughout her young childhood, and he was leery of catering to her needs.

When Catherine of Aragon passed away, Mary was faced with a very difficult decision. Henry requested that she sign papers agreeing that his marriage to Catherine of Aragon had been improper and that as a result, Mary was an illegitimate child! (An illegitimate child refers to one born out of wedlock. Mary was *not* illegitimate since Henry and Catherine were actually married.)

Mary couldn't win. If she signed the paper in agreement with her father, she would dishonor her mother and declare herself illegitimate. But if she didn't sign the paper, she would face great punishment from her father and be completely disowned. He could have had her head cut off! So, Mary did the unthinkable. She signed. What an agonizing experience that must have been. Henry was relieved and delighted. Mary was humiliated and tormented.

Now, if you'll remember, some of Henry's later wives were kind to Mary. They invited her to the royal castle to live and oversaw her education. Because Mary had signed herself off as an illegitimate child, she was hardly a threat to Henry anymore. He didn't seem to mind her being around unless, of course, he was visiting with Elizabeth, his *other* daughter, who was born of Anne Boleyn. During those awkward visits, Mary was locked in her bedroom.

It was difficult for Mary, to say the least. She was on pins and needles as long as her father was alive. She never knew if she was on his good side or his bad side. Mary's nerves were frequently shattered, and she regularly fought severe headaches. She was pale and weak most of the time from poor health and routine "bloodletting." On top of not feeling well most of the

Most of her life, Mary Tudor suffered from poor health and the burden of emotional pain.

time, Mary carried a huge emotional burden. By her mere presence, she was a constant reminder to Henry of the queen he put away.

As the Reformation grew in England, Mary also suffered religious persecution in her childhood. She was, as you know, Roman Catholic. The celebration of a Catholic Mass was forbidden in England. Mary requested that Mass be said in her private quarters. For a time this was allowed, but freedom of worship was eventually taken away from her. The priest who said her Mass was taken away from her, too.

Keep in mind that to the Roman Catholic, taking part in the celebration of the Mass is sacred and necessary for salvation. When the Eucharist (also called communion) is served during Mass, it is believed to be the literal body and blood of Jesus under the appearance of bread and wine. Without this ritual and many others, Mary's worship experience would have felt empty and bewildering. These sacred rituals were all she had ever known growing up in Catholic Spain.

Now let's go back to Lady Jane Grey. In keeping with Edward's dying wishes, she claimed to be the queen of England. At the same time, Mary also claimed to be the queen of England! One of them had to go. Well, as much as England was getting used to becoming Protestant, when it came time to support one queen or the other, guess whom they chose? It was Mary! The English had adored Mary's mother, Catherine of Aragon, who had been dethroned and humiliated to make room for Anne Boleyn. Catholic or not, to the English it seemed only fair to put Mary on the throne out of respect and honor for her mother.

Troops gathered to carry out the wishes of the people. Mary prevailed and was officially made queen. Lady Jane Grey was immediately put in the Tower of London, along with family members who were part of the conspiracy to make her queen. It's sad, really. Young Lady Jane Grey had been queen for only nine days. Six months later she was beheaded for a crime of treason she never wished to commit! At her execution, she didn't cry but confessed she had been wrong to try to take Mary's place. I find it a curious story.

## *Mary's Reign Begins*

It was a historic event in **1553**, when Mary took the throne, since England had been ruled by a single queen only one other time in history. Mary's first years on the throne were relatively good ones. Though she was frequently ill and weak, she was capable. Mary lowered taxes and reduced corruption, trimmed the royal budget, and improved the system of elections. She was extremely generous to the poor and on occasion snuck out of the castle in ordinary clothes just to mingle with housewives. Mary enjoyed needlework and played the lute. And

Mary greatly hoped for happiness in marrying Philip II, the young Catholic king of Spain.

oddly enough, she proved at first to be tolerant of the Protestants around her.

But Mary took a turn against the English that would mark the beginning of her unpopular reign. Mary pursued a royal marriage to **Philip II**, the king of Spain and the son of Charles V, who was the Holy Roman Emperor. Philip was 11 years younger than Mary, but he was eager to join Spain and England through this union with Mary. His greatest hope was for a son to be born to them who could inherit *both* nations and keep them joined together. The English were furious at the idea of the marriage but could do little to stop the queen.

For Mary, marriage was at last a chance for real happiness — something she had not had much of. In Philip, it would appear that she had everything to gain. He was young, powerful, rich, Spanish, and Catholic. Mary believed their union would strengthen her Catholic influence over England. A child born to them would be even better. Mary was nearly 40 years old but behaved like any young bride would. She relished every detail of the royal wedding and doted endlessly on her new husband. She wrote to her father-in-law, Charles V, that she was "happier than I can say, as I daily discover in the King my husband so many virtues and perfections that I constantly pray God to grant me grace to please him."[2]

All I can say is, Mary tried. It sounds to me like she loved her husband and tried to please him. But I don't think Philip ever really loved Mary in return. He only stayed in England for a year or so after their wedding before he found official "business" elsewhere. Before he left, Mary thought she was expecting a child. It was announced all over England. But sadly for Mary, it was a false pregnancy. She was crushed and embarrassed. Like scattered leaves in the fall, gossip swirled around the country, adding to Mary's shame. Without a baby, Mary must have known she was close to losing Philip for good. Without an heir to the throne, he found no reason to stick around.

Before Philip left, Mary had already begun to make changes in England. She had used her position as the head of the English church to bring back a few Roman Catholic practices. I think that was expected, considering her faith. But Mary went a step further and replaced Protestant bishops with Catholic ones. Of great importance, she imprisoned in the Tower of London Thomas Cranmer, Hugh Latimer, and Nicholas Ridley — all Protestant leaders. She freed Bishop Bonner and Bishop Gardiner — two Catholics who had been locked up in the Tower during the reign of Henry VIII.

## The Turning Point

The release of Bonner and Gardiner was the turning point of Mary's career. With Philip hardly around, the two bishops and a cardinal of the Roman Church served as advisers to Mary. I'm not sure of their motives. On the one hand, I think they sincerely loved the Roman Church — believed it was the only true church — and wanted to see it return to

England for the glory of God. On the other hand, I think they were also out for revenge. Remember, the two bishops had spent a long time waiting for release from the cold, dark dungeon of the Tower of London.

The bishops and the cardinal advised Mary in every situation to arrest those who were a threat to her reign and a threat to the Roman Church. They convinced Mary that without a heavy hand, she would lose her crown and her country to Protestants. She was advised to restore the old monasteries, bring back all the Catholic customs, and place the pope back in charge of England. She obliged.

Mary was happy once again. She was happy to experience Mass in the churches and to see holy relics and pictures adorn the walls. As part of a religious ritual, she washed and kissed the feet of old women and gave money to the poor. She had failed at marriage and motherhood, but she would do her best not to fail at restoring the Roman Church. It became her highest goal.

Okay. So here comes another sad part of the story. To accomplish her goal, Mary began to persecute Protestants. I mean, ruthlessly persecute Protestants. It started when Bishop Gardiner arrested six Protestant preachers. Four were burned at the stake. Gardiner quickly learned that he didn't have the stomach for these cruel executions and withdrew his involvement. Bishop Bonner took his place and sent more Protestant preachers to the stake. At least one Spanish friar tried to stop the killings. He declared that the burning of heretics was contrary to the teachings of Christ. But he was overruled and they continued.

Nearly 300 people were burned at the stake during the last years of Mary's short reign. Some were arrested for preaching, some for teaching, and some for merely reading the Word of God. Though "Bloody" Bishop Bonner was the cruel-minded one behind most of the trials, Mary upheld the rulings and allowed the massacre. At any time, she had the authority to stop the burnings, but she didn't. The English grew to despise Mary, and the nickname of "Bloody" was passed on to her. Plots abounded to end her short reign.

Of all the deaths, there is just one that I will describe in detail. It is the execution of Thomas Cranmer, the strong Protestant leader of England. Of great meaning to English Protestants, Cranmer had written a prayer book to guide them in their faith. But after three years of prison, Cranmer weakened in his own faith. He knew his friends Latimer and Ridley had already been executed. He was worn out and scared. When asked to take back his Protestant beliefs, he did. Cranmer signed papers saying that he had been wrong about his views toward the Roman Church and the pope.

Thomas Cranmer, a leader in the English Protestant Reformation, spent three years in prison before facing execution.

The queen and Bishop Bonner were excited to hear that at least one of the accused recanted. However, they still planned to execute him. (Remember, it was Thomas Cranmer who had given Henry VIII his annulment from Mary's mother!) The queen and the bishop intended to make Thomas Cranmer an example and planned that he would read his recantation at his execution.

Well, Thomas Cranmer's accusers underestimated his faith. When the time came for him to read the things he had signed, he read something else instead. He read an apology. Thomas Cranmer took back his recantation and added to it that he would burn his hand first for having signed anything that dishonored his Lord. He said, "And forasmuch as my hand hath offended, writing contrary to my heart, therefore this my hand shall first be punished; for when I come to the fire, it shall first be burned."[3]

Thomas Cranmer lived up to his word. When the fire was lit, he stretched out his right hand and allowed it to burn in front of the gawking crowd. He then stepped into the fire to face death and deliverance. His actions were shocking to Protestants and Catholics alike.

The strange thing about persecuting Christians is that it doesn't stop them. As the Holy Spirit gives strength to the accused, it only reflects His glory. Protestants were inspired when Latimer said to Ridley at their dual execution, "We shall this day light such a candle, by God's grace, in England as I trust shall never be put out."[4] There are so many heroic stories of men and women who died under the reign of Mary Tudor. I wish I had time to honor each and every one. But another author has already done that for us. His name was **John Foxe**. John Foxe wrote the book commonly known as *Foxe's Book of Martyrs*. Foxe lived during the reign of Mary Tudor and was able to capture firsthand the gruesome but inspiring details. If it interests you, read the book yourself. Just be warned, it may make you cry.

As for Queen Mary, her final year on this earth was filled with more disappointment. Philip visited to talk her into a war against France. She agreed to it, but the war failed. In the process, England lost the last city it held in France. It was the city of **Calais** (Ke LAY), the only English claim to France since the days of Joan of Arc. All Mary really wanted was to have a baby with her husband. But that failed, too, and Philip left Mary again. Mary was described as nearly insane by this time. She would curl up on the floor for hours at a time and wander through the palace, overcome with grief and despair.

One of England's crown jewels is a decorative orb symbolizing the sovereign's role as Defender of the Faith.

In 1558, a plague that Mary could not resist swept through England. Her immune system might have been weakened from other illnesses or from a tumor that caused her false pregnancy. Some believe she had cancer. Knowing she was dying, Mary did a strange thing. She sent Elizabeth, her half sister, the crown jewels. Why? Because Mary knew that Elizabeth was rightfully the next queen. Mary also knew that Elizabeth was a strong Protestant. In recognizing her sister, Mary gave up her dreams of restoring England as a Catholic nation. She yielded her strong-felt faith to grant England a period of peace. It tugs at my heart to imagine this gracious gesture at the end of such a tragic life.

According to legend, there is a common nursery rhyme that sums up the life of Mary I. It reads,

Mary, Mary quite contrary,
How does your garden grow?
With silver bells and cockleshells,
And pretty maids all in a row.

Though interpretations vary, some would say that "silver bells" and "cockleshells" were symbols worn on the robes of devout Catholics on holy pilgrimages, and that "pretty maids" refers to the nuns brought back to England under Mary's influence. Others claim that silver bells and cockleshells were nicknames for torture devices, and maids in a row were guillotine-type structures! Regardless of the intention of the author of the nursery rhyme, it has been well remembered. We will pick up this fascinating story in our next lesson when Elizabeth I becomes queen.

## Lesson 38 1558–1603

# Elizabeth I

If history itself could take a breath and sigh, I think it would do so after the death of Mary Tudor. Her "bloody" reign had left the English bewildered, both Protestant and Catholic alike. Conflict between the groups was far from over with Mary's death, but for a time all were weary of the persecution. So, when **Elizabeth I** took Mary's place as the next queen of England, she did so very carefully. She remained neutral on religion, as well as on marriage, for as long as she could. In fact, Elizabeth was probably the most cautious, coy, and cunning queen ever to rule over England. Her reign was extraordinary and lasted almost 50 years, from **1558** to her death in **1603**. Personally, I'm quite fond of Elizabeth and would love the chance to meet her.

When I consider what to tell you about Elizabeth, I realize that I can't begin to fit it all into one lesson. Her remarkable reign overlapped the lives of so many big names in history such as Sir Francis Drake; Mary, Queen of Scots; and William Shakespeare. A span of 140 years has been named after this woman because of her significance. It's called the **Elizabethan Age**. We'll get to that later. For now, we'll look at Elizabeth's peculiar childhood, her path to the throne, her religious influence, and her numerous courtships. That will be plenty!

### *Elizabeth's Peculiar Childhood*

As you know, Elizabeth was the daughter of Henry VIII and *Anne Boleyn*. (In this review, the names of Henry's wives will appear in italics.) Elizabeth had her father's reddish-blond coloring and her mother's enchanting eyes. Though she was a beautiful baby, her entrance into this world was disappointing to Henry. He wanted her to be a boy — a male heir to the throne of England. Elizabeth would always have to fight for her father's love.

Windsor Castle, an enormous fortress and palace in Windsor, England, was one of many homes to both Mary and Elizabeth.

Henry especially shunned Elizabeth after he grew tired of Anne Boleyn. Poor Elizabeth. She was only 2 years old when her father ordered the execution of her mother. How does a child ever deal with a tragedy such as that? Elizabeth was removed from Henry's sight to help him forget what he had done to Anne Boleyn. Though Elizabeth was too young to understand it then, the stories of her mother would haunt her for the rest of her life.

As Henry went from one wife to the next, Elizabeth and her half sister, Mary, would have four stepmothers. (Ironically, *Catherine of Aragon* and Anne Boleyn died the same year, leaving each child without a mother.) First to step in was *Jane Seymour,* Henry's third wife. Jane was good to both Mary and Elizabeth and brought them to live at the royal court. She tried her best to make them a happy family. But if you remember, Jane died after giving birth to Edward. Elizabeth was about 4 when that happened. She and Mary were both thrilled to gain a little brother, but in the process they lost their kind stepmother.

When Elizabeth was 7, Henry married *Anne of Cleves,* the unattractive princess from Germany. Anne adored Elizabeth as if she were her own child. Mary was old enough to be Anne's good friend. But Anne didn't last long as their stepmother. In only six months, her marriage to Henry was annulled. Anne remained friends with the girls the rest of her life.

Next in line, Henry married *Catherine Howard*. She was too young and immature to be a very good stepmother. She and Mary never got along well. When Elizabeth was just 9, Catherine Howard was accused of cheating on Henry and, like Anne Boleyn, was executed. Her beheading was yet another tragedy in Elizabeth's life. Catherine Howard's screams throughout the castle would leave a lasting impression on Elizabeth's young heart. She must certainly have wondered if marriage was *ever* a good thing.

A year later, Henry married the sensible and loving *Catherine Parr*. Elizabeth was about 10 years old and in desperate need of a mother. Catherine Parr proved to be that and more. Catherine welcomed all of Henry's children into her life. She doted on Mary, Elizabeth, and Edward by overseeing their education and teaching them good manners. Elizabeth was given the best tutors and gleaned a good education from Catherine herself.

Elizabeth studied Greek all morning and Latin all afternoon. Her Greek studies included the New Testament and influenced her Protestant faith. Elizabeth mastered French and Italian, and she had beautiful handwriting. She inherited musical ability from her father and graced the court with her wit and charm. To demonstrate just how bright she was, at a young age Elizabeth translated a poem, written by Margaret of Navarre, from French into English. (Margaret of Navarre was a poet and writer I mentioned in Lesson 29.) Young Elizabeth dedicated the poem, titled "A Godly Meditation of the Soul," to Catherine Parr, who filled a special place in her life.

Elizabeth and Edward were together when the news came that their father had died. Elizabeth was 14 and Edward was 9. They openly wept. Throughout all these years, Elizabeth had been in and out of her father's favor. At times, Henry showed much love and concern for her. Other times, he had her banished from his presence. Both Mary and Elizabeth were "disowned" when their birth mothers were put away and "reinstated" when Henry grew older. It must have been peculiar and confusing to be the daughter of Henry VIII.

Speaking of peculiar, let's stop and look at the relationship between Mary and Elizabeth. Mary was 17 years old when Elizabeth was born. If you put the pieces together, you'll see that Elizabeth was the daughter of the woman who appeared to ruin Mary's life. That woman was Anne Boleyn of course. It was a strain on Mary to welcome this little sister into her life, but most of the time she did. When Mary was a young girl and brought under the care of Jane Seymour, she insisted that Elizabeth join them for Christmas. Both Mary and Elizabeth were at Edward's christening as a baby and watched him grow up. They shared many of the same experiences in knowing that they were both "in line" to be queen if anything would ever happen to Edward.

## *Elizabeth's Path to the Throne*

When Henry VIII died, Edward did become king — but his reign was a short one. He died at 15. This put Mary on the throne when she was 37. Elizabeth was 20. Unfortunately, that is when Mary and Elizabeth's relationship began to unravel. Soon after Mary ascended the throne, she was advised to remove all threats from around her. One of those threats was Elizabeth! She was a threat because she was inclined toward the Protestant cause. Besides that, Elizabeth was young and attractive, a sure threat for gaining the love of the English. Mary was advised to have Elizabeth locked up. It had to have been an excruciating decision for Mary to make. But from what you already know of her, you have probably guessed that she followed the guidance of her advisers. Mary hardened her heart against Elizabeth and had her put into custody in the Tower of London.

Elizabeth was terrified of the Tower. It was the same eerie place where her mother, as well as many others, had been executed. On the day of her delivery to the Tower she sat down in the rain, refusing to enter. She was afraid she would never make it out alive. She didn't know what to think of her sister, who was a friend and an enemy, a relative and a rival.

Elizabeth plotted that her only way out of the Tower of London was to convince Mary that she was *not* a threat and was indeed a Catholic at heart. I don't know if Elizabeth was sincere or not about changing the tone of her faith. But she embraced the Catholic traditions, including Mass. Mary, who then had no solid reason to keep her sister confined, released Elizabeth after two months of captivity. Elizabeth was kept under house arrest for another year and was closely watched.

As you know, Mary's reign didn't last long. Elizabeth was 25 when Mary died. It was a new day for England in 1558 when Elizabeth I inherited the throne. Her only apparent threat was a beautiful young Catholic cousin who also had ties to the throne. That cousin was Mary, Queen of Scots. But her story is so interesting that I'm saving it for later.

On her coronation day, Elizabeth I, with long red hair, posed in a fur-lined robe with a scepter in one hand and a sovereign orb in the other.

## *Elizabeth's Religion*

Elizabeth waited six months after becoming queen to make her religious beliefs obvious. In 1559, the Act of Supremacy declared her the "governor" of the Church of England. The point of being only a governor was to lessen the strain between Protestants and Catholics. It seemed less harsh to be a governor than to be the "head."

Elizabeth was not bent toward persecuting anyone for what they believed (at least at first). Having seen the horror of bloodshed between Catholics and Protestants, she let things sit for awhile without making drastic demands or changes. Elizabeth would say, "There is only one Christ, Jesus, one faith. All else is a dispute over trifles." She would also say that she had "no desire to make windows into men's souls."[5] She meant that she would not play the judge of men's hearts and condemn them for their beliefs.

In time, however, Protestant traditions replaced Catholic ones. It was made illegal to celebrate Mass, but no one was immediately burned at the stake for it. Eventually, the established Church of England became the **Anglican Church of England**. (In America, the Anglican Church would be called the **Episcopal Church**.) To Elizabeth, the Anglican Church was an acceptable blend of faith and tradition that she believed would keep Catholics and Protestants happy. Of course, it really didn't. There were ardent Protestants, called the "Puritans," who wished to see more pure reform in the Anglican Church. And then there were ardent Catholics, like the Jesuits, who still expressed loyalty to the pope. Both ends of the spectrum would at times suffer persecution for upsetting the balance that Elizabeth thought she had created.

To complicate matters, in 1570 the pope excommunicated Elizabeth! He hoped to see Elizabeth's cousin take the crown and restore Catholicism to England. Catholics were torn between their loyalty to Elizabeth and their loyalty to the pope. Those were tough times indeed. Elizabeth ignored the excommunication, and eventually the Anglican Church won out. It has been the state church of England ever since.

> *"I have no desire to make windows into men's souls."*
> *–Elizabeth I*

## *Elizabeth's Numerous Courtships*

I'm going to transition now to Elizabeth's many courtships. Being a young, pretty, and intelligent queen, Elizabeth was quite a catch. She had at least 20 serious suitors over the course of her lifetime. It's a fascinating piece of history because when all was said and done, Elizabeth chose to marry — no one! It was unheard of back then for a queen to do such a thing. All expected her to marry and have children to carry on the Tudor legacy. Elizabeth baffled the world with her indecisiveness or independence — or perhaps her complete fear of marriage.

One of Elizabeth's first suitors was none other than Philip II of Spain, the widower of Mary Tudor. I doubt that Philip missed Mary when she died, as he had never really loved her. But he did miss the connection he had with the throne of England. So Philip immediately tried his hand at courting Elizabeth. She used the attention to keep good relations between England and Spain, but she never gave in to Philip or to his son, who would later court her also. In fact, to show her true colors, Elizabeth would later go to war *against* Philip II and Spain and shape history in doing so! We will definitely come back to that story in another lesson.

Many other suitors would come and go. They came from Denmark, Sweden, and France. They were princes, kings, and dukes. Elizabeth flirted and played their games. She used the courtships to mend foreign relations as well as to break them. She dangled her hand in marriage when it was convenient to do so and retracted it when it wasn't.

Elizabeth even used her lavish wardrobe as an expression of her fickle heart. Her gowns were so fancy they seemed to say, "Please look, but don't come near me." Elizabeth was the queen of image — dressing splendidly at all times to maintain a look of purity and dignity. Pearls were one of her favorite adornments. She also used white makeup on her face to give an impression of glamor and royalty.

Elizabeth's love life was the talk of England. Every new suitor brought a potential heir to the throne. If the suitor was Protestant, it brought joy to the Protestants. If the suitor was Catholic, it brought joy to the Catholics. But no one seemed to bring real joy to Elizabeth except a man named **Robert Dudley**.

Elizabeth had been friends with Robert Dudley since she was a child. He was an English nobleman, and one of the few men in her life who appeared to care more for her than for her crown. But Dudley was a married man. His close friendship to the queen would create gossip for centuries. Elizabeth seemed to truly love the man but was never in the position to marry him. Dudley's father and grandfather had both been beheaded for treason. Robert Dudley himself had spent time in the Tower of London for the conspiracy involving Lady Jane Grey. If that weren't scandalous enough, Dudley's wife died from a fall down a flight of stairs. Many suspected that she was murdered. If she was or not, the mystery of it would destroy what little hope Dudley had of marrying Elizabeth. He was far too much of a risk. Elizabeth would ignore her heart for the sake of England and abandon Robert Dudley in the process.

One of Elizabeth's last serious suitors was **Francis, the duke of Alencon**. He was from France. If Elizabeth married the duke, it would have given England strong ties to France and protected her from Spain. But that was both good and bad. The French and the English had warred for centuries. The thought of uniting their crowns was deplorable to many. To make matters more complicated, France was in the middle of a religious war at that time between Protestants and Catholics. The last thing Elizabeth needed was to drag more of *that* battle to England!

With pearls, adornments, and stiff lace, Elizabeth's extravagant wardrobe portrayed an image of purity, dignity, and royal wealth.

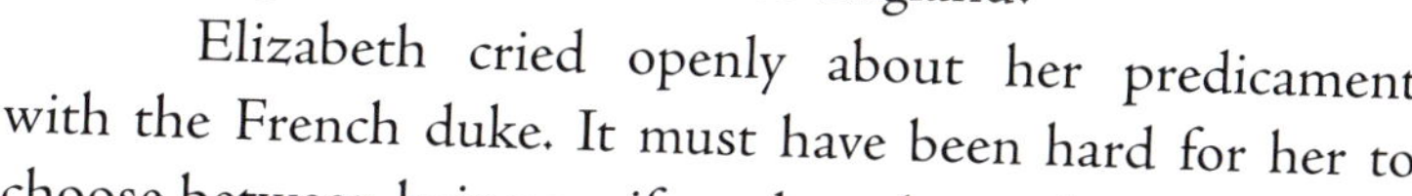

Elizabeth cried openly about her predicament with the French duke. It must have been hard for her to choose between being a wife and mother or being single the rest of her life. As I already told you, she chose to remain alone on the throne and unattached in her heart. Some think that Elizabeth decided early in life not to marry. Growing up in the Tudor household, she certainly had seen her share of trouble over love and romance.

As Elizabeth grew older and the prime years for motherhood slipped away, she proudly called herself the "Virgin Queen." The state of "Virginia" in the United States is named in her memory. Others would remember her as "Good Queen Bess" for steering England successfully for such a long time and at such personal cost. She said of herself, "I know I have but the body of a feeble woman, but I have the heart of a King and a King of England, too."[6] I'll save the rest of Elizabeth's story for later. She truly had the heart of a king and used it to love her country.

## Lesson 39 — 1559

# John Knox and the Scottish Reformation

"I fear John Knox's prayers more than an army of ten thousand men!"[7] Those were the words of Mary, Queen of Scots. I think she really meant them. Mary, Queen of Scots, and **John Knox** were bitter enemies. Like so many, they violently disagreed over religion. Mary, the queen of Scotland, was Catholic. John Knox, a reformer, was a firm Protestant. To cloud

When she was 16 years old, Mary, Queen of Scots, married Francis at the famous Gothic cathedral of Notre-Dame in Paris, France.

king was in love with a woman 20 years his elder. This older woman was Diana and she was always by his side. Catherine tried her best to be a good wife despite the humiliation of having Diana around the court. Catherine provided the king with as many as 10 children. One of her sons was Francis, the dauphin who was promised in marriage to Mary, Queen of Scots.

You would think that Catherine de' Medici would be pleased to have her son engaged to a young queen. But Catherine wasn't the least bit pleased with this arrangement. For one, Mary, through her mother, was of the Guise family. The Guise family was a huge threat to the French royal throne. Second, Francis, the young dauphin, was a weakly boy. Catherine feared that her nation would actually suffer under Francis if he ever were to become king. She had more confidence in her other sons.

Nonetheless, when Mary turned 16, she and Francis were married as promised. The grand wedding took place in the cathedral of Notre-Dame in 1558. Mary loved every detail of it. She loved Francis, too. Theirs was a genuine love that started as a friendship in childhood.

The young couple would be forced to grow up fast, though, because not long after their wedding, tragedy struck the royal family. Henry II, the king of France, died quite unexpectedly from an accident. His death immediately made Francis the new king of France. His title became **Francis II**. Through marriage, Mary, his young bride, became the new queen of France! Some considered Mary also to be the queen of England because her grandmother was the sister of Henry VIII! (We will come back to that fact later.) Almost everyone was excited to see the newlyweds advance to the status of king and queen. That is, except for Catherine de' Medici. She was usurped by Mary, who now outranked her as queen! This reshuffling of status was an awkward strain between the two women who were never close to begin with.

But Mary soon had a much bigger problem than that. Just two years into their reign, her husband Francis died of a simple ear infection. It might have been a tumor that actually killed him. He was only 18 years old. Nonetheless, his death made Mary a very young widow. It also caused her to lose her position as the queen of France. Catherine de' Medici gladly stepped in as regent to the throne of France until one of her other sons was old enough to rule.

Some thought that Mary should remarry one of Francis's brothers to retain her position as queen. But Catherine would never allow that to happen. It left Mary in a strange predicament under the heavy hand of the mother-in-law who despised her. In the same year, Mary received news that *her* mother, Mary of Guise, had died in Scotland. It would appear that her best option was to return to Scotland, where she was still the rightful queen. She only hoped to be well received there. As Mary's ship pulled away from France, she whispered, "Farewell dear France, I believe never to see you again."[1] Mary was right. She never would see France again.

## *Mary Assumes the Scottish Throne*

By ship, it was a six-day journey from France to Scotland. Mary landed on the shores of her homeland at the city of **Leith** (Leeth) on August 19, **1561**. Being nearly 6 feet tall with brownish hair and dark eyes, Mary was an elegant-looking queen. She was well known for her fair, lovely skin and long, slender hands. But on the day Mary landed in Scotland, the weather was dreary and the sky drizzled rain. John Knox believed the bad weather was a sign of rough times to come. He suspected that Mary would attempt to return Scotland to the Catholic faith.

Knox and many others were surprised that Mary did *not* arrive with any such plans on her mind. Mary was young, fun loving, and frivolous. She preferred the outdoors and golf to talking about religion. In matters of faith, all she requested was the right to celebrate Mass in her private chapel. She was granted that right and left the matter alone.

Mary spent her first years in Scotland traveling from one city to the next visiting with her new people. It would appear that all was well in her kingdom. But, of course, that wasn't really the case. All kings and queens have troubles to deal with and Mary was no exception. Her first problem was that the son of Philip II wanted her hand in marriage. His name was **Don Carlos**. When word of that got out, John Knox threw a fit. He and many others did *not* want their queen married to a Catholic Spaniard. John Knox met with Mary to share his strong opinions on the matter. In defense, she accused Knox of treason! However, he was never convicted. This was the first of many run-ins between them. And as it turned out, Mary did NOT marry Don Carlos, but it was her choice and not the choice of John Knox.

Mary's next problem was with the man she *did* choose to marry in 1565. He was **Henry Stuart**, her cousin. He was also known as Lord Darnley. (I will call him Darnley to avoid confusing him with other Henry's.) Darnley turned out to be a pitiful husband. He was a poor leader and unfaithful in his marriage. Mary grew to despise him and hardened her heart against him.

Out of despair, Mary made another poor choice. She grew very close to an Italian musician named **David Riccio**. He was her private secretary. It has never been proven that the two were more than friends, but they spent entirely too much time together. One night, while Riccio was dining alone with the queen, Lord Darnley and his associates burst into the queen's chambers. They dragged Riccio from the table and killed him right in front of Mary! She was six months pregnant with Darnley's child at the time and might very well have been innocent of any misconduct. Regardless, David Riccio was dead and Mary was bewildered.

To escape any wrath against her, Mary fled for safety. Things quieted down for awhile and she gave birth to her son. He was named **James**. (Incidentally, he would later be the same James who authorized the "King James" version of the Bible.)

Lord Darnley continued to disappoint Mary as a husband, but for self-preservation, she kept her feelings hidden. Well, sort of. A suspicious-looking series of events took place that would haunt the rest of Mary's life. It seems that Lord Darnley fell extremely ill and was moved to a special house in order to recover. Mary visited her husband every night and read out loud by his side. One night she paid Darnley a visit as usual and then left to join the wedding party of one of her attendants. It would be the last time she ever saw Lord Darnley.

At two o'clock in the morning, a large stash of gunpowder exploded at Darnley's dwelling! He was found dead in the courtyard, naked and strangled! Oh, what a scandal the incident proved to be! Though Darnley's death was never traced directly to Mary, many suspected she was involved. She looked particularly guilty when only three months later, she married again.

Mary's third marriage was to the **earl of Bothwell**. Most believe *he* was responsible for the death of Lord Darnley. Some suspect that Bothwell abducted Mary and coerced her into the whole thing. Regardless, the two were wed. This poor choice by Mary, if indeed it was her choice, would be one of her greatest mistakes. Unlike Henry VIII, who would appear to "get away with murder," Mary would not escape suspicion in this murder.

## *Mary Deposed*

In 1567, Mary was forced to abdicate the throne to James, her young son. That means she was fired! Her husband, the earl of Bothwell, was arrested for conspiracy in the murder of Lord Darnley. Found guilty, he was sentenced to prison and chained to a pole half his height. He spent 10 years in that crouched position in the pit of a dark Danish dungeon! The Scottish imprisoned Mary at **Loch Leven Castle**. She was only 24 years old. Her son James was a 1-year-old toddler. You can only imagine Mary's anger, despair, and humiliation. She claimed she was completely innocent of the death of Lord Darnley. To this day, her involvement remains a deep mystery.

Pictured here is a view from Loch Leven. Though the castle setting was lovely, Mary, Queen of Scots, tried more than once to escape from her prison home there.

Mary tried to escape from Loch Leven dressed in the clothes of a washerwoman. But a guard recognized Mary's long, lovely hands, and she was returned to her dreadful captivity. In 1568, Mary tried again to escape her prison home, this time with the help of friends. Her plan succeeded, but you won't believe where she fled for help. If you think about it, where *does* a queen run? In this case, Mary turned to Elizabeth I, her cousin and the queen of England. Though the two had never met, Mary thought Elizabeth was her best chance to regain her life and her throne.

But by now you know how fickle and capricious Elizabeth was. Let's look back at their remote relationship. When Mary first sailed for Scotland in 1561, she had asked Elizabeth for permission to pass through England on the way. Elizabeth said no. Then she said yes. But the answer came too late and Mary had already set sail. For years, Mary made efforts to try to meet Elizabeth. They were related. Do you remember how? Mary's grandmother was the sister of Henry VIII, who was the father of Elizabeth. Though distant, the women were cousins.

For years Mary hoped to establish some connection with Elizabeth I. But the hope was not felt both ways. Elizabeth failed to see the benefit of becoming "friendly" with her cousin. There were many who believed that Mary had more right to the throne of England than Elizabeth did! Why? As you know, Elizabeth's mother was Anne Boleyn. Supporters of Catherine of Aragon always believed that Henry's marriage to Anne was not legitimate. If that were the case, it made Elizabeth an "illegitimate" child and disqualified her as queen. Besides that, Mary was Catholic and Elizabeth was Protestant. The pope, and many other Catholics, wished for Mary, Queen of Scots, to have the throne of England instead of Elizabeth.

With all those issues between them, Mary really didn't stand a chance of winning Elizabeth's favor. In 1568, a pitiful trial was held in England to try to get to the bottom of Lord Darnley's murder. In that trial, Mary was refused a lawyer and had her legal papers taken away. Some believe that letters she had sent to Bothwell were "forged" (meaning faked) to make her look guilty. The evidence was inconclusive but convincing enough to keep Mary a prisoner.

Mary would pay a great price for her supposed crime. Elizabeth, who was never in a rush to decide on anything, kept Mary a prisoner for years. In fact, she remained captive for 19 years, being moved from one English castle to another. As time dragged on, Mary grew more and more ill. She lost her health, her hair, her youth, and her beauty. But Mary never quite lost her hope for freedom.

Over the years, supporters of Mary schemed marriages and rescues to try to set her free. All the while, her enemies plotted ways to prove her guilty of treason. But efforts failed on both sides. The years marched on and Mary grew older and weaker. A final plot to free Mary appears to have been a farce and a setup. Mary was framed for treason against Elizabeth I! Guilty or not guilty, it would cost her her life.

Under the advice of her counselors, Elizabeth I was faced with the agonizing duty of signing the death warrant for Mary, Queen of Scots. Though the two women had still never met, Elizabeth openly wept over the matter. I suppose it was to Mary's detriment that they had never spoken face-to-face because although Elizabeth was torn over the issue, she ultimately followed her head over her heart. To protect her throne and her kingdom, she signed the dreadful papers, and Mary was sentenced to death after 19 years of captivity.

The night before her execution, Mary settled her will and sent letters to loved ones. Her attendants wept as they tried to prepare her for the next day. By this time, Mary was 44 years old. Her health was poor, and she had suffered a horribly long time in prison. Perhaps death came as a welcome relief.

**Note to Teacher:** *Sensitive students will want to skip the next paragraph. The details of Mary's execution are heartfelt and interesting, but may be disturbing to some.*

On February 8, 1587, Mary was escorted to the chopping block wearing a long black gown with a red petticoat and a white veil. As was custom, Mary forgave the executioner and handed her last belongings to her loyal maids. Keeping great composure, her eyes were covered and she stooped to her death. As if she had not suffered enough, the executioner did a poor job of putting her to death. The first blow hit Mary in the back. She whispered, "Sweet Jesus." The second blow was as incomplete as the first. The executioner had to swing a third time to finish his gruesome task. Between 9:00 and 10:00 in the morning, the ordeal was finally over. When the executioner lifted her head, it tumbled to the ground, as he had grasped only her wig.

(**Resume reading.**)

Much to the shock of the crowd, just after Mary was executed, her dress began to rustle about! What could it be? It was Mary's little dog that had apparently been hiding beneath her long gown. The small terrier crawled out from under the dress, but was said never to eat again after the death of his mistress. Legend says that purple thistles grew where Mary wept that day. They are called "Mary's Tears." The prickly flower grows abundantly in Scotland and is, in fact, a national emblem.

Legend says that purple thistles grew where Mary's tears fell on her day of execution. The thorny flower is the national emblem of Scotland.

There is a lot we know about Mary, Queen of Scots, but there is a lot we don't know. I believe it is the unknown that lures people into her sad story. Did she plot the death of Lord Darnley? Did she scheme to overthrow Queen Elizabeth? Did she deserve the punishment she received? We may never know, but I suspect the mystery will remain a fascinating one.

## Lesson 41 — 1562

# *Jeanne d'Albret*

I am unusually fascinated with our main character today. Her name is **Jeanne d'Albret** (dahl BRAY). She was both the **queen of Navarre** and **the countess of Béarn**. (Navarre and Béarn were small kingdoms formerly situated just between France and Spain.) I think I'm fascinated with Jeanne d'Albret because of her courage and conviction. She was a strong Christian woman who brought reform to her tiny kingdoms in the midst of war, illness, separation, and betrayal. I find Jeanne d'Albret to be a truly remarkable woman, but strange to me is that very few history books feature her at all! I'm honored to include her in mine.

Jeanne's mother was Margaret of Navarre. I've already introduced you to her. She was one of the well-educated Renaissance women discussed in Lesson 29. You may remember that Margaret was a people lover who protected Protestants and Catholics alike. You'll find out that Jeanne was a lot like her mother but even more courageous. Because of all she faced, she needed to be!

You may or may not remember, but Margaret of Navarre was also the sister of Francis I, the king of France. As king, he insisted that Jeanne, his young niece, leave her mother in Navarre and live with him in Paris. He thought she would receive a stronger Catholic education in France. He also thought it would keep young Jeanne away from Philip II of Spain. Philip was always conniving to marry *someone* to further his kingdom! Francis wasn't interested in giving his niece away to Spain.

Though it was heartache for Margaret, she sent Jeanne to Paris when she was about 9. With Jeanne in Paris, Francis I continued to meddle in her life. When she was only 12, Francis demanded that she marry the German duke of Cleves. The marriage was in France's best interests, not in Jeanne's. It was in that situation that Jeanne's strong character first began to show itself. She fought against the arranged marriage with everything in her. No one would listen to her pleading so, on her wedding day, she had to be physically carried to the altar. Some say she was dragged. As soon as the ceremony was over, Jeanne ran away! She went back to her parents in Navarre where she was welcomed and spoiled. She took care of that marriage! In a few years, it was annulled.

Back under the care of her mother, Jeanne learned more about the Protestant faith. Though her mother never claimed to be Protestant, she surrounded herself with Protestant teachings. She befriended John Calvin and invited his pupils to Navarre. She also surrounded Jeanne with Protestant tutors who taught her the Bible. It would shape the rest of her life.

Though small in stature, Jeanne had matured by age 20. She was ready then to seriously consider marriage. Though *somewhat* arranged, Jeanne was happy to walk down the aisle for this wedding. No one had to drag her! But her happiness was not to last more than a few years. Her husband, **Anthony of Bourbon**, would disappoint her in many ways. He was wishy-washy in matters of religion as well as marriage. He wasn't loyal to one faith *or* to his wife.

If you recall, Mary, Queen of Scots, was once in the same predicament. She, too, had married a disappointing husband. But her actions and those of Jeanne d'Albret would be very different. Mary, Queen of Scots, turned to other men when her heart was broken. Jeanne turned to the Lord. For the rest of her life, He would be her source of strength.

## *Jeanne Becomes Queen*

In 1555, Jeanne d'Albret's father died. It made her the official queen of Navarre. She was 27. By marriage, her husband Anthony became the king of Navarre. But Jeanne didn't have much confidence in his leadership. She ruled Navarre much on her own, which seemed to be fine with him. She gave birth to five children, though only two survived. They were Catherine and Henry. (I know, these names are all the same and hard to keep straight!) Jeanne's job wasn't an easy one. It was especially difficult with Spain and France threatening her tiny kingdoms on both sides.

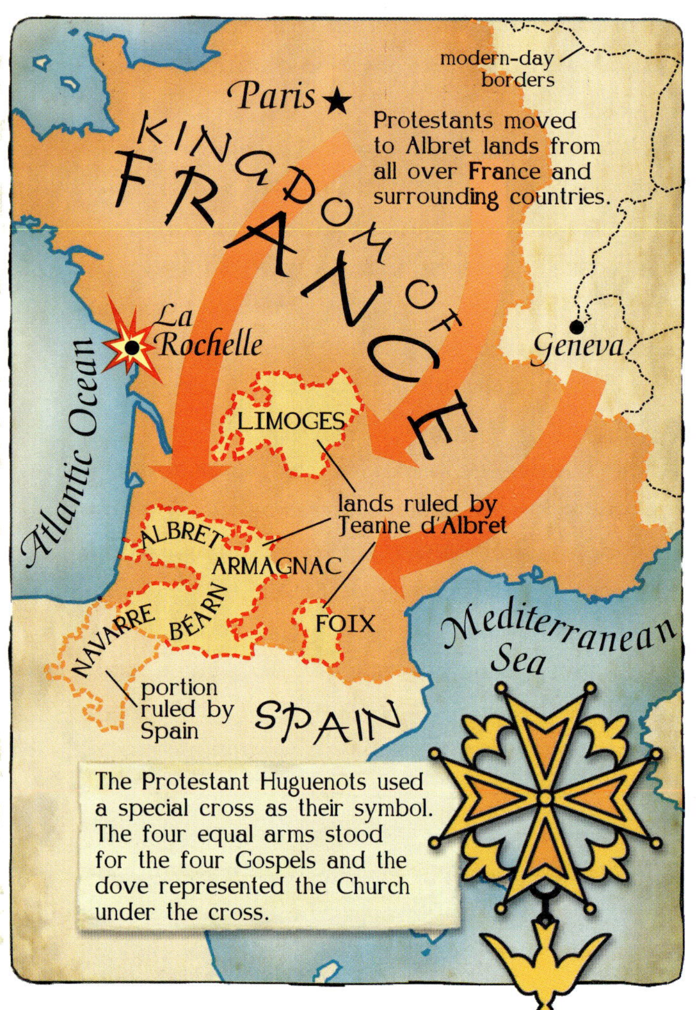


Why were Spain and France "threatening" her kingdoms? Well, as mentioned before, the small states of Navarre and Béarn sat right at the border between Spain and France. Both of the larger countries were eager to swallow up Navarre and Béarn and make them their own. But besides that, Navarre and Béarn had grown to be a safe refuge for Protestants. Jeanne, like her mother, extended them freedom. Protestants flooded in from all across Europe. The Huguenots poured in from France; the Reformed came from the Netherlands; and zealous Calvinists moved there from Geneva. For these reasons, both Spain and France kept a watchful eye on Jeanne d'Albret. They feared the spread of Protestantism into their own Catholic territories. Jeanne faced a great challenge in keeping her kingdoms safe.

But as I said earlier, Jeanne was a rather courageous woman. Despite her small frame, she stood tall and bold. In 1560, she publicly declared herself a follower of the Protestant faith. Her profession of faith was blasphemous to those in Rome who heard of it. Jeanne now had France, Spain, *and* Rome breathing down her neck. She did her best to stand up against them in defense of her strong beliefs.

## *Betrayal and Illness*

Over the years, Jeanne and her husband, Anthony, visited Paris many times. It was important for them to keep good relations with their "neighbor." Jeanne had spent three of her growing-up years there under Francis I. Through her father, Jeanne had some connection to the throne of France — should it ever be vacant. As you know, for a time Catherine de' Medici served as regent in France while waiting for her son to grow up and serve as king. With her own political interests, Catherine wasn't easy to get along with. Her policies toward Protestants were always changing. Jeanne had to tread carefully around Catherine, who was both friend and foe.

While Jeanne and Anthony were visiting Paris in **1562**, the religious winds shifted again. For political reasons, Catherine de' Medici, who had once allowed Protestants freedom, swung firmly to the Catholic cause. Anthony, Jeanne's husband, also took sides with the Catholic Church. He was a brilliant general and joined Catholic forces to fight for France. Jeanne must have felt completely betrayed! Her own husband, who once strongly shared in her *Protestant* beliefs, was going to war for the *Catholics*.

To worsen matters, Anthony asked Jeanne for a divorce. If that weren't difficult enough, Anthony forced her to go home to Béarn and leave 9-year-old Henry behind in Paris where he could be tutored by Catholics. Jeanne's family crumbled. Some say young Henry was treated more like a hostage in Paris than a prince. He was there against his will.

It was hard for Jeanne to accept Anthony's change of heart toward her and her faith. But it was harder still to leave her son in Paris. Jeanne begged young Henry to never forget his Protestant upbringing. (You'll learn in the next lesson how he fared in keeping his mother's wishes.)

To complicate this sad situation, Jeanne was diagnosed with tuberculosis. As mentioned, she was small and frail to begin with. The disease weakened her so much that doctors felt she might not survive the trip from Paris to Béarn. They had no idea how strong she really was.

Ironically, it was Jeanne's husband, Anthony, who would die first. Just a year after he went to war for the Catholic cause, he was fatally wounded in battle. On his deathbed, his wishy-washy nature revealed itself again. In dying, he asked to be reinstated as a member of the *Protestant* church! It seems he never knew exactly where he stood on matters of faith.

As for Jeanne, she was left to rule Béarn completely alone. Despite fighting her disease, she did a remarkable job. Through the difficulties of running a small kingdom, her faith and courage soared. Let me tell you what she accomplished.

## *Reformation in the Kingdoms*

For about seven years, Jeanne studied ancient and modern laws, seeking ways to improve her kingdoms. The code of laws she drafted remained in effect until the 1800s! She leaned heavily on the Calvinists for direction in making Béarn a Protestant state and began the same in Navarre. In the transition, rather than confiscate or take Catholic property solely for herself, she divided it three ways. She gave one-third of the spoils to schools, one-third to the poor, and one-third to Protestants.

Though Jeanne d'Albret clearly set up Béarn to be Protestant, she abolished the persecution of those who weren't. Finally there would be a more civilized approach to religious differences. In the kingdom of Béarn, there were no arrests and no trials, and there was no Inquisition. Though Catholic worship was restricted, private opinions were respected. It was some progress toward religious freedom.

In the midst of all the changes, an interesting saga was going on behind the scenes. Remember Philip II of Spain who was always trying to marry his way into another country? He approached Jeanne to consider marrying his son. Do you think she was interested? Not at all! Marrying the upcoming king of Spain would have been a disaster. Her small kingdoms would have been completely swallowed up by Spain, and all she had done to make them Protestant would have been undone.

I find that Jeanne's reply to Philip testifies to her strong convictions. She said, "Although I am just a little Princess, God has given me the government of this country so I may rule it according to His Gospel and teach it His Laws. I rely on God, who is more powerful than the King of Spain."[2] It would appear that Philip struck out again!

Soon after that, the pope came knocking at Jeanne's door. Well, not literally. He sent a representative to meet her and persuade her to recognize his authority over Béarn. She didn't. Like so many others, Jeanne faced excommunication from the church in Rome. For standing against the pope, it was rumored that she would be kidnapped and placed before the Inquisition in Spain! It never happened, but the threat of it must have been terrifying.

In 1567, Jeanne made some peace with Catherine de' Medici and was finally allowed the return of her son from Paris. Henry was 14 by then. His presence in the court of Béarn probably brought Jeanne much comfort. Her situation was growing more intense by the day as war was drawing closer.

In 1568, a third civil war broke out in France between Catholics and Protestant Huguenots. This one was close to home and Jeanne could not avoid it. She and her son and daughter fled Béarn to the city of La Rochelle where Jeanne would continue to demonstrate great strength in times of peril.

Still battling tuberculosis, Jeanne gave aid to Protestant troops for three years from La Rochelle. She offered military strategy and funding to troops — even to the point of trading her crown jewels for a loan. She wrote letters and manifestos for help; she oversaw the influx of thousands of Huguenot refugees; and she personally held the hand of a soldier during an amputation. On top of that, she helped start a Protestant college by paying the salaries of the professors. Her contribution was amazing. Though frail, Jeanne was unwavering in protecting the rights of Protestants and furthering the teaching of the Bible.

Peace negotiations raged on between the Huguenots and the French Catholics. At one point, the Huguenots were instructed to lay down their arms to make peace. Jeanne replied, "We have come to the determination to die, all of us, rather than to abandon our God, and our religion, which we cannot maintain unless permitted to worship publicly, any more than a human body can live without meat and drink."[3]

*". . . we cannot maintain unless permitted to worship publicly, any more than a human body can live without meat and drink."*

*–Jeanne d'Albret*

For a time, the war was suspended and troops took a break. In August of 1570, the **Peace of Saint-Germain** was signed by Charles IX, who was old enough by then to serve as the king of France. The Peace of Saint-Germain actually extended a great deal of freedom to

Jeanne d'Albret agreed to the arranged marriage of her son, Henry of Navarre, to Marguerite, the daughter of Catherine de' Medici.

Huguenots in France. With the war subsided, by 1571, Jeanne was safe in returning to Béarn. She worked even harder there at securing true reform for her kingdom.

In the meantime, Catherine de' Medici was keeping a close eye on every move that Jeanne made. Somewhere along the way, she concluded that a royal marriage would help smooth relations between France and Béarn. The marriage on her mind was not one for Jeanne. It was Jeanne's son, Henry of Navarre, that Catherine was interested in. She wanted to see him marry her youngest daughter, Marguerite.

It's curious to me that Jeanne agreed to the plan. Catherine's daughter was obviously Catholic. Henry was obviously Protestant. Their marriage was sure to be a risk for either side of the religious war. I think each queen assumed that her child was the stronger and would sway the other to his or her cause. I don't know the outcome Jeanne envisioned with this marriage.

But Jeanne would never see it take place. Just two months before the wedding, her disease finally caught up with her. For four days she was bedridden with her illness. Her attendants sat by her side, reading her favorite Bible passages out loud. Among many verses, they read Psalm 31 and John 14–18. Excerpts from Psalm 31 include these verses:

> Have mercy on me, O Lord, for I am in trouble;
> My eye wastes away with grief,
> Yes, my soul and my body!
> For my life is spent with grief,
> And my years with sighing; . . .
>
> But as for me, I trust in You, O Lord;
> I say, "You are my God."
> My times are in Your hand; . . .
>
> Blessed be the Lord,
> For He has shown me His marvelous
> kindness in a strong city!
>
> –from Psalm 31:9–10; 14–15; 21

After many perilous years, Jeanne died at age 44. Some suspect she was poisoned, but it was probably tuberculosis that killed her. While Rome and Spain were relieved at her passing, the Huguenots wept in great sorrow. Jeanne d'Albret had been their strongest leader.

It may sound tactless, but it may have been best that Jeanne died when she did. For by dying, she was spared inevitable heartache of a different kind. Had she lived just a few months longer, she would have seen the religious winds shift again in France. And this time, it would lead to a massacre so brutal and so tragic, it's hard to put into words. But I will seek to find those words for our next lesson in which we will pick up the life of Catherine de' Medici.

# St. Bartholomew's Day Massacre

I prepared you ahead of time that this lesson would be hard to put into words. As the title would indicate, it involves a massacre. According to Webster's dictionary, a massacre is "the act or an instance of killing a number of usually helpless or unresisting human beings under circumstances of atrocity or cruelty."[4] The word *massacre* couldn't be more fitting for what happened to the Huguenots starting on **St. Bartholomew's Day** in **1572**. Before I get to the gory details, let me review what was going on in France beforehand.

The last we looked at France, Catherine de' Medici was planning a wedding. She had arranged a royal wedding between Marguerite, her youngest daughter, and Henry of Navarre, the son of Jeanne d'Albret. Recall that while wedding plans were being made, Jeanne d'Albret took a sudden turn for the worse and died — probably from tuberculosis — before the wedding ever took place. She also died before the massacre that we're going to learn about. It was probably for the better.

It was Jeanne's wish that her son, Henry of Navarre, would carry on her fight for Protestants and Huguenots. (As a reminder, Huguenots are "French Protestants.") Henry carried a huge load on his shoulders. He was marrying a Catholic girl and making Catherine de' Medici his mother-in-law. Could he keep his beliefs under those circumstances? Would he? You'll soon find out.

As you know, between the years 1562 and 1598, France was viciously torn by bloody warfare between Protestants and Catholics. That may be hard to grasp in present times. But the Reformation was still "fresh." Both sides in the conflict believed they were defending the true faith. They believed it to the point of killing each other through three gruesome religious wars, a sad but true part of the history of Christendom. In just a 10-year span in France, the war between the faiths included 18 attacks on Huguenots, 5 attacks on Catholics, and at least 30 assassinations.

In Paris, France, a massacre against Huguenots started on August 24, 1572, coinciding with the feast day of St. Bartholomew.

In the 1530s, Protestants like John Calvin fled France because of the brutal persecution. But others stayed and Protestantism grew. As early as 1559, the French Protestant Church had been established. Seventy-two Protestant churches were set up in and around Paris. An untold number met in hiding to worship in the wilderness. Most pastors of these flocks were graduates of Calvin's academy in Geneva. Due to the severity of the religious wars, their life expectancy was only about six weeks!

In and out from behind the scenes, the French royal family was a part of it all. In 1570, Charles IX signed the Peace of Saint-Germain, granting Huguenots control over four towns in France. The moody personality of the royal family certainly had something to do with the ever-changing status of religion in France.

## *Catherine de' Medici*

I've already given you some background on Catherine de' Medici, the figurehead of this French family. But she is so important to this story that I'm going tell you a little more about her. As you know by her name, Catherine was "a Medici." You should have some idea what that means. Catherine was descended from the rich Italian family of Cosimo and Lorenzo de' Medici. When it came to fine taste and loving the arts, she was just like them.

Catherine had unquestionable flair in a wide range of interests. Like Elizabeth I, she was greatly concerned with image and appearances. She dressed lavishly and made it fashionable in France to wear tight-fitting corsets. Though painful, it gave women tiny waistlines and straight posture. Catherine was a firm believer in table manners and loved elaborate ceremonies. She introduced ballet dancing, and the grace that comes with it, to France. Like her ancestors, she appreciated fine architecture and saw to the raising of many fine structures. Because she was frequently homesick for Italy, Catherine de' Medici hired cooks and chefs from her homeland to bring their culinary skills to France. All these things would change the nation. France is still known for its taste in fine food and high fashion.

So, there is that side of Catherine to know. By her wide interests in the arts, she was a true "woman of the Renaissance." Another side of her to know is that she was not particularly religious. Like the Medicis before her, she was a humanist. She was far more interested in the accomplishments of her family than in the advancement of *any* faith. For that reason, she wore well the image of a "woman of the Renaissance." She grew up with the traditions of the Roman Church but was also surrounded by Protestants. For years she avoided following either group too closely. Differences in doctrine and theology never appeared to interest her much.

What did interest Catherine was power. After her husband died, she oversaw three of her sons as kings of France. The first was Francis II, who married Mary, Queen of Scots, and died rather young. The second was Charles IX, who was so young upon becoming king that Catherine filled in for him as regent. (The third son who became king is not relevant to us now, but Catherine *tried* to marry him to Elizabeth I! Of course, she had no luck there.) All along the way, Catherine was known for being power hungry. It was rumored that she used palace trapdoors and secret stashes of poison for doing away with her enemies.

Some would say that Catherine de' Medici had "Machiavellian" tendencies. I hope you remember what that means. Machiavelli wrote in *The Prince* that the use of evil, ruthless politics was permissible (meaning okay) if it prospered the country. Evidently, Catherine believed the same. She was always looking for ways to secure the throne. Remember that when I get to the part about the massacre.

## *Weddings, Plots, and Massacres*

Let's go now to the royal wedding that Catherine was planning in 1572 between her daughter Marguerite and Henry of Navarre. Outwardly, it would appear to be a peaceful union, as weddings usually are. On the day of the ceremony, all were smiling and looking quite lovely. In attendance were Catholics and Protestants, all hoping to make it through the day without a brawl. Inwardly, all were nervous, including the bride and groom. Like statues carved of ice, the two stood still through the ceremony, hardly looking at one another! Their marriage could easily have triggered yet another religious war and everyone there knew it.

As feared, the peace of the union between Protestants and Catholics didn't last even a month. Within weeks, there was a serious problem. It seems that a Jesuit priest was particularly fearful of Henry's strong Protestant upbringing. He feared that Henry of Navarre would one day be king and persecute Catholics. This Jesuit priest began to counsel Catherine de' Medici to take action. He meant serious action.

Catherine, as you know, wasn't so concerned about the faith of France. But she was concerned with losing royal power. So, under the guidance of the Jesuit priest, she plotted the murder of a Huguenot admiral named **Coligny** (Caw li NYAY; the "g" is silent). Coligny was well liked and respected, particularly by Charles IX. Catherine dreaded the influence he might have on her son and proceeded to plan Coligny's death on August 22.

But something went wrong on August 22, and the assassination plot failed. It left the royal family in an embarrassing situation with guilt written all over Catherine. Supposedly, Charles IX responded to his mother in jest saying, "If you're going to kill Coligny, why don't you kill all the Huguenots in France, so that there will be no one left to hate me?"[5] His words were taken far too seriously.

In haste and panic, Catherine responded by reordering the execution of Coligny — and of *all* the Huguenot leaders in Paris! Many of these leaders had just recently attended the royal wedding. The killing started at four o'clock in the morning of August 24, 1572. It coincided with St. Bartholomew's Day, which was a feast day of the Catholic Church. Thus, the event I'm about to describe has been remembered by that name.

The first man killed was Coligny, murdered while on his knees in prayer. Then, other Huguenot leaders were led out into the city and shot one by one. Charles IX watched in horror as what he had implied to his mother in jest was coming true. It's hard to say what happened after that, but it was no less than a true massacre. Once a few Huguenots were killed by the army, members of the lower class joined in the violence. Apparently, many of the lower class resented the more successful Huguenot businessmen. They went after them with a vengeance. Homes of Protestants were marked with white crosses and the residents slain. Men, women, and children were torn from their homes and slaughtered. In the melee, a bookmaker was burned to death along with his seven children. His own books were used for the fire.

The riot spread from Paris to the provinces. The massacre went on for days and weeks. In the city of Lyon, Huguenots were forced into a monastery and transferred to a prison. The prison was attacked by mobs and the Huguenots killed. Anywhere from 30,000 to 100,000 people were butchered. Rivers were clogged with the dead. Survivors were enslaved. It was pure bedlam and madness.

Even Catherine de' Medici was shocked and appalled. What started as the botched-up murder of just one man had turned into a gargantuan bloodbath. To try to cover up the mess, she desperately had Charles issue a statement that the assassination of Coligny was necessary because of his involvement in a conspiracy — not because he was a Huguenot. But it was too late. The damage was done. For years she would try to make up for the massacre through ploys and policies, but none of her efforts were lasting. Charles would suffer from nightmares of the event. In less than two years he died at the age of 24, still tormented by memories of the tragedy.

Old tombstones in Lyon, France, mark the graves of thousands who were buried after the St. Bartholomew's Day Massacre.

France was nearly ruined after the St. Bartholomew's Day Massacre. For five more years, civil war raged on. After Charles IX died, his brother Henry III became king. In January of 1589, Catherine de' Medici died. Not long after her death, Henry III was assassinated. Then lo and behold, guess who ascended the throne of France? It was Henry of Navarre, the son of Jeanne d'Albret. As the husband of Marguerite, his turn to rule France finally came in 1589. He was crowned **Henry IV**. But by then, France was a mess. What was he to do to clean up the disaster he inherited?

It might surprise you. Though Henry's mother, Jeanne d'Albret, had begged him to never leave the Protestant faith — he did. To make peace for France, Henry of Navarre, now Henry IV, declared himself Roman Catholic. He said, "Paris is well worth a Mass," meaning that the city was worth his change of faith.[6] To try to keep peace with Huguenots Henry issued the **Edict of Nantes** (Nantz) in 1598. It gave some religious freedom but not enough to keep Huguenots safe in their homeland.

In time, thousands of Huguenots spread to other parts of Europe and finally to the shores of North America. All were seeking freedom of worship. After studying the Reformation, I think you will never see the settling of America quite the same again. You see, many of America's forefathers were descendants of the Huguenots. Do you think they ever forgot what had happened in France? I don't think so. It would be difficult to forget.

"Paris is well worth a Mass."
–Henry of Navarre

# Semester II

## The Growth of Nations

### Quarter 3

### The Age of Reason 1572 – 1632



### Quarter 4

### The Age of Resolve 1632 – 1707

*Historically, the Pillars of Hercules at the Strait of Gibraltar were symbolic of mythology and the ancient world. Francis Bacon updated the symbol with this sketch of a ship sailing through the Pillars of Hercules and a motto stating "Many will pass through, and knowledge will be increased." Francis Bacon was referring to the Age of Reason and the era of discovery that were replacing the Renaissance.*

# *The Age of Reason*
## *1572–1632*

Congratulations! You've made it halfway through *The Mystery of History*, Volume III, and completed one semester. By now, you've had quite a sampling of *The Renaissance and Reformation.*

In this second semester, titled the *Growth of Nations*, we will begin to see a few significant countries take shape. France will be firmly and "extravagantly" ruled by *Louis XIV*. The *Netherlands* will emerge united as they struggle out from under the heavy hand of Spain. And then Spain itself will withdraw to heal from the defeat of their *Armada*. (Elizabeth I had something to do with that.) Other rising nations this semester will include *Japan, Russia, England, Australia,* and the *colonies of North America.*

Of course, the United States of America won't take shape until later in history, but through the Pilgrims and other settlers, the seeds of democracy and freedom will begin to take root. After all our study on the bloodshed of the Reformation, I think you'll find the idea of religious freedom to be particularly meaningful.

As for this quarter, I'm borrowing the title "The Age of Reason" to describe 1572–1632. (I say I'm "borrowing" this term because others coined it a long time ago.) There were two things that helped push man toward "reason" as he moved into the 1600s. For one, the discovery of the New World led men and women to wonder if the ancient Greeks and Romans were as smart as Europeans thought they were! You know, the Renaissance was largely based on the rebirth of Greek and Roman thought. But if the New World was really new, then what else might the ancient thinkers have missed? What else was there to learn and to discover by reason? The ideas of the Renaissance would fade as scholars of the seventeenth century would no longer look to the past for answers.

A second thing to push man toward reason had to do with the problems found in religion. Europeans had certainly grown weary of all the wars and fighting that went on between Protestants and Catholics. And so, some men and women searched beyond religion for answers. *Francis Bacon* was one scientist of this time period who encouraged others to consider the answers found in science and reason. He himself believed in God, as did *Galileo* and *René Descartes*, other great minds we will study this quarter. But these thinkers would advance scientific methods to promote understanding. This new wave of thinking would usher in an era labeled "The Age of Reason."

If you think about it, in some ways man has never left the Age of Reason. He is always looking for ways to "rationally" understand life and the mysteries it contains. I am so thankful that we have science to explain many, many things about our material world. But for those things that cannot be explained, I'm so grateful the Lord provided us with His Word to give us guidance and inspiration. I hope you enjoy this quarter.

# WEEK 15

## Lesson 43 1572

# *Tycho Brahe and Johannes Kepler: Stargazers of the Renaissance*

When I was a child, I wanted to grow up to be an astronaut. It's true. I was a little girl when the first man walked on the moon. I remember watching it with my family on black-and-white television in the living room. I don't think I realized how historic that first moonwalk was, but it must have burned something deep into my heart because in high school, I looked into joining the space program at NASA. Things didn't work out for me in that field, but I've always loved outer space and wished I could walk on the moon!

Knowing this about me, you'll better understand why I like today's lesson. Our two main characters, **Tycho Brahe** (TIE koh *or* TEE koh Brah) and **Johannes** (YO hahn) **Kepler**, were space lovers, too. These men dedicated their lives to studying the moon, the stars, and the planets. Had there been a NASA program back then, I imagine they, too, would have looked into joining.

### *Tycho Brahe*

First we will look at the life of Tycho Brahe. He was Danish, which means he was from Denmark. (Denmark juts into the North Sea near Germany and almost touches Sweden.) Tycho invested many years into his education, attending five universities. He first knew he was interested in astronomy when, in 1560, he observed a solar eclipse (that's when the moon passes in front of the sun and eerily blocks its light). The shadowy phenomenon would stir a curiosity in him that lasted the rest of his life.

In 1560, Tycho Brahe witnessed the phenomenon of a solar eclipse. It inspired a curiosity for astronomy in him that lasted his entire life.

While attending a university in Rostock, Germany, Tycho had an unfortunate accident. He entered a sword duel with a Danish nobleman and lost part of his nose in the event. Being a scientist at heart, Tycho came up with a solution to his disfigurement. He crafted a fake nose piece out of silver and gold. To make it look more lifelike, he dabbed it with face powder that he carried with him at all times in a small container. Tycho Brahe's metallic nose was one of his claims to fame.

Of far more significance, Tycho grew famous for being the first to accurately observe a **supernova**. To understand what that is, let me tell you a little bit about stars. Stars are not constant lights suspended in the sky. It is believed that stars have a life cycle where they form, they age, and they die. A supernova is a large star in the *final* stages of dying. (By large, I mean a star bigger than our sun.) Because it is dying, a supernova is an unstable mass of gas, dust, and other material. When it dies, it appears to explode, letting off as much light as a whole galaxy! This kind of violent explosion may last for days or weeks, but the light it emits can travel for years.

So when Tycho sighted a supernova on November 11, **1572**, he had quite an amazing observation on his hands. The star he saw was located in the constellation *Cassiopeia*. The discovery of it launched Tycho's career in astronomy. At a lecture in 1575, Tycho quoted **Ovid**, a Roman poet, and said, "*God has given mankind a face that looks upwards and has commanded us to stay at our feet and turn our eyes upwards to see the stars.*"[1] I think that's a beautiful way to view Creation.

To further his studies, Tycho appealed to the king of Denmark for help. The king agreed to sponsor Tycho in building an amazing observatory on the island of **Hven** (Ven *or* Veen ), a small island located in the channel between Denmark and Sweden. The observatory was extraordinary for the time period. It started as a small castle but grew to be a spectacular observatory sunk partially into the ground. It was surrounded by beautiful Renaissance gardens. The settlement included a paper mill and print shop. Many visited to marvel at Tycho's work. A map of Hven from the 1570s still exists to testify to the brilliance of Tycho's design.

For almost 20 years at his island observatory, Tycho watched the movement of the stars, the planets, and at least one comet. His comet observations were especially important because they broke the "rules" of astronomy that existed back then. Tycho realized that the comet came from outside the earth's atmosphere, which meant that the heavens were moving and not fixed in space. Night after night Tycho recorded his findings in great detail. In 1588, he published the second volume of a three-part series. The amazing part of his observations is that he made them without a telescope. All his work was done with the "naked eye." The precision of the instruments he used with his naked eye was exceptional. For this reason, some would call Tycho Brahe the most amazing astronomer that ever lived!

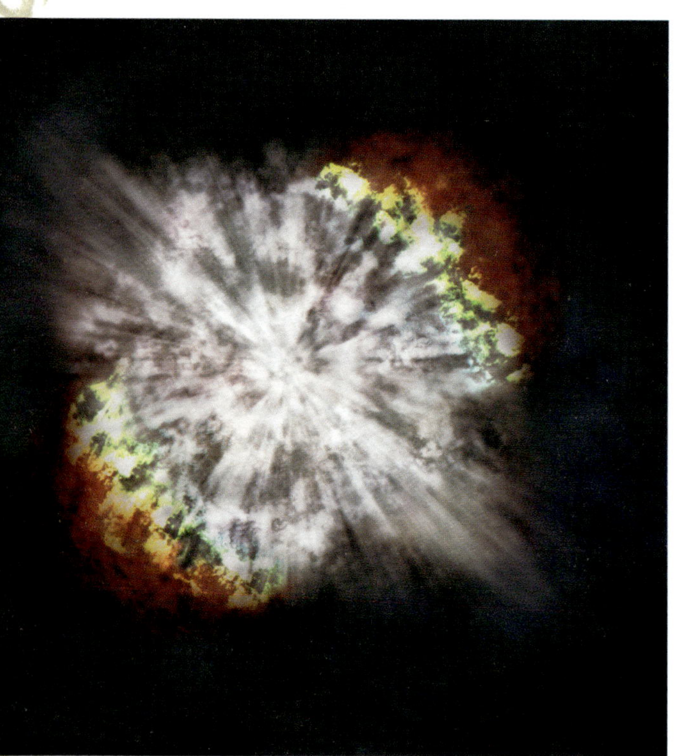

A supernova is the explosion and collapse of a massive star at the end of its life cycle.

As amazing as he was, Tycho never fully accepted the theories of Copernicus. Do you remember Nicolaus Copernicus? He theorized that the earth revolved around the sun. Tycho held on to the ancient idea that the earth was the center of the solar system.

But he modified it this way: Tycho thought that five other planets (Mercury, Venus, Mars, Jupiter, and Saturn) each revolved around the sun. And that along with the sun, these planets revolved around the earth as it stood still in the heavens! His theory was a mathematical nightmare that he was never able to solve.

After nearly 20 years on the island of Hven, Tycho was forced to move out. The king of Denmark died and was replaced by someone far less interested in Tycho's work. For a time, Tycho traveled and wrote his autobiography. Finally, in 1600, Tycho settled in Prague and was appointed the "Imperial Mathematician" by the Holy Roman Emperor. It was one of the highest honors of the land.

It was there in Prague that Tycho found the solution to his mathematical problems. He found Johannes Kepler. Actually, it was Kepler who found Tycho. And it was Kepler who solved the math problems. Let me tell you his story.

## *Johannes Kepler*

Johannes Kepler was a German astronomer and mathematician. He grew up poor, serving tables at an inn with his mother and grandparents. His father was killed in a war. Johannes was strong in his Christian faith and attended a Protestant university in Germany.

At this time in history, the ideas of Copernicus were talked about only in secret at the universities. Literally. Kepler's astronomy professor taught the ancient ideas of the solar system in his classroom. But at special seminars, he taught the theories of Copernicus to those he thought could handle it. Kepler was one of those who could. His understanding of mathematics was exceptional, though he made "A's" in everything *but* math! He probably wondered about too many things.

As delighted as Kepler was with the theories of Copernicus, he had questions. He once wrote Tycho Brahe for answers. By the nature of his questions, Tycho recognized that Kepler was a gifted mathematician, and this was just what he needed. So Tycho Brahe invited Johannes Kepler to Prague to serve as his assistant. Kepler accepted.

I wish I could write that the two scientists I put in the same lesson were great friends. But they really weren't. Tycho never fully trusted his young new assistant and withheld parts of his research from him. However, Tycho did turn over to Kepler his volumes of work on the planet Mars. These volumes proved to be a gold mine of information. As a better mathematician than an astronomer, Kepler kept his nose in the books rather than looking up at the stars. He deciphered Tycho's notes and formulated some interesting ideas.

Before I go on with Kepler's ideas, let me tell you the fate of Tycho Brahe. In 1601, only one year after Kepler joined him, Tycho Brahe died. He was only 54. For years it was believed that he died from bladder problems because he was too polite to excuse himself to go to the bathroom at a dinner party. A few years ago, however, it was proven differently. Hair samples taken from Tycho's corpse showed high levels of mercury in his system. Mercury is toxic!

Was Tycho poisoned with mercury? He was but probably not on purpose. Tycho had been known to experiment with making his own medicines out of mercury (not knowing it was harmful). Most likely he gave himself a good dose of mercury-based medicine to treat his bladder problem. Rather than help, the mercury probably made his situation worse, causing him to die a painful death.

After Tycho died, Johannes Kepler was chosen to replace him as the Imperial Mathematician. It was helpful to his career, which was taking off. Now, let's get back to Kepler.

## *The Three Laws of Kepler*

As a mathematician, Johannes Kepler struggled with making sense of all the ideas of Copernicus. His first problem was with the shape of orbits. Up until this time, it was believed that orbits were completely round like a circle. Kepler finally realized that planets revolve in oval-shaped orbits. He called them ellipses. This new fact became known as Kepler's "first law of planetary motion." But, for the record, had Johannes not had all the data that Tycho gave him about Mars, he could never have proved his first law! Tycho's paperwork on Mars was so massive that Johannes referred to his calculations kiddingly as "my war with Mars."[2]

A second law of planetary motion proved by Kepler says that as a planet revolves, it moves faster when it whips around the sun. It's more difficult to explain the science behind this law, but Kepler was right. The path that a planet takes around the sun "sweeps" out the same amount of space in a given time period. So when it is closer to the sun, it speeds up. Picture it like this: The sun is so hot that when a planet gets close to it, it speeds up to avoid getting burned!

After 17 more years of study, Kepler discovered a third law. Not all of you will understand it, but I'll write it out anyway. Kepler discovered that "the squares of the periods of the planets are proportional to the cubes of their semimajor axes."[3] Whether that makes sense to you or not, the bottom line is that the solar system is an incredible mathematical device! It surely attests to the greatness of the One who created it. And these planetary laws would lay the foundation for other scientists to build on, leading to even more understanding of the heavens. One of those scientists was Isaac Newton, whom we'll study later.

Johannes Kepler formulated planetary laws and used his understanding of the human eye to improve the telescope.

Kepler did more in his life than create these planetary laws. He worked on better understanding the lens of the human eye. He was first to grasp that an image is projected upside down on the retina of the eye. This information helped in the development of the telescope. Kepler used a basic telescope to see the satellites of Jupiter. (I wish Tycho Brahe had lived long enough to see that!)

In 1612, the Holy Roman Emperor was deposed and Johannes Kepler lost his position as the Imperial Mathematician. But it didn't stop his work. In 1613, Kepler worked on improving the calendar and was the one who realized that the date for the birth of Christ was off by five years. The new date put his birth at 4 B.C. Though it sounds strange to us that Jesus was born four years "before Christ," it was easier to make that adjustment than to change every date on the Julian calendar after Jesus was born. Kepler also worked on proving logarithms that no one else could and on developing calculus. When all was said and done, he had calculated the most accurate astronomical tables of the time.

Nonetheless, in between all of Kepler's publications and observations, he had a difficult personal life to contend with. In 1611, his 7-year-old son died. Kepler wrote to a friend that his son's death was especially painful because the curious boy reminded him so much of himself. A year later, his wife, whom he had loved greatly, died. Johannes remarried for practical reasons and had six more children, but three of them also died very young.

On a lighter note, Johannes's second wife was quick to learn how obsessed with science her new husband really was. At their wedding, Johannes was greatly distracted by a group of wine barrels. He observed the manner in which they were measured by a rod, which had something to do with Archimedes' theory of displacement. He would later write articles about the phenomenon, which is part of "infinitesimal" calculus today. It goes to show that even at his wedding, his brilliant mind could not turn off.

Brilliant or not, Johannes had other struggles. For a time, he was excommunicated by the Roman Catholic Church *and* was in disfavor with the Lutherans. He wasn't sure if he fully agreed with their doctrine. But his personal faith in God never wavered. He wrote of Him in all his works, pointing out God's marvelous creation of the heavens.

At the end of his life, Kepler had to grapple with the Thirty Years' War. Protestants in his region were persecuted, and he was forced to flee. For a time he had no salary and no position. He died a few years later without much reward for his brilliance.

On a closing note, both Tycho Brahe and Johannes Kepler have statues standing in Prague in memory of their fine work. And believe it or not, I discovered that Tycho Brahe has a fan club on the Internet. Apparently, Tycho has "fans" who want to remind the world that Johannes Kepler would never have been successful without the achievements of Tycho Brahe.

## Lesson 44 — 1577

# *Sir Francis Drake*

The English would call **Sir Francis Drake** a splendid *navigator*. The Spanish would call him a *pirate*. Why such differing views? I think it's a matter of perspective. In the name of England, Sir Francis Drake skillfully navigated a ship all the way around the world. But along the way, he stole vast amounts of treasure from Spanish ships laden with silver! Coincidentally, he was secretly commissioned to do so by Queen Elizabeth, who, as you know, had an ongoing rivalry with Spain. The story of Sir Francis Drake is an intriguing drama between kings and queens and sailors and thieves.

Francis was born in Devonshire, England, to a large family with 12 children. His father was a farmer and later a Protestant preacher. As the second male in the family, Francis wasn't in the position to inherit his father's farm, so he set out to find his own career at sea. At 13, he landed his first job aboard a ship that sailed around the North Sea. When the captain of that ship died, Francis was made the new captain. He was only about 20 years old when given that title.

In 1572, Francis Drake set out on his first major expedition. With two ships and 73 men, Drake sailed to the waters of the Caribbean and the islands of the West Indies. Do you remember why these islands were called the "Indies"? It was because Christopher Columbus thought he was near India when he first landed on those shores.

On this particular expedition, Francis Drake wasn't interested in exploring. He was interested in looting Spanish ships loaded with silver. His target was a number of ships leaving **Nombre de Dios** (Nom bray day DEE ohs), a port in Panama. Now the odd thing about this act of piracy is that the silver that Drake was after didn't belong to the Spanish any more than it belonged to Francis Drake. The Spanish were mining it from the mountains of Peru and packing it on mules to be carried to Nombre de Dios. There it was loaded on ships that sailed back to Spain.

Queen Elizabeth knew about the silver mines that Spain was claiming as their own. I don't know if she was jealous, greedy, or just seeking revenge against Philip II of Spain. But she wanted that silver and commissioned Francis Drake to get it — or should I say, steal it!

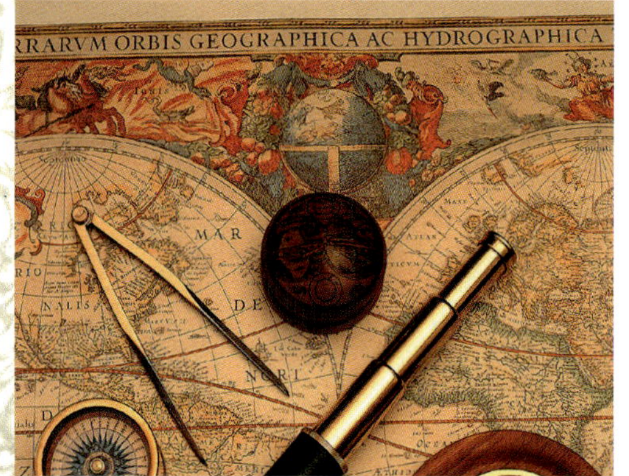

To protect her name and her interests, Elizabeth I kept her pirating arrangement with Francis Drake secretive and "off the books."

Of course, this "commission" was off the books. That means it was unofficially sanctioned by the queen. Had Drake, or any other ship captains, gotten into trouble on the open sea, Elizabeth would not have acknowledged that she was behind the venture. You could say it was a secret mission. Others would say it was piracy!

Regardless of what you call it, in 1572, Francis Drake not only intercepted ships leaving Nombre de Dios, but he ambushed the entire town. Drake filled his ships with so much gold that he was forced to leave behind loads of valuable silver. Though the historical record is unclear, some would say that the Spanish nicknamed him "the Dragon" for his antics. In England, however, he was hailed as a hero. He and 30 of his English crewmen were rewarded with riches to last them a lifetime. Meanwhile, Queen Elizabeth had signed a truce with Philip of Spain. So she could not "officially" acknowledge anything that Drake had accomplished — and, as was typical of Elizabeth, she didn't.

## *Sailing Around the World*

Five years later, Francis Drake returned to the sea, but this time on a far more serious expedition. He set out to circumnavigate the world! As you know, Ferdinand Magellan is often given credit for being the first European to circle the globe. He didn't really make it of course, but Francis Drake would.

Shrouds of mysteries, however, hang over the famous voyage of Francis Drake and his crew. The biggest mystery lies in what the *true* intention of the journey was. The crew first believed that they were going to Africa for trade. They soon found out otherwise as their ships were steered across the Atlantic and headed for Brazil. Some questions still remain about the direction in which the ships were steered. Was Francis Drake secretly sent by the queen to loot more Spanish ships or was that his own doing? Was he planning to be the first Englishman to circle the world or did he accidentally do so because he couldn't find a northern passage around America? No one knows for sure. As before, the "business" of the voyage seems to have remained "off the books" and secret, leaving much to speculation.

Drake's trip around the world started in Plymouth, England, in **1577**. Drake and two other captains made up the "Queen's Corsair," as it was called. The Queen's Corsair didn't fare very well. On the first day of the trip, a storm forced Drake's ship, the *Pelican*, to abandon its mast. Giving up a mast is one way to survive a storm but no way to travel. All were forced back to Plymouth to start over again. On their second attempt, the fleet left with six ships and 164 men.

The journey of the Queen's Corsair would be a familiar one because they followed the previous route of Ferdinand Magellan across the Atlantic Ocean to South America. After eight horrendous months at sea, Drake sailed his three remaining ships through the Strait of Magellan, the passage across the southern tip of the continent. It would be a smooth journey through the Strait of Magellan but a disaster upon entering the Pacific Ocean. Severe storms destroyed one of the three ships. Another was forced back through the strait to return to England in disgrace. Drake's ship (which he renamed the *Golden Hind*) was blown south of the Strait of Magellan. As a result, Drake realized that Tierra del Fuego was a freestanding island and was *not* attached to a continent, as some had thought.

Eventually Francis Drake maneuvered the *Golden Hind* up the western coast of South America. Along the way, he again raided rich Spanish settlements like **Valparaíso** in Chile and **Lima** in Peru. He also captured ships loaded with treasure, including the one named *Cacafuego*. He stole Spanish sea charts, too, hoping to find a northern passage back to England. That he never found.

The mountains of Peru are rich with natural resources such as copper, silver, gold, petroleum, timber, iron ore, and coal.

## *More Mystery*

What happened next remains another mystery regarding Francis Drake. This mystery centers on just where he landed next. It is certain that somewhere north of Spanish territory on the western coast of North America, Drake sailed into a comfortable harbor to make repairs to the *Golden Hind*. But just where was this harbor? Some speculate that it was around San Francisco Bay on the coast of California. Others claim it was near San Jose or as far north as Canada. Drake claimed that the waters of the port were icy, which means either he was a great deal farther north than San Francisco or it was terribly cold there at the time. Since it was July, it's hard to believe there was ice in the water!

You may wonder why it even matters. Well, to many people it matters a great deal. For one, Francis Drake claims he and his crew partook of the Lord's Supper at the place where they made harbor. This makes him the first to bring Protestant practice to the western coast of the New World. It would be nice to know just where that took place.

Over the next few years, it mattered a great deal to mapmakers as to where Francis Drake claimed to stop in the New World. It would alter the claims of both the English and the Spanish for a long time as they battled for territory in the New World. The situation was so hostile that the Spanish supposedly tortured Francis Drake's brother in South America to try to learn exactly where Drake had been! (But this story may be an exaggeration.)

Other than that, there are landowners and park commissioners today who, for the sake of tourism and fame, would like to claim *their* harbor as the one where Drake made his home for about five weeks. Being the hero that he was to the English, this location would be something to brag about.

Wherever that location was, Drake made a brass plate monument of his stop and claimed the harbor for England.[4] He named the harbor *Nuevo Albion*, which is Latin for "New Britain" or "New England." (That's a little strange to Americans who think of New England as being on the East Coast, not the West!) Well, in the 1930s, the supposed brass plate was "found." Years later, the plate was declared a fraud. For the sake of publicity or as a prank, the plate had been fabricated to try to prove that Drake landed near San Francisco. This fraudulent incident is a sad reminder of what some people will do for fame!

After three years at sea, Francis Drake and the crew of the *Golden Hind* entered the port of Plymouth, England, on September 26, 1580, having circled the entire globe!

As for Francis Drake, once repairs were made and provisions refilled, he and his crew left the western coast of the New World and sailed west toward home. Drake made a few stops along the way, including the Moluccas Islands where of course he picked up rare spices. He wouldn't think of returning to England without them.

In a few months, Francis Drake rounded the Cape of Good Hope. On September 26, 1580, the *Golden Hind* slipped into the port of Plymouth after having circled the entire globe! It had been three years since the men left England. The first thing that Drake wanted to know was whether Queen Elizabeth was alive. Her fate was certainly his fate. What he learned, of course, was that Elizabeth was very much alive and well. This meant he would be widely recognized.

With great ceremony, Queen Elizabeth herself boarded the *Golden Hind* and made Francis Drake a knight. (That is why his name starts with "Sir.") She awarded him a green silk scarf with Latin words meaning "The Almighty be your Guide and your Protector to the End." Drake was also named the mayor of Plymouth and given a seat in Parliament. Not a bad deal for a "sea dog," as Francis was often called.

In later years, Drake would surface again to aid Elizabeth in her rivalry against Spain. But I'll save that story for later. After fighting against Spain, Francis Drake would sail many more times. It eventually cost him his life. His body was submerged into the depths of the ocean in a lead casket. Historians bicker today as to whether or not the body should be retrieved from its watery grave and returned to England. I think the debate has something to do with whether you see him as a gifted navigator or a ghastly pirate!

## Lesson 45 1581

# *William the Silent Leads the Dutch Revolt*

I don't know of any other king in history nicknamed "the silent." It doesn't sound to me like a flattering term for a leader, but in the case of **William the Silent**, it was good.[5] William wasn't silent so much in his words as he was in his actions. As a leader in the **Dutch Revolt**, he was cautious, sly, and slow to advance on his enemies. Who were his enemies? I'm glad you asked. They were the Spanish. For about 80 years, the Dutch and the Spanish waged war over who was in charge of the Netherlands.

For centuries, the Dutch have harnessed nature using large, graceful windmills to pump low-lying water and push back the sea.

Before going on with my story of William, I want to straighten out some confusing terms. The terms are: the **Netherlands**, the **Low Countries**, **Holland**, and the **Dutch**. The Netherlands is a country in western Europe. It is north of Belgium and west of Germany. The term *Netherlands* means the "Low Countries." This region of Europe was and is nicknamed the Low Countries because of how low the land is to sea level. Situated on the edge of the North Sea, the Netherlands is in fact *below* sea level in many places. That's why the Netherlands is famous for large, beautiful **windmills** and **wooden shoes**. The wind-driven mills were designed to help pump water out of low-lying areas, and since the farmers in these areas worked in damp, muddy farmlands, wooden shoes were invented to keep their feet dry.

As for Holland — it is actually the name of two provinces found in the Netherlands. People often use the term wrongly by referring to *all* the provinces of the Netherlands as Holland, when in fact it refers to only two. (It would be like someone saying California when they meant the entire United States.) The people of the Netherlands call themselves Nederlanders, but most English-speaking nations call them the Dutch. For convenience, I'll do the same.

Okay, now that we have our terms straight, I want to tell you how the Netherlands evolved into a proud, independent nation. William the Silent had a lot to do with it. He's considered the father of his country. But we've got to step back a little in history to understand how this came to be.

## *A Short History of the Netherlands*

Do you remember **Charles V**? He was the Holy Roman Emperor who declared Martin Luther a heretic at the famous Diet of Worms. Well, Charles V was from the family of the **Hapsburgs**, a wealthy European family that supplied the Holy Roman Empire with most of its emperors. I bring up the Hapsburg family because in the early 1500s, the powerful Hapsburgs inherited the Netherlands. Thus, Charles V — who was a Hapsburg — inherited the Netherlands when he became the Holy Roman Emperor. (Now, all of this may sound trivial, but I'm building the case for why the Dutch and the Spanish eventually went to war. So hang in there and pay attention.)

The Duke of Alba, who tried to put down the Dutch Revolt with great brutality

Charles V was especially fond of the city of **Brussels** in Belgium, which at that time was part of the Netherlands. Of all the places in his empire, Brussels became one of his favorite places to live. So although the Dutch weren't always happy with the policies of Charles V, they considered him one of their own because he made his residence among them.

But trouble began to brew between Charles and the Netherlands as it became more and more Protestant. Charles, having already lost parts of Germany to the Lutherans, wasn't happy to find out that Protestantism was growing rapidly in the Netherlands. To try to stop it, he brought in the Inquisition.

By now, you know what that means. Many Dutch were found guilty of heresy by the courts of the Inquisition and burned at the stake for their Protestant beliefs. As a matter of fact, as many as 5,000 Protestants were put to death in the Netherlands during the reign of Charles V!

As bad as that sounds, things got worse in 1556 when Charles retired and passed part of his empire over to his son. Do you know who his son was? You might know from other lessons that Charles's son was **Philip II of Spain**. Yes, I'm referring to the same Philip who was the husband of Bloody Mary and who tried to marry Elizabeth I. Philip inherited the Netherlands from his father.

But Philip II never loved the Netherlands as his father had. He never learned to speak Dutch, and he didn't set foot in the Netherlands past the year 1559. Philip only looked at the Netherlands as a place to conquer and control. He wanted "in" on the growing trade business there, and he wanted to utterly destroy the Protestant movement. It eventually led to war. That is where today's story *really* begins. So let's look now at William the Silent and how he fits into this growing plot.

## *William, the Prince of Orange*

William the Silent, long before he was nicknamed the silent, was born into nobility in Germany and became the Prince of Orange at age 11. **Orange** is an area in southern France.[6] As a very young man, William was noticed by Charles V and became his favorite page. Though William was raised in a strong Protestant family, Charles insisted that William receive Catholic training in his court. When he was old enough, William was put in charge of Catholic troops in France in 1555. Remember that. William was on the side of the Catholics.

William was climbing the ladder of success in the Holy Roman Empire. He had mastered several languages and was a strong statesman. He was good pals with Charles V and gaining more respect every year. But then, as I described earlier, Charles stepped down as emperor in 1556 and his son, Philip II, inherited parts of the empire. (He did *not* become the next Holy Roman Emperor, however.) Philip II was good to William — at first. In 1559, Philip appointed William to be the governor of four provinces in the Netherlands. But things slowly changed between Philip and William. Like most of the Dutch, William became distrustful of Philip and didn't care for his persecution of Protestants.

While accompanying Philip on a royal hunt, William learned that Philip was conspiring with France to annihilate as many Protestants as possible! Three million Dutch Protestants were at stake. Disturbed by that, William switched sides in the war between the faiths! (This didn't happen very often back then.) William joined the cause of the Protestants and rallied *against* Philip II of Spain. He hoped to end the tyranny and the harsh persecution.

Bear in mind that Spain at this time was quite a world power. In size and strength, the Spanish far exceeded the Dutch. But the more that Philip oppressed the Dutch, the more they resisted. And the more they resisted, the stronger they got. By 1576, the brewing revolt *against* Spain was official. In history it has been remembered as the Dutch Revolt. As far as revolts go, it is one of the more historic.

Though small in number, the Dutch rose up against the Spanish in 1576 in what historians have labeled the *Dutch Revolt.*

Leadership of the Dutch Revolt fell into William's hands. This is ironic because William had once been so close to Charles V. Now he was waging war against Charles's son! William was not so much a religious leader as he was a military leader. He fought for freedom — freedom of the Netherlands from the tyranny of Spain. Religion, politics, and economics were all at stake.

William once said, "The privileges [meaning rights] are no free grants of the sovereign [meaning king] to his subjects, but form contracts binding both prince and people."[7] (Words in brackets are mine.) In other words, a king ought not to have the right to do anything he pleases to his people, but he should be in contract with his people for their good. What William never realized was that his ideas for freedom would one day resonate across the Atlantic and onto the shores of the United States. There are many parallels between the two nations in history as each fought for their independence. More on that later.

As for leading the Dutch Revolt against Spain, William really didn't do a very good job. Many times he failed on the battlefield. Many times he failed in his policies. He upset the Dutch by having to ask France for help. He upset the Calvinists by failing to attend church regularly. He upset the Catholics by never being able to squelch riots among the commoners who destroyed statues, churches, and altars of the Roman Catholic Church. To top it all off, William tragically lost his own brothers in battle.

But William was extraordinarily patient and didn't give up his fight. Many would say it was his passion for religious freedom that most spurred him on. He wept for those who had suffered persecution, both Protestant and Catholic alike. In instructions to a deputy he wrote, "First of all, . . . deliver the towns of that Province from Spanish slavery, and . . . restore them to their ancient liberties, rights and privileges, and . . . take care that the Word of God be preached and published there, but yet by no means to suffer that those of the Romish Church should be in any sort prejudiced, or that any impediment should be offered to them in the exercise of their religion."[8]

I hope you understood those words clearly. William wanted to see the Word of God preached and published as Protestants desired. But he did not want to bring suffering to those of the Roman Catholic Church. Would he live to see peace between the faiths in the Netherlands? Please keep reading to find out.

## *The Council of Troubles*

William's greatest obstacle was the **duke of Alba**. The duke was sent to the Netherlands by Philip to set up the **Council of Troubles**. The Council's job was to investigate and persecute those who were *not* loyal to Philip of Spain or the Roman Catholic Church. Well, thousands were guilty of both. It's been recorded that under the duke of Alba, 50 to 70 Dutchmen were executed per day. Some 8,000 died! Thirty thousand people were stripped of their property, and at least 100,000 Dutch fled to other countries because of the Council of Troubles. Because so many died, the Dutch called this council the "Council of Blood."

In retaliation for the dreadful Council of Troubles, the Dutch flooded the dikes of the Netherlands to help overcome Spanish trading ships.

As bad as it was, the Council of Troubles (or Council of Blood) served a purpose in the history of the Dutch. It gave them reason to fight. And they did. The Dutch weren't very successful on land, but they were outstanding on the sea. Dutch sailors rose to the occasion. They manipulated the dikes to flood out the enemy, and they took their fury out on Spanish trading ships. The loot helped pay for the war that raged on for 80 years. By 1573, the duke of Alba left his post in the Netherlands — ultimately defeated by his own ruthlessness. His brutal methods did more harm than good to Philip's cause as the Catholics also grew to despise Alba.

The final straw for the Dutch occurred in November of 1576. The city of **Antwerp**, at that time in the southern Netherlands, was savagely attacked and pillaged by Spanish soldiers who weren't receiving their pay. The soldiers went berserk. In what has been called the **"Spanish Fury,"** thousands of Dutch were massacred in Antwerp. The bodies of men, women, and children filled the streets while Dutch homes were looted for money.

Up until this time, the northern and southern provinces of the Netherlands had been sorely divided. For years, they had been divided by terrain, customs, and religion. The northern provinces were strongly Protestant; the southern provinces were Catholic. The horrible incident in Antwerp swung the Catholics in the south to join the Protestants in the north against the tyranny of Spain. They came together to sign the **Pacification of Ghent**. Under William the Silent, *all* 17 provinces of the Netherlands were united — at least for a time.

But William was unable to keep them together. Through pressure and politics, Spain won back the southern provinces. It left the north on its own. So in 1579, seven northern provinces joined together at the **Union of Utrecht**, vowing to remove Spain from the northern Netherlands and to give religious freedom to all. They renamed themselves the **Republic of the United Netherlands**. The southern provinces eventually pulled away altogether and became the nation of **Belgium**. They remain largely Catholic today. (There was much detail in those last few paragraphs. I suggest you reread them before going further. Try to keep the northern and southern provinces straight in your mind.)

## The Dutch Declaration of Independence

Do you remember my statement about parallels between the Netherlands and the United States? It was probably most obvious in the signing of the Declaration of Independence. When hearing that term, most of us think of the one signed on July 4, 1776, when the

United States declared its independence from England. But on July 26, **1581**, the northern Dutch provinces declared freedom from Spain through the **Dutch Declaration of Independence** (officially called the **"Act of Abjuration"**). In essence, the declaration stated, "The people were not created by God for the sake of the Prince . . . but, on the contrary, the Prince was made for the good of the people."[9] It was a bold step toward democracy that would live on even until today.

The tragic death of William the Silent served to fuel the passion of the Dutch for political freedom, which by their persistence they achieved.

As you can imagine, Philip of Spain wasn't very happy with William the Silent. In 1581, he issued a ban against William and offered a reward to see him dead. As a result, numerous attempts were made to kill William. He was shot at, nearly poisoned, and almost blown up. William survived these ordeals until a half-crazed Frenchman took the challenge. The Frenchman was named **Balthasar Gérard**. He pretended to be in need of a job and weaseled his way into William's home in the city of **Delft**. With two pistols he crouched in a stairwell while William dined with his family. As William got up to leave, Gérard rose to his feet, shot William dead, and fled.

You may not have been expecting this tragic ending to the life of William the Silent. I gave no hint throughout the lesson that he would die by assassination. He was only 51 when he was murdered. But strangely, he did almost as much for the Netherlands in his death as he did in his life. The tragedy caused the Dutch to rise up all the more strongly against Spain. They had a true martyr for their cause. Though war raged off and on until 1648, the Dutch ultimately won. Under William's sons, and with some help from England, the Netherlands eventually became a free nation, and a proud and free nation at that for having fought against such odds.

The Dutch have never forgotten William the Silent, their fallen hero. A memorial statue stands in the city of Delft. In honor of William, the Prince of Orange, the color orange remains a national color and is worn by Dutch athletes. The national anthem contains words about William, and the coat of arms bears his motto. In French, it is *Je maintiendrai*, meaning "I shall persist." In Dutch, it is *Ik zal handhaven*, which translates as "I shall stand fast." Both refer to William's steadfastness through adversity.

So did William live to see religious freedom in the Netherlands? Not completely. But progress was made and something significant was started through the Dutch quest for independence. I wish William could have known that. I wish he could have known that future nations would be influenced by his ideas of freedom.

# WEEK 16

## Lesson 46 1584

# *Sir Walter Raleigh*

Potatoes and tobacco. These are two things that **Sir Walter Raleigh** introduced to Ireland and England. He found them in North America on one of his many voyages away from home. But that fact is but a fraction of the story. Sir Walter Raleigh was quite a character. Some would say he was the best example of an "Elizabethan man" there ever was. If you don't know what an Elizabethan man is, don't worry. After this lesson on Sir Walter Raleigh, you'll have a good picture of one.

Just like Sir Francis Drake, Walter Raleigh was born in Devonshire, England. When he was about 15, Walter's adventuresome spirit lured him to France to fight with the Huguenots. He barely escaped the massacre on St. Bartholomew's Day. The horrible experience gave him a taste of the Reformation that he didn't particularly care for. He grew to despise Roman Catholics and stayed distant from "religion."

Walter Raleigh returned to England and enrolled in college in Oxford, England. He studied law and the works of Aristotle, but he never graduated. His restless soul sent him on a voyage of discovery and piracy with his half brother, **Sir Humphrey Gilbert**. I say he was involved in "piracy" because as you learned in our lesson about Francis Drake, Queen Elizabeth encouraged her captains to scourge the seas for treasure. In the name of England, Walter Raleigh and his half brother did just that.

Walter Raleigh became, in fact, one of the queen's most preferred sea captains. And like the others, he did his share of ruthless plundering. In Ireland, Raleigh got involved in putting down a revolt that killed thousands. But he was handsomely rewarded by Queen Elizabeth with 12,000 acres in Ireland! For 17 years, Raleigh would go back and forth to Ireland, at times making it his home.

But there was more to this "gift" of land than politics. Walter Raleigh was 6 feet tall, very handsome, and extremely charming. With blue-gray eyes and a strong build, he grew to become Queen Elizabeth's favorite courtier (KOR tee er). A courtier is one who attends the royal court and practices

Elizabeth I awarded Walter Raleigh 12,000 acres of beautiful green countryside in Ireland for putting down a revolt and for serving as one of her favorite sea captains.

flattery. It describes Raleigh very well. Although Walter Raleigh was 20 years younger than Elizabeth, he paid her a great deal of attention. In return, she showered him with all kinds of special favors and gifts, including castles, estates, and eventually, 42,000 more acres in Ireland! In **1584**, Elizabeth officially made him a knight, thus giving him the title of "Sir" Walter Raleigh. (Coincidentally, 1584 was the same year that William the Silent was assassinated and Ivan the Terrible died.)

Sir Walter Raleigh played a dangerous game as the queen's favorite courtier. Others were jealous of him, and should he ever slip out of favor with the queen, it would cost him his life. He played the game anyway. For years, Sir Walter Raleigh strutted about England doing just about anything he pleased. Though it may only be a tale, someone once wrote that Walter Raleigh first gained the attention of the queen by valiantly dropping his velvet coat over a mud puddle for her to cross. True tale or not, this grand gesture sounds like something he would do. Sir Walter Raleigh flattered Elizabeth all the days of her life to keep in her royal favor.

With the favor of the queen, one of Walter Raleigh's ambitions was to start an English colony in North America. He approached the queen with the idea, and she agreed to sponsor his first expedition. Though it wasn't a successful expedition, during this first voyage Raleigh named the east coast of the New World "Virginia" in honor of the virgin queen. Knowing how vain Elizabeth was, I imagine she loved it.

Another voyage to Virginia was planned by Walter Raleigh, but as it turned out, he did not take part in this one. Elizabeth agreed to sponsor the trip only if Walter stayed home. (She wanted Walter nearby.) It's probably a good thing that he stayed put. The ultimate fate of the voyage remains an unsolved mystery even today. Let me sidetrack and tell you this intriguing story about what has been named the "Lost Colony."

## *The Lost Colony*

In 1587, 150 settlers left England for North America. This time, there were 17 women included. These folks weren't gold hunters as previously had been the case. They were true colonists, hoping to establish a new home on **Roanoke Island** (off the coast of North Carolina). One event they celebrated at Roanoke was the birth of **Virginia Dare**, the first English baby known to be born in the New World. But other than that, the colonists didn't fare well. They weren't prepared for the harsh conditions of the coastal life. The land was rich and fertile in strips but overall, difficult to tame. Storms and hurricanes off the Atlantic Ocean were regular threats. Their governor, **John White**, who was also Virginia Dare's grandfather, decided it would be best if he sailed back to England for fresh supplies and better provisions.

His voyage proved to be a bad choice. You see, the year John White returned to England was the year the English were fighting the Spanish Armada. Because of the war, he was forbidden to sail back to North America. For that reason, and numerous others, it would be three long years before John White made it back to Roanoke.

When, in 1590, John White *did* finally make it back, he found the settlement at Roanoke deserted. No one was there. Over one hundred colonists had disappeared! Other than ruins of the colony, the only clues to their fate were two carvings on a tree. One read "CROATOAN." The other read only "CRO." Some believe the short inscription implies that the settlers were suddenly overcome by the Croatoan Indians and couldn't finish writing.[1] Others believe that the settlers went voluntarily to live farther inland with the friendly Croatoans where they had a better chance of survival.

One bit of evidence to support this theory is the unusual fact that some descendants of the Croatoans have blue eyes, light hair, and English names. It could be that there is truth in both theories. Some colonists may have been captured and killed; others may have surrendered or joined the natives. It's quite a mystery. And Walter Raleigh might have been part of the mystery had Elizabeth not forbidden his departure!

## *Meanwhile, in England*

Meanwhile, back in England, Sir Walter Raleigh was still chasing adventure. He built a ship and joined the fight against the Spanish Armada. He was quite successful, too. (We'll learn more about the Spanish Armada in another lesson.) By 1590, Sir Walter Raleigh was at the height of his career. He was adored by Elizabeth and successful in many ventures. He governed Ireland for a time and sponsored a famous poet named **Edmund Spenser**, who wrote *The Faerie Queene* about Elizabeth I. But something happened that nearly ruined Sir Walter Raleigh. He fell in love.

Walter Raleigh fell deeply in love with a young woman named **Elizabeth Throckmorton**. He called her Bess. The problem? The problem was that young Bess worked for Queen Elizabeth as one of her royal maids. What a predicament. As one of the queen's favorite courtiers, Walter was not able to make his love public. Queen Elizabeth would never have approved. So, in secret, Walter married his sweetheart. Or so he thought it was in secret. Elizabeth found out about the matter and was very upset. No one from her court was allowed to marry without her permission. Walter and Bess had dared to do so and made Elizabeth look like a fool.

For insulting and humiliating her, Elizabeth I locked the couple in the Tower of London, where they spent their honeymoon. With his usual finesse, Walter wrote a flattering letter to Elizabeth I telling her that she was still, without a doubt, the most perfect queen the world had ever known. Whether he meant it or not, the sweet letter worked. Sir Walter Raleigh was released, and in time, Bess was too, though she obviously lost her job as a maid in the court.

Sir Walter Raleigh continued his adventures. To try to win back his favor with Elizabeth I, in 1595, he sailed to South America in search of **El Dorado**, the legendary city of gold. Like other Europeans, he was duped by Native Americans into believing that such a place existed. Of course, the hunt for gold was a failure. But Walter informed Queen Elizabeth that when he showed her miniature picture to the South American natives, they were in awe of her beauty and far more compliant. I suspect it warmed the queen's heart to hear that, but by then, Elizabeth had other courtiers to spoil her.

In 1596, Walter Raleigh went back to Ireland and introduced the potato. In case you didn't know, potatoes are to Ireland what corn is to Iowa. (That means they are a main crop!) Despite this stroke of genius, because of financial debt Raleigh was forced to sell his property in Ireland. He went back to adventuring on the sea.

Sir Walter Raleigh learned of hearty potatoes from his voyages to North America and introduced them to Ireland, where they became a successful main crop.

## *Imprisonment*

But Sir Walter Raleigh's adventuring was to come to a sudden, screeching halt. In 1603, Elizabeth I died. Her cousin, **James VI** of Scotland, took her place as James I of England. James was nothing like Elizabeth. He had no attachment to Sir Walter Raleigh and no room for him in his court. Raleigh was suspiciously condemned for treason and once again locked up in the Tower of London.

Walter Raleigh surely realized that this time, there was no way out of the Tower. He knew a flattering letter to James wasn't going to rescue him. So, instead of writing to James, he wrote a deeply moving letter to his wife, Bess. Thinking he was soon to die, Walter Raleigh showed a side of himself in writing that few had known. He shared his deep love for his wife, his concern for their child, and his faith in God. Since Walter had not lived the life of a religious man, few knew that his faith ran as deep as it did. In facing death, he seemed to develop a new love for his Creator. He wrote:

> Love God, and begin betimes to repose your selfe upon him, and therein shall you finde true and lasting riches, and endlesse comfort . . . Teach your son also to love and feare God whilst he is yet young, that the feare of God may grow with him, and then God will be a husband to you, and a father to him; a husband and a father which cannot be taken from you . . . The everlasting God, powerfull, infinite, and omnipotent God, That Almighty God, who is goodnesse it selfe, the true life and true light keep thee and thine: have mercy on me . . . and send us to meet in his glorious Kingdome. My deare wife farewell. Blesse my poore boy . . . let my good God hold you both in his armes.[2]

But an amazing thing happened. Walter Raleigh didn't face death at that time! King James kept Raleigh alive for 13 more years. Yes, he was kept a prisoner in the Tower — but a very privileged prisoner. Walter's wife and son were allowed to live with him in a small residence. He was given books, experiments, servants, and the opportunity to write. In fact, he wrote poetry and *The History of the World*, a book covering ancient history. Always witty, Walter acknowledged in his book that without having been a prisoner, he never would have found time to write. He was grateful for the opportunity.

But time in prison is still time in prison. It grew old, as did Walter. His spirited soul eventually schemed a way out of his confinement. He promised King James that if given the chance, he could find gold in South America. Believe it or not, the chance was granted.

Sir Walter Raleigh was released and allowed to lead an expedition to South America — but on one condition. He and his men were *not* to touch the Spanish or any of their territories.

James was seeking peace with Spain and didn't want any piracy on the open sea. Raleigh agreed to the conditions and sailed off. His son accompanied him.

> *"Love God, and begin betimes to repose your selfe upon him, and therein shall you finde true and lasting riches, and endlesse comfort . . ."*
> *–Sir Walter Raleigh*

Tragically, the expedition was jinxed from the beginning. For one, there really wasn't any El Dorado. And second, Walter's men just couldn't keep their hands off the Spanish. While Walter protected his ships in port, his men went scourging the land for gold. They came upon a Spanish settlement and completely violated the conditions that King James had asked them to keep. In an attack, Walter's young son was shot and killed.

Walter Raleigh was emotionally spent. His treasure hunt was a failure. His son was dead. He sadly wrote to his wife back home, "God knows I never knew what sorrow meant till now. Comfort your heart dearest Bess, I shall sorrow for us both."[3] Indeed he did.

Walter Raleigh headed home, knowing this time he faced certain death. As predicted, King James scolded him for violating the conditions of the expedition and ordered his execution. The once flamboyant Elizabethan man was doomed to die a traitor's death.

On the day of his execution, Sir Walter Raleigh held his head high. Legend says he was allowed one last smoke of the tobacco he made famous, which may have been the start of a long tradition of offering a final cigarette to the executed. Raleigh walked bravely to the scaffolding and joked with his executioner. He examined the blade that was about to take off his head saying, "This is sharp medicine . . . that will cure all my diseases."[4] Then, without wearing a blindfold, he himself signaled the ax to fall.

Sir Walter Raleigh sailed back to England with a heavy heart for losing his son and facing probable execution for his failed expedition.

It seems to me that Sir Walter Raleigh accepted his fate well. I suppose after all those years in the Tower of London, he had time to reflect on his more lavish days. He knew he had lived well by the hands of Queen Elizabeth. He knew he genuinely loved his wife, Bess. And he assumed it was his turn to die because he and his men had failed on their expedition.

Bess lived for 29 more years in England. It is said that she kept the embalmed head of her beloved in a cupboard for admirers to see. It's a strange way to honor the dead, but there is no doubt Bess loved her husband very much. As a captain, businessman, governor, soldier, explorer, poet, and historian, Sir Walter Raleigh was loved by many and in my opinion, was a true Elizabethan man.

# England Defeats the Spanish Armada

You could have predicted that this lesson was coming. I've made several references to it already. In **1588**, the English proudly defeated the **Spanish Armada**. An armada is a fleet of warships. This means that on the sea, the English beat the Spanish once and for all. The result was significant. The embarrassing defeat brought the Spanish down from being the dominant world power that they were. The details are fascinating.

As you've already learned, there was serious rivalry between England and Spain. One root of this rivalry was the fact that Henry VIII divorced Catherine of Aragon. She was a Spanish princess, you know, and she was Catholic. I'm not sure if the Spanish ever forgave Henry for humiliating the princess-turned-queen or for turning his back on the Roman Catholic Church. Another root of rivalry was the awkward marriage between Bloody Mary of England and Philip II of Spain. She married for love; he married for power. They never had children. This bothered Philip because without heirs to the throne, the Spanish were losing their foothold in England. Catholics were losing their foothold, too.

Do you remember when Philip began to court Elizabeth I? He failed, as did so many others, in making Elizabeth his wife. But he dared not make her his enemy — at least not an *obvious* enemy. As you know, Philip was already in trouble with the Netherlands because of William the Silent. Things were also touchy with France. A war with one nation was sure to trigger war with another. So Philip patiently kept peace with Elizabeth for years.

But there were at least four things that would ultimately disrupt that peace. For one, Elizabeth made things as difficult as possible when she allowed sea captains like Sir Francis Drake to pillage and plunder Spanish ships and settlements! Philip pretended not to notice when he probably knew exactly what was going on.

Second, Elizabeth scared Philip when she flirted with the idea of marrying a duke from France. Had Elizabeth married the French duke, it would have bound England and France together. That was something Philip couldn't afford because they would probably have united against Spain.

Third, Elizabeth gave help to the Dutch in 1585 when they were fighting for their independence from Spain. That was a deep blow to Philip. I don't think he ever expected to lose his grip on the Netherlands. But as you know, he did.

Fourth, Elizabeth finally had Mary, Queen of Scots, executed in 1587. I'm sure you remember that tragic story. Spain had hoped that Mary would one day take the throne of England and restore the Catholic Church. Her death was sad news for Spain and the Roman Catholic Church.

Facing war against Philip II, Elizabeth I stated before her troops, "I have but the body of a feeble woman . . . but the heart of a King."

All these events added together were more than Philip could take. He no longer could avoid a war against Elizabeth. But just as war "stirred up" the Dutch in their revolt, so war would prove to stir up the English, too. When they knew that a great armada of warships was being formed against them, Elizabeth herself rode out before her troops and gave this noble speech: "I am come among you at this time being resolved . . . to lay down for my God, and for my Kingdom, and for my people, my honour and my blood, even in the dust . . . I have but the body of a feeble woman, . . . but the heart of a King."[5] The pending war was sure to be a showdown between the strong heads of Elizabeth I and Philip II.

But before I get into the details of the war, I want to shed a different spotlight on Philip II. I've certainly made him out to be a monster thus far for bullying his way around Europe. And to most Europeans, he was deplorable. But as is the case with most people, there was another side to his character. The Spanish *loved* and *adored* their Philip. The following will help explain why.

## *Philip II, the Man and the Mission*

Philip was only 16 when he became the regent of Spain. He hardly had a youth. What little youth he had was spent under the guidance of priests and nuns. His mother died when he was only 12. All his life, he was surrounded by obligations. He took those obligations very seriously and lived more like a priest than a king.

Philip had several marriages, but all were political. None seemed to be for love. The only real love he knew was for his church and his country. For those, he would sacrifice all the luxuries and frills normally associated with being a king.

For example, Philip built an incredible palace home, the **Escorial**, that included a monastery, a seminary, and a church. But he himself slept in one of the smallest chambers of the building. It was similar to the quarters of a monk. Philip in fact dressed so plainly — like the monks did — that a visitor once mistook him for hired help.

Though he was the king of Spain, Philip II maintained a humble lifestyle. He dressed in plain clothes, enjoyed good laughter, and played the guitar.

Enemies of Philip would say that he only smiled when he heard about the massacre on St. Bartholomew's Day. But closer friends would say that Philip enjoyed music, pranks, good laughter, and playing the guitar. He kindly tended to the needs of one of his wives on her deathbed, and he wrote tender letters to his daughters. (Philip did, however, fail to have good relations with his sons. One he locked up for being rebellious and half mad!)

But all in all, Philip was extremely devout. He hated to go to war, and he put it off as long as possible. Philip truly believed that his calling in life was to protect the Roman Catholic Church. He did so all his life by fighting the Islamic Turks, the Protestant Dutch, and finally, the English.

So as you can see, the Spanish had reason to love Philip. In their eyes, he was strong, pious, and adoring. As their leader, he was calm and calculating. The Spanish believed Philip would certainly lead them to triumph when it was finally time to wage war against England. But as you learned from the title of this lesson, Philip wasn't the one who triumphed. The English did. Now that you've seen this other side of Philip, let's move on to the details of his war.

## *The Attack of the Armada*

By May of 1588, Philip had built one of the largest navies ever assembled. His armada, nicknamed the **"Invincible Armada,"** consisted of 130 ships, 2,500 guns, and more than 30,000 men. Almost 200 of those men were priests and friars who viewed war against England as a "holy" calling. They were not only fighting for Spain, they were fighting for the Roman Catholic Church, which was quickly diminishing in England.

The English, on the other hand, had a small navy of only 82 warships. The rest of the navy was made up of fishing boats and merchant vessels eager to go to war. The admiral of the English navy was **Charles, Lord Howard of Effingham**. The vice admiral was Sir Francis Drake, who I'm sure you remember. Sir Walter Raleigh was also involved and in fact, funded his own ship for the undertaking. When armed and ready, the small English fleet waited at the port of Plymouth. Both sides said their prayers.

Spanish ships were built large and bulky to hold lots of soldiers for grappling and man-to-man combat. English ships were small, easy to maneuver, and loaded with gunpowder!

It was July of 1588 when the Spanish Armada was first seen entering the English Channel. The Spanish idea of a sea battle was to come alongside an enemy ship, attach to it with large iron grapples (which are giant hooks), then board and fight man to man. Thus, Spanish ships were built large and bulky to hold as many soldiers as possible. The English, however, weren't looking for man-to-man combat. With fewer ships and fewer men, they hoped to sink the Spanish fleet with fire and gunpowder. So their ships were built small and easy to maneuver.

As the armada approached, the Spanish hoped to lure the English to the open sea for large-scale grappling and combat. But, like swarming bees, the small English ships darted around the Spanish — firing at them broadside with all they had. The Spanish ships were so tall that when they tried to return fire, they shot over the low-lying English ships — hardly damaging them at all. By nightfall, Sir Francis Drake captured one Spanish ship; one was blown up; and at least one was completely wrecked.

The fighting went on for days. The Spanish sent for soldiers they had stationed in the Netherlands, but the Dutch (who were siding with the English) blocked the ports. One Spanish captain wrote, "The enemy pursue me, they fire on me from morn till dark, but they will not grapple . . . There is no remedy, for they are swift and we are slow."[6]

After more days of fighting, Francis Drake came up with a brilliant strategy. He set fire to eight small, tar-covered vessels and sailed them directly into the armada! (Of course, he and his crew jumped before crashing.) In fright, the Spanish fled toward the coast of France. Drake followed them the next day, as did the admiral, Lord Howard. The English fleet poured all their firepower into the thick-hulled Spanish ships until the large craft were barely afloat. The Spanish Armada lost 4,000 men that day; nearly as many men were wounded. The Spanish could bear no more and retreated.

Even in retreat, the winds were against the Spanish. To get home, the armada was forced to sail north around the island of Great Britain. The badly battered ships weren't fit for such a trip around the jagged coastline. By the time they hit the coast of Ireland, 17 ships were splintered to pieces. Spanish soldiers washed ashore begging for aid, but most were denied. Only 54 ships returned safely to the harbor in Spain. Out of 30,000 Spaniards, only 10,000 survived the defeat.

Philip II, upon hearing of this great loss, locked himself up in a small room at the Escorial. For a very long time, he spoke to no one. Elizabeth, however, was in all her glory. She continued to send out war fleets against Spain, even past the death of Philip in 1598. Not all her fleets were victorious, but by then it was not as important. The English had won the big one by defeating the "Invincible" Armada, and history was changed because of it.

How was history changed? Well, the weakening of Spain did many things. For one, it helped the Dutch in their battle for independence. Second, it gave strength to the Protestant cause in England. Third, it opened the door for the English to colonize North America, rather than the Spanish. Some would say that Europe and North America would be far more Spanish and Roman Catholic had the Spanish Armada not been stopped that year. Who's to say for sure?

The defeat of the armada certainly changed the tone of both Spain and England. The Spanish withdrew to tend their wounds. The English entered their Golden Age under poets like **William Shakespeare** and transported their luxuries, their customs, and their language to North America. So war, good or bad, appears to have an undeniable influence on the course of mankind and history.

# *Michel de Montaigne and* Essays

The life of **Michel de Montaigne** (mih SHELL duh Mon TANE) was not particularly eventful. He wasn't an artist, an explorer, or a ladies' man. Nor was he a monk, a martyr, or a king. Michel de Montaigne was, however, a significant writer. From the comfort of his study, he spent years writing personal essays. Montaigne's honest style was refreshing to those who had grown weary of the classics. And his "skeptical" approach to life drew much attention. I'll explain skepticism later in our lesson.

Michel de Montaigne was born in France and spent most of his life there. He was born during the era when France was warring over religion. The Catholics and Huguenots were at odds and both sides had resorted to bloodshed. This fact would be one of many influences on Montaigne.

Montaigne's family had a mixed heritage. His father was Roman Catholic; his mother was by blood a Spanish Jew but by faith, a Protestant; his siblings were strong zealous Calvinists. This diverse background would also have a great influence on Montaigne, who later would not know what to believe.

Montaigne's education was an unusual one. During his first three years of life, his father sent him away from their wealthy home to live with a poor family. He hoped it would teach Michel to appreciate the lower working class. Once older, Michel was brought home to his rich estate and reared by a Latin-speaking tutor. Though French was his native tongue, no one, including the servants, was allowed to speak to the boy except in Latin.

Michel naturally mastered Latin, but he never cracked a book to learn it. In much the same way, he learned everything useful through games and experience, not by studying books. A zither player followed him around day and night to play music. He was given free rein to learn everything but was never forced to learn anything. You could say he was a "non-schooler" of sorts. This upbringing also influenced the views of Montaigne.

Later, after attending boarding school, Montaigne studied law. But the tediousness of the subject was suffocating to his free spirit. He moved on to serve in Parliament where he met the closest friend he would ever have. His friend was a kindred spirit and a humanist at heart. He opened Montaigne's mind to all kinds of philosophies. But, without much warning, his friend died, and Montaigne would say he was never the same. A part of him died, too. This loss would also influence Montaigne.

## Essays

In 1571, Michel de Montaigne retired from his short career in government and began to write. He isolated himself in the study of his castle for nearly 10 years and made it his place of refuge from the world around him. His inward journey resulted in a collection of writings titled ***Essays*** that are still talked about today.

When Montaigne began to write, he broke away from all tradition. He formalized what is known as the "personal essay." In essay form, Montaigne felt he could be transparent and share a lot about himself as well as his philosophies. He did so brilliantly. Though a little self-absorbed, Montaigne was honest. He wrote, "I never speak of others, but that I may the more speak of myself."[7] Montaigne would admit that his interest in philosophy was selfish in nature. He said, "If I study, I only endeavor to find out the knowledge that teacheth or handleth the knowledge of myself, and which may instruct me how to die well and how to live well."[8]

For nearly ten years, Michel de Montaigne huddled in the study of his castle to write *Essays*, which, because of its personal and transparent style, broke away from all tradition of that era.

So, in *Essays*, Michel de Montaigne explored the depths of several topics as they related to himself. He wrote on friendship, books, cruelty, and repentance. He discussed anger, education, human will, and honesty. People enjoyed what Montaigne had to say because his writings were genuine. Then as now, many people found the essay to be livelier than a textbook or encyclopedia and a better tool for learning. About dry, factual knowledge, Montaigne would say, "Mere bookish sufficiency is unpleasant."[9] I think most of us would agree!

In style, Montaigne wrote to his readers as if they were there. We call that using the "first person." My own style of writing is similar and might be defined as a narrative essay because I'm writing as if I'm talking directly to you. Like Montaigne, I use the word "I" and pretend you're right next to me. (And just like I'm doing right now, I use a lot of parentheses to whisper extra little things to you.) Montaigne did much the same thing but with fancier words and much longer sentences.

Now, Montaigne wasn't the first writer to master the essay. Some would categorize the ancient works of Plato, Cicero, and Marcus Aurelius as essays. But Montaigne was the first to make the essay a respected literary form. Many famous writers would copy him — writers such as Thomas Paine, Ralph Waldo Emerson, Edgar Allan Poe, and Henry David Thoreau. Today, newspaper columnists write in essay form, as do the authors of most magazine articles. It's a personable style of writing that most people enjoy.

## Skepticism

But unique to Michel de Montaigne would be his reputation as a **Skeptic.** A skeptic is a person who has a difficult time believing in something. It often refers to a person with little or no faith in God. But Montaigne's skepticism was broader than that. He was part of a philosophical movement known as Skepticism, whose followers doubted that anything was certain. Because of his own background and many difficult circumstances, Montaigne found it hard to believe in much at all.

For one, Montaigne didn't believe that love had much to do with marriage. So he married a practical woman and had five children with her. Only one survived. Montaigne was faithful to his wife, but he seldom spoke of her. Theirs was a marriage of convenience.

Second, Montaigne was skeptical toward education. He thought that memorizing facts and figures was a waste of time compared to learning by experience, as he had done as a child. He thought the end result of education is what matters. He wrote, "I would not only have him [a student] to demand an account of the words contained in his lessons, but of the sense and substance thereof . . . not by the testimony of his memory, but by the witness of his life."[10] (Words in brackets are mine for clarity.) He makes a good point!

Third, Montaigne was definitely skeptical toward religion. He wrote, "How many things served us but yesterday as articles of faith, which today we deem but fables?"[11]

Montaigne had seen the worst side of the religious wars in France and had family members on opposite sides of Christendom. Though he wrote and spoke about God, the Lord seemed distant and not personal to him at all. Montaigne's distance from the Lord would be picked up by others and increase their skepticism. As the Age of Reason was on the rise, Montaigne fed the mind-set of godlessness with his doubts about faith.

Last, of life in general, Montaigne seemed uncertain of absolutes. He wrote, "I have my own laws and tribunal to judge of me . . . None but yourself knows rightly whether you be demiss and cruel, or loyal and devout."[12] And Montaigne questioned his own goodness when he wrote this: "When I religiously confess myself unto myself, I find the best good I have hath some vicious taint."[13]

Well, after nine years of straight writing, Michel de Montaigne left his private study to travel. In the years 1580 and 1581, he visited France, Austria, Switzerland, Germany, and Italy. One of his ambitions was to find a cure for his kidney stones, which caused him great personal pain. Throughout his travels, Montaigne kept a travel diary that he later had published.

While traveling, Montaigne learned that he was elected mayor of Bordeaux in France. So he went home to try to keep peace between the warring Catholics and Protestants. In particular, he gave support to Henry of Navarre. (Remember him?) But, to complicate matters, the plague broke out in Bordeaux, disrupting the lives of everyone, including Michel de Montaigne. He died in **1592** at the age of 59.

Because of the challenges that Montaigne faced, many would sympathize with his skeptical views toward life. In hard times, many would naturally grow skeptical and question life. But consider this: The Bible says that our faith can be strengthened in trials and tribulations! Romans 5:3–5 says, ". . . but we also glory in tribulations, knowing that tribulation produces perseverance; and perseverance, character; and character, hope. Now hope does not disappoint, because the love of God has been poured out in our hearts by the Holy Spirit who was given to us." Through all his observations, I wish Montaigne could have better understood the hope found in Christ.

*"When I religiously confess myself unto myself, I find the best good I have hath some vicious taint."*

*–Michel de Montaigne*

# WEEK 17

## Lesson 49 1592

# *The Works of William Shakespeare*

All the world's a stage,
And all the men and women merely players:
They have their exits and their entrances;
And one man in his time plays many parts.

(*As You Like It*)

To be, or not to be: that is the question.

(*Hamlet*)

Shall I compare thee to a summer's day?
Thou art more lovely and more temperate.
. . . . . . . . . . . . . . . . . . . . . . . . . . . .
So long as men can breathe or eyes can see,
So long lives this, and this gives life to thee.

(Sonnet 18)

But, soft! what light through yonder window breaks?
It is the east, and Juliet is the sun!

(*Romeo and Juliet*)

I don't know how else to start this lesson except with some of the most famous words of **William Shakespeare**. Aren't they beautiful? He wrote over a million such words in his deep and complex works. There is no doubt that Shakespeare is considered England's greatest poet and playwright. I'm sure I can never do him justice in the space I'm provided, but I will try.

Traditionally, it is believed that William Shakespeare grew up in **Stratford-upon-Avon**, a village near London, England. He probably attended grammar school there, where he would have been heavily instructed in Latin. In fact, classes could last from 6 or 7 A.M. to 5 or 6 P.M., if you can imagine! William's father held many respectable jobs in Stratford, but at one point in his career he struggled to make ends meet. So, because of financial problems, William dropped out of school and became an apprentice.

According to tradition, William Shakespeare made his fortune from the Globe Theatre. A replica of the theater stands in London today and continues to draw crowds and tourists.

When he was 18, William married a woman named **Anne Hathaway**. She was 26 years old. In a short time, she gave birth to a daughter, and twins followed soon thereafter. The historical record is unclear as to exactly what William was up to during those years in Stratford. He was quite possibly a schoolteacher. It is known through court documents that he got into trouble for hunting on someone else's property and was arrested for it.

In **1592**, it is certain, and unfortunate, that William moved to London without his wife or children. Why did he leave them? No one knows for sure. Some speculate that he moved 80-plus miles away for a better job and visited back home from time to time. Others believe he separated from his wife and had little to do with his family for the next 20 years.

Once in London, William pursued acting and writing. Neither job was considered worthy of high wages, but the theater was a growing business in London for all walks of life. William eventually made a great deal of money, but it was not from his acting or written works. He made money by investing in the theater itself. In particular, he helped build the famous **Globe Theatre** in the suburbs of London. Or so the story goes. There may be more to it than that.

Some suspect that the man I just described to you was not the poet or playwright who penned the great works of Shakespeare! The man named William Shakespeare who was born in Stratford-upon-Avon may have been used as a cover-up. And the money he supposedly made from the Globe Theatre? It just might have been a payoff to keep secret the true identity of the real author. Sound a bit bizarre? Perhaps it is, but I believe it is worth our consideration.

## *The Real William Shakespeare?*

Apparently, it is the very depth of the works of William Shakespeare that has caused some to think the man from Stratford wasn't capable of writing it. As early as the 1700s, scholars began to question the authorship of Shakespeare's plays and sonnets. Because he grew up in a small village with little schooling beyond his teen years, some think that the Stratford man could never have produced the masterpieces that bear his name. But if it was not him, then who was it? And why would someone else let Shakespeare take the credit for his work? There are some fascinating theories.

Some speculate that **Francis Bacon** was Shakespeare's ghostwriter. He was highly educated, brilliant, and well versed. But Francis Bacon was also a very busy man. He had his own works to publish and might not have had time to write plays on the side. He also had no reason to "hide" behind the name of William Shakespeare.

But there were two men who did have reason to hide who are a bit more suspicious. There was a man named **Christopher Marlowe**, who was supposedly killed in action as a spy. Secretly, he was kept alive — perhaps like someone under a witness-protection plan. Nonetheless, Marlowe had at one time been a talented playwright. But since he was "dead," he couldn't publish his works. It may be that he did so under the name of Shakespeare.

A far more convincing theory centers on **Edward de Vere, the earl of Oxford**. He was an accomplished gentleman, an educated writer, and personal courtier to Queen Elizabeth. In his lifetime, it wasn't considered "proper" for a courtier to write for the theater because it was a crude and rowdy place. De Vere supposedly wrote some incredible plays, but *none* exist under his name! So where did they go? Some speculate that the plays of de Vere were attributed to Shakespeare to protect de Vere's family and reputation. Ghostwriting was very common in the English court. And as you've learned, Elizabeth was certainly one to concern herself with image. Perhaps she preferred that her courtier be discreet with his talent for the theater.

In studying the life of Edward de Vere, one can't help but find some amazing parallels to the works of William Shakespeare. What I mean is that Edward de Vere seemed to live out every play and poem ever written under the name of Shakespeare. De Vere had a strong classical education and he traveled around Europe. In real life, he experienced a love triangle, a troubled marriage, problems with in-laws, endless debt, and widowerhood. Plays and poems under the name of William Shakespeare just may be a collection of Edward de Vere's personal memoirs and a chronicle of his experiences close to the throne of England. The play titled *Hamlet*, for example, seems practically an autobiography of de Vere. And the character of Lady Macbeth in the play *Macbeth* is a possible representation of Elizabeth I when she struggled with the beheading of Mary, Queen of Scots.

If Edward de Vere was the true author of Shakespeare's works, who then was William Shakespeare from Stratford-upon-Avon? Some believe that William Shakespeare was a common actor at the Globe Theatre who agreed to live a lie. It is thought that he accepted money to allow de Vere to hide behind his name. In public, Shakespeare from Stratford claimed to have written all the poems and plays of Shakespeare, even though no one ever saw him doing it or has proof that he did.

There is much speculation surrounding the true authorship of the works of William Shakespeare.

As convincing as the evidence might sound, William Shakespeare of Stratford has many fans who don't agree that there was a ghostwriter behind the scenes. No one to date has absolute proof of Shakespeare's authorship. So for now, all intriguing theories remain just that — theories. (For ease of reading, I will use the name of William Shakespeare to refer to whoever it was that wrote his works!)

## *The Plays of William Shakespeare*

Let's look now at the vast works attributed to William Shakespeare. As for his plays, they can generally be divided into three categories: historical plays, comedies, and tragedies. The historical plays certainly would have stirred the patriotic hearts of the English. These plays covered the lives of Henry the Fourth, Fifth, Sixth, and Eighth. Shakespeare also wrote plays on King John, Richard II, and Richard III. In *Richard III*, he embellished the mysterious disappearance of Richard's nephews that we learned about in our lesson on the Wars of the Roses. It seems the English never grew weary of seeing their history acted out on the stage.

When it came to comedy, William Shakespeare was notorious for poking fun at the roles of men and women. Apparently, the themes of these comedies are timeless because high schools, civic groups, and amateur theaters are still drawing crowds today with their performances. Titles of Shakespeare's comedies include *As You Like It, The Merchant of Venice, A Midsummer Night's Dream, Much Ado About Nothing, Twelfth Night,* and *The Taming of the Shrew*. The last is a pun about keeping a woman "in line."

In total, William Shakespeare produced 17 comedies, which appeal to the whims of human nature and cross all boundaries of race, religion, and the sexes. In the most pleasant of ways William Shakespeare could scold mankind for their vices and sympathize with their weaknesses. Jealousy, pettiness, and tests of true love are common underlying themes. Shakespeare frequently switched his boys into girls and his girls into boys to test or conceal true love. This was easier to do on the stage in Shakespeare's day because women were not allowed to be actresses. Only young boys, dressed like girls, played the parts of females!

As for tragedies, Shakespeare's most famous would probably be *Romeo and Juliet* — a masterpiece about two "star-crossed lovers" whose families were bitter enemies. In the end, the young lovers end their lives to end their miseries. Though the tragic plot of *Romeo and Juliet* originated in ancient Greece, no one put the story together quite like Shakespeare did. "O Romeo, Romeo! Wherefore art thou Romeo?" This line, spoken by Juliet, is timeless.

Other tragedies include *Hamlet, Macbeth, Othello,* and *Antony and Cleopatra*. Shakespeare's characters, both historical and fictitious, are profound and deep. The themes of the plays cover racial issues, death, and madness. His scripting is superb and thought provoking. For example, it is Hamlet who speaks the famous phrase, "To be, or not to be: that is the question." I don't believe anyone has answered him yet.

And on a somber note, those who follow the Edward de Vere theory believe that the closing lines of *Hamlet* are a confession of de Vere's secret authorship near his death. They read,

> O good Horatio, what a wounded name,
> Things standing thus unknown, shall live behind me!
> If thou didst ever hold me in thy heart,
> Absent thee from felicity awhile,
> And in this harsh world draw thy breath in pain
> To tell my story.

## *Shakespeare's Sonnets*

In between acting and writing 37 plays, Shakespeare wrote 154 poems. He wrote in the form of **sonnets**, which are poems that follow certain rules in rhythm and rhyme. Had he never written a single play in his life, I think he would have still been famous for his sonnets. Like his plays, Shakespeare's sonnets shed light into the soul of man. He expresses deep love, deep loss, and deep regard for death. Here are a few lines from various sonnets. Read them slowly and with meaning.

On love:

. . . . . . . . . . . . . . . . . . . . . . . . . .
. . . Love is not love
Which alters when it alteration finds,
Or bends with the remover to remove.
O, no! it is an ever-fixed mark
That looks on tempests and is never shaken;
It is the star to every wandering bark,
Whose worth's unknown, although his height be taken
Love's not Time's fool, though rosy lips and cheeks
Within his bending sickle's compass come;
Love alters not with his brief hours and weeks,
But bears it out even to the edge of doom.
  If this be error and upon me proved,
  I never writ, nor no man ever loved.

(Sonnet 116)

On aging:

That time of year thou mayst in me behold
When yellow leaves, or none, or few, do hang.
Upon those boughs which shake against the cold,
Bare ruin'd choirs, where late the sweet birds sang.
In me thou see'st the twilight of such day
As after sunset fadeth in the west,
Which by and by black night doth take away.
Death's second self, that seals up all the rest.
. . . . . . . . . . . . . . . . . . . . . . . . . .

(Sonnet 73)

On death:

Poor soul, the centre of my sinful earth.
. . . . . . . . . . . . . . . . . . . . . . . . . .
Shall worms, inheritors of this excess,
Eat up thy charge? Is this thy body's end?
. . . . . . . . . . . . . . . . . . . . . . . . . .
  So shalt thou feed on Death, that feeds on men,
  And Death once dead, there's no more dying then.

(Sonnet 146)

It is Sonnet 81, thought to be one of Shakespeare's last, that many believe describes his hope that his words would live on. The last lines read:

> Your monument shall be my gentle verse,
> Which eyes not yet created shall o'er-read,
> And tongues to be your being shall rehearse
> When all the breathers of this world are dead,
> You still shall live — such virtue hath my pen —
> Where breath most breathes, even in the mouths of men.

For centuries, admirers of Shakespeare have tried to figure out whom William was writing to. It is still unclear. Part of the confusion has to do with the question of who was really doing the writing! No matter whom Shakespeare wrote to, he wrote with great depth, using brilliant vocabulary.

In fact, it is the vocabulary — or choice of words — that Shakespeare used that makes him stand unique among English writers. You see, in Shakespeare's time, the English language wasn't as well formed as it is today. So, when the poet/playwright couldn't find a word to match a rhyme, he made up words using parts of other languages and his own imagination. Whimsical words that Shakespeare made up include *barefaced, bumps, fitful, fretful, frugal, gloomy, gnarled, hurry, puke, recall, spurring,* and *suspicious.* More serious words that he formed include *assassination, courtship, critical, disheartened, dwindle, exposure, fumitory, impartial, lonely,* and *monumental.* These words did not exist until Shakespeare brought them to life. And he gave complete new meaning to the use of metaphors, alliterations, and puns. Some famous phrases include *dead as a doornail, heart of gold, sorry sight, elbow room,* and *full circle.*

The author of the works of Shakespeare greatly influenced the English language by making up whimsical words and phrases of his own imagination.

Some of you aren't quite ready to read through the works of William Shakespeare. The language is challenging; the plots are complicated; and a few parts are crude in nature. But one day you'll undoubtedly read a Shakespearean play or watch it on the stage. I hope you'll appreciate whoever it was that wrote the works of William Shakespeare. He was a literary genius whose works have stood the test of time.

# Tokugawa Japan

Japan is a land of great beauty and intriguing culture. It's beautiful for bonsai trees, origami art, and cherry blossoms. It's intriguing for sumo wrestlers, ninja fighters, and samurai. But during the 1600s, Japan closed its doors to the rest of the world. For nearly 200 years it remained isolated. For that reason, Japan "grew up" a little differently from the rest of the world. Today we will peek into what was going on behind those closed doors during this interesting time period, which is commonly referred to as **Tokugawa** (Toe koo GAH wah) **Japan**.

During the Tokugawa period of Japan, the art form of *bonsai* (the sculpting and miniaturizing of plants and shrubs) grew popular in landscape gardening.

Before we get to sumos or ninjas, I want to give you a quick review of the history of Japan. In ancient times it was inhabited by the **Ainu** (I noo), people who didn't — and still don't — look at all like the modern Japanese. About 600 years before Christ, **Jimmu Tenno** was one of the first emperors of Japan. Two hundred years later, the **Yamato clan** gained control of the islands and to this day, they claim to have descendants on the throne.

During the *early* Middle Ages, clans on the islands of Japan warred against one another until **Prince Shotoku** centralized the government. (Do you remember him from Volume II?) Shotoku has been remembered as the "founder of the Japanese civilization." Besides pulling the island clans together, Prince Shotoku introduced **Buddhism** to Japan. Before Buddhism, the Japanese practiced **Shinto**, a religion found only in Japan because it believes that the Japanese are a sacred people. Most Japanese today practice a blend of these two religions.

Samurai knights were known for their swordsmanship and unwavering loyalty to the ruling shogun.

It was during the *later* Middle Ages that Japan came under the rule of the **shoguns** (SHOW gnz) and **samurai** (SAH mooh rye). A shogun was a feudal lord (or military commander) who served under the name of the emperor. In reality, he ran the country. The emperor, or **mikado**, remained a figurehead. The shogun was protected by samurai knights who were known for their sharp swords and unwavering loyalty. The tradition of the samurai lasted well into the 1800s.

## *Tokugawa Ieyasu*

So what happened to Japan in the 1600s that made it close its doors to the rest of the world? I'm getting to that. It had to do with one man, named **Tokugawa Ieyasu** (Toe koo GAH wah YAY ah sue). Though listed first, *Tokugawa* was the surname (meaning family name) of Ieyasu. *Ieyasu* was his personal name. Therefore, in history, the time period that started under his leadership is called *Tokugawa Japan* and it extended from **1603 to 1867**.

Ieyasu spent most of his life in battle. When only 6 years old, Ieyasu lived as a hostage under the care of his enemies. Between ages 9 and 15, he became hostage to another clan. He thus grew up knowing nothing but conflict and wanting revenge for his family. With patience and cleverness, Ieyasu eventually fought clan after clan and battle after battle until he finally took leadership of Japan.

Tokugawa Ieyasu was 60 years old in 1603 before he was named the new shogun of Japan. He made **Edo** his capital, which is now the city of **Tokyo**. There he improved the famous **Edo Castle**, now known as the Imperial Palace. His favorite pastimes were hawking (hunting birds with a trained hawk) and swimming. Even later in life, he was known to swim the moat that surrounded his castle. Ieyasu was the official shogun for only two years, but through his son, he continued to rule Japan as if it were his own. Some would consider him a dictator because of his strict policies. Ieyasu was not well liked, but he was greatly respected.

Under Ieyasu, Japan was slowly made a closed country. It *had* been open to outsiders for the exchange of goods and ideas. If you remember, Francis Xavier traveled to Japan with the Gospel message of Christ in the 1500s, and thousands of Japanese converted to Christianity. The Portuguese traded all kinds of goods between the East and the West. But Ieyasu grew suspicious of outsiders. He was afraid that Christian ideas and Western products would break down the traditions of Japan. He feared that the class system of Japan would unravel under the Christian teaching that all men are created equal. In an arrogant way, Ieyasu was probably afraid, too, of losing his power to outsiders and their ideas.

So, in 1612, Ieyasu made it illegal to be a Christian in Japan. Years later, it led to a period of terrible persecution. I'm sad to report that the persecution was so severe, it forced Christians to abandon their faith or die. Thousands of Japanese Christians did die. Thousands more were hushed, and the spread of Christianity was stopped in Japan for a long, long time.

As for the Portuguese traders, for a while they were allowed to trade in one city — the city of **Nagasaki**. But after many years, that port was closed too, and Japan was cut off from most of the world for a period of 200 years. No one was allowed in, and no one was allowed out. Even books from the outside world were banned until 1720.

This long period of isolation transformed Japan. Because the Japanese were cut off from trading with outsiders, they traded more intently from one island of Japan to another.

The islands competed and specialized to make the best goods. This led to greater prosperity among the middle-class merchants. As the economy boomed, so did the population. In fact, the population tripled in Japan during the Tokugawa period. Four times more rice had to be grown to keep up with feeding everyone. Rice was, and still is, the main staple in the Japanese diet. In fact, properly translated, the words for breakfast, lunch, and dinner in Japanese literally mean "morning rice, noon rice, and evening rice."

Though isolated from most of the world, the population of Japan tripled under the prosperity of the Tokugawa period.

## The Social Structure of Japan

While talking about rice, let me tell you a little bit about the farmers of Japan and the social structure of the country. Though they were a poor class of people, the farmers of Japan were considered second only to the nobility. Farmers, especially rice farmers, were an honored class of individuals because without them, no one would eat! Strangely to us in the West, the Japanese social structure looked like this:

- First were the nobility, which included the emperor, the shogun, and the samurai.
- Second were the poor working farmers.
- Third were the craftsmen who made things like swords and cloth.
- Fourth were the rich merchants who sold and traded goods.
- Fifth was a mixed group of people who didn't fit in the other classes. These would include priests, entertainers and artists, and the very, very poor, who were named the **"burakumin."**

It was extremely important to the Japanese that each person fulfill his or her role in society and be loyal to the government. For this reason, movement from one class to another was practically forbidden. Oddly enough, though merchants were the wealthiest class, they were *not* highly respected. The merchants were looked down on for not working as hard as farmers and craftsmen. Nonetheless, this class grew and enjoyed their great wealth.

In contrast, members of the burakumin class suffered. They were shunned by other classes. Much like the "untouchables" in India, the burakumin became the outcasts of society. Their nickname (which I won't write here because it is so offensive) means "much impurity" or "much dirt." This derogatory (meaning bad) nickname originated because the burakumin commonly had jobs that the Shinto religion viewed as "impure," such as handling the dead.

Though laws have been passed to protect the rights of the burakumin, great prejudice still exists in Japan, and many remain trapped in a cycle of poverty. The Ainu people, who are also a minority, are often trapped in the same cycle and treated as unfairly as the burakumin. This kind of prejudice is an unpleasant reminder that mankind can be terribly cruel and that racism can be found all over the world.

## *Sumo Wrestlers and Ninjas*

On a completely different note, the isolation of Japan led to the development of interesting customs and traditions that aren't found anywhere else in the world. For example, during the Tokugawa period, the Japanese invented the famous sport of **sumo wrestling**. Weighing up to 400 pounds, sumotori wrestlers, called sumo for short, are still valued for their enormous size and strength. These wrestlers spend years in intense training to gain weight and learn the skills and tradition of the sumo.

One Shinto tradition of sumo wrestling is to stomp around the ring to scare away evil spirits and sprinkle salt on and around them for purification. Sumo wrestlers still wear topknots on their heads like samurai warriors of the past. Using mass and muscle, the sumo wrestler's goal is to wrestle his opponent out of the ring without being taken down to the ground.

The weight a sumo wrestler carries is so great that it could kill him. So most sumo wrestlers today retire at 30, lose weight, and take on regular jobs. But their fame may last the rest of their lives.

Another fascinating development in Japan was **ninja** fighting. Though ninja fighters weren't like the superheroes seen today in films and books, they were a specialized group of people. Ninja were created far back in history to serve as a type of "secret police" to the emperor or shogun. By the Tokugawa period, they were hired by local lords as well to spy, fight, and assassinate under complete disguise.

Most ninja were probably outcasts to begin with, though some believe they were disowned samurai warriors who had lost their honor. Both men and women ninja stayed hidden among the peasants by appearing to be gardeners or servants. Because they were always "undercover," they learned to master all kinds of disguises and carry secretive weapons like throwing blades, hand claws, and iron spikes. They also mastered martial arts like karate and judo. For this reason, modern legend portrays the ninja as having superhuman abilities, such as being able to fly and to become invisible! Though fun to imagine, ninja, of course, couldn't fly or disappear. But they may have seriously dabbled with fireworks to pull off some of their stunts.

The root word for ninja means "to do quietly." The term has evolved from another Japanese word that means "skilled in the art of stealth." The ninja were so good at being secretive that their history remains mysterious today. Very little has been written about their past, but there is no doubt they were real. The ninja may have existed well into the 1900s, though it is hard to know for certain because fact and fiction have run together over time.

## *Purely Japanese*

During the Tokugawa period, Japan developed much more than specialized wrestling and fighting. On an intricate level, the Japanese developed **origami**, which is a precise and delicate way to fold paper into artistic creations. You may have tried origami yourself using special paper and instructions to make the shape of a bird or animal. It's a fun skill to learn.

Traditional origami involves the mathematics of folding and creasing paper into ingenuous shapes without the use of glue or scissors.

In a style of theater called the **bunraku**, the Japanese created an interesting way to deal with changing characters. They built large-sized puppets to portray the different actors and used only one narrator to read all the parts. The puppets were so elaborate that at least three men were needed to manipulate each one. These puppeteers dressed all in black and moved about as if they were invisible. Some think that for that reason, the ninja are commonly shown in black to resemble the stealth-like stagehands of the theater.

On a different note altogether, the Japanese have always been known for flying **kites**. I don't mean ordinary kites but rather, large festive works of art. Kite flying was probably brought to Japan by Buddhist priests in the tenth century as a way to ask their gods for blessings and thank them for a good harvest. But kite flying grew to be an amusing sport and a favorite Japanese pastime.

Last, I want to mention the literature of Tokugawa Japan. In the late 1600s, a poet named **Matsuo Bashō** made famous a form of poetry called the **haiku** (HIGH koo). A haiku is a short poem with only 17 syllables. The poem has three lines and contains at least one word relating to nature or the seasons. The first and third lines contain 5 syllables, but the second line has 7. It is hard to translate Japanese haikus into English. In the examples below, the Japanese syllables are numbered as they should be, but they don't exactly add up in English.

| | |
|---|---|
| ***Te wo uteba*** | *as I clap my hands* |
| ***kodama ni akuru*** | *with the echoes, it begins to dawn —* |
| ***natsu no tsuki*** | *the summer moon* |
| | |
| ***kirishigure*** | *in the misty rain* |
| ***Fuji wo minu hi zo*** | *Mount Fuji is veiled all day —* |
| ***omoshiroki*** | *how intriguing!* |

As you can tell, the Tokugawa period was rich and prosperous. It was as if Japan was experiencing its own Renaissance — privately from the rest of the world. Because peace was prevalent, the samurai spent less time fighting and more time appreciating poetry, the arts, and long tea ceremonies. Under Ieyasu, the Japanese also returned to ancient Shinto beliefs to promote strong nationalism. All were taught that the emperor was divine and worthy of respect. What we'll learn later in history is that it was this strong sense of pride and nationalism that drove the Japanese to fight the way they did in World War II. But that's another story for another volume when we'll learn of Japan reopening her doors to the world and shaping history.

## Lesson 51 — *1605*

# *Sir Francis Bacon and the Age of Reason*

After all we've learned about the influence of the Renaissance, you'd think it was going to last forever. But you know what? It didn't. Philosophers and scientists like **Francis Bacon** began to unravel the ideas of the Renaissance and replace them with the **Age of Reason**. What was the Age of Reason? I'll try to explain it in this lesson as we study the philosophies of Francis Bacon more closely. And just to let you know, Francis Bacon was no relation to **Roger Bacon**, an English scientist I wrote about in Volume II. The two "Bacons" did have a lot in common, though. Both were famous; both were English; and both promoted the **scientific method**.

Francis Bacon was born in London, England. He was schooled at home during his younger years. At the young age of 12, he entered Trinity College at Cambridge. He later went to law school. While Elizabeth I was alive, Francis held a few minor offices in the government and was given a seat in Parliament. One of many things he did in Parliament was to vote for the execution of Mary, Queen of Scots. Their lives briefly overlapped. But what interested Francis more than law was philosophy. In fact, it consumed him. You could say that what sculpting meant to Michelangelo, philosophy meant to Francis Bacon. It was his passion.

By writing *The Advancement of Learning* in 1605, Sir Francis Bacon drew attention to himself as a budding philosopher and promoted "reason."

As you know, Elizabeth I died in 1603 and James of Scotland became the next king of England. That same year, James I "knighted" Francis Bacon because he was very fond of him. It was two years later, in **1605**, that Francis drew even more fame. By writing ***The Advancement of Learning***, he brought attention to himself as a budding philosopher.

In this work, Francis Bacon began to formulate his ideas of "reason." Generally, Francis was tired of seeing brilliant men and women revert to *ancient* philosophers for the answers to life. Remember, that's what the Renaissance had been about — it was the "rebirth" of the ideas of the ancient Greeks and Romans. Francis Bacon believed in looking to sound reason, not the past, for understanding. In particular, he believed that answers could be found to just about anything through systematic learning and **science**. He once said that his goal in life was "To bring about the better ordering of man's life . . . by the help of sound and true contemplations [meaning science] — this is the thing I aim at."[1] (Words in brackets are mine.)

Well, Francis Bacon's goal in life was certainly a lofty one. I think he truly believed that man could be made "better" through reasoning and science because he also wrote the famous phrase that "knowledge is power." But Francis would live through some serious ups and downs before he could advance his theory.

## The Fall of Francis Bacon

In 1606, when Francis was 45 years old, he married for the first time, though apparently not for love. He had no children and continued to devote himself to his career. In an eight-year span, he was promoted under King James to attorney general, the Privy Council, Lord Keeper of the Great Seal, the baron of Verulam, and the viscount (VYE kaunt) of St. Albans. (A *viscount* was a social ranking just below an earl but above a baron.) With the addition of all these titles, Francis Bacon grew extremely wealthy. According to others, he spoiled himself like a prince and kept himself in debt.

It may be that his love for luxury is what first got Francis Bacon into trouble. It seems that in 1621, the same year he was appointed a viscount, Francis was accused of taking bribes while serving as a judge. (To "take a bribe" is to take money or a favor in exchange for doing something unethical or illegal.) The worst part of the accusations was that Francis Bacon admitted they were true! Some historians wonder if Francis was innocent of bribery charges but confessed to them out of loyalty to the king. Francis himself claimed that he was *forced* to plead guilty to the charges. Others theorize that Francis was simply as corrupt as the other judges of his day. Regardless, taking bribes was wrong, and Francis knew he would suffer for it.

For his crimes, Francis was thrown into the Tower of London and slapped with a hefty fine. But, being that King James was his good friend, Francis was let out within four days and his fine canceled! Though Francis was freed, his reputation was ruined. He kept his fancy titles but was not allowed to serve in the Parliament or hold any office in England.

## A Philosopher of Science

It was after this embarrassing episode that Francis Bacon poured himself into that which he really loved — the philosophy of science. Apart from his masterpiece titled *Novum Organum*, his greatest works came *after* he was disgraced. Funny how that works. It was in 1624 that Francis Bacon wrote *The New Atlantis*. It was a fanciful story, written like Thomas More's *Utopia*. In the same way that Thomas More imagined a perfect island with a perfect *social order*, Bacon imagined a perfect island with perfect *science*.

Lesson 52 1605

# *Cervantes Writes* Don Quixote

The last we looked at Spain, she was recovering from war with England. The Spanish Armada had been sorely defeated by Queen Elizabeth's navy, which meant that Philip II was knocked out of the race to rule the Western world. But Spain was not completely destroyed by the loss of its navy. The nation still had a beating heart. This was especially evident in Spanish art and literature. In fact, one of the world's greatest novels was written by a Spaniard of this time period. The novel was called *The Life and Adventures of the Renowned Don Quixote de La Mancha.* I'll call it ***Don Quixote*** (Don Key HO tee) for short. The writer was **Miguel de Cervantes** (Mi GELL day Sair VAHN tays). If you like stories of crusty old knights with a lot of imagination, you'll like *Don Quixote.*

Most would agree that the life and times of Miguel de Cervantes had much to do with the creation of *Don Quixote*. So let's start there. Miguel was the son of a poor traveling doctor. He went from town to town with his father, treating broken bones and minor ailments. Most young men of Miguel's day received a good education and were well read. But there is no record that he ever attended a university. He never immersed himself in the classics as most would expect of a great writer. No, Miguel was the kind of person who learned from his own life experiences. And some of those experiences were tough.

Miguel de Cervantes spent five years in the Spanish army. Fighting against the Turks in the Battle of Lepanto, he received a permanent wound to his left hand. On his return home to Spain, Miguel and his brother were intercepted by Moorish pirates, captured, and sold into slavery! Slave masters found that Miguel was carrying important letters and so believed him to be a prominent citizen. They kept Miguel for a high ransom and let his brother go. For five agonizing years, Miguel remained captive to the Moors in Algiers (Al JEERZ), a city in northern Africa.

Several times Miguel tried to escape from Algiers — but he failed every time. His mother sold belongings in hopes of buying him back. His sisters sold even their wedding dowries for money to trade for their brother. But it wasn't until they received help from some monks that a ransom was accepted for Miguel. In 1580, he was set free.

Though the timeline of his life is a little unclear, most think that Miguel tried his hand at writing as early as 1569. It seems that a schoolmaster in Madrid published six poems written by Miguel de Cervantes. His next work would not appear until 1584 when he wrote a romance for the woman he loved. It was titled *Galatea*. It was not a successful book, but it touched the woman he wrote it for. She agreed to marriage and to adopting Miguel's one illegitimate daughter.

Before Philip II declared war against England, Miguel de Cervantes helped stock ships for the Spanish Armada.

For the next 25 years, Miguel de Cervantes would be pretty unlucky with writing. He wrote at least 30 plays, but not one of them became famous. He had a hard time making a living this way and chose to work again for his country. He helped stock ships for the Spanish Armada — that is, before the war against England. You know how that turned out. After the armada was defeated, Miguel roamed about Spain, writing here and there, and serving time in jail for debt.

Strangely enough, it was while he was broke and in jail that Miguel de Cervantes was inspired to begin writing *Don Quixote*. It was published in **1605**. After all those years of bad luck, Cervantes finally struck gold. Many would say that *Don Quixote* is the most entertaining novel ever written. As recently as 2002, "one hundred major writers from fifty-four countries voted *Don Quixote* the best work of fiction in the world."[1] I find that impressive. So let's move on to getting to know the characters of this amusing, heartfelt story.

## Don Quixote and Sancho Panza

In the first chapter of the book, it is clear that Don Quixote, an old gentleman, is just a little bit senile. (That means he's losing his senses.) After years of reading tales of romance and chivalry, the old gentleman is confused as to what is real and what isn't. He imagines that every young girl is a damsel in distress and every old inn is a castle. As valiant as any knight of the Middle Ages, the old gentleman leaves his home to seek adventure and fame. He believes it his duty to right the wrongs and free the captives of his land — that is, if he can find any.

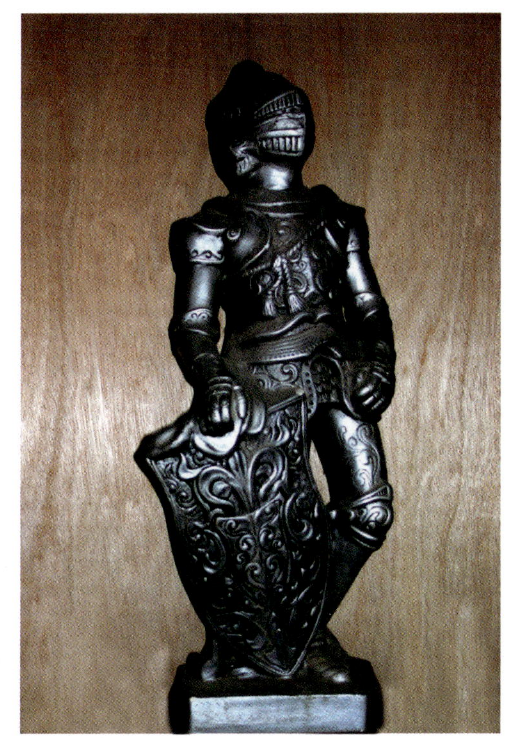

Miguel de Cervantes wrote *Don Quixote* when chivalry was dead and knights in shining armor were a remnant of the past.

The funny part about this quest is that Don Quixote lives in a time when chivalry is dead. The Middle Ages have passed and knights in shining armor are no longer needed to police the land. So the people he passes on the road snicker at his armor and lance and wonder just what the old coot is up to. Despite being elderly, Don Quixote is up to a lot! In one way or another, he creates knightly adventure, though most of the time he attacks innocent bystanders — mistaking them for bandits or thieves!

The literary balance of the book is found in Don Quixote's sidekick. You see, every good knight needs a squire, so Don Quixote coaxes a common villager to leave his family and accompany him on his great quest. The round little man's name is **Sancho Panza**. Together, the two set off but with very different mind-sets.

Don Quixote is a dreamer, an idealist, and a romantic. Sancho is practical, a realist, and down-to-earth. They represent two completely different ways to view life. Most of us have a little of both of them in us.

It is probably the blending of the two personalities that makes the book a classic. One funny example of their differences would be Don Quixote's attempt to fight a windmill, one that he perceives to be a "giant." With an air of properness, Don Quixote informs his companion that he sees 30 giants in the distance. Sancho replies that they are but large windmills. Not seeing the truth of the matter clearly, Don Quixote proceeds to attack a windmill with his lance. As the sails of the windmill turn, they scoop Don Quixote and his horse off the ground and drop them back just as hard! Sancho doesn't laugh at his master, but in a practical, caring way, he helps Don Quixote back on his horse to move along to their next adventure.

Amusing and tragic scenes like these are found over and over throughout the book as each man "battles" the world in the way he sees it. Neither is completely victorious. Neither is completely defeated. But both are beaten up and bruised on their journey. Some would say that the two characters represent the old Spain of medieval times and modern Spain after the Renaissance. Like Don Quixote, medieval Spain dreamed of dominating the world in a romantic kind of way. Like Sancho Panza, modern Spain was more sensible and calculating after the sinking of the Spanish Armada.

As for the author, Miguel de Cervantes, he cleverly keeps himself in the background of *Don Quixote* as a spectator of sorts. It adds to the feeling that the characters are quite real. Cervantes writes about the characters like a reporter on the scene, finding clues about their whereabouts and mishaps.

In a humorous scene, Don Quixote mistakes a windmill for a giant. As he attacks it with his lance, he and his horse are scooped up, then thrown back onto the hard ground.

## *Later Years*

After publishing Part I of *Don Quixote*, Miguel de Cervantes took a break from writing. It would be 10 years later that he published the second half. It was just long enough to create a demand for the book and finally help Cervantes make a living. Cervantes still tried writing other things, but nothing was very successful.

Unlike Shakespeare, Miguel de Cervantes didn't die a wealthy man. In fact, he never was. But he predicted that his great novel would sell at least 30 million copies. It far surpassed that! *Don Quixote* has been outdone only by the Bible in the number of languages into which it has been translated. It is enjoyed worldwide. I hope one day you'll read *Don Quixote* for yourself.

## Lesson 53 1605

# Australian Aborigines

As you probably know, there are seven continents on our planet earth. But only one of these continents is also considered a country. That would be **Australia**, the "land down under." Australia is called the land down under because the entire continent falls "under" the equator. This extraordinary land is like no other place in the world. But it wasn't until **1605** that Europeans were certain it existed. They learned of it when a Dutch navigator named **Willem Janszoon** (YAHNS zone) landed there. I'm going to tell you a little bit about Janszoon and how it was that he sailed to Australia, but most of this lesson will be on Australia itself and the original people who lived there. They are the **Australian Aborigines** (A buh RIH juh nees).

### Willem Janszoon

Little is known about Willem Janszoon before he became a ship captain except that he was probably born in the Netherlands. What we do know is that in 1603 he sailed east from the Netherlands toward the Indonesian islands, or East Indies, in order to trade. You already know how valuable the spice trade was to Europeans. They risked their very lives for it.

Willem Janszoon's ship was named the *Duyfken*, which means "Little Dove." It was one of 12 ships bound for the East Indies. Upon reaching the islands, Janszoon was commissioned by the **Dutch East India Company** to sail farther east to explore **New Guinea**, a large island *north* of Australia. But there may be more to that story.

Some speculate that Janszoon was sent toward New Guinea and beyond in search of gold and a great southern continent. You see, it had been rumored that King Solomon of the Old Testament had hidden gold somewhere around New Guinea. I don't know how or why this rumor was started, but it was. Furthermore, long before Willem Janszoon became a ship captain, Europeans suspected there might be a vast continent in the southern hemisphere. They called it *terra australis incognita*, which in Latin means "unknown southern land." Of course, the term *australis* has stuck around ever since and is the root word for "Australia."

As for Willem Janszoon, it would seem that the hope of finding both gold *and* land sent him to sea. He never found storehouses of King Solomon's gold, but he did find a great southern land. It happened like this: In 1605, after landing on the western shores of New Guinea, Janszoon turned his ships and sailed south into the **Gulf of Carpentaria**. (You might want to find that on a map right now. The Gulf of Carpentaria is the notched-out body of water on the northern shore of Australia.) Willem and his crew soon landed on the western shore of the Cape York Peninsula in Australia. He was near the present-day town of Weipa, Australia.

Though others may have beaten them to it, Willem Janszoon and his crewmen were, as far as historians know, the first Europeans to set foot on the continent of Australia. Though Willem knew he was onto something big, it is doubtful that he knew how big, how curious, and how amazing the place was. He stayed only a short time because the land there was swampy and the native people were hostile. Nine or ten of his men were attacked and killed by locals. So, after carefully charting hundreds of miles of the coastline, Willem Janszoon sailed back home with some rather wild stories to tell. His adventure changed the way maps were drawn for years to come.

## *Amazing Attributes*

So, had Willem Janszoon stayed awhile longer in Australia, what would he have found that makes this continent one of the most remarkable places in the world? I don't have room to tell it all. But here are a few things. I'll start with the attributes of the land.

At almost three million square miles, Australia is the sixth largest country in the world. And out of these three million square miles, two-thirds are dry, rocky, and hard to live in. Folks have nicknamed this harsh region the **"Outback."** The most famous landmark of the Outback is a huge rock named **Uluru** (or Ayers Rock). Uluru stands 1,142 feet high, but it is believed that most of the rock lies far beneath the earth and can't be seen! What can be seen is spectacular because tiny specks of feldspar in the rock reflect the sun and glow at dawn and dusk.

But not all of Australia is dry and rocky. In the east, there are snowy mountains, and in the west, there are stunning beaches. Of course, since Australia is in the *southern* hemisphere, the months of the summer and winter seasons are opposite what they are in the *northern* hemisphere. This means that the continent is coldest in June, July, and August — and warmest in December, January, and February.

Uluru stands 1,142 feet high and glitters in the sun from specks of feldspar. But most of the rock structure is buried deep in the earth and hidden from sight.

The crystal-clear waters along the edge of Australia contain the longest coral reef in the world. It's called the **Great Barrier Reef**, and it stretches for 1,250 miles. The reef is home to green turtles, dolphins, whales, and 1,500 species of fish. I imagine if I were a sea creature, I wouldn't want to live anywhere but around the beautiful coral of the Great Barrier Reef.

## *Amazing Animals*

The Great Barrier Reef off the coast of Australia stretches for 1,250 miles and is home to at least 1,500 species of fish.

The most unusual animal group in Australia is the **marsupial** (mar SOO pee uhl). Marsupials are mammals that carry their newborn babies in pouches where they nurse and develop. Believe it or not, there are about 260 different species of marsupials. But the most well-known ones — found only in Australia — include kangaroos, koalas, wombats, wallabies, bandicoots, and Tasmanian devils. At 6 feet high, the male red kangaroo is the largest marsupial and one of the most amusing. The shrew-like ningauis is the smallest marsupial, weighing less than one-tenth of an ounce!

My favorite marsupial is the cuddly koala. He is often mistakenly called a bear, but he is not one. The koala is known for its thick fur and lazy lifestyle. Koalas appear lazy because they sleep up to 18 hours a day. Their slow metabolism helps them digest the leaves of the eucalyptus (yoo kuh LIP tuss) tree, which are poisonous to most animals.

Other species unique to Australia are wild dingoes, frill-necked lizards, kookaburras, echidnas, and platypuses. The echidna and the platypus are the only mammals in the world that lay eggs. For this feature, they are truly peculiar. Australia is also home to giant crocodiles; 13-foot-long earthworms (called Gippsland giants); 10 of the world's deadliest snakes; and the *most* poisonous spider in the world — the funnel-web spider. (So be careful if you ever visit!)

Australia's most cuddly marsupial, the koala, is perfectly suited to digest the poisonous leaves of the eucalyptus tree.

## *Amazing Aborigines*

And now I get to introduce you to the Aboriginal people of Australia. *Aboriginal* means the "very first" and reminds us that the Australian Aborigines were indeed the *very first* to inhabit the strange but marvelous land of Australia. Before the arrival of Europeans in Australia, there may have been one to three million Aboriginal people. They lived within five or six hundred distinct groups, and each group had its own language, politics, territory, and social structure. Because of this diversity, it will be hard for me to accurately describe the Aboriginal people, but I'll try.

The Aborigines of Australia are a very spiritual people. Within their belief system they refer to **Dreamtime** as being how and when the world was created. Each Aboriginal group has its own version of Dreamtime that involves its favorite "spirit." As in Greek mythology, these spirits were believed to be both kind and cruel and were thought to influence and guide mankind. (Though a large percentage of Aborigines embrace other religions today, including Christianity, many still hold to their traditional beliefs.)

Of great importance, it was believed that the Dreamtime spirits designated the territories of the Aboriginal groups. For this reason, groups did *not* normally war with each other over boundaries and resources. On the contrary, Aboriginal groups usually cared for each other in times of drought or famine. A visitor once wrote, "I always noticed how open-handed and generous the Aborigines were. Some of us would do well to learn from them in that respect. If there were unfortunates who had been unlucky in the hunt for food, it made no difference — they did not go without but shared equally with the others."[2]

Sharing came naturally to the Aborigines because they had respect for one another and for their land. Rather than build permanent homes or plant crops, they traveled around their territories hunting, fishing, and living off the land. And they did so quite well. Aborigines were clever enough to survive in the wild, or the "bush" as they would call it. In the harsh, dry Outback they learned how to dig for water, lay traps, and carefully eat poisonous plants. Besides a diet of fruits, vegetables, grains, and meats, they also ate ants, bees, moths, and grubs. (Grubs, by the way, are supposed to be high in protein and taste like almonds — but I've never tried one!)

Most Aborigines hunted kangaroo and emu for meat, fur, and feathers. And they invented the famous boomerang for hunting. Did you know that a boomerang can travel nearly 300 feet? The returning boomerang, which is still made for sport, is a marvelous demonstration of aerodynamics.

Like cultures all over the world, the Aboriginal Australians still enjoy their own style of music, games, and ceremony. They gather at *corroboree* (core uh BORE ee) festivals several times a year for singing, dancing, and celebrating their heritage. Men decorate their bodies with paint and emu feathers and spread ash on their skin — like hunters did in the past. Music is played using click sticks and the didgeridoo (did jer ih DOO). The didgeridoo is a fascinating instrument made from a long, hollow branch first carved out by termites. To finish it, Aborigines smooth out the hollow tube, paint it, and add a rim of beeswax around the mouthpiece to make a mesmerizing wind instrument.

At a gathering called a *corroboree*, these Aboriginal children are celebrating their heritage by learning the music and dance of their ancestors.

During the Renaissance period, Aboriginal artists may not have painted like Leonardo da Vinci, but they were elaborate rock painters and carvers. They frequently illustrated the human body, both inside and out, as if they had X-ray vision. Their paintings often told stories related to their Dreamtime myths. But some animals were considered too sacred to put into art. Most groups carved totem poles to tell their stories, which were memorized from generation to generation for thousands of years.

### *Devastation and Reconciliation*

Knowing now how important the land was to the Aborigines of Australia, you can only imagine how devastating it was when the Europeans came along. Europeans were of the mind to explore, conquer, and claim the land of Australia that was new to them. Europeans of the seventeenth and eighteenth centuries disregarded the customs of the Aborigines and did not respect their natural boundaries and territories. Much like Native Americans in the United States, the native people of Australia were hurt by the newcomers. Their populations dropped because of new diseases brought by explorers and the loss of hunting grounds. Only 2 to 3 percent of Australians today are Aborigines! This number includes the **Torres Strait Islanders**, another minority group of original Australians. Like the Aborigines, these seafaring islanders have their own distinct culture and heritage.

As bizarre as it may sound, it was not until 1967 that the Aborigines of Australia were granted the right to vote in Australia and recognized as "citizens." Can you believe that? The very first people of Australia, who lived there for thousands of years, were not considered citizens of the land down under. It goes to show how differently people think.

Fortunately, things are improving in Australia for the Aboriginal people. They, along with the Torres Strait Islanders, have been speaking up for their rights for decades. As an example, in 1988, Aborigines marched in protest *against* "Australia Day" — a festive day set aside by most Australians to remember the arrival of Europeans. In 1993, the Native Title Act was passed to help restore land to the Aborigines and the Torres Strait Islanders. It is a step toward reconciliation between all the inhabitants of Australia.

And one last thing I find special is this: In 2000, an Aboriginal athlete named **Cathy Freeman** lit the torch for the Olympic Games that were being hosted in Sydney, Australia. Cathy Freeman went on to win the gold in her racing event. In other words, an Aboriginal Australian was chosen to represent the land down under before the entire world — and won the gold in doing so! I hope it is an indication of better things to come for all Australian Aborigines as they are recognized for their special heritage and home "down under."

## Lesson 54 — *1607*

# *The Founding of Jamestown*

In 1607, three ships sailed from England to the shores of North America. You could say that of *all* the ships that sailed to the New World, these ships would have the greatest impact. For you see, these ships carried a fiery redhead named **John Smith**, who was going to change history. By his tough and stubborn character, he was going to help a band of weary men survive the difficult founding of **Jamestown**, the first permanent English settlement in the United States. His success had something to do with the kindness and compassion of a young Indian princess named **Pocahontas**.

Sponsored by the London Company, Captain Newport and his settlers named Jamestown in North America after King James I of England. This is James I's coat of arms.

At 16, John Smith left home to seek adventure. He quickly found it by enlisting in the armed forces. He fought in numerous battles across Europe, suffering injury and captivity. I imagine those experiences were part of what made this man so tough.

It was in 1606 that John Smith first learned of three ships sailing to the New World. They were the *Discovery*, the *Godspeed*, and the *Susan Constant*. They were being sponsored by the **London Company**, a group of English merchants. As an adventurer, John Smith wanted to join — and did. However, halfway between Europe and the New World, John Smith was accused of plotting a mutiny! He was shackled in chains by Captain Christopher Newport, who was in charge of the expedition. Smith remained in chains for some time and barely escaped execution because he was *not* well liked. Nor was he trusted.

When the ships reached North America in **1607**, they landed on the coast of Virginia. If you remember, earlier in history Sir Walter Raleigh had named the east coast of the New World "Virginia" in honor of Elizabeth I, the Virgin Queen. In keeping with tradition, Captain Newport's settlers named their new home "Jamestown," in honor of King James I of England.

The London Company hoped that Jamestown would bring profit to England through gold or lumber. A few sincere souls hoped, too, to share Christ among the native peoples of North America. I'm not sure if any of the settlers then had a vision for starting a new *nation* in North America, but they had a big part in doing so. This is how: The king of England sent a secret box containing seven names with Captain Newport to the New World. The names of these men were not to be read until they reached their destination. The seven named men were selected to govern the new settlement under the authority of the king of England. Keep that in mind. Though people were *already* living in North America (and had been for thousands of years), the English believed that they had the right to claim the New World and rule it. Eventually they did both. Right or wrong, it was in a way the very beginning of the history of the United States of America.

Well, when the time came for the names to be read out loud, almost all were shocked to hear the name of John Smith. Though still in chains, Smith was one of the men chosen by the king of England to rule the New World! The captain of the expedition acknowledged Smith but chose to leave him in chains for at least the first month or two of their landing in the New World. John Smith was that unpopular.

When John Smith was finally released, it proved to be for the better of the colony. You see, the settlers weren't getting along at all, their supplies were short, and they had no strong leadership. Furthermore, a form of socialism was in place that allowed everyone to eat from the common storehouse, whether they collected food or not. The problem with that system was that at least 50 of the 100 men were "gentlemen" and didn't believe in hard labor. They preferred instead to laze about and search for gold. When John Smith got out of confinement, he changed all of that.

Though his tactics were nothing to be proud of, John Smith bullied his way into leading the entire colony. Some report that he resorted to poisonings, floggings, and assassinations of troublemakers. John Smith quickly saw that it would require hard labor from *every* man there to survive the upcoming winter. He issued a policy that if a man didn't work, he didn't eat! And he meant it. This policy changed the entire social structure of the community. Socialism was out, and private labor was in. (It was a form of **capitalism**.) Through private labor, the gentlemen with hungry stomachs were soon motivated to do their share of work in order to eat.

Regardless of everyone's work, times were terribly hard on the settlers. Food remained scarce because the men weren't equipped with good hunting and fishing supplies. Clumsy rifles only scared the deer away, and there were no nets for fishing. Jamestown sat near a swampy area infested with mosquitoes and low on pure drinking water. With the men now weakened by starvation and dehydration, sicknesses like typhoid, malaria, and dysentery raged through the camps, killing men left and right.

Jamestown was founded near a swampy area low on fresh water and infested with bloodthirsty mosquitoes.

John Smith, in taking charge of things, remained very unpopular. But some would admit that, by his forcefulness, he kept them alive. One of his ideas was to aggressively seek the Native Americans for help with food.

## *Pocahontas*

So let's talk about the Native Americans here. There were at least 18,000 **Powhatan Indians** living in the region of Virginia. Most spoke the Algonquian language. At that time, 30 tribes were united by one chief who went by the name Wahunsonacock. The settlers called him **Powhatan** (POW uh tann) because it was the name of the chief's town and empire — and it was easier to pronounce. I'll call him by the same.

Chief Powhatan was a negotiator. Though he never fully trusted the settlers, he tried to. At times, he and his braves were kind and friendly. They were impressed with the white man's magic needle and talking paper, better known as the compass and written language. Other times, the Native Americans were fearful and hostile. This leads us to the legendary story of Powhatan's daughter, the Indian princess named Pocahontas.

According to John Smith's version of the story, he was exploring territory of the Native Americans when they captured him and took him to the camp of Powhatan. On that occasion, according to Smith, Powhatan was not feeling friendly. He called for a stone block and club and laid John Smith's head on it with the intention of killing him right then and there! John Smith claims that Powhatan's young daughter Pocahontas, who was between

10 and 13 years old, was watching the event and threw herself over his head — crying and pleading for his life. Powhatan, out of love for his daughter, stopped the execution to appease her.

Some wonder if this story of Pocahontas is true. John Smith was suspected of exaggerating the truth and telling tall tales. I don't know. But there is evidence that Pocahontas was indeed a real Native American girl and the daughter of Powhatan. We know that because there is more to the story.

Over the next few months, Pocahontas remained loyal to John Smith and the settlers. She brought them corn and other food to help keep them alive. Why did she do this act of kindness? I wish I knew. It made her father nervous because he still did not trust the white man. I would like to believe that Pocahontas was just one of those rare people who had a heart of compassion that extended beyond race or color or beliefs. She took great risks in being nice to the settlers. But they were glad she did.

Powhatan continued to distrust the settlers more than he trusted them. On one occasion when John Smith demanded corn, Powhatan refused to give it. Smith in return offered Powhatan gifts from the king of England. Powhatan was given a luxurious bed, a basin and pitcher, and a purple cape. When the Englishmen offered Powhatan a crown, they had a hard time placing it on his head because he refused to bow down for the ceremony! Powhatan was a proud chief. Reluctantly, he gave up some corn in exchange for the gifts.

## *Surviving the Starving Time*

As for John Smith, from 1608 to 1609, he continued to lead the settlers through good and bad times until he suffered a terrible injury. A bag of gunpowder that he carried around his waist accidentally blew up on him. His pain was awful, and so he decided to sail back to England for proper medical care. He didn't know it then, but when he left the New World, he had not seen the last of Pocahontas. (I'll tell you the rest of her amazing story in another lesson!)

John Smith led the settlers of Jamestown for two years before he suffered a gunpowder injury and returned to England for medical care.

After John Smith left Jamestown, things went downhill for the settlers. New Europeans arrived but not with enough supplies. Without strong leadership, the men grew lazy, quarreled, and made poor decisions. They suffered from fires, Indian attacks, and drought. When winter set in, it nearly killed them all. Food supplies were far too low for fighting the sickness and disease that ravaged the camp. The settlers nicknamed that winter "the starving time." Indeed it was that, since only 60 out of 500 settlers survived until spring!

Fortunately, things improved in 1610 when a new governor named **Thomas West, Lord de la Warre**, took charge. (By the way, it is from his name that the name of the state of "Delaware" is derived.) Under Thomas West and others, Jamestown eventually found a way to survive. Though they tried and failed to harvest silkworms and grapes, they were successful at raising hogs, Indian corn, and a sweet-tasting tobacco. These products were shipped back and forth to England, bringing more and more settlers to North America with hopes and dreams of a new life.

One shipload of settlers was a little more significant than the rest. It was the ship that brought 90 "young, handsome and honestly educated maids" to Jamestown. In other words, young, available women were brought to Jamestown to become wives. They were significant because they gave the men incentive (meaning good reason) to settle, farm, and make a living. The new wives — and eventually the arrival of children — changed everything in Jamestown. The seeds of individualism and "free enterprise" were planted. Free enterprise is a term referring to the right to make a living through a private business. It allowed the men to better provide for their families. Free enterprise is a fundamental value of North Americans that still exists today.

Another value of Americans is the right of representation. This means that when decisions and laws are made, Americans want to have a voice in the matter. They want to be "represented." As early as 1619, a representative body was started in the New World. It was called the **House of Burgesses**. This house of individuals met to make laws for the bigger group of people on the basis of *representation*.

## *Seeds of Injustice*

As good as I make that sound, seeds of injustice were also being planted. Representation and the spirit of free enterprise had its problems. As with the Aborigines of Australia, the early Europeans did not understand what they were doing to the Native Americans. I'm sure some cared. But many didn't. Every pasture that was cleared for farming and business took away hunting grounds of Native Americans. Europeans drove Native Americans farther west or drove them to hostility. War was inevitable.

Furthermore, laborers were needed in the New World to make business boom. Tragically, a quick fix to meet this need came through the slave trade. Africans sold other Africans to Dutch sailors, who in turn shipped them to the New World to work. There was no freedom for these laborers. There was no fair representation. They would be enslaved for many years to come, causing wounds that have yet to be fully healed in the Americas.

Of course, I'm getting way ahead of myself here. The history of slavery in America is an issue we'll explore many more times. As you can see, both good and bad seeds were planted in America when Jamestown survived those early winters. By 1624, the king of England did away with the privately owned London Company and made Virginia a "royal colony" under his rule. In 1699, the town relocated a few miles away in **Williamsburg**, which became the capital city in the historic colony of Virginia. We've a lot yet to learn about the early American colonies — Jamestown was really just the beginning.

Lesson 55 1608, 1611

# Samuel de Champlain and Henry Hudson Explore Canada

Do you remember Jacques Cartier? He was the French explorer to Canada. Though he didn't establish a lasting settlement in Canada, he did establish a lasting trade. It was the fur trade. And this trade would lure other Frenchmen to explore Canada. The most famous was **Samuel de Champlain**. Today we'll look at Champlain and also at **Henry Hudson**, an Englishman who explored Canada and died a mysterious death after his crew mutinied against him!

## Samuel de Champlain

Samuel de Champlain was a gifted man. Of all the brave explorers we've looked at, he was probably one of the more "balanced." He had a good mind for trade, geography, exploration, navigation, and relating to natives, most commonly called the "First Nations" people of Canada. He was incredibly ambitious but not brutal, as many before him were.

Samuel de Champlain's greatest ambition was to settle the city of **Quebec**. He first arrived there in **1608**, about the same time that John Smith was taking charge of Jamestown. To fortify Quebec, Champlain set up permanent buildings and surrounded them with a 15-foot-wide moat. Like other early settlers, these pioneers suffered horrible conditions. Only 9 out of 28 people survived the first winter because of scurvy, smallpox, and the bitter cold.

While exploring Canada, Samuel de Champlain became personally acquainted with the First Nations people and their customs.

In the summer of 1608, Champlain tried to associate with the First Nations people of that region but not with all of them. He chose to join the **Huron** (sometimes called the Wyandot [WHY an dot]) and the Algonquians in battle against their enemies, the Iroquois. Unfortunately, this move would turn the Iroquois against the French in a war that lasted almost 100 years. But that's another story.

An important thing to remember about Samuel de Champlain is that he sincerely tried to understand First Nations people. With their animal-skin clothing, bark-covered longhouses, and unfamiliar hairstyles, the natives were very different from the French settlers. But this didn't prevent Champlain from getting to know them. He joined the Huron on hunting trips and rode the rapids with them for fun. He invited priests along to share the Christian faith. Champlain was intent on exploring Canada, but he respectfully involved native inhabitants on nearly every expedition he took.

Champlain's home country of France was still determined to find a northern passage to Asia. The French had yet to grasp how big Canada was and how remote was their dream of reaching China by this route. But they were beginning to realize that this new land was abundant with resources that just might be as valuable as spices. They were right about that. North America was "the land of plenty," as others would say.

Over the course of several years, Samuel de Champlain explored many corners of Canada and re-established a strong fur trade. The fur trade was largely based on the abundance of beaver in Canada. The fur of this large rodent was perfect for making felt-top hats, which were extremely popular in Europe. In fact, the beaver was so important to Canada's trade that it became a national emblem and remains on the Canadian nickel.

Expanding the fur trade all along the way, Champlain would travel to Montreal, the Ottawa River, Lake Nipissing, and Lake Huron. He continued to befriend the Huron, battle the Iroquois, and work on a peace treaty between them. The Huron insisted that Champlain spend a winter with them, during which time he learned firsthand about their customs and ways of life. Eventually he would write about all these things.

In one of his writings, Samuel de Champlain explained his ambition for navigation. He wrote:

> Navigation has always seemed to me to occupy the first place. By this art we obtain a knowledge of different countries, regions, and realms. By this we attract and bring to our own land all kinds of riches; by it the idolatry of paganism is overthrown, and Christianity proclaimed throughout all the regions of the earth. This is the art . . . which led me to explore the coasts of a portion of America, especially those of New France, where I have always desired to see the lily flourish, together with the only religion catholic, Apostolic and Roman.[1]

One obstacle to Champlain's mission would be the English. They wanted a corner of the growing fur trade, and so the English captured Quebec! During the capture, Champlain was taken prisoner and shipped to England. After some negotiations between France and England, Champlain was ultimately released. He was then reassigned as lieutenant governor of "New France," as it was called in Europe. Many still today refer to Samuel de Champlain as the "Father of New France," which is the French-speaking part of Canada.

On one of his many trips back and forth to the New World, Champlain brought his young wife, Helene. She was but 14 years old and Champlain was in his thirties. The teenage bride must not have adapted well to the New World because she visited only once. Samuel de Champlain, on the other hand, died in the New World on Christmas day in 1635. Through all his journeying, what he had accomplished was to start the first *permanent* European settlement in Canada.

## *Henry Hudson*

Now we'll shift gears to the English and the strange disappearance of Henry Hudson. His is an interesting story. Henry Hudson made four journeys to the New World. The first two journeys were under the sponsorship of the **English Muscovy Company**, which, like other merchant companies, was interested in finding a passage to Asia. They were called the Muscovy Company because of their trade with the Russians.

Henry's first journey was in 1607 aboard a ship named the *Hopewell*. He traveled with only 10 men and a boy. He hoped to sail across the frigid North Pole to reach China. This didn't work though, and they reached Greenland and Spitsbergen instead. The trip was treacherous in the icy cold waters, but the crew was amused with sightings of whales and whiskery walruses.

In 1608, Henry sailed again from England to North America looking for a northern passage to Asia. Of all things, on this trip Henry Hudson recorded seeing a mermaid! It is doubtful that there was any truth to this tale, but it sure made the trip more interesting. In the end, this second attempt to find a passage was a failure just like the trips before it.

In 1609, Henry Hudson tried a new trading company. He went to work for the Dutch East India Company, the same company that sponsored Janszoon on his voyage to New Guinea and ultimately, to Australia. At that time in England, it was considered treason to sail for another country. But Henry did it anyway. Could he have been hired by the English to sail for the Netherlands as a spy? We don't know, but some suspect that this is true because, although he was arrested for treason, Henry was never convicted of it. (That means he never served time for it.) But back to his journey . . .

Aboard a ship named the *Half Moon*, Henry Hudson sailed from Amsterdam in the Netherlands toward the North Pole, hoping again to reach China. Like his other voyages, he failed to find a shortcut. But this time, rather than suffer defeat, he changed direction and headed south. In doing so, Hudson reached the Chesapeake Bay and South Carolina. He then turned north and eventually entered what is now the Hudson River (later named after him). This river led him all the way to present-day Albany, New York. Though New York wasn't then what it is now, it was a great success to explore the region.

In 1610, Henry Hudson started his fourth and final voyage to the New World on a ship named the *Discovery*. This is the interesting voyage. For one, Henry was again being sponsored by an English company, leading some to wonder what his Dutch-sponsored voyage had been about. Second, rather than sail northerly as he always had, Henry entered the Hudson Strait when he reached North America. The strait then led him to Hudson Bay. (Of course, both the Hudson Strait and the Hudson Bay were later named after him.) It was his expedition around Hudson Bay that ended in mystery.

It seems that Henry Hudson's crew was baffled as to why they were continuing to sweep the edges of the bay. They were led to believe that they were still looking for a northwest passage to Asia. But Henry didn't carry onboard the *Discovery* any letters to introduce himself, any trade items for the Asians, or any of the other things one would expect of a crew seeking passage to the East. This leads some to think that Henry was on another mission — a secret one.

Some think that Henry Hudson had been sponsored to find the perfect harbor for a trading port in Hudson Bay. If he was, it would better explain his actions because he didn't just sail across the bay, he meticulously combed the coast charting his observations. He may have been comparing ancient maps to his modern ones.

Henry Hudson's behavior might have been acceptable with the crew had they not been starving, cold, and fighting disease. But they were! To worsen the tension, some crewmen suspected Henry of hiding a food stash! Henry accused them of the same. It was recorded that he cried when he passed out some of the very last food rations. So who knows who was really starving? The crew begged Henry to abandon the mission altogether and sail them back to safety. But he refused. Furthermore, when questioned by his crew, Henry would not reveal a thing about the purpose of their voyage. This made his men even more suspicious of him and less willing to cooperate.

As a result, on a cold morning in June of **1611**, the crew of the *Discovery* declared a full-fledged mutiny! Disillusioned with their leader, the crew forced Henry Hudson, his 19-year-old son John, and seven sailors loyal to Henry onto a small boat. They were set adrift in the Hudson Bay where some would say they were never heard from again.

The crew of the *Discovery* set Henry Hudson, his son, and seven sailors adrift in a small boat on Hudson Bay. Their fate remains a mystery.

There are legends and rumors about the fate of Henry Hudson and his small band of drifters. Some natives tell a story of a handful of European men who settled to live among them and marry. Others claim to have found skeletons of white men among the ruins of a small boat. Still others claim to have found the initials "H. H." carved up and down the Ottawa River, giving possible evidence of Henry's survival. By the insistence of Henry's wife, one rescue mission was sent out to look for Hudson and his crew, but they were never found. As compensation for her loss, Henry's wife received a trading post from the East India Company that made her a great deal of money after Henry's disappearance.

It may be impossible to ever know for sure what happened to Henry Hudson, his son, and those seven sailors. The possibilities are endless and intriguing. As for the crew of the *Discovery*, they struggled to return home safely. Some men died from starvation. Once in England, the survivors were arrested for declaring mutiny, but none were ever convicted of the crime. I can't help but wonder what Henry Hudson would have thought of that.

## Lesson 56 — *1608*

# *John Smyth: A Separatist of England*

History is full of controversy. I think you'll agree after this lesson. You see, some people would write that **John Smyth** was the founder of the **Baptist** denomination. Others would strongly disagree. I decided that I would include this lesson to remind us all to be careful of who we follow and what we believe. I also included this lesson because a lot of people are members of the Baptist denomination and will be interested in this part of history. (John Smyth, by the way, was not the same John Smith who was rescued by Pocahontas. You can tell them apart by the different spelling of their last names.)

John Smyth (with a *y*) was first ordained as a priest in the Anglican Church. To review, the Anglican Church was the Church of England. Though many would say that Henry VIII started the Anglican Church, he really didn't. He did, however, break away from the Roman Catholic Church because he wanted a divorce. It was Henry's daughter, Elizabeth I, who "formally" established the Anglican Church (though others before her laid the foundation). I hope you remember the long reign of Queen Elizabeth I. After the death of Bloody Mary, Elizabeth tried to keep both Protestants and Catholics "happy" with the doctrines of the Anglican Church.

Of course, neither devout Protestants nor devout Roman Catholics were satisfied. They did not see the Anglican Church as an acceptable middle ground. And so divisions over faith continued in England.

## The Puritans and the Separatists

Before I go any further, I need to explain more about these divisions — because there were divisions within the divisions! Let's pause for a minute and get some terms straight. Within the Protestant movement in England, there grew to be two main factions. They were the **Puritans** and the **Separatists**.

The Puritans believed that the Anglican Church needed to be "purified." They saw problems within the Anglican Church but didn't want to leave it. Their desire was to improve the church that existed. They were opposed to some Anglican ceremonies and to the use of symbols such as crosses and wedding rings.

The Separatists, on the other hand, also saw problems in the Anglican Church, but they wanted to "separate" from it altogether. Their desire was to start a new church, one that they believed would be true to the Word of God. Though a smaller group than the Puritans, the Separatists were the most persecuted. Thousands died cruel deaths for holding to their strong beliefs.

Just to let you know, the Puritans and the Separatists didn't call themselves by these names. These names were given to them as derogatory (meaning bad) terms by others who didn't share their beliefs. To complicate things, the Separatists were sometimes called **Independents, Congregationalists**, and **Brownists** (after Robert Brown, one of their more ambitious leaders). All of this is to say that because of name-calling and differing terms, the history of the Puritans and the Separatists can be confusing and the lines between them, fuzzy. Just remember that when we begin to study the **Pilgrims** — a group that included *both* Puritans and Separatists seeking religious freedom!

## John Smyth and Baptism

Now, to get back to John Smyth . . . as I said before, he was a priest in the Anglican Church. But he was an unhappy priest. John Smyth held to deep convictions that were not part of Anglican tradition. Therefore, around 1606, he "separated" himself from the Anglican Church. Because of this, John Smyth was considered by most to be a Separatist.

As a Separatist, John Smyth set up an independent church in Gainsborough, England. But it was not to last long. Persecution of Separatists was intense at this time. So, in **1608**, the congregation fled to Amsterdam, a city in the province of Holland in the Netherlands. It was a historic event.

Because of persecution, John Smyth and his Separatist congregation fled England in 1608 for the safety of Amsterdam, a city in the province of Holland in the Netherlands.

In Holland, John Smyth tried to set up a church that he believed was close to the church described in the New Testament. He strongly believed in personal salvation by faith through acceptance of the work of Christ. He also believed that baptism was *only* for those who had experienced personal salvation. We often call that "believer's baptism." Like many Christians today, Smyth would state that the baptism of infants was not according to Scripture (since they were too young to "believe"). For this, John Smyth would be labeled by some as a "Baptist." In fact, some would go so far as to say that Smyth's church was the first Baptist church because of his strong emphasis on believer's baptism.

Of course, I already told you that this is a controversial piece of history. Here's why. For one, Christians today are not in agreement over the baptism of infants. Some baptize babies; some don't. I'm not going to defend either side here but just say that this controversy exists, as do many others in Christianity.

But to complicate matters in John Smyth's time, he would change his mind about how and when baptism should be performed. This led to confusion among his followers. Because of this confusion, John Smyth was asked to leave his church in Amsterdam! John Smyth and 24 of his members did leave and sought acceptance in a Mennonite church in Amsterdam. Soon afterward, in 1610, John Smyth died while still living in Holland.

Now that you know that part of the story, let's look at the history of the Baptists. You can probably see why some Baptists today would NOT consider John Smyth their founder. He never called his church a "Baptist" church. Furthermore, for changing his ideas on baptism, he was asked to leave that church.

On the other hand, because John Smyth *originally* taught believer's baptism, many would say he *was* an early Baptist and his church in Amsterdam was a Baptist church. It's a bit confusing. Some historians think that it was actually members of the Amsterdam church who went *back* to England who first called themselves Baptists. They may have done so to distinguish themselves from other Protestants in England. Regardless, this doesn't give us the full history of Baptists.

There are yet those who would say that the Baptist denomination existed in one form or another since the days of the apostles, through the Donatists and the Waldensians. Early Christians may not have called themselves Baptists, but some believe they were practicing the same things that Baptists do today. These same believers would profess that they were never a part of the Roman Church and did *not* spring out of the Reformation.

Some would label John Smyth a Baptist for originally teaching believer's baptism. Over time, however, he would change his teachings.

You may be wondering, does all of this really matter? I think it does. I think Christians need to be very careful in stating their beliefs and doctrines. Whatever one's denomination or faith, it should be taken seriously. Because men and women will make mistakes, I believe it's important that Christians look above all else to the Holy Spirit and the Holy Scriptures for knowledge and understanding of God.

# The Marriage of Pocahontas

The last we looked at **Pocahontas**, she supposedly saved the life of John Smith when she dramatically threw herself over him and begged that he be spared. Well, there is still much debate as to whether or not that story is true. But what *is* true about Pocahontas is that when older, she was sold out, kidnapped, and married. She gave birth to a baby in the New World, then traveled to England to see the Old World for herself! I find it an intriguing story of love and adventure that brought two very different worlds together.

As you learned before, Pocahontas was the daughter of Chief Powhatan. Because he was the "king" of many native tribes, most would consider Pocahontas a "princess." But that title is questionable. We are not sure if she or her people would have given her this exalted title.

You see, the birth name of Pocahontas was **Matoaka**. But the Native Americans nick-named her "Pocahontas," which means the "naughty one," the "spoiled child," or the "one who plays." Her winsome nickname gives us the clue that she had a mischievous character and may not have been what others would consider "proper" princess material. For myself, I would very much like to have known this brave little Native American girl. (To stay with tradition, I'll call her Pocahontas, too.)

Going back in time a bit, it was 1609 when John Smith was injured from a gunpowder explosion and sailed back to England. After he sailed, the settlers told Pocahontas that John Smith was dead. I don't know why she was misled. But she was. Still, she continued to interact with the settlers of Jamestown. She carried messages to and from her tribe, traded furs and food for English tools, and practiced cartwheels with the boys just for fun. Some believe that somewhere along the way, she married a Native American warrior.

## Captured!

Well, it was in 1613 that the life of Pocahontas would dramatically change. It seems that both Native Americans and Europeans would have a hand in her demise. A ship captain named Samuel Argall bribed a Native American couple with a shiny copper kettle if they would help him lure Pocahontas onboard his ship. The couple agreed. I don't know why they would sell out and betray one of their own, but they did.

The captain's intention was to capture Pocahontas and use her for ransom in negotiating with Chief Powhatan! The plan didn't exactly work. Powhatan would *not* give the ship captain everything that he wanted in exchange for Pocahontas. That, too, is hard to believe. It may reflect that Powhatan had lost faith in his daughter after she first befriended the white man. It's hard to say.

For a year, Pocahontas remained in captivity with the European settlers. She was moved from Jamestown to a secondary English settlement named Henricus. It is believed that she was treated well and taught English and the basics of the Christian faith by Alexander Whitaker, a theologian from England who had started two churches near the Jamestown colony. I don't know exactly what Pocahontas thought of the story of Jesus Christ, which would have been new to her, but she professed to become a Christian and was baptized. She took the English name of Rebecca.

As if those changes weren't drastic enough, Pocahontas went a step further. On April 5, **1614**, she married a kind English widower named **John Rolfe**. Native Americans speculate that she only married to gain her freedom. We don't know if she married for love or self-preservation. But in a letter that John Rolfe wrote, it would appear that he truly loved her. He wrote, "It is Pocahontas to whom my hearty and best thoughts are, and have been a long time so entangled, and enthralled in so intricate a labyrinth that I could not unwind myself thereout."[2]

I find myself extremely curious about this wedding in the New World. I wonder if Pocahontas wore flowers in her hair or carried them in a bouquet. I wonder if she followed the wedding traditions of her native people or of the Europeans or both. Apparently, many friends and family rejoiced over the marriage of this couple and attended the wedding — that is, except for Chief Powhatan. I suspect that he did not approve. But the marriage helped create peace between the Native Americans and the European settlers — at least for some time. Even Chief Powhatan must have warmed up to the idea for he did allot the couple property for a cottage along the James River.

Just about a year later, Pocahontas and John Rolfe had a baby boy, whom they named **Thomas**. With parents of the Old World and the New, I wonder what he looked like and how his mother bundled him. Did she carry her son in warm animal skins like a Native American papoose or wrap him in soft woven blankets like an English newborn? I wonder if she whispered softly to him in her language or if she sang to him newly learned lullabies in English. We may never know these details.

From letters written by John Rolfe, it would appear that he married Pocahontas for true love. He claimed to have "hearty and best thoughts" for her.

## *Traveling to England*

Well, as time passed, John Rolfe decided to take his wife and child back "home" to England. The English were excited at the idea, as was Chief Powhatan. But there was probably political motivation on both sides. For the English, showing off Pocahontas in England would surely create excitement and support for settlers to the New World. For Chief Powhatan, it was a chance to send his warriors to scope out the homeland of their white "invaders" and learn what the white man was capable of. So, when the time came to sail, Pocahontas was joined by 12 of her own people. Uncertain of their future, they were brave to leave home.

Once in England, Pocahontas fully adopted the ways of the English. She dressed in high style with long, frilly dresses and pulled up her hair with pins and curls. It must have felt peculiar to dress like European women and walk in high-heeled shoes! But she did. Imagine Pocahontas seeing castles and cathedrals for the first time, hearing harps and church bells, and smelling sugar-coated pastries and puddings. I hope she enjoyed the new sights and sounds and scents. The English adored her and treated her like royalty. Pocahontas was invited to balls, banquets, dances, and plays, including one written by William Shakespeare. I can hardly imagine what she thought of that.

In adopting English customs, Pocahontas would have traded in her soft leather moccasins for high-heeled shoes!

I mentioned in a previous lesson that John Smith had not seen the last of Pocahontas. If you remember, he returned to England to heal from his wounds. It is said that the two saw one another at least twice in public. Apparently their encounters were awkward. Maybe because Pocahontas had been told that John Smith was dead! Or maybe John Smith was concerned she might tell stories that were a little *different* from the ones he told about the New World. Many suspected that he fibbed a lot about his North American adventures to make himself more of a hero than he was.

Regardless of their strained encounters, John Smith wrote to the queen of England to say that Pocahontas had been kind to him and once saved his life. It prompted the queen to invite Pocahontas to her court! At least, that's how the story goes. We may never know exactly what transpired between Pocahontas and John Smith.

The saddest part of this story is that as Pocahontas and her husband and toddler prepared to travel back to North America, Pocahontas fell ill — deathly ill. At only 21 or 22, she suffered from a bad case of either pneumonia, tuberculosis, or smallpox. She never boarded the final ship that sailed back to the New World. She never crossed the sea to embrace her own people again. Pocahontas died in England and was buried there at St. George's Church in Gravesend. Many grieved the loss of this special young woman who had shown so much courage in her lifetime.

As for John Rolfe and Thomas, they lived most of their lives in North America. Unfortunately, peace with the Powhatan nation did not continue. After Chief Powhatan died, fighting broke out between the settlers and the Native Americans. The Powhatan nation would not survive.

As an interesting side note, some have tried to trace the descendants of Pocahontas and John Rolfe to modern times. One descendant was **Edith Wilson**, the second wife of Woodrow Wilson (America's 28th president). For a time, some believed that the family of President George W. Bush was related, but that theory has been disproved.

In closing, I want to discuss the way that Pocahontas has been portrayed in films and books. She is certainly a well-loved figure. But recent films and many children's books are hardly accurate from a historical perspective. In a romantic way, Pocahontas is usually shown as a young woman when she rescues John Smith, rather than as the child she was (if it happened at all). Then, in fairy-tale style, the two supposedly fell in love! Well, when you come across this legend, try to remember the real story. Remember that Pocahontas, when just a little girl, really did show kindness to the European settlers of Jamestown by bringing them corn from time to time. But rather than live happily ever after, Pocahontas was kidnapped and used as a pawn between the English and her Native American people. Eventually, and tragically, she died in England at a young age, leaving behind her husband and baby son. Hers is a brave but tragic story of two very different worlds coming together and shaping history.

The real story of Pocahontas is a brave but tragic account of two very different worlds coming together and shaping history.

# WEEK 20

## Lesson 58 — 1618–1648

# *The Thirty Years' War*

The **Thirty Years' War** was nothing simple. I guess wars never are. What complicated this war was the fact that it involved *several* nations across Europe in a total of 40 battles. And unfortunately, it started as a battle between the faiths — that is, the faith of the Protestants and the faith of the Catholics. The good news is that this would be one of the last *major* wars between Christian groups in Europe.

The Thirty Years' War, which lasted from **1618 to 1648**, is so complicated that I will never be able to cover it all in a few pages. What I'll try to do is break it down into four major phases according to who was fighting whom. In this order, we'll study what I'm subtitling *The Bohemian Revolt*, *The Danish Invasion*, *The Swedish Charge*, and *The French Involvement*. Last, I will focus on the damage and effects of the agonizing war. As you will learn, it is often the common people who suffer the most from war.

The Thirty Years' War won't make any sense until I clarify the makeup of the Holy Roman Empire. So I'm going to start with that. The Holy Roman Empire was not necessarily holy. Nor was it Roman. It was not even a country. The Holy Roman Empire was a region that *included* several nation/states in Europe who agreed to fall under the leadership of the Holy Roman Emperor. These nation/states included Austria, Bohemia, Franche-Comté, Germany, Lorraine, Luxembourg, Moravia, Switzerland, and part of Hungary.

The Thirty Years' War sprawled across Europe, involving several nations in 40 battles. Many suffered from the damage left behind.

For almost 400 years, the Holy Roman Emperor came from the same powerful family. It was the family of the **Hapsburgs** (also known as the Habsburgs). Remember that! And note that Bohemia and Germany were two nation/states that were *part* of the Holy Roman Empire. You'll soon see why this is important information.

It was in Bohemia that the Thirty Years' War would have a rather "unusual" start. You see, it happened twice in Bohemia's history that unhappy citizens threw their officials out of windows as a means of punishment or death! The second time was on May 23 in **1618**. It seems that a group of Protestant citizens (including some Calvinists) were upset with their Catholic rulers for taking away their religious rights and freedoms.

*Fenestra* means "window" in Latin, and *de* means "out of." So the *De-fenestration of Prague* refers to a historic event in Prague when individuals were tossed from a window.

In particular, a new king of Bohemia, named **Ferdinand II**, wanted to close Protestant churches and forbid their members to gather. As a result, a mob of angry Protestants rallied together in the city of Prague. Eyewitnesses claim that some people in the mob tossed two governors and a secretary out of a 50-foot-high window! Surprisingly, the three who were tossed survived. The Catholics claim it was divine intervention. Protestants claim the officials' lives were spared only because they landed in a heap of manure — which in fact they did! (Seems there are always two sides to a story.)

This messy event was labeled in history as the **Defenestration of Prague**. What does *defenestration* mean? I'm glad you are wondering that. In Latin, the word for "window" is *fenestra* and *de* means "out of." So *de-fenestration* refers to tossing something out of a window — in this case, several people! Regardless of the term, this single event would spark a war that was to last for the next 30 years and nearly ruin Germany for two centuries to come.

## *Phase One — The Bohemian Revolt*

The first phase of the Thirty Years' War lasted about five years, from 1618 to 1623. It occurred in Bohemia where the war started to begin with. After Ferdinand II became king, Protestants rose up in a revolt because they were so unhappy with the king's policies. And in fact, they were so unhappy that they elected their own king. His name was **Frederick**. He was a strong Calvinist.

The Protestants' plan to depose (meaning to get rid of) Ferdinand II and replace him with Frederick might have been more successful except for one serious problem. Shortly after being deposed, Ferdinand II was elected by *other* nation/states to be the *emperor* of the Holy Roman Empire! Remember, Bohemia was just a little part of the Holy Roman Empire. In becoming emperor, Ferdinand now ranked *higher* than the king of Bohemia. You could call it a promotion.

So Ferdinand II, now acting as the "Holy Roman Emperor," quickly ordered Frederick to leave the throne of Bohemia. Frederick refused and so an army of 25,000 men crossed from Austria to Bohemia to physically remove him. The army was led by the **count of Tilly**. (Most people refer to him simply as Tilly.) In the **Battle of White Mountain**, Tilly won that part of the war near Prague. He overthrew Frederick and restored Catholicism in Bohemia. Frederick was nicknamed "the winter king" for having lasted only a few winter months on the throne.

Had things stopped with the removal of Frederick, there might not have been any more to the Thirty Years' War. But word soon spread through the Holy Roman Empire that Ferdinand II, the new emperor, was *not* going to be tolerant of Protestants. Ferdinand II was indeed a devout Catholic who was trained by Jesuits. But he is not to be blamed for the rest of the war. *Both* Protestants and Catholics were guilty of bashing each other. Neither side extended grace to the other. By the year 1618, there were 1,800 publications written back and forth between the faiths. These publications were full of lies, bad names, and gross exaggerations. These tabloid-style writings added deadly fuel to the flames of the Reformation. The Protestant Reformation — which had started 101 years earlier with Martin Luther — was still alive.

## *Phase Two — The Danish Invasion*

The second phase of the Thirty Years' War started in 1625 and lasted about four years. In this case, it was the king of Denmark who acted. His name was **Christian IV**. He was a strong Lutheran. Due to the location of his country *near* the Holy Roman Empire, he feared the policies of Ferdinand II and rose up in arms. In 1625, Christian IV of Denmark led 20,000 men to war. It wasn't going to go well for him.

For one, Christian IV had to deal with Tilly, who had already squelched the Protestants in Bohemia. But besides that, Christian IV had to contend with the very best general that Ferdinand II had. His name was **Albrecht von Wallenstein** (AL breckt von WALL en stine). Wallenstein was a military genius with a greedy army. I say greedy because they fought for the emperor in exchange for the spoils and the booty they could keep. Wallenstein's army was an unusual mix of Protestants *and* Catholics, but Wallenstein himself was educated by the Jesuits, passionate about Catholicism, and very rich. Christian IV could not compete with Wallenstein's fury and strength. Christian IV was forced to give up his fight against the empire after losing a series of battles. In order to keep his throne as the king of Denmark, Christian IV signed the **Treaty of Lübeck** in 1629.

Once again, the war could have ended there. Many wish it had. But Ferdinand II allowed politics to interfere. He was urged by a group of Catholics to take back property that had fallen into the hands of the Protestant Lutherans. In what has been called the **Edict of Restitution**, Ferdinand II demanded that a great amount of wealth and property be returned to the Roman Catholic Church. According to Catholics, it was property that was rightfully theirs. This edict didn't go over very well across the Holy Roman Empire, which was already painfully divided by the warring faiths.

## *Phase Three — The Swedish Charge*

This leads to the next phase of the Thirty Years' War. The third phase occurred between 1630 and 1635. It involved the Swedish. Why the Swedish? Well, while they were not *part* of the Holy Roman Empire, they were close enough to be *affected* by the empire. A popular king of Sweden named **Gustavus II Adolphus** (Goo STAH voose *or* GOO stah voose Aye DOLL fuss) — also known as Gustav II Adolf — chose to lead a charge against the Holy Roman Emperor. For his strong character, he was nicknamed the "Lion of the North."

Flintlock guns, first developed about 1610, were more common by 1630. Compared to other guns, they were lighter, easier to keep steady, and quicker to reload.

King Gustavus Adolphus, like Christian IV, was concerned with the growing power of the emperor. He thought his best *defense* was to establish an *offense*. In other words, to avoid being taken over, he tried to gain a foothold on the mainland of Europe. It would take an army to do so.

King Gustavus Adolphus had just the right army in mind. He meshed the troops of several nations together to build an army of 40,000 men. These men were swift and mobile because they used newly developed flintlock guns instead of old-style matchlocks. These new weapons were lighter to carry, easier to keep steady, and quicker to reload.

Besides that, King Gustavus Adolphus created a strong army by demanding high morals of his men. Women were forbidden to visit unless they were the wives of the soldiers. Every morning and evening was dedicated to prayer, and worship services were held on Sundays. What I appreciate about King Adolphus is that, wherever he conquered, he allowed freedom of religion. He did not force his own convictions on others. That's not what he was fighting for.

In the **Battle of Breitenfeld** (1631), Tilly's army was hit hard and defeated by the Swedes. A year after this, Tilly himself was injured in battle and later died of his wounds. It turned the tide in the Thirty Years' War in favor of the Protestants. It also left King Adolphus, the Lion of the North, to meet face-to-face with Wallenstein, who was still the best general the Holy Roman Emperor could put forth in his defense.

It was November 16, 1632, when the face-off occurred. In this famous battle, called the **Battle of Lützen**, King Adolphus had 25,000 men and Wallenstein, 40,000. Wallenstein was given extra help from Spain. Though the Swedes were outnumbered, the troops of King Adolphus were victorious. However, in the midst of the battle, King Adolphus — the Lion of the North — was shot and stabbed to death. That night, the winners of the battle cried — for losing their hero. The losers of the battle rejoiced — for losing their main enemy. It was a mixed victory for the Protestant army and a mixed defeat for the Catholics.

In the Battle of Lützen in 1632, the Swedes successfully defeated Wallenstein, but they lost their leader, King Gustavus Adolphus, the Lion of the North.

## *Phase Four — The French Involvement*

Okay. So we have just one more phase of the Thirty Years' War to cover. Hang in there. The last phase involves the French. At this time in history, the country of France was being run by a cardinal of the Roman Catholic Church. He "ran" France, so to speak, because the king of France was too young to take the throne. The odd thing about this cardinal, whose name was **Richelieu** (REE shuh LYOO), is that he decided to support the *Protestant* army of the Swedish and Dutch in their final sweep against the Holy Roman Empire. What? Why would a Catholic support a war against a Catholic emperor? Well, the war no longer had to do with religion. It had more to do with power. Let me explain.

As a final twist to the Thirty Years' War, Richelieu, a devout Catholic, gave his support to the Protestant Swedish army to suppress the powerful family of the Hapsburgs.

Richelieu was devout in his Catholic faith but not vicious toward Protestants. He never tried to take away freedom of worship from the French Protestants (the Huguenots). His issue was power. He was most concerned with keeping the strong Hapsburg family in their place. He feared that one day the Hapsburgs of the Holy Roman Empire would join with Spain and take over France. It was a threat he could not afford to deal with. So Richelieu (a Catholic) gave his financial support to the *Protestant* Swedish army to keep the Hapsburg family under control. It meant that the fighting of the Thirty Years' War would continue on.

Ferdinand II's son, who served next as the Holy Roman Emperor, was not as tough as his father had been in military matters. When he was handed the Thirty Years' War, he looked for ways to end it. As I stated before, by this time the war was no longer about religion. Nor was it simply one nation against another. The war had grown to involve Calvinists, Lutherans, and Catholics in six nations, including Germany, Denmark, Bohemia, Spain, Sweden, and now France. Most of the fighting had taken place on German soil, though the Germans weren't the initiators of the battles. The new emperor had inherited quite a mess. His name, by the way, was **Ferdinand III**.

## *The Peace of Westphalia*

Ferdinand III was not the first to want peace in the Holy Roman Empire. The Germans were more than worn out from the war. They were exhausted. (I'm exhausted just trying to write about it all!) By then, the country had been ripped to pieces from the fighting that sprawled from one village to the next. Farms were ruined; businesses were abandoned; and the commoners were hungry, as were the soldiers who ravaged the countryside begging for bread. In some cases, they begged for horses, dogs, and rats to eat. Things were horrifically bad. Two-thirds of all property was destroyed, and perhaps one-third of the population was dead. (I say "perhaps one-third" because it's hard to count how many died from war wounds and the disease and famine that followed.)

Finally, the decision was made to hold a meeting and try to end the war. The delegates were so filled with hatred toward one another that they didn't think they could meet face-to-face. They opted instead to meet in two different cities in the state of **Westphalia**, Germany. The French attended both locations. You won't believe how long the "meeting" took. Just to get started, it took six months for everyone to agree on who would sit where! (Too many egos, I suppose.) Then, it took another three and a half years for negotiations to take place. Finally, after four long years, the **Peace of Westphalia** was agreed upon in 1648. Almost everyone signed the treaty — except the pope and some other unhappy individuals. (Because of this, the pope's power in Europe was never quite the same.)

But here are a few important things that were decided through the Peace of Westphalia. *First,* the Calvinists living in the Holy Roman Empire were recognized and given rights equal to those of the Lutherans. That was a big deal for Calvinists who were growing in number. *Second,* Sweden was given control over the mouths of three rivers, which would help Sweden stay in the trade business no matter how powerful the Holy Roman Empire grew to be. *Third,* France was allotted portions of land to ensure that they would not be run over by the empire. The French gained the most from the treaty.

Well, I think I've done it. I've given you the *basic* story of the Thirty Years' War in a few pages. It's a lot of information to absorb and may require some rereading. As for the *effects* of the war, it would do more to Europe than anticipated. I'll sum it up with these three things. *First,* the war would leave the Europeans helpless in many ways and open to the leadership of some very powerful kings. Just wait till you learn about Louis XIV of France! *Second,* the bitter taste of this religious war would steer some toward the New World in hopes of religious freedom. That's a whole story in itself that we will look at next. *Third,* the war would lead others away from faith altogether. Remember the Age of Reason we discussed? It would be more appealing than ever for some people to look toward reason rather than toward God to better their lives. In my opinion, that would be the saddest result of all.

## Lesson 59 — 1620

# The Pilgrims Land at New Plymouth

"Are we there yet?" I wonder how many times the children on board the *Mayflower* asked this question. Their voyage across the Atlantic was as expected — smooth at times and tumultuous at others. When bad storms hit, the ship was tossed to and fro. In one such storm, lightning struck the crossbeam of the mast. There were lots of days and nights when the children were forced below deck along with the other passengers. The stench was awful, but it was far too dangerous to be outside on those bad days. One crewman had already fallen off the deck and been rescued. He was lucky to have survived.

The *Mayflower* made its historic voyage from Plymouth, England, to New Plymouth, Massachusetts, with 102 passengers and a crew of about 30 men. Thirty-two passengers were children.

As far as the Separatists were concerned, it wasn't luck that was keeping them alive. It was prayer. The Separatists, as you know, were those people who wanted to "separate" from the Church of England. They held deep convictions regarding the Word of God. For this, they were seeking religious freedom in the New World.

## *Persecution in England*

The story of the Pilgrims really begins in the early 1600s when a group of Separatists (and some former Puritans) started their own congregation in Scrooby, England. Members included **William Brewster**, a postmaster and tavern keeper; **William Bradford**, a 12-year-old orphan; and **John Robinson**, who later became a pastor. At this time, James I was the king of England. Under his reign, there was a great deal of hostility toward anyone opposed to the Church of England. It led to persecution.

The Separatists were forced to meet secretly at the Scrooby manor. Authorities were suspicious. William Brewster was fired as postmaster (or perhaps resigned), and church members were being spied on day and night. A few were tortured and imprisoned. So the congregation of Scrooby decided to pack their belongings, sell their homes, and move to Holland in the Netherlands.

The Separatists' first attempt to flee in 1607 ended in disaster. Their plot was discovered, and most of the congregation was thrown in jail for a month! The second attempt was equally difficult when authorities once again found out their plans. As the men escaped by ship, the women and children were held back from joining them. There was great distress, and many tears were shed! But the women and children were released and in 1608, the families reunited in Amsterdam, Holland. This was near the time that John Smyth moved *his* congregation to Amsterdam. (I hope you remember the controversial John Smyth.) For a short time, the two congregations merged. But eventually, about 100 of the Scrooby churchmen moved to **Leiden** (LYE den), Holland. Though Leiden wasn't "home," it was a place to freely worship God.

The Separatists would have stayed in Leiden, Holland, a long time I suppose, except that things weren't going as smoothly as they hoped. The Separatists had been farmers back in England. But in Holland, they were forced to work in factories. It was so difficult to make a living that even the children were working in the factories and falling behind in their schoolwork. Furthermore, after 11 years in Holland, the young people were forgetting their English customs; they were forgetting English and speaking Dutch; and they were picking up bad habits. William Bradford wrote this of the youth: ". . . of all sorrows most heavy to be borne, was that many of their children . . . were drawn away by evil examples into extravagant and dangerous courses, getting the reins off their necks and departing from their parents."[1]

Besides that, William Brewster was a "wanted" man in Holland for printing and shipping religious materials to England. And on top of it all, Spain remained a constant threat to the Dutch. (Remember the Dutch Revolt?)

Through all these difficult circumstances, many Christians believe it was the Lord who led the Separatists to relocate. But where? Well, as difficult as things had been for the settlers of Jamestown, the New World was still inviting. The land was ripe, abundant, and wide open. Yes, there were reports of friction with Native Americans living there, but some had proven to be friendly. The Separatists were eager to share Christ, to settle, and to spread out in a new land. After all the trials, the bloodshed, and the persecution of the Reformation, the Separatists were willing to move again for the sake of freedom.

## *Heading to the New World*

William Brewster was one of the leaders who arranged the voyage across the Atlantic Ocean. London merchants agreed to finance the trip using an old boat named the *Speedwell*. Brewster and members of his church boarded the *Speedwell* and sailed first to England. Pastor John Robinson stayed behind with the rest of the church, hoping to join them later. I wonder what it was like when these brothers and sisters in Christ said good-bye. Did they exchange gifts and goods for the trip? Did they exchange hugs and prayers? William Bradford wrote in his account, ". . . truly doleful was the sight of that sad and mournful parting, to see what sighs and sobs and prayers did sound amongst them, what tears did gush from every eye, and pithy speeches pierced each heart."[2]

There were many uncertainties ahead for the travelers, not to mention great danger. John Robinson led church members in a day of prayer and fasting before they divided the church in two. For inspiration, he read Ezra 8:21, asking the Lord for the "right way for us and our little ones and all our possessions."

Once they made it to England, the Separatists were joined by **"Strangers."** That's what the Separatists called them. The Strangers were a mix of Englishmen seeking adventure and new business. According to William Bradford, "They left that goodly and pleasant city which had been their resting place near twelve years; but they knew they were *pilgrims*" when they first left Holland.[3] (Italics in quotation are mine.) He was referring to the Separatists who were on a *pilgrimage* to the New World. But over time, the *entire* group — Separatists and Strangers alike — came to be called "the Pilgrims."

*"They left that goodly and pleasant city which had been their resting place near twelve years; but they knew they were pilgrims."*
*–William Bradford*

In England, the Pilgrims filled the old *Speedwell* and a larger ship named the *Mayflower*. (You've probably heard of it before.) Unfortunately, the *Speedwell* was unstable on the sea. It had to return to port twice. It was finally abandoned. And with it, several passengers had to abandon their plans and return home.

When at last the *Mayflower* was boarded, it carried about 30 sailors, and 102 Pilgrims. Only 35 of the Pilgrims were Separatists from Leiden. Most of the Pilgrims were traveling as families, so there were 32 children onboard (if you can imagine!). But that number changed when two babies were born on the *Mayflower*! One, named *Oceanus Hopkins*, was born at sea and cleverly named after the event. Another baby, named *Peregrine White*, was born while the ship was anchored in the harbor of the New World. With everyone's belongings and supplies, a few favorite pets, and crying newborns, the ship was far more cramped than planned.

Fortunately, the Strangers and the Separatists got along well. Though they ventured across the ocean for different reasons, they had much in common. All were courageous folks. All had hopes for starting new lives in North America. They would cling together through difficult times yet ahead. I imagine that those new babies were rocked and held by most of the women onboard.

After 65 days at sea, land was finally in sight. (I'm sure the children shrieked with delight!) The first obstacle the Pilgrims faced was where to set ashore. You see, they had been granted passage to the territory of Virginia, but they didn't exactly land there. The storms in the Atlantic drove them farther north than Jamestown. They were at **Cape Cod** in present-day Massachusetts. The Pilgrims tried to turn the *Mayflower* south, but the rocky shoreline and strong currents wouldn't allow for it. A historic decision was then made.

The Pilgrim men gathered onboard the *Mayflower* to sign the **Mayflower Compact.** It was an agreement among all of them that they were to be "self-governed." Since they weren't in Virginia, they weren't under its laws and needed to make their own. The Mayflower Compact stated that each man would do his best according to God's will and would protect the rights of others. This would help prevent any one man from ruling over all the rest and restricting freedom — the very thing they were striving for. At this time, **John Carver** was elected the first governor.

Now, the signing of the Mayflower Compact may not seem like a big deal. But it really was. You have to remember the state of things back in Europe. The Thirty Years' War was raging between Protestants and Catholics under the weight of heavy-handed kings and

When Pilgrim men gathered to sign the Mayflower Compact, they agreed to be self-governed by following God's will as they understood it and protecting the rights of others.

emperors. The Pilgrims didn't want the same problems in the New World. The Separatists therefore did *not* impose their faith and religion on the Strangers among them. Nor did the Strangers restrict the worship of the Separatists. All the men sought to be represented and protected under this newly formed charter. (The women did not participate.) The Mayflower Compact represented baby steps toward democracy in the New World.

Before I tell you about making landfall, let me introduce you to one of the heroes of the Pilgrims. His name was **Myles Standish.** (His first name is sometimes spelled Miles.) His wife was named Rose. Myles was a short, stout redhead with a fiery temper. Myles Standish met the Separatists back in Leiden. He never joined the church of the Separatists, but he had great respect for these god-fearing people. The Separatists voted him in as the first captain of the colony. They knew that to tame the land, they needed his bravery and expertise. Unfortunately, Myles had hostile encounters with the Native Americans that ended in bloodshed. The Native Americans quickly learned to leave the short redhead alone.

## *New Plymouth*

After scouting the area for five weeks, Myles Standish and others found a place with a clearing, good water, and a high hill for scouting. The area had been home to a Native American tribe that had since died out. The Pilgrims named their settlement **New Plymouth**, after a city in England. The official date of their landing was December 26, **1620**. There sits a piece of a rock at Plymouth today that marks the spot where the Pilgrims supposedly stepped from their ship to the shore. All I can picture are the children hitting the beach and running — after their long and dreary confinement!

William Bradford describes the scene for us this way, "Being thus arrived in a good harbour, and brought safe to land, they fell upon their knees and blessed the God of Heaven who had brought them from all the perils and miseries thereof, again to set their feet on the firm and stable earth, their proper element."[4]

Unlike the gentlemen of Jamestown, the Pilgrims were hard workers. They immediately went about their chores of building, hunting, and gathering wood. The women had loads of foul laundry to wash. Even with all their hard work, the Pilgrims' first winter in Plymouth was miserable. It was so cold that their clothes froze on their bodies. Food was scarce and disease raged. The Pilgrims called the winter of 1620 to 1621 "the Great Sickness." Everyone lived under the same roof of a fort that soon turned into a hospital.

Over the years, Plymouth Rock has been moved, broken, and sold off in pieces. Today a small piece is preserved for display at Pilgrim Memorial State Park in Plymouth, Massachusetts.

At one time, only seven Pilgrims were healthy enough to tend to all the others. One of the healthy Pilgrims was Myles Standish. He cooked, nursed the sick, and did laundry. Despite the efforts of everyone, by springtime, 42 Pilgrims were dead, including Rose Standish. This means that half the Pilgrims perished that first winter in Plymouth! I do wonder what the Pilgrims thought of the desperate situation. Had they heard the Lord clearly? Would they survive?

In mid-March of 1621, the Pilgrims were startled to hear in broken English, "Welcome, Englishmen, welcome, Englishmen!"[5] These words were spoken by a Native American named **Samoset**. According to the Pilgrims, Samoset was a gift from God. He spoke some English and introduced them to two very important people. First, he brought them **Squanto**, a Native American who spoke almost perfect English! Second, Samoset brought them **Chief Massasoit** (Mass eh SOIT). Massasoit was a kind Native American chief who was visiting in the region. He was the leader of the *Pokanoket* Indians who lived in southeastern Massachusetts. They were also called the **Wampanoag** (Wom peh NO ag), which means "people of the early light." On the east coast of North America, they were the first people to see the sun rise each morning.

Squanto was so important to the survival of the Pilgrims that I'm going to tell you his incredible story in the next lesson. (I think you'll like Squanto.) As for Chief Massasoit, after getting to know the Pilgrims, he agreed to sign a peace treaty with them that lasted for 50 years. The peace treaty greatly helped the Pilgrims survive their hardships.

In April of 1621, Governor Carver died. It was decided then that William Bradford would be the new governor. Bradford carried a great amount of responsibility on his shoulders, but he relied on the Lord for strength and held his position for 30 years. William Bradford was a godly man and provided the spiritual leadership that the Pilgrims desperately needed. He wrote, "the whole country, full of woods and thickets, represented a wild and savage hue. If they looked behind them, there was the mighty ocean . . . What could now sustain them but the Spirit of God and His grace?"[6] I suspect that with every new grave that was made, many prayers were said. I believe the Lord was listening.

As you may already know, the Pilgrims celebrated a time of Thanksgiving that first fall. After all they had been through, they were *very* thankful to be alive. I'll give you the details of that historic event in our next lesson about Squanto. He had a lot to do with the bountiful harvest that is still commemorated every late November in the United States.

## Lesson 60 — *1621*

# *Squanto*

As I promised in our last lesson, let me now tell you more about **Squanto**. I think you'll agree that his story is worthy of an entire lesson. Though his life was short, it was full of adventure and hardship. Much like Pocahontas, Squanto was caught between the New World and the Old.

## *Captured by Europeans*

The first historical reference to Squanto is found in 1605. That was a couple of years before Jamestown was founded by English settlers. As the story goes, a ship captain by the name of **George Weymouth** was sent to the New World under the leadership of **Sir Ferdinando Gorges**. Captain Weymouth captured five Native Americans on his voyage to the New World. They were **Manida, Skidwarres, Nahanada, Assacumet**, and **Tisquantum**. Although they may be difficult names for English speakers to pronounce, I like listing them out to acquaint us with Native American culture and to remind us that these young men were not just part of a tale. They were real. And they were captive! The last one, Tisquantum, is the one who later became known as Squanto. He was probably about 20 the first time he was captured by Europeans.

Tisquantum, better known as Squanto, was about 20 years old the first time he was captured by Europeans and carried across the Atlantic to the Old World.

Captain Weymouth promptly delivered his five captives to Ferdinando Gorges in England. The Native Americans were used for promotional purposes and trained as guides. Supposedly, Gorges treated the Indians well. Two were returned home on the next voyage back to North America. Squanto, however, was *not* one of them. He remained under the care of Gorges for nine years in England. In that time, Squanto learned to speak very good English. It would affect the rest of his life.

In 1614, Squanto met someone you already know. It was John Smith, the captain who helped establish Jamestown. (Coincidentally, the year of their meeting in England was the same year that Pocahontas married John Rolfe back in Jamestown.) As you know, John Smith was recovering from wounds in England. He was always hoping to return and in fact, did. He invited Squanto to go with him, with the promise that he would be returned "home."

Now, you know the reputation of John Smith. He wasn't the most trustworthy guy. I don't know if he ever planned on setting Squanto free or not. But this is what happened in the New World: Squanto and John Smith spent a lot of time together in the New England area, including the area of Squanto's original home. Squanto continued to serve as an interpreter for Smith and helped him maneuver around his homeland. But at the end of the trip, John Smith's associate captain, **Thomas Hunt**, lured Squanto and 20 of his tribesmen aboard his ship — and then took off! Squanto was being kidnapped a *second* time — stolen from his homeland and sent across the ocean. I can't imagine how his heart sank when the wind caught the sails and swept him away again.

Thomas Hunt wasn't kind to his prisoners. He took his "cargo" of Indians to Spain with the intention of selling every one of them into slavery for 20 pounds apiece. His plan would have made him some extra money except that some kindly monks found out about it. The monks interfered and took the Indians into their custody.

Squanto spent about two years living with these monks in Spain. As they worked together and ate together, the monks taught the Christian faith to their new friends by both word and deed. Who knows what Squanto thought of these prayerful men who dressed and acted so differently than the ship captains Squanto had come to know. I hope they had a lot of laughs as they got acquainted with one another's customs.

In 1616, Squanto was befriended by an Englishman who took him to London. At least there he was back in familiar territory. For about a year, Squanto lived with another Englishman named **Sir John Slaney**. Slaney happened to be the treasurer of the Newfoundland Company, a trading company to North America. It was beginning to look like Squanto *might* have a chance to get back to North America.

As hoped, Squanto was invited to accompany a ship that sailed to Newfoundland in 1617. At last he was back on his home continent. But wouldn't you know, Squanto was recognized by a sea captain who used to work for his old master, Ferdinando Gorges! The sea captain's name was **Thomas Dermer**. Dermer wasn't a cruel man, but he wrote to Gorges back in England to say that he had found "his Indian" and asked what Gorges would like him to do with the Indian. Apparently, Ferdinando Gorges was thrilled to hear of Squanto's whereabouts and told Dermer to bring him back to England. And so he did.

It is not clear whether Squanto returned to England under his own free will or in chains. If you remember, Ferdinando Gorges, his first master, had treated him well. Maybe Squanto wanted to go back. Maybe he didn't. Regardless, if you add up the years, it would seem that as a young man, Squanto had spent more time in Europe than in North America. It is no wonder that the Pilgrims later found his English to be nearly perfect!

In 1619, Squanto was given another chance to cross the ocean and return home. Let's see, in my count, he had already made the trip five times. This would be his sixth and last voyage across the Atlantic. This time he was traveling with Thomas Dermer, the captain who recognized him in Newfoundland. Squanto and Dermer were sent to scout the area of Plymouth, which happened to be Squanto's original home. He was from the **Pawtuxet** tribe. It was the Pawtuxet who first occupied the hill and the clearing of Plymouth before the Pilgrims arrived.

What Squanto learned in 1619 was devastating. After 14 years away from his own people, he came home only to learn that every man, woman, and child of his tribe had died in 1617 from a mysterious plague! Apparently, this plague had wiped out thousands of Native Americans, including the Pawtuxet, in a few short years. Oddly, the same plague never affected the Europeans.

I don't know exactly what Squanto felt. But I can imagine what I would feel to find nobody at "home." I would feel angry, empty, and lost. Squanto had no one. No aunts or uncles, no brothers or sisters, no parents or grandparents. He was the only Pawtuxet known to be alive. It's a sad thought.

Do you remember Samoset? He was the Indian who spoke broken English to the Pilgrims. Samoset was originally from Maine but was visiting in the Wampanoag territory. He befriended Squanto and invited him to live among the Wampanoag. And so Squanto did. For a year he stayed among the Wampanoag Indians who were under Chief Massasoit.

Well, you can probably connect the dots now to the story of the Pilgrims. After Samoset met the friendly Pilgrims, it only made sense that he would introduce them to Squanto, who spoke the white man's language so well. It must have been a delightful encounter on both sides because once Squanto met the Pilgrims, he never left.

Do you remember that first terrible winter for the Pilgrims in 1620 to 1621? That's when nearly half of them died from the Great Sickness. Well, it was in the spring of **1621** that Squanto came to join them. Squanto taught them many things — like how to find eel and clams and how to sneak up on deer, turkey, and bear. He taught the Pilgrim children where to find wild berries and nuts. It was probably something he grew up doing as a young Indian boy.

But probably the most famous gesture by Squanto was teaching the Pilgrims how to improve their crops of corn, beans, and pumpkins. (I love this part of the story.) In particular, Squanto taught the settlers to fertilize the ground with fish. Yes, fish. Squanto showed them that every seed or kernel planted should be surrounded by three small alewives, or tiny fish. (Alewives are fish in the herring family.) The decomposing fish nourished the ground and helped the crops grow stronger.

## *The First Thanksgiving*

Squanto's tips and tricks would pay off. That fall, in 1621, the Pilgrims had an extremely bountiful harvest. Governor Bradford declared it a time of "thanksgiving." The feast lasted three days and included worship, Bible readings, and games. I think you already know who was invited. The Pilgrims invited Chief Massasoit, who brought about 90 Native Americans with him to the first Thanksgiving. They in turn brought more deer to eat. It was only fitting.

Fortunately, we have written accounts of that first Thanksgiving, so we don't have to use our imagination. Edward Winslow wrote a letter to a friend in England describing the great feast. He wrote:

In 1621, Squanto taught the Pilgrims how to fertilize their crops with decomposing fish. This bountiful harvest contributed to the first Thanksgiving.

> Our harvest being gotten in, our Governor sent four men on fowling, that so we might . . . rejoice together, after we had gathered in the fruits of our labors. They four in one day killed as many fowl as . . . served the Company for almost a week, at which time, amongst our recreations, we exercised our arms, many of the Indians coming amongst us, and amongst the rest their great king the Massasoit, with some ninety men, whom for three days we entertained and feasted.[7]

Beyond the full bellies, I hope there were full hearts on that first Thanksgiving. I hope the Pilgrims and the Native Americans were warmed by the presence of one another. I hope they saw beyond their differences in color and creed. I imagine the boys were being "boys" and having fun competing in their games. In my mind, the girls were probably being "girls" and trading homemade dolls and bracelets and flowers for their hair. I would love to have been there.

I wish I could end the story here and say that all lived happily ever after. But that is not the case. The next winter and spring were terribly difficult. Again the Pilgrims were short of food, and a severe drought nearly killed their crops. Ships from the New World arrived with more hungry settlers and few supplies. There just wasn't enough to go around. At one time, each Pilgrim was allotted no more than five kernels of corn to eat per day. Regardless, the Pilgrims continued to pray and place their faith in God. They would survive to celebrate more Thanksgivings, but it wasn't without hardship.

As for Squanto, he had only a few adventures left that give us a little insight into his character — both good and bad. He heard that Captain Thomas Dermer was captured by other Native Americans. As a good gesture, Squanto rescued his European friend and helped to set him free. As another good gesture, Squanto joined a search party for a lost Pilgrim boy. Fortunately, the young boy was found! But on a bad note, we know that Squanto was accused of spreading rumors of an Indian attack on Plymouth! His intentions in this matter are unclear. Governor Bradford dropped any charges against him and allowed him to stay on with the Pilgrims.

In the end, Squanto suffered quite unexpectedly. In the fall of 1623, Squanto fell ill with a high fever and nosebleed. He knew he was dying. Squanto asked William Bradford to pray for him that he would be taken to heaven by the white man's God. He then gave his few belongings to the Pilgrims. Squanto died at about age 38.

William Bradford wrote a lot about how much Squanto had meant to them. I'll end with an excerpt from what he wrote (the words in brackets are mine for clarity):

> . . . But Squanto continued with them [the Pilgrims] and was their interpreter and was a special instrument sent of God for their good beyond their expectation. He directed them how to set their corn, where to take fish, . . . and was also their pilot to bring them to unknown places for their profit, and never left them till he died.[8]

WEEK 21

Lesson 61 | 1628

# René Descartes

"I think, therefore I am." These are the words that made **René Descartes** (Re NAY Day KART) one of the most well-known philosophers in history. But what do these words mean, and why did they make him famous? I'll try to answer these questions today as we study the life of René Descartes, who was not only a French philosopher but also a brilliant scientist and mathematician.

"I think, therefore I am."
–René Descartes

## A Frail Childhood

As a boy, René was very frail. He fought tuberculosis, a lung condition that took the life of his mother when he was just a baby. His father wasn't around much. René might not have survived babyhood except that a nurse took a special liking to him and made sure that he was properly nourished. She couldn't have known then, but her tender care would influence the thoughts of the Western world for centuries to come!

Around age 8, René Descartes was placed in the care of the Jesuit priests for his education. Because he was still not strong, he was allowed to lie in his bed beyond the normal time of rising. There he had much time to read and think deeply about many things. He grew stronger in time but never stopped the practice of deep thinking.

After studying law in Paris, René joined the army in Holland in 1618. (Can you think of something important that started in 1618? It was the Thirty Years' War.) Descartes never saw face-to-face combat, but he experienced great adventure traveling around Europe, which seemed to be his intent.

In his travels, René Descartes met a gifted mathematician named Isaac Beeckman. His friendship with Beeckman would influence Descartes for years. In all his thinking, he wondered if mathematics could explain the unexplainable things of the universe. He even dreamed about it. Over his lifetime, Descartes contributed a great deal to what we call *analytic geometry*. It's a step of mathematics that falls somewhere in between algebra and calculus. Analytic geometry seeks to measure things and break them down. Remember this because René Descartes would do the same with philosophy.

There is an interesting legend about René Descartes, that may or may not be true, but it will help you remember one of his major contributions to mathematics — the **Cartesian**

**coordinate system.** ("Cartesian," by the way, is a derivative of Descartes' last name.) The story goes that one day while René was resting in bed (as the Jesuits allowed him to do), he noticed a fly on his ceiling. As he studied it, he realized that he could mathematically plot the location of the fly through the use of two numbers. The numbers represented the distances from the fly to the edges of the room. Middle and Older Students will recognize these numbers as the *x* and *y* coordinates of a point on a graph. Yes, the Cartesian coordinate system was invented by René Descartes. The story of the fly will help you remember it.

The Netherlands offered René Descartes a peaceful place to study math, science, and philosophy. His favorite subject was philosophy.

After his army experiences, Descartes moved to the Netherlands in **1628** for a peaceful place to study. The Netherlands must have suited him well because he lived there for more than 20 years, burying himself in the study of math, science, and philosophy. He performed endless experiments in physics and optics and drew countless diagrams and equations. Once in a while, he had to dodge the Inquisition, which was suspicious of his sciences. He also tried to evade a group of strong Calvinists who disagreed with him about predestination. All of this is to say, he moved 24 times in 20 years! I'll try now to summarize Descartes' great contribution to philosophy, but it won't be easy. Philosophy never is.

## *Philosophies*

When René Descartes looked at his generation, he was not impressed with their philosophies. He found French intellects to be "skeptical," or doubtful, that anything was certain. We call these doubting philosophical thinkers **Skeptics.** With religious wars and the Age of Reason growing, skepticism *was* on the rise. Skeptics wondered, too, if the ancient philosophers really had been all that smart since they didn't even know the New World existed!

But René Descartes disagreed with the Skeptics. He thought there were some things that were "certain." He decided to break all philosophy down to the most basic thought as he had done in mathematics. But what was the most basic thing he knew? Descartes decided that it was himself.

René Descartes believed that he could doubt everything he saw around him, but he *could not* deny his own existence. If he doubted he existed, then he didn't exist! But he *knew* he existed because he could think about it. (Did you follow that?) His existence was the one thing he knew to be true. In two of his publications (*Discourse on Method* and *Principles of Philosophy*), Descartes wrote his famous line, "I think, therefore I am." In Latin, it reads *Cogito ergo sum* and may be more properly translated as "I am thinking, therefore I exist."[1]

By observing the properties of a wax candle, René Descartes formulated the basic idea of dualism, which separates the body from the mind.

To René Descartes, his own existence was the first block of all philosophy. From that, he built convincing arguments for the existence of the material world around him *and* the existence of God. Some would say that the idea of man being the start of all things was an example of humanism. Humanism was still popular from the Renaissance. But, according to Descartes, God *had* to exist because a good God would never create man to think God existed if He didn't! Descartes also thought that a perfect God could not have come from the mind of imperfect men. No, Descartes was *not* a humanist who placed God aside. I don't know how deep his personal faith was, but René believed in a Divine Creator.

Besides the quote "I think, therefore I am," René Descartes is also famous for his idea of **dualism**, or the separation of the *body* from the *mind*. He saw them as two distinct things (thus the term *dual*-ism, which means two). Let me explain, using wax as an example. When René Descartes observed cold wax, his bodily senses would tell him that wax was hard and takes a certain shape. But when he placed the wax by a flame, his senses would tell him that wax was soft and liquid. So his senses (or what we will call the *body*) could not be trusted to *explain* the wax. René concluded that he would have to rely on his *mind*, not his *body* or senses, to give him the truth about wax. His mind could understand the changes that the wax went through when warmed.

René Descartes applied this reasoning to philosophy. He suggested that the body, or the things we sense, is different from what our minds know. He called it dualism — the distinction between body and mind. Descartes went so far as to theorize that the body and mind had a special place of interaction in the *pineal gland* in the brain. He called it the "seat of the soul." He wasn't completely right about the function of the pineal gland.

Regardless of that, Descartes promoted *methodical reasoning* of the mind (or deduction) to understand the world we live in — since the senses themselves can't be trusted. Reread that slowly for understanding if you need to and ponder the following quote by René Descartes: "This 'me,' that is to say, the soul by which I am what I am, is entirely distinct from the body."[2]

You may have noticed that I've not mentioned the family of René Descartes. That's because he never married. He did, however, father a child who died at a young age. He wept greatly at his loss, showing us the soft side of his genius. Though he was a genius, he demonstrated tenderness in his old age by tutoring two women of royalty. He tutored the princess of Bohemia through a series of delightful letters. But for the queen of Sweden, he moved to Stockholm to give her person-to-person instruction. Some would say it cost him his life.

Apparently Queen Christina of Sweden was used to rising very early and insisted that her lessons be taught at five o'clock in the morning. If you remember, René grew up rising later than most people. Some believe that these early morning classes throughout the cold Swedish winter caused him to catch pneumonia. Others believe that he caught pneumonia from taking care of a soldier friend who had the illness. Perhaps it was a combination of both. Regardless of the cause, René Descartes died just one week after coming down with pneumonia. He was 54.

Now you may be wondering what philosophy has to do with us. Well, philosophy is part of history, and man is greatly influenced by it! According to René Descartes, "Philosophy is a perfect knowledge of all that man can know, as well for the conduct of his life as for the preservation of his health and the discovery of all the arts."[3] That ranks philosophy rather highly and in turn, René Descartes. As a matter of fact, a man named Michael H. Hart ranked Descartes as #49 in a list of the most influential figures in history![4] I think that says a lot about what he contributed to Western thought.

## Lesson 62 — 1630

# John Winthrop and the Puritans

I hope you remember my introducing you to the **Puritans** and the **Separatists**. Both groups were unhappy with the Anglican Church of England. The Separatists were the ones who "separated" themselves entirely from the Church of England. A precious number of them sailed to the New World aboard the *Mayflower* and became known as the Pilgrims. I'm sure you remember them.

John Winthrop, a godly Puritan leader, was born the same year that the English defeated the Spanish Armada.

Well, today we're going to look at the Puritans. They are the group who hoped to "purify" the Anglican Church from practices they believed were unbiblical. Just like the Separatists, many Puritans sailed to the New World for religious freedom. They found their freedom in **Boston, Massachusetts**. They did so with the help of **John Winthrop** (WIN thrup), a godly Puritan of impeccable character.

John Winthrop grew up in a Puritan family in England. He was born the same year that the Spanish Armada attempted to defeat the English. Elizabeth I was queen. As you know, James I was the next king and after him came Charles I. Unfortunately, Charles was terribly intolerant of anyone outside the Anglican Church. The Puritans were *not* outside the Anglican Church — but they were quite a bother to King Charles with their ideas of "purifying" the Anglican Church. The king, in fact, despised the Puritans for tampering with tradition. Charles persecuted the Puritans almost as much as he did the Separatists.

Now, John Winthrop and the Puritans were in a real dilemma. They did *not* want to separate from the church. But to stay in it, they would suffer. So the idea of relocating became more and more attractive. The Puritans sincerely hoped that by moving to the New World, they could build a pure church that would influence the church back in England. John Winthrop's desire to serve God was sincere. At only 24 he wrote, "I do resolve first to give myself — my life, my wits, my health, my wealth — to the service of my God and Savior who by giving Himself for me and to me, deserves whatsoever I am or can be, to be at His commandment and for his glory."[5]

Puritans held strongly to the Golden Rule of the New Testament. Their gentle lifestyle reflected genuine love and concern for one another.

## A Proposal for the King

Winthrop and a group of Puritan businessmen approached King Charles and proposed the idea of joining a small fishing village in the New World at **Salem, Massachusetts**. It was about 50 miles north of Plymouth. Of course, the Puritans wanted to do much more than fish in the New World, but the details were not important to the king. He agreed to sign a charter to form the **Massachusetts Bay Company**. It probably made him happy to see some Puritans leaving England and thus leaving him alone.

The truth is, the Puritans were the happy ones. They were happy to leave England, given the state it was in. You see, morally, England had lapsed into a rather permissive society. It was nicknamed *Merrie England* for catering so much to the pleasures of the world. One very conservative Puritan named William Prynne blamed high immorality on the theater. He said, "Most plays are blasphemous and obscene, full of . . . lust-arousing music, song, and dance; all . . . is devilish."[6] (Some would say that times haven't changed much!)

Before the Puritans ever set sail for the New World, they elected John Winthrop as their governor. Their choice was a good one. In the spring of **1630**, more than 700 Puritans boarded 11 ships under the leadership of Winthrop. That's a huge fleet! Their group was the largest yet to sail from the Old World to the New. Imagine the number of dishes and shoes and tools to pack. Imagine the number of boys and girls and aunts and uncles who made that voyage. Imagine the cheers, the tears, *and* the fears of leaving home. Persecution or not, it must have been hard to leave what was familiar. The Puritans were brave — as well as determined — to leave England.

The determination of the Puritans was rooted in their deep love for the Word of God. Puritans in general took the teachings of Scripture to heart. They were known for their disdain of sin — first in their own lives and then in the lives of others. Puritans held strongly to the Golden Rule of caring for one another, as found in Matthew 7:12. It reads, "Therefore, whatever you want men to do to you, do also to them . . ." This spirit of brotherly love would carry them for a long time.

Exactly one day before setting sail for the New World, John Winthrop preached a message onboard his ship, the *Arbella*. In his message, Winthrop reminded the Puritans of their mission. He said, "We shall be as a city upon a hill, the eyes of all people are upon us . . . we shall be made a story and a by-word through the world."[7] He was absolutely right. Many would watch the Puritans and follow in their footsteps.

In one of his writings, titled *A Model of Christian Charity*, John Winthrop also reminded the Puritans that they were in a covenant (meaning a promise) with God to build a holy community. It could only be done through the Puritans' commitment to brotherly love. On this voyage to the New World, the Puritans' commitment was put to a test!

You see, after 72 days at sea, when the Puritans entered the harbor of Salem they were shocked to find nothing more than huts and tents on the beach. This was the fishing village of Salem? It didn't offer much to the 700 sea-weary travelers. The former governor explained to John Winthrop that disease and starvation had killed 80 of the first settlers. Out of about 250, only 85 remained. The rest had either died or gone back to England, and more were thinking about leaving.

## *Surviving and Growing*

Here, then, was the test. Could the Puritans themselves survive? Could they pull together and work hard enough to salvage this dying village? The answer would be yes! The Puritans had a strong work ethic. All would work; none would slack. They believed it their God-given duty. Unlike previous settlers who were too "gentlemanly" to lift a hand, the Puritans were devoted to labor. It would make a huge difference in the settlement.

Motivated by a strong work ethic, the Puritans salvaged the dying village of Salem and spread to other towns where they built homes and schools.

The Puritans were, in fact, so successful in Salem that they soon began to spread to other towns and villages. By September of 1630, John Winthrop himself moved to a village that he renamed Boston. You've probably heard of Boston, Massachusetts. It's a very large city today.

You've probably also heard of **Harvard University**. (If you haven't heard of it, Harvard is one of *the* most prestigious schools in the world!) Harvard was the first college established in the New World. But most people don't know that it was started by the Puritans only six years after they arrived. And you know why? They started it for the training of young men in the ministry. The purpose of this early Christian college was: "Let every student be plainly instructed, and earnestly pressed to consider well, the main end of his life and studies is, to know God and Jesus Christ which is eternal life (John 17:3) and therefore lay Christ in the bottom, as the only foundation of all sound knowledge and learning."[8]

Education was, in fact, so important to the Puritans that it was required. By 1642, parents were required to teach their young children to read so they could know the Scriptures. By 1657, if a town had at least 50 families, it was required to hire a teacher for the students. The purpose of teaching was to learn the Word of God and defeat Satan, who was the deluder (meaning the liar). So the law to teach was called the "Old Deluder Satan Act." As a Christian educator, I find this very interesting!

In fact, I find the Puritans themselves very interesting. Some would portray them as always being somber and serious because they dressed in black. While at church, they used a "tithingman" to poke the people who fell asleep! But the Puritans liked to play, too. The women congregated for quilting, sewing, and visiting. The children played games and competed in spelling bees. If a barn needed fixing, the men all came together to help.

According to William Prynne, who didn't approve of the theater, the Puritans found their entertainment in nature. Prynne wrote, "If they need diversion, they have . . . the sun, the moon, the planets, the stars, with all the infinite variety of creatures to delight their eyes. They have music of all birds . . . to please their ears . . . the pleasures that orchards, rivers, gardens, ponds, woods . . . can afford them."[9] Four hundred years later, I think many of us would agree with William Prynne that there are fewer things more entertaining than a day at the beach or a hike in the woods. God has given us much to enjoy in nature.

As we near the end of this lesson, you may be wondering how well the Puritans did in interacting with the Native Americans. Well, I can't speak for all of them. But I can share an example of one Puritan whose heart I think was right toward the local inhabitants. His name was **John Eliot**. John Eliot was so intent on sharing Christ with Native Americans that he spent years learning their speech and translating the Bible into the Algonquian language! In fact, the first Bible ever printed in North America was one for the Native Americans.

So did the Puritans survive? For a very long time they did. They elected John Winthrop 11 more times to serve as their governor. Some of their ideas worked, and some didn't. Still, they played a large role in the founding of the United States, with 25,000 more Puritans arriving by 1642. Did you catch that? In only 12 years, the number of Puritans in the New World grew to more than 25,000! For this staggering growth, the event has been labeled the **Great Migration**. It would change the course of history as 13 colonies began to take shape and grow in North America.

# Galileo Galilei

I have a physics question for you. If you stood at the top of a tall tower and dropped a 10-pound ball and a 1-pound ball at the exact same time, which one would hit the ground first? I'm not going to give you the answer yet. But I am going to tell you that the *correct* answer escaped scientists for centuries. It was not until the 1600s that the basic laws of gravity were understood. One man who contributed a great deal to this was **Galileo Galilei** (Gal uh LEE oh Gal uh LAY). He was an Italian genius whom most people call simply "Galileo."

Galileo was born on the same day that Michelangelo died. You could say that as one great mind exited this world, another entered. As a boy, Galileo had many talents, including music, the arts, Latin, and Greek. His father taught him these things at home. But as time went by, he built clever toys and machines, showing that he had a greater mind for science than anything else.

When he was about 20, Galileo supposedly was sitting in church when he noticed the gentle swing of a lantern suspended from a high cathedral ceiling above him. He was intrigued. He measured the rhythm of the swing against his own pulse. From that simple observation, Galileo showed he was a budding genius when it came to understanding physics. Determining the precise swing of a pendulum and the complicated science behind it was just the beginning of his career.

Galileo Galilei was an Italian genius who contributed a great deal to the understanding of physics. Most simply call him Galileo.

Galileo was born in **Pisa, Italy**, and attended the University of Pisa. His first studies were in medicine and philosophy. But his family didn't have the money for him to finish his education. This didn't stop Galileo from learning. He switched from medicine to a self-study of math and soon invented the hydrostatic balance, an instrument that measures the specific gravity of objects in water. Sounds cool, doesn't it?

## The Law of Falling Bodies

When Galileo was 25, he returned to the University of Pisa — but not as a student. He returned as a professor of mathematics, even though he never received his own degree. He apparently proved himself smart enough. It was during this time that he developed his most famous law of physics — the law of falling bodies. I already introduced it with a physics question about dropping heavy and light things at the same time. Let me explain further.

Legend says that Galileo dropped objects of various weights from the famous Leaning Tower of Pisa to test his theories in physics.

Long before Galileo, there was a Greek philosopher named Aristotle who thought that heavy objects fell faster than light ones. So, in my earlier question about dropping a 10-pound ball and a 1-pound ball at the same time, Aristotle would have said that the 10-pound ball would hit the ground first. But he was wrong. Galileo proved otherwise.[10]

Legend says that Galileo experimented with his theories by dropping different weights from the famous **Tower of Pisa.** (You probably know it better as the "Leaning Tower of Pisa" because over the years, its unstable foundation has caused it to slowly tilt.) I don't know if Galileo really used the tower or not because he never wrote about it. (One of his biographers did.) But Galileo *did* write about rolling differently weighted balls on a slanted board. Perhaps the results were easier to measure this way.

Whatever his method, Galileo's point was made regarding the law of falling bodies. In an airtight vacuum without wind or other resistance, objects are drawn toward the earth at the same rate. So in an airtight vacuum, a bowling ball and a penny would hit the ground at the *same* time if dropped from a skyscraper. (But don't try it! It could hurt someone below.)

Unfortunately, Galileo's law wasn't fully accepted. For a time he was forced to leave the University of Pisa by those who clung to the old theories of Aristotle. So, in 1592, Galileo moved to the University of Padua and remained there for 18 years as a professor of geometry, astronomy, and mechanics. Surpassing Francis Bacon (who focused on causes and effects), Galileo quantified and calculated the things he philosophized about. He tried to measure the speed of light and the frequency of sound. Studying parabolas (puh RAB uh las) and the law of squares, he *related* math to science more than anyone else had before him. Galileo was so in love with mathematics, he would state in his lifetime that "natural philosophy . . . was written in the language of mathematics."[11]

## Advancements with the Telescope

It was in 1609 that Galileo significantly improved the telescope. Building on the ideas of others, Galileo made the telescope strong enough to see stars that had never been seen before, and he made a number of significant discoveries. For one, he determined that the

Milky Way is not just a blur in the sky but rather, a galaxy of stars "so numerous as to be almost beyond belief."[12]

Second, with use of the telescope, he discovered four of the numerous moons of Jupiter. You just won't believe whom he named them after — it was the Medici family.[13] Yes, the descendants of Cosimo and Lorenzo de' Medici were still ruling over provinces in Italy. Like their ancestors, the Medicis of Galileo's day were great patrons of the arts and sciences. Cosimo II sponsored much of Galileo's work. (I think Cosimo I and Lorenzo would have been proud!)

Galileo greatly improved the telescope in 1609 to discover that the Milky Way is much more than a blur in the sky. It is a galaxy of stars!

Third, it was with a telescope that Galileo recognized that our moon does not give off its own light but rather, reflects it from the sun. This was a revolutionary idea in the 1600s! He noticed, too, that the moon was rough with craters and mountains rather than smooth, as Aristotle had claimed it was.

Taking what he knew about telescopes, Galileo also created the first compound microscope in 1624. Imagine the things he saw both near and far that no one had ever seen before! This brilliant man also worked on practical things for his day and age, such as an automatic tomato picker, a combination fork and comb, and something similar to a ballpoint pen. On a more difficult level, he invented a thermometer using air compression, and he improved the accuracy of cannons using proper mathematics. His interests knew no limits. Even his style of writing was admired as being one of the best in Italian prose.

As brilliant as he was, Galileo didn't get everything right. He observed the rings of Saturn but never fully grasped what they were. He failed to understand the *elliptical* orbits of planets (as described by Johannes Kepler) and thought them to be *round*. He saw Neptune but thought it was only a star, and he never understood what the moon had to do with the high and low tides of the ocean. But Galileo *did* accurately detect sunspots and the phases of Venus and Mars. Supposedly he allowed Pope Urban VIII himself to view these things through one of his powerful telescopes.

Using a telescope, Galileo realized that our moon reflects light from the sun and has a rough surface, with numerous craters and mountains.

## *Conflict Develops*

Speaking of the pope, let me remind you that Galileo lived at a time when the Roman Catholic Church still had a lot of power. A conflict developed between some of Galileo's ideas and the church. Why? Well, Galileo, like Copernicus, thought the earth revolved around the sun. But devout theologians were afraid that this idea contradicted the Scriptures and forbade the teaching of it. I want to remind you that though the theologians were wrong, they were seeking to preserve what they believed to be true and were trying to protect the credibility of God's Word. We discussed this when we studied Copernicus. With that in mind, what were they to do with Galileo?

Well, in **1632**, things came to a head when Galileo published a work titled *Dialogue Concerning the Two Chief World Systems*. This work was exactly what it sounds like. It was an imaginary conversation among three people about the earth revolving around the sun, and vice versa. The pope had requested that the book be published to explain the two controversial views (geocentric and heliocentric). He requested that Galileo *not* draw conclusions on either view. The problem with the dialogue was that Galileo made Pope Urban look rather foolish as one of those involved in the conversation (although under a different name), and he made a strong case for the heliocentric theory. That didn't go over very well with the authorities.

Galileo was put on trial by the Inquisition for his teachings that were contrary to those of the Roman Catholic Church. His ideas were considered heresy. Generally speaking, the church urged him to present his heliocentric ideas as *only* theories or hypotheses, rather than as facts. Galileo refused. For taking this stance, some would call him the "Father of Science."

Fortunately for Galileo, church officials were "lenient" in his sentencing. He was confined for only about a year, forced to write a recantation in 1633, then kept under house arrest for the remainder of his life. His works were banned by the church for 200 years. Compared to years past, when heretics were burned and beheaded, it was progress.

Galileo spent his final years writing on the laws of motion and force in a book called *Dialogues Concerning Two New Sciences*. The outstanding work labeled him as the "Father of Modern Physics." He understood the principles of *inertia*. (Inertia is the idea that things keep going until stopped by an outside force.) Both **Sir Isaac Newton** and **Albert Einstein**, two brilliant scientists, would benefit greatly from the works of Galileo. Newton's famous first law of motion would be based on Galileo's understanding of inertia. And Einstein's theory of relativity was based on Galileo's understanding of motion. (Don't worry if you don't understand this part. Just remember the names of Newton and Einstein.)

> *"This universe that I have extended a thousand times . . . has now shrunk to the narrow confines of my own body. Thus God likes it; so I too must like it."*
> *–Galileo Galilei*

In closing, there is one more significant story to share about Galileo that I find quite sad. In the last five years of his life, Galileo lost his sight and became blind. After all those years of staring into the far distance of space, he couldn't see a thing on earth. Galileo turned to the enjoyment of music and then began to lose his hearing, too. His last years were quiet as well as dark. But he kept an amazing attitude about his losses. Galileo once said, "This universe that I have extended a thousand times . . . has now shrunk to the narrow confines of my own body. Thus God likes it; so I too must like it."[14]

*In his final self-portrait, painted in 1669, Rembrandt depicted himself as rather weathered and resigned. He was a man resolved to follow his heart and his artistic instincts despite the personal cost. Though famous now, Rembrandt died with little recognition from his peers.*

# The Age of Resolve 1632–1707

This quarter was the hardest of all for me to title. It was difficult to name because the events of it are so varied. I could hardly think of one "r" word to describe it all. Do you remember our other quarter titles using "r" words? In this order, we've studied the Age of *Rebirth*, the Age of *Reform*, and the Age of *Reason*. Well, after much thought, I've chosen to name Quarter 4 "The Age of *Resolve*." Here's why . . .

The word *resolve* means to settle on doing something with great determination. I find this kind of resolve in the *Jews* of the sixteenth and seventeenth centuries who were determined to survive despite all kinds of horrible treatment. I also find great resolve in the *Scottish Covenanters*. You will learn that even through serious persecution, they stood their ground for Christ, determined to die for their Lord if need be. Theirs is a sad but inspiring story.

Individual men of resolve would include *George Fox* and *Jacob Amman*, Christians who broke away from tradition to start their own movements of faith. In nations abroad, we'll learn of two determined leaders, *K'ang-hsi* and *Peter the Great*. And closer to home (for most of us) were *Thomas Hooker* and *William Penn*, who resolved to settle North America under the banner of freedom. Though they didn't know it then, they helped to shape the very core of the United States, a nation that would later emerge from the colonies.

However, not everyone in North America would know freedom. While seeds of democracy were being planted, the wicked weeds of slavery were growing, too. You see, through the opening of the *trans-Atlantic slave trade*, Europeans began to "buy" people from West Africa to labor in the New World. It was the beginning of a long struggle with racism, still tender in the United States today.

England would also suffer turmoil in the seventeenth century. The *Cavaliers* and the *Royalists* would go to war against one another — each side determined to sway the other. One side would win the civil war in England, but the victory wouldn't last. England would restore one king to the throne, appoint another, and then scheme a revolution to give the crown to *William and Mary*! It's a wild story of politics that would end with the writing of the English Bill of Rights, a very important document in history.

This final quarter, spanning 1632 to 1707, will cover 75 years of world history. We'll just step into the eighteenth century to hear the sounds of something beautiful. But I won't give that away just yet. When it's all over, I hope you leave this volume of history feeling more inspired than when you began. One reason I love world history is because it *can* inspire. I believe it can teach and remind us that we are all part of the same amazing storyline, an epic of the ages written by the author of all Creation. So enjoy to the fullest these last seven weeks of *The Mystery of History*, Volume III!

# WEEK 22

## Lesson 64 — *16th–17th Centuries*

# *The Jews of the Renaissance and Reformation*

The history of the Jewish people is like none other. There is an amazing reason for that. According to the Bible, the Jews are a "chosen" people. (See Is. 44:1–5.) They were chosen to reveal God's marvelous plan of redemption through Jesus Christ. Jesus was a Jew himself and of the house of David, a fact that fulfilled prophecy. (See Ps. 89:3; Matt. 1:1.) Despite this glorious plan, the history of the Jews has been difficult. Jews have suffered a great deal in the last few centuries. With this in mind, we will look at two things today. First, in Part I of this lesson, we'll look at the treatment of Jews during the Renaissance and Reformation that spanned the **sixteenth and seventeenth centuries**. Second, in Part II of this lesson, we'll look at what the Bible says about God's covenant plan with the Jewish people. (**Note to Teacher**: Part II may be too difficult for Younger Students and some Middle Students. Feel free to stop with Part I. There will be no quiz or test questions from Part II.)

**Part I**

### *Treatment of the Jews*

To review, it was in the first century that the Jews lost their homeland of Israel. In A.D. 70, the Romans destroyed the Jewish temple in Jerusalem. Some of you will remember from Volume II that at that time thousands of Jews fled to **Masada** as a place of refuge. But they didn't survive. In the second century, thousands of other Jews revolted against the Romans under a man named **Bar-Kokhba**, who claimed to be the Messiah. Few survived. Those who did were homeless and scattered abroad.

During the Middle Ages, Israel was occupied by Muslim Turks. This led to the **Crusades** in the eleventh century — a time when Christians fought Muslims for the Holy Land of Israel. The Crusades failed miserably, and Muslims *kept* control of Israel for a very long time. Without a homeland of their own, Jews remained scattered. Some Jews prospered, but most Jews didn't. Some lands welcomed them, but most lands didn't.

This brings us to the Renaissance and Reformation. What was life like for the Jews of this period? Well, it varied. Just like the time period of the Middle Ages, some Jews prospered, but most Jews didn't. Some lands welcomed them, but most lands didn't. Those that didn't were deplorable in their treatment of the Jews (deplorable means bad or wretched).

In A.D. 66, the fortress of Masada near the Dead Sea became home to about a thousand Jewish refugees. Tragically, they chose mass suicide rather than surrender to the Romans.

To make my point, I have several examples to share, but they are too detailed for some of you. **Younger Students:** I suggest that you read just a few examples below and move on. **Middle and Older Students:** Read all the examples I've provided. Read them slowly enough to absorb what was really going on.

- In 1506, Jews were massacred in **Portugal** by zealous Dominican monks.
- In 1516 in **Venice, Italy**, the *Ghetto Nuovo* was created and the idea spread to France and Germany. The ghetto was designed as a place for Jews to live *separate* from Christians and under harsh restriction.[1]
- In 1519, 800 Jews were forced to leave **Regensburg, Germany**. Five thousand Jewish gravestones were demolished and used for other building projects.
- In 1523 in **India**, a Jewish community was demolished, forcing most to flee as refugees.
- In 1535, the city of **Tunis** in **northern Africa** was sacked by the Spanish who then destroyed the Jewish community there.
- In **Russia**, Ivan the Terrible would *not* allow Jews to live in his kingdom. In 1563, he ordered the drowning of 300 Jews who refused to convert and be baptized.
- In 1555, Pope Paul IV created a ghetto system in **Rome** and added stringent rules to it. Communities were not allowed more than one synagogue, and Jews were locked in the ghettos at night. The pope also forced Jews to wear special garments for quick identification — something that would later be repeated by the Nazis. Apart from Pope Sixtus V (1586), decades of popes were cruel in their policies toward Jews.

- In 1569, Philip II of Spain ordered the establishment of the Inquisition in the New World. **Mexico** was the first to follow the order and burned at least 200 Jews at the stake. Two hundred more were imprisoned for being Jewish.
- In 1595, in Lima, **Peru**, 10 people were found guilty of practicing Judaism. Four were punished and one Jew was burned alive.
- In 1615, Louis XIII of **France** forced all Jews to leave his country or face death.
- In 1630, Ferdinand II insisted that the Jews in **Prague, Czechoslovakia**, were to sit through church services every Sunday. Those who refused or fell asleep in church were fined.
- William Prynne, the Anabaptist who verbally attacked the English theater for its loose morals, also attacked the Jews. He wrote in *A Short Demurrer to the Jews* that Jews were guilty of counterfeiting money and murdering children. His accusations distressed those who believed in him and caused slanderous rumors to spread among the English.
- Between 1648 and 1658, reckless torture and killings took place under the Cossacks (Russians). Jews in **Poland, Lithuania**, and **Russia** suffered the most, and about 34,000 died in one decade.

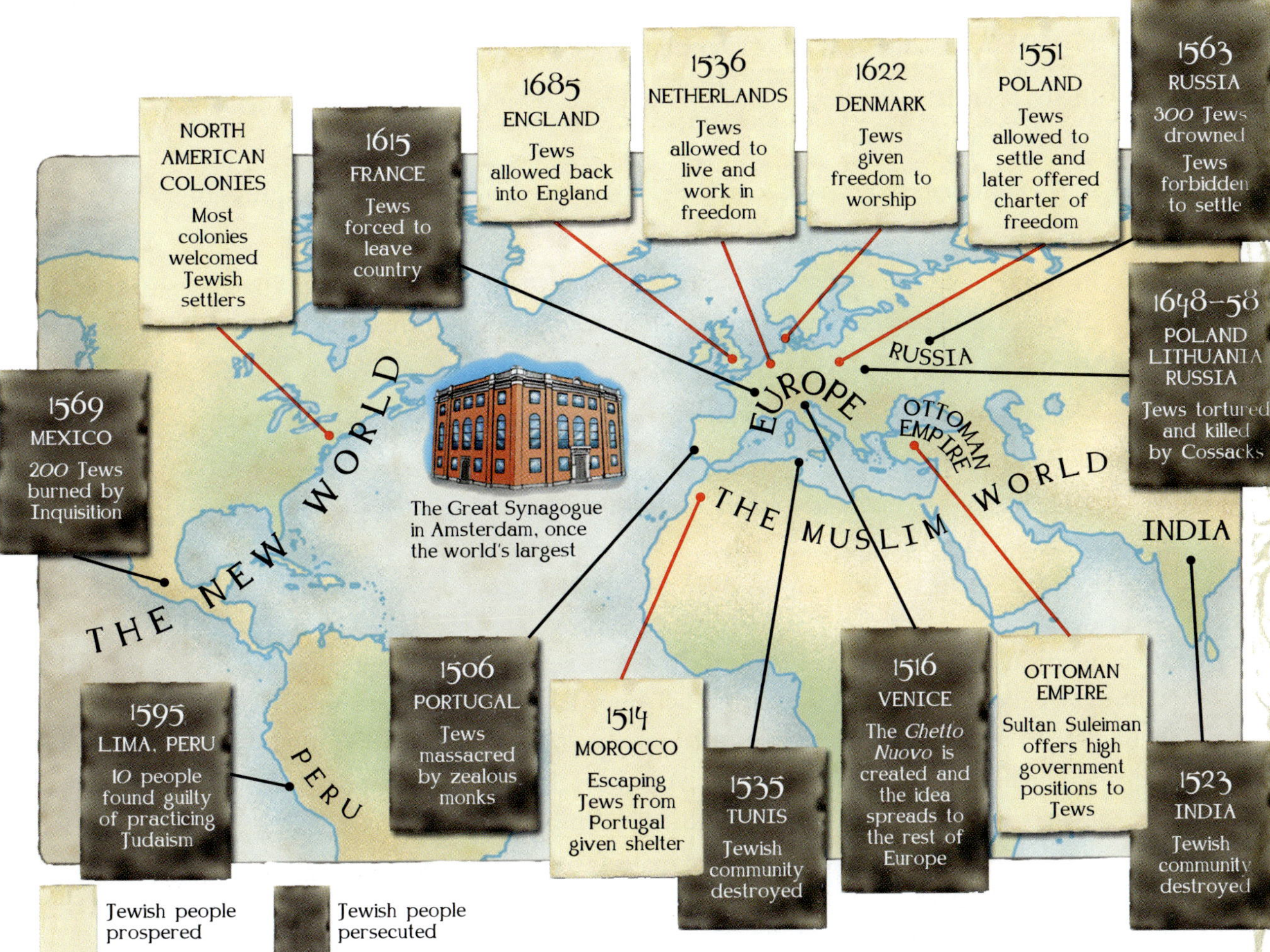

These are just a few examples of mistreatment that went beyond Europe and included India, Russia, North Africa, Mexico, and South America. There are many more, but I think I've shared enough to show how difficult it was in *some* places to be Jewish.

On a different note, there were other places in the world where Jews were free to settle and prosper. And there were many Jews who contributed to the arts and sciences of the Renaissance. **Younger Students:** Read a few examples and move on. **Middle and Older Students:** Please read all the examples below.

- In 1514, Azemmour, **Morocco**, provided shelter to Jews escaping Portugal.
- Salamone de' Rossi was a Jewish-Italian composer who had his own orchestra.
- In 1536, Charles V (the Holy Roman Emperor) allowed Jews the freedom to live and work in the **Netherlands**.
- Jose Solomon Delmedigo was a successful Jewish student under Galileo.
- In 1551, Sigismund II allowed Jews to settle in Vilna, **Poland**, and later offered them a charter of freedom. As a result, half a million Jews lived in Poland by 1648.
- Suleiman the Magnificent of the **Ottoman Empire** was generous in his treatment toward Jews, offering them numerous positions in his government.
- David Gans was a Jewish historian and astronomer who worked alongside Johannes Kepler.
- In 1622, King Christian IV of **Denmark** gave freedom of worship to Jewish residents.
- In 1655, Jewish architect Baldassare Longhena rebuilt a beautiful synagogue for the wealthier Jews of **Venice**.
- Portuguese Jews who resettled in **Amsterdam** were able to build a magnificent synagogue that Christians helped to dedicate.
- In 1685, Jews were allowed back into **England**, where years before they had been banned. A Jewish man named Manasseh ben Israel helped fight for that, but he died before seeing any success.
- Most of the **North American colonies** welcomed Jewish settlers. By the early 1700s more than 10,000 Jews made North America their home.

Persecuted or not, there were some commonalities among the Jews that helped hold them together. First, the Jews as a whole had a very strong work ethic and sought to be prosperous despite their circumstances. And many were. Second, the Jews held tightly to family and to customs passed from one generation to the next. Third, Jews clung to the writings of their great rabbis. They had, of course, the Old Testament, but they also studied traditional writings of the **Talmud** and the **Kabbalah** (mystical interpretations of the Old Testament). Fourth, Jews of Central Europe developed their own language called **Yiddish**. It was a mesh of German, Hebrew, and Slavic languages. And last, the Jews drew strength from the idea that the Messiah was still to come to deliver them from their sufferings.

As you continue in your studies of history, try to remember this bigger picture. Remember God's plan for salvation for Jews and Gentiles alike. Though we do see the oppression of God's chosen people and though we do see Jews suffer persecution, God is still at work.

**Part II**

## *God's Chosen People*

With that in mind, let's look now at what the Bible says about God's chosen people and his covenant relationship to them. In Exodus 19:5–6, God told Moses that the Israelites would be special. The Lord said, "Now therefore, if you will indeed obey My voice and keep My covenant, then you shall be a special treasure to Me above all people; for all the earth is Mine. And you shall be to Me a kingdom of priests and a holy nation."

Under the conditions of this covenant, the Jews were required to bring blood sacrifices to the altar for the atonement or removal of sin. Priests of the temple were given very specific instructions on how, when, and where these sacrifices were to take place.

Why Israel you ask? Deuteronomy 7:7 helps answer that question. It says, "The Lord did not set His love on you [the Israelites] nor choose you because you were more in number than any other people, for you were the least of all peoples; but because the Lord loves you, and because He would keep the oath which He swore to your fathers . . ." (Words in brackets are mine.)

Over the ages, Jews have clung to traditions to help preserve their faith. A candlestand called a menorah is used during Hanukkah to remember God's miraculous provision of oil for the rededication of the Temple in Jerusalem in 165 B.C.

The important part of that passage is that God chose the Israelites because they were at one time the *fewest* of all peoples. They were a small nation. God's point? He knew His glory would be best seen through their weakness. Unlike the dreadful Assyrians or the powerful Romans, the ancient Israelites could never say they were a mighty nation by their own strength. Rather, they were made strong by *God's* hand. They would bear testimony to *His* grace and mercy.

The Old Testament is full of stories that demonstrate the power of God based on His covenant with Israel. But unfortunately, the people of Israel did *not* remain faithful to God. They rebelled against Him. God then declared that He would make a *new* covenant. He said, "Behold, the days are coming, says the Lord, when I will make a new covenant with the house of Israel and with the house of Judah—" (See Jer. 31:31.) And do you know how the new covenant was made? It was made through the blood of Christ!

Hebrews 9:15 helps explain. It says, "And for this reason He is the Mediator of the new covenant, by means of death, for the redemption of the transgressions under the first covenant, that those who are called may receive the promise of the eternal inheritance."

Matthew 26:27–28 tells us, "Then He [Jesus] took the cup, and gave thanks, and gave it to them, saying, 'Drink from it, all of you. For this is My blood of the new covenant, which is shed for many for the remission of sins.'" (Word in brackets is mine.) This is great news!

In Exodus 24:7, Moses referred to the written words of the Lord as the Book of the Covenant. A Torah, as pictured here, is used by Jews today to hold the Book of the Law of Moses (the first five books of the Old Testament, also called the Pentateuch).

The new covenant was made to *complete* the faith of the Jews! It was made to redeem them and provide forgiveness for their sins once and for all. (See also Heb. 10:1–10.) But were the Jews the only ones needing salvation? Of course not. The Bible says, "for all have sinned and fall short of the glory of God." (See Rom. 3:23.) So Jesus came ultimately for *all* whom He would choose to have mercy on. Paul, a Jew and a follower of Christ, said, "For I am not ashamed of the gospel of Christ, for it is the power of God to salvation for everyone who believes, for the Jew *first* and also for the Greek." (See Rom. 1:16. Italics are mine for emphasis.)

If this is true, that the gospel was first for the Jews, then why didn't the Jews follow Jesus? Well, many of them did. Christ's first followers *were* Jews! His family was Jewish, his disciples were Jewish, and Paul — who wrote most of the New Testament — was Jewish. But as non-Jews, or Gentiles, also came to follow Christ, they changed their names to identify with Christ. In time, believing Jews *and* Gentiles all began to call themselves "Christians."

It seems there's been some confusion ever since. Jews who did *not* embrace Christ as the Messiah came to distrust those who did. In fact, the Jews even persecuted them. Ironic, isn't it? And those who *did* follow Christ came to distrust those who didn't. Generally speaking, Jews and Christians grew in opposition after the resurrection.

To make some sense of this tragedy, let's look again at what the Bible says about the Jews who did not believe that Christ is the Messiah. Paul wrote, "Concerning the gospel they [the Jews] are enemies for your sake, but concerning the election they [the Jews] are beloved for the sake of the fathers. For the gifts and the calling of God are irrevocable." (See Rom. 11:28–29. Words in brackets are mine for clarification.)

What all of this means, my friends, is that God has a plan that *includes* the salvation of the Jews! The Bible says clearly, "God has not cast away His people whom He foreknew . . . But through their fall, to provoke them to jealousy, salvation has come to the Gentiles . . . blindness in part has happened to Israel until the fullness of the Gentiles has come in. And so all Israel will be saved, as it is written . . ." (See Rom. 11:2, 11, 25, 26.) When does it say that the Jews will be saved? The answer is — when the full number of Gentiles has come into the kingdom!

This is deep stuff, and I realize that. It means that Gentiles have the responsibility to share the Gospel and further God's kingdom. When that job has been done, the Jews will be saved. Are the Gentiles doing their job? I hope so. First, the Gentiles must accept the Gospel and then trust God to work through them.

I love what Paul said about this to the Christians in Rome. He wrote, "How then shall they [the Jews] call on Him in whom they have not believed? And how shall they believe in Him of whom they have not heard? And how shall they hear without a preacher? And how shall they [the Gentiles] preach unless they are sent?" (See Rom. 10:14–15. Words in brackets are mine.) I believe this is a clear message to Christians that we are to preach the Gospel.

Exciting to me is the fact that there are many Jews today professing Jesus as the Messiah. They refer to themselves as **Messianic Jews** and they refer to Jesus as **Yeshua**. These are crucial times as more and more Jews call on Jesus for salvation. Pray for Jews to understand the new covenant made through the blood that was shed through Jesus Christ.

## Lesson 65 — 1634

# Rembrandt

**Rembrandt** was a giant in the history of art. But he is hard to categorize. He is *not* considered a master of the Renaissance — because he lived about a hundred years after Leonardo, Michelangelo, and Raphael. *Nor* is he considered one of the great **Baroque** (Ba ROKE) painters of his day — because he refused to follow that trend. (I'll explain the Baroque style of art later.) I guess you could say that Rembrandt was simply — Rembrandt! He had a style all his own that goes beyond time and location. Following the highs and lows of his own perilous life, Rembrandt captured the very heart and soul of mankind with great depth. For that, he is well loved (especially by me).

Rembrandt painted more than a hundred portraits of himself. He did so probably as a means of experimentation rather than out of vain conceit.

Rembrandt's full name was **Rembrandt Harmenszoon van Rijn**. He was born in Leiden, Holland. His father added *van Rijn*, or "of the Rhine," to their family name to distinguish it from others. He was a miller and hoped the distinction would help the family business. Rembrandt's parents were humble folks of humble means living in Holland after the religious wars. Protestantism had taken hold and was a great influence in Rembrandt's life.

As a youngster, Rembrandt attended Leiden Latin School. His older siblings didn't have that opportunity, for none were as gifted as Rembrandt. At 14, he entered the University of Leiden. But it didn't suit him well. In less than a year, he dropped out to follow his passion for painting. Though his parents may have been disappointed at first, they supported his love for the arts. The rest of his life was devoted to painting. Rembrandt was probably the least educated of the master artists but not the least passionate. Painting consumed him.

One of Rembrandt's favorite subjects to paint was himself. Since he was the shy, quiet type, I don't think he painted himself out of vain conceit. I think he was simply the most "available" subject on which to practice. In his lifetime, Rembrandt painted more than a hundred self-portraits that serve as a visual diary of his life. Other favorite subjects were his sister, his first and second wives, and his mother reading Scripture. I suspect these women were kind and patient enough to sit as models on quiet afternoons and evenings. Or perhaps they just couldn't get away from his paintbrush!

## *Baroque Style of Art*

Before I go on, let me pause and introduce you to the Baroque style of art. The word *baroque* probably comes from the Portuguese noun *barroco,* which is an *irregular*-shaped pearl. It was first used in a derogatory (meaning insulting) way to describe the *irregular* style of painters who came after the great masters of the Renaissance. When you think about it, how were new artists to compete with the works of Leonardo or Michelangelo? They couldn't. So French, Spanish, and Italian artists began to break away from the classical style. Straight lines in art became curved; circles became ovals; and calm, simple scenes were replaced with overly dramatic ones.

The result? Baroque works are extremely elaborate in detail. (Some would call them "overdone.") Though beautiful, Baroque works tend to be busy and flamboyant. In paint form, great examples would be *Aeneas' Flight from Troy* by Federico Barocci and *Adoration of the Magi* by Peter Paul Rubens. Both are full of colorful detail and movement. In sculpture, a great example of Baroque style would be Gian Lorenzo Bernini's statue *David*. Unlike Michelangelo's *David,* Bernini's is caught in intense action. It's really quite breathtaking.

Most historians believe that the Baroque style took off because of the Counter-Reformation. Do you remember that? That was a time *after* the Protestant Reformation when the Roman Catholic Church made attempts to "reform" itself from within. As it always had, the Catholic Church used works of art to teach Bible stories to men and women who couldn't read. This continued into the 1600s through the employment of Baroque-style artists who painted and sculpted with more flair and passion than ever. (This style is so distinctive that the term *Baroque* has come to mean almost anything that is extravagant.)

## *The Netherlands and Rembrandt's Career*

Now, let's get back to Rembrandt by thinking about his homeland, the Netherlands. Was the Netherlands a Catholic nation? No. Its provinces had been divided. Most of Holland (a province of the Netherlands and the home of Rembrandt) was Protestant. It was only natural, then, that the style of art found there would be different from that of its Catholic neighbors. And it was. Rembrandt was the most famous of those artists who resolved within themselves *not* to follow the trend of Baroque-style painting. Unfortunately, it would cost him. But I'll get to that part later.

Rembrandt's greatest interest was in creating *realistic* portraits and drawings. He didn't hide the bumps or warts or wrinkles of his models. And most importantly, he didn't hide their feelings. Rembrandt tried more than most to draw out the emotions of those he painted. It's quite a challenge to make a single scene in time full of emotion *without* using busy and exaggerated movements. But Rembrandt did it using explicit light and shadow. Let's look at his career and some of his most famous works.

For about six months, Rembrandt moved to Amsterdam to study under other artists. At 19, he moved back home to Leiden as a master himself. He was considered very young to be his own boss. A self-portrait done about 1629 shows him looking young, unrefined, and naïve. At the same time, his eyes and brows are intense and furrowed because he was quite serious about his new profession. Distinctive to his portraits is the use of light on the face of his subject, with darkness in the background. This gives a viewer the warm feeling of sitting by the subject in the dim light of the evening.

In 1631, Rembrandt moved to Amsterdam again. It was a growing trade city where tulip bulbs and paintings were the rage. Rembrandt was quickly employed by groups and guilds that wanted portraits of their profession. The best example of this is *The Anatomy Lesson of Dr. Nicolaes Tulp*.[2] This eerie scene of a doctor dissecting a corpse was a real-life event. The corpse in the picture was a 28-year-old hoodlum who had been executed. Dr. Tulp was the anatomist who invited Rembrandt to paint the classroom scene of the dissection. You see, the government allowed one criminal a year to be dissected for learning more about the human body. The painting was a huge success, as the light captured each man's awkward but curious attention toward the cold corpse lying in front of them. Remember, Rembrandt was famous for capturing feelings.

Dr. Tulp, an anatomist in Amsterdam, invited Rembrandt to capture this classroom scene of an actual dissection in *The Anatomy Lesson of Dr. Nicolaes Tulp.*

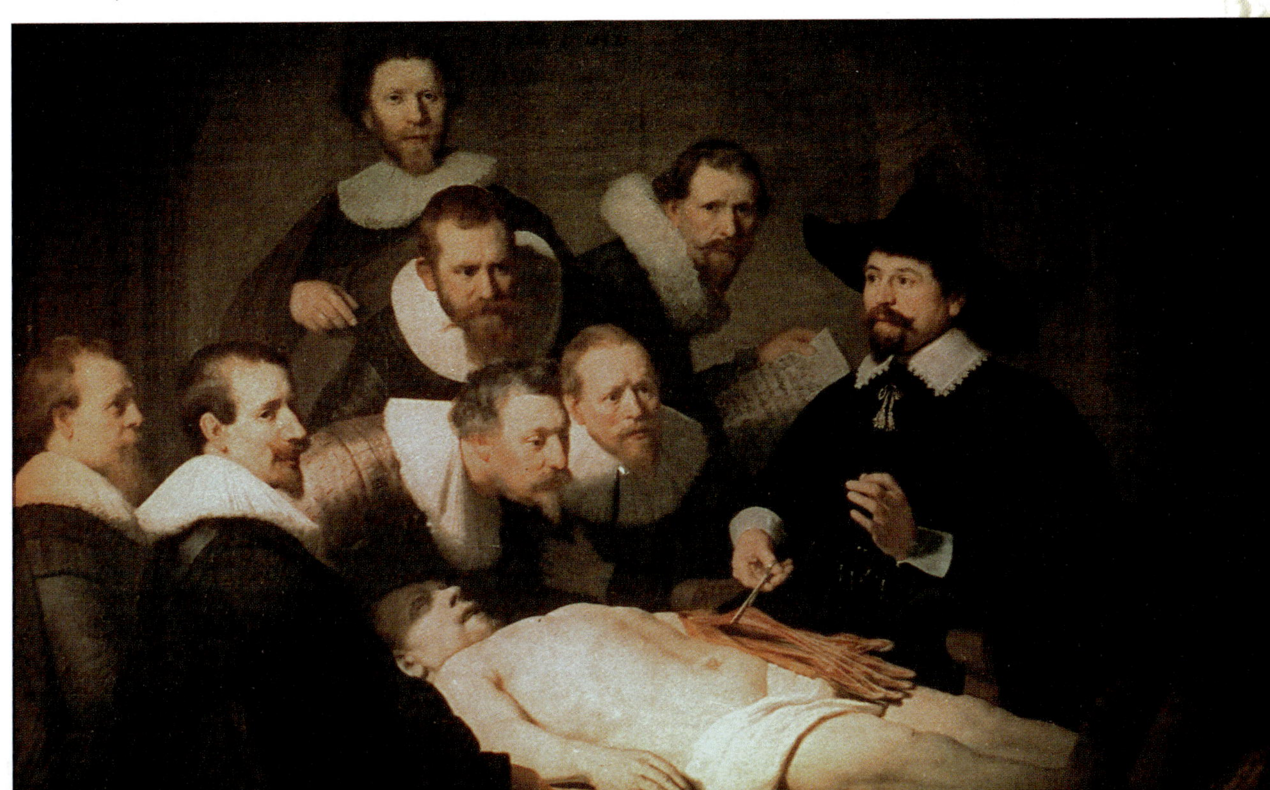

As Rembrandt's fame spread, he experienced the typical problems of an artist. He discovered that high-paying customers could be very demanding. They usually wanted to be painted in a stiff, formal style — one that Rembrandt didn't really care for. So, when he had the chance to paint scenes from the Bible, he did so with great passion. In *Presentation in the Temple,* Rembrandt conquered the problems of air, space, depth, and drama. He makes the family of Jesus look small in the Temple of Solomon as they were in contrast to the baby king at hand. He also made them look Dutch to draw his own people to the timeless message of the Gospel.

While in Amsterdam, Rembrandt met a sophisticated young woman named **Saskia** (ZA skee uh), and the two fell very much in love. With this change of heart came a new mood and style to Rembrandt's works. In a simple sketch titled *Saskia,* he captured the flirty adoration of his bride-to-be. After their wedding in **1634**, Rembrandt caught his wife in everyday poses — doing her hair, lying in bed, and playing with the baby. These natural scenes were a far cry from the Baroque artists of the day! But Rembrandt was at the height of his career. He grew wealthy and enjoyed the prestige of his wife, who was social and fashionable. In the painting *The Prodigal Son in the Tavern* (also known as *Saskia and Rembrandt*), the happy artist gives a toast to life while bouncing his wife on his knee.

Unfortunately, Rembrandt and Saskia's children didn't live long. Three babies died within weeks of their birth. This, too, changed the mood of Rembrandt's works. In *Woman Carrying a Child Downstairs,* Rembrandt shows us his own tenderness and longing as the woman in the sketch kisses and caresses the child in her arms. There is movement in the sketch but not at the expense of being distracting. It only adds to the realism of the sweet scene. The viewer knows that the next step of the woman is down the stairs, and so Rembrandt captured an ongoing scene rather than a frozen portrait. He would do this over and over again.

Something else happened in Amsterdam that would influence Rembrandt's works. He moved to a new home in a different part of town. In doing so, he found himself surrounded by Jewish immigrants fleeing persecution. In getting to know some of these Jews personally, Rembrandt grew to better understand the Jewish life led by Jesus Christ himself — and it showed in his works. Rembrandt no longer used Dutch people as models for his Bible stories. He used his Jewish neighbors, who had the same features and complexion as the characters of the Bible. Abraham, Mordecai, David, and Jesus were all painted after Jewish models. It brought a new sense of realism to Rembrandt's works for which he remains famous.

Despite his success, tragedy was to haunt Rembrandt. His dear wife died shortly after the birth of their son, **Titus**. In *Widower,* Rembrandt captures the desperate emotion of a father trying to feed a baby on his own. It was an experience he lived through and something that would harden him over the next few years — making him very difficult to work with. It is amazing that during this mournful time, Rembrandt managed to paint one of his most famous masterpieces, *The Night Watch.*

*The Night Watch* depicts a company of soldiers receiving their marching orders. The name is misleading. In the 1800s, the painting was found to be so darkened by varnish that it was thought to be a night scene and so was renamed *The Night Watch*. But it had nothing to do with nighttime. In 1642, Rembrandt was commissioned to do a painting of a company of soldiers that would hang in the banquet hall of the civic guard. It is one of Rembrandt's largest paintings. The people loved it — probably because it was more like the Baroque style of art that was so popular across Europe. The huge painting *is* busy and full of movement.

But as you know, Rembrandt loved simple emotion. He turned to nature to soothe this desire and painted *The Three Trees* and *The Mill*. Both landscapes are masterpieces in and of themselves, giving great peace to the viewer. It was probably just what Rembrandt needed.

## *Love and Loss*

What Rembrandt didn't know then was that his heart would be given another chance at love. A young woman named **Hendrickje** (HEN drih kwuh) moved in as an assistant to his housekeeper. She was to steal Rembrandt's heart. *Girl in a Doorway* was the first of many paintings of the young redhead whom Rembrandt clearly loved. He took her as his common-law wife, and together they had a baby girl.

Things brightened up with Hendrickje in the home, but she couldn't solve Rembrandt's financial problems. It seems that Rembrandt was terrible with money. He spent his wealth on rare antiques and props to use in his paintings and insisted on the most expensive paints and brushes. It caused him to fall into a great amount of debt, for which his friends struggled to forgive him. They got tired of loaning him money that he rarely if ever repaid. This debt was the beginning of Rembrandt's downfall — but he painted through it all.

In absolute perfection, Rembrandt painted *Titus* (his son) and a portrait titled *Girl with a Broom*. Both children have the face of an angel illuminated against a dark background. In the spirit of realism, he painted *Beggar Seated Warming His Hands* and inspired one of his pupils to paint *Old Woman Cutting Her Nails*. Neither scene is glamorous, but both are familiar to us all.

In *Girl in a Doorway*, Rembrandt painted Hendrickje, the youthful redhead who would steal his heart and become his wife.

Very popular during the Age of Reason was Rembrandt's painting titled *Aristotle Contemplating a Bust of Homer*. It was ironic that Rembrandt painted Aristotle thinking about Homer when in actuality, Rembrandt himself pondered Homer a great deal. He did so because Homer was blind, and it was Rembrandt's greatest fear that he, too, would lose his sight. For this reason, the blind are a theme of many of Rembrandt's last works.

Rather than suffer blindness, Rembrandt instead suffered the loss of his second wife. That he seemed to never get over. A few years later his son, Titus, died as well, leaving Rembrandt with only a young daughter. He didn't seem up to the task of raising her, and in his grief, never chose to paint the girl. Instead, shortly before he died, he painted a portrait of himself as a weathered, seasoned, and resigned

Rembrandt painted *Aristotle Contemplating a Bust of Homer* to depict the unanswered questions of ancient minds and to satisfy his personal interest in the blind.

old man. (See his 1669 self-portrait in the Around the World section of Quarter 4.) In one of his last paintings, he depicted himself in the crowd of those who had crucified Christ. He seemed to understand that Christ had died for *his* sins as He died for the sins of the world.

Sadly, by the time Rembrandt died in 1669, he was all but forgotten by the Dutch. His realistic paintings were pushed aside for the popular works of flashy Baroque artists. Though Rembrandt finished 600 paintings, 300 etchings, and 1,400 drawings, few attended his funeral. Few hailed him as great — at least in that century. Almost four hundred years later, the Dutch, as well as the rest of the world, hold Rembrandt dear for his talent and ability to capture the soul of man.

## Lesson 66 — 1639

# Thomas Hooker Founds Connecticut

A few lessons back I introduced you to John Winthrop. He was the Puritan who governed a booming settlement in Boston under the Massachusetts Bay Colony. Well, John Winthrop had a very good friend named **Thomas Hooker**. Winthrop and Hooker were a lot alike. Both were God-fearing men with a vision for settling the New World. However, they disagreed on one thing. Because of their disagreement, which I'll explain later, Thomas Hooker relocated to start *another* important colony in North America. That colony became **Connecticut**, which is now one of 50 states in the United States of America. For some of you, this lesson will feel close to home.

Thomas Hooker was born in England to a Puritan family. It was while he attended college that a fellow student challenged him to a personal relationship with Christ. Hooker responded and grew quickly in his faith. He soon became a popular Puritan preacher in England.

But Thomas Hooker didn't have it easy. He lived during a time when the Anglican Church of England was still at odds with the Puritans. I'm sure you remember the ordeal

Escaping Anglican persecution, Thomas Hooker fled to the Netherlands. But like the Pilgrims before him, he later journeyed to the New World.

of the Puritans who tried to "purify" the Anglican Church. They regularly faced persecution in England. Hooker's biggest enemy was the archbishop of Canterbury, a fervent Anglican.[3] The archbishop put so much pressure on Hooker that he resigned as a preacher. For a time, Thomas Hooker opened a school for children in his home. Even then, Hooker *still* faced persecution by the archbishop, who tried to have the preacher arrested.

Finally, it was in 1630 that Thomas Hooker fled to the Netherlands. The Netherlands was at that time a safe place of refuge for Protestants. But, like the Pilgrims before him, Thomas wasn't content in the Netherlands. He heard stories of the New World that beckoned him to settle there among other English colonists seeking religious freedom.

In 1633, Thomas Hooker boarded a ship named the *Griffin* to sail for North America. Do you want to guess who pursued him even as the ship cast off? It was the archbishop of Canterbury! Even as the *Griffin* pulled away from the shore, the archbishop was on Hooker's heels. But Thomas hid out with others who were in danger until the ship was well out to sea. Miles out in the Atlantic Ocean, Thomas finally found peace and rest from those who pursued him.

It was a long voyage for Thomas Hooker and the other settlers on board the *Griffin*. It took them almost eight weeks to reach North America. It must have been inspiring to see the New World for the first time. I do wonder how that felt. After years of hassle in England, the settlers were free.

Thomas Hooker first settled in **Newtown** in the Massachusetts Bay Colony. Newtown was later named **Cambridge**. Hooker became the first minister of the First Parish of Cambridge, a church that remains standing today. His home was on the plot of land where Harvard University is now. Hooker might have lived the rest of his life in Massachusetts — but as I've already told you, he didn't. Thomas Hooker had a disagreement with John Winthrop that caused him to relocate to Connecticut. Let's stop and look at their disagreement. It was to shape the history of America!

## The Puritans Disagree

John Winthrop, as you know from another lesson, was a very good governor. He was godly in manner and well liked by the Puritans in Boston. They re-elected Winthrop 11 times to be their governor. There was no problem there. But Thomas Hooker was wise enough to see that there *could* be problems in the future. Let me explain.

Under John Winthrop, *only* the members of the Puritan church were allowed to vote for the governing leaders of the community. People who were not members of the church were *not* allowed to vote. Why? John Winthrop believed that the government should be in the hands of godly men of the church. He thought that this would work best if only church

Depicted here are Pilgrim Fathers leading their first public worship service. Under Thomas Hooker, Puritan policies regarding the right to vote would change.

members could vote. Now, when Boston was small and contained, this policy worked. Almost everyone was a member of the Puritan church anyway.

But stop and think this through. From what we have studied, what happens when the church and the government are the same? It often leads to persecution. Do you remember the persecution the Puritans faced in England? That persecution existed because the head of the church and the head of the government were the same. The Anglican Church was ruled by the monarchy of England. And it was a royal mess! The government decided how people ought to worship and punished those who didn't agree. It limited the freedom of religion and perpetuated persecution.

Thomas Hooker was wise enough to think through this matter of allowing only church members the right to vote. Though he was a Puritan like John Winthrop, he disagreed on Winthrop's policy. Hooker wanted to see *all* men given the right to vote — whether they were members of the church or not! He wanted to keep the church and the government separate.

John Winthrop and Thomas Hooker never saw eye to eye on this issue. But they parted as friends and wished one another well. With the blessings of John Winthrop, Hooker left the Massachusetts Bay Colony. He left with 100 settlers from three different congregations to start another colony.

## *Connecticut*

It was friendly Native Americans who first steered Thomas Hooker and his settlers toward an area they called *Quin-nequk-tu-cut,* meaning "long river." The area offered good farmland and fishing to anyone who could settle there. Hooker and his people made the long journey together by starting and ending every day in prayer. Hooker's wife had to be carried for the trip because she was very ill. I imagine they prayed for her, too.

It was worth the difficult trek because the pioneers found the land as good as promised. The three congregations settled **Hartford**, **Wethersfield**, and **Windsor**. Because these settlements were out of the jurisdiction of the Massachusetts Bay Colony, they merged to become their own colony. The colony was officially chartered by King Charles of England, but he was far away and the colonists felt much on their own. They named the colony Connecticut after the original Indian name of the area.

In time, Thomas Hooker went a step further to settle the new colony. In **1639**, he and others wrote down their ideas of freedom in the **Fundamental Orders of Connecticut**. The orders spelled out the rights of men to vote and other important matters. Many would say that this document was the first constitution of America and that Thomas Hooker was the "Father of American Democracy." A man named John Fiske stated, "It was the first written Constitution known to history, that created a government, and it marked the beginnings of American democracy, of which Thomas Hooker deserves, more than any other man, to be called the father."[4]

Others would say that this was a bit of an exaggeration, but nonetheless, the ideas of the Fundamental Orders certainly caught on and were influential in the formation of the free nation to come. By the way, John Winthrop's idea of limited voting didn't last.

Thomas Hooker seemed to not let ingenuity go to his head. On his deathbed at the age of 61, his friend said to him that surely he would receive great reward in heaven for his hard labors. Thomas replied, "Brother, I am going to receive mercy."[5] He clearly saw himself in need of the Savior despite his fine reputation.

As good as things were in Connecticut, there was an unfortunate incident that took place there. It had to do with the Native Americans. One tribe of Native Americans called the **Pequot** (PEE kwot) **Indians** did not welcome the settlers. In their hostility, the Pequots murdered nine colonists. Though tragic, the worst part of the story is this: In revenge for the murders, the colonists of Connecticut burned the village of the Pequots to ashes, killing 400 men, women, and children! Those who survived were sold into slavery.

This was a tragic response by the colonists. Rather than working toward peace with the Pequots, they annihilated them. There was nothing fair about that. Even with the wisdom of Thomas Hooker, the New World had a long way to go in becoming "the land of the free and the home of the brave."

You know, time and time again we see man in conflict. We see it in all nations, tribes, and religions. I believe it is a reminder of what the Bible says in Romans 3:23. It reads, "for all have sinned and fall short of the glory of God." Jeremiah 17:9 says, "The heart is deceitful above all things, and desperately wicked; who can know it?" We see a lot of wickedness in history. Thanks be to God that He sent us a Savior, who is Christ, the Lord!

Lesson 67 1641

# John Amos Comenius: The Father of Modern Education

Think back with me about the Thirty Years' War. Do you remember where it started? It started in Bohemia with the Defenestration of Prague. That was when Protestants pushed three Catholic rulers out of a window in revolt! This event triggered the Thirty Years' War, which spread to nearly all parts of Europe. I bring this up because our lesson today is about one man who was caught up in the Thirty Years' War and driven from his homeland. The man's name is **John Amos Comenius**. I would have had much in common with this guy because he was a teacher, a Christian, and the author of a textbook for children. This is his story of faith, courage, and dedication.

John Amos Comenius was born in Moravia. Like Bohemia, Moravia was a small nation under the umbrella of the Holy Roman Empire. In 1618, the same year that the Thirty Years' War broke out, John Comenius was starting a new job as a pastor and a school principal in Moravia. His church was that of **The Unity of the Brethren** (or ***Unitas Fratrum***), who were descendants of the followers of John Huss (HOOS). John Huss was an early reformer whose story you will find in Volume II.

The Unity of the Brethren church was Protestant. This means that when the Thirty Years' War broke out, they were in trouble. As Catholics gained ground in Bohemia and Moravia, Protestants suffered persecution. To be more specific, it was 1620 when Ferdinand II ousted Frederick from the throne of Bohemia. After victory at the Battle of White Mountains, Ferdinand II restored Catholicism in Bohemia, and it spread to Moravia.

The Unity of the Brethren church descended from John Huss, who was burned at the stake in 1415 for seeking reform of the Medieval Church.

If you recall, those were bitter days between the faiths. Though Protestants and Catholics both claimed to be "Christians," they fought to the death over religious freedom. For seven years, John Amos Comenius was forced to live on the run for his faith. As pastor for The Unity of the Brethren, he was under attack and his home burned to the ground. He hid from farm to farm and found refuge in caves and hollow trees while ministering to members of his church. Even on the run, John wrote a story, titled *The Labyrinth of the World and the Paradise of the Heart*. It was an allegory about the difficulties of life. He knew much about difficulties because John's wife and children died from the plague during his seven years of wandering.

By 1628, the danger was too great for John Comenius and members of his church. They fled for their lives over the mountains in Moravia to Poland. It's been said that while in flight, John Comenius paused to look back at his homeland and pray that a "hidden seed" of faith would remain with his people. You will learn later that his prayer was answered though he never set foot in Moravia again.

## *Improving Education*

John Comenius and his followers settled in **Leszno,** Poland. While there, Comenius was free to resume his interest in education. Remember, he had once been a school principal. In 1632, Comenius published some of his ideas about learning. Keep in mind that at this time period 80 percent of Europe was still illiterate. This means that more than half of all Europeans couldn't read or write. In many places, school was available only to the wealthy, and education focused greatly on the mastery of languages. To Comenius, education seemed narrow, impractical, and difficult to come by. So, in summary, he proposed these ideas to improve it:

1. Education should be available to all children whether they are rich, poor, male, or female.
2. Education should be realistic and use concrete objects or nature whenever possible to teach abstract things.
3. Education should include the training of the body as well as of the mind through outdoor play and sports.
4. Education should be practical and teach things that help with the ordinary business of life.
5. Education should include the study of science.
6. Education should ultimately improve one's character and produce order and happiness for others.

Besides these principles, John Comenius believed that the only truth was God's truth. He thought that all reason should be based on obedience to God. Comenius also believed that teaching should be started in the home by parents who could rely on nature to teach Christian values. Overall, he looked at education as more than the retention of facts but rather, as a method for learning to think.

In my opinion, Comenius had some excellent ideas on education. The Parliament of England thought so, too. In **1641**, the Parliament invited John Comenius to England to present his ideas as recorded in his book *The Way of Light*. Unfortunately, civil war broke out in England that same year. The civil war put a stop to John's project and halted the start of a new school. He went to Sweden instead, where he tutored the queen.

In 1642, John Comenius returned to Poland. A few years later, the Peace of Westphalia ended the Thirty Years' War. But the results were not good for Comenius and The Unity of the Brethren. Though the war was over, the Brethren were *not* allowed to return to Moravia! Comenius would remain more or less a wanderer the rest of his life, visiting remnants of his church that were scattered across Europe. Coincidentally, his second wife died at a young age, leaving him with four children to rear alone.

In 1655, John Comenius expressed his support of Protestants in Sweden. After all, he had spent some time there tutoring the queen. In doing so, he provoked enemies in Poland. The following year these enemies burned down his home and destroyed his possessions. One of the items lost in the fire was an encyclopedia that Comenius had been working on for years. It was a great loss.

## A Textbook for Children

But John Comenius was yet to be defeated. At age 64, he fled to Amsterdam, Holland, and wrote some more. In 1658, he put together the first textbook for children that contained almost as many pictures as words. It was the first of its kind and titled *Orbis Pictus*, meaning the "World in Pictures." Comenius created this text based on his belief that concrete objects, or pictures of them, were helpful in teaching abstract things to the young.

For example, when teaching the virtue of *justice*, Comenius provided a picture of a woman and named her "Lady Justice." Lady Justice holds scales in her hands to teach the idea that justice "weighs out" what is fair. In the picture, Lady Justice is also shown blindfolded to teach that justice should *not* be influenced by what is seen with the eyes.

I think you'll agree that John Amos Comenius had some wonderful ideas and was dedicated to education. But he was not always listened to. At the age of 75, he had the chance to stand before a peace council between England and Holland. Having suffered much from war, Comenius had ideas for keeping peace through improved education. But he was not heard. His ideas at that time were pushed aside.

However, the prayer of John Comenius *was* heard. If you remember, he prayed that a "hidden seed" of faith would one day sprout from his homeland. It did. Many years later, members of the Brethren church migrated to Herrnhut, Germany, and started a spiritual revival there.

Though Comenius remained poor most of his life and didn't receive much recognition, he has been remembered today. After writing 154 books on education, he is considered by many to be the "Father of Modern Education." The face of Comenius appears on one of the money bills of the former country of Czechoslovakia. Schools and awards are named after him, and Teacher's Day is celebrated on his birthday in the Czech Republic. After all his efforts and hardships, I think John Amos Comenius would be honored to know that he is indeed remembered.

Though John Amos Comenius didn't receive much recognition in his lifetime, his face was later added to currency in the former country of Czechoslovakia.

# The English Civil Wars

War can be cruel and dreadfully ugly. When nations rise up against other nations, people get hurt and many die. But worse than that in my opinion, is *civil* war — when nations rise up against their *own* people, and their *own* people get hurt and die. Today's lesson is about such a series of wars, spanning the years **1642 to 1651**. They are usually referred to as the **English Civil Wars** and are rather complicated.[1] To try to make it simple, we'll follow the lives of two men — **King Charles I** and **Oliver Cromwell**. The first man tried to be a dictator but failed. The second man tried *not* to be a dictator but failed as well! It's a complex story.

As you know, James I became king of England after the long reign of Elizabeth I. When James died, his son Charles became the next king of England. Charles I was a lot like his father. He believed in the "divine right of kings." That means he saw himself as appointed by God to be the king, and he believed that whatever he said was right.

Well, Charles couldn't have been more wrong! England wasn't about to bow down to that kind of a king, or **absolute monarch** as it is also called. The English had positioned themselves long before then to have some say in government affairs. They did so by establishing the **Parliament**, which is an advisory council to the king. In fact, the word *Parliament* comes from the French word *parler* (par LAY), which means "to speak."

Like his predecessors, Charles I supported the "divine right of kings." But because he ignored the Parliament, his stance would lead to civil wars in England.

The kings of England were supposed to work *with* Parliament to make important decisions — especially decisions that involved money, taxes, and war. Under normal circumstances, the Parliament was called into session by the king a few times a year. But Charles I ignored the Parliament for 11 years and made decisions on his own. In particular, he spent a lot of money on religious wars in France and Scotland and raised new taxes to cover it. He also raised taxes for his navy and called it "ship money." Charles did all of this without calling Parliament into session even once between 1629 and 1640! That was a mistake.

When Charles *did* call the Parliament together in 1640 to ask for money, it was a disaster. His policies had divided the members of Parliament into two groups — those who were for him and those who were against him. The division was so serious that it led to civil war. Let's examine these groups more closely to understand why.

## The Cavaliers and the Roundheads

Members of Parliament who were in *favor* of the king were called **Royalists**. They were nicknamed the ***Cavaliers*** because many of them were well-trained horsemen who rode in "cavalries." The Cavaliers were known for dressing like gentlemen and wearing their hair in long ringlets. As owners of large estates, the Cavaliers (or Royalists) preferred the heavy hand of the king. They believed a strong king, or absolute monarch, would protect their wealth and interests.

Members of Parliament *against* the king were called the **Parliamentarians**. Most were Puritans and nicknamed the ***Roundheads***. Why Roundheads? Well, the term referred to the simple bowl-style haircut common to Puritan men who stayed away from long curly wigs and fancy clothes. About one-third of the Parliament was made up of Puritans, who (as you already know) were at odds with the king and suffered persecution under him.

Cavaliers (on the left) were known for their horsemanship, fine dress, and ringlet hairstyles. Roundheads (on the right) were nicknamed for the bowl-style haircut of most Puritans, who avoided fancy clothes and wigs.

So, let's summarize. When Charles I clashed with Parliament, it caused division between the Cavaliers and the Roundheads. The Cavaliers supported the king — the Roundheads didn't. By 1642, the groups positioned themselves for war. As for the Parliament itself, the Roundheads succeeded in taking it over and kept it in session for the next 20 years! It has thus been nicknamed the **Long Parliament**. Charles I had no power over the Long Parliament because most of its members schemed against him through the civil wars that followed.

## *The First and Second English Civil Wars*

The **First English Civil War** started on a small scale in 1642. Neither side had more than a few thousand men. Ordinary folks didn't know which side to join in the war and tried to stay out of it. But as time went on, more and more got involved, and more and more fought and died. The Roundheads recruited farmers and herdsmen and taught them to fight like soldiers. The Cavaliers recruited nobles, Irishmen, and Catholics. (The king's wife was Catholic, so most Catholics were on the side of the king.) War raged on for the next four years. It's been estimated that 10 percent of the English population perished in the process.

In 1643, the Scottish joined the fighting. Do you want to guess which side they were on? They gave help to the Roundheads because they held similar religious views. (If you remember, the Scottish had gone through strict religious reform under John Knox many years before. They called themselves *Covenanters* or *Presbyterians*.) With the help of the Scottish Covenanters, the Roundheads grew stronger. After a series of battles, including the **Battle of Naseby** (NAZE bee) in 1645, the Cavaliers were weakened. Charles I was defeated and forced to flee to Scotland. His surrender in 1646 ended the First English Civil War.

While in exile, Charles tried to make peace with the Scots and rally them back to his side. He was, after all, Scottish himself. His grandmother was none other than Mary, Queen of Scots! But this didn't help him. The Scottish Covenanters distrusted Charles because he was set on imposing the rules of the Anglican Church on their clergy and churchmen. So, generally speaking, the Scottish turned against Charles I.

Regardless, in 1648, Charles managed to gain some strength and lead troops in what was called the **Second English Civil War**. But it lasted less than a year. In the end, the second civil war ended the same as the first. The Roundheads were the victors. But unlike the first war, Charles didn't get away. He was captured by the Scottish Covenanters and handed over to the English who proceeded to have him arrested.[2]

A remnant group of Parliament called the **Rump Parliament** met in a special session to decide the fate of their former king. Their sentence? Death. Yes, Charles I, the king of England, was sentenced to death for crimes against his own country! It's a rare event in history that a country executes its own king. (It happens but not often.) Charles I was declared a "tyrant, traitor, murderer and public enemy." On January 30, in 1649, Charles was beheaded in front of the Palace of Whitehall. It was a clear message that the English were *not* going to tolerate an absolute monarch or a dictator on the throne.

## *Oliver Cromwell*

Though Charles I was dead, the English Civil Wars weren't quite over. There was still division between the Cavaliers and the Roundheads over the rights of kings. Problems and wars existed with Scotland and Ireland, too. (Generally speaking, the Scottish backed the Roundheads and the Irish backed the Cavaliers.) Knowing this, it's time now to follow the life of Oliver Cromwell, the next main character of our lesson.

Oliver Cromwell was born into an ordinary Puritan family. He grew up in the country and had little education. But at 27, he came into a personal relationship with Christ and felt a divine calling on his life. Oliver was a quiet, serious man who spent much time in prayer and fasting. He had no ambition for politics, but his Puritan friends had great respect for him and sent him to Parliament as their representative.

So Oliver Cromwell was both a Puritan and Parliamentarian. That means he was one of the Roundheads. Cromwell wasn't trained as a soldier, a general, or a statesman, but as his reputation grew, he served as all three. When it came to serving as a general, Oliver Cromwell was brilliant. He believed that the strength of an army depended on the strength of the soul. Weapons were important, he would say, but Cromwell felt that the real power of an army was in the moral fiber of the troops.

Oliver Cromwell grew up an ordinary Puritan but served England through its civil wars as a soldier, a general, and a powerful statesman.

With that view in mind, Cromwell disciplined his army like no other. Cursing and drunkenness were forbidden. Prayer and worship were mandatory. As if Cromwell's troops were an army of ancient Israelites, they sang the Psalms of David while in battle. These measures proved to make Cromwell's army strong. Though usually outnumbered, they were never beaten. The reputation of Cromwell's regiment spread, and it was nicknamed the "Ironsides." It was later named the **New Model Army**. It was actually the New Model Army that won the Battle of Naseby and ended the First English Civil War.

As noble as Oliver Cromwell was, he had a revengeful streak. This was apparent in 1649 went he led his troops against the Irish. Do you remember that Irish Catholics had supported the Cavaliers in the civil war? Well, Cromwell set out to punish them for that and for having persecuted Protestants (which they had). Though the attack on Ireland was called the **Cromwellian Conquest**, it was more like a massacre.

The term *massacre* is usually used to describe the killing of a lot of innocent people. Remember the St. Bartholomew's Day Massacre led by Catholics? The reverse occurred in Ireland under Oliver Cromwell, who was a Protestant. Rather than army fight against army, Cromwell's troops attacked civilians, or ordinary people. In the town of Drogheda, every Catholic priest was slain. In the city of Wexford, 1,500 residents were slaughtered. By 1652, two-thirds of Ireland's property was put in the hands of Englishmen after 600,000 of the Irish perished from war, the plague, or starvation. According to Cromwell, it was God's judgment. To others it was a scary sign of Cromwell's growing power.

## *Lord Protectorate or Dictator?*

With his military successes, Oliver Cromwell's leadership grew. He helped lead Parliament in establishing a **Commonwealth**, which is a system *without* a king. The Commonwealth was an "experiment," really, because England had been run by kings for so long that it hardly knew what to do without one. The Commonwealth was a good temporary solution, but it wasn't perfect. So, in 1653, Oliver Cromwell and his Puritan army overthrew the Commonwealth and tried something else.

First, Oliver Cromwell dismissed the Long Parliament that had been in session for 20 years. Second, he and his army formed a new government called a **Protectorate**. They based it on a written constitution. And to oversee this new government, guess who was named **"Lord Protectorate of England, Scotland, and Ireland"**? It was Oliver Cromwell, of course. Believe it or not, a Puritan was holding the highest office of the land.

Ultimately, Oliver Cromwell would be titled Lord Protectorate of England, Scotland, and Ireland. To some, he would appear no different than a king.

The Puritans of England were glad to have a Puritan in power. Under Cromwell's leadership, many Puritan ideas were put in place. Theaters were closed for being indecent, and Wednesdays were set aside for fasting. Shops were closed on Sundays and games and sports were forbidden. Even travel on Sundays was shunned. Moral laws like these were traditionally printed on blue paper and thus nicknamed "blue laws."

Some would say the blue laws helped to improve the morals of England. In legislating righteous living, the Puritans were as effective as any other group in history. But the Puritan rules and blue laws were only outward expressions of faith. In and of themselves, they couldn't change the hearts of sinners. According to the Bible, only the spirit of God can do that. (See John 1:12–13; Phil. 2:12–13.)

As for Oliver Cromwell, his rule as Lord Protectorate was both good and bad. On a good note, Cromwell was able to drive pirates from the sea, and he kept peace with France and Spain. But on a bad note, Oliver Cromwell began to look and act a whole lot like a strong king, or absolute monarch. It wasn't his intention. He was a Roundhead through and through and had fought hard to rid England of having a king at all. But when it came down to it, *somebody* had to be in charge. He may have been called Lord Protectorate, but Cromwell was living a lot like the new king of England. Some went so far as to call him a dictator. Isn't that ironic?

Oliver Cromwell kept his position for 15 years. With mixed feelings from the public, it wasn't an easy position. In legislating morality, he found it nearly impossible to keep everyone happy. Cromwell gave freedom to some and yet persecuted others. He hated taxes but raised them. He faced more war than he could stomach with Holland and Scotland.

Many grew to despise Oliver Cromwell, and plots to assassinate him were whispered on the streets of England. One source says of Oliver Cromwell, "The rule of Cromwell became hated as no government has ever been hated in England before or since."[3] Oliver Cromwell said of his troubles, "I can say in the presence of God . . . I would have lived under my woodside, to have kept a flock of sheep, rather than undertook such a government as this is."[4]

What you will learn in a few lessons is that *after* the experiment of the Commonwealth and the Protectorate, England went back to having a king! But before that would happen, there would be one more English Civil War. You might be surprised when you learn who it was that finally became the king of England after all the wars were over.

## Lesson 69 — 1645

# Robert Boyle: The First Modern Chemist

As you've already learned, the English Civil Wars were complicated. But in the midst of them, there were men who rose above the fighting and delved into other matters. One of those men was **Robert Boyle**. He was an Irish scientist who moved to England in **1645** to further his studies in chemistry and physics. As much as Robert Boyle loved science, he loved the Lord and sought to use one love to explain the other. This is a refreshing story of one man's faith and intellect.

Robert Boyle was born in Munster, Ireland. He was one of 14 children! His father encouraged his education and sent him to school at the age of 8. Young Robert easily mastered Latin, Greek, and algebra. When he proved he could do these subjects without pencil and paper, he was moved to a higher level of education. At 12, Robert was sent to school in Switzerland where he added fencing, dancing, and tennis to his studies. He grew tall and lean but struggled with bad health.

According to his biography, it was in Geneva that Robert Boyle came into a personal relationship with Christ. When he was about 17, he was caught in a thunderstorm so severe that he thought it might be the end of the world. Robert didn't feel then that his soul was ready to stand before Christ. After a contemplative night, Robert gave his life to Jesus. He dates as his conversion the morning of December 31, 1641. Robert Boyle would cling to a strong faith in Christ the rest of his life.

With an inheritance in place, Robert Boyle was free to study the science he loved and to join the "Invisible College" of like minds.

In 1645, which was the same year as the Battle of Naseby, Robert Boyle's father was hospitalized. In his old age, he left his son a manor in Ireland and several estates. With this inheritance to lean on, Robert was free to pursue his love of science. He did so with great passion.

One of Robert Boyle's steps to recognition was to join what was called the "Invisible College." This was a group of like-minded scientists and philosophers who gathered often in London, England, to cultivate their ideas. The Invisible College grew to become the **Royal Society of London** — a prestigious group, to say the least. Boyle's connections led him to build a laboratory in Oxford in 1654.

## *Discoveries*

From this laboratory, Robert Boyle made many amazing discoveries in the field of chemistry. So let's think science and examine them. For one, Robert Boyle helped explain the difference between **compounds** and **elements**. You see, it was believed for a long time that all matter was made up of one of four elements — air, water, fire, or earth. Robert argued that these four things were *not* elements but rather, compounds because they could be broken into smaller parts called atoms.[5] For example, he saw water as a *compound* made up of the *elements* of hydrogen and oxygen. (In other words, elements are the "ingredients" of compounds.) Robert Boyle was right. Properly defining elements was a big step in chemistry and in understanding matter.

Robert Boyle also studied the rusting effect of metals and the difference between an **alkali** and an **acid**. Do you know what those are? Alkalis and acids describe the pH (or "potential of hydrogen") level of solids, liquids, and gases. On a scale of 1–14, a "1" is a strong acid, and a "14" is a strong alkali. For example, a car battery is a strong acid and has a pH level of 1. Baking soda is an alkali with a pH of 8. Levels of hydrogen are a fascinating tool of measurement.

Boyle's other interests included the study of color, crystals, refraction, and hydrostatics (which deals with the properties of liquids). The only medieval idea Robert Boyle held onto was the hope of making gold from other metals. We call that the field of **alchemy**. Since no one had yet been able to make gold, alchemy had been made illegal under Henry IV. Boyle worked to have the law reversed, believing it still possible to manufacture gold. Obviously it wasn't.

One of Robert Boyle's many interests was the field of alchemy. Alchemists hoped they could make gold from other base metals.

Robert Boyle was particularly intrigued with the results of putting pressure on liquids and gases. He studied the barometer and experimented with the compression and expansion of air. A short story has been told that during one of Robert's experiments with air, a mouse fainted for lack of oxygen. Supposedly, Robert Boyle stopped the experiment to revive the little creature!

On a more serious note, it was Robert Boyle's experiments with air pressure that led to the discovery of **Boyle's Law**. In simple words, this important law states: *At a constant temperature, the volume of a fixed amount of gas varies inversely with pressure.* This means that if pressure increases, the volume of gas *decreases*. If pressure decreases, the volume of gas *increases*.

Robert Boyle published the discovery of this law in 1662. Two other men, **Robert Hooke** and **Edmé Mariotte** realized the law at about the same time, and so all have received some credit for it.

The important thing about Robert Boyle's works is that he used the scientific method to back up his findings. In his most famous publication, *The Sceptical Chymist*, Boyle wrote about the importance of methods. Many in his day were still relying on mysticism to understand the world we live in. But Boyle was a true scientist with a bent toward order and experimentation to prove his ideas. For this, many would call him the **"First Modern Chemist."**

## Devotion

*"The world behaves as if there were diffused throughout the universe an intelligent being."*
*—Robert Boyle*

As devoted as Robert Boyle was to science, he was equally devoted to God. In fact, he saw science and nature as windows into the study of God. He once wrote, "The world behaves as if there were diffused throughout the universe an intelligent being."[6] Robert Boyle believed that the goal of science was to know and worship God.

With his wealth, Robert Boyle arranged the translation of God's Word into Irish, Turkish, Welsh, Malaysian, and Indian. As director of the East India Company, he supported missionaries who were dedicated to spreading the Gospel of Christ to the corners of the earth.

Robert Boyle never married but lived his last 20 years with his sister. When his health began to fail in his old age, he dedicated himself to writing lectures about his Christian beliefs and science. The **Boyle Lectures**, as they were called, were powerful statements used as items of debate between atheists and Christians.

Robert Boyle died on December 30, 1691, almost exactly 50 years from the time of his conversion to Christ. In his lifetime, Robert named himself "Philatetus," which is Greek for "lover of virtue." It is a fitting description, I think, of this fine man who maintained a virtuous character in all his pursuits.

# WEEK 24

## Lesson 70 1648

# George Fox and the Quakers

The Word of the Lord is powerful. **George Fox** would agree. He once told a British judge that the judge ought "to *tremble* at the word of the Lord." As a result, the stern judge accused George Fox of being a "trembler," or a "quaker." And so the nickname of the **"Quakers"** came to be. The Quakers were the followers of George Fox, but they named themselves the **Society of Friends.**

George Fox was raised in Puritan England. His life spanned some of the years that Oliver Cromwell was in power. The Puritans were happy to have a strong Puritan leader in Cromwell. It certainly freed them from Anglican persecution.

But as the heart of mankind can be deceptive, so not all the Puritans were sincere and godly. Some practiced the "outward" appearance of their faith but failed to experience "inward" transformation. This bothered George Fox, who took great offense at hypocrisy. (Hypocrisy, in the spiritual sense, is *pretending* to be righteous by words or deeds but not really being right with God.)

George referred to these hypocrites as "professors" for *professing* to believe one thing but doing another. Even in childhood he found it hard to play make-believe games because he thought it was deceitful to pretend! I don't agree with him that make-believe games are harmful, but I appreciate how very much he valued honesty and sincerity.

When he was about 19, George Fox began to travel around England in hopes of finding a more sincere Christian experience than he had observed. It's not that he claimed to be without fault. In fact, George Fox would describe himself as struggling greatly with temptations. But he found few around him with genuine faith who could help him understand his spiritual condition. Well-meaning friends and priests suggested he try marriage, tobacco, singing hymns, or joining the military to soothe his troubled spirit. George Fox chose instead to turn solely to the Lord in quiet places. He wrote these words in his journal:

> I fasted much, walked abroad in solitary places many days, and often took my Bible, and sat in hollow trees and lonesome places till night came on; and frequently in the night walked mournfully about by myself; for I was a man of sorrows in the time of the first workings of the Lord in me.[1]

It was in 1647, when he was 23 years old, that George would claim the Lord spoke to his sorrowful spirit saying, "There is one, even Jesus Christ, who can speak to thy condition."[2] From that time on, George Fox felt his sorrow turn to joy. He grew to understand that in embracing what Christ had done for him on the cross, his sinful condition could bring glory to God! In his journal, he wrote:

> Then the Lord let me see why there was none upon the earth that could speak to my condition, namely, that I might give Him all the glory. For all are concluded under sin, and shut up in unbelief, as I had been; that Jesus Christ might have the pre-eminence who enlightens, and gives grace, and faith, and power.[3]

*"For all are concluded under sin, and shut up in unbelief, as I had been; that Jesus Christ might have the pre-eminence who enlightens, and gives grace, and faith, and power."*

—George Fox

## *Public Ministry*

After that experience, George Fox couldn't be hushed. Though not trained to be a pastor, he began a public ministry in **1648**. He preached to outdoor crowds and at the close of Puritan services. Fox encouraged others to follow a simple faith in Christ and heed the "inner light" of the Holy Spirit. He urged his listeners to be more honest in business and compassionate to the needy. He taught simplicity in dress, at meals, and in worship. He concluded from his own experience that formal training wasn't what made a preacher but rather, experience in knowing and loving God.

So when the followers of George Fox began to gather for worship, there were no priests or rituals or formal sermons. There were "meeting houses" rather than fancy churches. The rich and the poor sat side by side, and men and women shared equally in expressing their faith in public. The Quakers sometimes practiced silence as they waited for the spirit of God to speak to them. One Quaker described a meeting like this:

> The power of God will break forth into a whole meeting, and there will be such an inward travail, while each is seeking to overcome the evil in themselves . . . every individual will be strongly exercised as in a day of battle, and thereby trembling and a motion of the body will be upon most . . . as the Power of Truth prevails . . . with a sweet sound of thanksgiving and praise.[4]

As you can imagine, the sincere teachings of George Fox were appealing since the English were in the middle of a civil war that had a lot to do with organized religion. Fox taught against war, churchy rituals, and formalities of any sort.

Furthermore, George Fox didn't believe in taking oaths because of Christ's words found in Matthew 5:33–37. Fox also did not believe in "tipping his hat" to others in false respect. (Fox believed that all men are equal and none more important than another. So Quakers forbid tipping one's hat as a sign of honor.) For those tired of bloodshed and hypocrisy, the message of George Fox was refreshing. By 1660, 50,000 would join the society and call themselves "Friends."

Though the Society of Friends grew quickly, George Fox remained humble. He credited his fame as the work of the Lord. He wrote in his autobiography:

> A report went abroad of me, that I was a young man that had a discerning spirit; whereupon many came to me, from far and near, professors, priests, and people. The Lord's power broke forth, and I had great openings and prophecies, and spoke unto them of the things of God, which they heard with attention and silence, and went away and spread the fame thereof.[5]

## *Oppression*

Of course, not everyone in Puritan England appreciated George Fox's calling to what *he* understood of genuine faith. On several occasions, he was tossed down church steps and beaten with sticks. Critics of the Quakers (both then and now) would state that while George Fox was a sincere man, he went too far in breaking away from the Bible's teaching on the importance of the church. Being led by a lot of feeling and emotion from Fox, the Quakers were left with very little solid doctrine to guide them.

Many misunderstood George Fox's refusal to tip his hat to others. Though he was a godly, peaceful man, some considered Fox a threat to the government.

Apart from that, within English society few understood why George Fox wouldn't tip his hat to others. Many took great offense to the lack of this gesture and considered it a form of disrespect. Quakers were shunned, too, for refusing to take oaths. This was viewed as a stance against the government itself! For shaking up so many ways of thinking, Fox was thrown into prison several times. His followers suffered, too. More than a thousand were put in jail for assembling illegally. At least 450 Quakers died while in prison.

Another reason the Puritans feared George Fox was that they were afraid he would try to overthrow Oliver Cromwell. Remember, devoted Puritans were happy to see England in the hands of a Puritan. But George Fox had no interest in politics or in overthrowing Cromwell. He met with Cromwell only to encourage his personal faith in Christ. Though Oliver Cromwell *was* strong in his faith, the two men never did see eye to eye on the role of the church and other matters. They parted as friends — at least for a time.

Oliver Cromwell would later oppress the Quakers for appearing to be a threat to his cause. It is ironic that the Puritan leader who fought for the religious freedom of *his* people would persecute the Quakers! I can't explain it because it doesn't make sense to me. It didn't make sense to George Fox either. He sent Quakers to visit other Quakers in prison and gather their testimonies. He hoped that their desperate stories would one day help end religious persecution. Quakers today still gather at a **Meeting for Sufferings** to bring light to social injustices that exist around the world.

As for George Fox, in 1669, he married a widow and earned the love of her children. He would later travel abroad to tell the good news of Christ. He went to Ireland, Scotland, the Netherlands, the West Indies, and North America. It was in 1677 that George Fox made it to the New World. He was impressed by the tender spirit of many Native Americans and urged others to make the Gospel known to them. One of his companions, **William Penn**, would have a great influence on the founding of the colony of Pennsylvania. But that's a story I'll save for later.

When George Fox returned to England, he was thrown into prison again. So was his wife. They were yet to be completely free of persecution. George Fox used some of those years to write and was later released. In 1689, a few years before Fox died, the Quakers were finally recognized in England as a valid denomination under the **Act of Toleration**. By this act, the Quakers received limited freedom of worship, and many were released from prison. They had by then demonstrated the genuineness of their faith. The Quakers opened schools and hospitals and ministered to the mentally ill. By their honesty, the Quakers greatly contributed to the business world.

Upon George Fox's death in 1691, the Quakers numbered 100,000 in England, Scotland, and North America. Though George Fox would say he never meant to start a sect, he had. His ideas and interpretations of Scripture were firmly planted. Not all Christians would believe the same as George Fox on matters of war, oaths, election, or baptism. But his personal integrity and teachings influenced thousands to examine their faith in Christ, which was the ultimate aim of George Fox.

## Lesson 71 — 1654

# *Blaise Pascal*

When **Blaise Pascal** (Blaze pas KAL) died, his servants were left to tend to his belongings. In doing so, one of them found something bulging in the lining of his master's coat. Curiously, the servant tore open the lining and found an aged and folded piece of paper. It was dated "the year of grace **1654**" and read:

> God of Abraham, God of Isaac, God of Jacob, . . . He can only be found by the ways taught in the Gospels . . . "O righteous Father, the world had not known thee, but I have known thee" . . . Let me not be cut off from Him forever! "And this is life eternal, that they might know thee, the only true God, and Jesus Christ whom thou hast sent" . . . Let me never be cut off from Him![6]

What the servant found was the handwritten testimony of Blaise Pascal. Pascal had come into a personal relationship with Christ just eight years before his early death. The experience of knowing Christ was so meaningful to him that he wrote it down and kept it close to

Blaise Pascal carried his handwritten testimony of knowing Jesus Christ close to his heart in the lining of his coat.

his heart in the lining of his coat. Apparently, he moved two copies of the paper from coat to coat over the last few years of his life. Let's look at the earlier years of Blaise Pascal and what led to his heartfelt conversion.

Blaise was born in France. His mother died when he was only 3 years old. His father took over his education. In doing so, Blaise's father insisted that his son master the study of languages before moving on to math. But Blaise couldn't be stopped from discovering geometry on his own. When he was 12, his father caught him solving geometry problems using charcoal on the wall! In particular, Blaise proved that the sum of the angles of a triangle is equal to two right angles. Rather than scold him, Blaise's father gave him a geometry book by **Euclid** (YOU klid) to further his love for mathematics. It did just that.

At only 16 years of age, Blaise wrote an essay on the geometry of cones. It was so impressive that the famous mathematician René Descartes doubted the lad wrote it. But he did. Blaise was a mathematical genius. Though most of his original essay has since been lost, one of his ideas still bears his name. We call it **Pascal's Theorem.**

(**Younger Students: You can move on to the next paragraph. Middle and Older Students: Keep reading.**)

Pascal's Theorem basically states this: In a hexagon (inscribed in a conic section), if you were to extend the lines of opposite sides until they intersect, the three points where the opposing lines intersect would form a straight line when connected. It's cool geometry when you see it illustrated.

In 1639, Blaise Pascal's family moved to Rouen, France, where his father took a new job as a tax collector. This job would influence Blaise at 19 to invent a simple calculator. He wanted to simplify the job of totaling long columns of numbers for his father. His invention contained eight notched wheels and dials that could carry digits from one column to the next and display numbers in little boxes. Pascal spent years perfecting his mechanical device, which he called the **Pascaline.** The Pascaline didn't take off in Blaise's lifetime because some thought it would make people grow lazy or cause unemployment by replacing accountants! But Blaise was onto something big with the idea of a calculator! It would just take some time for it to be appreciated. (You can still find one of Pascal's 50 original calculators in the Zwinger Museum in Germany.)

Something that *was* appreciated in the lifetime of Pascal was his understanding of pressure. He concluded, in **Pascal's Law,** that liquids in a confined vessel carry pressure in all directions at the same rate. That knowledge helped to improve pumps, compressors, and elevators, all of which work on the principles of equal pressure. A unit of measurement called a "Pascal" was named after him. It is abbreviated "Pa" and used in scientific equations.

But one thing that stumped Pascal was the mystery of air pressure in a barometer. To solve the mystery, in 1648, he had his brother-in-law take a barometer reading at the base of a mountain and then again at the top of the mountain and compare the readings. The experiment was repeated several times. As Pascal suspected, the barometers had different readings because air pressure *decreases* with an increase in altitude. For discovering this, Pascal was hailed in Europe as a genius.

## Changes

Unfortunately, not all was well in the Pascal household. In 1651, Blaise's father died, and one of his two sisters moved into a convent — against Blaise's wishes. These changes left Blaise Pascal wealthy but very much alone. To fill the void in his life, Blaise indulged in the lifestyle of the rich and famous in Paris. He would later describe these as his "worldly" years.

Pascal worked with gamblers in Paris and used his mind to determine the *probable* outcome of card games. You see, he was asked by two friends to figure out the probable end of a card game that they wished to end in the middle. They wanted Pascal to determine who would *probably* have won the game. With the help of others, Pascal refined the **Theory of Probabilities** to help them with their answer. The theory applies to a lot of things and is still used today.

Never stopping his curious mind, Pascal supposedly was first to invent the wrist-watch by securing his pocket watch to his wrist with a string. He also worked on inventing a coach line of carriages in Paris and flaunted himself about the city in a four-horse carriage of his own. Ironically, those fancy horses would have something to do with his change of heart.

You see, one day Blaise Pascal lost control of his horse-drawn carriage. His horses tumbled over a steep bridge, leaving him and his companions dangling for their lives in his carriage! They barely survived. Blaise fainted from the shock and remained unconscious for some time. From this terrifying encounter, Pascal's perspective on life was changed.

Upon recovering, Blaise Pascal turned to the book of John in the New Testament and began to read. In the middle of the night, the Word of God gave new meaning to his life. It was then that he wrote out his precious testimony on two pieces of paper that he sewed into the lining of his coat and kept close to his heart.

From that year on, Blaise Pascal changed his focus from math and science to matters of the heart and spirit. He joined his sister in her convent at Port Royal and absorbed the teachings he found there. Let me stop and describe the teachings of this particular convent. They were not traditional ones of the Roman Catholic Church.

## The Jansenists

The convent at Port Royal was made up of **Jansenists**. Who are the Jansenists, you ask? They were a group of Roman Catholics who believed in grace and predestination, as did the Protestant Calvinists of that time period. The Jansenists ridiculed the Jesuit priests of the Catholic Church for their emphasis on works and discipline. You could say that the Jansenists were to the Catholic Church what the Puritans were to the Anglican Church. They were believers of sincere faith seeking to reform the church they belonged to. Much like the Puritans, the Jansenists were shunned for their efforts most of the time. But they managed to operate out of the convent at Port Royal, which was about 15 miles from Paris.

When Blaise Pascal joined the convent, he was quickly identified as a person with great intelligence. The Jansenists believed Pascal's brilliance could help their cause. They insisted that he write a defense of their beliefs in grace. He did, and all of France came to know it.

Blaise Pascal penned 18 Provincial Letters designed to stir the personal faith of the Jesuits. Written in beautiful prose style, the letters became best-sellers in France.

As things went, Blaise Pascal penned a group of letters that became best-sellers in France. They were called the **Provincial Letters**. There were 18 in all. Each letter was cleverly written to challenge the Jesuits and encourage a more personal expression of faith. Though the king and the pope condemned the letters, they are considered some of the best French prose ever written. Blaise had done well in expressing his personal faith in God.

**(Middle and Older Students: This next section is for you. Younger Students: Resume reading as directed below.)**

And do you remember Pascal's theory of probabilities? In an interesting way, he used the same idea of probabilities to defend having faith in God. He called it a wager (or taking a chance believing), and it went like this:

- If I wager (or take a chance believing) that there *is* a God, and I'm *right*, then I **gain** eternity for having believed in Him.
- If I wager that there *is* a God, and I'm *wrong*, then I **lose** nothing for having believed in Him.
- If I wager that there is *no* God, and I'm *right*, then I **lose** nothing for having not believed in Him.
- If I wager that there is *no* God, and I'm *wrong*, then I **lose** eternity for having not believed in Him!

Pascal's conclusion? It is best to wager that there is a God! It is the only chance that brings a *gain* for eternity. All other options result in a *loss*. Reread the wager statements a few times until they make sense. The statements are a good discussion starter.

**(Younger Students: Resume reading here.)**

The touching part of Pascal's strong faith is the fact that he suffered a great deal of physical pain. From about age 18 on, he fought bad headaches, a weak stomach, and numerous aches and pains that put him on crutches at times. Some said of Pascal that his pain made him grumpy and that he rarely smiled. That may be true. But his pain did not interfere with his faith — it made his faith stronger. Many were encouraged by his experience and acceptance of his condition.

Blaise Pascal suffered the most in his final years. His health was so poor that he managed to write only fragments of thoughts on paper. But those fragments were exceptional. Years after he died, friends published them in a book called ***Pensées***, which is a French word meaning "thoughts." They were the thoughts of a man who knew pain and suffering as well as the joy of the Lord. Personally, my favorite reading of this time period has been *Pensées*. Something about Pascal resonates with my soul and makes my heart fond of him. Below are several thoughts Pascal wrote.[7] Please read according to your age group.

**(Younger, Middle, and Older Students)**

- "God alone is man's true good." (p. 45)
- "We do not know of ourselves what we are, we can learn it only from God." (p. 49)

**(Middle and Older Students)**

- "It is vain that you seek within yourselves the cure for your miseries. All your intelligence can only bring you to realize that it is not within yourselves that you will find either truth or good." (p. 48)
- "Jesus Christ is the object of all things, the centre towards which all things tend. Whoever knows him knows the reason for everything." (p. 141)

**(Older Students)**

- "All things have come out of nothingness and are carried onwards to infinity. Who can follow these astonishing processes? The author of these wonders [God] understands them: no one else can." (p. 61. Word in brackets is mine.)
- "Nature has nothing to offer me that does not give rise to doubt and anxiety. If I saw no sign there of a Divinity I should decide on a negative solution: if I saw signs of a Creator everywhere I should peacefully settle down in the faith." (pp. 134–135)
- "It is good to be tired and weary from fruitlessly seeking the true good, so that one can stretch out one's arms to the Redeemer." (p. 209)
- "Montaigne's faults are great . . . One may excuse his somewhat free and licentious views on certain situations in life, but his completely pagan views on death are inexcusable; for all hope of piety must be abandoned if we are not at least willing to die as Christians." (p. 215)

> "It is good to be tired and weary from fruitlessly seeking the true good, so that one can stretch out one's arms to the Redeemer."
> —Blaise Pascal

**(All Students resume reading here.)**

Blaise Pascal died in 1662, just shortly after turning 39 years old. An autopsy showed that he suffered from strange indentations in his brain and that he probably died from stomach cancer. But Blaise Pascal's contributions to science live on, and his legacy of faith remains. As the Age of Reason was dawning in Europe, Pascal boldly proclaimed that faith in God alone was the answer to life.

## Lesson 72 1661

# Louis XIV: The Sun King

Of all the kings who reigned over Europe, none were more "kingly" than **Louis XIV**. He believed he was born to be the king of France and that the "divine right of kings" applied to everything he did and said. From his heavy rule and love of war, to his sumptuous clothing and festive parties, Louis XIV was an *absolute monarch* from head to toe. And you know what? The French loved it — at least in the beginning.

Now if you remember, the English didn't care for this kind of king. They put Charles I to death for demanding the divine right of kings and for trying to be an absolute monarch! So why did the French allow it? How did Louis win their admiration? Well, it happened slowly.

### A Rocky Childhood

When Louis was only 5 years old, his father died. His father had been the king of France, and so Louis inherited the title. Of course, since Louis was only 5, his mother became the real ruler of France. Her name was **Anne of Austria.**

Anne of Austria had a difficult time ruling France. The French Parlement had their eyes on England. They observed how the English Parliament overthrew Charles I and had no king at all. It crossed their minds to do the same.

There was a revolt in Paris over this very matter when Louis was just a boy. Angry mobs gathered *against* Anne of Austria and her chief minister in hopes of bumping them out. The mob threw things toward the royal palace in slings called *frondeurs* (frawn DEWRZ). Because of the frondeurs, the revolt has been nicknamed the **"Fronde"** (Frond). There were two Frondes in a few years.

During both revolts, Louis and his mother were forced into hiding. They traded their jewels for food and slept on straw beds. It was hardly the life they were used to. In between the uprisings, Louis was neglected at the royal court. His mother was too busy trying to maintain the peace to tend properly to his needs. Louis dressed in shabby clothes and scavenged for his meals. His education was practically ignored. Louis would never forget those hard times.

When Louis turned 13, he ended the regency of his mother. A year later the second Fronde was stopped, and it was safe for Louis to re-enter Paris. He was only 14 at that time, but he was confident, handsome, and a great horseman. When he entered Paris, the crowds chanted *Vive le roi*, meaning "The king lives." With great dignity Louis strode into the city like he owned it. In reality, he did.

When the chief minister died in **1661**, Louis was expected to replace him with someone else. But he didn't. When his officers asked Louis whom they were to report to, his simple but profound answer was, "To me!" At 23, Louis wanted to be in charge of everything. The Parlement and the people allowed it. Louis took full control of the throne from 1661 until his death. Counting his childhood years, his was one of the longest reigns in history.

The *fleur-de-lis*, which resembles three petals of an iris, is a symbol of French royalty and signifies life, light, and perfection.

So why did the French back down from their revolt? Why did they so eagerly welcome the young king to the throne? I suppose they were just worn out. After having fought in the Thirty Years' War and after two failed revolts, the French accepted their absolute monarch. It must have felt like the right time for a king to be a king and take control of the nation. Louis did so like none other.

Now keep in mind that France was no small country at this time. With 20 million residents, France had four times the number of people that England, Spain, or Italy had. (They each had 5 or 6 million people.) With 21 million residents, the Holy Roman Empire was larger than France, but the empire was sorely divided by its individual states. France then was the largest and most bustling *single* nation in Europe. Some would say it "needed" an absolute monarch as much as Louis wanted to be one.

With such a large population, Louis wanted to expand the borders of France. He believed its natural boundaries were the Pyrenees mountains, the Alps, and the Rhine River. For better or worse, he would spend decades trying to reach those borders and keep them. Louis enlarged his army to three or four hundred thousand. He grew the navy from 20 to 270 warships. With all that manpower, Louis XIV oversaw four wars in all. None were extremely successful, but none were complete failures. They all, however, put a dent in Louis's budget.

Speaking of budgets, one of the wisest moves Louis XIV ever made was to put a man named **Jean-Baptiste Colbert** (Coal BARE) in charge of finances. Colbert was shrewd with money. He put high taxes on imports and created a demand for goods within the country. Business boomed under Colbert, who also enforced **mercantilism** (MER can teel ism). One facet of mercantilism is the idea that a colony started by a country owes its profits to the mother country. This meant that French colonies in the New World and abroad were *supposed* to send raw resources back home to France. This didn't go over very well in the colonies, but it kept France a prosperous nation for a long time. In fact, the ideas of mercantilism were prominent in Europe through the eighteenth century.

## *The Palace of Versailles*

Louis XIV took full advantage of the prosperity that Colbert helped to create. He wined and dined like you wouldn't believe. His extravagance was most clearly seen by his decision to build the magnificent *Château de Versailles,* or in English, the **Palace of Versailles** (Ver SIGH). He could have settled for the famous *Louvre* (Loove) in Paris as his home. But Louis never quite got over what the residents of Paris had done to him and his mother when he was a boy. So he chose to build his palace nine miles *outside* Paris on a marshy site that had been his father's hunting lodge. Furthermore, by putting everything under one roof Louis gained even more control of the government.

Louis XIV abandoned the Louvre in Paris for the Palace of Versailles. The Louvre has since become the world's most renowned art museum.

It took 47 years and 30,000 laborers to complete the building project at Versailles. I'm not surprised. It has walls and floors of marble and 1,400 fountains. The front of the palace is a quarter of a mile wide. In Louis's time, it was lit at night by thousands of candles that glittered off watery canals. One of the most famous rooms is the *Hall of Mirrors,* which contains 357 large mirrors within 17 arcades. Another famous room is the *Salon of Apollo,* which holds a throne of solid silver for the king. Everything was designed in the

The Hall of Mirrors is the biggest room in the Palace of Versailles and one of the most ornate. It is named for the 357 mirrors that decorate the arched windows.

baroque style, making the palace as ornate as was possible. Many an architect has attempted to copy the palace, but few can compare.

Louis hardly needed to leave his grand palace. With 15,000 courtiers, or attendants, why would he need to go anywhere at all? To employ this ridiculous amount of help, he hired even his nobles for the slightest duties. One had the job of handing him his wig — another his coat — and another his napkin. Louis truly lived like a king. During the day, he handled six to eight hours of business at his desk. But during the night, he danced and partied to his heart's content.

Between servants, nobles, and bureaucrats, there were 10,000 people living at the Palace of Versailles with Louis and his queen. He did his best to entertain them all. There were balls, masquerade parties, and water pageants. There were grand ballets, concerts, and operas. I guess that dressing up for these splendid events was half the fun because even the men got caught up in it. They wore lacy shirts with short trousers, silk stockings, elegant gloves, and large soft hats topped with feathers. Men's coats were short in the front and long in the back, with fancy buttons, embroidery, and turned-up cuffs.

The women of this period flaunted themselves, too, with tight-fitting corsets, high heels, and long, bustling gowns. If their hair couldn't hold ribbons or perfume or curls, it was replaced with a wig that could. Image was everything, and Paris issued the first fashion magazine in 1672 to promote the glamor.

But no one was more glamorous or vain than Louis himself. His coats were trimmed with real gold and studded with genuine diamonds. He wore large hats and high heels to look taller and layers of lace for fluff. Louis enjoyed his nickname as *Le Roi-Soleil*, or "The Sun King," because he likened himself in importance to the sun! Like Queen Elizabeth I of England, Louis always posed for his portraits in regal attire. Both loved the pomp and the ceremony of the crown. It was said of Louis XIV that he was "the greatest actor of majesty that ever filled a throne."[8] It certainly would appear that way. Louis's only faux pas (meaning social blunder) was that he preferred to eat with his fingers rather than use a fork!

## The Downside of Glitter and Glamor

Now, are you wondering if there was perhaps a downside to all the glitter and glamor of the palace life? The answer is yes, there was. For one, Versailles was so large that by the time the king received his food from the kitchen, it was usually stone cold. And as grand as the palace was, it had very few bathrooms! Most residents wore a lot of perfume because showers were hard to come by.

On a more serious note, the palace was so enormous that it was hard to monitor all that went on there. Behind closed doors, morals were overlooked. There was so much flirting and frolicking going on that adultery became acceptable around the palace. The king himself kept several mistresses and fathered children from them all. He was a poor role model for the French until near the end of his reign when he honored his queen by marital faithfulness.

But another problem was this — the more time Louis spent at his palace, the less time he spent with ordinary people. He grew indifferent to the needs of the common man and ignored the desperation of the poor. The poor grew to resent their fine king. He ran the

Louis XIV enjoyed the glamor and pageantry of being a king, but because of his self-indulgent ways, he failed to be a very good one.

country into debt with wars and parties while peasants groveled for food in the streets. It was said of the peasants of France that they were like "sullen animals, male and female, filthy, blackened and scorched by the Sun, living in hovels on black bread, water, and grapes."[9] It sounds to me like Louis had so much fun playing king that he failed to be a very good one.

The same could be said of Louis's bureaucrats, who failed to be the best they could be. The term ***bureaucrat*** comes from the word *bureau*, which means "desk." It refers to men who sit at desks to make important decisions. Louis's men did too much of that. They sat around their desks at the glorious Palace of Versailles growing more and more out of touch with the real people of France.

But one of Louis's greatest downfalls, in my opinion, was his terrible treatment of the Huguenots, or the French Protestants. Louis XIV was Roman Catholic by faith and wished the whole nation to be the same. Politically, it was easier for him to control those of the Catholic Church. So, in 1685, he revoked the Edict of Nantes! The Edict of Nantes was the document that had given Huguenots the freedom to worship. This freedom was taken away, and France was sent back a hundred years in time. Louis's terms were steep and included these five things:

1. All Huguenot churches were destroyed.
2. No public or private worship by Huguenots was allowed.
3. Huguenot children were to be baptized by Catholic priests and raised in the Roman Catholic Church.
4. Huguenot ministers who joined the Roman Catholic Church would receive a lower pension.
5. Huguenot ministers who would *not* convert to the Roman Catholic Church were to leave the country in 10 days or be put to death!

Needless to say, thousands resisted the terms by hiding or fleeing the country. Nearly half a million left France for Germany, the Netherlands, and elsewhere. Some, like the parents of Paul Revere, went as far as North America. (I think you've heard of him before.)

Well, it's hard to summarize the reign of Louis XIV since it was both good and bad. On the good side, Louis brought a great deal of stability and prosperity to the large, growing nation of France. On the bad side, he allowed luxury to distance him from his people. Some would say he was ruined by self-absorption. Good or bad, his total reign of 72 years was one of the longest in European history. Despite all his wealth and luxury, Louis died from a painful case of gangrene just before his 77th birthday. All in all, I think Louis XIV's nickname, the Sun King, suited him well because he certainly lived as if the world revolved around him!

Lesson 73 1661

# The Scottish Covenanters

I have grown weary of sad lessons about religious persecution. They break my heart. But we have one more significant wave of persecution to study in this book. We're going to look at the **Scottish Covenanters** and their severe oppression under **Charles II**. Who was Charles II and why did he oppress the Scottish? To answer those questions, we'll have to go back to the confusing events of the English Civil Wars.

During the English Civil Wars, England was divided between the Cavaliers and the Roundheads. Remember them? The Cavaliers supported the king. The Roundheads supported the Parliament. The Roundheads basically won the civil war and in the process, Charles I was beheaded. Oliver Cromwell then stepped in as the Lord Protectorate of England.

Well, before Charles I was executed, he was helped in battle by his 15-year-old son. His son was Charles II, whom we're studying today. Some folks claimed upon the execution of Charles I, that Charles II was the next rightful king of England and Scotland. But it was hard for Charles II to claim the throne. In fact, it was nearly impossible. For having helped his own father in battle, Charles II was considered an enemy — at least by the Roundheads. After losing a battle to Oliver Cromwell, Charles II was forced into hiding. A price was put on his head, and he became a "wanted" man.

Stonehenge, a megalithic structure built about 2700 B.C., served as one of many outdoor hideouts for Charles II before he fled England for France.

The time that Charles II spent in hiding was to shape his life. Unlike most kings, he ate and slept among commoners while on the run. Though an Anglican, he found refuge among Catholic families who had supported his father. Charles II hid from home to home and barn to barn. He camped out in the woods and among the ruins of Stonehenge. He cut his long hair and disguised himself as a traveling servant and a woodsman. His servant role was convincing to the peasants who sometimes spoke to him face-to-face, not knowing he was Charles II!

On one occasion, to flee enemy soldiers, Charles spent the night hiding in an oak tree! This unusual story — of the king hiding in a tree — burned itself deep into the English memory. To remember the perilous escape, it became customary for the English to pin oak leaves on their clothes on Charles's birthday. This custom lasted nearly 200 years! But back to our story.

After 40 days on the run, Charles II made safe passage to France where he joined his mother in hiding. Louis XIV had mercy on him and gave him money and protection. He eventually moved to Brussels. For nine years Charles laid low, until 1658, when Oliver Cromwell passed away. When Cromwell died, *his* son tried to be the next Lord Protectorate. But he didn't do a very good job and offered to resign from the position.

And so, the highest place of leadership in England was vacant. That wasn't good. Do you want to know what happened as a result? After *all* those years of turmoil in the Parliament over having a king, and after *all* those years of civil war, the Parliament voted a king *back* into the position! You know who that king was, don't you? It was Charles II.

It must have been an unreal experience for Charles to cross back over the sea from Brussels to England. After years in hiding, he was now being welcomed home like a hero. On May 25, 1660, thousands stood on the banks of England with tears in their eyes, hailing the arrival of the king. Church bells rang in London as Charles made his way there through the fanfare. Banners were hung, flowers were thrown, and toasts were made. It was a huge turn of events in England. The people called it the **English Restoration** because a king was being "restored" to the throne. It was almost as if the civil war had never happened.

Does this event sound a bit familiar? It does to me. It reminds me of the French welcoming Louis XIV into Paris when he was 14. The English were submitting to an absolute monarch in much the same way the French had submitted to Louis. Like the French, they were tired and worn out from wars and went right back to having a king. Isn't history a mystery?

Charles II enjoyed playing the role of king. Like Louis XIV, he dressed extravagantly and flirted and flaunted himself regally about his court. But unlike Louis, Charles connected with the common people. He remembered the peasants who had helped him escape England years before. The ordinary English folks delighted in Charles, who seemed kind and down-to-earth. They called him "the good-natured king." The Parliament liked Charles, too, because he wasn't very interested in politics, and he allowed them to carry on as they pleased. They did just that.

## *Persecution of the Scottish*

If all was well in England, then why is this lesson about persecution? Well, I'm getting to that. You see, though Charles was at first tolerant of the various religions in England, he was *not* tolerant of the Scottish Presbyterians. For one, it was the Scottish who had captured his father, Charles I, and placed him in the hands of the English for execution. Charles II was brimming with revenge for this act. But secondly, since the Scottish were officially under Charles's rule, he believed he was the head of their church.[1] He couldn't have been more wrong.

According to the Presbyterians, Christ alone was the head of their church. As far back as 1581, Presbyterians agreed to sign "covenants" stating their faith in Christ and were then nicknamed the "Covenanters." In 1638, 60,000 Scots gathered to sign a **National Covenant** put on display at Greyfriars Church in Edinburgh. By 1640, the Scottish Parliament made the Covenant system official. (Or so they tried.)

Underestimating the faith of the Scottish Covenanters, Charles II revoked the National Covenant in 1661. It led to dreadful persecution and bloodshed.

In seeking control over the Covenanters, Charles II did something in **1661** that would begin a reign of terror in Scotland. He *officially* established himself as the head of the Church of Scotland and declared it *illegal* to hold a covenant that stated otherwise. This means he revoked, or undid, the National Covenant that thousands had already signed! (**Older Students:** In legal terms, Charles was reinstituting the law of **prelacy** [PRELL uh see] whereby "prelates," or bishops, were assigned to the churches by discretion of the king. Prelacy grossly violated the individual rights and freedom of churches.)

I don't know if Charles II realized what he was up against. He was up against the deep, solid, personal faith of the Covenanters. They would rather die than submit to anyone other than the Lord Jesus Christ.

There are many sad parts to this story. But one sad part to me is the fact that Charles II was unmoved by the faith of the Covenanters. He himself was not a man of faith or one to practice religion, and so it was doubtful that he understood their devotion to Christ. Though the English called Charles "the good-natured king," he seemed to *not* be good-natured toward the Covenanters. Similar to Louis XIV's persecution of the Huguenots, Charles began to persecute the Covenanters for the sake of *political* power. And as mentioned earlier, Charles was also motivated to avenge the death of his father. He was as willing to *kill* for his cause as the Covenanters were willing to *die* for theirs. And so the conflict erupted.

By 1662, the Scottish Covenanters attempted to outsmart the law. Since they were forbidden to congregate in the churches, they met outdoors in open fields. They called these worship gatherings **conventicles**. By 1670, authorities had caught on to these meetings and declared it illegal for preachers to hold outdoor services. It was, in fact, made a capital crime, which means it was punishable by death. Even this did not stop the Covenanters from gathering or the preachers from preaching.

The Covenanters gathered by the thousands in the hills, the marshes, the moors, and the woods. They armed themselves with lookout guards while mass numbers were secretly baptized or married in Christian ceremonies. Large rocks were their altars and streams their baptismals. They didn't need steeples or pews or walls to make their church. The church was in their hearts. At one such conventicle in 1670, 6,000 worshipers gathered to hear preaching. Boulders were lined up as tables to distribute communion to 3,000 believers. The large stones still stand today as testimony to this brave gathering.

There were times when the Scottish Covenanters tried to rise up in rebellion against their persecutors. They fought at Rullion Green, Drumclog, Bothwell Bridge, and Ayrsmoss. Twice they won and twice they lost. **Richard Cameron**, one of the Covenanters' strongest leaders, was killed at Ayrsmoss. For being considered a traitor, his head and hands were severed (meaning cut off) and put on public display.

## The Killing Times

As bad as these times were, they actually got worse under the next king. Charles II was followed by his brother, **James VII.**[2] James held fast to the divine right of kings and set out to rid Scotland of *all* Presbyterians. The reign of James VII was so horrible, and his methods so barbaric, that a few months in 1685 have been nicknamed the "Killing Times." They were called this because the Covenanters were flushed out and hunted down like animals. Lists of church members were collected, trials were skipped, and God-fearing men and women were tracked down and killed on the spot for their faith in Christ. Some were sold into slavery or shoved into dark dungeons for the rest of their lives. Many inspiring stories have emerged from this dreadful time. They are inspiring because *through* the lives of the martyrs, we see faith triumph over fear.

The Bible comforts us with these words: "Blessed are those who are persecuted for righteousness' sake, for theirs is the kingdom of heaven." (Matt. 5:10)

(**Younger Students and/or those who are sensitive to these things:** You may want to end this lesson here and simply remember the few months called the "Killing Times." Remember that as many as 18,000 Scottish believers died for their devotion to Christ and according to Matthew 5:10, "theirs is the kingdom of heaven." But if you would like to be familiar with the personal names and stories of a few of these martyrs, please keep reading.)

## John, James, and the Two Margarets

Though each life lost during the Killing Times was special, there are four that stand out in Scottish history. The first is the life of **John Brown.** John Brown was a strong Christian who probably would have been a preacher except that he had a speech problem. It was hard for him to talk without a stutter. So rather than preach, he served the body of Christ by hosting meetings and hiding Covenanters in his home.

As the story goes, on May 1, 1685, soldiers came to John Brown's home. They pressed him to swear his allegiance to the king of England. John Brown refused. It's been said that when he spoke out for his faith, his stutter disappeared! Nonetheless, his refusal cost him his life. After saying his prayers, he was shot at his front door in front of his wife and children. The man who ordered the shooting suffered with nightmares for his cruelty.

The second story involves two women. Both were named **Margaret**. One Margaret was a 67-year-old widow. The other was an 18- or 19-year-old maidservant. Both stood firm in their faith and suffered for it. The two women were found in hiding and arrested in 1685 for refusing to give up the Covenant. Unlike some, they were given a trial. But it did not help. The judge ordered them to be executed by the manner of drowning.

Stakes were hammered into a sandy beach at low tide and the women strapped down. Both were offered the chance to save their lives by submitting their faith to the rules of the king. Even as the tide came in, neither of them would falter. One sympathetic soldier killed the older Margaret before the rising waters would steal her last breath. The younger Margaret recited Psalm 25 until she was suffocated by the sea.

Last, I will tell you about **James Renwick**. James Renwick was an ordained preacher who had studied theology in Holland. He knew when he returned to his home in Scotland that he would be persecuted for his faith. He preached anyway and baptized hundreds of children who professed their faith in Christ. For his open preaching apart from the government church, he was identified as a traitor. For at least three years he lived in hiding.

The day came, however, when he could hide no more. He was arrested and condemned to death. The night before he died, he wrote to his loved ones, "He has strengthened me to outbrave man and outface death, and I am now longing for the joyful hour of my dissolution, and there is nothing in the world I am sorry to leave but you."[3]

As he stood at the gallows, James Renwick quoted Psalm 103 and Revelation 19. He prayed out loud, "Lord, I die in the faith that Thou wilt not leave Scotland, but that Thou wilt make the blood of Thy witnesses the seed of Thy church, and return again and be glorious in our land. And now, Lord, I am ready."[4] James Renwick was 26 years old when he prayed that prayer. What he didn't know then was that his execution would be the last public killing of that awful time. And he didn't know then how specifically his prayer would be answered. I'll get to that in a few lessons when we study the "glorious" reign of **William and Mary**.

## Lesson 74 — 1662

# *K'ang-hsi the Manchu and the Ch'ing Dynasty*

I don't think most 13-year-olds are qualified to serve as emperors of nations. But I stand to be corrected with a young man named **K'ang-hsi** (Kang SHEE).[5] K'ang-hsi was the second emperor of the **Ch'ing dynasty** of China. Strangely enough, though, K'ang-hsi wasn't Chinese! He was a **Manchu** (Man CHOO) from the country of **Manchuria**. Let me explain how a young Manchu became one of China's greatest emperors.

We first need to review some geography. You need to know that Manchuria is a great plain located in northeast China. Today Manchuria is part of China, but it wasn't in the 1600s. Manchuria was a large neighbor of China's and under its own ruler.

From 1368 to 1644, China was ruled by emperors of the Ming dynasty. Like most dynasties, it had its highs and lows. But it was during the early 1600s that the Ming dynasty began to crumble from the inside out. In shame, the last Ming ruler committed suicide along with his wife. He left a note saying, "I am ashamed to meet my ancestors. Therefore I myself take off my crown, and with my hair covering my face await dismemberment at the hands of the rebels. Do not hurt a single one of my people."[6]

Upon the death of that Ming emperor, the Manchu swept down from their great plain, overcame Chinese rebels, and in the course of a few years set up the Ch'ing dynasty. It would last until the 1900s! That's a long-lasting dynasty — especially since it was composed of foreigners.

The first Ch'ing emperor was **Shun-chih**. He was only 7 when he obtained the throne, so he relied on his uncle to rule for him. His uncle introduced an unusual custom to the Chinese. He insisted that Chinese men shave the front of their heads and wear a single long pigtail called a **queue**, just like the Manchu! He also insisted that they dress in Manchu fashion. Women weren't told how to dress or style their hair, but they were forbidden to practice foot-binding, which was an old custom among the upper class.

In establishing the Ch'ing dynasty, Shun-chih insisted that Chinese men adopt Manchu clothing and wear a *queue*, which is a single long pigtail.

As you can imagine, the Chinese didn't appreciate being told how to groom their feet, wear their clothes, or cut their hair. The Chinese believed that hair was a gift from their parents and ancestors. So head shaving to them was quite demeaning. It was one of many things that would reflect the humiliation the Chinese felt for a very long time under the Manchu.

Shun-chih grew up and ruled China better than his uncle did. But, in 1661, Shun-chih died suddenly at a young age. After his death, his 8-year-old son inherited the throne. That son was K'ang-hsi, our focus of study today, and that is how he came to rule China in **1662**.

## The Industrious Emperor

As mentioned earlier, K'ang-hsi was only 13 when he took official control over China. Most would not expect a boy that age to be ready for such a job. But apparently he was. K'ang-hsi was a very hard worker. He rose before sunup every morning to start his day and held meetings as early as five o'clock in the morning. He oftentimes worked until midnight. What was he up to all those hours? A lot!

Like most emperors, K'ang-hsi had to bring local uprisings under control. He did so with success through an eight-year battle with three feuding regions. After that, he invested his time into expanding the borders of his empire in every direction. By 1683, he took Taiwan. A few years later he pushed back the Russians and the borders of Outer Mongolia. From all of this, K'ang-hsi made China larger than it had ever been before. (And it was pretty big to begin with!)

Part of K'ang-hsi's success was due to his well-organized army. The Manchu before him had organized the army into eight banners, or divisions. Each banner was color coded and ranked in importance. K'ang-hsi expanded the banner system and made it even better. The bannermen, as they were called, were amazingly loyal to the emperor.

Though K'ang-hsi was an absolute monarch through and through, he cared a great deal for the people of China. Yes, he took high control of things, but he did so with care. For one, he respected the Chinese and their customs more than his ancestors had. He gave the native Chinese the lands that had been taken from them, and placed more Chinese in the government. In a unique system, both Manchu and Chinese officials worked side by side, with the Manchu having the most power.

For the common people, K'ang-hsi lowered taxes and improved public services. He knew how things were around his empire because he regularly left his palace to visit the people in the countryside. Now remember, this emperor was a foreigner! It was an amazing show of skill on his part that the Chinese grew to trust him. But in time they did.

When it came to the arts and sciences, few were as interested as K'ang-hsi. Under his rule, painting and porcelain making reached new heights, as did the harvesting of pearls and ginseng (JIN sing), a popular root. Though an emperor, K'ang-hsi attended hours of academic classes and insisted that his officials be well educated, too. He even went so far as to invite Jesuit priests to China. They were well known for their brilliant scholarship, and K'ang-hsi welcomed it.

To further prove his devotion to the Chinese, K'ang-hsi sponsored three massive literary projects that would preserve Chinese tradition. First, he hired scholars to write the history of the Ming dynasty. Second, he compiled a Chinese dictionary holding 50,000 characters. And third, he sponsored the compilation of a 5,000-volume encyclopedia that included the teachings of Confucius and other important Chinese philosophies.

The tedious production of porcelain eluded Europeans for centuries because only the Chinese knew the secrets of the craft.

Does K'ang-hsi sound too good to be true? In some ways, he really was. He has gone down in Chinese history as one of the greatest emperors ever born. His fine reputation spread to Europe, and K'ang-hsi was the envy of his contemporaries for having the largest, richest empire in the world. Even Louis XIV was impressed by the Manchu monarch whose reign was long and prosperous.

### *Separation*

But of course, as you might suspect, some policies of the Ch'ing dynasty were unfair. Though the Chinese outnumbered the Manchu by the millions, the Manchu were encouraged to have an attitude of superiority over the Chinese. For one, they shut the doors of Manchuria to all Chinese and would not allow them in. Now that's interesting, isn't it? It's like saying, "We'll invade your country, but you can't come into ours." In fact, Manchu officials were required to regularly vacation back "home" in Manchuria to keep themselves distinct from the Chinese.

In the banner army, too, there was separation between Manchu and Chinese. The Upper Banners were primarily Manchu. The Lower Banners were primarily Chinese and not as well equipped. On top of that, the Manchu kept their language and legal documents separate from the Chinese. And Manchu were forbidden to marry Chinese until the 1900s.

Speaking of forbidden, the famous **Forbidden City**, which was the capital and home of the emperor, was off-limits to the Chinese but not to the Manchu. When foreign diplomats were allowed to see the emperor, they were expected to show their respect by kowtowing before him. Kowtowing was the gesture of knocking one's head on the floor in humility before the emperor. It was intended to show how high the emperor was respected above all others.

So the Ch'ing dynasty had its strengths and weaknesses. Some of these weaknesses would in time hurt the vast empire. Separatism would keep China practically behind closed doors and cause them to fall behind the rest of the world in some areas of progress. In fact, the Ch'ing dynasty would be the last dynasty to rule China. But we won't be studying that story until we're well into the 1900s, which is a long way off from the Renaissance and Reformation.

The magnificent Forbidden City in the middle of Beijing, China, was the daunting government seat and palace home of emperors for about five centuries.

# Sir Isaac Newton

Though it may be just legend, there is a story about **Isaac Newton** that will help you remember his most famous contribution. Supposedly, Isaac Newton was sitting in a garden drinking tea when he saw an apple fall to the ground. From that simple observation, which most would not have thought about twice, Newton concluded that **gravity** is the force that holds the entire universe together! The implications of this were to shape human history.

There is no doubt that Sir Isaac Newton was a genius. But you would never have known it when he was a kid. For one thing he was born so prematurely that he barely survived babyhood. Then, in his youth, Isaac did poorly in school. Rather than study, he spent time tinkering with gadgets and building sundials, water clocks, and windmills.

Isaac Newton did poorly in school as a youth, but he tinkered with building sundials, which are complicated devices that must be accurately aligned with the sun.

Isaac Newton quit school for a time to help his widowed mother with the family farm. But he wasn't much help. He spent more time reading than doing his chores. An uncle sent him back to school, hoping to make something good of him. On his second try at school, Isaac performed much better.

But in college, Isaac Newton failed to prove that he was extraordinary. He graduated without any special awards. However, a retiring math professor at Cambridge University recommended that Newton take his place because he saw a glimpse of the genius that was in him. Newton took the position as a math professor but, wouldn't you know, few attended his classes. He apparently spoke so far over the heads of his students that most couldn't understand him. On the days his classroom was vacant, he lectured to the walls.

I imagine that Isaac Newton was the epitome (meaning great example) of an absent-minded professor. He frequently forgot to eat and held a grudge against sleeping for being a waste of his time. He was known to wander around in messy clothes and unkept hair, talking out loud to himself. He didn't make friends very easily.

Though he might have lacked social skills, Isaac Newton possessed thinking skills like few others. By **1666**, at just 24 years of age, he formulated some incredible ideas relating to calculus, gravity, and light. Each is so important that we'll spend most of this lesson addressing them.

## *Newton's Three Major Ideas*

1. *Calculus.* First, when it comes to calculus, it is Isaac Newton who has been given the most credit for inventing it. I say the "most" credit because another mathematician, named **Gottfried Leibniz** (GOT freet LIPE nitz), claimed to be first to develop calculus. Unfortunately, the two men argued over the matter, and it dampened both their careers. It may be that Leibniz was first to *publish* his ideas on calculus, but Newton was first to discover them. Newton was notorious for waiting years before publishing most of his great ideas.

Though Sir Isaac Newton was brilliant in mathematics, he is probably most famous for his three laws of motion, which help to explain the phenomenon of gravity.

If you don't know, calculus is one of the highest forms of mathematics. It seemed to come easily to Newton. His advancements in math helped prove the elliptical theories of Tycho Brahe and Johannes Kepler. I hope you remember those guys. (**Older Students:** Newton was particularly known for infinitesimal calculus, the binomial theorem, Newton's identities, and Newton's method. He also discovered a new formula for *pi* and used fractional indices to solve Diophantine equations. Don't ask me to explain!)

2. *Gravity.* As important as calculus is, it was Newton's ideas on gravity that have made him truly famous. Going back to the example of an apple falling to the ground, Newton was first to realize that the force that causes an apple to fall is the same force that attracts the moon to the earth, the earth to the sun, and the sun to the universe. It's all gravity!

The difference between an apple and a planet is, of course, its size, or **mass**. Newton realized that the greater the mass of an object, the stronger its gravitational pull. Look at it this way: A boulder has more mass than a pebble. That's obvious. So the force of gravity on a boulder is *stronger* than on a pebble. We would say the boulder had more "weight," but in reality, it has a stronger gravitational pull toward the earth! That's not so obvious, but it's an interesting way to view the mass of things.

(**Middle and Older Students: Read this paragraph.**)

Besides mass, **distance** also determines how gravity works. The farther away an object is, the less gravitational pull it has. In Newton's words, "every particle of matter in the universe attracts every other particle with a force varying inversely as the square of the *distance* between them and directly proportional to the product of their *masses*."[7] All of this together helped Newton explain many things, including the bulge of the earth at the equator and the pull of the sun and the moon on the tides of the earth. (Again, it's all gravity!)

(**All Students: Resume reading here.**)

In summary, Newton contributed **three laws of motion** to science with his understanding of universal gravity.[8] They are as follows:

- First Law (the law of inertia): This law states that an object in motion stays in motion unless it is acted on. And an object at rest stays at rest unless acted on.[9]
- Second Law: The force on an object is equal to mass times acceleration. (A simplified equation form is $F = ma$, where $F$ stands for force, $m$ stands for mass, and $a$ stands for acceleration.)[10]
- Third Law: For every action, there is an equal and opposite reaction.

Newton's first and third laws are the easiest to explain with examples, so I'll try. Newton's first law, the law of inertia, is at work when you're spinning around on a merry-go-round and try to jump off. It's not that easy to do! When you jump, it's almost impossible to land in a certain spot and remain on your feet because your body is *still* in motion from the merry-go-round. Right? Have you ever done that before? Your body is fighting inertia, the force that put you in motion.

As for an object's staying "in motion unless it is acted on," it's hard for us to see that on earth because we have friction to slow things down. If you roll a ball on your lawn, the grass will eventually slow it down. But not in outer space! An object would "float" or stay in motion if there were nothing to stop it.

As for Newton's third law, imagine that you and a friend are standing face-to-face on ice skates on a frozen pond. If you place your hands on your friend's shoulders and push away, your friend will move, too. The action of the push causes an *equal* push in the *opposite* direction. Try it sometime. It's much less painful than falling off a merry-go-round.

3. *Light*. It's time now to look at Newton's ideas regarding light. For one thing, he recognized that white light is made up of a spectrum of colors. You can see this phenomenon when light passes through a prism and is divided into red, orange, yellow, green, blue, indigo, and violet. This spectrum is best seen in rainbows when we see light passing through raindrops on a sunny day. Newton was the first to clearly explain the beautiful colors of the rainbow.

Beyond that, Newton recognized that the color of an object is not the color we see with our eyes. Instead we see the color the object is *reflecting* and not absorbing. Consider a green bowl. Our eyes would tell us the bowl is green when in reality, the bowl is absorbing every color in the spectrum of light — except green! The color green is bouncing off the bowl and returning to our eyes. Isn't that thought amazing? As true as it is, we usually refer to things as the color we see them. It's much easier to say that a pumpkin *is* orange than to say, "a pumpkin is absorbing every color except orange and reflecting that back to our eyes"!

Newton used his ideas of light to figure out some incredible things. By studying the color of stars, he could calculate their distance from earth. He also used light to invent the reflecting telescope that used mirrors rather than lenses to study the heavens. This invention greatly advanced astronomy.

From all his brilliant ideas, you would think that Isaac Newton was confident. But confidence was one thing he lacked. For that reason, he waited as long as 20 and 30 years to write about his breakthrough discoveries. He waited so long because he feared the scrutiny or criticism of others. In fact, it took the persistence and funding of a scientist named **Edmond Halley** to put Newton's works into print in 1687. Newton's masterpiece on gravity is titled *Principia* (Prin SIP ee uh). The ideas in *Principia* would stand unchallenged until **Albert Einstein** refined them with his famous *theory of relativity*. But that's another story in history.

## The Faith of Isaac Newton

With all Newton did for science, it might surprise you to know that he wrote more about theology than he did about physics or math. It's true. As magnificent as his contribution to science was, Newton was more fascinated with God and the Bible. Isaac Newton was a member of the Anglican Church in England and influenced by the Puritans. He read the Bible every day and spent his life seeking ways to better understand it. Some would say he was one of the first to try to decipher a code out of all the words in the Bible. He never did find a special code, but he was intrigued by the concept, as are many today who comb the Scriptures for hidden words in mathematical sequences.

Religious folks of Newton's day were concerned with his profound explanation of gravity in the universe. They feared that in naming the force of gravity, people would think less of God and more of gravity for appearing to hold all things together. The truth is that Isaac Newton was a strong believer in God. He believed it was God who created gravity and everything that held up the heavens. He was in awe of God's creation and gave Him full credit for it. Newton said, "Gravity explains the motions of the planets, but it cannot explain who set the planets in motion. God governs all things and knows all that is or can be done."[11]

> *"Gravity explains the motions of the planets, but it cannot explain who set the planets in motion. God governs all things and knows all that is or can be done."*
>
> –Sir Isaac Newton

As a final note on his life, you might wonder why Isaac Newton was given the title "Sir." The title was given to him by Queen Anne of England in 1705 — but not for science or theology! Queen Anne dubbed Isaac Newton a knight for his excellent work in the mint of England. (A mint is a place that manufactures money.) During Newton's day, there were many counterfeiters trying to make fake money. Through his knowledge and interest in alchemy, Newton was far slyer than they were and had many counterfeiters arrested. To find criminals, he was known to disguise himself and hang out in taverns. I think it's an interesting side job in the life of this genius.

Sir Isaac Newton lived to be 85. He never married, but he was generous to the extended family he had. He was fortunate during his lifetime to be recognized for his achievements. He spent numerous years as president

As a sign of great honor, Sir Isaac Newton was buried at Westminster Abbey, which is the final resting place for 17 of England's monarchs.

of the Royal Society and was buried in the fashion of a king at Westminster Abbey.

It is undeniable that Sir Isaac Newton forever changed the way mankind would view the world in motion. He made sense of the "world machine," as it was called. Yet he remained a humble man. Near his death, Isaac Newton said this of himself, "I do not know what I may appear to the world, but to myself I seem to have been only like a boy playing on the seashore, and diverting myself in now and then finding a smoother pebble or a prettier shell than ordinary, whilst the great ocean of truth lay all undiscovered before me."[12]

# WEEK 26

## Lesson 76 — 1667, 1678

# *John Milton and John Bunyan: Puritan Authors of the Seventeenth Century*

We have studied a good deal of England from the outside. We've looked closely at her kings and queens and the civil wars in between. Today, we're going to look at England from the inside. We're going to study two Puritan authors of the seventeenth century who, by their writings, gave us a more personal glimpse into the mind and heart of the English. The famous writings we'll focus on are *Paradise Lost* by **John Milton**, and *The Pilgrim's Progress* by **John Bunyan**. Both books are well-loved classics.

### *John Milton*

John Milton was raised in Puritan style before the break of the English Civil Wars. He was about 12 years old when fellow Pilgrims set sail on the *Mayflower*. But John Milton was not the stereotypical Puritan that was somber and serious minded. He loved music and enjoyed Greek and Latin classics. He mastered those languages, as well as Italian and French. You could say that words and language were his love. With that love, John Milton traveled to mainland Europe and spent months in Italy appreciating the achievements of the Renaissance. While abroad, he heard news of the terrible civil war back home and so returned to England. There in his homeland, he poured himself into politics.

John Milton poured himself into the study of Italian and French, and he enjoyed Greek and Roman classics. His love of languages would shape his future.

Because of John Milton's extensive knowledge of Latin, he was chosen by the Roundheads to write for their cause. The Roundheads wanted their ideas written in Latin and circulated to other nations in Europe — who still had that language in common. Milton responded to the task. Like a soldier, he joined the civil war — but his weapon was his pen. He spent years writing fiery tracts and pamphlets defending the ideas of freedom. He was a strong believer in democracy and freedom of speech.

But in 1652, tragedy struck Milton's personal life. First, at only 44, he lost his eyesight. He was born with weak eyes to begin with, but he had probably made them worse from years of writing late into the night by candlelight. That same year, his wife died and left him with three young daughters to oversee.

If that weren't difficult enough, Milton's second wife died during childbirth in just their second year of marriage. The baby was stillborn, which means that the baby died, too. It was very tragic. On top of that, John Milton was arrested for his Puritan beliefs after Charles II took the throne! Some wished to see Milton hang for writing against the royalty, but his suffering in prison was relatively mild and his sentence was short. In his old age, he retired and tried marriage a third time.

I share these personal tragedies with you because they certainly had something to do with shaping John Milton's "perspective" on life. Through his own trials and heartaches, his perspective grew to be less and less on this world — and more and more on the life to come. As a firm believer in the Word of God, Milton looked toward heaven for hope and Christ for deliverance. It led him to write *Paradise Lost*, a creative allegory of heaven and hell. (An allegory is a story that uses imaginary things to tell about real things.) Let me share with you a little of this beautiful story.

## Paradise Lost

*Paradise Lost* is a long epic poem written in blank verse. That means it doesn't rhyme. Through the delicate arrangement of thousands of words, Milton paints a picture of eternity for us. He starts with the fall of Satan, who almost stands out as the hero of the story for his power and determination. But the reader is quickly reminded of the devil's surroundings and sufferings and that hell is something absolutely deplorable. As if Satan were speaking about leaving heaven, Milton wrote:

> "Is this the region, this the soil, the clime,"
> Said then the lost Archangel, "this the seat
> That we must change for Heaven? — this mournful gloom
> For that celestial light? Be it so, since he
> Who now is sovereign can dispose and bid
> What shall be right: farthest from him is best,
> Whom reason hath equaled, force hath made supreme
> Above his equals. Farewell, happy fields,
> Where joy forever dwells! Hail, horrors! hail,
> Infernal World! and thou, profoundest Hell,"
>
> (Book I, Lines 242–251)

I want to remind you that this poem is written as an allegory. We don't have any record in the Bible of Satan really saying these things. Milton used his imagination to describe what he thought Satan would say about leaving heaven. The words are still powerful. To describe hell itself, as Milton imagines it to be, he wrote the following:

A dungeon horrible, on all sides round,
As one great furnace flamed; yet from those flames
No light; but rather darkness visible
Served only to discover sights of woe,
Regions of sorrow, doleful shades, where peace
And rest can never dwell, hope never comes
That comes to all; but torture without end
Still urges, and a fiery deluge, fed
With ever-burning sulphur unconsumed.

(Book I, Lines 61–69)

As you think about this literary masterpiece, I want you to remember that John Milton was blind at the time he composed it. Perhaps it was his very blindness that fueled his imagination of seeing heaven and hell. Regardless, there were physical challenges. It was Milton's three daughters who had to actually write down the words he dictated at odd hours of the day and night. According to them, it was awful. The daughters had been trained to read and write other languages for their father, but they only understood English. They themselves were not well educated and in fact, despised the books that their father so loved.

This arrangement probably added to Milton's grumpiness and impatience in his later years. He was known to spit out 40 sentences in a minute and then beg for them to be rewritten after hearing them out loud. It would take seven laborious years of this method of writing and rewriting to complete *Paradise Lost* in **1667**.

As difficult as it was, Milton didn't end his career with *Paradise Lost* but kept composing. He spent his last years on *Paradise Regained* and a story about Samson. Can you imagine his interest in the biblical character of Samson? He, too, knew the misery of blindness, the turmoil of politics, and the loss of love. Milton so identified with Samson that he wrote Samson's story as if it were his very own.

## *John Bunyan*

Let's turn our thoughts now toward our other Puritan author of interest. That is John Bunyan. His story is not at all like John Milton's, but the two men share this time in history as famous writers in England.

John Bunyan was raised the son of a poor tinker, one who goes from home to home with a cart to repair pots and pans and utensils. He didn't get much schooling, but he learned enough to read and write. You'll soon see it was all he really needed for what he believed the Lord had in store for him.

For two years, John Bunyan served as a soldier in the English Civil War. According to him, he was one of the rowdiest soldiers in England. He had no concern for spiritual things but was very much in love with the world. He spoke with foul language and swore loudly at the taverns and pubs where he usually drank too much.

In his own words, Bunyan wrote, "I had but few equals both for cursing, swearing, lying, and blaspheming the holy name of God. Yea, so settled and rooted was I in these things that they became as a second nature to me."[1]

Against all odds, at 19 John married a young woman of good reputation. She owned very little except two theology books given to her by her father, who was a godly man. The books would in time intrigue John Bunyan as he began a long journey toward coming to know Christ.

At the start of his journey, Bunyan was skeptical that God would love a man like him. He knew he was worldly and doubted that God had a place for him in heaven. But something, or rather Someone, drew him to the faith. As he finally embraced God's love, he wrote:

> Then I began to give place to the word which with power, did over and over make this joyful sound within my soul, "*Thou art My Love, thou art My Love, and nothing shall separate thee from My Love.*" And with that my heart was filled full of comfort and hope, and now I could believe that my sins should be forgiven me; yea, I was now so taken with the love and mercy of God, that I remember I could not tell how to contain till I got home: I thought I could have spoken of His love, and have told of His mercy to me, even to the very crows that sat upon the ploughed lands before me, had they been capable to have understood me.[2]

After converting to Christianity, John Bunyan was bombarded by evil thoughts, which he believed were from the devil. In these thoughts, John was tormented to give up the precious faith he had come to know! He would later believe it was merely the deception of the devil that led him to think such things. In time, and through much prayer and study of the Bible, John Bunyan stood on solid ground in his faith. After all his doubts and struggles, he devoted the rest of his life to helping others along in their faith.

In helping others, John became an active preacher. He was not well educated in Hebrew, Greek, or Latin, but he spoke from his heart. It was his life experiences that seemed to qualify him for the ministry rather than a school or seminary. But consider the times in which John Bunyan lived. His life spanned the "Restoration," when Charles II was restored to the throne of England. It was a difficult time for anyone *outside* the Anglican Church to flourish. For openly preaching as he did, Bunyan was thrown into jail.

Unlike Milton, Bunyan served a long time in prison. He was so kindhearted to all who knew him that even his jailers were lenient in their treatment toward him. His wife and children were allowed to visit him every day. His friends came around to see him, too, and on occasion he was let out. Still, over the course of 12 years, John Bunyan was in and out of prison for his faith. It could not have been easy.

During those 12 years, John Bunyan wrote books. First he wrote *Grace Abounding to the Chief of Sinners*, which is his autobiography and testimony of coming to know Jesus Christ. It is easy to read and fascinating in thought. In the plain language of an ordinary man, he tells of the wonder and joy of knowing Jesus. One of my favorite lines is this: "I was made to see, both again and again, that God and my soul were friends by His blood."[3] What beautiful words these are to those who understand grace.

> *"I was made to see, both again and again, that God and my soul were friends by His blood."*
>
> *–John Bunyan*

### The Pilgrim's Progress

But a far more popular book is John Bunyan's story titled *The Pilgrim's Progress*, published in **1678**. Like *Paradise Lost, The Pilgrim's Progress* is also an allegory. (An allegory, again, is a story using imaginary things to tell about real things.) With great creativity, John Bunyan brought his characters to life by their names. The main character is *Christian*. He leaves home in rags, with a Book in his hands and a Burden on his back, to find the Celestial City of the King.

In *The Pilgrim's Progress*, John Bunyan portrays the ups and downs of a character named *Christian* on a spiritual journey to the Celestial City of the King.

I hope you can identify the symbolism John Bunyan uses. *Christian* represents a person seeking God. His book is the Bible and his burden is his sin. The Celestial City of the King is, of course, heaven.

But like people in real life, *Christian* encounters many obstacles on his journey. He meets a character named *Obstinate*, who refuses to join him in his journey. He also meets *Mr. Worldly Wiseman*, who tries to sidetrack *Christian* to find comfort in things of the world. *Christian* is nearly led astray by many things on his journey, but he is encouraged by his friends, *Evangelist*, *Help*, and *Faithful*. They help steer *Christian* through imaginary places like the *Doubting Castle*, the *Valley of Humiliation*, and the *Town of Stupidity*.

I won't give away the end of the story because I hope you will take time to read it one day. *The Pilgrim's Progress* will inspire you because you might just see yourself in the life of *Christian*. Like him, we are all distracted by trials and temptations on our journey to spend eternity with the King. And like him, we are indebted to the encouragement of other brothers and sisters in Christ who help us along our way.

## Lesson 77 — *1681*

# *William Penn and the Founding of Pennsylvania*

In **1681**, **William Penn** was granted land between New York and Maryland on the North American continent. That may not sound like a very big deal, but keep reading. William Penn said something almost prophetic about this new land. When it was given to him, Penn said, "My God that has given it to me . . . will, I believe, bless and make it the seed of a nation."[4] Well, the land *did* become the seed of a nation. The land was **Pennsylvania** where, in years to come, the Declaration of Independence would be drafted, the Constitution would be signed, and the first capital of the United States would be located! I don't know if William Penn realized in his lifetime how special his role in establishing freedom in the United States would be, but his ideas still influence Americans today.

William Penn was born in England. He was the son of an admiral in the English navy. But William Penn was nothing like his father. William was drawn to spiritual matters rather than to war. He was expelled from college for holding on to Puritan beliefs. To try to shake off his son's religious views, William's father sent him to study in Europe.

For a time, William was distracted from spiritual matters by the things of the world. After traveling to France, he enrolled in law school and then, in 1667, he visited Ireland. Against his father's wishes, William came to know some Quakers living in Ireland. They drew him back to his interest in spiritual matters and at age 22, William joined the Quaker faith. His father was outraged.

If you recall, one of the Quaker beliefs was to avoid war. William's father was a naval officer! He just couldn't understand William's resistance to war. On a minor note, William's father was offended that his son would not tip his hat to him, as was the Quaker custom. William's father was concerned and afraid for his son. He knew William would face persecution.

For following Quaker customs and beliefs, William Penn caused strain on the relationship with his father and was frequently put in jail. While in prison he wrote *No Cross, No Crown*.

William Penn did face persecution. For his Quaker beliefs, he spent time in and out of jail the rest of his life. But like many faithful ones before him, he made the most of his confinement and used the time to write. While spending eight months in the Tower of London, William Penn wrote a book titled *No Cross, No Crown*. It is a tremendous work on the cost of following Jesus Christ.

On one of his leaves from prison, William Penn was able to join George Fox (the founder of the Quakers). Together they traveled to Germany and the Netherlands with their message of simple faith and simple doctrine. If you remember, the Quakers put great emphasis on personal devotion to Christ. They did not complicate their faith with rituals or formalities. Many in Europe were hungry for the simple but hopeful message of the Quakers and joined the movement.

## *Pennsylvania*

About this time, William Penn had his eye on North America. He wondered if freedom could be found there for the Quakers, but he didn't have the money to invest in a colony. When his father died, an opportunity was created that solved the problem. You see, Charles II (the king of England) owed a great deal of money to William's father. Upon the father's death, the king's debt was transferred to William. (That means the king owed William a lot of money!) William asked the king to pay him with land in America — rather than with cash. The king agreed, thinking the gesture would be an easy way to get out of debt and rid England of a few thousand Quakers! (They were not a popular group. Even the Puritans oppressed them.)

So, in 1681, Charles II granted a charter to William Penn for a tract of land between New York and Maryland. It was almost as large as England itself. Penn first wanted to name it "New Wales" for the many Welsh Quakers living there. But *Sylvania* was chosen, which in Latin means "wooded land." The king's council insisted on adding *Penn* to the beginning of *Sylvania* to honor William's father.[5] William didn't like the name *Pennsylvania* for fear others would think he proudly named the land after himself. He wrote, "I feared lest it should be looked upon as a vanity in me, and not as a respect of the King, as it truly was, to my father, whom he often mentions with praise."[6] William was right — many *have* mistakenly given him credit for the name, though Pennsylvania was really named for his father!

So, being so humble, how do you think William Penn handled his new land? I'm happy to say that he handled it like a gentleman. Though as governor he was given almost absolute power in Pennsylvania, William would *not* become a dictator. He wrote, "I purpose . . . to leave myself and successors no power of doing mischief; *that the will of one man may not hinder the good of a whole country*. It is the great end of government to secure the people from the abuse of power."[7] (Words in italics are italic in source document.) William Penn set limits to his authority as governor by having a Council and a General Assembly. His miniature "country" had a three-pronged balance of power similar to the United States government today.

Besides that, William Penn did something quite extraordinary. In his first three weeks of visiting the continent, he set up a meeting with the Native Americans who lived there. They gathered under a large elm tree for business. His point? In following the Golden Rule found in Matthew 7:12, William Penn wanted to *buy* the land from the people who lived there — not just take it! Of course, the Native Americans had no use for English money, so Penn offered them things they could use. He actually "paid" for

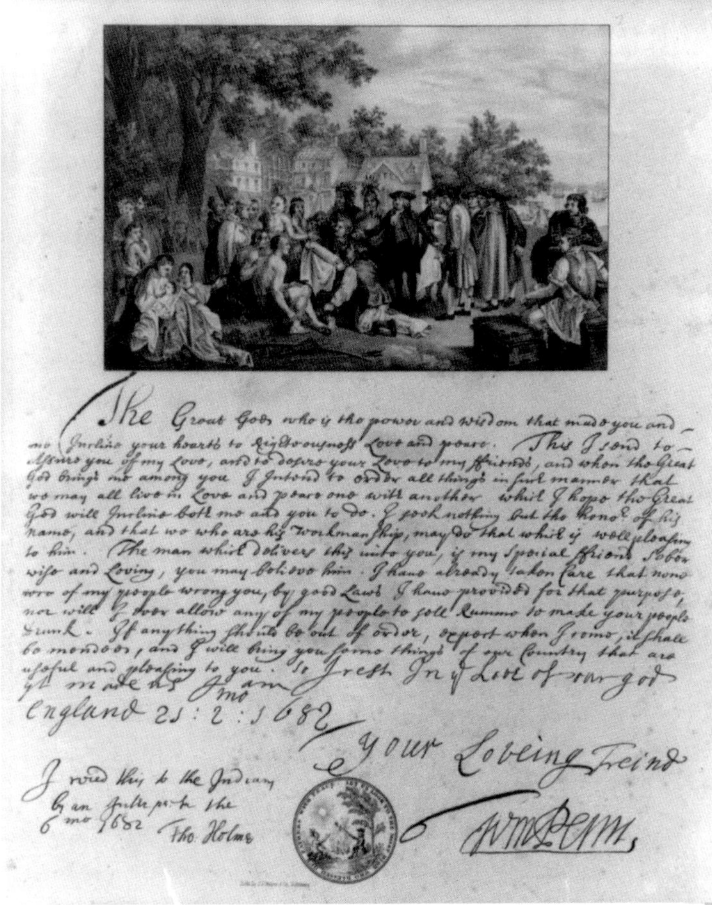

The Great God who is the power and wisdom that made you and me incline your hearts to righteousness love and peace. This I send to assure you of my love, and to desire your love to my friends, and when the Great God brings me among you I intend to order all things in such manner that we may all live in love and peace one with another which I hope the Great God will incline both me and you to do. I seek nothing but the honor of his name, and that we who are his workmanship, may do that which is well pleasing to him. The man which delivers this unto you, is my special friend sober wise and loving, you may believe him. I have already taken care that none of my people wrong you, by good laws I have provided for that purpose, nor will I ever allow any of my people to sell rumme to make your people drunk. If anything should be out of order, expect when I come, it shall be mended, and I will bring you some things of our country that are useful and pleasing to you. So I rest in ye love of our God yt made us. I am

England 21:2:1682

your Loveing Freind

Wm Penn

I read this to the Indians by an interpreter the 6 mo 1682 Tho. Holme

William Penn wrote a treaty with Native Americans to purchase land and assure them of peace among the Quakers. The treaty was a great success.

Pennsylvania with items such as blankets, needles, combs, scissors, coats, and the like. I wish other colonists had been so just.

But there's more to the story of Native Americans than this purchase. William Penn made it clear to these people that the Quakers did not believe in war. Because the Quakers had no soldiers, no guns, and no swords, Penn assured the Native Americans that they were safe among the new arrivals. And they were! Penn created a law to provide for a fair trial should there be a claim that a Native American was mistreated. These trials were to include a jury with equal numbers of colonists and Indians. Penn knew a lot about the jury system as he had fought for a fair jury during his *own* confinement in England.

Furthermore, William Penn was one of the few pioneers who made it a point to recognize the differences among Native Americans. He realized there were three tribes in his area: the **Susquehannock**, the **Shawnee**, and the **Lenni-Lenape**. He strove to learn their dialects and ways of life. As a result, the Native Americans would say, "We will live in love with William Penn so long as the sun gives light."[8] The Indians were true to their word as Penn was true to his, and there was no bloodshed between them. No other colonists experienced as much peace with the Indians as did those in Pennsylvania. It's been said that Indian children and European children played side by side while their mothers and grandmothers took turns babysitting.

Of course, a peaceful place like this was bound to attract more people. As word spread, thousands immigrated to Pennsylvania in the late 1600s, making it the first American "melting pot." One of the main attractions was religious freedom. You see, William Penn had known religious persecution firsthand and would not allow it. He encouraged faith in God but did not dictate it. So the masses who came to Pennsylvania were of all faiths and from all nations. They were Roman Catholics, Huguenots, Jews, Lutherans, Mennonites, and Moravian Brethren. They traveled from England, Ireland, Germany, Holland, Sweden, and Switzerland.[9] William was willing to welcome all and called it a "Holy Experiment." As part of his experiment, taxes were kept as low as possible, and women were given equal rights with men. For his insight and integrity, Thomas Jefferson would later say that William Penn was "the greatest lawgiver the world has produced."[10]

As a side note, the Germans who migrated to Pennsylvania called themselves the *Deutsch* (Doich), which means "German." However, many others mistook the term *Deutsch* for *Dutch*. As a result, the Germans were called the *Pennsylvania Dutch*. Don't be confused. They were not the Dutch from Holland. Just thought I'd clear up that misconception. Now back to William Penn.

## *Philadelphia*

One of the few criticisms William experienced in America came from the Quakers who thought his mansion on the Delaware was a bit overdone. Perhaps it was. William worked hard on creating a beautiful home to match his beautiful city. You see, he personally designed the city of **Philadelphia**. The Greek origin for the name *Philadelphia* means "brotherly love" and accurately describes what Penn was trying to accomplish.

Philadelphia grew quickly to cover 1,200 acres. In three years, it was as busy as New York, which had been around for 50 years. Carefully laid out in a rectangular grid, it had more than 600 homes, a school, and a printing press. For convenience, the important buildings were placed in the center of town. But they were not crowded together as in most cities. Penn had seen in London that a crowded city was not a healthy city. Overcrowding led to the spread of disease and fire. So, in Philadelphia, the homes and buildings were strategically spaced far enough apart to allow for big gardens and to prevent fire from taking out whole city blocks at a time.

William Penn implemented "green space" to keep Philadelphia free of congestion. The idea quickly spread to nearby towns, creating a beautiful landscape in New England.

The streets of Philadelphia were made wide for safety, and trees were kept in place wherever possible. Today, we call that "green space." Penn may never have used that term, but green space was very important to him — he wanted his city to look and feel more like the country, with large estates and plenty of fresh air to breathe. Trees were so important that the streets were named Walnut, Cherry, Chestnut, and Pine. Philadelphia became a model city that every little town would try to duplicate. If you live in the United States, you probably have streets in your city named after trees, too! By copying the layout and the laws of Philadelphia, the typical American town was born, and the ideas of freedom followed right along with it. (Though I will say that the Puritan colonies were not so quick to adopt the ideas of liberty. They were still practicing intolerance, which included persecuting the Quakers in America.)

As for William Penn, his later years were not so smooth. Upon returning to England in 1684, he was accused of being friends with the duke of York, who became James II, the next king of England. James II was overthrown by the government! Because of this friendship, Penn was forced into hiding in the slums of London for years. He would go back to Pennsylvania once more to enjoy his well-planned city and the freedom it offered. But he didn't stay. He returned to England and, believe it or not, was imprisoned again! This time it was for debts he owed. Unfortunately, he didn't handle his money very well and was taken advantage of by others who ruined him financially.

William Penn would not recover from his last experience in jail. He suffered two strokes. The last one left him unable to speak or take care of himself. He lived six years in that condition and died in his home in England. In the United States, he has been memorialized in two major places. First, there is a bronze statue of William Penn in Philadelphia on top of City Hall. Until the 1980s, no other building was allowed to stand taller than William Penn's statue. Second, there is a frieze in Washington, D.C., at the U.S. Capitol that portrays William Penn making a treaty with Native Americans. His just deeds would not be forgotten.

I greatly admire the work of William Penn. But as a lead into our next lesson, I must say he had one serious oversight. He, like many colonists in America, was a slave owner! As much as he cared for freedom, he failed to extend it to *all* men. He was kind to his slaves, but nonetheless, he "owned" them and traded them like property. I will say ahead of time that the history of slavery in America is a difficult topic because there are wounds that still need healing in the United States. But, as best as we can, we will begin to look at slavery in our next lesson. We will approach this topic carefully and together try to unravel the roots of this dark and painful part of American history.

## Lesson 78 — *Late 17th Century*

# *The Atlantic Slave Trade*

As I mentioned at the end of our last lesson, the history of slavery in America is a difficult topic because the wounds from it are still felt today. But I think it's necessary to begin to address the pain of the past. I say "begin to address" because we won't even come close to finishing our study of slavery in this volume. We will only look at the *beginning* of the **Atlantic slave trade** that grew strong in the **late seventeenth century**. Did you know that slavery in America had a lot to do with sugar? It did. I'll tell you about that in this lesson. In the next volume, we will look more closely at personal stories of slavery, those who bravely fought against it, and how it was finally abolished in America.

Slavery goes back to the earliest of times. In ancient history, people were oftentimes forced into slavery upon losing a war. People were sometimes made "indentured servants," or temporary slaves, for debts they couldn't pay. And people were frequently made slaves for labor. Remember the ancient Israelites? They were pushed into slavery by the Egyptians. They were despised for being foreigners and forced into making bricks for building projects.

In America, laborers weren't needed for making bricks, but they were needed for the production of sugar, tobacco, cotton, and coffee. Unfortunately, this need for labor led to 350 years of unbelievable cruelty in America as humans were captured, sold, and traded to provide manpower. The first people to be enslaved were the native population who already lived in the Americas. But many Native Americans died from disease brought by white Europeans. When that supply of native manpower ran low or ran out, Europeans turned their eyes toward enslaving the peoples of West Africa.

The first West African slaves were captured as far back as 1441 during the Middle Ages. It was the Portuguese who kidnapped these people and took them as slaves to their own country. In that case, the African people were hunted and caught firsthand by Europeans through the use of chains, swords, and other weapons. But half a century later, the acquiring of slaves looked entirely different. By the 1500s, it was more common that Africans themselves sold *other* Africans into slavery to make a profit! Why would they do that? It's a great question that many still ponder.

To help understand, you should know that the nation/states and kingdoms of Africa were *not* united. Each had its own customs, language, and form of government. They regularly warred against each other for land and resources. In doing so, kingdoms acquired prisoners of war and found them easier to sell than to take care of. This means, sadly enough, that some Africans *contributed* to the slave trade by selling their enemies, or their own criminals, to greedy Europeans! It became so profitable that even the kingdoms that were *not* at war sometimes abducted each other for the business of trade.

This slave castle in Africa was a holding place for those taken captive and sold in the slave trade. Africans, Arabs, and Europeans participated in the brutal slave business.

The king of Dahomey, Africa, for example, was reported to be five times wealthier than any duke of England because he sold his neighboring Africans into slavery. The king of the Asante empire grew rich from trading cola nuts, gold, and African slaves. Both Europeans and Arabs from northern Africa set up trading posts along the Gold Coast, as it was called, where African kingdoms did business. I doubt that the Africans involved in the capture and selling of slaves could have foreseen the ripple effect of their actions. For who could have imagined then how quickly the colonies of America would grow? Who could have imagined then the oppression that followed? Who could have known then that the slavery of Africans would cause damage for centuries to come?

The first African slaves were brought to the Americas by the Spanish. They were taken to Hispaniola (Hees span YOLE uh) in 1502 to harvest sugar and molasses from sugar cane. Do you remember Hispaniola from our studies of the explorers? This Caribbean island is present-day Haiti (HAY tee) and the Dominican Republic. When gold mines ran low in Hispaniola, the Spanish turned to growing sugar cane for profit. That's when they ran low of laborers and brought in African slaves to do the work. You see, sugar is tedious and complicated to make. Seventy percent of all African slaves taken to America were used to produce sugar! Let's stop and look at the sugar-refining process to help understand the high demand for labor that was created.

## *The Sugar Industry*

In the seventeenth century, the cultivation of sugar began in August or September when fields were first planted with sugar cane. This required laborers to dig holes 5 or 6 inches deep to plant old pieces of cane stalk. When new shoots emerged from the soil, they needed tending for 7 to 22 months. Once ripe, the mature sugar cane reached 10 to 15 feet high.

It needed to be cut within 24 hours to prevent spoiling. So, from dawn to dusk, in the scorching heat, workers harvested the sticky cane by hand. They chopped down the stalks, stripped off the leaves, and gathered the stalks into 100-pound bundles to take to the mill.

Once at the mill, more laborers were needed to produce sugar and molasses. Though not as backbreaking as the field work, the work at a mill was extremely dangerous. Laborers called "feeders" were needed to supply the cane to large rollers that crushed the stalks. If an arm or a finger were caught in the process, the rollers were strong enough to pull and crush a person to death! That gruesome fact is known because it happened.

Juice was extracted from the crushed cane and channeled to a boiler room. Workers called "boilermen" labored through the night in temperatures over 100 degrees. After hours of boiling and skimming the cane juice, large ladles were used to transfer the hot liquid to small containers where the raw sugar crystallized. Molasses was collected from the drippings and used to make rum. In the dim light of the boiler rooms, it was difficult to avoid getting burned!

As you can see, there are many steps involved in the manufacturing of sugar. Today machines do a lot of the work. But in the seventeenth century, before machinery, millions of slaves were used — and abused — in the production process. The life of a sugar slave was probably worse than we can imagine. To keep up the assembly, most slaves were beaten, starved, and punished. It actually cost a sugar farmer less to buy a new slave than to take care of an old one. After about six years of work, the average slave died of exhaustion and malnourishment.

So the difficulty of sugar production had something to do with *why* slavery was started in the Americas. Of course, this doesn't justify it but only helps shed light on the mindset of those who instituted it. Slavery started with the Spanish in the Caribbean. It spread to the Dutch, who jumped in on the trade, and it was later used by the English who would enslave the greatest number of Africans in all. Why were the English involved? The answer goes back to sugar. The English were *the* largest consumers of the sweet stuff we call sugar. Seventy-five percent of *all* the sugar made in the seventeenth century went to London to supply the newly popular coffeehouses with something delicious. But, oh, at what a tragic price!

The irony of slavery in North America is that the founding fathers of the United States believed in freedom! It was freedom of religion, freedom of livelihood, and freedom of speech that drew so many to the shores of the new continent. Interestingly, in 1776, Thomas Jefferson wanted to *condemn* slavery in the Declaration of Independence, but others thought it was "too divisive" an issue. How slavery then slipped in is hard to grasp. But once it did, it was even more difficult to shut the system down. The economy of the Americas quickly grew addicted to the toil, sweat, and labor of the slaves.

## The Slave-Trade Triangle

The slave trade to America became so common that it developed a name of its own. It was called the Atlantic slave trade (or trans-Atlantic slave trade). As explained on the next two pages, there were three parts to this trade that on a map took the shape of triangle.

1. On the first leg of the trade route, ships left Europe for Africa carrying MANUFACTURED GOODS such as weapons, rum, jewelry, textiles, and metalware. These items were traded *to* Africans in exchange for human slaves. It is believed that about half of the enslaved died in confinement camps *before* they were ever traded because of harsh, starving conditions!

2. On the second leg of the trade route, ships left Africa for America with hundreds of shackled HUMAN SLAVES at a time. Cramped conditions were so brutal, with little to eat or drink, that untold thousands, maybe millions, died during this "middle passage," as it was called. Sharks actually followed the ships to eat the dead bodies that were regularly tossed overboard. Without sanitation, the stench and disease were unbearable. John Newton, a former slave-ship captain who later came to Christ and wrote the words to the hymn "Amazing Grace," wrote this as an eyewitness:

> . . . this height is divided toward the middle for the slaves to lie in two rows, one above the other, on each side of the ship, close to each other like books upon a shelf. I have known them so close that the shelf would not easily contain one more. The poor creatures, thus cramped, are likewise in irons for the most part which makes it difficult for them to turn or move or attempt to rise or to lie down without hurting themselves or each other. Every morning, perhaps, more instances than one are found of the living and the dead fastened together.[11]

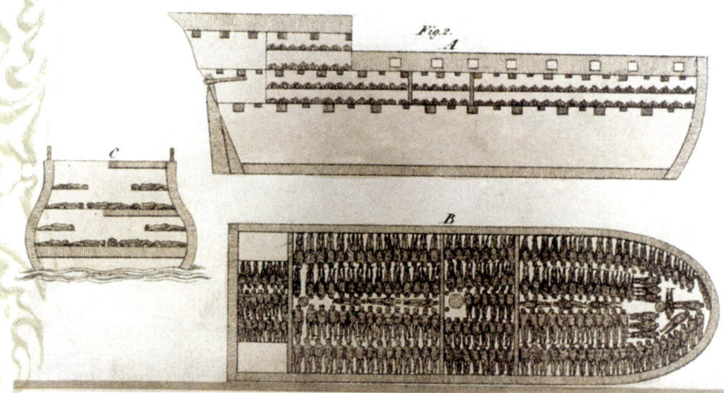

This eighteenth-century engraving of the cross-section of a slave ship displays the vile and cruel conditions that slaves were forced to endure when taken across the Atlantic Ocean.

3. On the third leg of the trade route, ship captains sold slaves at the ports of North, South, and Central America.[12] (It is believed that many thousands died in American slave camps *before* they were sold or auctioned.) After slaves were unloaded, the empty ships were reloaded with RAW GOODS from America such as tobacco, cotton, coffee, indigo plants, and of course, sugar. These items were sailed across the Atlantic and sold at high prices to the Europeans. (The items didn't grow so well in the chilly climates of Europe.) Then the triangular trade route started all over again when those ships sailed to Africa with MANUFACTURED GOODS.

Of course, not all the trading followed this exact pattern, but most of it did. The perceived value of the triangular trade was that ship captains could make money on *every* leg of their long journey. Winds and currents, particularly the **Gulf Stream**, encouraged this pattern as nature helped move ships on every leg of the journey. The worst threats facing these ships were the pirates of the Caribbean who stalked the seas for treasures and gold.

How long did the Atlantic slave trade last? Too long. This particular trade business started in 1502. Slavery itself was not made illegal in the United States until 1863 when **Abraham Lincoln** signed the **"Proclamation of Emancipation."** How many suffered from the slave trade? No one could accurately count the number of lives that were lost or ruined. But it has been estimated that millions upon millions were involved in the trade from beginning to end. One source states that 12 to 13 million Africans were enslaved over 350 years.[13] For every one slave that survived, probably one or two died from poor treatment.

Is that alarming? It should be. The Atlantic slave trade was a terrible episode in the history of mankind. Some today call it "Maafa," or the African Holocaust. The term *maafa* comes from a Kiswahili word meaning "disaster" or "great tragedy."[14] It was a great tragedy indeed because it's about real people. It's about real moms and dads or brothers and sisters who were torn from their loved ones or captured as whole families. This tragedy is about real people who lost dreams and struggled to maintain dignity. It was a horrific era that most of us cannot comprehend — but for the sake of reconciliation and healing, we must try.

The Atlantic slave trade, or "Maafa" as it is called by some, was a tragedy that devastated Africans of all ages. Slaves lost not only their freedom but their dreams and ambitions as well.

To help a little, I'll close with something the Bible says to believers in Christ. Colossians 3:10–11 reads, "... put on the new man who is renewed in knowledge according to the image of Him who created him, where there is neither Greek nor Jew, circumcised nor uncircumcised, barbarian, Scythian, slave nor free, but Christ is all and in all."

# WEEK 27

## Lesson 79 — 1689

# *William and Mary and the Glorious Revolution*

You should be primed and ready for this lesson. I think that even you younger students are going to understand what has been called the **Glorious Revolution**. The reason you are so ready for this is because we have already spent a lot of time on England and its fight against absolute monarchs. Do you remember who was beheaded in England for ruling like a dictator? It was Charles I. Do you remember the English Civil Wars? They were fought over disagreements in the Parliament involving the rule of kings.

What you'll learn today is that through a royal couple named **William and Mary**, England finally got straight what it really wanted in a king, a queen, and the Parliament. What England wanted was a "balance of power." This chapter in English history is an important one because many other nations would seek the same balance of power in their governments.

To review a little, after Charles I was put to death, Oliver Cromwell served England as Lord Protectorate. He had so much power, that some thought him a dictator. So after Cromwell died, the English "restored" a Stuart king back on the throne of England. That was Charles II. In England, Charles II was not so cruel, but in Scotland, he severely persecuted the Covenanters. You could say that a "healthy" balance of power had not yet been achieved.

Well, when Charles II died, he left no sons to reign after him. So the English chose his brother James, the duke of York, to be the king.[1] He was crowned James II in 1685. (As a reminder, this is the James whom the Scots refer to as James VII. It was this James who brought on the "Killing Times" described in our lesson on the Covenanters.) James was a lot like his brother except in one matter. James was a strong Catholic. As you should know by now, that was a problem in England.

Do you remember Henry VIII? He broke England *away* from the Catholic Church. His daughter, Bloody Mary, tried to bring it back. Elizabeth I tried to keep both Protestants and Catholics happy by strengthening the Anglican Church. It didn't really work, and England grew steadily more Protestant, or Anglican, and less Catholic over time. The fact that James II was Catholic was unnerving to the English, who feared he would force his beliefs on everyone.

The most ironic thing about James II is this — he promoted religious tolerance (meaning freedom) in England! One of the first things he did in taking the throne was to sign the **Declaration of Indulgence**. It allowed freedom of religion to Catholics and all kinds of

Presently, the Parliament of the United Kingdom meets for business at the enormous Palace of Westminster located on the bank of the River Thames in London.

Protestants. If you recall, James had been a longtime friend of William Penn, a strong Quaker. So James was lenient toward Quakers, Puritans, and other Protestant "dissenters" who had at one time been thrown in jail for *not* being part of the Anglican Church. James let them all out! (Except in Scotland where he tried to flush out the Covenanters. That was revenge for how the Scottish had turned against his father, Charles I.)

So what, then, was the problem in England? Well, James moved too fast. He was already 52 when he became king and didn't think he had much time. His hasty actions scared the English because he granted religious freedom *without* the consent of the Parliament! Let me say that again: James II made a decision as the king of England *without* the consent of the Parliament. In his defense, James didn't arrest members of the Parliament or dissolve the Parliament like his father, Charles I, did. But he did act *apart* from the Parliament. It was a grave mistake.

Now let me clarify something. I wouldn't say it was a "mistake" that James gave the English freedom in worship. That was a good thing. His mistake was in how he went about doing it. In the spring of 1688, James forced a document to be read from every Anglican pulpit in the land. The document was the Declaration of Indulgence mentioned earlier. Bishops who refused to read it out loud were arrested. All feared that if James did *one* thing without the permission of the Parliament, then he might do more. What was to stop him from making other decisions behind Parliament's back? What was to stop him from one day making England or Scotland Catholic?

## The Formation of the Whigs and the Tories

Before I go on with the rest of the story, I need to describe two political parties that emerged, or rose up, about this time in history. You see, some members of the Parliament began to meet separately — and sometimes in secret — to try to solve problems in the government. They met at a London tavern and called themselves the **Green Ribbon Club**. They wore green ribbons in their hats to identify themselves on the streets of London.

The Green Ribbon Club was open to those who were interested in debating the rights of kings and other important matters. Their motto was "life, liberty, and property." They were freedom fighters for the rights of mankind. In the pursuit of liberty, they were labeled "Liberals." (The term *liberal* has a different connotation today.)[2]

Included in the Green Ribbon Club were Scottish Covenanters who, for obvious reasons, were interested in freedom and liberty from the king. They had suffered a long time under both Charles II and James II. I bring up the Scottish Covenanters because they were nicknamed the **Whigs** for the way they called their horses. The Covenanters, when fighting, would use the word *whiggam* to urge their horses forward. In time, *all* those in the Green Ribbon Club were nicknamed the "Whigs" for short. Maybe you've heard of them before.

In contrast, another political party rose up. They were called the **Tories**. The motto of the Tories was "the king, the church, and the land." These men were more loyal to the king than the Whigs were. They believed a strong central government was good for all. We won't be focusing a great deal on the Whigs and the Tories, but I wanted to introduce them to you now because they *were* influential in creating a "balance of power" in England. (In the United States, political parties like the Democrats and Republicans still exist to help create balance in the government. Americans can thank the English for that.)

## *William and Mary*

Now, let's return to our story line of James II. So, he came to power in England and promoted religious freedom for the sake of his fellow Catholics and the persecuted. But he went behind the back of Parliament to do so. Besides that, he placed Catholics in powerful positions and built up a large army. The army made the English very suspicious. No one quite knew what James was up to.

Furthermore, because James had no son, it was assumed that the daughter from his first marriage would one day take the crown. Her name was Mary, and she was a Protestant. She was no threat to England. But in 1688, James and his second wife gave birth to a son. It was then assumed that this boy would grow up and take the crown *instead* of Mary. And everyone knew he would be Catholic.

As happy as James was to have a son, the English were unhappy. At least the majority of the English were unhappy. The Catholics of England were excited. They saw it as a sure way to regain their rights.

You can only imagine the rumors that must have been flying around London in those days. Those suspicious of James rumored that he started the Great Fire of London (a tragedy that occurred in 1666) and that he poisoned his brother. People were nervous about the future. It led a small group of Englishmen to form a conspiracy. Members of both the Whig party and the Tory party got together to decide the fate of the nation. Behind the king's back, they decided to invite James's daughter, Mary, and her husband, William, to be the king and queen of England! This small group of Whigs and Tories risked being arrested for treason.

Now think about this awkward situation for a minute. Mary was being invited to take the throne from her father. That had to be strange. But she agreed to it. Her husband, William, was eager for the arrangement as long as he was appointed an equal ruler with Mary. He was, after all, the nephew of James II. (William and Mary were cousins.) William was also the ruler of the Netherlands and hoped that by joining the English, he could better keep Louis XIV in his place in France.[3]

There was one condition, however, to William and Mary's being accepted as king and queen. They had to agree to the English **Bill of Rights**. In this bill, there were important limits placed on the monarchy. For example, the bill stated that the king could not override the laws of the land; that Parliament was needed to approve monies used by the king; that Parliament was allowed freedom of speech; and that Parliament was to meet often. The Bill of Rights ultimately abolished the "divine right of kings," or the threat of an absolute monarch. It was brilliant — at least to most of the English.

To claim the throne that he was offered, William and his army landed on the coast of England in November of 1688. James wasn't at all prepared for this. He tried to assemble his army to fight, but his own men refused to defend him. In fact, some of his soldiers defected to the side of William! (That means they traded sides.) James's other daughter, Anne, chose also to side against her father. With so many against him, James fled to France. He was taken in by Louis XIV.

By February of **1689**, William and Mary were crowned the official king and queen of England — without a drop of blood shed! For that reason, some call it the **Bloodless Revolution**.[4] The truth is, some blood was shed later when James rallied troops in Ireland to try to take England back. But he failed at the Battle of Boyne and went back to France. James remained exiled the rest of his life and never saw England again. He had been the king of England for only three years.

As for William III and Mary II, as were their official titles, they served England well. They took seriously their role of staying in balance with the Parliament that was made up of both Whigs and Tories. English "cabinets," or committees, were put in place to distribute the work. England was never again to have an absolute monarch! And the world would take notice of that.

William and Mary were crowned the king and queen of England in 1689. They stayed "in balance" with the Parliament and ended absolute monarchy in England.

One ironic thing about William was that he was a Presbyterian Calvinist who could hardly speak English. He wasn't an Anglican at all. But the English were okay with that as long as William and Mary maintained the Anglican Church as the Church of England. They did.

In 1690, William and Mary went a step further. They reinstated the Presbyterian Church as the Church of Scotland. (Remember the Covenanters who died under Charles and James?) But it was not mandatory to be a member of the state churches of England or Scotland! This gave religious freedom to *almost* everyone. William did place limits on Jews and forbade Catholics to serve in the government. He was also harsh toward Irish Catholics who had backed James II. But, under William and Mary, the English were at least on their way toward a balanced government that was designed to serve the people without the heavy hand of a king.

# John Locke

Now that you've learned about the Glorious Revolution, I'm ready to introduce you to **John Locke**. John Locke was an Englishman who wrote some very important works *defending* the Glorious Revolution. These things will make more sense now that the story of the revolution is behind us. The most important piece Locke wrote was titled *The Second Treatise of Government*. It defended England's stance against absolute monarchs, or the divine right of kings. Locke also wrote a piece titled *An Essay Concerning Human Understanding*. Together, John Locke's essay and treatise would have a great influence on the world to come.

John Locke was born to Puritan parents. He was very smart and attended Christ's College at Oxford University. One of his friends was the scientist, Robert Boyle. Boyle helped Locke with his laboratory experiments. Locke studied many things, including philosophy and medicine. Though he never completed his medical degree, John's knowledge of the subject would shape his future.

You see, John Locke knew just enough about medicine to perform a life-saving operation on a good friend. This good friend was **Anthony Ashley Cooper, the earl of Shaftesbury**. The earl was so impressed with Locke that he invited Locke to live and work at his estate. This arrangement paved the way for John Locke to get into the "political world" of the earl of Shaftesbury.

After some time abroad, John Locke returned to England and was an eyewitness to living history when William and Mary ascended the throne.

The political world of Shaftesbury was that of the Whigs. In fact, he helped found the Whigs! Do you remember them? The Whigs were one of two political parties that emerged during the Glorious Revolution. The Whigs were the ones who greatly opposed the absolute monarchy. Because of this, the earl of Shaftesbury and John Locke were under suspicion by the king of England. It led John Locke to flee the country for a few years. He traveled to France and the Netherlands where he met other important thinkers who spurred him on.

John Locke returned to England from Holland in 1688 (or 1689) on the same ship that carried Mary, the soon-to-be queen of England! They both arrived in England about the time the Glorious Revolution was complete. This made John Locke an eyewitness to history when James II fled, when William and Mary were invited to take the throne, and when the divine right of kings was abolished in England forever.

John Locke immediately joined the Whigs to defend the revolution on paper. He wrote so that people like us might understand and learn from what happened in England. In **1689** (or 1690), Locke published the two important writings that I mentioned earlier. Each is so full of historical ideas that we'll spend most of this lesson examining them.

**(Younger Students may want to skip to the last subhead, "Other Ideas.")**

## An Essay Concerning Human Understanding

As the title would suggest, Locke wrote *An Essay Concerning Human Understanding* to try to explain how man understands life. According to Locke, men and women are born with minds that are blank slates. He would say our minds are empty like a soft tablet, or as he would write it in Latin, a *tabula rasa*. Locke believed that like a soft tablet, our minds are written on by "experience" and like pages in a book, we are filled by our senses.

In fancier language, this is the concept of **empiricism**. Empiricism is the school of thought that man is mainly shaped by his experiences. According to empiricism, new ideas are formed by associating them with old ideas. Empiricists would say that knowledge is *perception* (using our senses) plus *reflection* (using our experiences). Even in choosing right from wrong, empiricists would say, experience is our guide. Locke would write, "Reason must be our last judge and guide in everything."[5]

Though man *is* greatly shaped by experience, many would disagree with John Locke's summary of mankind. Critics of John Locke would say that because man is created in the image of God, his mind in infancy is far more than a blank slate. Critics would also point out that according to God's Word, there does exist absolute truth — rather than experience — to guide mankind in choosing right from wrong. (See Ex. 20:1–17; Ps. 119:105; Gal. 1:6–12; 2 Tim. 3:14–17.) Nonetheless, Locke's philosophies would be influential. You could say that Locke was to psychology what Newton was to science.

I do want to point out that John Locke did claim to believe in God. When he read the New Testament, he was overwhelmed with the perfection of Christ's teachings and believed Him divine. So, even though Locke's ideas would foster liberal thought and "secularism" (thinking that separates religion from man), he himself believed in God.

## The Second Treatise of Government

In *The Second Treatise of Government*, John Locke tackled some other major issues. He first addressed what he called man's "natural rights." He believed it is natural for man to protect his *life*, his *liberty*, and his *property*. He called these rights "inalienable," meaning that they can't be separated, isolated, or transferred to someone else. Have you heard that term before? **Thomas Jefferson** borrowed the term *inalienable rights* when he drafted the Declaration of Independence. It's a very important concept to the free world today.

Let me restate this important concept in the words of John Locke. He wrote, ". . . no one ought to harm another in his life, health, liberty or possessions; for men being all the workmanship of one omnipotent and infinitely wise Maker."[6]

> "... *no one ought to harm another in his life, health, liberty or possessions; for men being all the workmanship of one omnipotent and infinitely wise Maker.*"
>
> –John Locke

John Locke expanded on this by saying that in man's natural state, he can't be completely safe because there is no one in charge. That makes sense, right? In nature, there is nothing to stop or protect men from violating the rights of other men. Locke concludes that government is necessary to create laws that protect the life, liberty, and the property of mankind. He wrote, "Where there is no law there is no freedom. For liberty is to be free from restraint and violence from others, which cannot be where there is no law."[7]

On the same note, Locke would point out that it is man's duty to obey the government that seeks to protect him. The Bible supports this principle. (See Matt. 22:17–21; 1 Pet. 1:13–17.) Man *ought* to follow the laws of the land that were created to protect him. Locke would call this two-way agreement between man and government a "social contract."

Now, stay with me here because these ideas are all going to come together. Consider this: When a man or woman breaks the social contract and fails to follow the law, an obvious consequence follows if he is caught. He is removed from society and put in jail — or at least given a fine to pay. But what happens when the government fails to keep *its* end of the social contract? What happens when an absolute monarch — with unlimited power — fails to protect the life, liberty, and property of his people? This was John Locke's main concern.

In *The Second Treatise of Government,* John Locke answered this difficult question. He claimed it was ultimately the role of the government to protect man's inalienable rights. When the government "failed" to uphold its end of the contract, it was the right *of the people* to overthrow the government! In fact, he would say it was their obligation. Ah, hah! This is where the Glorious Revolution comes into play.

John Locke brilliantly justified the Glorious Revolution that took place in England in 1688. Philosophically, he laid the groundwork for why it was the right of the people to overthrow an absolute monarch. Locke believed that Charles I, Charles II, and James II all failed as absolute monarchs to protect the inalienable rights of the English. So the English were "allowed" to replace them and the system of government that supported them!

Are you beginning to see how significant John Locke was? You know, Locke was not the first to promote the idea of a government existing "for" the people and "by" the people. Aristotle said some similar things about democracy during the Golden Age of Greece. But John Locke was the person most successful in making the idea popular — especially with the middle class of England. And this idea of government would one day carry over to the shores of North America where colonists would fight for "life, liberty, and the pursuit of happiness."

## *Other Ideas*

Now that we've tackled the two most important writings of John Locke, I want to mention a few last things. John Locke had no wife or children to provide for and so poured himself into improving society. He wrote pieces on education, Christianity, and a constitution for the newly formed Carolinas in North America. He helped Isaac Newton improve the money system of England; he served on trade boards; and he joined the Royal Academy of Science.

One of John Locke's greatest ambitions was to settle the issue of religious freedom. He wrote and rewrote *A Letter Concerning Toleration*. In the same way that he defended the Glorious Revolution, he defended religious freedom. Remember the term *inalienable rights?* Locke would suggest that faith is a personal choice and does not fall under the category of the government's responsibility. Some would call that a "wall of separation" between the church and state. Locke did much to promote that idea. After all the bloodshed we've studied in this volume over the matter, it's refreshing to know that by the late seventeenth century, religious freedom was being grasped — at least to some degree — in England.

But on a sour note, John Locke, like many others, would fail to practice what he preached when it came to slavery. He overlooked the "inalienable rights" of both Native Americans and African Americans. I don't know why, except that perhaps he was merely a product of his times. He was of an era that grew dependent on the workforce provided by slavery and ignored the cruelty behind it. Freedom was, as the expression goes, taking "one step forward and two steps back." You could say that with the help of John Locke's ideas, man was making progress toward freedom, but he wasn't quite there yet.

With words from the Constitution inscribed around it, the Jefferson Memorial in Washington, D.C., bears witness to the influence of John Locke on American history.

Most prefer to remember John Locke's achievements rather than his shortcomings — and for good reason. John Locke would go on to influence important men in Europe like Montesquieu (MON teh skew), Rousseau (Rue SO), and Voltaire (Vol TARE). In North America, he influenced Alexander Hamilton, James Madison, and Thomas Jefferson. I suppose you've heard of some of these guys but not all of them. That's okay. We'll study them all in Volume IV when *The Mystery of History* continues.

# The Salem Witch Trials

In **1692**, darkness and confusion shrouded the village of Salem, Massachusetts. In less than one year, 19 people were hung at the gallows, 5 died in prison, and one man was pressed to death. Why? There was a witchcraft scare. There are many theories as to what went on in Salem that year. We'll look at the facts that led to the famous **Salem witch trials** and draw on what the Bible says about witchcraft.

You learned in Lesson 62 that Salem is located about 50 miles north of Plymouth, Massachusetts, where the *Mayflower* Pilgrims had settled. In 1630, John Winthrop led 700 Puritans to settle Salem. They were seeking religious freedom in the New World. When they arrived, Salem was in poor shape. Disease and starvation had hit the small fishing village very hard.

But in a few years, the Puritans, with their strong work ethic, turned things around. Salem was thriving. The Puritans elected and continually re-elected John Winthrop as their governor. Winthrop preached that Salem would be "as a City upon a Hill" for all eyes to see the Christian love that was among the Puritans. How little did he know that 62 years later, the reputation of the Puritans would be stained.

So what happened to tarnish this little town? Well, it seems that the trouble started during the winter of 1691 with two young girls who were being disobedient. The girls were 9-year-old **Elizabeth Parris** (sometimes called Betty) and 11-year-old **Abigail Williams.** The girls were cousins. Betty and Abigail were being disobedient because they were listening to "forbidden" stories about witchcraft and magic. It was forbidden by the church to tell these stories.

Keep in mind that in those days, Puritan children weren't even allowed to have toys because playing was considered an "idle" use of time. Children were encouraged to be sensible, to work hard at their chores, and to be students of God's Word. So when Betty and Abigail began to meet secretly in the evening to hear scary stories, they really were doing something they were taught not to do.

The stories they gathered for were being told by a servant girl named **Tituba.** Tituba was brought to Salem as a slave. She was probably from South America and sold into slavery in the West Indies. Betty's father, a minister in Salem, took Tituba to be his servant. His wife was sickly, and he relied on Tituba to care for his children.

Having lived in the West Indies, Tituba had been exposed to voodoo, a pagan religion that involves the use of magic. Allegedly, Tituba used magic to liven up the evil stories she told at night. Betty and Abigail were enticed and invited their friends to join them in their secret meetings around a fire. More than likely, this circle of friends included **Ann Putnam, Mercy Lewis, Elizabeth Hubbard, Mary Walcott, Susannah Sheldon**, and **Mary Warren.** I say "allegedly" above because some say that Tituba's "storytelling" is only a story itself.

Whether the storytelling was a real event or not, in January of 1692, young Betty and Abigail began to show signs of strange behavior. They screamed, had convulsions, hid under furniture, and went into trance-like spells. Soon other girls in the circle of friends had the same kind of "fits," as these episodes were called. Seven girls in all were reported to have similar symptoms, including contortions of the body and the sensation of pinching and biting on their skin. No one could explain what was happening. I'm sure it was frightening.

Unfortunately, the fear of the unknown led to some drastic conclusions. A doctor examined the girls and stated that they were "bewitched." He did not claim that the girls themselves were witches but rather, that witches in Salem were "afflicting" the young girls. Many villagers turned to prayer and fasting.

## The Accused

As problems persisted, the girls were asked to point out who it was that afflicted them or drove them into their fits. The girls accused three women. Naturally, one of the accused was Tituba — who had supposedly filled the girls' minds with witchcraft. The other women were **Sarah Good** and **Sarah Osborne**. Sarah Good was a middle-aged homeless woman known to mumble under her breath when out begging. Sarah Osborne was an outcast for having married her servant. These three women were not very popular in Salem, and so they all became easy targets for rumors and lies.

It was March 1, 1692, when these women were officially arrested. Both Good and Osborne claimed to be innocent. But Tituba — after being beaten — confessed to practicing witchcraft. She claimed, too, that other witches were at work in Salem. This confession sent shock waves through the community, and the girls began to point fingers at others! Soon everyone was under suspicion, and two "fine" women of good reputation were accused and arrested as well. They were **Martha Corey** and **Rebecca Nurse**. The women were good friends, and both were members of the local church. Along with them, little **Dorothy Good**, the 4-year-old daughter of Sarah Good, was put in prison!

In 1692, two women of the local church in Salem, Massachusetts, were arrested for supposed witchcraft. It led to fear and distrust in the town and to many more accusations.

The arrests of Martha, Rebecca, and young Dorothy were alarming to the community. It led the town to madness. No one knew whom they could trust or whom they could talk to for fear of being accused. In time, about 150 men and women in Salem and nearby towns were accused and arrested for witchcraft and wizardry.

In May, a special court was set up to try the suspects. It was called the **Court of Oyer and Terminer**, which in French means "to hear" and "to determine." The court was designed to listen and decide the special cases brought before it. Unlike our legal system today, in the Court of Oyer and Terminer, *no one* was given a lawyer. And in Puritan New England, the punishment for witchcraft was death! For several months through 1692 the court met and tried supposed witches and wizards.

Oddly enough, Sarah Good, who claimed to be innocent, was eventually sentenced to hang. Tituba, who admitted guilt, was exiled out of the community! The system in place was arbitrary and grew to be worse. The accused were subjected to examinations of moles and spots on their bodies that were thought to be marks of the devil. Now, don't be frightened if you have moles and spots! I have plenty. No one today thinks these are a sign of evil. But in 1692, the colonists were not so sure.

One explanation of the hysteria is that the colonists of Massachusetts had been greatly influenced by a local preacher who wrote books and tracts against witchcraft. His name was **Cotton Mather**. He was a strong preacher and greatly respected around town. At least three of the judges on the Court of Oyer and Terminer were Cotton Mather's friends and had read his books on witchcraft. Mather's writings probably kept the notion of witchcraft fresh in many people's minds — and fueled the fear of it.

One fear of witchcraft was the possibility of seeing a ghost. The girls of Salem claimed to "see" ghost-like visions of people taunting them. The court considered a vision of this sort "spectral evidence," and spectral evidence *alone* was enough to have someone arrested, accused, and condemned as a witch! Some would simply call it "finger-pointing."

I find spectral evidence to be a good example of extreme superstition. Superstition is an irrational fear or belief meant to give an explanation to the unknown or the mysterious. For example, it is superstitious to think that a black cat brings bad luck. There is no scientific, logical, or biblical reason for that belief. In the case of the Salem witch trials, a lot of superstition was used as evidence in court! Folks were beginning to blame any illness or tragedy on witchcraft. Ultimately, it would bring tragedy to the community.

Through the Court of Oyer and Terminer, witch trials were held in Salem in the fall of 1692. Those found guilty were executed at Gallows Hill.

The witch trials continued in Salem between May and October of 1692. Nearly everyone accused claimed to be innocent. Some appeared to confess to witchcraft under enormous pressure to do so and the promise that it would save their lives! Those found guilty were hung at a place called Gallows Hill. The executions were spread out over four dates and included 13 women and 6 men. Four or more died in prison from poor conditions. One man, the husband of Martha Corey, refused to stand trial. For that, he was pressed to death by having stones piled on a board across his body. All the executed were denied proper burials.

After the last Salem witch trial of that fateful year, the Court of Oyer and Terminer was dissolved. A law was eventually passed in Massachusetts stating that "spectral evidence" could no longer be used in court. A few families tried to sue the courts for the loss of their loved ones and their loss of reputation. Some financial settlements were made, but most who survived the trials or imprisonment suffered hardship the rest of their lives.

As for the seven girls who had supposedly been "afflicted," only one would make a public apology in the years to follow. It was Ann Putnam. In 1706, she confessed to a church congregation that she had not meant to cause harm to the innocent but was deluded by Satan to accuse others of witchcraft. She was particularly sorry for the death of Rebecca Nurse, who Ann admitted was *not* a witch. As recently as 2001, the Massachusetts House of Representatives officially declared that all the people executed in the Salem witch trials were innocent and cleared their names in the record books!

Skeptics of witchcraft have tried to come up with theories for the strange behavior of the girls of Salem. Ergot poisoning, a fungus found in rye, was once thought an explanation because it can produce drug-like hallucinations. Others theorize that encephalitis of the brain or a similar condition called *Huntington's chorea* might have been responsible for what happened in Salem. Some think the girls were simply acting out of imagination, peer pressure, or rivalry in the community.

Both the Old and the New Testament of the Bible clearly teach the avoidance of witchcraft and define it as sin. In 1 Samuel 15:23, the Bible says, "For rebellion is as the sin of witchcraft."

## *"As Innocent as Doves"*

No one really knows what caused the girls of Salem to behave so strangely. But I think it is important to consider what the Word of God says about witchcraft. In Deuteronomy 18:10–12 (NIV), the Lord says to the people of Israel, "Let no one be found among you who sacrifices his son or daughter in the fire, who practices divination or sorcery, interprets omens, engages in witchcraft, or casts spells, or who is a medium or spiritist or who consults the dead. Anyone who does these things is detestable to the Lord."

In the New Testament, the Bible says, "The acts of the sinful nature are obvious: sexual immorality, impurity and debauchery; idolatry and witchcraft; . . . and the like. I warn you, as I did before, that those who live like this will not inherit the kingdom of God." (See Gal. 5:19–21, NIV.) These passages clearly state that God does not approve of witchcraft. That would imply that witchcraft is real; it is evil; and it is to be avoided.

I don't know if Betty or Abigail or any of the other girls of Salem were truly influenced by witchcraft or not, but in my opinion, it is probable. If they were, it seems that the tragic trials could have been prevented if the girls had heeded God's Word to begin with and avoided the stories of witchcraft. When it comes to evil, Jesus said, "be as shrewd as snakes and as innocent as doves." (See Matt. 10:16, NIV.) I interpret that to mean we are to be shrewd enough to recognize evil — but innocent enough to stay away from it! That's a good lesson for all of us.

Lesson 82 1693

# Jakob Amman: Founder of the Amish

There are few things as picturesque as an Amish horse and buggy trotting down a country lane, especially against the backdrop of burnt orange and red autumn leaves. We have lived in Ohio near "Amish country," where it is not uncommon to see a pretty sight like this on a fall day. Nearly every time we pass one of these buggies in our gasoline-powered car, I wonder what the Amish think about us. Politely, we exchange smiles. Out of curiosity, the younger children wave and stare as we drive past. And then our worlds drift back apart. I drive off into my world — a hurried one of the twenty-first century. The Amish journey into theirs — a simpler world that appears to be locked in the past.

Because of their opposition to the use of modern technology, such as the automobile, the Amish are distinctively known today for traveling by horse and buggy.

Today we're going to examine the founder of the **Amish**. His name is **Jakob Amman**. We'll look at his faith and the practices he adopted that have shaped the Amish of today. Some of you might even be Amish. I hope you enjoy this lesson about your unique heritage.

It is difficult to gather a lot of information on Jakob Amman because the written records of the Amish are scarce (meaning they're rare). But it's believed he was born in Switzerland and moved to France. Jakob was raised among the Swiss Brethren and/or the Mennonites. Let me refresh your memory as to who the Swiss Brethren and Mennonites were because we learned of them way back in Lessons 23 and 24.

The Swiss Brethren were a group of believers who broke away from the teachings of Ulrich Zwingli, an early reformer from Switzerland. These Christians differed from Zwingli in their beliefs toward baptism, church discipline, and the separation of church and state. Because of their views on believer's baptism, the Swiss Brethren were nicknamed the "Anabaptists." It was not a name they cared for, but it was widely used.

The Swiss Brethren, or Anabaptists, were greatly persecuted — even by Ulrich Zwingli! It led many of the Swiss Brethren to flee Switzerland. The Brethren went in many different directions under different leaders — some good and some bad. In time, Menno Simons provided godly leadership to many of the Brethren in Germany. His followers, the "Mennonites," grew in great numbers and remain a large movement today.

## *Division Among the Swiss Brethren*

Now, getting back to Jakob Amman — he grew up among the Swiss Brethren (and/or Mennonites). But he had some issues with his fellow churchmen. In particular, Jakob disagreed with a fellow minister named **Hans Reist** over "banning" members of the church.[1] The ban is called *Meidung* and means "to shun" or excommunicate.

Hans Reist had a relaxed view of the ban and wasn't quick to enforce it — but not Jakob Amman. It seems he was a very strict man. Jakob Amman believed that if church members were spiritually out of line, it was the church's responsibility to ban them and cut them off from the rest of the congregation. He would suggest that any person who left the church should be shunned, as should anyone marrying a person who was not a member of the church. Shunned members were not to buy, sell, trade, or even eat with church members! This strict practice of *Meidung* was supposed to encourage church members to obedience. Sometimes, though, it backfired.

In the case of Jakob Amman, the issue of shunning, and a few other things, led to a split in the Swiss Brethren church. Between **1693** and 1696, Jakob broke away from Hans Reist's congregation, taking many followers with him. Jakob would say that it was not a difference in fundamental "beliefs" but rather, a difference in "method and spirit" that separated the congregations.[2]

Years later, Jakob Amman would regret dividing the Swiss Brethren and offer to ban himself if it would bring reconciliation or peace. But it was too late. Jakob's followers had adopted many other practices that made them distinct, and the "Amish," as they were called, came into being. Because they were followers of Jakob Amman, they were naturally named the "Amish."

## *Amish Practices Then and Now*

The practices of the Amish were strict then and are strict now. Jakob Amman believed it was very important for his church members to be plain and unified in their dress, so as not to draw vain attention to themselves. So married men wore untrimmed beards and wide-brimmed hats. Women wore long dark skirts and bonnets. They still do. The most conservative Amish today (those of the **Old Order Amish**) still use hooks and eyes instead of buttons to keep their garments "plain."

It was from the Dutch Mennonites that Jakob Amman borrowed the biblical custom of foot washing and made it a regular practice. He also encouraged the partaking of communion more than once a year. The Amish would say that their main text is the Bible. Jakob encouraged the direct reading of the Scriptures. Rather than build churches, the Amish traditionally worship in homes. Each congregation has a bishop, a deacon, and two ministers.

Additionally, the Amish refer to the *Ordnung*, which is a set of unwritten rules of the church. Though not in print, these rules are greatly respected and provide the basis for Amish customs and practices. Upon baptism, a member of the Amish church is obligated to uphold the rules of the *Ordnung* or face excommunication.

Pictured here is a one-room Amish schoolhouse located in Nappanee, Indiana. In keeping with Amish tradition, notice the horse-drawn school bus and wood-burning stove.

Like the Mennonites, the Amish are opposed to the taking of oaths and to military service. The Amish would also choose not to vote or to attend school beyond the eighth grade. The most obvious distinction of the Amish is their stand against the use of modern inventions such as electricity, automobiles, and the telephone. They believe that inventions of this type lead to laziness and worldliness. The Amish prefer hard work by hand over technology. If you were to drive past an Amish farm today, you would see hay bales stacked by hand like teepees rather than rolled with modern equipment.

To avoid worldly entertainment, the Amish place great value on useful hobbies and handicrafts. With impeccable woodworking skills, Amish men are famous today for sturdy handcrafted furniture. Amish women are known for their beautiful hand-sewn quilts and fresh baked goods. (When we lived in Ohio, we could buy these delicious goods on the roadside.)

Still, as part of Amish custom, church members separate themselves as far as possible from the outside world. One reason for the distance is that Jakob Amman believed that no one outside the Anabaptists could receive Christ's salvation. Therefore, the Amish do not recruit members from the outside because they believe it would be pointless. Neither do they regularly associate with the "unsaved" and the shunned for fear of being stained by worldliness.

Though evangelical Christians greatly respect the wholesome values of the Amish, they would fault them for not reaching out to the lost and unsaved. Because of their strict practice of separation, it would appear that the Amish do not seek to fulfill the Great Commission as spelled out in Matthew 28:19–20 and Acts 1:8.

As for Jakob Amman, he died of natural causes at an old age. He himself never migrated outside of Europe. But his followers did. As persecution came and went, the Amish of Europe rejoined their neighboring Mennonites — or fled. There are no Amish settlements in Europe today. Those who fled went to the New World, where there was the promise of freedom. Do you want to guess which colony in 1710 was the first to receive the Amish? It was Pennsylvania, the home of the Quakers who welcomed *all* faiths. From there, the Amish migrated west to Ohio and Indiana, and north to Ontario, Canada. Presently, the Amish also live in Delaware, Illinois, Iowa, Kansas, Nebraska, and South Dakota, with a few scattered settlements elsewhere.

It is difficult to determine the number of Amish today, but estimates range from 34,000 to 134,000. It is hard to know because only adults are counted as church members. Regardless of the numbers, the Amish are a thriving group. Their simple lifestyle, which comes straight out of the seventeenth century, will always be intriguing to outsiders. The Amish are naturally admired for their work ethic and family values. And they are equally scorned and misunderstood for their separation. Outsiders like me may never fully comprehend the Amish, but I know I'll keep smiling and waving when we meet on country roads.

The Amish spend a great deal of time on useful hobbies such as quilting and woodworking. Handcrafted Amish furniture is simple, sturdy, and practical.

## Lesson 83 — 1696

# Peter I: Czar of Russia

Imagine a tough and rambunctious little boy playing war games with model ships. Can you see him? Now imagine that little boy growing up to be the czar (zar) of Russia — and creating a full-scale navy for war! If you can envision that in your mind, then you are seeing **Peter I**. Standing 6 feet 8 inches tall, Peter I was one of the strongest and most intimidating leaders Russia ever had. And he was one of the most determined to build a navy. But his character was a strange one. Peter I was curious and crude; a genius and a buffoon. Though Peter I did much to try to improve Russia, most of his people despised him.

After the death of Ivan the Terrible, Russia slipped into a period of chaos and confusion. The Russians call it the **Time of Troubles**. To end the period, representatives from 50 cities gathered together and voted **Michael Romanov** (ROW mah noff *or* Ruh MAH noff) into power. He started the Romanov dynasty that would last up to the twentieth century.

By 1696, Peter I had become the sole czar of Russia. He sought absolute power and confidently referred to himself as "Peter the Great."

As you might have guessed, Peter I was of the Romanov family. At just 10 years of age, he and his half brother, **Ivan**, gained access to the throne of Russia. Ivan was nearly blind and partially insane. Their older sister, **Sophia**, led a small bloody rebellion to rule as a regent in place of her brothers. But by the time Peter turned 17, he felt confident in his abilities to rule without her. So, in 1689, he had Sophia confined to a convent where she was given luxury and attendants but absolutely no freedom! Ivan, with his feeble mind, was easily pushed aside. Seven years later he died. All of this is to say that, by **1696**, Peter I became the *sole* czar of Russia. Russia would never be quite the same.

Peter had three main goals for Russia. First, he wished to "westernize" the nation and make it more like Europe. Second, he wished to give landlocked Russia an outlet to the sea. And third, Peter wished to make the role of the czar one with *absolute* power. Through his amazing ability, he accomplished all three. Because of his ambition, he called himself "Peter the Great."

## *Western Reforms*

To westernize Russia, Peter did something quite out of the ordinary. He traveled "incognito" (meaning in disguise) across Europe with an entourage of 250 Russians. It must have been hard to miss this boisterous group with their thick accents and 7-foot-tall leader. But Peter did his best to appear a common "giant." He wore the clothes of a peasant and labored among the poor. Peter rose as early as 4 A.M. to walk to the docks and the shipyards in Holland. With an axe on his shoulder and a pipe in his mouth, Peter "blended" in with the local shipbuilders. His royal hands grew calloused and what few manners he had disappeared altogether.

Why did the king of Russia choose to work so hard and live so rough? It goes back to his love of the sea. Peter, from childhood on, was fascinated with shipbuilding. It was his obsession. He must have thought he was the luckiest king in the world to be able to shed his crown and his robe for a hammer and a saw — at least for awhile.

For 18 months, Peter traveled to Germany, Austria, England, France, and the Netherlands. He investigated every dimension of building boats and observed the crafts, the habits, and the politics of the West. He even found time for conversation with William Penn, who tried his best to explain the beliefs of the Quakers. When it suited his fancy, Peter I revealed his true identity as the czar of Russia and wined and dined with the kings and queens of Europe. They found him rather gross and lacking in all social graces. Peter knew nothing of proper dancing or using a fork or knife. He ate with his fingers, told coarse jokes, and amused himself by excessive drinking.

Peter's adventure came to an end when he heard of an uprising back home. In 1698, he returned to Russia more confident than when he left. To settle the uprising, Peter had thousands of the *streltzi*, or palace guards, put to death. He personally decapitated many members of the *streltzi* and seemed to enjoy doing it! It marked the beginning of his outlandish style of leadership.

One of Peter's first reforms back in Russia was to insist that his countrymen cut off their beards! Wearing a beard was far more than a fashion statement to the Russians. Members of the Russian Orthodox Church believed that God wore a beard and that men, created in God's image, should do the same. In other words, a beard was considered sacred. Peter didn't seem to care. He wanted his citizens to look as modern as Europeans, with clean-shaven chins. The only way to keep one's whiskers was to pay a high tax. The tax payment entitled a man to wear a bronze token around his neck that protected him from the scissors of the king! Literally. Without a token, someone wearing a beard could be stopped by the king and groomed on the spot.

Peter also set out to change the wardrobe of the Russians. He thought the long flowing robes of the older people were outdated and impractical. If he felt like it, he would cut the sleeves of those in his company! He insisted that coat lengths be raised like those in the West and that women dress fancier, too. Women were also encouraged to attend social events and receive an education. That to me sounds like a positive reform.

Speaking of social events, Peter had some funny ideas for entertainment. He enjoyed surrounding himself with midgets and dwarfs and once acted out *Gulliver's Travels* with a cast of little people. (He was, of course, Gulliver, and the little people were the Lilliputians.) For fun, he forced a friend to eat tortoise and another to consume vinegar until it made him sick. For sport, Peter smacked his friends in the face and held drinking contests to see who could hold the most liquor. He usually won.

As rowdy as that sounds, there was a more serious side to Peter. When it came to the church, he considered himself the head. Much like Henry VIII of England, Peter gave himself final authority over the church in Russia. He also took the land of the monasteries for his own benefit. Behind his back, the priests whispered among themselves that Peter the Great was perhaps the "anti-Christ." But to keep their heads, they kept those thoughts to themselves and submitted to Peter's rules.

In the late 900s, Vladimer I brought the Eastern Orthodox Church from the Byzantine Empire to Russia. Peter I made himself the head of this church, which by then was called the Russian Orthodox Church.

As for the army, Peter completely revised it. It was out with the old and in with the new. The *boyars*, or nobles, were dismissed and replaced. Peter instituted a type of draft that forced boys of 15 to join the army for a few years. There was no choice in the matter. Coincidentally, though Russia was at war during most of Peter's reign, more soldiers died from cold weather, disease, and malnourishment than from battle wounds. Peter was notorious for overworking and underpaying his troops — or just about anybody else who worked for him.

Even when dining, Peter I was cheap. He invited his friends to picnics rather than to royal dinners so that his guests could each pay their own way. And he taxed just about everything in sight. Under Peter, taxes were placed on boots, hats, births, beehives, chimneys, cellars, and marriages. It was a bit ridiculous.

Peter was always looking for ways to increase production at a lower cost. To supply the cities with enough labor, serfs and peasants were channeled away from the farms and forced to work in factories. It was a lifetime of drudgery for the masses, with no hope for a better way of life. No matter how hard the serfs toiled or how well they did their jobs, their quality of life remained the same. Without incentive (which means motivation), production suffered while the lives of the serfs deteriorated. Begging became so common and bothersome on the streets that it was deemed a crime.

On a more positive note, some of Peter's reforms were quite valuable. He worked as hard as any peasant on improvements. He sent cobblers to the West to learn better ways to make shoes. He revised the Russian alphabet and started the first Russian newspaper. Peter opened a free museum and offered complimentary snacks to those who came. And though Peter was in control of the Russian Orthodox Church, he allowed Calvinists, Lutherans, Roman Catholics, and Jews to worship freely in his country. I find that extraordinary, considering Peter's heavy hand in everything else.

Vitus Bering was sent by Peter I to explore what was thought to be land connecting North America and Russia. It proved to be a waterway and was named the Bering Strait.

Another positive reform was that Peter I tried to advance education by bringing in expert teachers from the outside and updating Russians to the Julian calendar.[3] Because of his great curiosity, he promoted the **Russian Academy of Sciences** and commissioned **Vitus Bering** to explore the land between North America and Russia. Have you ever heard of the **Bering Strait**? It is a 58-mile-wide channel of water separating Asia and North America. It was named for Vitus Bering, who confirmed that the two continents were not attached — though many believe they were connected by a land bridge during the Ice Age.[4]

## *An Outlet to the Sea*

Let's discuss now Peter's goal to find an outlet to the sea. A port city in Russia's possession was important for trade and commerce. Without it, Russia would never be able to compete in the markets of the world.

So Peter looked at every border he owned for an opening. In the south, he battled the Turks for the port city of **Azov** on the edge of the **Black Sea**. He won that city but later lost it.

In the north, he sent explorers to the frigid coast of Siberia. The water was too icy to deal with. To the southeast, Peter fought with the Persians for access to the **Caspian Sea**. His success helped him open trade to China, but Peter was far more interested in what the Europeans had to offer. This left the far western border of Russia as *the* most desirable for a port. But there was a problem. The Swedish owned the strip of land that would give Russia access to the **Baltic Sea**.

The Russians, the Swedes, and a few of their neighbors would fight for 20 years over this land. The struggle was called the **Great Northern War**. In 1703, before the war was finished, Peter was confident enough to begin building a port city at the mouth of the **Neva River** that poured into the Baltic Sea. The city was **St. Petersburg**. It was both a marvel and a headache for the Russians. Let me explain why.

The land at the mouth of the Neva River was a soft, marshy delta. To build a city there, timbers had to be imported and driven into the ground for support. Forests had to be cleared and hills flattened. Food and supplies had to be brought in from Moscow, which was miles away. Thousands of soldiers died trying to transform the marsh into a port.

Though St. Petersburg was difficult to build, Peter I loved the new city and considered it the "window to the West" that he had dreamed of.

The residents of Moscow resented the building of St. Petersburg. They watched the new city slowly replace Moscow as the capital and center of Russian life. But Peter couldn't have been more pleased. He adored his new city and made his own residence there at a grand palace named *Peterhof*. The beautiful Neva River wound through the city like "Main Street," with ferries to carry citizens from one side of the river to the other. To Peter I, St. Petersburg was his own "Venice" and became the "window to the West" that he dreamed of.

## *The Czar*

We'll close by looking at Peter's last goal for Russia, which was to strengthen the role of the czar. I think you would agree that he was successful. Peter exerted his authority on every level of Russian life from making himself the head of the church to shaving off the beards of his countrymen. Peter got what he wanted. By title, Peter was acclaimed the **Emperor of All Russia** in 1721 after defeating the Swedes. But not everyone was keen on this. Some European kings feared that the title of "emperor" was higher than that of "king" and refused to use the term.

The greatest misuse of Peter's power was probably against his own son. Peter feared that his son **Alexei** would undo the "progress" he had made. As a result of his distrust, Peter allowed for his son's arrest and torture, which led to Alexei's early death. Tragic, isn't it! Without other sons to follow Peter on the throne, Russia fell back into some confusion when Peter I died at the age of 52.

So, was Peter the Great that "great" for Russia? Opinions of him are mixed. Some of his reforms were lasting; others were not. Some found him entertaining; others thought him despicable. Peter didn't view himself as a tyrant but rather, as a servant of his nation. Whether he was successful or not, there is no question that Peter I tried to improve Russia and that he will be remembered for it.

## Lesson 84 1707

# Isaac Watts

It's been a long journey through "The Renaissance, Reformation, and Growth of Nations." But at last we are on the final lesson of Volume III. There are many places where I could have ended this volume, but I chose this date for a reason. This date coincides with the life and times of **Isaac Watts**. Isaac Watts was a hymn writer. His love for the Lord and his love of music would come together to influence Christians for centuries to come. As the writer of one of my favorite hymns, Isaac Watts still influences me. I think his story is a pleasant one on which to close this volume and celebrate the study of God's hand in history. And before this lesson is over, I'll tell you about my favorite hymn. Even today, the words bring tears to my eyes.

The close of our study coincides with the life of Isaac Watts, who loved the Lord and wrote hundreds of inspirational hymns. Many are still treasured today.

Isaac Watts was born in England. His father went to prison at least twice for his faith because he was a dissenter during those turbulent times in England that we have so long studied. His simple "crime" was not worshiping in the style of the Anglican Church. Isaac's mother took him as a baby to visit his father in prison. She took him again when Isaac was 9 years old. Isaac would grow up under much less persecution than his father, but he was very aware of what his father had suffered for the sake of worship. Isaac's mother was part Huguenot and had probably known persecution in her family as well.

Young Isaac was very smart. By the age of 4, he learned Latin; at 9, he knew Greek; at 11, he studied French; and by 13, he knew Hebrew. It wasn't common for an English boy to learn French, but Isaac's community in Southampton was made up largely of French Huguenots who had fled France under persecution. Isaac wanted to be able to talk to his neighbors, and so he learned their language. (If you remember, Louis XIV revoked the Edict of Nantes in France. This caused many Huguenots to flee to England.)

Because of Isaac's brilliance, a rich man offered to put him into a fine university. But for Isaac to attend, he would have to conform to the Anglican Church. He refused. Isaac would stand strong for his beliefs. He later attended an academy for dissenters. It suited him much better. He excelled in science, language, and philosophy.

At some point when he was just out of college, Isaac Watts complained to his father about the poor quality of music in his church. His father's reply was simple. He challenged Isaac to produce something better. Isaac did! Isaac wrote a hymn that was sung the very next Sunday in his home church. It was titled "Behold the Glories of the Lamb." It was the beginning of a lifelong career of hymn writing. Isaac Watts would write more than 600 hymns before his death.

## *Hymns and Spiritual Songs*

To appreciate the impact of these hymns, let me tell you this: Before the time of Isaac Watts, there was very little singing in the churches in England. The Lutherans in Germany sang a great deal in their churches because of their founder, Martin Luther. He loved music and wrote many hymns. But they weren't available in England. The Anglicans had the *Book of Common Prayer* to recite, but there was no music to it. In 1562, the Anglicans added the *Old Version,* which were Psalms put to music — but they were not very pretty. The *New Version* of 1696 was more pleasant but still lacked any real quality. This was the music that Isaac wanted to improve.

People are funny, though. They find it so hard to agree. You see, though many people loved the new worshipful hymns, there were many who didn't. Conservative Anglicans feared that the hymns would replace the reciting of the Psalms — the inspired Word of God — in the church. I can appreciate their concern. Man's poetry and songs should never replace God's Word. But I don't think that was Isaac's plan. His goal was to inspire worship *through* song.

According to the Bible, Christians are to worship using God's Word *and* hymns and spiritual songs! Ephesians 5:18–19 says: "And do not be drunk with wine, in which is dissipation; but be filled with the Spirit, speaking to one another in psalms and hymns and spiritual songs, singing and making melody in your heart to the Lord." Those are beautiful instructions, aren't they? Nonetheless, it would be 154 years before Anglicans would produce a hymnbook. In Isaac Watt's lifetime, churches were divided over the issue — the most notable being John Bunyan's former church. It was mainly the dissenting churches (like the Baptists and Independents) that appreciated the hymns of Isaac Watts.

*". . . but be filled with the Spirit, speaking to one another in psalms and hymns and spiritual songs, singing and making melody in your heart to the Lord."*

*–Ephesians 5:18–19*

Now let me tell you a little more about Isaac Watts so that *you* might appreciate the praises of his heart. Isaac faced physical challenges all his life. For one, his stature was awkward because he had an oversized head on a body only five feet tall. Wigs, which were common then, made his head appear even bigger. Besides that, Isaac had a frail body and a weak voice.

At 38, he fell very ill and went to a friend's home to recuperate. But he never did. Isaac remained sick for the next 36 years of his life! He was not so sick that he was dying, but he was not well enough to live on his own. He slipped in and out of good spells when he could preach and teach as he desired. During bad spells, he nearly lost his mind.

Though Isaac fell in love once, his poor health interfered with plans for marriage. Instead, gracious friends adopted him as part of their family and cared for him until the day he died. Out of great love for the little man, Isaac's church continued to pay his salary through his illness. (Isaac generously tithed one-fifth of his salary right back to his church and to missions.)

## The Accomplishments of Isaac Watts

Knowing his limitations, you might agree that Isaac Watts was extraordinary for what he *did* accomplish. You see, he did far more than write hymns during all those years. When he felt well, Isaac tutored children, was pastor of a church, and wrote on a wide range of topics. Did you know that he wrote a university level philosophy book *and* wrote books for children? He did. His book titled *Logic* was circulated for a century in the highest universities, and his book *Divine Songs* for children was the first of its kind. Isaac Watts also wrote books on astronomy and geometry, published 10 volumes of sermons, and wrote books on teaching children. Isaac had the ability to span all age groups with his pen. That's a gift!

But the greatest gift Isaac Watts had, in the opinion of many, was his talent for writing hymns. I'm sure you know the hymn "Joy to the World." That was written by Isaac Watts. Read or sing the first and last verse.

Joy to the world, the Lord is come!
  Let earth receive her King;
Let every heart prepare Him room,
  And Heaven and nature sing,
  And Heaven and nature sing,
And Heaven, and Heaven, and nature sing.

He rules the world with truth and grace,
  And makes the nations prove
The glories of His righteousness,
  And wonders of His love,
  And wonders of His love,
And wonders, wonders, of His love.

–from "Joy to the World"

Isaac also wrote "Our God, Our Help in Ages Past"; "Alas! and Did My Saviour Bleed"; and "Jesus Shall Reign Where'er the Sun." In **1707**, these and 600 others would be published for all to enjoy. The collection was titled simply *Hymns and Spiritual Songs*. These songs would inspire Christians for centuries, even to the present day.

Though Isaac Watts wrote on several topics, his 1707 publication of *Hymns and Spiritual Songs* would be one of his greatest gifts to Christian believers.

And now I get to share with you my favorite hymn written by Isaac Watts — the one that oftentimes brings tears to my eyes. It is "When I Survey the Wondrous Cross." Read or sing it slowly to absorb the meaningful lyrics.

When I survey the wondrous cross
On which the Prince of glory died,
My richest gain I count but loss,
And pour contempt on all my pride.

Forbid it, Lord, that I should boast,
Save in the death of Christ my God!
All the vain things that charm me most,
I sacrifice them to His blood.

See from His head, His hands, His feet,
Sorrow and love flow mingled down!
Did e'er such love and sorrow meet,
Or thorns compose so rich a crown?

His dying crimson, like a robe,
Spreads o'er His body on the tree;
Then I am dead to all the globe,
And all the globe is dead to me.

Were the whole realm of nature mine,
That were a present far too small;
Love so amazing, so divine,
Demands my soul, my life, my all.

–from "When I Survey the Wondrous Cross"

I can't think of a better way to close our study of this time period than to dwell on the wondrous cross. When you consider history — the good, the bad, and all that's in between —

it makes more sense in light of the cross. By God's design, man is so obviously wretched on his own. (See Rom. 3:23.) We've seen that, haven't we? We've studied the worst of mankind through stories of war, persecution, and the selfish ambitions of kings and nations. But in the hands of a forgiving, merciful God, man can be redeemed through faith in Christ. He can be saved! (See Matt. 1:21, 18:11; John 10:9; Rom. 5:10; Eph. 2:8; 1 Tim. 1:8–9.) We've seen that, too, through our study of God's Word and the stories of the faithful saints of Jesus Christ.

Until we meet again, I pray that you will be one of the faithful. I pray that you will consider God's marvelous plan of redemption and be a good steward of this mystery. As Paul challenged his friends, I challenge you: "Let a man so consider us, as servants of Christ and stewards of the *mysteries* of God." (See 1 Cor. 4:1. Italics are mine for emphasis.)

# Would You Like to Belong to God's Family?

We all belong to a family, but did you know that God has His own family, too? If you are a member of His family, He will always be there for you. To belong to God's family, you have to know four facts:

## FACT 1: *God loves you and has a plan to make you part of His family.*

God's Word, the Bible, says:

**God loves you.**

*God loved the world so much that He gave His only Son [Jesus] . . . so that whoever believes in Him may not be lost, but have eternal life* (John 3:16).

**God has a wonderful life planned for you.**

*(Jesus speaking) I came to give life — life in all its fullness* (John 10:10).

But why aren't we part of God's family already?

## FACT 2: *Your sins keep you from being part of God's family.*

**What is sin?**

Sin is something we do or say or think that does not please God. The Bible says that *everyone* has sinned. What are some sins? (Fighting, bad thoughts, lying, stealing, disobeying parents, bad words)

*All people have sinned and are not good enough for God's glory* (Romans 3:23).

Even though God made us and loves us, sin causes us to be far away from God. Because of our sin, we deserve punishment for doing wrong things. But God doesn't want to see anyone punished. He wants to give us a gift instead. That gift is a new kind of life.

*When someone sins, he earns what sin pays . . . But God gives us a free gift — life forever in Christ Jesus* (Romans 6:23).

This picture shows how our sin keeps us from knowing and pleasing God. Many people try to please God by doing good things, such as going to church, praying more, and helping others. Doing these things makes you a nicer person, but they can't erase your sin or make you part of God's family.

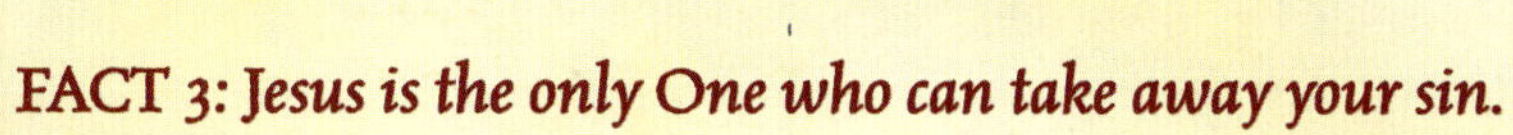

## FACT 3: *Jesus is the only One who can take away your sin.*

**Jesus was punished in your place by dying on a cross.**

*[Jesus] died for us while we were still sinners. In this way God shows His great love for us* (Romans 5:8).

**And Jesus came back to life!**

*[Jesus] was buried and was raised to life on the third day* (1 Corinthians 15:4).

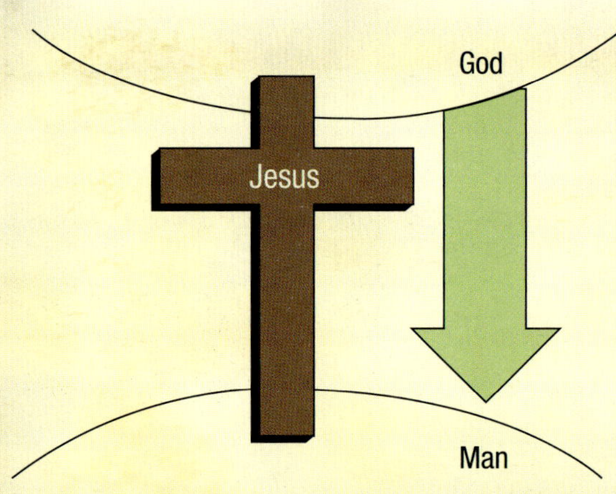


**Jesus is your way to God.**

*Jesus answered, "I am the way. And I am the truth and the life. The only way to the Father is through Me"* (John 14:6).

Jesus made a way for us to come to God, our heavenly Father, and be a part of God's family. Jesus did this by paying for your sin when He died on the cross. But just knowing this is not enough . . .

**FACT 4: *To become part of God's family, you must accept God's gift. Jesus is God's gift to you. When you accept Jesus, God's Son, you become God's child.***

*Some people did accept [Jesus]. They believed in Him. To them He gave the right to become children of God* (John 1:12).

**How do I accept God's gift?**

You accept God's gift by asking Jesus to forgive you of your sins. Right now, Jesus is waiting to forgive your sins and come into your life.

***(Jesus speaking) Here I am! I stand at the door and knock. If anyone hears My voice and opens the door, I will come in*** **(Revelation 3:20).**

God's book, the Bible, tells us that there are two kinds of people. Some people run their own lives. Others let Jesus control their lives.

You can accept God's gift right now by asking Jesus to forgive your sins. Talking to Jesus is called prayer. If you pray this prayer, you will belong to God's family!

***Dear Jesus:***

***I need You. Thank You for dying on the cross for my sins. Thank You for forgiving my sins and making me part of God's family. Take control of my life and make me the kind of person You want me to be.*** **Amen.**

If you prayed this prayer — and really meant it — you are part of God's family **right now!**

But what happens if you sin again? Will you still be part of God's family?

**Yes!**

When you disobey your parents, you make them unhappy. But you are still their child. To make things right, you tell them you are sorry for what you did. When you disobey God, He is not pleased, but you are still part of His family. He still loves you. But you need to tell Him you are sorry for what you did.

***If we confess our sins, He will forgive our sins. We can trust God. He does what is right. He will make us clean from all the wrongs we have done*** **(1 John 1:9).**

As soon as you sin, tell God you are sorry. Then God will forgive you and things will be right again between you and God.

---

From the booklet, "Would YOU Like to Belong to GOD'S FAMILY?" Published by Campus Crusade for Christ and Bright Media Foundation. Used by permission (www.campuscrusade.com).

# Endnotes

## Endnotes for Week 1, Lessons 1–3

1. We can thank William Shakespeare for the term *Wars of the Roses*. He was the first to draw attention to the roses in a fictional play about Henry VI.
2. Will Durant, *The Renaissance*. Vol. V of *The Story of Civilization*. (New York: Simon and Schuster, 1953), 102.
3. *World Book Encyclopedia*, 50th Anniversary ed., s.v."Torquemada." (Chicago: Field Enterprises Educational Corp., 1966).
4. E. Michael and Sharon Rusten, *The One Year Book of Christian History*. (Wheaton, IL: Tyndale House Publishers, 2003), 430–431.

## Endnotes for Week 2, Lessons 4–6

1. Crane Brinton, John B. Christopher, and Robert Lee Wolff, *A History of Civilization*, Vol. I: Prehistory to 1715, 3rd ed. (Englewood Cliffs, NJ: Prentice-Hall, Inc., 1967); 372; quoting A. J. Toynbee, *Civilization on Trial* (New York, 1948), 171.
2. Ibid., quoting F. Adelung, *Kritisch-literarische Ubersicht der Reisendan in Russland*. (St. Petersburg and Leipzie, 1846), I, 153.
3. Will Durant, *The Renaissance*. Vol. V of *The Story of Civilization*. (New York: Simon and Schuster, 1953), 113.
4. Ibid.
5. As a side note, read Numbers 11:16–17 and Luke 10:1 to find examples of Moses and Jesus choosing 70 elders and preachers.
6. Durant, *The Renaissance*, 117.
7. Brinton, Christopher, and Wolff, *A History of Civilization*, Vol. I, 408; quoting Machiavelli, *Florentine History*. W. K. Marriott, trans. (New York, 1909), 359–360.

## Endnotes for Week 3, Lessons 7–9

1. According to translator John Cummins, Columbus wrote to his heirs,"work always to enhance the reputation, welfare and growth of the city of Genoa . . . for I came from there and there I was born." (See *The Voyage of Christopher Columbus: Columbus' Own Journal of Discovery*, newly restored and trans. by John Cummins. (New York: St. Martin's Press, 1992), 20.
2. The variations of the name of Columbus include Christophorus Colonus (Latin), Cristoforo Columbo (Italian), and Christopher Columbus (Anglican/English).
3. "Columbus and Christianity: Christian History," Issue 35 (Carol Stream, IL: Christianity Today, Inc., 1997). Accessed on the *Christianity Today* Web site: http://ctlibrary.com/3890.
4. It is believed that Columbus and his crew departed from the port of Palos rather than the more common port of Cadiz because Cadiz on that date was packed with thousands of Jews who had been ordered to leave Spain under the Edict of Expulsion. The edict (to leave in three months or convert) was written on March 31 but issued on May 1. Thus, thousands left Spain on August 2, coinciding with the date of Columbus's departure.

5. *The Voyage of Christopher Columbus: Columbus' Own Journal of Discovery*, (Cummins trans.), 84. Log entry of August 9.
6. Neither original journal survives today. However, Bartolomé de Las Casas and Fernando Columbus (the second son of Columbus) separately reconstructed the journal of Columbus's first voyage. The translation by Las Casas is difficult to sort through because the author fluctuates between first and third person, referring frequently to Christopher Columbus as "the Admiral." Translator John Cummins, in *The Voyage of Christopher Columbus: Columbus' Own Journal of Discovery*, rewrote a compilation of these two resources and removed all third-person references to the Admiral. For the sake of easier reading, I chose in my text to quote from the version by Cummins. The original log re-created by Las Casas is easily accessible through the Internet and varies somewhat from my quotations here.
7. *The Voyage of Christopher Columbus: Columbus' Own Journal of Discovery*, (Cummins trans.), 85.
8. Ibid., 92.
9. Ibid., 93.
10. San Salvador Island in the Bahamas (formerly Watling Island) did not officially receive its name until 1986 when the island was declared the place of Columbus's first landfall. Since then, other locations are suspected. Do not confuse the island of San Salvador with the city of San Salvador, which is the capital of El Salvador in Central America.
11. *The World's Great Letters*, ed. by M. Lincoln Schuster. (New York: Barnes and Noble Books, 2003), 64.
12. Both quotes in this paragraph are from *The Voyage of Christopher Columbus: Columbus' Own Journal of Discovery*, (Cummins trans.), 94.
13. Ibid., 105.
14. *The World's Great Letters*, 67.
15. *The Voyage of Christopher Columbus: Columbus' Own Journal of Discovery*, (Cummins trans.), 127
16. Ibid., 106.
17. Ibid., 111.
18. Ibid., 157.
19. Ibid.
20. About 40 sailors stayed behind to settle the fort/town of Navidad.
21. *World Book Encyclopedia*, 50th Anniversary ed., s.v. "Columbus." (Chicago: Field Enterprises Educational Corp., 1966).
22. The three quoted Bible verses written here **are as they appear in the English translation of the** *Book of Prophecies*. From *Repertorium Columbianum Volume III, The Book of Prophecies edited by Christopher Columbus*, ed. by Roberto Rusconi and trans. by Blair Sullivan. (Eugene, OR: Wipf and Stock Publishers, 1997).
23. Ibid., 75.
24. Philip Koslow, *Mali: Crossroads of Africa*. (New York: Chelsea House Publishers, 1995), 12.
25. Sean Sheehan, *The Ancient World: Great African Kingdoms*. (Austin: Raintree Steck-Vaughn, 1999), 9.
26. Ibid., 43.

27. Louise Minks, *Traditional Africa* (World History Series). (San Diego: Lucent Books, 1996), 26.

**Endnotes for Week 4, Lessons 10–12**

1. Crane Brinton, John B. Christopher, and Robert Lee Wolff, *A History of Civilization*, Vol. I: Prehistory to 1715, 3rd ed. (Englewood Cliffs, NJ: Prentice-Hall, Inc., 1967), 454.
2. Will Durant, *The Renaissance*. Vol. V of *The Story of Civilization*. (New York: Simon and Schuster, 1953); 148.
3. Ibid., 150.
4. Ibid., 156.
5. Brinton, Christopher, and Wolff, *A History of Civilization*, Vol. I, 454.
6. Durant, *The Renaissance*, 161.
7. The term *Imam* is also used by the Sunnis, but in their sect, it has a different meaning.
8. Because "da Vinci" refers to the place that Leonardo is from, it is incorrect to use the term "da Vinci" as his last name.
9. T. Walter Wallbank and Alastair M. Taylor, *Civilization Past and Present*, Vol. 1. (New York: Scott, Foresman and Co., 1949), 481.
10. Brinton, Christopher, and Wolff, *A History of Civilization*, Vol. I, 439.
11. Durant, *The Renaissance*, 209.
12. Ibid., 208.
13. Richard Muhlberger, *What Makes a Leonardo a Leonardo?* (New York: The Metropolitan Museum of Art [Viking], 1994), 39.
14. Durant, *The Renaissance*, 227.

**Endnotes for Week 5, Lessons 13–15**

1. Gilles Neret, *Michelangelo*. (New York: Taschen, 1998), 18.
2. Ibid., 23.
3. Ibid.
4. Ibid.
5. Ibid., 83.
6. David Larsen, *The Company of the Creative*. (Grand Rapids, MI: Kregal Publications, 1999), 77.

**Endnotes for Week 6, Lessons 16–18**

1. All quotes that follow are from Niccolò Machiavelli, *The Prince*, trans. by George Bull. (New York: Penguin Books, 1999).
2. The full title is *Discourses on the First Ten Books of Titus Livy*.
3. *Merriam-Webster's Collegiate Dictionary*, 11th ed. (Springfield, MA: Merriam-Webster).
4. Ross King, *Michelangelo and the Pope's Ceiling*. (New York: Walker and Co., 2003), 180.
5. Ibid., 182.
6. Ibid.
7. Giorgio Vasari, *The Lives of the Artists*, trans. by Gaston DuC. de Vere. Accessed at http://members.efn.org/~acd/vite/VasariRaphaelS3.html.
8. "Raphael Sanzio." Accessed at http://totallyhistory.com/raphael-sanzio.

9. Will Durant, *The Reformation*. Vol. VI of *The Story of Civilization*. (New York: Simon and Schuster, 1957), 338.
10. Peter N. Herdon, "The Ideas and Ideals of Man, From the Renaissance to the Reformation." Accessed on the Web site of the Yale-New Haven Teachers Institute: www.yale.edu/ynhti/curriculum/units/1986/3/86.03.04.x.html.
11. Durant, *The Reformation*, 343.
12. A. Kenneth Curtis, J. Stephen Lang, and Randy Petersen, *The 100 Most Important Events in Christian History*. (Grand Rapids, MI: Fleming H. Revell, 1991), 96–97.
13. James Akin, "A Primer on Indulgences." Accessed on the Catholic Information Network Web site: www.cin.org/users/james/files/indulgen.htm.
14. *Catechism of the Catholic Church*, 2nd ed. (New York: Doubleday, 1997), Pt 2, Sect 2, Chap 2, Art 4.X. "Indulgences," para. 1478.

**Endnotes for Week 7, Lessons 19–21**

1. Jackson J. Spielvogel, *Western Civilization*, 5th ed., Comprehensive Vol. (Wadsworth/Thompson Publishing, 2003), 378.
2. T. Walter Wallbank and Alastair M. Taylor, *Civilization Past and Present*, Vol. 1. (New York: Scott, Foresman and Co., 1949), 556.
3. Laurence Bergreen, *Over the Edge of the World: Magellan's Terrifying Circumnavigation of the World*. (New York: Harper Perennial, 2004), 282.
4. Ibid., 340.
5. Will Durant, *The Reformation*. Vol. VI of *The Story of Civilization*. (New York: Simon and Schuster, 1957), 360.
6. Crane Brinton, John B. Christopher, and Robert Lee Wolff, *A History of Civilization*, Vol. I: Prehistory to 1715, 3rd ed. (Englewood Cliffs, NJ: Prentice-Hall, Inc., 1967), 463.
7. E. Michael and Sharon Rusten, *The One Year Book of Christian History*. (Wheaton, IL: Tyndale House Publishers, 2003), 217.
8. Robert G. Shearer, *Famous Men of the Renaissance and Reformation*. (Lebanon, TN: Greenleaf Press, 1996), 98.

**Endnotes for Week 8, Lessons 22–24**

1. Will Durant, *The Reformation*. Vol. VI of *The Story of Civilization*. (New York: Simon and Schuster, 1957), 704.
2. *Grossmünster* means "Great Minister."
3. Roger L. Berry, *God's World: His Story*. (Harrisonburg, VA: Christian Light Publications, Inc., 1976), 363.
4. Ibid., 379.

**Endnotes for Week 9, Lessons 25–27**

1. *The World's Great Letters*, ed. by M. Lincoln Schuster. (New York: Barnes & Noble Books, 2003), 80.
2. Allison Weir, *The Six Wives of Henry VIII*. (New York: Grove Weidenfeld, 1991), 423.

3. Ibid., 75.
4. G. Roger Huddleston, "St. Thomas More." From *The Catholic Encyclopedia*, Vol. XIV. (New York: Robert Appleton Co., 1912). Accessed on the New Advent Web site: www.newadvent.org/cathen/14689c.htm.
5. Sir Thomas More, *Utopia*, ed. by George M. Logan and Robert M. Adams. (New York: Cambridge University Press, 1975), 60–61.
6. Robert G. Shearer, *Famous Men of the Renaissance and Reformation*. (Lebanon, TN: Greenleaf Press, 1996), 145.

**Endnotes for Week 10, Lessons 28–30**

1. Will Durant, *The Renaissance*. Vol. V of *The Story of Civilization*. (New York: Simon and Schuster, 1953), 432.
2. Ibid., 585.
3. Philip Schaff, *History of the Christian Church*, Vol. 8: The Swiss Reformation, 1519–1605. (Peabody, MA: Hendrickson Publishers, Inc., 1996), 310–311.
4. E. Michael and Sharon Rusten, *The One Year Book of Christian History*. (Wheaton, IL: Tyndale House Publishers, 2003), 227.
5. A. Kenneth Curtis, J. Stephen Lang, and Randy Petersen, *The 100 Most Important Events in Christian History*. (Grand Rapids, MI: Fleming H. Revell, 1991), 104.

**Endnotes for Week 11, Lessons 31–33**

1. Some would count Ivan III, better known as Ivan the Great, as the first tsar of Russia.
2. Will Durant, *The Reformation*. Vol. VI of *The Story of Civilization*. (New York: Simon and Schuster, 1957), 655.
3. V. V. Raman, "Society of Jesus and Jabir ibm Hayyam." Accessed on the Web site of Metanexus: The Online Forum on Religion and Science: www.metanexus.net/magazine/ArticleDetail/tabid/68/id/7243/Default.aspx.

**Endnotes for Week 12, Lessons 34–36**

1. Some of the New Testament was written in Aramaic but most was in Greek.
2. E. Michael and Sharon Rusten, *The One Year Book of Christian History*. (Wheaton, IL: Tyndale House Publishers, 2003), 340.
3. Antwerp is now in the country of Belgium, which became independent of the Netherlands in 1830.
4. The Matthew's Bible (sometimes referred to as the Matthew-Tyndale Bible) was actually the compilation of three men's work. In the order of their contribution, they were William Tyndale, Miles Coverdale, and John Rogers. John Rogers used the fictitious name of Thomas Matthew (a name that Tyndale secretly used for a time), thus giving the Bible its name and giving some hidden credit to Tyndale. John Rogers died a martyr's death under the reign of Bloody Mary.
5. Rusten, *The One Year Book of Christian History*, 341.
6. John Foxe, *Foxe's Christian Martyrs of the World*. (Westwood, NJ: Barbour and Co., Inc., 1985), 361.

7. Copernicus actually thought that the center of the universe was *near* the sun, not the sun itself. It was an odd idea that went away in time.

**Endnotes for Week 13, Lessons 37–39**

1. Mary "Tudor" is also the name of Henry VIII's *sister*, who married Louis XII, the king of France. You will not find her story in this textbook, but you may come across it in others. Do not confuse the two. The Mary Tudor of this lesson is also considered "Mary I of England." I will refer to her as both *Mary Tudor* and *"Bloody Mary."*
2. Will Durant, *The Reformation*. Vol. VI of *The Story of Civilization*. (New York: Simon and Schuster, 1957), 594.
3. John Foxe, *Foxe's Christian Martyrs of the World*. (Westwood, NJ: Barbour and Co., Inc., 1985), 503.
4. George T. Thompson and Laurel Elizabeth Hicks, *World History and Cultures in Christian Perspective*. (Pensacola, FL: A Beka Book, 1985), 219.
5. Both quotes in this paragraph are from Heather Thomas, "Elizabeth I Quotes." Accessed on the "Elizabeth R" Web site: www.elizabethi.org.
6. T. Walter Wallbank and Alastair M. Taylor, *Civilization Past and Present*, Vol. 1. (Chicago: Scott, Foresman and Co., 1949), 539.
7. Thompson and Hicks, *World History and Cultures in Christian Perspective*, 221.
8. *Great Leaders of the Christian Church*, ed. by John D. Woodbridge. (Chicago: Moody Press, 1988), 248.
9. E. Michael and Sharon Rusten, *The One Year Book of Christian History*. (Wheaton, IL: Tyndale House Publishers, 2003), 656–657.

**Endnotes for Week 14, Lessons 40–42**

1. Jean Plaidy, *Royal Road to Fotheringhay: The Story of Mary, Queen of Scots*. (New York: Three Rivers Press, 2004), 137.
2. Marilyn B. Manzer, "Reformed Royalty: The Strength of Queen Jeanne d'Albret." Accessed on the Center for Reformed Theology and Apologetics Web site: www.reformed.org/webfiles/antithesis/v1n2/ant_1n2_royalty.html.
3. Ibid.
4. *Merriam-Webster's Collegiate Dictionary*, 11th ed. (Springfield, MA: Merriam-Webster, Inc., 2004).
5. A. Kenneth Curtis, J. Stephen Lang, and Randy Petersen, *The 100 Most Important Events in Christian History*. (Grand Rapids, MI: Fleming H. Revell, 1991), 112.
6. Crane Brinton, John B. Christopher, and Robert Lee Wolff, *A History of Civilization*, Vol. I: Prehistory to 1715, 3rd ed. (Englewood Cliffs, NJ: Prentice-Hall, Inc., 1967), 517.

**Endnotes for Week 15, Lessons 43–45**

1. Swami Chandresh, "Tycho Brahian Days," trans. by Flemming Ravn Neft. Accessed on http://neft.dk/tycho.htm.

2. J. V. Field (London), "Johannes Kepler." Accessed on the MacTutor Web site: www-groups.dcs.st-and.ac.uk/~history/Biogaphies/Kepler.html. If you have trouble accessing this Web site, type: Kepler + "my war with Mars" into an Internet search engine.
3. *World Book Encyclopedia*, 50th Anniversary ed., s.v. "Kepler, Johannes." (Chicago: Field Enterprises Educational Corp., 1966).
4. The story of the plate originated from a written account of the voyage by Francis Pretty, one of Drake's gentlemen-at-arms.
5. There is another theory as to the nickname of William the Silent. Supposedly, when asked how he felt about the Inquisition and the persecution of Protestants, he remained silent, to not give away his true feelings to those who were increasingly becoming his enemies.
6. Our William was technically William I of Orange-Nassau and the only one called "the Silent," although there are others named William of Orange in history.
7. T. Walter Wallbank and Alastair M. Taylor, *Civilization Past and Present*, Vol. 1. (Chicago: Scott, Foresman and Co., 1949), 536.
8. Herman, Hanko, "Portraits of Faithful Saints (Chap. 32. William the Silent: Father of the Netherlands)." Accessed on the unofficial home page of the Protestant Reformed Churches in America: www.prca.org/books/portraits/william.htm.
9. Wallbank and Taylor, *Civilization Past and Present*, Vol. 1, 537.

### Endnotes for Week 16, Lessons 46–48

1. The Croatoan were previously named the Hatteras or Lumbee tribe.
2. *The World's Great Letters*, ed. by M. Lincoln Schuster. (New York: Barnes and Noble Books, 2003), 83–84.
3. Christopher Smith, "Sir Walter Raleigh (Part 19: Raleigh's Execution)." Accessed on the Britannia Web site: www.britannia.com/bios/raleigh/executio.html.
4. Ibid.
5. T. Walter Wallbank and Alastair M. Taylor, *Civilization Past and Present*, Vol. 1. (Chicago: Scott, Foresman and Co., 1949), 539.
6. Will and Ariel Durant, *The Age of Reason Begins*. Vol. VII of *The Story of Civilization*. (New York: Simon and Schuster, 1961), 36.
7. Michel de Montaigne, *Essays*, trans. by John Florio. (New York: Prometheus Books, 2005), 39.
8. Ibid., 161.
9. Ibid., 46.
10. Ibid., 43.
11. Ibid., 90.
12. Ibid., 227.
13. Ibid., 195.

### Endnotes for Week 17, Lessons 49–51

1. Will and Ariel Durant, *The Age of Reason Begins*. Vol. VII of *The Story of Civilization*. (New York: Simon and Schuster, 1961), 172.

2. Ibid.
3. "Francis Bacon." Accessed on the Web site of Wikipedia: The Free Encyclopedia: www.en.wikipedia.org/wiki/Francis_Bacon.
4. The three quotes in this paragraph are from Francis Bacon, *The Essays*, ed. by John Pitcher. (New York: Penguin Books, 1985), 111, 83, and 165, respectively.

### Endnotes for Week 18, Lessons 52–54

1. Miguel de Cervantes, *Don Quixote*, new trans. by Edith Grossman. (New York: Harper Perennial, 2005), xix.
2. Mal Garvin, *Us Aussies*. (Carnegie, Victoria [Australia]: Hayzon Pty Ltd., 1987), 96.

### Endnotes for Week 19, Lessons 55–57

1. Arthur G. Doughty, "Samuel de Champlain," transcribed by Joseph P. Thomas. Quoting *Les voyages du Sieur de Champlain*, Pt. V; publ. Paris, 1613. From *The Catholic Encyclopedia*, Vol. III. (New York: Robert Appleton Co., 1908). Accessed on the New Advent Web site: www.newadvent.org/cathen/03567a.htm.
2. "Pocahontas." Accessed on the Web site of Wikipedia: The Free Encyclopedia: en.wikipedia.org/wiki/Pocahontas.

### Endnotes for Week 20, Lessons 58–60

1. William Bradford, *Of Plymouth Plantation 1620–1647*, intro. by Francis Murphy. (New York: Modern Library College Editions, 1981), 25.
2. Ibid., 50.
3. Ibid.
4. Ibid., 69.
5. Ashbel Steele, *Chief of the Pilgrims, or the Life and Times of William Brewster*. Original from the New York Public Library. (Philadelphia: J. B. Lippincott and Co., 1857), 257.
6. Timothy Keesee and Mark Sidwell, *United States History for Christian Schools*, 2nd ed. (Greenville, SC: Bob Jones University Press, 1993), 23.
7. Bradford, *Of Plymouth Plantation 1620–1647*, 100.
8. Ibid., 89.

### Endnotes for Week 21, Lessons 61–63

1. Jeremy Strangroom and James Garvey, *The Great Philosophers*. (New York: Barnes and Noble Books, 2006), 42.
2. David L. Larsen, *The Company of the Creative*. (Grand Rapids, MI: Kregal Publications, 1999), 91, quoting from the *Discourse of Method* by René Descartes.
3. T. Walter Wallbank and Alastair M. Taylor, *Civilization Past and Present*, Vol. 2. (Chicago: Scott, Foresman and Co., 1949), 46.
4. Michael H. Hart, *The 100: A Ranking of the Most Influential Persons in History*. (New York: Citadel Press, 2000), 248.

5. E. Michael and Sharon Rusten, *The One Year Book of Christian History*. (Wheaton, IL: Tyndale House Publishers, 2003), 238.
6. Roger L. Berry. *God's World: His Story*. (Harrisonburg, VA: Christian Light Publications, Inc., 1976), 417.
7. Timothy Keesee and Mark Sidwell, *United States History for Christian Schools*, 2nd ed. (Greenville, SC: Bob Jones University Press, 1993), 25.
8. Kurt A. Grussendorf, Michael R. Lowman, and Brian S. Ashbaugh, *America: Land I Love*, (Teacher Edition). (Pensacola, FL: A Beka Book, 1994), 37.
9. Berry, *God's World: His Story*, 417.
10. In 1553, a less famous scientist named *Giambattista Benedetti* came to the same conclusion as Galileo in regard to falling bodies. *John Philoponus* also thought the law true centuries earlier, but he failed to demonstrate it.
11. Will and Ariel Durant, *The Age of Reason Begins*. Vol. VII of *The Story of Civilization*. (New York: Simon and Schuster, 1961), 586.
12. *World Book Encyclopedia*, 50th Anniversary ed., s.v. "Galileo." (Chicago: Field Enterprises Educational Corp., 1966).
13. Later astronomers renamed the *Medicean stars* as the *Galilean satellites*.
14. Durant, *The Age of Reason Begins*, 612.

### Endnotes for Week 22, Lessons 64–66

1. *Ghetto Nuovo* means "New Foundry." The basis for the Ghetto Nuovo came from the Third Lateran Council of the Roman Church in 1179, which stipulated that Jews and Christians should not live together. The Ghetto Nuovo was established by the Venetian government in 1516 as a compromise between allowing Jews to live freely throughout Venice and expelling them from Venice.
2. Dr. Nicolaes Tulp adopted the tulip for his family shield, thus many would write his last name as Tulip. In reference books, you'll find it written as both Tulp and Tulip.
3. The archbishop of Canterbury at that time was William Laud, who served as archbishop to Charles I from 1633 to 1645.
4. Alice Porter, "Thomas Hooker." Published in *Connecticut Magazine*, July–August 1906. Accessed on http://history.rays-place.com/ct/thomas-hooker.htm.
5. Barbara Cross, "Thomas Hooker." Accessed on the Britannia Web site: www.britannia.com/bios/hooker.html.

### Endnotes for Week 23, Lessons 67–69

1. Because of the involvement of Scotland and Ireland in the English Civil Wars, recent historians are calling them the Wars of the Three Kingdoms.
2. It is important to understand now that the Scottish Covenanters turned *against* Charles I and aided the English in his capture. I point this out because later in history, his sons, Charles II and James II, would seek revenge for their father and horribly persecute the Covenanters. More on that in Lesson 73.

3. Will and Ariel Durant, *The Age of Louis XIV*. Vol. VIII of *The Story of Civilization*. (New York: Simon and Schuster, 1963), 201.
4. Ibid.
5. Most agree that the ancient Greek named Leucippus (480–420 B.C.) was first to recognize the concept of atoms.
6. Durant, *The Age of Louis XIV*, 529.

### Endnotes for Week 24, Lessons 70–72

1. "George Fox: An Autobiography." Accessed on the Street Corner Society Web site: www.strecorsoc.org/gfox/ch01.html.
2. A. Kenneth Curtis, J. Stephen Lang, and Randy Petersen, *The 100 Most Important Events in Christian History*. (Grand Rapids, MI: Fleming H. Revell, 1991), 122.
3. "George Fox: An Autobiography." Street Corner Society Web site.
4. Will and Ariel Durant, *The Age of Louis XIV*. Vol. VIII of *The Story of Civilization*. (New York: Simon and Schuster, 1963), 196.
5. "George Fox: An Autobiography." Street Corner Society Web site.
6. Blaise Pascal, *Pensées*, trans. with an Introduction by A. J. Krailsheimer. (New York: Penguin Books, 1995), 285–286.
7. All the quotes that follow are from Pascal, *Pensées*, endnote 6. (A reference page number is given in parentheses after each quote.)
8. T. Walter Wallbank and Alastair M. Taylor, *Civilization Past and Present*, Vol. 2. (Chicago: Scott, Foresman and Co., 1949), 89.
9. *The Kingfisher Illustrated History of the World*. (New York: Kingfisher Books, 1992), 438.

### Endnotes for Week 25, Lessons 73–75

1. Scotland was joined to England when James I of the House of Stuart took the throne after Elizabeth I. He was of Scottish and English descent, thus bridging the nations together.
2. James has two names in history. According to the Scottish, he was James VII because the Scottish did not approve of the union of Scotland and England. Thus, they counted their Stuart line of kings differently than the English did. According to the English, James was James II. To them, he was the second James to rule over both Scotland and England. Don't be confused. James II and James VII are the same person. I will use his Scottish title (James VII). In my lessons on England, I will use his English title (James II). But I'll remind you that he was both.
3. E. Michael and Sharon Rusten, *The One Year Book of Christian History*. (Wheaton, IL: Tyndale House Publishers, 2003), 97.
4. Ibid.
5. This name is sometimes spelled Kangxi.
6. Will Durant, *Our Oriental Heritage*. Vol. I of *The Story of Civilization*. (New York: Simon and Schuster, 1954), 767.
7. T. Walter Wallbank and Alastair M. Taylor, *Civilization Past and Present*, Vol. 2. (Chicago: Scott, Foresman and Co., 1949), 45.

8. As accurate as Newton's laws were, they would not hold up for extremely minute (meaning very small) objects or extremely fast-moving objects. These problems would later be solved by quantum mechanics and the theory of relativity.
9. The law of inertia was not recognized solely by Newton. Other scientists recognizing inertia include Mo-tzu (470?–391? B.C.), a Chinese philosopher; Galileo; and René Descartes.
10. This formula, implied by Newton, was a huge breakthrough in science because it disputed Aristotle's teaching that force equals mass times velocity, or $F = mv$.
11. J. H. Tiner, *Isaac Newton: Inventor, Scientist and Teacher*. (Milford, MI: Mott Media, 1975).
12. *World Book Encyclopedia*, 50th Anniversary ed., s.v. "Newton, Isaac." (Chicago: Field Enterprises Educational Corp., 1966).

### Endnotes for Week 26, Lessons 76–78

1. John Bunyan, *Grace Abounding to the Chief of Sinners*. (Westwood, NJ: Barbour and Co., Inc., 1988), 18.
2. Ibid., 57–58.
3. Ibid., 69.
4. Mark A. Beliles and Stephen K. McDowell, *America's Providential History*. (Charlottesville, VA: Providence Foundation, 1989), 90.
5. The Welsh Quakers claim that the prefix *pen-* means "head" or "top" and that William agreed to *Penn-sylvania* to identify the region as the "head woodlands" or "top woodlands."
6. Susan Coolidge, "A Short History of the City of Philadelphia, from Its Foundation to the Present Time (1880)." Accessed on the Web site of Fairfield University: www.faculty.fairfield.edu/faculty/hodgson/courses/city/philadelphia/PHILHISTORY.html.
7. Ibid.
8. Ibid.
9. Before William Penn ever settled in Pennsylvania, there were about 1,000 Europeans in the area from Holland, Finland, Germany, and Sweden. Naturally, some resisted the new government. In time, the original settlers were absorbed into the new colony or made their own colony in nearby Delaware.
10. Beliles and McDowell, *America's Providential History*, 90.
11. Rev. Earl Carter, *No Apology Necessary*. (Lake Mary, FL: Charisma House, 1997), 47.
12. Overall, South America (particularly Brazil) took the most African slaves captive. The Caribbean Islands took second place and North America third place as consumers in the slave trade.
13. Carter, *No Apology Necessary*, 48. (See also http://en.wikipedia.org/wiki/Atlantic_slave_trade.)
14. See the African Holocaust Web site: www.africanholocaust.net/html_ah/holocaustspecial.htm.

### Endnotes for Week 27, Lessons 79–81

1. In 1664, a Dutch colony in North America named New Amsterdam was taken by the English. In honor of James, the duke of York, it was renamed New York. New York became one of the busiest and most well known of all the 50 states of the United States of America.

2. A "liberal" in seventeenth-century England referred to one who *opposed* a strong central government. A "liberal" in modern America generally refers to one who — among other things — *favors* a strong central government.
3. William III was the great-grandson of William the Silent, who fought in the Dutch Revolt against the Spanish. If you remember, William the Silent also advocated religious freedom and fought against absolute monarchy. It is an interesting thread to follow in history!
4. Modern historians lean toward retitling this event the Revolution of 1688 since the terms *glorious* and *bloodless* render a certain bias. During this Revolution, Protestants rioted against Catholics and were cruel in looting Catholic homes and tearing down churches. To the Catholics in England, it was not a "glorious" time period. And the term *bloodless* is not entirely accurate because as many as 15 may have died in an early skirmish.
5. Will and Ariel Durant, *The Age of Louis XIV*. Vol. VIII of *The Story of Civilization*. (New York: Simon and Schuster, 1963), 589.
6. John Locke, *The Second Treatise of Government*, intro. by Joseph Craig. (New York: Barnes and Noble Books, 2004), 4. Originally published 1690.
7. Ibid., 32.

**Endnotes for Week 28, Lessons 82–84**

1. Some sources would state that the Anabaptists divided into three groups: the Dutch/Prussian Mennonites, the Hutterite Brethren of Austria, and the Swiss Brethren. In that scenario, Hans Reist would identify himself as a Swiss Brethren and not a Mennonite. If so, it would be more accurate to say that Jakob Amman broke away from the Swiss Brethren. However, tradition labels the Amish as the "Amish Mennonites" and therefore closely associates the movements.
2. Carol Hepburn, "Amish-Mennonite History" (Somerset County, Pennsylvania, Genealogy). Accessed on http://www.rootsweb.com/~pasomers/amish.htm. (Be sure to type in the "http://" when accessing this URL.)
3. At the time that Peter updated the Russians to the Julian calendar, most Europeans were adopting the Gregorian calendar, which was more accurate. Russia would remain on the old Julian calendar until 1917. For this reason, the dates of Russian events and European events do not easily coincide.
4. Incidentally, the International Date Line runs through the Bering Strait. This means that if you stand in Alaska and look across the strait to Russia, you are looking into tomorrow! If that doesn't make any sense, talk about the date line with your teacher.

# Bibliography

Bacon, Francis. *The Essays*. Edited by John Pitcher. New York: Penguin Books, 1985.

Beliles, Mark A., and Stephen K. McDowell. *America's Providential History*. Charlottesville, VA: Providence Foundation, 1989.

Bergreen, Laurence. *Over the Edge of the World: Magellan's Terrifying Circumnavigation of the World*. New York: Harper Perennial, 2004.

Berry, Roger L. *God's World: His Story*. Harrisonburg, VA: Christian Light Publications, Inc., 1976.

Bradford, William. *Of Plymouth Plantation 1620–1647*. Introduction by Francis Murphy. New York: Modern Library College Editions, 1981.

Brinton, Crane, John B. Christopher, and Robert Lee Wolff. *A History of Civilization*, Vol. I: Prehistory to 1715, 3rd ed. Englewood Cliffs, NJ: Prentice-Hall, Inc., 1967.

Bunyan, John. *Grace Abounding to the Chief of Sinners*. Westwood, NJ: Barbour and Co., Inc., 1988.

Bunyan, John. *The Pilgrim's Progress: From This World To That Which Is To Come*. Westwood, NJ: The Christian Library, 1984.

Burton, Rosemary, and Richard Cavendish. *Wonders of the World*. New York: Barnes and Noble Books, 2003.

Canta, Lillo, and Carol Volk. *The Renaissance: The Invention of Perspective*. New York: Chelsea House, 1995.

Carter, Rev. Earl. *No Apology Necessary*. Lake Mary, FL: Charisma House, 1997.

*Catechism of the Catholic Church*, 2nd ed. New York: Doubleday, 1997.

Cervantes, Miguel de. *Don Quixote*. New translation by Edith Grossman. New York: Harper Perennial, 2005.

Cole, Alison. *Renaissance*. New York: Dorling Kindersley, 1994.

Curtis, A. Kenneth, J. Stephen Lang, and Randy Petersen. *The 100 Most Important Events in Christian History*. Grand Rapids, MI: Fleming H. Revell, 1991.

Dale, David. *The 100 Things Everyone Needs to Know About Australia*. Sydney, Australia: Pan Macmillan Australia, 1997.

Damkani, Jacob. *Why Me?* Jaffa, Israel: Trumpet of Salvation, 1997.

Darian-Smith, Kate. *Australia and Oceania*. Austin: Raintree Steck-Vaughn, 1997.

Davis, Kevin. *Look What Came from Australia*. Danbury, CT: Franklin Watts, 1999.

Dor-Ner, Zvi. *Columbus and the Age of Discovery*. New York: William Morrow and Co., Inc., 1991.

Durant, Will. *Our Oriental Heritage*. Vol. I of *The Story of Civilization*. New York: Simon and Schuster, 1954.

Durant, Will. *The Renaissance*. Vol. V of *The Story of Civilization*. New York: Simon and Schuster, 1953.

Durant, Will. *The Reformation*. Vol. VI of *The Story of Civilization*. New York: Simon and Schuster, 1957.

Durant, Will and Ariel. *The Age of Reason Begins*. Vol. VII of *The Story of Civilization*. New York: Simon and Schuster, 1961.

Durant, Will and Ariel. *The Age of Louis XIV*. Vol. VIII of *The Story of Civilization*. New York: Simon and Schuster, 1963.

Dyson, John. *Columbus: For Gold, God, and Glory*. New York: A Simon and Schuster/Madison Press Book, 1991.

Flowers, Sarah. *The Reformation* (World History Series). San Diego: Lucent Books, 1996.

Foxe, John. *Foxe's Christian Martyrs of the World*. Westwood, NJ: Barbour and Co., Inc., 1985.

Galilei, Galileo. *Discoveries and Opinions of Galileo*. Translated with an Introduction and Notes by Stillman Drake. New York: Doubleday Anchor Books, 1957.

Garvin, Mal. *Us Aussies*. Carnegie, Victoria (Australia): Hayzon Pty Ltd. 1987.

Gray, Shirley W. *Australia* (First Reports – Countries Series). Minneapolis: Compass Point Books, 2001.

*Great Leaders of the Christian Church*. Edited by John D. Woodbridge. Chicago: Moody Press, 1988.

Greenblatt, Miriam. *Iran: Enchantment of the World*. New York: Children's Press (Division of Scholastic, Inc.), 2003.

Grussendorf, Kurt A., Michael R. Lowman, and Brian S. Ashbaugh. *America: Land I Love* (Teacher Edition). Pensacola, FL: A Beka Book, 1994.

Harpur, James and Jennifer Westwood. *The Atlas of Legendary Places: A Guide to the World's Most Mystical Locations*. Old Saybrook, CT: Konecky and Konecky, 2003.

Hellemans, Alexander, and Bryan Bunch. *The Timetables of Science*. New York: A Touchstone Book, published by Simon and Schuster, 1988.

*Illustrated Dictionary of British History, The*. Edited by Arthur Marwick. Norwich, Great Britain: Thames and Hudson, 1980.

Keesee, Timothy, and Mark Sidwell. *United States History for Christian Schools*, 2nd ed. Greenville, SC: Bob Jones University Press, 1993.

*Kingfisher Illustrated History of the World, The*. New York: Kingfisher Books, 1992.

King, Ross. *Michelangelo and the Pope's Ceiling*. New York: Walker and Co., 2003.

Koslow, Philip. *Mali: Crossroads of Africa*. New York: Chelsea House Publishers, 1995.

Kuhne, Heinz. *Leonardo da Vinci: Dreams, Schemes, and Flying Machines*. New York: Prestel Verlag, 1999.

Larsen, David L. *The Company of the Creative*. Grand Rapids, MI: Kregal Publications, 1999.

Locke, John. *The Second Treatise of Government*. Introduction by Joseph Craig. New York: Barnes and Noble Books, 2004. Originally published 1690.

Lyle, Gary. *Iran*. Philadelphia: Chelsea House Publishers, 1999.

MacDonald, Fiona. *The World in the Time of Leonardo da Vinci*. Parsippany, NJ: Dillon Press, 1997.

Machiavelli, Niccolò. *The Prince*. Translated by George Bull. New York: Penguin Books, 1999.

Marshall, Diana. *Aboriginal Australians*. New York: Weigl Publishers, Inc., 2004.

Marshall, Peter, and David Manuel. *The Light and the Glory for Children*. Grand Rapids, MI: Fleming H. Revell, 1992.

*Merriam-Webster's Collegiate Dictionary*, 11th ed. Springfield, MA: Merriam-Webster, Inc., 2004.

Milton, John. *Paradise Lost*. London: Capella (Arcturus Publishing Ltd.), 2007.

Minks, Louise. *Traditional Africa* (World History Series). San Diego: Lucent Books, 1996.

Montaigne, Michel de. *Essays*. Translated by John Florio. New York: Prometheus Books, 2005.

More, Sir Thomas. *Utopia*. Edited by George M. Logan and Robert M. Adams. New York: Cambridge University Press, 1975.

Morris, Charles, Michael J. McHugh, and Edward J. Shewan. *A Child's Story of America*. Arlington Heights, IL: Christian Liberty Press, 1998.

Muhlberger, Richard. *What Makes a Leonardo a Leonardo?* New York: The Metropolitan Museum of Art (Viking), 1994.

Neale, J. E. *Queen Elizabeth I: A Biography*. Garden City, NY: Doubleday Anchor Books, 1957.

Neret, Gilles. *Michelangelo*. New York: Taschen, 1998.

Pascal, Blaise. *Pensées*. Translated with an Introduction by A. J. Krailsheimer. New York: Penguin Books, 1995.

Peters, Edward. *Inquisition*. New York: The Free Press (Division of Macmillan, Inc.), 1988.

Pickersgill, Howard. *Great Paintings*. Secaucus, NJ: Albany Books, 1979.

Plaidy, Jean. *Royal Road to Fotheringhay: The Story of Mary, Queen of Scots*. New York: Three Rivers Press, 2004.

Pryor, Felix. *Elizabeth I: Her Life in Letters*. Los Angeles: University of California Press, 2003.

*Repertorium Columbianum Volume III, The Book of Prophecies edited by Christopher Columbus*. Edited by Roberto Rusconi and translated by Blair Sullivan. Eugene, OR: Wipf and Stock Publishers, 1997.

Rusten, E. Michael and Sharon. *The One Year Book of Christian History*. Wheaton, IL: Tyndale House Publishers, 2003.

Schaff, Philip. *History of the Christian Church*, Vol. 8: The Swiss Reformation 1519–1605. Peabody, MA: Hendrickson Publishers, Inc., 1996.

Shearer, Robert G. *Famous Men of the Renaissance and Reformation*. Lebanon, TN: Greenleaf Press, 1996.

Sheehan, Sean. *The Ancient World: Great African Kingdoms*. Austin: Raintree Steck-Vaughn, 1999.

Shelley, Bruce L. *Church History in Plain Language*. Nashville: Thomas Nelson Publishers, 1995.

Simpson, Robert. *Martyrland: A Tale of Persecution from the Days of the Scottish Covenanters*. Birmingham, AL: Solid Ground Christian Books, 2006.

Spence, Jonathan D. *Emperor of China: Self-Portrait of K'ang-hsi*. New York: Vintage Books (Division of Random House), 1988.

Spielvogel, Jackson J. *Western Civilization*, 5th ed. (Comprehensive Vol.). Wadsworth/Thompson Publishing, 2003.

Stearns, Monroe. *Rembrandt and His World*. New York: Franklin Watts, 1967.

Steele, Ashbel. *Chief of the Pilgrims, or the Life and Times of William Brewster*. Original from the New York Public Library. Philadelphia: J. B. Lippincott and Co., 1857.

Strangroom, Jeremy, and James Garvey. *The Great Philosophers*. New York: Barnes and Noble Books, 2006.

Thompson, George T., and Laurel Elizabeth Hicks. *World History and Cultures in Christian Perspective*. Pensacola, FL: A Beka Book, 1985.

Tiner, J. H. *Isaac Newton: Inventor, Scientist and Teacher*. Milford, MI: Mott Media, 1975.

Vasari, Giorgio. *The Great Masters*. Translation by Gaston Du C. de Vere. New York: Hugh Launter Levin Associates, Inc., 1986.

*Voyage of Christopher Columbus, The: Columbus' Own Journal of Discovery*. Newly restored and translated by John Cummins. New York: St. Martin's Press, 1992.

Wallbank, T. Walter, and Alastair M. Taylor. *Civilization Past and Present*, Vols. 1 and 2. Chicago: Scott, Foresman and Co., 1949.

Weir, Allison. *The Six Wives of Henry VIII*. New York: Grove Weidenfeld, 1991.

West, Ruth, and Willis Mason West. *The New World's Foundations in the Old*. Norwood, MA: Norwood Press, 1934.

Wingate, Philippa. *The Usborne Book of Kings and Queens* (Famous Lives Series). Tulsa: Educational Development Corp., 1995.

*World Book Encyclopedia*. 50th Anniversary ed. Chicago: Field Enterprises Educational Corp., 1966.

*World Book Looks at Australia*. Chicago: World Book, Inc., 1998.

*World Book of Science Power, The*, Vols. I and II. Chicago: World Book, Inc., 1994.

*World's Great Letters, The*. Edited by M. Lincoln Schuster. New York: Barnes and Noble Books, 2003.

Yip, Dora, and Maria O'Shea. *Welcome to Iran*. Milwaukee: Gareth Stevens Publishing, 2001.

Zeri, Federico. *Titian: Sacred and Profane Love*. Richmond Hill, Ontario: NDE Publishing, 2000.

# Index

## PHOTO CREDITS

**2:** © The Gallery Collection/Corbis; **13:** © Arte & Immagini srl/CORBIS; **15:** ©Erich Lessing / Art Resource, NY; **20:** © Demetrio Carrasco/JAI/Corbis; **26:** Courtesy of the Library of Congress/LC-USZ62-112535; **28:** © National Gallery Collection; By kind permission of the Trustees of the National Gallery, London/CORBIS; **30:** Courtesy of the Library of Congress/LC-USZ62-103980; **37:** Courtesy of the Library of Congress/LC-USZ62-105452; **57:** © The Granger Collection, New York; **58:** © Visual Arts Library (London) / Alamy; **59:** © The Gallery Collection/CORBIS; **60:** © The Granger Collection, New York; **61:** © National Gallery Collection; By kind permission of the Trustees of the National Gallery, London/CORBIS; **64:** © Araldo de Luca/CORBIS; **66:** © Design Pics Inc. / Alamy; **67:** © Gianni Dagli Orti/CORBIS; **68:** © The Granger Collection, New York; **69:** © National Gallery Collection; By kind permission of the Trustees of the National Gallery, London/CORBIS; **70:** © Francis G. Mayer/CORBIS; **71:** © Bettmann/CORBIS; **72:** © The Granger Collection, New York; **75:** © Stapleton Collection/Corbis; **82:** © Fine Art Photographic Library/CORBIS; **83:** © Alinari Archives/CORBIS; **84:** © Ted Spiegel/CORBIS; **86:** © Arte & Immagini srl/CORBIS; **95:** Courtesy of the Library of Congress/LC-USZ62-43530; **97:** Courtesy of the Library of Congress/LC-USZ62-104354; **98:** © John and Lisa Merrill/Corbis; **103:** © NASA/Corbis; **135:** © The Print Collector / Alamy; **138:** © Visual Arts Library (London) / Alamy; **143:** © The Granger Collection, New York; **147:** © The Granger Collection, New York; **148:** © The Granger Collection, New York; **150:** © Francis G. Mayer/CORBIS; **151:** (bottom) © Historical Picture Archive/CORBIS; **153:** © Scala / Art Resource, NY; **161:** © Steven Vidler/Eurasia Press/Corbis; **169:** Courtesy of the Library of Congress/LC-USZ62-2977; **170:** Courtesy of the Library of Congress/LC-USZ62-45582; **171:** Courtesy of the Library of Congress/LC-USZ62-9097; **173:** Courtesy of the Library of Congress/LC-USZ62-38775; **177:** © The Granger Collection, New York; **180:** © Denis Scott/Corbis; **185:** © Bertrand Gardel/Hemis/Corbis; **195:** © The Gallery Collection/Corbis; **197:** © The Gallery Collection/Corbis; **198:** © Richard Elliott/getty images; **206:** © Riccardo Spila/Grand Tour/Corbis; **220:** © Image Select / Art Resource, NY; **224:** © Science Source / Photo Researchers, Inc.; **244:** Courtesy of the Library of Congress/LC-USZ62-49872; 270: © Ludo Kuipers/Corbis; **279:** Courtesy of the Library of Congress/LC-USZ62-128969; 284: Courtesy of the Library of Congress/LC-USZ62-5242; **286:** Courtesy of the Library of Congress/LC-D416-18753; **295:** Courtesy of the Library of Congress/LC-USZC4-7155; **306:** Courtesy of the Library of Congress/LC-USZC4-4290; **314:** © Visual Arts Library (London) / Alamy; **318:** © Atlantide Phototravel/Corbis; **325:** © The Granger Collection, New York; **327:** © Erich Lessing / Art Resource, NY; **328:** © The Granger Collection, New York; **330:** Courtesy of the Library of Congress/LC-USZ62-17892; **334:** © Stockbyte (RF); **353:** (bottom) © Authors Image / Alamy; **375:** Courtesy of the Library of Congress/LC-USZ62-3933; **382:** (top) © The Granger Collection, New York.

**From Editor's Toolkit 1,** Digital Juice, Inc.: pp. 47, 290 (bottom), 307, 390, 407. From **Editor's Toolkit 2,** Digital Juice, Inc.: pp. 73, 127, 132, 164, 176, 191, 228, 240, 243 (bottom), 247, 254, 259, 260, 266, 269 (top, bottom); 273, 285, 290 (top), 300, 304, 311 (top, bottom), 321, 322, 337, 341, 349, 356, 359, 364, 369, 384, 392, 394, 399.

## INDIVIDUAL PHOTO CREDITS

**Alicia Balyeat:** p. 102. **Vicki Del Boccio:** p. 398. **Alicia Divers:** p. 131. **Monica Farling:** pp. 119, 149. **Billy Grobe:** p. 193. **Tim Harrison:** p. 9. **Heather Hobar:** pp. 33, 40, 255 (bottom), 362, 401. **Linda Hobar:** pp. 31, 265 (bottom), 296. **Ron Hobar:** pp. 11, 19 (top), 303, 403. **Shelly Hobbs:** pp. 5, 10 (bottom), 141, 208, 368. **J. B. Hogan:** pp. 52, 54. **Maggie Hogan:** pp. 202, 250. **Ray Lacour:** p. 96. **Caroline Laing:** pp. 39, 99, 229. **Dale McClure:** p. 396. **Sarah Mercer:** pp. 106, 146, 204, 310, 353 (top). **Joel Rakes:** pp. 112, 123, 156, 217, 237. **Herman Rumpke:** pp. 80, 118, 255 (top), 257. **Ray Shaw:** p. 268. **Kendra Thomae:** pp. 42, 43, 44, 379. **Carol Topp:** p, 363.

## ILLUSTRATION CREDITS

**Amy Pak:** From *History Through the Ages: Resurrection to Revolution; History Through the Ages: Creation to Christ; History Through the Ages: Napoleon to Now; History Through the Ages: America's History* (all Copyright © 2003 Amy Pak - Home School in the Woods); and from *History Through the Ages: Bonus Figures* (Copyright © 2004 Amy Pak - Home School in the Woods), the following illustrations are used by permission.

Quarter 1: pp. 7, 8, 10 (top), 17, 18, 19 (bottom), 22, 24 (top), 41, 46, 49, 51, 74, 77, 79, 88, 89, 93, 94, 100, 108, 110.

Quarter 2: pp. 116, 121, 128, 130, 139, 151 (top), 158, 163, 165, 166, 175, 179, 181, 184, 188, 189, 190, 200, 213, 214.

Quarter 3: pp. 223, 226, 230, 234, 236, 241 (bottom), 243 (top), 251, 265 (top), 272, 274, 276, 282, 287, 288, 291, 292, 298, 305, 309.

Quarter 4: pp. 323, 329, 332, 335, 338, 340, 345, 347, 355, 358, 361, 365, 373, 374, 382 (bottom), 386, 387, 393, 400, 402, 404.

Also, **Nicole Petersen:** p. 336.

## MAP CREDITS

**John Ott:** pp. 24, 53, 117, 210, 232, 278, 319, 381.